THE WAITE GROUP'S

Visual Basic 6®

D0988737

How-To

Eric Brierley
Anthony Prince
David Rinaldi

SAMS

A Division of Macmillan Computer Publishing
201 West 103rd St., Indianapolis, Indiana, 46290 USA

The Waite Group's Visual Basic® 6 How-To

Copyright © 1998 by Sams Publishing

International Standard Book Number: 1-57169-153-7

Library of Congress Catalog Card Number: 98-84685

Printed in the United States of America

First Printing: September 1998

00 99 98   4 3 2 1

Trademarks

All terms mentioned in this book that are known to be trademarks or service marks have been appropriately capitalized. Sams cannot attest to the accuracy of this information. Use of a term in this book should not be regarded as affecting the validity of any trademark or service mark.

Visual Basic is a registered trademark of Microsoft Corporation.

Windows is a registered trademark of Microsoft Corporation.

Warning and Disclaimer

EXECUTIVE EDITOR
Brian Gill

ACQUISITIONS EDITOR
Ron Gallagher

DEVELOPMENT EDITOR
Scott Warner

MANAGING EDITOR
Jodi Jensen

PROJECT EDITOR
Maureen Schneeberger McDaniel

COPY EDITORS
Lisa Lord
Geneil Breeze

INDEXER
Erika Millen

TECHNICAL EDITOR
Robert Stokes

SOFTWARE DEVELOPMENT SPECIALIST
Andrea Duvall

PRODUCTION
Mike Henry
Tim Osborn
Staci Somers

CONTENTS AT A GLANCE

TABLE OF CONTENTS

Eric Brierley is an independent consultant, trainer, and Microsoft Certified Professional. His company SoftForge was founded in 1992 and is based in central North Carolina. He is currently teaching courses on the development of multitier client/server Web applications with ASP and Visual Basic. He has been building computing solutions since the mid 1970s for many segments of business and industry including financial services, high-volume data handling, manufacturing, and textiles. Eric has been writing applications with Visual Basic since the release of version 2. This is the third Visual Basic programming book Eric has written for The Waite Group, and his technical articles have appeared in several trade journals. He and his wife homeschool their children, and they are all involved with their church. The family enjoys life on their small backyard farm where they garden and raise chickens, honeybees, rabbits, sheep, and pygmy goats. His other interests include golf, photography, and bird watching. Eric can be reached at the Internet at `eric.b@usa.net`.

Anthony Prince lives near Huntsville, Alabama. A software developer for the last 11 years, Anthony has spent the last nine years working on Electronic Design Automation software. Before that, he developed tax and agricultural software for a southern university. Over the years, Anthony has programmed in C, C++, dBASE, Clipper, FORTRAN, Pascal, and, of course, BASIC. He is also a Miata enthusiast and an active participant in the local Miata club. When not coding, he can be found traveling the curvy backroads of the Tennessee Valley.

David Rinaldi is a Senior Systems Analyst with Crestar Bank in Richmond, Virginia where he is involved in converting two-tier client/server applications to a distributed multitier intranet platform. He has been a software developer for the past 10 years, and has specialized in barcoding, inventory management, employee timekeeping, productivity analysis, and telephony systems. David began developing software with Microsoft Macro Assembler, BASIC PDS, and C. He has worked with Visual Basic since version 3 and is a Microsoft Certified Professional. In his spare time, he enjoys composing and recording music with his MIDI system. David lives in central Virginia with his wife and four children.

DEDICATION

To my wife Martha and our children Miriam, Tesea, Calin, and Hannah, for loving me and being here to enjoy life together.

–Eric Brierley

In loving memory of my mother.

–Anthony Prince

To my lovely wife Tracey who endured many weeks without me, and to my four beautiful children Anthony, Andrew, Michael, and Ahnna.

–David Rinaldi

ACKNOWLEDGMENTS

On behalf of the authors involved on this book project, I would like to thank all of our editors. Their understanding, graciousness, and constructive advice played a large role in the overall quality of this book. There are a number of people who provided support in ways that are not always obvious. The students in my classes may not know it but they helped a lot. Dealing with questions from developers who have different perspectives and challenges has helped to broaden my own views.

There are two people that deserve special mention. My wife Martha is a true blessing and the love of my life. When we met in high school and became friends and neighbors, who knew that years later the Lord would build on that foundation and weld us together as husband and wife. Now after almost 20 years of marriage, I am still amazed at how He blesses us as we walk together. Also, Pastor David continues to be a treasured friend, Godly counselor, and encourager. Thanks, brother.

I owe a lot of hugs and evenings and weekends to my wife and children. Daddy's "second job" cost them some of Daddy. Thank you for sharing me with the book. I'm done feeding the dragon that lived downstairs.

Finally, I am compelled to thank the Lord. Not because I have to, but because I delight in it. He is my center, and the sweetest and greatest gift of all. I thank God for His blessings beyond measure, the sometimes difficult and often delightful paths that He has lead me down, and the joy and promise of eternity with Him.

—Eric Brierley

TELL US WHAT YOU THINK!

As the reader of this book, *you* are our most important critic and commentator. We value your opinion and want to know what we're doing right, what we could do better, what areas you'd like to see us publish in, and any other words of wisdom you're willing to pass our way.

As the Executive Editor for the Programming team at Macmillan Computer Publishing, I welcome your comments. You can fax, e-mail, or write me directly to let me know what you did or didn't like about this book—as well as what we can do to make our books stronger.

Please note that I cannot help you with technical problems related to the topic of this book, and that due to the high volume of mail I receive, I might not be able to reply to every message.

When you write, please be sure to include this book's title and author as well as your name and phone or fax number. I will carefully review your comments and share them with the author and editors who worked on the book.

Fax: 317-817-7070

E-mail: `prog@mcp.com`

Mail: Executive Editor

        Programming

        Macmillan Computer Publishing

        201 West 103rd Street

        Indianapolis, IN 46290 USA

INTRODUCTION

Microsoft Visual Basic 6 is a powerful and potent new release of Visual Basic. We'll introduce you to it here. Then we'll tell you what this book, *Visual Basic 6 How-To*, is all about and how to make the best use of it. We'll explain what's in the book and what's on the CD-ROM. Finally, we'll tell you how to load and run, browse, install, and use the projects on the CD.

About Visual Basic 6

Visual Basic comes in several different variations. Each of these adds more functionality than the previous. At this time, the following six versions of Visual Basic are available:

- ✔ Learning Edition—Demonstration version
- ✔ Control Creation Edition—Full features, but only builds executable ActiveX controls
- ✔ Professional—Creates all types of 32-bit executables for Windows
- ✔ Enterprise—Same as professional, plus all of the tools necessary to create enterprise-wide client/server applications
- ✔ Application Edition—Embedded macro language in Microsoft Office applications
- ✔ Scripting Edition—Provides server- and client-side scripting in Web pages

Lots of New Features

There are a lot of new features available in Visual Basic 6. You don't need the Professional or Enterprise editions to get the new stuff. The following are a few goodies that are available in all of the editions:

- ✔ ActiveX Data Objects are now included with Visual Basic
- ✔ File System Objects offer drive and folder navigation and text file creation without the use of controls or the `DIR$` command

✔ Format objects provide data conversion and formatting as data moves between a database and bound controls

✔ There are many new features and enhancements to support Internet integration including HTML page design with drag-and-drop control placement, and support for Dynamic HTML code authoring

✔ The `ImageList` control now supports GIF files

✔ The new `Validate` event allows data to be verified before a `LostFocus` event fires

New language features and statements include the following:

✔ Passing User Defined Types (UDT) as arguments and return values for properties and methods

✔ Functions can now return arrays

✔ New string functions include `Filter`, `InstrRev`, `Round`, `Replace`, and `Split`

✔ There are now `Drive`, `Folder`, and `File` collection objects

✔ New formatting statements include `FormatCurrency`, `FormatDateTime`, and `FormatPercent`

✔ New built-in constants cover date formats and `TriState` values

✔ `CallByName` enables properties and methods to be invoked using variable contents instead of explicitly coding the names

New controls include the following:

✔ ADO data control

✔ `DataGrid` Unicode-enabled version of older `DBGrid`

✔ Hierarchical Flexgrid updated version handles structured data from multiple tables

✔ `DataList` and `DataCombo` allow dynamic runtime switching of data sources

✔ `ImageCombo` is similar to the regular `ComboBox` but allows graphics for the list items

✔ Lightweight versions of `CheckBox`, `ComboBox`, `Command`, `Frame`, `ScrollBars`, `ListBox`, `Option`, and `TextBox`

The "What's New" section of the Visual Basic 6 help file is huge. The following are some of the new features and enhancements found in the Professional and Enterprise editions:

✔ ActiveX controls can be built that support apartment threading

✔ New features have been added to the `ListView`, `MSChart`, `ProgressBar`, `Slider`, `TabStrip`, and `TreeView` controls

✔ User controls can be built that support data binding

✔ Lightweight user controls are supported

✔ The new Data Interface Wizard replaces the Data Form Wizard

New controls include the following:

✔ `DataRepeater`

✔ `Coolbar` provides an Internet Explorer–style toolbar

✔ `DatePicker` offers drop-down date selection

✔ `FlatScrollBar`

✔ `Header` supports header items for tabular data

✔ `MonthView` lets users select dates and date ranges

✔ `Script` control allows you to add VBScript capabilities to any program

All of these new features should get you thinking about the great new applications that you can build. You will really enjoy working with Visual Basic 6. Use the How-Tos in this book to start your journey of exploration into the features and capabilities of this rich language.

About This Book

Following in the footsteps of earlier editions of *Visual Basic How-To*, this book has a wide diversity of examples and techniques for pushing Visual Basic 6 to its limits and beyond. You'll learn to create self-contained form objects. You will build an ActiveX control. You will use object-oriented class files to build customized container controls. Also, how to create tables from code, attach tables to a database, and access data in a Web page are some of the database techniques you will learn. In addition, there are details on how to subclass forms with the Windows API, evaluate the performance of your applications, build Windows 95/NT logo-compliant applications, and interact with the Internet.

Uses Windows APIs Extensively

Visual Basic has internalized a number of the Windows Application Program Interface (API) routines. For example, resource files can be added directly to projects, and text and graphics can be pulled from them and used directly in your applications. We will show you how to do this, and compare it with other methods for working with resources. But we've still found occasion to use dozens of Windows API calls in our How-Tos. Among other tasks, we will show you how to use Windows APIs to get disk drive characteristics, accept and process dropped files, and interact directly with registry entries.

Question-and-Answer Format

Don't worry, we wouldn't consider changing the format that worked so well in the earlier bestselling editions. You'll find questions and answers arranged by categories: controls, forms, class and object fundamentals, building ActiveX controls, Internet integration, performance, Windows API utilization, socket programming, database, logo compliance, extending Visual Basic, ActiveX Data Objects (ADO), and multitier Web applications. Each How-To contains a program solution with complete construction details. All the code, bitmaps, icons, forms, classes, and files are contained on the enclosed CD-ROM.

Expected Level of Reader

This book is for you, no matter what your level of expertise with Visual Basic. We've marked each How-To with a complexity level: Easy, Intermediate, or Advanced. If a How-To is marked Easy, it should be quick and simple to follow. Try these first if you're just starting out with Visual Basic. The ones marked Intermediate will be a bit longer and will often use a few simple Windows API commands. If you're more experienced using Visual Basic, you'll want check these out. If you're very comfortable in Visual Basic and want to see it and the Windows API really get a workout, check out some of the Advanced How-Tos.

What You Need to Use This Book

In order to use this book, you'll need a computer running Windows 95, Windows NT 4.0 Workstation, or Windows NT Server. And, of course, you will need Visual Basic 6. Most of the projects will run with the Professional Edition of Visual Basic. A few require the Enterprise Editions. Some of the projects will also run in previous versions of Visual Basic, and these are noted in the book.

How This Book Is Organized

This book is divided into 16 chapters, as follows:

✔ **Chapter 1: Extending Control Features**

This chapter takes you through examples of extending control functionality. You learn how to extend and build upon the standard features and capabilities of multiline text boxes, drop-down lists, list boxes, and common dialogs.

✔ **Chapter 2: The View Controls**

This chapter provides instruction on the use of the most interesting of the graphical controls shipped with Visual Basic 6. Specifically, you'll work with the `ListView` and `TreeView` controls, as well as the `ImageList` control, which helps manage the graphics you use with the `ListView` and `TreeView` controls.

✔ **Chapter 3: Class Fundamentals**

Although Visual Basic is not a truly object-oriented language, it is getting closer. By taking advantage of the available object-oriented techniques in Visual Basic, code can be created that is easier to understand and maintain. This chapter explores the basic principles for working with class modules and using them effectively in applications.

✔ **Chapter 4: Object Fundamentals**

There is a great deal of latent power in object-based development when building applications. Creating self-contained and reusable software components leverages the time and skills of software developers. This chapter introduces the fundamental concepts and terminology of object-oriented programming. These concepts are then applied to the development of some standard application dialogs. You will also learn how to integrate your own form-level components into the Visual Basic Application Wizard.

✔ **Chapter 5: ActiveX Controls**

This chapter shows how to build, use, and distribute custom ActiveX controls. The developer defines how the controls look; how they interact with the user; and what properties, methods, and events they will have.

✔ **Chapter 6: Internet Integration**

This chapter shows how to use Microsoft Visual Basic 6 to create applications that interact with the Internet and create robust Web pages. This is demonstrated by constructing an ActiveX document, creating a distributable CAB file, and including the component on a Web page. You will also learn how to use the WININET API functions and create your own Dynamic HTML DLL.

✔ **Chapter 7: Application Performance**

This chapter shows various techniques to evaluate some of the factors that contribute to overall application performance. Aspects of computational and graphics performance are explored. Two general-purpose utilities are also constructed in this chapter. The first analyzes characteristics of the source code. The second tool provides routines to profile the execution of a program.

✔ Chapter 8: Using the Win32 API

This chapter explores several different aspects of using the Win32 Application Program Interface, or API. The Win32 API is a feature-rich set of functions and subroutines that you can use to extend and add features to your program. In addition, many of the API calls can provide you with information about the system that cannot be obtained in any other way.

There are two specific aspects of the API that were not directly available to Visual Basic developers in previous versions of the language: callbacks and subclassing. Now, with version 6, you can call API functions that use callbacks and set hooks for subclassing. Examples of the use of both of these techniques are included in Chapter 8.

✔ Chapter 9: Windows Socket Programming

This chapter starts by building a simple socket-based task monitor. The initial How-To also establishes baseline code that is used as the foundation for the other examples. The baseline code is used to build a simple time server that synchronizes the local system times of multiple systems. A simple object pool manager is also constructed using the same socket management techniques. Finally, sockets are used to check for electronic mail on a POP3 server.

✔ Chapter 10: Forms

This chapter shows how you can add custom events and properties to a form. You also learn how to add icons to the Windows 95 and Windows NT desktop tray, and how to animate the tray icon.

✔ Chapter 11: Databases

This chapter introduces some of the basic concepts behind using Visual Basic to work with databases. The native database for Visual Basic is the Microsoft Access database, which is accessed through the Jet Engine. You can also access other types of databases using ISAM (Indexed Sequential Access Method) or ODBC (Open Database Connectivity) drivers. This chapter covers using the Jet Engine in its default mode to access a native database, as well as introduces you to using ISAM drivers to access other types of data. You will also learn to access data from an HTML Web page, and how to use the new `DataRepeater` control.

✔ **Chapter 12: Logo-Compliant Applications**

Many developers seek to have their applications certified to carry the *Designed for Microsoft Windows NT and Windows 95* logo. Building compliant applications is still desirable even if the certification is not sought or obtained. Building compliant applications ensures that the programs behave in a manner consistent with user expectations. This chapter shows how to build applications that provide the major logo-compliance features.

✔ **Chapter 13: Extending VB and Managing Development**

Microsoft provides a powerful extensibility object model that lets you add to the Visual Basic integrated development environment (IDE). It allows manipulation of form objects, user interface objects, code objects, project and component objects, and add-in management objects, as well as provides the capability to respond to events in the IDE such as project saves. Also included is the repository, which is used by tools such as the Visual Component Manager to provide persistent object storage and manipulation capabilities. In this chapter, you will see how you can use these tools to manage team development, to enhance code reuse, and to simplify advanced tasks such as code generation by writing add-ins and wizards.

✔ **Chapter 14: Advanced Data Objects**

ActiveX Data Objects (ADO) is a very thin and fast object layer that sits on top of ODBC. This chapter explains the differences between ADO and the older data object layers, DAO and RDO. You learn to interact with ADO recordsets and manage the data structures returned by the ADO methods. A simple database front-end is also built using the new ADO data control.

✔ **Chapter 15: Building Multitier Web-Based Applications**

This chapter introduces you to the Microsoft Solutions Framework (MSF) Application Model for building multitier applications. This new architecture utilizes a services-based paradigm with three primary layers. The introduction in this chapter walks you through the architecture and the component design process. You then learn to build data and business objects, and applications that use these remote objects. The final How-To explains how to write components that recognize and support the features of Microsoft Transaction Server (MTS).

✔ Chapter 16: Miscellaneous Topics

There are a few examples we wanted to include that did not fit in any specific category. They are included in this chapter. The examples include exposing an object to multiple applications, getting Web server data from an ActiveX control, and information on using the Class Builder Utility.

About the CD-ROM

The included CD-ROM is packed with all the files you'll need to run the projects in this book. Actually, there are more than 80 projects on the CD.

You'll find that the projects on the CD are organized by chapter and How-To. There's a folder for each chapter and, within each chapter, a folder for each How-To. In the How-To folder, you'll find the Visual Basic Project file and all the forms, classes, graphics, files, and general modules needed to run the project.

Ready to Run in Visual Basic 6

The projects are ready to run directly from the CD. You can just start Visual Basic, open a Project file (.VBP), and run it. But be aware that if you load and run a project from the CD without copying it to your hard drive, you won't be able to save changes. Some How-Tos attempt to write to the project folder and this will result in a runtime error. You will need to copy these projects to your hard drive to run them.

Read the License Agreement

You'll find a License Agreement at the back of this book. Please read it first to review your installation options. Any minor code changes made to a project after the book goes to print will be listed in a errata file on Macmillan's Web site at `http://www.mcp.com/info`.

CHAPTER 1

EXTENDING CONTROL FEATURES

1

EXTENDING CONTROL FEATURES

How do I...

1.1 **Integrate the Open/Save common dialog box into an application?**

1.2 **Extend the functionality of the multiline textbox control?**

1.3 **Extend the functionality in the combo and list box controls?**

1.4 **Use drag and drop to implement a sort order tool?**

With each release of Visual Basic, the number of controls provided with the product increases. In addition, as more applications take advantage of ActiveX technologies, controls used by these applications are also installed on your system, and you can sometimes use these controls in your Visual Basic applications. You can also find dozens of controls advertised for purchase in any Visual Basic magazine or on Visual Basic Web sites.

Most of the control functionality you need to implement in your Visual Basic applications, however, can be achieved with the stock controls shipped with the product. You needn't look beyond the shipping Visual Basic toolbox to find all the tools you need. With some creativity and sharp Visual Basic code, you can extend the functionality of almost every Visual Basic control. Opportunities are available, from the mundane textbox control to the tired option button control, and you can develop working solutions to real programming problems.

This chapter takes you through numerous examples of extending control functionality. You will learn how to extend and build on the standard features and capabilities of the edit, drop-down list, list box, command button, and common dialog box controls.

1.1 Integrate the Open/Save Common Dialog Box into an Application

Applications sometimes require the user to specify a file to be opened in the application, or perhaps the name of a file to which data in the application can be saved. Building the interface in which the user specifies the name of the file, the directory location of the file, as well as extra pieces of functionality, can be time-consuming and produce unneeded code overhead. In addition, users are accustomed to the standard Open and Save dialog boxes used in all of today's most popular commercial applications. Integrating the Open common dialog box control in an application saves time, reduces code overhead, and presents a familiar interface to users of your application.

1.2 Extend the Functionality of the Multiline Textbox Control

Next to the label control, the textbox control is probably the most used of all the Visual Basic controls. By setting the `multiline` property of the textbox control to `True`, however, you can use the control to present and edit large amounts of text. Working with large files in the control, however, can be tedious. For example, you might need to retrieve a certain line of text from the control or simply evaluate how many lines of text fill up the control. The multiline textbox control provides enhanced functionality over the standard textbox control, and you can extend its power with a handful of programming tricks.

1.3 Extend the Functionality in the Combo and List Box Controls

The two controls that provide lists of items to the user, the combination drop-down list and the standard list box, can be thought of as the neglected siblings of all the Visual Basic controls. Although new controls are developed and features are added to existing controls, the list box and combination drop-down list have changed very little over the course of the five major versions of Visual Basic. Developers have been forced to work around and provide creative solutions to solve and address some of the long-standing complaints. You will learn in this chapter how to enhance the functionality of these two useful controls.

1.4 Use Drag and Drop to Implement a Sort Order Tool

The drag-and-drop functionality enables the Visual Basic developer to create visually interesting and very easy-to-use applications. Although most drag-and-drop implementations involve moving a picture control across a form or moving an item from one list box to another, you can create drag-and-drop solutions involving any control. As an example, you can build a drag-and-drop solution to enable the user to specify a sort order for some data in your application. This chapter shows you how to use drag-and-drop techniques to build a custom hierarchy presentation in order for the user to construct a sort order.

COMPLEXITY
BEGINNING

1.1 How do I...
Integrate the Open/Save common dialog box into an application?

COMPATIBILITY: VISUAL BASIC 3, 4, 5, AND 6

Problem

Some applications require the user to specify the name of a file. This filename might be specified so that the file can be opened in the application or so that data can be written to the file. The user might also have the opportunity to specify the location of the file.

To maximize usability for the application, it makes sense that the user interface for selecting a file be similar to that provided by many popular applications with which the user might already be familiar. The problem is, however, that implementing a file selection dialog box from scratch requires much control and code overhead. In addition, providing some of the extra features that users have become accustomed to, such as filtering the list of files by type displayed in the dialog box or prompting users if they supply the name of a file that doesn't exist, also can be time-consuming.

Technique

The technique required to address this problem is simple. Starting with version 3.0 of Visual Basic, developers can integrate any standard Windows dialog boxes into their applications. These dialog boxes include the familiar Open, Print, Color Selection, Font Selection, and Save. To implement these dialog boxes, the Visual Basic developer adds the special common dialog box control to any form in the project. Next, the developer programs the control, assigning it properties that specify which type of dialog box should appear, such as the Open or Font Selection dialog boxes, as well as any dialog-specific behavior, such as the contents of the Files of Type drop-down list found in most file selection dialog boxes.

Steps

Open and run the OPEN_DLG.vbp project. Choose File, Open from the menu. Notice that the standard Open dialog box appears, as shown in Figure 1.1. Notice also that the Files of Type drop-down list is empty.

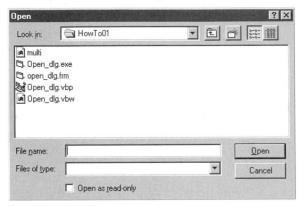

Figure 1.1 You can integrate the standard Open dialog box into a Visual Basic application.

Click the Cancel button and notice that a message box appears, reporting that no file was selected. Choose File, Open and this time choose a file in the dialog box. Change directories, if required, in order to find a file to select. Click the OK button and notice that a message appears, reporting the name of the file you selected. Click OK to clear the dialog box.

In the File Spec, enter any file specification mask, such as *.*. Next, enter a phrase that describes the mask in the Description textbox control. Click the Add to List button, and the mask and its description are added to the list on the right side of the dialog box. Add as many file specification masks and descriptions as you like. When complete, choose File, Open. Notice that each mask description appears in the Files of Type drop-down list, and when you select one, the mask is applied to the list of files. Click the Cancel button and then click the Remove from List button to remove masks from the list.

To continue the demonstration, choose the Allow Multi-File Select option. Next, choose File, Open and select more than one file by pressing Shift for a contiguous file range or Ctrl for a noncontiguous file range. Click Cancel and then clear the Allow Multi-Select option. Choose File, Open again and notice that you can select only one file at a time.

Choose both the Path Must Exist option and the File Must Exist option. Next, choose File, Open. Enter the name of a nonexistent path and filename in the File control and click OK. Notice that you are informed that the path you supplied doesn't exist. Click OK to clear the message and then click Cancel.

Clear the Path Must Exist option and then choose File, Open. This time, enter the name of a nonexistent file into the File Name box and then choose Open. Notice that you are informed that the file doesn't exist.

Next, choose the Raise Error on Cancel option. Choose File, Open and then immediately choose Cancel. Notice that you're no longer informed that no file was selected, only that Cancel was selected. Next, choose the Force Current Directory and try to change directories in the Open dialog box. Notice that this isn't possible as long as the Force Current Directory option is selected.

Choose the Hide Read-Only check box. Choose File, Open and notice that the Open As Read-Only check box no longer appears in the Open dialog box. Here are the steps required to create this project:

1. Create a new standard exe project named OPEN_DLG.VBP. Choose Projects, Components from the menu and then choose Microsoft Common Dialog Control 6.0 from the list box that appears under the Controls tab. If the control doesn't appear in the list, choose Browse to locate the MSCOMDLG.OCX file.

2. Add the objects listed in Table 1.1 to **Form1**, using the properties shown in the table.

Table 1.1 Objects and Properties for Form1

OBJECT	PROPERTY	VALUE
Form	Name	frmOpen_dlg
	Caption	VB 6 How-To 1.1
	Height	4395
	Left	2115
	Top	2205
	Width	8595
	LinkTopic	Form1
	ScaleHeight	4395
	ScaleWidth	8595
Frame	Name	Frame1
	Caption	File Spec Options
	Height	1935
	Left	120
	TabIndex	9
	Top	120
	Width	8415

continued on next page

continued from previous page

OBJECT	PROPERTY	VALUE
CommandButton	Name	cbRemoveFromList
	Caption	Remove from List
	Height	375
	Left	5160
	TabIndex	5
	Top	240
	Width	1575
TextBox	Name	txtSpec
	Height	285
	Left	1440
	TabIndex	1
	Top	360
	Width	735
TextBox	Name	txtDesc
	Height	285
	Left	1440
	TabIndex	2
	Top	720
	Width	3015
CommandButton	Name	cbAddFileSpec
	Caption	Add to List
	Height	375
	Left	1440
	TabIndex	3
	Top	1080
	Width	1215
ListBox	Name	lbFileSpecs
	Height	1035
	Left	5160
	TabIndex	4
	Top	720
	Width	2895
Label	Name	Label1
	Caption	File Spec
	Height	255
	Left	360

OBJECT	PROPERTY	VALUE
	TabIndex	11
	Top	360
	Width	735
Label	Name	Label2
	Caption	Description
	Height	255
	Left	360
	TabIndex	10
	Top	720
	Width	855
Frame	Name	Options
	Caption	Options
	Height	2055
	Left	120
	TabIndex	0
	Top	2160
	Width	8415
CheckBox	Name	ckRaiseCancelError
	Caption	Raise Error on Cancel
	Height	255
	Left	3480
	TabIndex	18
	Top	1320
	Width	2175
CheckBox	Name	ckForceCurrentDirectory
	Caption	Force Current Directory
	Height	255
	Left	3480
	TabIndex	17
	Tag	cdlOFNNoChangeDir
	Top	1080
	Width	2175
CheckBox	Name	ckHideReadOnly
	Caption	Hide Read Only Check Box
	Height	255

continued on next page

continued from previous page

OBJECT	PROPERTY	VALUE
	Left	3480
	TabIndex	15
	Tag	cdlOFNHideReadOnly
	Top	600
	Width	3135
CheckBox	Name	ckDiffDefaultExtension
	Caption	Notify If Different Than Default Extension
	Height	255
	Left	3480
	TabIndex	13
	Tag	cdlOFNExtensionDifferent
	Top	360
	Width	3375
CheckBox	Name	ckFileCreation
	Caption	Prompt for File Creation
	Height	255
	Left	480
	TabIndex	12
	Tag	cdlOFNCreatePrompt
	Top	1320
	Width	2055
CheckBox	Name	ckFileMustExist
	Caption	File Must Exist
	Height	255
	Left	480
	TabIndex	8
	Top	820
	Width	2295
CheckBox	Name	ckPathMustExist
	Caption	Path Must Exist
	Height	195
	Left	480
	TabIndex	7
	Top	620
	Width	2055

OBJECT	PROPERTY	VALUE
CheckBox	Name	ckAllowMultiSelect
	Caption	Allow Multi-File Select
	Height	255
	Left	480
	TabIndex	6
	Tag	cdlOFNAllowMultiselect
	Top	360
	Width	2295
CommonDialog	Name	CommonDialog1
	Left	9120
	Top	5280
Menu	Name	mnuFile
	Caption	&File
Menu	Name	mnuOpen
	Caption	&Open

3. Switch to the form created in step 1 and add the following code to the Declarations section of the form. The first three lines of the code declare module-levels variables used throughout the project. The first variable, m_FileSpec, stores the string that's used by the common dialog box control to populate the Files of Type drop-down list. The second variable, m_sSelectedFile, stores the name of the file chosen by the user. The third variable stores the value of the **Flags** parameter that is passed to the control. This variable stores the sum of all the flag values, and it's calculated just before the dialog box appears. **Flags** is the term used to describe the different options you can use with the common dialog box control, such as those described earlier in this How-To.

```
Dim m_sFileSpec As String
Dim m_sSelectedFile As String
Dim m_Flags As Long
Const ADD_SPEC = 1
Const REMOVE_SPEC = 2
```

4. Add the **CalcFlags** subroutine to **Form1**. This routine sets the value of the m_Flags variable by checking the state of each check box on the form. Each check box corresponds to a specific flag appropriate to the Open dialog box component of the common dialog box control.

```
Private Sub CalcFlags()

    m_Flags = 0
```

```
    If ckAllowMultiSelect.Value Then
        m_Flags = m_Flags + cdlOFNAllowMultiselect
    End If
    '
    If ckDiffDefaultExtension.Value Then
        m_Flags = m_Flags + cdlOFNExtensionDifferent
    End If
    '
    If ckFileCreation.Value Then
        m_Flags = m_Flags + cdlOFNCreatePrompt
    End If
    '
    If ckFileMustExist.Value Then
        m_Flags = m_Flags + cdlOFNFileMustExist
    End If
    '
    If ckForceCurrentDirectory.Value Then
        m_Flags = m_Flags + cdlOFNNoChangeDir
    End If
    '
    If ckHideReadOnly.Value Then
        m_Flags = m_Flags + cdlOFNHideReadOnly
    End If
    '
    If ckPathMustExist.Value Then
        m_Flags = m_Flags + cdlOFNPathMustExist
    End If
    '
End Sub
```

5. Add the following code to the **Click** event of the **cbAddFileSpec** control. This subroutine fires the **ManageFileSpecList** subroutine. The routine receives the following parameters: the action that is being taken on the list (in this case, adding an item to the list) and the item in the list that is being acted on (**Null**, the item being added to the list).

```
Private Sub cbAddFileSpec_Click()
    '
    ManageFileSpecList ADD_SPEC, Null
    '
End Sub
```

6. Add the following code to the **Click** event of the **cbRemoveFromList** control. This subroutine, like the subroutine described in step 5, fires the **ManageFileSpecList** routine.

```
Private Sub cbRemoveFromList_Click()
    '
    If lbFileSpecs.ListCount > 0 Then
        If lbFileSpecs.ListIndex > -1 Then
            ManageFileSpecList REMOVE_SPEC, lbFileSpecs.ListIndex
        End If
    End If
    '
End Sub
```

7. Add the `ManageFileSpecList` subroutine to `Form1`. This routine manages the population of the list that the demonstration program uses to show the different file spec masks and descriptions. The first parameter determines whether an item should be added or removed from the list. If the first parameter specifies that an item should be removed from the list, the second parameter specifies the item's index.

The second function this subroutine performs is creating the string that the common dialog box control requires for populating the Files of Type drop-down list in the Open dialog box. Because the list in the demonstration programs combines the file spec mask and the description with a hyphen symbol, the following routine must first parse each string in the list to determine the mask portion and the description portion of each combination. When parsed, the routine combines the description and the mask together in a string, each element separated by a pipe (¦) symbol. Every combination of description and mask is also separated by a pipe symbol. This string is set as the `Filter` property of the common dialog box control just before it appears.

```
Public Sub ManageFileSpecList(Action As Integer, Spec As Variant)
    '
    Dim sSpec As String
    Dim sDesc As String
    Dim iHyphen As Integer
    Dim iDescLength As Integer
    '
    If Action = REMOVE_SPEC Then
       lbFileSpecs.RemoveItem Data
    Else
        '
        If txtSpec.Text <> "" Then
            lbFileSpecs.AddItem txtSpec.Text & "  -  " & _
txtDesc.Text
            txtSpec.Text = ""
            txtDesc.Text = ""
        Else
            txtSpec.SetFocus
        End If
    End If
    '
m_sFileSpec = ""
    For iCounter = 0 To lbFileSpecs.ListCount - 1
        lbFileSpecs.ListIndex = iCounter
        iHyphen = InStr(1, lbFileSpecs.Text, "-")
        sSpec = Left$(lbFileSpecs.Text, iHyphen - 3)
        sDesc = Right$(lbFileSpecs.Text, (Len(lbFileSpecs.Text) _
- (iHyphen + 2)))
        m_sFileSpec = m_sFileSpec + sDesc + "¦" + sSpec + "¦"
    Next
    m_sFileSpec = Left$(m_sFileSpec, Len(m_sFileSpec) - 1)
    '
End Sub
```

8. Add the following code to the `Click` event for the `ckRaiseCancelError` control. Unlike the options defined with the `Flags` value, the `CancelError` value is defined as a property for the control. When this property is set to `True`, a trappable error is raised when the user chooses Cancel from the common dialog box.

```
Private Sub ckRaiseCancelError_Click()
    '
    If ckRaiseCancelError.Value Then
        CommonDialog1.CancelError = True
    Else
        CommonDialog1.CancelError = False
    End If
    '
End Sub
```

9. Add the following code to the `Click` event for the `mnuOpen` menu control. The code in this subroutine sets the critical properties for the common dialog box control and then displays the dialog box. The `Flags` property is set to the module-level `m_Flags` variable, and the `Filter` property is set to the value of the variable storing the pipe-delimited string of file spec masks and descriptions. To display the Open dialog box, the `ShowOpen` method is used with the common dialog box control. The dialog box remains open until the user chooses Open or Cancel. At that point, the filename property is set, and you can execute whatever action on the file is required.

```
Private Sub mnuOpen_Click()
    '
    On Error GoTo ErrHandler:
    '
    CalcFlags
    CommonDialog1.Flags = m_Flags
    CommonDialog1.Filter = m_sFileSpec
    CommonDialog1.ShowOpen
    MsgBox "File(s) selected: " + CommonDialog1.filename
    Exit Sub
    '
ErrHandler:
    '
    MsgBox "Cancel was pressed"
    '
End Sub
```

How It Works

The common dialog box control is multipurpose. This means you can use the same control for selecting a file and for choosing a color or font. Using the common dialog box control for another purpose simply involves setting the proper flags and then calling the appropriate **Show** method. For example, to display the Color Selection dialog box, you set the flags specific to the Color dialog box, and then you call the **ShowColor** method for the control.

Comments

By using the common dialog box you can make your applications look and behave like other popular applications. This can be an important aspect of your product if it is competing against other products. The one that looks and acts like products the purchaser already owns or is familiar with will have an advantage over those that present their own way of doing common tasks.

COMPLEXITY

BEGINNING

1.2 How do I...
Extend the functionality of the multiline textbox control?

COMPATIBILITY: VISUAL BASIC 4, 5, AND 6

Problem

The multiline textbox control is helpful in presenting a large amount of textual data in a single control. Although ActiveX technologies present the possibility of interesting alternatives, such as embedding WordPad or some other editing control, using the multiline textbox control is the easiest.

Developers need help in working with the multiple lines in the control, however. Accessing a specific line of text stored in the control is difficult. Using an array to store all the lines or rereading each line in the file when text is shown in the control would require too much code, and the processing would be too slow. An even tougher task is retrieving the first visible line of text in the control.

Without special calculations, it's difficult to determine which line of text appears at the top of the control after the user has scrolled through the list. In addition, getting an accurate count of the number of lines in the file can also be tedious.

Technique

The Windows API solves lots of problems for the Visual Basic programmer, especially for the programmer looking to extend the functionality in some of the standard controls. The **SendMessage** function can be used to affect the behavior of the textbox control in many ways, each dependent on a specific parameter sent to the routine. For example, by sending an integer value signifying a line number in the control, **SendMessage** returns the text at that line number. The following steps show three examples of the **SendMessage** function as a technique to extend the functionality of the multiline textbox control.

Steps

Open and run the MULTILINE.VBP project. Click the Load button. The multiline textbox control at the bottom of the dialog box is populated with the content of the CHP1.TXT file, which can be found in the **Chapter1** directory. Notice also that the textbox control in the Retrieve Single Line of Text frame is populated with the first line of text shown in the multiline textbox control, as shown in Figure 1.2. Also notice that the textbox control in the Number of Lines frame shows the number of lines containing text in the multiline textbox control.

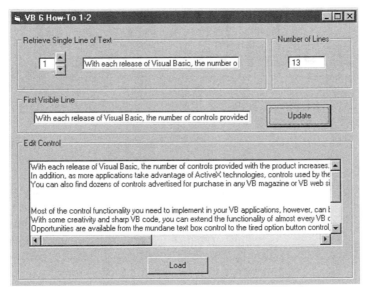

Figure 1.2 The SendMessage function can be used to extend the functionality of the textbox control.

Last, use the scrollbars to scroll through the text in the multiline textbox control. Be sure to scroll so that a line other than the first is shown at the top of textbox control. Next, click the Update button, and the first line visible in the multiline textbox control appears in the textbox in the First Line Visible frame. Scroll either up or down in the multiline textbox control and click the Update button again. Notice how the textbox control is updated to show the new line at the top of the multiline textbox control.

Complete the following steps to create this project:

1. Create a new standard exe project named MULTILINE.VBP. Choose Projects, Components from the menu and then choose Microsoft Common Controls-2 6.0 from the list box that appears under the Controls tab.

2. Add the objects listed in Table 1.2 to Form1, using the properties shown in the table.

Table 1.2 Objects and Properties for Form1

OBJECT	PROPERTY	VALUE
Form	Name	Form1
	Caption	VB 6 How-To 1-2
	Height	5745
	Left	2085
	Top	1230
	Width	7680
	LinkTopic	Form1
	ScaleHeight	5745
	ScaleWidth	7680
Frame	Name	Frame4
	Caption	First Visible Line
	Height	855
	Left	120
	TabIndex	9
	Top	1560
	Width	7455
CommandButton	Name	cmbUpdate
	Caption	Update
	Height	495
	Left	5520
	TabIndex	11
	Top	240
	Width	1455
TextBox	Name	txtFirstVisibleLine
	Height	285
	Left	360
	TabIndex	10
	Top	360
	Width	4815

continued on next page

continued from previous page

OBJECT	PROPERTY	VALUE
Frame	Name	Frame3
	Caption	Number of Lines
	Height	1215
	Left	5760
	TabIndex	6
	Top	240
	Width	1815
TextBox	Name	txtNumberofLines
	Height	285
	Left	360
	TabIndex	7
	Top	480
	Width	855
Frame	Name	Frame2
	Caption	Edit Control
	Height	3135
	Left	120
	TabIndex	4
	Top	2520
	Width	7455
CommandButton	Name	cbLoadFile
	Caption	Load
	Height	375
	Left	2880
	TabIndex	8
	Top	2640
	Width	1335
TextBox	Name	txtMultiLine
	Height	1935
	Left	240
	MultiLine	True
	ScrollBars	3 - Both
	TabIndex	5
	Top	480
	Width	6975

OBJECT	PROPERTY	VALUE
Frame	Name	Frame1
	Caption	Retrieve Single Line of Text
	Height	1215
	Left	120
	TabIndex	0
	Top	240
	Width	5535
TextBox	Name	txtLineNumber
	Height	285
	Left	480
	TabIndex	3
	Text	1
	Top	480
	Width	375
UpDown	Name	UpDown1
	Height	525
	Left	840
	TabIndex	2
	Top	360
	Width	240
	BuddyControl	txtLineNumber
	BuddyDispid	196618
	OrigLeft	855
	OrigTop	360
	OrigRight	1095
	OrigBottom	885
	Increment	1
	SyncBuddy	True
	BuddyProperty	0
	Enabled	True
TextBox	Name	txtLineFromFile
	Height	285
	Left	1440
	TabIndex	1
	Top	480
	Width	3495

3. Create a new module. Add the following code to the new module. The first line is the declaration for the **SendMessage** function. The three constant values are possible parameter values for the **SendMessage** function. How each of these parameters is used is covered later in this How-To.

```
Declare Function SendMessage Lib "user32" Alias "SendMessageA"
(ByVal hwnd As Long, ByVal wMsg As Long, ByVal wParam As Long, _
lParam As Any) As Long _
Public Const EM_GETFIRSTVISIBLELINE = &HCE
Public Const EM_GETLINE = &HC4
Public Const EM_GETLINECOUNT = &HBA
```

4. Switch to the form created in step 1 and add the following code to the Declarations section of the form. Each of the three lines declares a module-level variable that the project needs in order to help manage working with the Windows API calls.

```
Dim m_sLineString As String * 1056
Dim m_lngRet As Long
Dim m_sRetString As String
```

5. Add the following code to the **Click** event for the Load button. This code loads the content of the file CHP1.TXT into the multiline textbox control. The last two commands in the event procedure call two other routines that initialize a few other controls on the form. The functionality of these two routines, the **txtLineNumber_Change** and **CountLines** subroutines, is covered later in this How-To.

```
Private Sub cbLoadFile_Click()
    '
    Dim iHandle As Integer
    Dim iFileString As String
    Dim iLine As String
    '
    iHandle = FreeFile
    '
    Open "c:\vb6ht\chapter01\chp1.txt" For Input As #iHandle
    Do While Not EOF(iHandle)
        Line Input #iHandle, sLine
        iFileString = iFileString + sLine + vbCr + vbLf
    Loop
    Close #iHandle
    txtMultiLine.Text = iFileString
    '
    Call txtLineNumber_Change
    CountLines
    UpDown1.Min = 1
    UpDown1.Max = m_lngRet
    UpDown1.Value = 1
    '
End Sub
```

6. Add the `ReadLine` function to `Form1`. This is the first of the functions in this project that call the Windows API. The `ReadLine` function returns the text at the line in the multiline textbox control passed to the function. The `ReadLine` function achieves this by calling the `SendMessage` function in the Windows API. By passing `SendMessage` the handle to the multiline textbox control and other information, the function updates the variable passed in with the text of the line.

Of note is the first line of the routine, which fills in the string variable being passed to the `SendMessage` function with spaces. The variable's length is fixed and is specified in the declaration of the variable in the form's code module. The length of the string is fixed by the calling routine to keep the `SendMessage` function from writing over another piece of memory, which could crash the application.

```
Private Function ReadLine(iLine As Integer) As String
    '
    Dim m_intRet as Long
    m_sLineString = Space$(1056)
    '
    m_intRet - SendMessage(txtMultiLine.hwnd, EM_GETLINE, iLine, _
        ByVal m_sLineString)
    ReadLine = m_sLineString
    '
End Function
```

7. Add the `CountLines` subroutine to `Form1`. Like the `ReadLine` function described in step 6, the `CountLines` subroutine also calls the `SendMessage` function in the Windows API. When you use the `SendMessage` function to count the number of lines in a multiline textbox control, the only parameters required are the handle to the control and the message itself, `EM_GETLINECOUNT` in this case. Rather than write to a passed-in variable, however, as is the case with the implementation of the function in step 6, here the `SendMessage` function simply returns the number of lines used in the control. The `CountLines` subroutine performs double duty because the `txtNumberofLines` control is updated with the value returned from the `SendMessage` function.

```
Private Sub CountLines()
    '
    m_lngRet = SendMessage(txtMultiLine.hwnd, EM_GETLINECOUNT, 0, 0)
    txtNumberofLines.Text = Str$(m_lngRet)
    '
End Sub
```

8. The final code in this project that calls the `SendMessage` function is the `ReadFirstVisibleLine` function. The message sent to `SendMessage` in this function asks for the number of the line that appears at the top of the multiline textbox control. For example, if the control is loaded with a 100-line file, and because of scrolling, the 50th line appears at the top of the control, the **SendMessage** returns a value of **49** because the index of the list is zero-based. For the **SendMessage** to return this data, the handle of the multiline textbox control is passed along with the **EM_GIRSTVISIBLELINE** message.

```
Private Function ReadFirstVisibleLine() As Integer
    '
    ReadFirstVisibleLine = SendMessage(txtMultiLine.hwnd, _
        EM_GETFIRSTVISIBLELINE, 0, 0)
    '
End Function
```

9. Add the following code to the **Click** event for the **cmbUpdate** button. This code updates the **txtFirstVisibleLine** textbox control with the topmost visible line in the multiline textbox control. This is accomplished by calling the **ReadLine** function. The number of the line that **ReadLine** returns is based on the **ReadFirstVisibleLine** function, which returns the number of the line.

```
Private Sub cmbUpdate_Click()
    '
    txtFirstVisibleLine.Text = ReadLine(ReadFirstVisibleLine())
    '
End Sub
```

10. Use the following code to create the **Change** event for **txtLineNumber**. When this control's text is changed, a read takes place that updates the viewable text.

```
Private Sub txtLineNumber_Change()
    '
    txtLineFromFile.Text = ReadLine(Val(txtLineNumber.Text) - 1)
    '
End Sub
```

11. Add the following code to the **Change** event of the **Updown1** control. This code enables the user to change the line number displayed, triggering the **Change** event for the **txtLineNumber** control.

```
Private Sub UpDown1_Change()
    txtLineNumber.Text = Str$(UpDown1.Value)
End Sub
```

How It Works

Most of the interesting functionality in this project comes from the use of the **SendMessage** Windows API function. The **SendMessage** function is used by Visual Basic developers, as well as persons writing C and C++ code to develop Windows applications. Without diving too deep into the architecture of

Windows, applications and the operating system work by sending messages. When a message is received, a specific action occurs, such as painting an icon on the screen. The application shown in this How-To uses fewer than a half dozen `SendMessage` calls. Windows 95 and Windows NT make thousands of `SendMessage` calls for certain applications.

Comments

This How-To showed how to use the Windows API `SendMessage` function to enhance the textbox control. There are many Windows API functions available to Visual Basic developers. These functions can cut down on coding and provide functionality that is difficult or impossible to duplicate using just Visual Basic code. Using the Windows API viewer that comes with Visual Basic, you can look up API functions and get the declarations needed to access them from Visual Basic code. You can also look up type declarations that the functions will need.

COMPLEXITY
INTERMEDIATE

1.3 How do I...
Extend the functionality in the combo and list box controls?

COMPATIBILITY: VISUAL BASIC 4, 5, AND 6

Problem

Like the multiline textbox control described in How-To 1.2, the list box and combination drop-down list are used extensively in Visual Basic and other Windows applications. Standard functionality in the control provides most of what any Visual Basic developer needs in implementing the control, but some features are missing.

For example, it would be nice if the combination drop-down list automatically opened when the user tabbed to the control. Also, clearing either the drop-down list or the standard list box can take a long time if the method of stepping though the list and firing the `RemoveItem` method is used. A quick way to clear the list would be helpful. Also, it would be convenient to control the maximum length of text that a user could add to either type of list.

Technique

Although programmers who use the Win32 Software Development Kit (SDK) and C++ to build applications can extend functionality of these controls, it's difficult to do so with the support Visual Basic provides. Using the Windows API, however, it's possible to add functionality to any control or process in Visual Basic, such as the list box and combination drop-down list. The `SendMessage` control is used to add the functionality previously described in the "Problem" section. The `SendMessage` routine is extremely flexible and powerful. It's used with any control in Visual Basic, and the parameters passed to it determine its behavior, such as specifying what control to work on, what to do to the control, and any special data that the routine needs.

Steps

Open and run the EXT_LIST.VBP project. The two list boxes at the bottom of the dialog box are automatically populated with 500 items each. Later on in the demonstration, the list amount is set to 2000 and 5000 items. Choose the Slow button. Both lists are cleared, and the time to clear both is reported. After you click OK in the dialog boxes where the time was reported, both lists are repopulated. Next, choose the Fast button. Notice how much faster both lists are cleared, as shown in Figure 1.3.

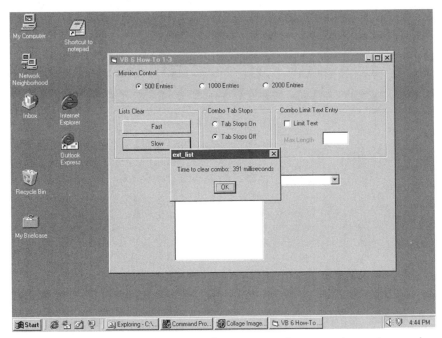

Figure 1.3 The speed of certain form operations can be enhanced through the use of Windows API functions.

Now, press the Tab key to move through the different controls on the form. Be sure to pass through the combination drop-down list. Notice that the control doesn't drop down. Press Tab until a control other than the drop-down list is selected. Choose the Tab Stops On option button and press Tab to move through the controls again. Notice this time how the combination drop-down list opens as you pass through it.

For the last part of the demonstration, choose the Limit Text option and then enter a value in the Max Length text box. Click the drop-down list and attempt to enter a value greater in length than the value you entered. Notice you are restricted from doing so.

To create this project, complete the following steps:

1. Create a new standard exe project named EXT_LIST.VBP.

2. Add the objects listed in Table 1.3 to Form1, using the properties shown in the table.

Table 1.3 Objects and Properties for Form1

OBJECT	PROPERTY	VALUE
Form	Name	frmTabStop
	Caption	Form1
	Height	6885
	Left	915
	Top	1695
	Width	7995
	LinkTopic	Form1
	ScaleHeight	6885
	ScaleWidth	7995Frame
Frame	Name	Frame5
	Caption	Combo Limit Text Entry
	Height	1455
	Left	4680
	TabIndex	9
	Top	1200
	Width	3135
CheckBox	Name	ckLimitText
	Caption	Limit Text
	Height	255
	Left	240
	TabIndex	15
	Top	360
	Width	1935

continued on next page

continued from previous page

OBJECT	PROPERTY	VALUE
TextBox	Name	txtMaxLength
	Enabled	False
	Height	375
	Left	1320
	TabIndex	10
	Top	720
	Width	735
Label	Name	lblMaxlength
	Caption	Max Length
	Enabled	False
	Height	255
	Left	240
	TabIndex	11
	Top	840
	Width	975
Frame	Name	Frame4
	Caption	Mission Control
	Height	975
	Left	120
	TabIndex	8
	Top	120
	Width	7695
OptionButton	Name	rb2000Entries
	Caption	2000 Entries
	Height	255
	Left	4200
	TabIndex	14
	Top	360
	Width	1335
OptionButton	Name	rb1000Entries
	Caption	1000 Entries
	Height	255
	Left	2400
	TabIndex	13
	Top	360
	Width	1335

OBJECT	PROPERTY	VALUE
OptionButton	Name	rb500Entries
	Caption	500 Entries
	Height	255
	Left	600
	TabIndex	12
	Top	360
	Value	True
	Width	1335
Frame	Name	Frame3
	Caption	Lists Clear
	Height	1455
	Left	120
	TabIndex	5
	Top	1200
	Width	2415
CommandButton	Name	cbFast
	Caption	Fast
	Height	375
	Left	240
	TabIndex	7
	Top	360
	Width	1935
CommandButton	Name	cbSlow
	Caption	Slow
	Height	375
	Left	240
	TabIndex	6
	Top	840
	Width	1935
Frame	Name	frm
	Caption	Combo Tab Stops
	Height	1455
	Left	2640
	TabIndex	2
	Top	1200
	Width	1935

continued on next page

continued from previous page

OBJECT	PROPERTY	VALUE
OptionButton	Name	rbTabOff
	Caption	Tab Stops Off
	Height	255
	Left	240
	TabIndex	4
	Top	720
	Value	True
	Width	1575
OptionButton	Name	rbTabOn
	Caption	Tab Stops On
	Height	255
	Left	240
	TabIndex	3
	Top	360
	Width	1455
ListBox	Name	ListBox1
	Height	2400
	Left	1800
	TabIndex	1
	Top	3120
	Width	2535
ComboBox	Name	Combo1
	Height	315
	Left	4560
	TabIndex	0
	Text	Combo1
	Top	3120
	Width	1935

3. Create a new module and add the following code to it. The **SendMessage** function is used to handle much of the functionality shown in this How-To. The **GetTickCount** is used for accurate timings. The four constant values are the different messages sent to the API with the **SendMessage** function.

```
Declare Function SendMessage Lib "user32" Alias "SendMessageA" _
(ByVal hwnd As Long, _
ByVal wMsg As Long, ByVal wParam As Long, lParam As Any) As Long
Declare Function GetTickCount Lib "kernel32" () As Long
```

```
Public Const CB_SHOWDROPDOWN = &H14F
Public Const CB_RESETCONTENT = &H14B
Public Const LB_RESETCONTENT = &H184
Public Const CB_LIMITTEXT = &H141
```

4. Add the following code to the Declarations section of `frmTabStop`. This code snippet includes two constants that define what speed to use when clearing the lists. In addition, a module-level variable is declared that stores the number of items in the two lists used in the project.

```
Const FAST_CLEAR = 1
Const SLOW_CLEAR = 2
Dim m_iAmount As Integer
```

5. Add the following code to the **Load** event for the Form control. The code sets the default number of list items and then calls the routine that populates the lists.

```
Private Sub Form_Load()      '
    'Set default amount of 2 lists,
    m_iAmount = 500
    PopulateLists'
End Sub
```

6. Add the following code to the **Click** events for the three option buttons. The routines set the value for the number of items in each list and then populate the lists.

```
Private Sub rb1000Entries_Click()      '
    m_iAmount = 1000
    PopulateLists
    '
End Sub
Private Sub rb2000Entries_Click()
    '
    m_iAmount = 2000
    PopulateLists
    '
End Sub
Private Sub rb500Entries_Click()
    '
    m_iAmount = 500
    PopulateLists
    '
End Sub
```

7. Add the **PopulateLists** subroutine to `frmTabStop`. This routine does nothing more than wrap the routines that populate the combination drop-down list and the list box, respectively.

```
Private Sub PopulateLists()      '
    PopulateCombo
    PopulateListBox
    '
End Sub
```

8. Add the `PopulateListBox` subroutine to `frmTabStop`. This is the first routine in this project that uses the Windows API `SendMessage` function. The main chore of this routine is to populate the list box with as many items as specified by the variable that stores this piece of data. Before populating the list box, however, the `SendMessage` function is used to clear the list.

Later in this chapter, this method is compared to the manual method of emptying a list. The only parameters required by the function when it is used to clear a list are the control handle and the appropriate message.

```
Public Sub PopulateListBox()
    '
    Dim iCounter As Integer
    Dim intRet As Integer
    '
    intRet = SendMessage(ListBox1.hwnd, LB_RESETCONTENT, 1, ByVal 0&)
    frmTabStop.MousePointer = vbHourglass
    For iCounter = 0 To m_iAmount
        ListBox1.AddItem "Item " + Str$(iCounter)
    Next
    frmTabStop.MousePointer = vbDefault
    ListBox1.ListIndex = 0
    '
End Sub
```

9. Add the `PopulateCombo` subroutine to `frmTabStop`. Like the code in step 8, this routine also populates one of the lists used in this project. Before populating the combination drop-down list, the `SendMessage` function is used to clear the list. Again, the only parameters required by the function to clear the list are the control handle and the message.

```
Public Sub PopulateCombo()
    '
    Dim iCounter As Integer
    Dim intRet As Integer
    '
    intRet = SendMessage(Combo1.hwnd, CB_RESETCONTENT, 1, ByVal 0&)
    frmTabStop.MousePointer = vbHourglass
    For iCounter = 0 To m_iAmount
        Combo1.AddItem "Item " + Str$(iCounter)
    Next
    frmTabStop.MousePointer = vbDefault
    Combo1.ListIndex = 0
    '
End Sub
```

10. Add the following code to the **Click** event for both the **cbFast** and
cbSlow control. The routines each clear both lists by using either the **Slow**
method or the **Fast** method, depending on the button chosen. After the
lists are cleared, the lists are repopulated.

```
Private Sub cbFast_Click()
    '
    ClearLists (FAST_CLEAR)
    PopulateLists
    '
End Sub
Private Sub cbSlow_Click()
    '
    ClearLists (SLOW_CLEAR)
    PopulateLists
    '
End Sub
```

11. Add the **ClearLists** subroutine to **frmTabStop**. This is the last piece of
code used to clear lists and is the routine that manages the clearing of the
two lists used in this project. Based on the parameter passed in, the lists
are cleared by using either the **Fast** method or the **Slow** method. When
the **Fast** method is chosen, the **SendMessage** function is used with the
RESENTCONTENT message. When the **Slow** method is chosen, the code fires
the **RemoveItem** method for each item in both lists.

```
Public Function ClearLists(intSpeed)
    '
    Dim lStart As Long
    Dim lEnd As Long
    Dim lElapsed As Long
    Dim lComboElapsed As Long
    Dim lListElapsed As Long
    Dim intRet As Integer
    Dim intListCount As Integer
    Dim intCounter As Integer
    '
    frmTabStop.MousePointer = vbHourglass
    Select Case intSpeed
        Case FAST_CLEAR
            'Clear the combo box
            lStart = GetTickCount
            intRet = SendMessage(Combo1.hwnd, CB_RESETCONTENT, 1, _
                    ByVal 0&)
            lEnd = GetTickCount
            lComboElapsed = lEnd - lStart
            'Clear the list box
            lStart = GetTickCount
            intRet = SendMessage(ListBox1.hwnd, LB_RESETCONTENT, _
                    1, ByVal 0&)
```

```
        lEnd = GetTickCount
        lListElapsed = lEnd - lStart

    Case SLOW_CLEAR
        'Clear the combo box
        lStart = GetTickCount
        intListCount = Combo1.ListCount
        For iCounter = 0 To intListCount - 1
            Combo1.RemoveItem intCounter
        Next
        lEnd = GetTickCount
        lComboElapsed = lEnd - lStart
        '
        'Clear the list box
        lStart = GetTickCount
        iCounter = 0
        For iCounter = 0 To intListCount - 1
            ListBox1.RemoveItem intCounter
        Next
        lEnd = GetTickCount
        lListElapsed = lEnd - lStart
        '
    End Select
    frmTabStop.MousePointer = vbDefault
    '
    MsgBox "Time to clear combo: " + Str$(lComboElapsed) + " _
        milliseconds"
    MsgBox "Time to clear list: " + Str$(lListElapsed) + " _
        milliseconds"
    '
End Function
```

12. Add the following code to the `Click` event of the `ckLimitText` control so that the user can set the maximum length of text added to the combination drop-down list control. This routine sets the enabled property of the label and the textedit controls in the Limit Text frame to the value of the check box, which can be only `True` or `False`. If the user has checked the option off, the `SendMessage` function is called to set the maximum length of text to 2048, a predefined default.

The `Changed` event for the `txtMaxLength` control, covered in the next step, manages the `SendMessage` event when a maximum of text is supplied other than the default. To use the `SendMessage` function in this context, you pass in the handle to the control, the `CB_LIMITEXT` message, and the length.

```
Private Sub ckLimitText_Click()
    '
    txtMaxLength.Enabled = ckLimitText.Value
    lblMaxlength.Enabled = ckLimitText.Value
    '
    If Not (ckLimitText.Value) Then
```

```
            intRet = SendMessage(Combo1.hwnd, CB_LIMITTEXT, 2048, _
                    ByVal 0&)
        End If
        '
End Sub
```

13. Add the following code to the `Changed` event for the `txtMaxLength`
control. When the user changes the control's value, which stores the
maximum length of text that can be added to the control, the
`SendMessage` function is called. The function sends a message that
establishes the maximum text length for the control. Like the
implementation of the `SendMessage` function in step 12, the control
handle is passed to the function, along with the appropriate message and
the maximum length.

```
Private Sub txtMaxLength_Change()
    '
    Dim iMaxLength As Long
    '
    iMaxLength = Val(txtMaxLength.Text)
    intRet = SendMessage(Combo1.hwnd, CB_LIMITTEXT, iMaxLength, _
            ByVal 0&)
    '
End Sub
```

14. Add the following code to the `GotFocus` event of the `Combo1` control to
automatically drop open the combination drop-down list when the user
tabs to the list. The code evaluates the `rbTabOn` control, which the user
selects to enable the automatic drop open of the control. If the control
evaluates to `True`, the `SendMessage` function is used to alter the behavior
of the control. As always with the `SendMessage` function, the control
handle is passed, along with the appropriate message and two unused
parameters.

```
Private Sub Combo1_GotFocus()
    '
    If rbTabOn Then
        '
        Dim intRet As Integer
        intRet = SendMessage(Combo1.hwnd, CB_SHOWDROPDOWN, 1, _
                ByVal 0&)
        '
    End If
    '
End Sub
```

How It Works

The `SendMessage` routine is used extensively in this project to alter the standard
behavior of the combination drop-down list and list box. Because some of the

code in this How-To is required for the purpose of demonstration, it's likely that you can use much less code to implement some of the behavior shown here.

In this example, the `SendMessage` routine was used to clear the `ListBox` and `ComboBox`. Both these controls have a `Clear` method that clears the lists with one call. The speed of this action is comparable to using `SendMessage`.

Comments

Be sure to review and understand the parameters passed to the `SendMessage` function, as well as the Windows API function. You must be exact in the data types you pass and in the spelling of any constants passed in.

COMPLEXITY
ADVANCED

1.4 How do I...
Use drag and drop to implement a sort order tool?

COMPATIBILITY: VISUAL BASIC 4, 5, AND 6

Problem

Database applications usually require the ability to use a sort order. This requirement is typically met through a combination of drop-down lists and textbox controls—a solution that isn't always usable and frequently doesn't match the level of graphical sophistication of the rest of the project. A more interesting and usable solution is necessary.

Technique

At its simplest level, the technique for implementing this feature involves managing the drag-and-drop events for different controls on the form, and it's possible to track the location of every control on the form. The technique is to use the information provided by Visual Basic about the controls being dragged and those being dropped on to manage the placement of other controls on the form. If controls, such as buttons, are used to represent fields, it's possible to know where each field is listed in the sort order, if at all.

The key to this application, then, is managing the drag-and-drop event procedures and tracking the location of the different controls on the form. The field names from our example database are presented as buttons on the form, and these buttons can be dragged to a tree structure on the form that is built with three frame controls and two line controls. The drag-and-drop operations occur when a button is dragged to some frame on the form or to some button (see Figure 1.4).

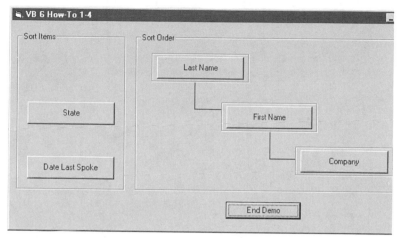

Figure 1.4 You can program other events to occur following a drag-and-drop event.

Steps

Open and run the DRAGDROP.VBP project, which is shown in Figure 1.4. Click the Last Name button and drag it to the top node of the tree on the right side of the dialog box. Drag the First Name button to the top node of the tree, on top of the Last Name button. Notice how the Last Name button is moved to the middle node of the tree and the First Name button appears at the top node of the tree.

Next, drag the State button to the top node of the tree, dropping it on the First Name button. Notice how the First Name button moves to the middle node of the tree and how the Last Name button moves to the bottom node of the tree. Experiment by dragging different nodes to different parts of the tree, as well as by dragging buttons back to the Sort Order frame.

Complete the following steps to create this project:

1. Create a new standard exe project named DRAGDROP.VBP.

2. Add the objects listed in Table 1.4 to Form1, using the properties shown in the table.

Table 1.4 Objects and Properties for Form1

OBJECT	PROPERTY	VALUE
Form	Name	frmSort
	Caption	VB 6 How-To 1-4
	Height	4590
	Left	1485

continued on next page

continued from previous page

OBJECT	PROPERTY	VALUE
	Top	1965
	Width	9120
	LinkTopic	Form1
	ScaleHeight	4590
	ScaleWidth	9120
Frame	Name	fraSortOrder
	Caption	Sort Order
	Height	3495
	Left	2760
	TabIndex	7
	Top	240
	Width	6015
Frame	Name	lblPosition3
	Height	735
	Left	3600
	TabIndex	10
	Top	2400
	Width	2175
Frame	Name	lblPosition2
	Height	735
	Left	1920
	TabIndex	9
	Top	1440
	Width	2175
Frame	Name	lblPosition1
	Height	735
	Left	360
	TabIndex	8
	Top	360
	Width	2175
Line	Name	Line4
	X1	3000
	X2	3600
	Y1	2760
	Y2	2760

OBJECT	PROPERTY	VALUE
Line	Name	Line3
	X1	3000
	X2	3000
	Y1	2160
	Y2	2760
Line	Name	Line2
	X1	1320
	X2	1920
	Y1	1680
	Y2	1680
Line	Name	Line1
	X1	1320
	X2	1320
	Y1	1080
	Y2	1680
Frame	Name	fraSortItems
	Caption	Sort Items
	Height	3495
	Left	120
	TabIndex	1
	Top	240
	Width	2415
CommandButton	Name	cbSortDate
	Caption	Date Last Spoke
	Height	495
	Left	240
	TabIndex	6
	Top	2760
	Width	1935
CommandButton	Name	cbSortCompany
	Caption	Company
	Height	495
	Left	240
	TabIndex	5
	Top	2160
	Width	1935

continued on next page

continued from previous page

OBJECT	PROPERTY	VALUE
CommandButton	Name	cbSortState
	Caption	State
	Height	495
	Left	240
	TabIndex	4
	Top	1560
	Width	1935
CommandButton	Name	cbSortLastName
	Caption	Last Name
	Height	495
	Left	240
	TabIndex	3
	Top	960
	Width	1935
CommandButton	Name	cbSortFirstName
	Caption	First Name
	Height	495
	Left	240
	TabIndex	2
	Top	360
	Width	1935
CommandButton	Name	cbEndDemo
	Caption	End Demo
	Height	375
	Left	4800
	TabIndex	0
	Top	3960
	Width	1695

3. Add the following code to the Declaration section of **Form1**. This code declares object variables, which are used as placeholders for each of the three pieces of the sort order. In addition, constants are declared that establish the fixed coordinates of the sort order components.

```
Dim Position1 As Object
Dim Position2 As Object
Dim Position3 As Object
Dim m_PositionTarget As Integer
Const POSITION1_TOP = 530
```

```
Const POSITION1_LEFT = 485
Const POSITION2_TOP = 1610
Const POSITION2_LEFT = 2045
Const POSITION3_TOP = 2570
Const POSITION3_LEFT = 3725
```

4. Add the following code to the **Click** event of the **cbEndDemo** control. This code ends the project.

```
Private Sub cbEndDemo_Click()
    '
    End
End Sub
```

5. Add the following code to the **MouseDown** event for each of the five field name button controls. The code simply enables the drag operation when the user clicks down on the control.

```
Private Sub cbSortFirstName_MouseDown(Button As Integer, Shift As _
    Integer, _
    X As Single, Y As Single)
    '
    cbSortFirstName.Drag 1
    '
End Sub
Private Sub cbSortLastName_MouseDown(Button As Integer, Shift As _
    Integer, _
    X As Single, Y As Single)
    '
    cbSortLastName.Drag 1
    '
End Sub
Private Sub cbSortState_MouseDown(Button As Integer, Shift As _
    Integer, _
    X As Single, Y As Single)
    '
    cbSortState.Drag 1
    '
End Sub
Private Sub cbSortDate_MouseDown(Button As Integer, Shift As _
    Integer, _
    X As Single, Y As Single)
    '
    cbSortDate.Drag 1
    '
End Sub
Private Sub cbSortCompany_MouseDown(Button As Integer, Shift As _
    Integer, _
    X As Single, Y As Single)
    '
    cbSortCompany.Drag 1
    '
End Sub
```

6. Add the following code to the **DragDrop** event of the **fraSortItems** control. The following code is called when the user drags a field name button to the Sortable Items frame. Occasions when this might occur are when the user removes a field from the sort order by dragging its button from the tree back to the Sortable Items frame or when the user attempts to move a field name button to a different location in the frame. This code ensures that the field name buttons are arranged properly after a drop operation.

```
Private Sub fraSortItems_DragDrop(Source As Control, X As Single, _
Y As Single)
    '
    Set Source.Container = fraSortItems
    Select Case Source.Name
        Case "cbSortFirstName"
            Source.Move 240, 360
        Case "cbSortLastName"
            Source.Move 240, 960
        Case "cbSortState"
            Source.Move 240, 1560
        Case "cbSortCompany"
            Source.Move 240, 2160
        Case "cbSortDate"
            Source.Move 240, 2760
    End Select
    CheckTreeForSource Source
    '
End Sub
```

7. Add the following code to the **DragDrop** event of each of three frames that store the three possible fields in the sort order. The code positions the button dropped into the frame and defines the container of the **Source** object. The **Source** object is the button that has been dropped onto the frame, and it sets the appropriate **Position** object to the **Source** object.

```
Private Sub lblPosition1_DragDrop(Source As Control, X As Single, _
Y As Single)
    '
    Source.Move POSITION1_LEFT, POSITION1_TOP
    Set Source.Container = fraSortOrder
    Set Position1 = Source
    '
End Sub
Private Sub lblPosition2_DragDrop(Source As Control, X As Single, _
Y As Single)
    '
    Source.Move POSITION2_LEFT, POSITION2_TOP
    Set Source.Container = fraSortOrder
    Set Position2 = Source
    '
End Sub
Private Sub lblPosition3_DragDrop(Source As Control, X As Single, _
Y As Single)
    '
```

```
            Source.Move POSITION3_LEFT, POSITION3_TOP
            Set Source.Container = fraSortOrder
            Set Position3 = Source
            '
    End Sub
```

8. Add the following code to the **DragDrop** event for each field name button. In each case, the **ManageReOrder** subroutine is called when an object is dropped on a button. The subroutine is passed the name of the button being dropped, as well as the target button. Details about the **ManageReOrder** subroutine are found in step 10.

```
Private Sub cbSortFirstName_DragDrop(Source As Control, _
    X As Single, Y As Single)
    '

    ManageReOrder Source, cbSortFirstName


    '
End Sub
Private Sub cbSortLastName_DragDrop(Source As Control, _
    X As Single, Y As Single)
    '

    ManageReOrder Source, cbSortLastName


    '
End Sub
Private Sub cbSortDate_DragDrop(Source As Control, _
    X As Single, Y As Single)
    '

    ManageReOrder Source, cbSortDate


    '
End Sub
Private Sub cbSortCompany_DragDrop(Source As Control, _
    X As Single, Y As Single)
    '

    ManageReOrder Source, cbSortCompany


    '
End Sub
Private Sub cbSortState_DragDrop(Source As Control, _
    X As Single, Y As Single)
    '


    ManageReOrder Source, cbSortState


    '
End Sub
```

9. Add the **CheckTreeForSource** subroutine to **Form1**. This code checks whether a field name button is being moved from the tree. It checks this by comparing the **Source** object to each of the three **Position** objects in the tree.

```
Private Sub CheckTreeForSource(Source As Control)
    '
    If Source.Name = Position1.Name Then
        Set Position1 = Nothing
    ElseIf Source.Name = Position2.Name Then
        Set Position2 = Nothing
    Else
        Set Position3 = Nothing
    End If
    '
End Sub
```

10. Add the `ManageReOrder` subroutine to `Form1`. This subroutine is the key to the entire application; it's used to determine the position of the control being dropped on. The case of the user dropping the control on the Sortable Items frame has been handled already, so this code handles drag-and-drop operations on the tree, exclusively. The first order of business is checking whether the button is being dragged from the tree control. If this is the case, as you learned in the preceding step, the **Position** object is set to **Nothing**.

The code then manages the tree in ascending order, starting with the bottom node. For each node in the tree, the code determines whether the target node already contains a button. If so, the button is moved down the tree to the next node. If that node is occupied, that button is moved down. If the target node is the bottom node, and that node is occupied, that button is moved back to the Sortable Items frame.

```
Private Sub ManageReOrder(Source As Control, Target As Control)
    '
    Dim TempPos As Object
    '
    CheckTreeForSource Source

    'If Position3 is empty, then target cannot be located there
    If Not (Position3 Is Nothing) Then
        If Position3.Name = Target.Name Then
            'Target is in Position3, so clear it, and move source
            Set Target.Container = fraSortItems
            fraSortItems_DragDrop Target, 240, 360
            Set Source.Container = fraSortOrder
            Source.Move POSITION3_LEFT, POSITION3_TOP
            Set Position3 = Source
            Exit Sub
        End If
    End If
    '
    'If Position2 is empty, then target cannot be located there
    If Not (Position2 Is Nothing) Then
        If Position2.Name = Target.Name Then
            'Target is in Position2
            If Position3 Is Nothing Then
```

```
                        Target.Move POSITION3_LEFT, POSITION3_TOP
                        Set Position3 = Target
                Else
                    Set Target.Container = fraSortItems
                    fraSortItems_DragDrop Target, 240, 360
                    End If
                    Set Source.Container = fraSortOrder
                    Source.Move POSITION2_LEFT, POSITION2_TOP
                    Set Position2 = Target
                    Exit Sub
            End If
    End If

    'Target must be in Position1
    If Position2 Is Nothing Then
        'Position2 is clear, so move target there
        Target.Move POSITION2_LEFT, POSITION2_TOP
        Set Position2 = Target

        Set Source.Container = fraSortOrder
        Source.Move POSITION1_LEFT, POSITION1_TOP
        Set Position1 = Source
    Else
        If Not (Position3 Is Nothing) Then
            'Clear out Position3
            Set TempPos = Position3
            Set TempPos.Container = fraSortItems
            fraSortItems_DragDrop TempPos, 240, 360
            Set TempPos = Nothing
        End If
        'Move 2 to 3
        Set TempPos = Position2
        TempPos.Move POSITION3_LEFT, POSITION3_TOP
        Set Position3 = TempPos

        'Move 1 to 2
        Target.Move POSITION2_LEFT, POSITION2_TOP
        Set Position2 = Target
        Set Source.Container = fraSortOrder
        Source.Move POSITION1_LEFT, POSITION1_TOP
        Set Position1 = Source
    End If
    '
End Sub
```

How It Works

Using objects in this technique reduces code, increases code reusability, and makes management of the entire application easy. Specifically, this project implements the target nodes as objects. Because the drag-and-drop events use objects to represent the source and targets, it becomes easy to determine and compare the buttons being dragged to the frames on which they are dropped.

You often see the comparison of the `Name` property used. In addition, because the logic comparisons are made as objects, setting the target nodes to `Nothing` makes it easy to determine whether the target is empty.

Comments

This How-To presents some rather simple operations but the fundamentals shown regarding drag and drop can be applied to other applications. For instance, you could have your program accept files that are dropped onto it and perform different functions on each file based on the file's extension.

CHAPTER 2

THE VIEW CONTROLS

2

THE VIEW CONTROLS

How do I...

2.1 Load and manipulate graphics with the `ImageList` control?

2.2 Load and manipulate graphics with the `ImageList` object?

2.3 Build an Explorer-style interface with the `ListView` control?

2.4 Present data objects with the `ListView` and `TreeView` controls?

The first Visual Basic applications built with version 1 were barely visual. Those applications were usually a mix of buttons, list boxes, radio buttons, and check boxes, but there were limited graphical controls. As Visual Basic has progressed through several revisions, the number of graphical controls available for application developers has increased significantly. Shipped now with Visual Basic 6.0 is a cornucopia of handy controls for displaying a variety of multimedia elements, as well as controls for presenting textual items in a graphical glitzy style. Application developers also can take advantage of a huge selection of third-party controls to enhance the visual impact of their applications.

This chapter provides instruction on the use of the most interesting of the graphical controls shipped with Visual Basic 6. Specifically, you'll work with the `ListView` and `TreeView` controls, as well as the `ImageList` control, which helps manage the graphics you use with the `ListView` and `TreeView` controls.

2.1 Load and Manipulate Graphics with the `ImageList` Control

Many Visual Basic applications use not just one but a number of different graphics. Consider any application that uses a toolbar. It's likely that six or more different graphics would be required for this type of application. Many applications use not only a toolbar but other graphically oriented controls, such as a picture box, image, or shape control. Managing the graphics used in an application is one function of the `ImageList` control. This control can be managed through either property pages or code. This How-To shows you how to manage graphics in your application with the `ImageList` through the control's property page interface.

2.2 Load and Manipulate Graphics with the `ImageList` Object

The `ImageList` control enables the application developer to maintain all the graphics used in an application in one place. The `ImageList` control acts as a repository for all the icons, bitmaps, and any other graphics used. The control can be managed by entering information using the control's property pages or from code. Using the code method gives the developer the option of making the control dynamic. For example, a user could specify the graphics he wanted to use in the application at runtime. The code in the application would load graphics specified by the user directly into the control.

2.3 Build an Explorer-Style Interface with the `ListView` Control

Windows 95 introduced a number of brand-new user interface elements. Perhaps the most popular is the Windows Explorer. In Explorer, the window is divided into two panes—the right pane is used to display the contents of whatever container the user selected in the left pane. Typically, the left pane shows a directory structure, and the right pane displays the contents of the directory. The contents pane can be formatted to show the files in either a list, a list with details about each, as large icons, or as small icons. This Explorer-style interface can be used to show any type of data, not just directories and files. This How-To shows you how to build an Explorer-style interface displaying files and directories.

2.4 Present Data Objects with the `ListView` and `TreeView` Controls

Using a tag team of Visual Basic 6's `TreeView` and `ListView` controls is a great strategy for presenting data stored in relational databases, such as Microsoft

Access. The `TreeView` control can be used to display the hierarchical aspects of a database, such as the relationship between the database, its tables, the fields in those tables, and the data in those fields. `ListView` can be integrated with the `TreeView` control to display details about the item selected in the `TreeView` control, such as displaying field information about a selected table.

COMPLEXITY
BEGINNING

2.1 How do I...
Load and manipulate graphics with the `ImageList` control?

COMPATIBILITY: VISUAL BASIC 5 AND 6

Problem

It's rare to find a Visual Basic application that doesn't use at least one graphic in its user interface. Considering the number of controls that require integration of graphics, this makes sense. Most users prefer to use an application that has a visually stimulating interface. Managing an application that uses many graphics, however, is time consuming, is a nuisance, and can lead to errors. Often, references to the physical location of the graphics files are scattered throughout the code. Also, different functionality and routines are required to manage the different types of graphics. This problem is exacerbated by the fact that many different controls use the same graphics, thus leading to rework and extra code.

Technique

The `ImageList` control is used to store images for use in your application. The `ImageList` behaves like a catalog for all your application's graphics, such as bitmaps or PCX files. Any control that requires images can use the `ImageList` control for its images instead of referencing a physical file since the control acts as a storehouse for the graphics.

Steps

Open and run the project IMGLIST1.VBP. Double-click the arc image beside Corporate Headquarters. The `TreeView` control expands to reveal the regional operations level for a fictitious corporation. Notice the standard send-to-front image beside each node in the second level of the tree. Double-click any of the send-to-front images to reveal the third and bottom branch of the tree, which shows the factories beneath the regional consolidations. Also notice the standard send-to-back image beside each node (as shown in Figure 2.1). Finally, take note of the different images on the toolbar.

Figure 2.1
Controls that
use the
`ImageList`.

End the project. From the Properties pull-down menu, select the `imlImages` `ImageList` control. Select the property labeled `Custom` to view the control's custom properties (see Figure 2.2). On the property page, click the Images tab. In the Images list box are the three images used in the tree control and the eight used on the toolbar. Click each of the images and take notice of the value displayed in the Key field.

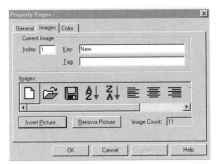

Figure 2.2 The `ImageList`
control's Images property tab.

Close the Property Pages dialog box for the `ImageList`, and then view the custom properties for the toolbar control. Notice the value of the `ImageList` field under the General tab, as shown in Figure 2.3. It contains the name of the `ImageList` control you just examined.

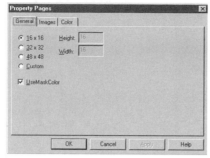

Figure 2.3 The `ImageList` control's General property tab.

Choose the Buttons tab, and then click the arrow buttons beside the Index field to scroll through each of the toolbar buttons. Examine the Image field for each toolbar button, and you'll find that the value in the field matches a Key field for an image in the `ImageList` control, as shown in Figure 2.4.

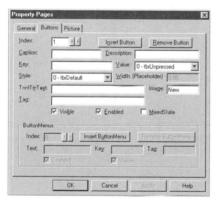

Figure 2.4 The toolbar buttons property tab.

Close the Property Pages dialog box for the toolbar, and open the Property Pages dialog box for the `TreeView` control (see Figure 2.5). You will also find the `ImageList` control referenced. Individual images are specified in code in the `Form_Load` event procedure.

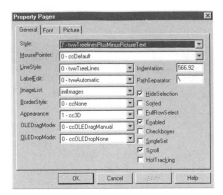

Figure 2.5 The `TreeView` property pages.

Complete the following steps to create this project:

1. Create a new standard EXE project named IMGLIST1.VBP. Choose Projects, Components from the menu, and then choose Microsoft Common Controls 6.0 from the list. If Microsoft Common Controls 6.0 does not appear in the list, choose Browse to locate the MSCOMCTL.OCX file.

2. Add the objects listed in Table 2.1 to `Form1`, using the properties shown in the table.

Table 2.1 Objects and Properties for `Form1`

OBJECT	PROPERTY	VALUE
Form	Name	Form1
	Height	4245
	Left	60
	Top	345
	Width	3135
	ScaleHeight	4245
	ScaleWidth	3135
	StartUpPosition	3 - WindowsDefault
Toolbar	Name	
	Align	1 - 'AlignTop
	Height	420
	Left	0
	TabIndex	0
	Top	0

OBJECT	PROPERTY	VALUE
	Width	3135
	ButtonWidth	635
	ButtonHeight	582
	Appearance	1
TreeView	Name	tvImageList
	Height	3855
	Left	0
	TabIndex	1
	Top	360
	Width	3135
	Style	7
	Appearance	1
ImageList	Name	imlImages
	Left	240
	Top	840
	ImageWidth	16
	ImageHeight	16

3. Right-click the `imlImages` control and choose Properties. When the Property Pages dialog box appears, click the Images tab.

4. Choose Insert Picture and select the following bitmaps: New, Open, Save, Sortasc, Sortdes, Lft, Cnt, Rt, Arc, Front, and Back. You can find the bitmaps in the **Chapter02** directory. The first eight bitmaps should appear in the Images list box as shown in Figure 2.6.

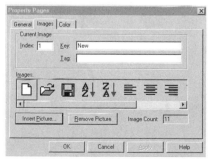

Figure 2.6 Specifying images on the `ImageList` control property page.

5. Click each of the images in the Images list and enter the filename of the bitmap in the Key field. For example, the Sort Descending image would have as its key *Sortasc*. The key is to identify the individual images in the **ImageList** control. Any text may be used as an image's key. Click OK when finished.

6. Right-click the **tbImageList** control and choose Properties. When the Property Pages dialog box appears, choose the **imlImages** control from the **ImageList** drop-down list.

7. Click the Buttons tab and then click Insert Button. A new, blank button appears on the toolbar. In the Image field, enter New. This value corresponds to the value of the Key field for the first image stored in **imlImages**. After entering New, choose Apply. The New image appears on the first button on the **tbImageList** control. The values entered for the keys are case sensitive and must match the values entered in step 5.

8. Using Table 2.2 as a guide, create nine more buttons for the **tbImageList** control, specifying images from the **imlImages** control. Note that a button with a style of **tbrSeparator** is used to create a visual break between groups of buttons. The Style column indicates where this type of button should be created. The Style field also appears on the Buttons tab. When you're finished, click OK.

Table 2.2 Creating Buttons for the tbImageList Control

BUTTON INDEX	STYLE	IMAGE
2	tbrDefault	Open
3	tbrDefault	Save
4	tbrSeparator	0
5	tbrDefault	Sortasc
6	tbrDefault	Sortdes
7	tbrSeparator	0
8	tbrDefault	Lft
9	tbrDefault	Cnt
10	tbrDefault	Rt

9. Assign the **imlImages** control to the **ImageList** property of the **tvImageList** control. To do so, right-click the **tvImageList** control. Choose Properties from the context menu, and then select **imlImages** from the **ImageList** drop-down list, as shown in Figure 2.7. After doing so, click OK.

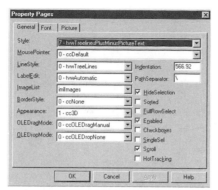

Figure 2.7 Selecting the
ImageList control for a TreeView
control.

10. Selecting images for the **tvImageList** control is not as easy as doing so for
a toolbar control, where a dialog box is used. The images used for a
TreeView control arc specified in code. To add an item to a TreeView
control, the Add method is used with the Nodes collection of the
TreeView control. The last two parameters of the Add method specify the
default image used with the node and the image that is used when the
node is selected. Coverage of the TreeView control is provided in section
2.3 of this chapter. For this How-To, add the following code to the
Form_Load event. Note that the last two parameters for each method
specify images you added earlier to the **imlImages** control.

```
Private Sub Form_Load()
'

    'Set up a node object
    Dim nNode As Node
'

    'Populate the tree
    Set Node = tvImageList.Nodes.Add(, , "Corp", "Corporate _
Headquarters", "Arc", "Arc")
    Set Node = tvImageList.Nodes.Add("Corp", 4, "Europe", _
"European Operations", "Front", "Front")
    Set Node = tvImageList.Nodes.Add("Corp", 4, "SA", "South _
America Operations", "Front", "Front")
    Set Node = tvImageList.Nodes.Add("Corp", 4, "NA", "North _
America Operations", "Front", "Front")
    Set Node = tvImageList.Nodes.Add("Corp", 4, "Mexico", "Mexico _
Operations", "Front", "Front")
    Set Node = tvImageList.Nodes.Add("Europe", 4, "Rome", "Rome", _
"Back", "Back")
```

```
    Set Node = tvImageList.Nodes.Add("Europe", 4, "London", _
"London", "Back", "Back")
    Set Node = tvImageList.Nodes.Add("Europe", 4, "Paris", _
"Paris", "Back", "Back")
    Set Node = tvImageList.Nodes.Add("SA", 4, "Peru", "Peru", _
"Back", "Back")
    Set Node = tvImageList.Nodes.Add("SA", 4, "Brazil", "Brazil", _
"Back", "Back")
   Set Node = tvImageList.Nodes.Add("NA", 4, "Wisconsin", _
"Wisconsin", "Back", "Back")
    Set Node = tvImageList.Nodes.Add("NA", 4, "Connecticut", _
"Connecticut", "Back", "Back")
    Set Node = tvImageList.Nodes.Add("NA", 4, "New York", "New _
York", "Back", "Back")
    Set Node = tvImageList.Nodes.Add("NA", 4, "Charlotte", _
"Charlotte", "Back", "Back")
'
End Sub
```

How It Works

Little mystery is associated with use of the **ImageList** control. You use a control to maintain a list of all the images used in the application. The list can contain images used by different controls, including controls of different types, such as icons and bitmaps. After you have decided on the images to use in your application, you specify them in the **ImageList** control and then reference both the **ImageList** and the images in it from the other controls in your application.

The **ImageList** maintains a key for each image, as well as an index, so it's easy to refer to each image uniquely. The index can be helpful when you are performing iterative operations, or when you need to track an image numerically. They key value can be used to refer to an image in a more familiar fashion.

Comments

The only caution regarding use of the **ImageList** control is that if a change must be made to the list of controls, you must first remove the reference to the **ImageList** from any controls already referencing it. This can be a nuisance, especially if all you want to do is add a control, or change its position in the list. It makes sense to completely spec out your application, especially the graphics to be used, before working with **ImageList** control.

COMPLEXITY
BEGINNING

2.2 How do I...
Load and manipulate graphics with the ImageList object?

COMPATIBILITY: VISUAL BASIC 5 AND 6

Problem

Applications tend to have numerous graphics. Managing these graphics during development of the application can be frustrating and time consuming. At the same time, the design of an application must not only account for the management of the many graphics used but also be flexible enough to support graphics specified at runtime, perhaps by the user. Also, it can be annoying switching to the property page of a control to retrieve a piece of information that is needed in code, such as the key of an image.

Technique

You can manage the ImageList control from code. As an alternative to entering the name, location, and key for a graphic on the ImageList control's property page, you can add images to the ImageList control in code, including assigning a key. The image can then be referenced anywhere in code. The technique exemplified in this How-To simply involves using the object associated with the ImageList control. For this How-To, you place an ImageList control on the form and then use the Add method to add images to the list. The elegance of this method is that the list of images can be managed dynamically. Code could be added that loads the list of images from the Registry or some other database that might store the user's preferences.

Steps

Open and run the project IMGLIST2.VBP. Double-click the arc image beside Corporate Headquarters. The tree control expands to reveal a number of corporate consolidation paths for some fictitious company. Click each of the plus signs in the TreeView control to fully expand all branches of the tree (as shown in Figure 2.8). Notice that the image associated with the top node in the tree is an arc, the image associated with any node that has children is the standard send-to-front image, and the image for any node without children is the standard send-to-back image. You may need to change the code that loads the bitmaps to point to the location where you loaded the chapter examples.

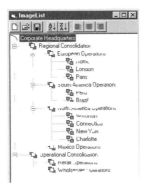

Figure 2.8 Using the ImageList control with the TreeView control.

End the project. From the Properties pull-down menu, select the imlImages ImageList control. Select the property labeled Custom to view the control's custom properties. Click the Images tab. Notice that no images are specified, which differs from the technique described in section 2.1 of this chapter. Close the Property Pages dialog box for the ImageList; then view the custom properties for the TreeView control. Notice the value of the ImageList field under the General tab; you'll find the name of the ImageList control you just examined. To create this project, complete the following steps:

1. Create a new standard EXE project and call it IMGLIST2.VBP. Choose Projects, Components from the Visual Basic menu, and then choose Microsoft Common Controls 6.0 from the list. If Microsoft Common Controls 6.0 does not appear in the list, choose Browse to locate the MSCOMCTL.OCX file. Click OK.

2. Add the objects listed in Table 2.3 to Form1, using the properties shown in the table.

Table 2.3 Objects and Properties for Form1

OBJECT	PROPERTY	VALUE
Form	Name	Form1
	Caption	ImageList
	Height	5430
	Left	0
	Top	0
	Width	4110
	ScaleHeight	5025
	ScaleWidth	3990
	StartUpPosition	3 - WindowsDefault
TreeView	Name	tvImageList
	Height	5415
	Left	0
	TabIndex	0
	Top	400
	Width	5175
	Style	7
	Appearance	1 - cc3D
ToolBar	Name	Toolbar1
	Left	0
	ShowTips	True
	Style	0 - tbrStandard
	Top	0
	Width	5160
ImageList	Name	imlImages
	Left	240
	Top	600

3. Add the following code to the General Declarations section of Form1's code module. Each of these variables stores the name and location of a bitmap image that is used in the application. Using a variable makes it easy to refer to a specific image with the **ImageList**. This way, the value of the variable can be managed from a single location in code rather than on the **ImageList** property page. Also, the fact that the value is stored in a variable makes it easy to change its value from some other module in the application, such as a module that presents an interface allowing the user to select images to use.

```
Dim m_strVBGraphicsDir as String
Dim m_strNewImg as String
Dim m_strOpenImg as String
Dim m_strSaveImg as String
Dim m_strAscImg as String
Dim m_strDescImg as String
Dim m_strLeftImg as String
Dim m_strCenterImg as String
Dim m_strRightImg as String
Dim m_strTopImg as String
Dim m_strParentImg as String
Dim m_strBaseImg as String
```

4. Add the following code to the **Form1 Form_Load** event. This code should precede any other code in the event procedure. This code declares some variables needed in the application, as well as specifies the default images to be used in the application. Change the directory structure to match the location that you loaded the example chapter file to.

```
'Declare Some variables
'
Dim imgThisImage As ListImage
Dim ndTVNode As Node
'
'Set-up variables to store name and location of graphics files
'
m_strVBGraphicsDir = "C:\VB6HT\CHAPTER02"
m_strNewImg = m_strVBGraphicsDir + "\NEW.BMP"
m_strOpenImg = m_strVBGraphicsDir + "\OPEN.BMP"
m_strSaveImg = m_strVBGraphicsDir + "\SAVE.BMP"
m_strAscImg = m_strVBGraphicsDir + "\SORTASC.BMP"
m_strDescImg = m_strVBGraphicsDir + "\SORTDES.BMP"
m_strLeftImg = m_strVBGraphicsDir + "\LFT.BMP"
m_strCenterImg = m_strVBGraphicsDir + "\CNT.BMP"
m_strRightImg = m_strVBGraphicsDir + "\RT.BMP"
m_strTopImg = m_strVBGraphicsDir + "\\ARC.BMP"
m_strParentImg = m_strVBGraphicsDir + "\FRONT.BMP"
m_strBaseImg = m_strVBGraphicsDir + "\BACK.BMP"
'
```

5. Add the following code to **Form1**'s **Form_Load** event below the code entered in step 4. This code adds images to the **ImageList** control. The **imgImageList** object that was declared at the top of the event procedure is reused here for each image added to the control. The **ListImages** collection is used in conjunction with the collection's **Add** method. The **Add** method requires three parameters, the first and third of which are the most relevant. The first parameter is the key. This is the value referenced by controls using images stored in the `ImageList`. The `Key` property in the example code is specified on the line following each instantiation of the `Image` object. The third parameter specifies the physical image that should be loaded with the `ImageList`. Notice that the `LoadPicture` function is used to set the image into the `ImageList`.

```
'Initialize ImageList
'
Set imgThisImage = imlImages.ListImages.Add(, , _
LoadPicture(m_strNewImg))
imgThisImage.Key = "New"

Set imgThisImage = imlImages.ListImages.Add(, , _
LoadPicture(m_strOpenImg))
imgThisImage.Key = "Open"

Set imgThisImage = imlImages.ListImages.Add(, , _
LoadPicture(m_strSaveImg))
imgThisImage.Key = "Save"

Set imgThisImage = imlImages.ListImages.Add(, , _
LoadPicture(m_strAscImg))
imgThisImage.Key = "Asc"

Set imgThisImage = imlImages.ListImages.Add(, , _
LoadPicture(m_strDescImg))
imgThisImage.Key = "Desc"

Set imgThisImage = imlImages.ListImages.Add(, , _
LoadPicture(m_strLeftImg))
imgThisImage.Key = "Left"

Set imgThisImage = imlImages.ListImages.Add(, , _
LoadPicture(m_strCenterImg))
imgThisImage.Key = "Center"

Set imgThisImage = imlImages.ListImages.Add(, , _
LoadPicture(m_strRightImg))
imgThisImage.Key = "Right"

Set imgThisImage = imlImages.ListImages.Add(, , _
LoadPicture(m_strTopImg))
imgThisImage.Key = "Top"

Set imgThisImage = imlImages.ListImages.Add(, , _
LoadPicture(m_strParentImg))
imgThisImage.Key = "Parent"

Set imgThisImage = imlImages.ListImages.Add(, , _
LoadPicture(m_strBaseImg))
imgThisImage.Key = "Base"
'
```

6. Add the following code to the **Form_Load** event procedure. This code populates the **TreeView** control. To add an item to a **TreeView** control, the **Add** method is used with the **Nodes** collection of the **TreeView** control. The last two parameters of the **Add** method specify the default image used with the node and the image used when the node is selected. Coverage of the **TreeView** control is provided in section 2.4 of this chapter. Note the last two parameters for each method specify the value of the **key** property you entered in step 5.

```
'Populate the tree
'
Set ndTVNode = tvImageList.Nodes.Add( , , "Corp", "Corporate _
Headquarters", "Top", "Top")
Set ndTVNode = tvImageList.Nodes.Add("Corp", 4, "Region", _
"Regional Consolidation",_
"Parent", "Parent")
Set ndTVNode = tvImageList.Nodes.Add("Corp", 4, "Operational", _
"Operational_
Consolidation", "Parent", "Parent")
'
Set ndTVNode = tvImageList.Nodes.Add("Region", 4, "Europe", _
"European Operations",_
"Parent", "Parent")
Set ndTVNode = tvImageList.Nodes.Add("Region", 4, "SA", "South _
America Operations",_
"Parent", "Parent")
Set ndTVNode = tvImageList.Nodes.Add("Region", 4, "NA", "North _
America Operations",_
"Parent", "Parent")
Set ndTVNode = tvImageList.Nodes.Add("Region", 4, "Mexico", _
"Mexico Operations",_
"Parent", "Parent")
'
Set ndTVNode = tvImageList.Nodes.Add("Operational", 4, "Retail", _
"Retail Operations",_
"Parent", "Parent")
Set ndTVNode = tvImageList.Nodes.Add("Operational", 4, "Whole", _
"Wholsesale Operations",_
"Parent", "Parent")
'
Set ndTVNode = tvImageList.Nodes.Add("Europe", 4, "Rome", "Rome", _
"Base", "Base")
Set ndTVNode = tvImageList.Nodes.Add("Europe", 4, "London", _
"London", "Base", "Base")
Set ndTVNode = tvImageList.Nodes.Add("Europe", 4, "Paris", _
"Paris", "Base", "Base")
'
Set ndTVNode = tvImageList.Nodes.Add("SA", 4, "Peru", "Peru", _
"Base", "Base")
Set ndTVNode = tvImageList.Nodes.Add("SA", 4, "Brazil", "Brazil", _
"Base", "Base")
Set ndTVNode = tvImageList.Nodes.Add("NA", 4, "Wisconsin", _
"Wisconsin", "Base", "Base")
```

```
Set ndTVNode = tvImageList.Nodes.Add("NA", 4, "Connecticut", _
"Connecticut", "Base", "Base")
Set ndTVNode = tvImageList.Nodes.Add("NA", 4, "New York", "New _
York", "Base", "Base")
Set ndTVNode = tvImageList.Nodes.Add("NA", 4, "Charlotte", _
"Charlotte", "Base", "Base")
```

7. Add the following code to the end of the **Form_Load** event procedure. This code adds buttons and assigns ToolTips to the **Toolbar** control. The **ImageList** control **imlImages** is used to provide the graphics for the toolbar.

```
Toolbar1.ImageList = imlImages
Set tButton = Toolbar1.Buttons.Add(1, , , , 1)
tButton.ToolTipText = "New"
Set tButton = Toolbar1.Buttons.Add(2, , , , 2)
tButton.ToolTipText = "Open"
Set tButton = Toolbar1.Buttons.Add(3, , , , 3)
tButton.ToolTipText = "Save"

Set tButton = Toolbar1.Buttons.Add(4)
tButton.Style = tbrSeparator

Set tButton = Toolbar1.Buttons.Add(5, , , , 4)
tButton.ToolTipText = "Ascending"
Set tButton = Toolbar1.Buttons.Add(6, , , , 5)
tButton.ToolTipText = "Descending"

Set tButton = Toolbar1.Buttons.Add(7)
tButton.Style = tbrSeparator

Set tButton = Toolbar1.Buttons.Add(8, , , , 6)
tButton.ToolTipText = "Left"
Set tButton = Toolbar1.Buttons.Add(9, , , , 7)
tButton.ToolTipText = "Center"
Set tButton = Toolbar1.Buttons.Add(10, , , , 8)
tButton.ToolTipText = "Right"
```

How It Works

Almost every control shipped with Visual Basic includes an object interface you can work with in code. By simply adding the control to the form, you can manage a control almost exclusively from code. This is possible because much of the **ListImage** can be manipulated programmatically. You can manage the list of images in the control using properties like **Index** and **Count** and methods such as **Clear** and **Add**.

Comments

You should be aware of a few other properties for the **ImageList** control. These properties can be managed from either the property page for the control or from code. The `UseMaskColor` property determines whether the color specified by the `MaskColor` property is used as a mask. When a color is used as a mask, the portion of the control that uses the color becomes transparent when the overlay method is used. This makes it easy to merge two images together. Because the `UseMaskColor` and `MaskColor` properties apply to all images in the `ImageList`, it makes sense to use a separate `ImageList` control to manage those images you will be merging. When the `UseMaskColor` property is set to `False`, the `MaskColor` property is not used, making merged images impossible. You can modify the `UseMaskColor` either in code or by checking or clearing the `UseMaskColor` check box on the General tab of the `ImageList`'s property page.

COMPLEXITY
INTERMEDIATE

2.3 How do I...
Build an Explorer-style interface with the `ListView` control?

COMPATIBILITY: VISUAL BASIC 5 AND 6

Problem

Most users have grown accustomed to the Explorer interface used in Windows 95 and Windows NT 4.0. Leveraging that familiarity, it makes sense to implement an Explorer-style user interface wherever appropriate. Up until Visual Basic 4, the only way to implement such an interface was through either a third-party control or the Win32 API. Visual Basic 6 also includes controls to build an Explorer-style interface, but using these controls takes some care and requires some expertise.

Technique

This How-To focuses on the `ListView` portion of the Explorer interface. The work involved in implementing the `ListView` control requires a few subtasks, such as populating the list. After you have solved the problem of populating the list, you must deal with the four different modes in which the items in the list can be displayed. List view is relatively easy, but for the Icon and Small Icon views you must set up `ImageList` controls to manage the two different sets of icons. For Report view, you must collect additional data for display in the additional columns that view uses. It is best to divide the project into smaller pieces, solving one problem at a time, before integrating all the code. This How-To shows one way to accomplish this objective.

Steps

Open and run the project LISTVIEW.VBP. Select a drive from the Drives drop-down list. Next, choose a directory from the Directories list by double-clicking the directory name. Be sure to choose a directory that contains both subdirectories and files. Notice that the contents of the directory appear in the Contents list on the right side of the dialog box. The list defaults to Large Icons View, as shown in Figure 2.9. The two icons used to display files and folders have already been set and are specified in code.

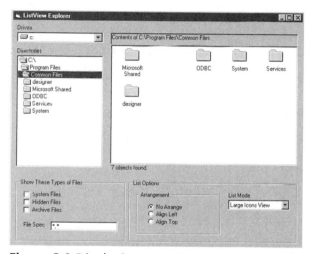

Figure 2.9 Displaying `ListView` items in Large Icons View.

Change to Small Icons View by selecting the second item in the List Mode drop-down box in the bottom-right corner of the dialog box. Notice the contents of the list are now displayed as small icons, as shown in Figure 2.10. These images are also specified at design time in code. Next, select List View from the drop-down list. Notice the contents of the list are now displayed in a list format, as shown in Figure 2.11.

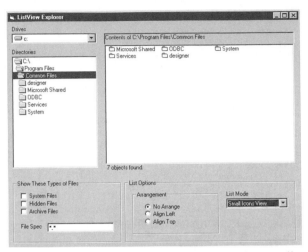

Figure 2.10 Displaying ListView items in Small Icons View.

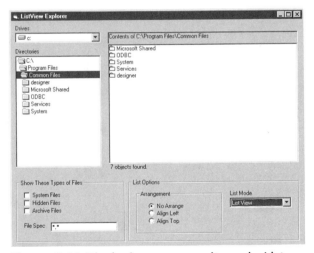

Figure 2.11 Displaying ListView items in List view.

Finally, choose Report View from the drop-down list. The list now changes to display the contents of the current directory with additional information displayed in columns, as shown in Figure 2.12. Click each of the column headers to sort the list by the contents of the column on which you click. You can also change the width of a column by dragging the column header left or right when the mouse cursor changes to a cross-hair shape.

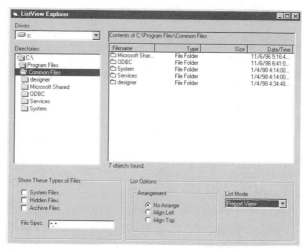

Figure 2.12 Displaying `ListView` items in Report View.

Some additional functionality that is worth discussing is included in the example program. With the list set to either Large Icons View or Small Icons View, choose from one of the different Arrangement options. The application defaults to No Arrange, but you can switch to top alignment or left alignment. Also, change the text in the File Spec edit box at the bottom-left corner of the dialog box to display files of your choice. For example, you could display all files with the extension TXT by entering `*.TXT`. The list is updated after you press Enter. Finally, you can specify whether certain types of files are shown in the list. You do this by either selecting or clearing the three check boxes in the Show These Types of Files frame. Complete the following steps to create this project:

1. Create a new project and name it LISTVIEW.VBP. Choose Projects, Components from the menu and then choose Microsoft Common Controls 6.0 from the list. If Microsoft Common Controls 6.0 does not appear in the list, choose Browse to locate the MSCOMCTL.OCX file. Click OK.

2. Add the objects listed in Table 2.4 to **Form1**, using the properties shown in the table.

Table 2.4 Objects and Properties for Form1

OBJECT	PROPERTY	VALUE
Form	Name	Form1
	Caption	ListViewExplorer
	Height	6960
	Left	60
	Top	345
	Width	9030
	LinkTopic	Form1
	ScaleHeight	6960
	ScaleWidth	9030
	StartUpPosition	3 'WindowsDefault
Frame	Name	Frame1
	Caption	ListOptions
	Height	1935
	Left	3600
	TabIndex	10
	Top	4920
	Width	5295
Frame	Name	Frame3
	Caption	Arrangement
	Height	1335
	Left	240
	TabIndex	12
	Top	360
	Width	2655
OptionButton	Name	rbAlignTop
	Caption	AlignTop
	Height	195
	Left	360
	TabIndex	15
	Top	840
	Width	1215
OptionButton	Name	rbAlignLeft
	Caption	AlignLeft

OBJECT	PROPERTY	VALUE
	Height	195
	Left	360
	TabIndex	14
	Top	600
	Width	1815
OptionButton	Name	rbNoArrange
	Caption	NoArrange
	Height	255
	Left	360
	TabIndex	13
	Top	360
	Value	True
	Width	2055
ComboBox	Name	cmbView
	Height	315
	Left	3120
	Style	2 - Dropdown List
	TabIndex	11
	Top	600
	Width	1935
Label	Name	Label2
	Caption	ListMode
	Height	255
	Left	3120
	TabIndex	16
	Top	360
	Width	1335
Frame	Name	Frame2
	Caption	ShowTheseTypesofFiles
	Height	1935
	Left	120
	TabIndex	4
	Top	4920
	Width	3375

continued on next page

continued from previous page

OBJECT	PROPERTY	VALUE
TextBox	Name	txtFileSpec
	Font	MSSansSerif
	Size	8.25
	Charset	0
	Weight	700
	Underline	0 'False
	Italic	0 'False
	Strikethrough	0 'False
	Height	285
	Left	1080
	TabIndex	8
	Text	*.*
	Top	1320
	Width	2055
CheckBox	Name	cbSystem
	Caption	SystemFiles
	Height	255
	Left	240
	TabIndex	7
	Top	360
	Width	1455
CheckBox	Name	cbArchive
	Caption	ArchiveFiles
	Height	255
	Left	240
	TabIndex	6
	Top	840
	Width	1335
CheckBox	Name	cbHidden
	Caption	HiddenFiles
	Height	255
	Left	240
	TabIndex	5
	Top	600
	Width	1215

OBJECT	PROPERTY	VALUE
Label	Name	Label1
	Caption	FileSpec
	Height	255
	Left	240
	TabIndex	9
	Top	1320
	Width	735
DirListBox	Name	dirListView
	Height	3465
Left	120	
	TabIndex	2
	Top	1080
	Width	2655
DriveListBox	Name	drvListView
	Height	315
	Left	120
	TabIndex	1
	Top	360
	Width	2655
ListView	Name	ListView1
	Height	3735
	Left	3000
	TabIndex	0
	Top	720
	Width	5895
	LabelWrap	True
	HideSelection	True
	BorderStyle	1 - ccFixedSingle
	Appearance	1
	NumItems	0
Label	Name	Label4
	Caption	Directories
	Height	255
	Left	120
	TabIndex	19
	Top	840
	Width	1695

continued on next page

continued from previous page

OBJECT	PROPERTY	VALUE
Label	Name	Label3
	Caption	Drives
	Height	255
	Left	120
	TabIndex	18
	Top	120
	Width	1215
Label	Name	lblObjectCount
	Height	255
	Left	3000
	TabIndex	17
	Top	4440
	Width	5775
ImageList	Name	imlSmallIcons
	Left	3960
	Top	1080
Label	Name	lblContents
	BorderStyle	1 - Fixed Single
	Caption	Label1
	Height	375
	Left	3000
	TabIndex	3
	Top	360
	Width	5895
ImageList	Name	imlIcons
	Left	3120
	Top	960
	_ExtentX	1005
	_ExtentY	1005
	BackColor	&H80000005&
	MaskColor	&H00C0C0C0&

3. Add the following constants to the General Declarations section of `Form1`. The constants are used to store the name and location of graphics managed by the `ListImage` control and referenced by the `ListView` control. You might need to change the directory location for the bitmaps.

```
'Constants for use with the ListImage control
Const SMALL_FOLDER = "c:\VB6HT\CHAPTER02\closed.bmp"
Const SMALL_FILE = "c:\VB6HT\CHAPTER02\Leaf.bmp"
Const LARGE_FOLDER = "c:\VB6HT\CHAPTER02\clsdfold.ico"
Const LARGE_FILE = "c:\VB6HT\CHAPTER02\drag1pg.ico"
```

4. Add the following variable statements to the General Declarations section of **Form1**. The comments preceding the statement indicate the use of the variable.

```
'Stores total attributes for types of files displayed
Dim m_intAtts As Integer
'
'Stores ListView mode
Dim m_intViewType As Integer
'
'Flag indicating whether combo box has been populated
Dim m_blComboPop As Boolean
'
'Flag indicating whether columns have been set for Report mode
Dim m_blnFlgColumnsSet As Boolean
```

5. Add the **PopulateList** subroutine to **Form1**. This subroutine contains the central functionality for the project. This subroutine populates the **ListView** control based on a setting specified elsewhere in the project, such as the current directory and types of file shown. It is called from a number of different spots in the application.

The **Dir** function is used to retrieve file and directory names from the target directory. Prior to the first time the **Dir** function is called, some string manipulation is performed to pass a properly formatted parameter to the **Dir** function, which includes the file spec (such as *.*). In addition, an original copy of the path is kept. The **Dir** function is called until it has returned every file or directory in the target directory.

When the **Dir** function returns a found object, the object is immediately added to the **ListView** control using the **Add** method for the **ListItems** collection of the **ListView** control. The **GetAttr** function is used to determine whether the object is a file or a directory, and based on the result, the appropriate **ImageList** key is specified. Remember, an image is assigned to a control from the **ImageList** through the individual image's key. The **SmallIcon** and **Icon** properties are used to specify what images are used in Icon and SmallIcon modes.

Next, if Report mode is being used, additional information is retrieved about the file or folder and that information is applied to the **SubItems** property of the **ListImage** object. **SubItem** properties are used to store columnar information for when the **ListView** control is in Report mode. To be sure the correct information is applied to the correct **SubItem** index, the index of the column matching the header specified is determined and that column index is used as the **SubItem**'s index. At the end of the routine, the text for use in the "x objects found" caption is created.

```
Private Sub PopulateList()
'

    Dim lvListItem As ListItem
    Dim strFileName As String
    Dim strSearchPath As String
    Dim strFileSpec As String
    Dim strItemType As String
    Dim intObjectCount As Integer
    '

On Error GoTo poperr

    'Empty items for the View control
    ListView1.ListItems.Clear
    '

    'Get the file spec value for the form
    strFileSpec = txtFileSpec.Text
    '

    strSearchPath = dirListView.Path
    '

    'Set the 'Content of' caption
    lblContents.Caption = "Contents of " & strSearchPath
    '

    'Remove trailing backslash in case current directory is
    'root directory (in which case the \ is added by the O/S)
    If Right(strSearchPath, 1) = "\" Then
        strSearchPath = Left(strSearchPath, 2)
    End If
    '

    'Store the path so we can locate the file later in order
    'to retrieve its attributes
    strAttributePath = strSearchPath
    '

    'Add the file spec to the search path
    strSearchPath = strSearchPath + "\" + strFileSpec
    '

    'Retrieve the first object from the directory using
    strFileName = Dir(strSearchPath, m_intAtts)
    '

    Do While (strFileName <> "")
        intObjectCount = intObjectCount + 1
        If strFileName <> "." And strFileName <> ".." Then
            Set lvListItem = ListView1.ListItems.Add(, , _
                        strFileName)
            '

            'This logic will trap all non-directory items found.
            'This saves me for
            'testing for all of the attributes associated with a
            'file
            If (GetAttr(strAttributePath + "\" + strFileName) <> _
                        'vbDirectory) Then
                lvListItem.SmallIcon = "File"
                lvListItem.Icon = "File"
```

```
                                strItemType = "File"
                        Else
                            lvListItem.SmallIcon = "Folder"
                            lvListItem.Icon = "Folder"
                            strItemType = "File Folder"
                        End If
                        '
                        If ListView1.View = lvwReport Then
                            lvListItem.SubItems(ListView1.ColumnHeaders _
                            ("Type").SubItemIndex) = strItemType
                                '
                            If strItemType = "File" Then
                                lvListItem.SubItems(ListView1.ColumnHeaders _
                                ("Size").SubItemIndex) _ = Str$(FileLen _
                                (strAttributePath + "\" + strFileName))
                            Else
                                lvListItem.SubItems(ListView1.ColumnHeaders _
                                ("Size").SubItemIndex) = " "
                            End If

lvListItem.SubItems(ListView1.ColumnHeaders("Date").SubItemIndex) _
= Str$(FileDateTime(strAttributePath + "\" + strFileName))
                        End If
                            '
                    End If
                        '
                    strFileName = Dir
                '
            Loop
            If intObjectCount = 1 Then
                lblObjectCount.Caption = Str(intObjectCount) + " object _
found."
            Else
                lblObjectCount.Caption = Str(intObjectCount) + " objects _
found."
            End If
                '
            Exit sub

poperr:
    Resume Next
End Sub
```

6. Add the following subroutine to **Form1**. This subroutine sets up the columns
for when the **ListView** control mode is set to Report View. This is
accomplished by adding **ColumnHead** objects to the **ListView** control.
Although up to five parameters can be passed to the **Add** method, only four
are relevant: an index for the **ColumnHeader**, a key that uniquely identifies
the column, the text to be used in the header, and a numeric constant that
specifies the alignment of the column.

```
Private Sub SetColumns()
    '
    Dim chListView As ColumnHeader
    '
    Set chListView = ListView1.ColumnHeaders.Add(1, "Filename", _
"Filename", , lvwColumnLeft)
    Set chListView = ListView1.ColumnHeaders.Add(2, "Type", _
"Type", , lvwColumnRight)
    Set chListView = ListView1.ColumnHeaders.Add(3, "Size", _
"Size", , lvwColumnRight)
    Set chListView = ListView1.ColumnHeaders.Add(4, "Date", _
"Date/Time", , lvwColumnRight)
    '
End Sub
```

7. Add the following subroutine to **Form1**. This subroutine populates the List Mode drop-down list from which the user selects the mode for the **ListView** control. Two items are worth noting with respect to this routine. The list is populated so that the index of each item in the list matches the corresponding value of the **View** property of the **ListView** control. The **View** property determines the view mode of the list. This technique enables the routine to refer to the index of the drop-down list to determine the mode of the **ListView** control.

The other item of note is setting of the **m_blComboPop** variable. This flag tells the application that the **Click** event for the drop-down list was generated because the subroutine was called. The second-to-last line of the subroutine sets the index of the list to 0, which generates the **Click** event. The **Click** event for the drop-down list naturally should force the **ListView** to be repopulated, but not when the drop-down list is initialized. The next step continues this discussion.

```
Private Sub PopulateViewCombo()
    '
    'Populate the View Type list box
    m_blComboPop = True
    With cmbView
        .AddItem "Large Icons View"
        .AddItem "Small Icons View"
        .AddItem "List View"
        .AddItem "Report View"
        .ListIndex = 0
    End With
    '
End Sub
```

8. Add the following code to the **Click** event for the **cmbView** control on **Form1**. This event code is used to repopulate the **ListView** list when the user changes the control's mode. As described in the last step, the list should not be repopulated simply when the drop-down list is initialized, so a trap is set for the **m_blComboPop** variable. Another task for this event procedure is to update the module-level variable that stores the current mode of the **ListView** list. Another critical part of this routine is setting the **View** property. Immediately upon setting the property, the view mode of the **ListView** control is changed. In this case, the appearance of the list changes as soon as the second line of this subroutine is executed. Care should be taken where and how often the **View** property is modified.

```
Private Sub cmbView_Click()
    '
    m_intViewType = cmbView.ListIndex
    ListView1.View = m_intViewType
    '
    If (m_blComboPop) Then
        m_blComboPop = False
        Exit Sub
    End If
    '
    PopulateList
    '
End Sub
```

9. Add the following code to the **Click** event for the **rbNoArrange** control on **Form1**. This subroutine is fired when the user selects no alignment of the items in the **ListView** list. This is done by selecting the **rbNoArrange** radio button in the Alignment group. In this subroutine, the **Arrange** property for the **ListView** control is updated, and the list is repopulated. Because simply changing the **Arrange** property does not automatically arrange the items in the list, the **PopulateList** routine must be called.

```
Private Sub rbNoArrange_Click()
    '
    ListView1.Arrange = 0
    PopulateList
    '
End Sub
```

10. Add the following code to the **Click** event of the **rbAlignLeft** control on **Form1**. This subroutine is fired when the user selects left alignment of the items in the **ListView** list. This is done by selecting the **rbAlignLeft** radio button in the Alignment group. In this subroutine, the **Arrange** property for the **ListView** control is updated, and the list is repopulated. Because simply changing the **Arrange** property does not automatically arrange the items in the list, the **PopulateList** routine must be called.

```
Private Sub rbAlignLeft_Click()
    '
    ListView1.Arrange = 1
    PopulateList
    '
End Sub
```

11. Add the following event subroutine to **Form1**. This subroutine is fired when the user selects top alignment of the items in the **ListView** list. This is done by selecting the **rbAlignTop** radio button in the Alignment group. In this subroutine, the **Arrange** property for the **ListView** control is updated, and then the list is repopulated. Because simply changing the **Arrange** property does not automatically arrange the items in the list, the **PopulateList** routine must be called.

```
Private Sub rbAlignTop_Click()
'
    ListView1.Arrange = 2
    PopulateList
'
End Sub
```

12. Add the following code to the **keypress** event for the **txtFileSpec** control on **Form1**. This routine traps the Enter key being pressed in the File Spec edit box. This indicates to the user that a filename mask has been specified for filtering the list of items in the **ListView** list.

```
Private Sub txtFileSpec_KeyPress(KeyAscii As Integer)
'
    If KeyAscii = vbKeyReturn Then
        PopulateList
    End If
'
End Sub
```

13. The next subroutine to be added to the application is similar to code used in the first two How-Tos in this chapter. As you'll see in this step, however, it is sometimes required to use two **ImageList** controls.

Add the following code to the General Declarations section of **Form1**. The **ListView** control has two properties that both require **ImageList** controls as values. One property, **Icons**, is used to specify what **ImageList** to refer to to retrieve images for when the **ListView** list is in Icon mode. The other property, **SmallIcons**, is used to specify what **ImageList** to refer to to retrieve images for when the list is in Small Icon mode. As you can tell from the code, the **ImageList** controls are identical except for the images in them. One **ImageList** stores large bitmaps, whereas the other **ImageList** stores small icon images.

```
'Private Sub InitImageList()
    '
    'Specifies images used for the 2 Imagelist controls used in
    'the project
    Dim liListView As ListImage
    Set liListView = imlSmallIcons.ListImages.Add(, "File", _
                    LoadPicture(SMALL_FILE))
```

```
        Set liListView = imlSmallIcons.ListImages.Add(, "Folder", _
                         LoadPicture(SMALL_FOLDER))
        '
        Set liListView = imlIcons.ListImages.Add(, "File", _
                         LoadPicture(LARGE_FILE))
        Set liListView = imlIcons.ListImages.Add(, "Folder", _
                         LoadPicture(LARGE_FOLDER))
        '
        ListView1.Icons = imlIcons
        ListView1.SmallIcons = imlSmallIcons
        '
    End Sub
```

14. The next subroutine is used to repopulate the **ListView** list when the current directory is changed. Add this code to the change event of the **dirListView** control on **Form1**.

```
Private Sub dirListView_Change()
    '
    PopulateList
    '
End Sub
```

15. Naturally, if the user selects a different drive, the directory must be synchronized to the new drive. This subroutine, which is added to the change event of the **drvListView** control on **Form1**, handles this scenario. In addition, the routine intuitively sets keyboard focus to the directory list.

```
'Private Sub drvListView_Change()
    '
    'Synchronize drive and directory controls
    'Also, set keyboard focus to directory list immediately after
    'drive change
    dirListView.Path = drvListView.Drive
    dirListView.SetFocus
    '
End Sub
```

16. The event subroutine in this step is used to manage the display of specific file types in the **ListView** control when the user sets or clears one of the File Type check boxes. When the user selects or deselects one of the file type options, the variable storing the attributes of file types that should be displayed is recalculated (this is done in a separate routine), and then the list is repopulated.

```
Private Sub cbHidden_Click()
    '
    ProcessFileAtts
    PopulateList
    '
End Sub
```

17. Add the following event subroutine to **Form1**. This event is fired when the user sets or clears the check box for display of the System files.

```
Private Sub cbSystem_Click()
    '
    ProcessFileAtts
    PopulateList
    '
End Sub
```

18. Add the following event subroutine to **Form1**. This event is fired when the user sets or clears the check box for display of the Archive files.

```
Private Sub cbArchive_Click()
    '
    ProcessFileAtts
    PopulateList
    '
End Sub
```

19. Add the following subroutine to the General Declarations section of **Form1**. This code is used to recalculate the attribute value of the file types that should be displayed in the **ListView** list. The variable in the subroutine is used by the **Dir** function in the **PopulateList** method to retrieve the desired files.

```
Private Sub ProcessFileAtts()
    '
    m_intAtts = vbNormal + vbDirectory
    '
    If cbSystem.Value = 1 Then
        m_intAtts = m_intAtts + vbSystem
    End If
    '
    If cbArchive.Value = 1 Then
        m_intAtts = m_intAtts + vbArchive
    End If
    '
    If cbHidden.Value = 1 Then
        m_intAtts = m_intAtts + vbHidden
    End If
    '
End Sub
```

20. Add the following code to the column **Click** event of the **ListView1** control on **Form1**. This subroutine manages the sorting of the columns of data when **ListView** mode is set to Report View. One of the properties of the **ListView** control is **SortOrder**. In the following code, the **SortOrder** is toggled between ascending and descending as the user clicks on the column header. Following the establishment of the sort order, the column on which sorting should occur is specified, and then the list is sorted by setting the **Sorted** property to **True**.

```
Private Sub ListView1_ColumnClick(ByVal ColumnHeader As _
ColumnHeader)
    '
    If ListView1.SortOrder = lvwAscending Then
        ListView1.SortOrder = lvwDescending
    Else
        ListView1.SortOrder = lvwAscending
    End If
    '
    ListView1.SortKey = ColumnHeader.Index - 1
    ListView1.Sorted = True
    '
End Sub
```

21. Add the following code to the **Form_Load** event. This routine populates the **ListView** based on default settings, such as the default sort order, and the default file types to be specified in the list. Other setup work is handled by functions that have been covered already.

```
Private Sub Form_Load()
    '
    InitImageList
    m_intAtts = vbNormal + vbDirectory
    PopulateViewCombo
    SetColumns
    PopulateList
    ListView1.SortOrder = lvwAscending
    '
End Sub
```

How It Works

Like the **ImageList** control described in section 2.2 of this chapter, the **ListView** control is powerful, flexible, and easy to implement because all its functionality can be controlled in code. As demonstrated in this How-To, the entire management of the list occurs in code. Items are easily added to the list with the **Add** method of the **ListItems** collection; column headers and sorting are managed through a smaller subset of objects; and changing how the items in the list are displayed is a matter of changing the **View** property of the control.

Comments

How this example works is more a matter of design and preparation rather than under-the-hood secrets. Take the time to design the functionality of the application using the **ListView** control. Set up discrete routines for handling the setup chores and list population, and your application will be in good shape.

COMPLEXITY
INTERMEDIATE

2.4 How do I...
Present data objects with the
`ListView` and `TreeView` controls?

COMPATIBILITY: VISUAL BASIC 5 AND 6

Problem

Providing user access to a database is a constant requirement and a constant challenge for application developers. Whether the user is interested in meta-data or data, there is a constant demand to provide a view of databases for all users. A simple method for solving the problem is to provide users with the application used to develop the database. For example, if a user is interested in seeing Human Resources data, simply give the user her own copy of Microsoft Access and the proper security. This isn't the most efficient method, however, because of the learning curve associated with relational database systems.

Technique

A solution for providing a view of a database might be to build an Explorer-style application in Visual Basic. Using the `ListView` and `TreeView` controls, an application can be built that lets the user browse through the meta-data of a database and then view either details about the schema or the actual data. Specifically, the user could select a database, open it, and present its schema in a hierarchical format using the `TreeView` control.

As the user selects tables in the `TreeView`, the `ListView` control can be used to display either the fields in the table selected or even records from the table. Using built-in `ListView` functionality, the user could switch between different views of the data, including a detailed report view.

Steps

Open and run the project LVDATA.VBP. Enter the name and location of any Access database in the edit box in the Database frame at the top-left portion of the dialog box. To browse through your system to locate a database, click the Browse button. The common Open dialog box appears, with the Files of Type drop-down list set to Access Database Files. When you installed Visual Basic, the option was presented to install sample files. If you did so, two sample databases were loaded onto your system, the NWIND.MDB (a.k.a. Northwinds) and BIBLIO.MDB databases, in the main Visual Basic directory. Try using either of these databases with the example program. After you have chosen a database, click the Load button. After doing so, the left pane in the dialog box displays tables and fields in the database you selected using the TreeView control. Figure 2.13 shows how the Northwinds database appears in the example program.

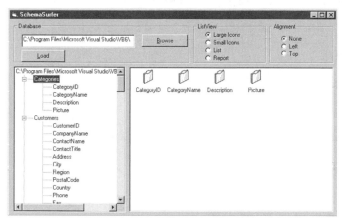

Figure 2.13 Displaying NWIND.MDB in the TreeView control.

Notice how the database appears as the top node of the tree. Also, notice how tables make up the second level in the tree, and how column names are displayed as dependents of each table. Click any table in the tree, and the ListView control in the right pane is updated to show the field names for the table you selected. Clicking a column name in the TreeView control has the same effect as clicking the table name.

With data displayed in the ListView control, select from the different List View options at the top of the dialog box; the default view is Large Icons. When you switch to Small Icons, notice how the icons for each column change, and each field shown in the list appears smaller. Next, switch to List view, and the field names are presented in a list format with small icons. Finally, switch to Report view. The appearance of the list changes dramatically, displaying information about fields from the table in columns. An X appears in the columns for any field with a matching attribute. Figure 2.14 shows how the Employees table of the NWIND.MDB database appears in Report view. The list could also be modified to display records for the table selected in the list.

Clicking any other table triggers an update to the contents of the list. In addition, choosing one of the Alignment options in the top-right corner of the dialog box also causes the list to be repopulated. Keep in mind that this option is only available when the list is not in Large Icon, Small Icon, or List views.

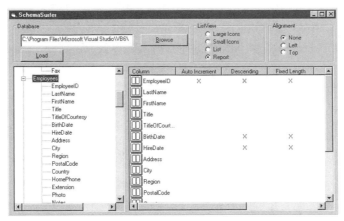

Figure 2.14 Displaying the Employees table in
Report View.

That's it for the tour of the example program. The following steps
demonstrate how to present data from a database in the `TreeView` control, and
then how to present some of the same data in the list. They also show how to
present attribute information about fields from the database in the list. Finally,
the application implements supporting functionality, such as using radio buttons
to help the user select the List view:

1. Create a new project and call it LVDATA.VBP. Choose Projects,
Components from the menu, and then choose Microsoft Common
Controls 6.0 from the list. If Microsoft Common Controls 6.0 does not
appear in the list, choose Browse to locate the COMCTL32.OCX file. Also,
add a reference to Microsoft DAO 3.51 Object Library. This library enables
your application to retrieve data from an Access database.

2. Add the objects listed in Table 2.5 to `Form1`, using the properties shown in
the table.

Table 2.5 Objects and Properties for `Form1`

OBJECT	PROPERTY	VALUE
Form	Name	frmTvData
	AutoRedraw	True
	Caption	SchemaSurfer
	Height	6435
	Left	60
	Top	345

OBJECT	PROPERTY	VALUE
	tWidth	10275
	LinkTopic	Form1
	ScaleHeight	6435
	ScaleWidth	10275
	StartUpPosition	3 - WindowsDefault
Frame	Name	Frame3
	Caption	Alignment
	Height	1335
	Left	8160
	TabIndex	11
	Top	120
	Width	2055
OptionButton	Name	rbTopAlign
	Caption	Top
	Height	195
	Left	360
	TabIndex	14
	Top	840
	Width	1455
OptionButton	Name	rbLeftAlign
	Caption	Left
	Height	255
	Left	360
	TabIndex	13
	Top	600
	Width	1455
OptionButton	Name	rbNoAlign
	Caption	None
	Height	255
	Left	360
	TabIndex	12
	Top	360
	Value	True
	Width	1455

continued on next page

continued from previous page

OBJECT	PROPERTY	VALUE
Frame	Name	Frame2
	Caption	ListView
	Height	1335
	Left	5760
	TabIndex	5
	Top	120
	Width	2295
OptionButton	Name	rbViewType
	Caption	Option1
	Enabled	False
	Height	255
	Index	1
	Left	360
	TabIndex	9
	Top	480
	Width	1335
OptionButton	Name	rbViewType
	Caption	Option1
	Enabled	False
	Height	255
	Index	2
	Left	360
	TabIndex	8
	Top	720
	Width	1335
OptionButton	Name	rbViewType
	Caption	Option1
	Enabled	False
	Height	255
	Index	3
	Left	360
	TabIndex	7
	Top	960
	Width	1335

OBJECT	PROPERTY	VALUE
OptionButton	Name	rbViewType
	Caption	Option1
	Enabled	False
	Height	255
	Index	0
	Left	360
	TabIndex	6
	Top	240
	Value	True
	Width	1335
TreeView	Name	tvData
	Height	4015
	Left	120
	TabIndex	4
	Top	1560
	Width	3495
	Style	6
	Appearance	1
Frame	Name	Frame1
	Caption	Database
	Height	1335
	Left	120
	TabIndex	1
	Top	120
	Width	5535
CommandButton	Name	cbLoad
	Caption	&Load
	Height	375
	Left	240
	TabIndex	10
	Top	840
	Width	1335
CommonDialog	Name	cmdTvData
	Left	480
	Top	1320

continued on next page

continued from previous page

OBJECT	PROPERTY	VALUE
CommandButton	Name	cbBrowse
	Caption	&Browse
	Height	375
	Left	3960
	TabIndex	3
	Top	360
	Width	1455
TextBox	Name	txtDatabaseName
	Height	405
	Left	240
	TabIndex	2
	Top	360
	Width	3495
ListView	Name	lvwData
	Height	4815
	Left	3720
	TabIndex	0
	Top	1560
	Width	6495
	LabelWrap	True
	HideSelection	True
	BorderStyle	1
	Appearance	1
ImageList	Name	imSmall
	Left	840
	Top	720
ImageList	Name	imLarge
	Left	120
	Top	720

3. Add the following code to the General Declarations section of Form1. The code declares a number of module-level variables needed throughout the application, as well as specifies values for two constants used for specifying ImageList graphics. You might need to change the location of the graphics files.

```
'Module Level variables we'll need throughout app
Dim m_dbTvData As Database
Dim m_tbTvData As TableDef
Dim m_intNumTables As Integer
Dim m_CurrentListTable As String
'
'Images for ImageList controls
Const SMALL_COLUMN = "c:\VB6HT\CHAPTER02\notebook.bmp"
Const LARGE_COLUMN = "c:\VB6HT\CHAPTER02\folder01.ico"
```

4. Add the following code to the **Click** event for the **cbBrowse** button. This code manages the common dialog box control used to help select a database.

```
'Populate the Files of Type dropdown in the Open dialog
'Also, set the default filter
cmdTvData.Filter = "Access Databases (*.MDB)¦*.mdb¦All Files _
(*.*)¦*.*"
cmdTvData.FilterIndex = 1
'
'Display the open dialog box
cmdTvData.ShowOpen
'
'Set the database name field to the return from the Open File db
If cmdTvData.filename <> "" Then
    txtDatabaseName.Text = cmdTvData.filename
End If
```

5. Add the following subroutine to the General Declarations section of **Form1**. This subroutine loads graphics into the **ImageList** control using **ListImage** objects; it is called when **FrmTvData** is loaded. The **ListView** control requires two **ImageList** controls to be used: one to store the graphics used for Large Icons view, and the other to store the graphics used for Report, List, and Small Icons views. Consequently, images are loaded into two different **ImageList** controls in this code. The last two lines of code in this subroutine specify the **ImageList** controls the **ListView** controls should use.

```
Private Sub LoadImages()
    '
    'Specifies images used for the 2 Imagelist controls used in
    'the project
    Dim liListView As ListImage
    Set liListView = imSmall.ListImages.Add(, "Small", _
    LoadPicture(SMALL_COLUMN))
    '
    Set liListView = imLarge.ListImages.Add(, "Large", _
    LoadPicture(LARGE_COLUMN))
    '
    lvwData.Icons = imLarge
    lvwData.SmallIcons = imSmall
    '
End Sub
```

6. Like the code added in step 5, the code added in this step handles some setup chores for the **ListView** control. This subroutine is called when the form is loaded. In Report mode, additional data about the item is displayed in the list. When the list is in Icon, Small Icon, or List view, only the item is displayed in the list. The code in the following subroutine defines the columns that appear when the list switches to Report mode.

```
Private Sub LoadColumns()
    '
    Dim lvcSchema As ColumnHeader
    '
    Set lvcSchema = lvwData.ColumnHeaders.Add(1, "Column", _
"Column")
    Set lvcSchema = lvwData.ColumnHeaders.Add(2, "AutoIncrement", _
"Auto Increment", , lvwColumnCenter)
    Set lvcSchema = lvwData.ColumnHeaders.Add(3, "Descending", _
"Descending", , lvwColumnCenter)
    Set lvcSchema = lvwData.ColumnHeaders.Add(4, "FixedLength", _
"Fixed Length", , lvwColumnCenter)
    Set lvcSchema = lvwData.ColumnHeaders.Add(5, "HyperLink", _
"Hyperlink", , lvwColumnCenter)
    Set lvcSchema = lvwData.ColumnHeaders.Add(6, "Updatable", _
"Updatable", , lvwColumnCenter)
    Set lvcSchema = lvwData.ColumnHeaders.Add(7, "VariableLength", _
"Variable Length", , lvwColumnCenter)
    '
End Sub
```

7. The next routine establishes captions for a control array of option buttons. These option buttons are used to specify the view type for the list. It is not an accident that the index of each button in the array matches the internal value for the corresponding view type. This way, the view type of the list can be set simply by setting the **View** property of the **ListView** control to the index of the selected option button. This is demonstrated in the **Click** event for the **rbViewType** option button control array.

```
Private Sub InitViewOptions()
    '
    rbViewType(0).Caption = "Large Icons"
    rbViewType(1).Caption = "Small Icons"
    rbViewType(2).Caption = "List"
    rbViewType(3).Caption = "Report"
    '
End Sub
```

8. The last of the routines called when **FrmTvData** is loaded is shown in this step. This routine controls whether the option buttons used to specify the alignment of items in the list are enabled. This helper routine either enables or disables the three option buttons based on a parameter passed to the routine.

```
Private Sub ManageAlignOptions(blEnabled As Boolean)
    '
    rbNoAlign.Enabled = blEnabled
    rbLeftAlign.Enabled = blEnabled
    rbTopAlign.Enabled = blEnabled
    '
End Sub
```

9. Now that the routines called when **FrmTvData** is loaded have been discussed, add the code that executes during the **Form_Load** event subroutine.

```
Private Sub Form_Load()
    InitViewOptions
    LoadImages
    LoadColumns
    ManageAlignOptions (False)
End Sub
```

10. One of the critical tasks in this application is to load a database the user chooses. Loading the database is the objective of one of three routines introduced in this step. To load the database and populate the **TreeView** control, the user clicks the Load button. The **Click** event procedure for the **cbLoad** control is shown as the last of the following three subroutines. Critical here, though, is the routine called when the button is clicked—the **LoadDatabase** subroutine.

The first chore of this subroutine is to check whether the user has entered a value in the **txtDatabase** control. The **GetDatabaseName** handles this work, and it returns the database name to the **LoadDatabase** routine. **GetDatabaseName** is the second of the following three routines.

After the name of the database is returned to **LoadDatabase**, a DAO call is made to open the database. The database object returned when the database is opened is then used to evaluate whether the database has tables. If no tables are found, the user is notified, and no more processing is required. If tables do exist, the option buttons showing the four view types are enabled, and a call is made to populate the **TreeView** control. Add the following three subroutines to **Form1**. The first two go in the General Declarations section, and the third is code that goes in the **Click** event of the **cbLoad** control.

```
Public Sub LoadDatabase()
    '
    Dim dbName As String
    Dim intNumTables As Integer
    '
    If Not (GetDatabaseName(dbName)) Then
        Exit Sub
    End If
```

```
    m_strDatabase = dbName
    '
    Set m_dbTvData = _
    DBEngine.Workspaces(0).OpenDatabase(m_strDatabase)
    '
    m_intNumTables = m_dbTvData.TableDefs.Count
    '
    If m_intNumTables < 1 Then
        MsgBox "Cannot find tables in specified database!", _
        vbCritical, "Database Explorer"
        Exit Sub
    End If
    EnableViewOptions
    PopulateTree

End Sub

Public Function GetDatabaseName(p_strDatabaseName As String) As
Boolean
    '
    If txtDatabaseName.Text = "" Then
        MsgBox "No database specified!", vbCritical, "Database _
        Explorer"
        GetDatabaseName = False
        Exit Function
    End If
    p_strDatabaseName = txtDatabaseName.Text
    GetDatabaseName = True
    '
End Function

Private Sub cbLoad_Click()
    '
    LoadDatabase
    '
End Sub
```

11. Add the following subroutine to the General Declarations section of **Form1**.
The routine added here simply enables the four option buttons that are
used to specify the view of the list. Because the view changes automatically
when any of the buttons is selected, the buttons are disabled until a valid
database is opened, which occurs at the end of the **LoadDatabase** routine.
Because the four buttons are implemented as a control array, the code
enables each of the buttons by simply looping through the array.

```
Public Sub EnableViewOptions()
    '
    Dim i As Integer
    For i = 0 To 3
        rbViewType(i).Enabled = True
    Next
    '
End Sub
```

12. The next piece of code to be added to the application is the subroutine that populates the `TreeView` control. The code may look complicated, but the objective of the subroutine is straightforward.

Using DAO concepts, the `TableDefs` collection of tables in the database is used to add each table to the `TreeView` control. This is done using the `Add` method of the `Nodes` collection. As the code iterates through each table in the database, the `Fields` collection is used to determine the fields in the table. As each field is returned, it is added to the `TreeView` control as a child of the current table. Because multiple fields in the database might have the same name, the table name is attached to the field's name when the key of the node is being set. A plus sign is used to join the two pieces of information. That plus sign also has another use. The `Expanded` method is used whenever a parent node is added to the tree; it expands the tree automatically. Add the following code to the General Declarations section of `Form1`.

```
Public Sub PopulateTree()
    '
    Dim ndData As Node
    Dim intCounter As Integer
    Dim intNumFields As Integer
    Dim intFldCntr As Integer
    Dim fld As Field
    '
    Set ndData = tvData.Nodes.Add(, , "db", m_dbTvData.Name)
    ndData.Expanded - True
    '
    'Walk through each of the tables in the database and
    'add each to the TreeView
    Do While m_intNumTables <> intCounter
        Set m_tbTvData = m_dbTvData.TableDefs(intCounter)
        Set ndData = tvData.Nodes.Add("db", tvwChild, _
                m_tbTvData.Name, m_tbTvData.Name)
        ndData.Expanded = True
        intNumFields = m_tbTvData.Fields.Count
        If intNumFields <> 0 Then
            intFldCntr = 0
            'Walk through each of the fields in the table and add
            'to the
            'TreeView control as dependents of the current table
            Do While intNumFields <> intFldCntr
                Set fld = m_tbTvData.Fields(intFldCntr)
                'Add the table name to the Key for the node in
                'case other fields
                'in other tables have the same name
                Set ndData = tvData.Nodes.Add(m_tbTvData.Name, _
                tvwChild, m_tbTvData.Name_
                        + "+" + fld.Name, fld.Name)
                intFldCntr = intFldCntr + 1
            Loop
        End If
        '
```

```
        intCounter = intCounter + 1
    Loop
    '
End Sub
```

13. The next step is to populate the `ListView` control. The list is only populated after a node in the `TreeView` is clicked. Considering this, the `NodeClick` event (which is a `Click` event reserved for the `TreeView` control and is used to trap a click on a node rather than a random click anywhere on a `TreeView` control) should be equipped with some intelligence. The routine should be capable of determining the node being clicked so that it might properly generate the population of the `ListView` control.

The following code determines the table whose fields populate the list by evaluating the key value for the node being clicked. If a plus symbol is found anywhere in the key, then the node is a field, and the text of the key up to the plus sign is extracted as the table name. Remember from step 12 that to guard against cases when a field in another table might have the same name, a plus sign is used to join the table name to the field name. Keep in mind that no two keys in the same `TreeView` can match, and the field name is being used as a key in this application.

After the routine has determined the table the user clicked on, a module-level variable is used to determine whether the user has simply clicked on a different field of the same table because then there would be no need to repopulate the list in this case. Finally, the name of the table whose fields populate the `ListView` control is passed to the `PopulateList` routine, and the module-level variable storing the name of the current table is updated. Add the following code to the `tvData_NodeClick` subroutine in `Form1`.

```
Private Sub tvData_NodeClick(ByVal Node As ComctlLib.Node)
    '
    Dim strTable As String
    Dim intPlus As Integer
    '
    'Evaluate what type of Node was selected and if
    'a base node, figure out the table name
    '
    'Do nothing if the top node is selected
    If Node.Key = "db" Then
        Exit Sub
    End If
    '
    'If a plus sign, then a base node, so extract parent
    intPlus = InStr(1, Node.Key, "+")
    If intPlus > 0 Then
        strTable = Left$(Node.Key, intPlus - 1)
    Else
        strTable = Node.Key
    End If
```

```
     '
     If strTable = m_CurrentListTable Then
         Exit Sub
     End If
     '
     PopulateList (strTable)
     m_CurrentListTable = strTable
     '
 End Sub
```

14. The workhorse of the application is the subroutine described in this step. The **PopulateList** routine adds items to the **ListView** control. What makes this routine a bit more interesting than normal is the processing of the database field attributes that must occur to support Report view. That code is discussed in a moment.

The routine kicks off by checking the table name to see whether it contains fields. If the table contains fields, the list is cleared, and the **Fields** collection is iterated through. Each field is added to the list through the **ListImage** object, and the icon and small icon images are assigned. Next, if the list is set to Report view, a bitwise comparison is made between the **Attributes** property of the field and the one of the seven attributes this application reports on in the list.

If the field matches any attribute, a **SubItem** object is added to the current **ListImage** object. A **SubItem** object is used to store and display any columnar data that appears in Report view. To ensure that the correct **SubItem** data is displayed in the proper column, the index of the column is retrieved by checking its key. This key was established in the **LoadColumns** routine, which is discussed in step 6. The routine wraps up by enabling the set of option buttons used to manage alignment of list items.

```
Private Sub PopulateList(strTableName as String)
     '
     Dim tbCurrentTable As TableDef
     Dim tmpField As Field
     Dim tmpImage As ListItem
     Dim intCounter As Integer
     Dim intNumFields As Integer
     Dim strFieldName As String
     '
     Set tbCurrentTable = m_dbTvData.TableDefs(strTableName)
     '
 lvwData.ListItems.Clear

     intNumFields = tbCurrentTable.Fields.Count
     If intNumFields = 0 Then
         Exit Sub
```

```
            End If
            '

        Do While intCounter <> intNumFields
                Set tmpField = tbCurrentTable.Fields(intCounter)
                Set tmpImage = lvwData.ListItems.Add(, tmpField.Name, _
tmpField.Name)
                tmpImage.Icon = "Large"
                tmpImage.SmallIcon = "SMall"
                intCounter = intCounter + 1
                '

            If lvwData.View = lvwReport Then
                If (tmpField.Attributes And dbFixedField) Then
                    tmpImage.SubItems(lvwData.ColumnHeaders _
                    ("FixedLength").SubItemIndex) = "X"
                End If
                '

                If (tmpField.Attributes And dbVariableField) Then
                    tmpImage.SubItems(lvwData.ColumnHeaders _
                    ("VariableLength").SubItemIndex) = "X"
                End If
                '

                If (tmpField.Attributes And dbAutoIncrField) Then
                    tmpImage.SubItems(lvwData.ColumnHeaders _
                    ("AutoIncrement").SubItemIndex) = "X"
                End If
                '

                If (tmpField.Attributes And dbHyperlinkField) Then
                    tmpImage.SubItems(lvwData.ColumnHeaders _
                    ("HyperLink").SubItemIndex) = "X"
                End If
                '

                If (tmpField.Attributes And dbUpdatableField) Then
                    tmpImage.SubItems(lvwData.ColumnHeaders _
                    ("Updatable").SubItemIndex) = "X"
                End If
                '

                If (tmpField.Attributes And dbDescending) Then
                    tmpImage.SubItems(lvwData.ColumnHeaders _
                    ("Descending").SubItemIndex) = "X"
                End If
                '

            End If
            '

        Loop
        ManageAlignOptions (True)
        '

    End Sub
```

15. This event routine is used to change the view of the list. When a user clicks one of the List View option buttons, the **View** property of the list is set to the index of the array button selected. Because the array index matches the relevant `View` property of the `ListImage` control, no special processing or parsing needs to occur. For example, to set the list to Report view, the `View` property must be set to a value of 3. The Report option happens to be last in the list, so its index in the array is 3.

```
Private Sub rbViewType_Click(Index As Integer)
    '
    lvwData.View = Index
    If Index <> 3 Then
        ManageAlignOptions (True)
    Else
        ManageAlignOptions (False)
    End If
    '
End Sub
```

16. The last routines to look at are those that manage the alignment of items in the list when the list is not set to Report view. Very simply, when the user selects any of three Alignment option buttons, the `Arrange` property of the `ListView` control is set, and the list is repopulated. Add the following three event procedures to the appropriate event handlers in the `Form1` code module:

```
Private Sub rbNoAlign_Click()
    '
    lvwData.Arrange = lvwNone
    PopulateList (m_CurrentListTable)
    '
End Sub

Private Sub rbLeftAlign_Click()
    '
    lvwData.Arrange = lvwAutoLeft
    PopulateList (m_CurrentListTable)
    '
End Sub

Private Sub rbTopAlign_Click()
    '
    lvwData.Arrange = lvwAutoTop
    PopulateList (m_CurrentListTable)
    '
End Sub
```

How It Works

The application in this How-To works by using DAO code in combination with properties, methods, and collections of the `TreeView` and `ListView` controls.

DAO returns objects, such as tables and fields, one at a time in code. This is demonstrated in instances where a loop is set up to iterate through each table in the databases' `TableDefs` collection, such as with this example:

```
Do While Counter <> NumTables
    Set MyTable = myDatabase.TableDefs(Counter)
Loop
```

In working efficiently with the `TreeView` and `ListView` controls, these controls require you to add `Node`s and `ListItem`s one at a time, as well. By using a series of loops, the application walks through the database's tables and `Fields` collections, adding `Node`s and `ListItem`s on-the-fly.

The use of the Key field for a `Node` item also comes in handy. By using a table's name as the value for the Key field when the table's node object is added to the tree, it becomes easy to specify the relevant node when a dependent field is added to the tree. When you have mastered the population of the two controls by using return values from the database's collection objects, you can easily add the support code required to finish the application. This support code could include routines to change the view of the list, load the database, populate the `ImageList`s, and more.

Comments

Using `TreeView` and `ListView` controls helps give your application the same look and feel as many popular programs. When you make use of common controls to perform the operations of your application, it makes it easier for users already familiar with the controls and their actions to adapt to your program. One thing you don't want to do is use common controls and program them to behave differently from the accepted behaviors.

CHAPTER 3
CLASS FUNDAMENTALS

3

CLASS
FUNDAMENTALS

How do I...

It is possible to transform most standard modules to class modules, but at times it will make your code modules awkward and difficult to use. Analyze the various components of the code routines that you are about to create. Determine how they will be used in your code. Based on how the routines will be used, you will be able to determine whether you should use a standard module or a class module.

To understand when to use a class module, it is important to realize the differences between standard modules and class modules. The primary difference is how data is stored. In a standard module, if one section of your program changes a public variable of the module and another section of your program then reads that variable, the new value is returned. Consider the following items when determining whether to use a class module or a standard module:

✔ How data is used—Data can exist independently for each instance of the class.

✔ Required lifetime code—Data exists in a standard module for the entire life of your program, whereas data in a class module only exists for the lifetime of the object that is instantiated from the class.

✔ Where is code called—Class modules should be used any time your program requires multiple instances of code or data.

3.1 Create a Simple Class with Properties and Methods

In this How-To, an employee class is created. The program creates three employees. By placing the employee-specific code into a class module, a separate instance of the employee class can be declared for each of the three employees. That makes the code much cleaner because each employee uses a separate instance of the same code.

3.2 Handle Events in a Simple Class

With Visual Basic 5 came the `RaiseEvent` statement. In previous versions of Visual Basic, the closest thing to this type of functionality was an idle loop that checked the status of a variable. If the variable changed, some code could do something such as canceling a long running operation. With the `RaiseEvent` statement, all this looping code is no longer required. Just raise an event when something needs to happen. This How-To demonstrates how to raise events in your class modules.

3.3 Migrate a Simple Class to Incorporate Polymorphism

As mentioned earlier, Visual Basic supports the `Implements` keyword. This feature enables a class to support multiple interfaces. This How-To demonstrates how to use the `Implements` keyword.

3.4 Create a Simple Container Control Using a Class

I want to add a status bar to my application. COMCTL32.OCX contains a lot of different functionality, including a status bar. I want my application to contain a status bar, but I do not need any of the extra functionality included in COMCTL32.OCX. This How-To shows how to create a Status Bar container control using a class.

3.5 Understand and Make Use of Apartment-Threaded Components

Visual Basic 6 inherited several features that were released in later service packs of Visual Basic 5. One feature that was introduced in Service Pack 2 of Visual Basic 5 is the Apartment-Threaded Model. This feature allows you to create multithreaded applications, and configure your ActiveX components to be compatible with other multithreaded applications. This How-To demonstrates the use of the Apartment-Threaded Model in a Visual Basic application.

3.6 Create a Dependent Object or Collection Within a Class

The technique of creating a dependent object within a class—combined with other techniques, design methods, and your own creative abilities—can be used to develop data and business object models that streamline your multitier applications.

COMPLEXITY
BEGINNING

3.1 How do I...
Create a simple class with properties and methods?

COMPATIBILITY: VISUAL BASIC 4, 5, AND 6

Problem

I have to track information on different employees. I do not want to repeat the code for each employee. How can I use the same code for each of the employees I want to track?

Technique

This How-To creates a class to keep track of employee information. This example also further demonstrates when to place code in standard modules and when to place code in a class module.

Steps

Open and run EMPLOYEE DATE.VBP. An example of the running program is shown in Figure 3.1. Select an employee from the employee list box. At this point, you can set the hire date, get the hire date, and determine the number of years the employee has been employed by clicking the appropriate command buttons.

Complete the following steps to create this project:

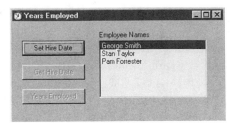

Figure 3.1 The main form at runtime.

1. Create a new project called EMPLOYEE DATE.VBP.

2. Add a form to the project and set the objects and properties listed in Table 3.1 for the form. Save it as EMPLOYEE.FRM.

Table 3.1 Project Form's Objects and Properties

OBJECT/CONTROL	PROPERTY	VALUE
Form	Name	frmMain
	Caption	"Years Employed"
	Icon	Timer01.ico
	StartUpPosition	2 'CenterScreen
CommandButton	Name	cmdSetHireDate
	Caption	"Set Hire Date"
CommandButton	Name	cmdGetHireDate
	Caption	"Get Hire Date"
CommandButton	Name	cmdYearsEmployed
	Caption	"Years Employed"
Label	Name	lblEmployeeNames
	Alignment	0 'Left Justify
	Caption	"Employee Names"
ListBox	Name	lstEmployees

3. Put the following code into the General Declarations section of the form. The code declares the instances of **clsEmployee** that are needed for the application and declares a constant for an empty string.

```
Option Explicit

Dim clsStanTaylor As New clsEmployee
Dim clsGeorgeSmith As New clsEmployee
Dim clsPamForrester As New clsEmployee
Dim clsCurrentEmployee As New clsEmployee

Const sEmptyString As String = ""
```

4. Add the following code to the form's **Load** event. This code adds the default employee names to `lstEmployees`.

```
'-- For demonstration purposes we will load three default names.
'-- If this was an actual application then these names should be
'   loaded either from a table or a text file.
lstEmployees.AddItem "George Smith"
lstEmployees.AddItem "Stan Taylor"
lstEmployees.AddItem "Pam Forrester"

'-- Ensure that one employee is always selected.
lstEmployees.ListIndex = 0
```

5. Place the following code in the `Click` event of the `cmdSetHireDate` `CommandButton`. When this code is executed, the user is prompted for the month, day, and year. These values are then validated to ensure that they are numeric. After validation, the date is converted to system format. The date in system format is obtained by calling the function `GetDateSystemFormat`. To finish this routine, the `HireDate` property of the current `clsEmployee` is set to be equal to the date in system format.

```
'-- This routine will set the date the employee was hired in
'   the system date format.

    Dim sCurrentEmployee As String
    Dim sDay As String
    Dim sMonth As String
    Dim sYear As String
    Dim sDateHired As String

    On Error GoTo error_cmdSetHireDate

    '-- Get the month, day, and year the employee was hired.
    sMonth = InputBox("Enter the month the employee was hired.")
    sDay = InputBox("Enter the day employee was hired.")
    sYear = InputBox("Enter the year the employee was hired.")

    '-- Ensure that a valid month, day, and year was entered.
    If IsNumeric(sMonth) = False Or _
       IsNumeric(sDay) = False Or _
       IsNumeric(sYear) = False Then
      MsgBox "You must enter a month, day, and year."
      Exit Sub
    End If

    '-- Get the date in system format.
    sDateHired = GetDateSystemFormat(CInt(sYear), CInt(sMonth),
CInt(sDay))

    '-- If sDateHired returns "" then an invalid date was entered.
    If sDateHired = sEmptyString Then
```

continued on next page

continued from previous page

```
        GoTo error_cmdSetHireDate
      End If

  clsCurrentEmployee.HireDate = sDateHired

    cmdGetHireDate.Enabled = True
    cmdYearsEmployeed.Enabled = True

  error_cmdSetHireDate:
    MsgBox "You have entered an invalid date"
```

6. Add the following code to the `Click` event of the `cmdGetHireDate`
`CommandButton`. This code displays the date that the currently selected
employee was hired via a `MessageBox`.

```
    '-- This routine will display the date the selected employee
    '    was hired.

  Dim sCurrentEmployee As String

  sCurrentEmployee = lstEmployees.List(lstEmployees.ListIndex)

  MsgBox sCurrentEmployee & " was hired on " &
  clsCurrentEmployee.HireDate
```

7. Enter this code into the `Click` event of the `cmdYearsEmployed`
`CommandButton`. This code calls a method of the currently selected
`clsEmployee` and displays the number of years the current employee has
been employed in a `MessageBox`.

```
    '-- This routine will display a message box indicating the
    'number of
    '    years the employee has been employed.

  Dim sCurrentEmployee As String
  Dim iYearsEmployeed As Integer

  sCurrentEmployee = lstEmployees.List(lstEmployees.ListIndex)

    iYearsEmployeed = clsCurrentEmployee.TimeEmployeed

  If iYearsEmployeed > 0 Then
    MsgBox sCurrentEmployee & " has been employed for " & _
      CStr(clsCurrentEmployee.TimeEmployeed) & " years."
  Else
    MsgBox sCurrentEmployee & " has been employed for less than _
                    one year."
  End If
```

8. Add the following code to the **Click** event of the **ListBox**. This routine checks the **Hiredate** property for the currently selected **clsEmployee** to determine whether the **cmdGetHireDate** and the **cmdYearsEmployed** CommandButtons should be enabled. If the **Hiredate** property of the selected **clsEmployee** is an empty string, then the **CommandButtons** are not enabled.

```
'-- This routine will ensure that the proper command buttons are
'enabled.

  Dim bStatus As Boolean

  Call SetCurrentEmployee

  If clsCurrentEmployee.HireDate <> sEmptyString Then
    bStatus = True
  Else
    bStatus = False
  End If

  cmdGetHireDate.Enabled = bStatus
  cmdYearsEmployed.Enabled = bStatus
```

9. Add the following subroutine, which is called when the user selects a name from the **lstEmployees** ListBox. This code sets the **clsCurrentEmployee** equal to the class associated with the selected name in the **ListBox**. By associating one common class to the name selected in the **ListBox**, you can refer to the common class throughout the code. Without this type of routine, you would have to have a similar **Select Case** statement in all the **CommandButtons** on the form.

```
Private Sub SetCurrentEmployee()

Dim sCurrentEmployee As String

'-- This routine will set the clsCurrentEmployee to the
'   employee that was selected in the list box.

sCurrentEmployee = lstEmployees.List(lstEmployees.ListIndex)

Select Case sCurrentEmployee
  Case "George Smith"
    Set clsCurrentEmployee = clsGeorgeSmith
  Case "Stan Taylor"
    Set clsCurrentEmployee = clsStanTaylor
  Case "Pam Forrester"
    Set clsCurrentEmployee = clsPamForrester
End Select

End Sub
```

10. Add a standard module to the project and save it as DATES.BAS. The
following routine returns a date in system format. This code is placed in a
standard module so that it can be used anywhere in the program. There is
no need to have multiple instances of this routine, so it is not placed in a
class module.

```
Public Function GetDateSystemFormat(iYear As Integer, iMonth As _
Integer, iDay As Integer) As String

'    -- This function will return a date in system format

    Dim sMonthNames(1 To 12)    As String
    Dim sSystemDateFormat       As String

    On Error Resume Next

    GetDateSystemFormat = ""

    '-- Populate the sMonthNames array with Jan, Feb, etc.
    GoSub LoadMonthValues

    '-- DateValue is a internal Visual Basic command.  If the date
    'is built
    '    using the format "Jul 10, 1997" Visual Basic is smart enough
    'to determine
    '    what the month, day, and year sections are.  DateValue
    'returns a date in
    '    system format.
    sSystemDateFormat = DateValue(sMonthNames(iMonth) & " " & _
            CStr(iDay) & ", " & CStr(iYear))

    '-- We have initialized GetDateSystemFormat to equal "".  If we
    'check the
    '    date value using IsDate and it returns false then
    'GetDateSystemFormat will
    '    return "".  We can check from the calling routine the return
    'value, if it
    '    is "" then an invalid date was entered.
    If IsDate(sSystemDateFormat) = False Then
        Exit Function
    End If

    GetDateSystemFormat = sSystemDateFormat

    Exit Function

LoadMonthValues:
    sMonthNames(1) = "Jan"
    sMonthNames(2) = "Feb"
    sMonthNames(3) = "Mar"
    sMonthNames(4) = "Apr"
    sMonthNames(5) = "May"
    sMonthNames(6) = "Jun"
```

```
       sMonthNames(7) = "Jul"
       sMonthNames(8) = "Aug"
       sMonthNames(9) = "Sep"
       sMonthNames(10) = "Oct"
       sMonthNames(11) = "Nov"
       sMonthNames(12) = "Dec"
       Return

    End Function
```

11. Select Add Class Module from the Project menu and add a new class module called **clsEmployee** to the project. In this program, there are multiple employees. By placing the following code in a class module, multiple objects can be created that have these same characteristics. The **HireDate** value is different for each employee because the data is encapsulated.

```
Option Explicit

Private DateHired As String

Property Get HireDate() As String

   HireDate = DateHired

End Property

Public Property Let HireDate(dHireDate As String)

   DateHired = dHireDate

End Property

Public Function TimeEmployeed()

   TimeEmployeed = DateDiff("yyyy", DateHired, Now)

End Function
```

How It Works

When the program is started, an object of the **clsEmployee class** is created for each employee in the system. The **HireDate** can then be set for each employee by selecting the employee from the **lstEmployee ListBox** and clicking the **cmdSetHireDate CommandButton**. The code in that event gets the hire date in system format by calling a routine in **modDates**. It then sets the property in the appropriate instance of **clsEmployee**.

When the user clicks the **cmdGetHireDate CommandButton**, the program gets the value of the **HireDate** property of the appropriate class and displays it in a **MessageBox**. The last portion of functionality in this program resides in the **cmdYearsEmployed CommandButton**. When this **CommandButton** is clicked, a method in the `clsEmployee` class is called, and the number of years the selected employee has been employed is displayed in a `MessageBox`.

Comments

This program has demonstrated code that should be implemented as a standard module and code that should be implemented as a class module. Because the code that returns the date in system format is not required to have any type of data persistence and is not required to have multiple instances, it is appropriate that it goes into a standard module.

The program is required to track the hire date for multiple employees. Because there could be any number of employees in a system, it makes sense that this code be implemented as a class module. The class itself is just a blueprint of the functionality required when creating an instance of this class. Each instance of the class has its own properties that are completely separate from the other instances of the employee class.

COMPLEXITY
BEGINNING

3.2 How do I...
Handle events in a simple class?

COMPATIBILITY: VISUAL BASIC 5 AND 6

Problem

I have an operation that uploads employee files to a remote server. This operation takes quite a bit of time to complete. I want to be able to display a percentage of files completed progress bar and give the user the option to cancel the operation.

Technique

Visual Basic is an event-driven programming language. Unlike conventional programming languages that implement a top-down structure, Visual Basic code does not execute until something happens. When a user clicks a command button, the code in the `Click` event of the command button is executed.

This How-To expands on the project created in the previous How-To. A method is added to the `clsEmployee` class that simulates uploading files to a remote server, which uses the `RaiseEvent` statement. By using the `RaiseEvent` statement, an event can be fired in the calling form to display the percentage of files transferred in a progress bar. This event also checks the status of a flag to determine whether the operation should be canceled.

Steps

Open and run Employee Date1.VBP. The running program is shown in Figure 3.2.

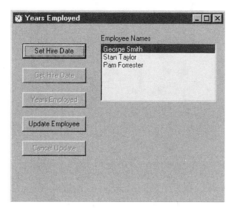

Figure 3.2 The main form at runtime.

This program looks similar to the program created in the preceding How-To with the addition of two `CommandButtons`, `cmdUpdateEmployee` and `cmdCancelUpdate`. When the `cmdUpdateEmployee` code is executed, a simulation of files being uploaded to a remote server is initiated. This process uses the `RaiseEvent` statement to cause an event to be fired in `frmMain`, which updates a progress bar indicating the percentage of files that have been uploaded to the remote server.

To create this program, complete the following steps:

1. Copy the files created in the preceding How-To to a new directory.

2. Set the objects and properties listed in Table 3.2 and save it as EMPLOYEE.FRM.

If you do not have the `ProgressBar` control available on your Visual Basic toolbar, select Project, Components. Scroll down and locate Microsoft Windows Common Controls 6.0 and put a check in the check box to the left of the selection. Then click the OK command button. This will make the ProgressBar control available on your Visual Basic toolbar.

Table 3.2 Project Form's Objects and Properties

OBJECT/CONTROL	PROPERTY	VALUE
Form	Name	frmMain
	Caption	"Years Employed"
	Icon	Timer01.ico
	StartUpPosition	2 'CenterScreen
CommandButton	Name	cmdSetHireDate
	Caption	"Set Hire Date"
CommandButton	Name	cmdGetHireDate
	Caption	"Get Hire Date"
CommandButton	Name	cmdYearsEmployed
	Caption	"Years Employed"
CommandButton	Name	cmdUpdateEmployee
	Caption	"Update Employee"
CommandButton	Name	cmdCancelUpdate
	Caption	"Cancel Update"
Label	Name	lblEmployeeNames
	Alignment	0 'Left Justify
	Caption	"Employee Names"
Label	Name	lblPercentCompleted
	Alignment	0 'Left Justify
	Caption	"Percentage of Files Transferred"
ListBox	Name	lstEmployees
ProgressBar	Name	pbarPercentCompleted
	Max	100
	Min	0

3. Add the following event to the General Declarations section of clsEmployee. Declaring the PercentCompleted event here enables access to the event from the calling form.

```
Option Explicit
Private DateHired As String
Public Event PercentCompleted(ByVal Percent As Single, Cancel As _
Boolean)
```

4. Add the following method to clsEmployee. This method simulates a transfer of files to a remote server. It takes one parameter that is the number of files to be transferred. Each time a simulated file transfer occurs, the RaiseEvent statement fires the PercentCompleted event. After returning from the event, the status of bIsCanceled is checked to determine whether the user canceled the operation. If the operation was canceled, then the code exits the method.

```
Public Function UploadEmployeeFiles(nNumberOfFilesToTransfer As
Integer)

    Dim bIsCanceled          As Boolean
    Dim sngStartTime         As Single
    Dim nNumberOfFilesCopied As Integer
    Dim bWaitCompleted       As Boolean
    Const nInterval          As Integer = 1

    '-- Upload the files to the server.
    For nNumberOfFilesCopied = 1 To nNumberOfFilesToTransfer
      sngStartTime = Timer
      bWaitCompleted = False

      '-- This is where each individual employee's file
      '   would be copied to the server.  For this example we
      '   will create a time delay to simulate a file being
      '   transferred to a server.
      Do
        If sngStartTime + nInterval < Timer Then
          bWaitCompleted = True
        End If
        DoEvents
      Loop Until bWaitCompleted = True

      '-- This will cause the event to be raised in frmMain.
      RaiseEvent PercentCompleted(nNumberOfFilesCopied / _
          nNumberOfFilesToTransfer, bIsCanceled)

      '-- If the user has clicked the Cancel CommandButton then the
      '   operation is finished.
      If bIsCanceled = True Then
        Exit Function
      End If

    Next 'nNumberOfFilesCopied

End Function
```

5. Add the following code to the General Declarations section of `frmMain`. A boolean variable is used to determine whether the user decided to cancel the file upload procedure. Also the `clsCurrentEmployee` declaration has changed. This is necessary to provide access to the `clsCurrentEmployee_PercentCompleted` event. The shell for this event is automatically created for you when the variable is declared. There is code that needs to be added to this event handler, which is discussed in the following steps.

```
Option Explicit

Const sEmptyString As String = ""

Dim clsStanTaylor As New clsEmployee
Dim clsGeorgeSmith As New clsEmployee
Dim clsPamForrester As New clsEmployee

Private mbOperationCanceled As Boolean
Private WithEvents clsCurrentEmployee As clsEmployee
```

6. Put the following code in the `clsCurrentEmployee_PercentCompleted` event. (The `PercentCompleted` event is available when specifying the `WithEvents` keyword for the `clsEmployee` class.) This code executes every time the `PercentCompleted` event is raised. The code sets the `pbarPercentCompleted` property of the `ProgressBar` to the value of `Percent`. It then checks to see whether the user has canceled the operation. If the operation has been canceled, the `Cancel` variable is set to `True`.

```
'-- This routine will update the ProgressBar and determine
'    if the user has canceled the operation.

pbarPercentCompleted.Value = CInt(100 * Percent)
DoEvents

If mbOperationCanceled = True Then
  Cancel = True
End If
```

7. Add the following code to the `cmdUpdateEmployee CommandButton`. When this code is executed, it sets the `Enabled` and `Visible` properties of the controls used during the upload procedure. It then initiates the upload procedure. When the upload procedure is completed, the controls are reset to their original values.

```
mbOperationCanceled = False

'-- Set proper enabled and visible properties
'    for controls during update procedure.
cmdCancelUpdate.Enabled = True
cmdUpdateEmployee.Enabled = False
pbarPercentCompleted.Visible = True
lblPercentCompleted.Visible = True
DoEvents

'-- Call the clsEmployee method to Upload 50 Employee files.
Call clsCurrentEmployee.UploadEmployeeFiles(50)

'-- Initialize controls to the original values
pbarPercentCompleted.Value = 0
```

```
pbarPercentCompleted.Visible = False
cmdCancelUpdate.Enabled = False
cmdUpdateEmployee.Enabled = True
lblPercentCompleted.Visible = False
DoEvents
```

8. Add the following in the `Click` event of the `cmdCancelUpdate` `CommandButton`. This code sets the variable `mbOperationCanceled` to `True`. This variable is checked every time the `PercentCompleted` event is fired. If it's `True`, the upload procedure is canceled.

```
mbOperationCanceled = True
cmdCancelUpdate.Enabled = False
cmdUpdateEmployee.Enabled = True
pbarPercentCompleted.Value = 0
pbarPercentCompleted.Visible = False
lblPercentCompleted.Visible = False
```

How It Works

This program simulates an upload of employee files. Each time an employee file is uploaded, the application is notified of the progress by updating a progress bar. To accomplish this, a `Public` event must be declared in the class called `PercentCompleted`. Each time an employee file is uploaded, the percent of the transfer that has been completed is calculated. When that reaches the proper percentage, the `RaiseEvent` keyword is used to fire the `PercentCompleted` event.

In the main form, `clsCurrentEmployee` is declared with the `WithEvents` keyword. When a class is declared in this manner, the framework for any events contained in that class is automatically included in our form declarations. That enables you to add the code to the event that needed to be executed every time the event was fired.

Comments

When the `RaiseEvent` keyword is used properly, it can make your code much more straightforward. When you contemplate using the `RaiseEvent` keyword, make sure to think through what you are trying to accomplish. Determine whether there would be a simpler way to accomplish the same thing. Under the proper circumstances, this new functionality has the capability of providing developers with a much greater degree of control over the programs that they create.

COMPLEXITY
BEGINNING

3.3 How do I...
Migrate a simple class to incorporate polymorphism?

COMPATIBILITY: VISUAL BASIC 5 AND 6

Problem

I now realize that I really have two separate types of employees—managers and workers. The methods that must be performed on each type of employee are different. I want to be able to use the same code to call the proper method depending on the type of object with which I am working.

Technique

This How-To expands on the example created in section 3.1. Using the new **Implements** keyword can provide polymorphism in a simple class. The simple class created here can support multiple interfaces by creating stub routines in the original class. These stub routines do not contain any code.

In separate class modules, corresponding stub routines are created to match each of the routines existing in the base class. By delegating an instance of the specific class to the base class, clients can execute methods and set properties of the base class. Clients can also call the proper method or set the correct property of the class that is associated with the base class. This should become much clearer when examining the following example.

Steps

Open and run Employee Date1.VBP. The running program is shown in Figure 3.3.

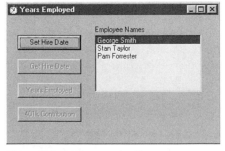

Figure 3.3 The main form at runtime.

Once again this program looks similar to the program created in How-To 3.1 with the addition of one `CommandButton` called `cmd401kContrib`. When the `cmd401kContrib` code is executed, the proper `Calculate401k` method is executed depending on whether the employee is a worker or manager.

Complete the following steps to create this project:

1. Copy the files created in How-To 3.1 to a new directory.

2. Set the objects and properties listed in Table 3.3 and save it as EMPLOYEE.FRM.

Table 3.3 Project Form's Objects and Properties

OBJECT/CONTROL	PROPERTY	VALUE
Form	Name	frmMain
	Caption	"Years Employed"
	Icon	Timer01.ico
	StartUpPosition	2 'CenterScreen
CommandButton	Name	cmdSetHireDate
	Caption	"Set Hire Date"
CommandButton	Name	cmdGetHireDate
	Caption	"Get Hire Date"
CommandButton	Name	cmdYearsEmployed
	Caption	"Years Employed"
CommandButton	Name	cmdUpdateEmployee
	Caption	"Update Employee"
CommandButton	Name	cmdCancelUpdate
	Caption	"Cancel Update"
CommandButton	Name	cmd401kContrib
	Caption	"401k Contribution"
Label	Name	lblEmployeeNames
	Alignment	0 'Left Justify
	Caption	"Employee Names"
Label	Name	lblPercentCompleted
	Alignment	0 'Left Justify
	Caption	"Percentage of Files Transferred"
ListBox	Name	lstEmployees
ProgressBar	Name	pbarPercentCompleted
	Max	100
	Min	0

3. Remove all the code from the **clsEmployee** class. This class now acts as a shell to access the routines associated with the specific worker type. In this example, there is a manager class and a worker class. The methods and properties defined in the following code are the methods executed from the calling procedure. Depending on worker type, **clsManager** or **clsWorker**, the proper code is executed.

```
Option Explicit

Public Sub Calculate401k()

End Sub

Property Get HireDate() As String

End Property

Public Property Let HireDate(sDateHired As String)

End Property

Public Function TimeEmployed()

End Function
```

4. Choose Project, Add Class Module from the menu to add another class module to the project. Name this class **clsManager** and save the class as MANAGER.CLS. Put the following code in this new class. The first line in the class is **Implements clsEmployee**. This line enables you to access this class through the base class **clsEmployee**. When this line is added, the framework for the property **Lets** and the property **Gets** is automatically added to the class. These properties do not have any code in them at this point. Code needs to be added to set the properties. Each of the methods and properties must be prefixed by **clsEmployee**.

```
Option Explicit

Implements clsEmployee
Private sHireDate As String
Const lSalary As Long = 45000
Const sngPercentContribution As Single = 0.06

Private Sub clsEmployee_Calculate401k()

  Dim sContribution As String
  Dim lTotalContribution As Long

  lTotalContribution = DateDiff("yyyy", sHireDate, Now) * _
                       lSalary * sngPercentContribution
```

```
    sContribution = Format(lTotalContribution, "#,000.00")
    MsgBox "Company 401k Contribution for this Manager is: $" &
sContribution

End Sub

Private Property Let clsEmployee_HireDate(DateHired As String)

   sHireDate = DateHired

End Property

Private Property Get clsEmployee_HireDate() As String

   clsEmployee_HireDate = sHireDate

End Property

Private Function clsEmployee_TimeEmployed()

   clsEmployee_TimeEmployed = DateDiff("yyyy", sHireDate, Now)

End Function
```

5. Choose Project, Add Class Module from the menu to add another class
module to the project. Name this class **clsWorker** and save the class as
WORKER.CLS. The following code is placed in this new class. It is similar
to the **clsManager** class created in the preceding step. The only real
difference is how the 401k contribution is calculated. All other aspects are
the same.

```
Option Explicit

Implements clsEmployee
Private sHireDate As String
Const lSalary As Long = 25000
Const sngPercentContribution As Single = 0.04

Private Sub clsEmployee_Calculate401k()
  Dim sContribution As String
  Dim lTotalContribution As Long

  lTotalContribution = DateDiff("yyyy", sHireDate, Now) * _
                      lSalary * sngPercentContribution
  sContribution = Format(lTotalContribution, "#,000.00")
  MsgBox "Company 401k Contribution for this Worker is: $" & _
         sContribution

End Sub

Private Property Get clsEmployee_HireDate() As String
```

continued on next page

continued from previous page

```
            clsEmployee_HireDate = sHireDate

    End Property

    Private Property Let clsEmployee_HireDate(DateHired As String)

        sHireDate = DateHired

    End Property

    Private Function clsEmployee_TimeEmployed()

        clsEmployee_TimeEmployed = DateDiff("yyyy", sHireDate, Now)

    End Function
```

6. The General Declarations section for `frmMain` must be changed. The specific employee classes need to be set to be either a worker or a manager. The following code goes in the General Declarations section of `frmMain`.

```
Option Explicit

Dim clsStanTaylor As New clsManager
Dim clsGeorgeSmith As New clsManager
Dim clsPamForrester As New clsWorker
Dim clsCurrentEmployee As New clsEmployee

Const sEmptyString As String = ""
```

7. The following line of code must be added to the `Click` event of `cmdSetHireDate` CommandButton. This CommandButton, along with `cmdGetHireDate` and `cmdYearsEmployed`, must be enabled if the `HireDate` property is successfully set for the current employee. The first two lines of the following code already exist; add the third line to this code module.

```
    cmdGetHireDate.Enabled = True
    cmdYearsEmployed.Enabled = True
    cmd401kContrib.Enabled = True
```

8. This next addition is similar to step 7. In the `Click` event of `lstEmployees` ListBox, the enabled status of all the command buttons needs to be set based on whether the currently selected object has a `HireDate` established. The first two lines of the following code are already in this code module; add the third line to complete the required changes.

```
cmdGetHireDate.Enabled = bStatus
cmdYearsEmployed.Enabled = bStatus
cmd401kContrib.Enabled = bStatus
```

9. Finally, you will need to execute the `Calculate401k` method of the `clsCurrentEmployee` class when the user clicks the 401k Contribution button. Enter the following code into the `Click` event of the `cmd401kContrib` CommandButton.

```
Call clsCurrentEmployee.Calculate401k
```

How It Works

When the program is started, a `clsWorker` or a `clsManager` is created for each employee in the system. When the employee is selected in the `lstEmployees` ListBox, the employee object (`clsWorker` or `clsManager`) is assigned to the `clsCurrentEmployee` object. The `clsCurrentEmployee` object is type `clsEmployee`. This generic object is associated with the class with the stub routines in it.

When methods are called or properties of this object are set, the appropriate code routines are called depending on what kind of object has been assigned to the `clsEmployee` object. After setting the `HireDate` for the currently selected employee, you can click the `Calculate 401k` CommandButton. At this point, the proper `Calculate401k` method is called depending on which type of object is in use.

Comments

This How-To demonstrates the power of the `Implements` keyword. This is a powerful feature of Visual Basic. If you want to add a programmer type of employee to this program, all that is needed is to add either the `clsManager` class or the `clsWorker` class to a new class called `clsProgrammer`.

At that point, you could make the required changes to the class that are unique to the programmer employee. Then in the calling form, you would simply define the appropriate employee to be a `clsProgrammer`, such as `Dim clsStanTaylor As New clsProgrammer`. By implementing code in this way, it is easy to make modifications to existing code without affecting any of the current functionality.

COMPLEXITY
INTERMEDIATE

3.4 How do I...
Create a simple container control using a class?

COMPATIBILITY: VISUAL BASIC 5 AND 6

Problem

I want to add a status bar to my application. A status bar control comes with Visual Basic, but I want to keep the size of my distribution disks down to a minimum. If I include the status bar custom control in my project, it increases the size of my project by including functionality that I do not require. How can I add a status bar without including COMCTL32.OCX?

Technique

This How-to uses a class module to create a status bar class. After the class is created, simply place a picture box on a form and use this picture box as a container control for the status bar. Declaring an instance of the **StatusBar** class in our program and then setting the **Initialize** property to be equal to the picture box does this.

This creates a link between the picture box on our form and the **StatusBar** Class. We can then call the methods and set the properties of the class to display text messages in the status bar and control what is displayed in the status bar. The status bar has the optional capability to display the time, date, or both.

Steps

Open and run Status Bar.VBP. The running program is shown in Figure 3.4.

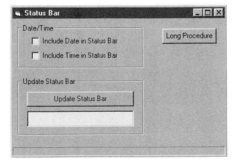

Figure 3.4 The main form at runtime.

Because this is used to create a specific object, a class module is used to encapsulate all the properties and methods of the status bar. That permits you to later change this into an OLE Object.

To build the project in this How-To, complete the following steps:

1. Create a new project called STATUS BAR.VBP.

2. Add a form to the project and set the objects and properties listed in Table 3.4 for the form and save it as STATUS BAR.FRM.

Table 3.4 Project Form's Objects and Properties

OBJECT/CONTROL	PROPERTY	VALUE
Form	Name	frmMain
	Caption	"Status Bar"
	Icon	Face02.ico
	StartUpPosition	2 'CenterScreen
CommandButton	Name	cmdLongProcedure
	Caption	"Long Procedure"
CommandButton	Name	cmdUpdateStatusBar
	Caption	"Update Status Bar"
Frame	Name	fraDateTime
	Caption	"Date/Time"
Frame	Name	fraUpdateStatus
	Caption	"Update Status"
CheckBox	Name	chkDateTime
	Caption	"Include Date in Status Bar"
	Index	0
CheckBox	Name	chkDateTime
	Caption	"Include Time in Status Bar"
	Index	1
TextBox	Name	txtStatusBar
	Text	""
PictureBox	Name	picStatusBar
	Visible	False
Timer	Name	timStatusBarUpdate
	Interval	10,000

3. Choose Project, Add Class Module from the menu to add a class module to the project. Name this class **clsStatusBar** and save the class as STATBAR.CLS. Add the following code to the General Declarations section of the newly created class module. This section defines all the variables and constants used in the class. It also declares the DrawText API. This function is a powerful API that can perform complex text formatting including word wrapping and handling of line breaks. In this example, the DrawText API is used to draw the text in the status bar.

Enumerations provide you with a way to work with sets of related constants and to associate constant values to names. By default, the first constant in an enumeration is 0; subsequent enumerations are one more than the previous constant. By assigning a specific value to an enumeration, you will change all the constant values from that point forward. For example, if you had an enumeration with five constants and you assigned a value of six to the third constant, then the constant values would be as follows:

PUBLIC ENUM	EXAMPLE
Value1	Would be equal to 0
Value2	Would be equal to 1
Value3 = 6	Would be equal to 6
Value4	Would be equal to 7
Value5	Would be equal to 8
End Enum	

In the following declarations, you will notice the use of an **Enum** statement that will be used to control the status bar state:

```
Option Explicit

Dim m_picStatus        As PictureBox
Dim miPanels           As Integer      ' Bit mask
Dim msCaption          As String
Dim mlLTColor          As Long
Dim mlRBColor          As Long
Dim mnTextHeight       As Integer
Dim mnPanelHeight      As Integer
Dim msDate             As String
Dim mdtLast            As Double
Dim mbVisible          As Boolean
Dim mbBusyActive       As Boolean


' Define an array for the coordinates of the panels
' where the panels are referenced as follows:
'    1 - Status text
```

```
'    2 - Busy panel
'    3 - Date panel
'    4 - Time panel

Dim mPanels(4)            As RECT

' Specific panel enabled status
Dim mbDate                As Boolean
Dim mbTime                As Boolean

' DrawText() Format Flags
Const DT_TOP = &H0
Const DT_LEFT = &H0
Const DT_CENTER = &H1
Const DT_RIGHT = &H2
Const DT_VCENTER = &H4
Const DT_BOTTOM = &H8
Const DT_WORDBREAK = &H10
Const DT_SINGLELINE = &H20
Const DT_EXPANDTABS = &H40
Const DT_TABSTOP = &H80
Const DT_NOCLIP = &H100
Const DT_EXTERNALLEADING = &H200
Const DT_CALCRECT = &H400
Const DT_NOPREFIX = &H800
Const DT_INTERNAL = &H1000

' Panel drawing metrics (in pixels)
Const PANEL_BORDERSIZE = 3         ' Margin between container and
                                   ' panels
Const PANEL_OFFSET = 5             ' Space between panels
Const PANEL_MARGIN = 2             ' Space between panel borders
                                   ' and text
Const TEXT_DRAW_FORMAT = DT_VCENTER Or DT_LEFT Or DT_SINGLELINE
Const DATE_DRAW_FORMAT = DT_VCENTER Or DT_CENTER Or DT_SINGLELINE

'***This is the beginning of the platform dependent section.***

Private Type RECT
    Left        As Long
    Top         As Long
    Right       As Long
    Bottom      As Long
End Type

Private Declare Function DrawText Lib "user32" _
    Alias "DrawTextA" _
        (ByVal hdc As Long, _
         ByVal lpStr As String, _
         ByVal nCount As Long, _
         lpRect As RECT, _
         ByVal wFormat As Long) As Long

' Panel type flags used to configure the status bar
  Public Enum PanelState
```

continued on next page

continued from previous page

```
        PANEL_STATUS            ' Status bar contains a status text panel
                                ' (always!)
        PANEL_DATE              ' Status bar contains a date panel (short
                                ' format)
        PANEL_TIME              ' Status bar contains a time panel (hh:mm
                                ' AM/PM)
    End Enum
```

4. Create the following subprocedure called `ComputeGeometry` and add the following code. This routine is responsible for calculating the size and locations of all the required panels in the status bar. There always needs to be at least one panel to display a status message. Optionally, there could be a panel for the time and a panel for the date. The location and size of the panels are determined in `ComputeGeometry`.

```
Private Sub ComputeGeometry()

' Calculate the panel locations

Dim nLoopCtr            As Integer
Dim lWidthConsumed      As Long
Dim lStatusWidth        As Long
Dim nPanelWidth         As Integer

lStatusWidth = m_picStatus.ScaleWidth
lWidthConsumed = 1

' Work backwards from right to left across the status bar
For nLoopCtr = 3 To 1 Step -1
    ' All panels have the same top and height settings
    mPanels(nLoopCtr).Top = PANEL_BORDERSIZE
    mPanels(nLoopCtr).Bottom = mPanels(nLoopCtr).Top + mnPanelHeight
- 1
    Select Case nLoopCtr
        Case 3              ' Time panel
            If mbTime = True Then
                mPanels(nLoopCtr).Right = lStatusWidth - _
                    lWidthConsumed
                ' Compute panel width
                nPanelWidth = m_picStatus.TextWidth("XX:XX XX") + _
                    (PANEL_MARGIN * 2) + 2
                mPanels(nLoopCtr).Left = mPanels(nLoopCtr).Right - _
                    nPanelWidth
                ' Adjust consumed space
                lWidthConsumed = lWidthConsumed + nPanelWidth +
PANEL_BORDERSIZE
            End If

        Case 2              ' Date panel
            If mbDate = True Then
                mPanels(nLoopCtr).Right = lStatusWidth - _
                lWidthConsumed
                ' Compute panel width
                nPanelWidth = m_picStatus.TextWidth(Format$(Now, _
                "Short Date")) +  _(PANEL_MARGIN * 2) + 8
```

```
                            mPanels(nLoopCtr).Left = mPanels(nLoopCtr).Right - _
                                    nPanelWidth
                            ' Adjust consumed space
                            lWidthConsumed = lWidthConsumed + nPanelWidth + _
                                    PANEL_BORDERSIZE
                    End If

            Case 1          ' Status text
                    mPanels(nLoopCtr).Right = lStatusWidth -
lWidthConsumed
                    mPanels(nLoopCtr).Left = 0
        End Select
Next nLoopCtr

End Sub
```

5. Add the following **Private** subroutine to the class module. This routine is declared as private because it should not be directly accessed from outside the class. Most subroutines in this class are declared as **Private** for the same reason. This is a good habit to get into if the routine should only be accessed by higher level routines of the class. By declaring this routine as private, another programmer using your class would not be able to accidentally call this routine.

This routine is responsible for drawing the status message that appears in your status bar. Drawing a solid box over the message text area blanks out the message section of the status bar. Then the message is drawn using the DrawText API.

```
Private Sub DrawPanelText(sText As String, nPanelID As Integer, _
nFormat As Integer)

Dim RECT_Text       As RECT
Dim lResult         As Long

RECT_Text.Top = mPanels(nPanelID).Top + 1
RECT_Text.Left = mPanels(nPanelID).Left + 1
RECT_Text.Bottom = mPanels(nPanelID).Bottom - 1
RECT_Text.Right = mPanels(nPanelID).Right - 1

' Blank the panel area by drawing a solid box
' using the background color of the container
m_picStatus.Line (RECT_Text.Left, RECT_Text.Top)- _
        (RECT_Text.Right, RECT_Text.Bottom), _
        m_picStatus.BackColor, BF

lResult = DrawText(m_picStatus.hdc, _
                sText, _
                Len(sText), _
                RECT_Text, _
                nFormat)

End Sub
```

6. Create the following subroutine called `DrawPanelFrame`. This subroutine draws the individual panels on the status bar. By adding dark lines to the top and left side of the panel and light lines to the bottom and right side of the panel, it gives it the appearance of being recessed, giving a 3D appearance.

```
Private Sub DrawPanelFrame(nPanelID As Integer)

' Draw a panel

' Blank the panel area by drawing a solid box
' using the background color of the container
m_picStatus.Line (mPanels(nPanelID).Left, mPanels(nPanelID).Top)- _
        (mPanels(nPanelID).Right, mPanels(nPanelID).Bottom), _
        m_picStatus.BackColor, BF

' Draw the panel frame to appear recessed
' The top and left side are dark
m_picStatus.Line (mPanels(nPanelID).Left, mPanels(nPanelID).Top)- _
        (mPanels(nPanelID).Right, mPanels(nPanelID).Top), _
        mlLTColor
m_picStatus.Line (mPanels(nPanelID).Left, mPanels(nPanelID).Top)- _
        (mPanels(nPanelID).Left, mPanels(nPanelID).Bottom), _
        mlLTColor

' The bottom and right side are light
m_picStatus.Line (mPanels(nPanelID).Left, mPanels(nPanelID).Bottom)- _
        (mPanels(nPanelID).Right + 1, mPanels(nPanelID).Bottom), _
        mlRBColor
m_picStatus.Line (mPanels(nPanelID).Right, mPanels(nPanelID).Top)- _
        (mPanels(nPanelID).Right, mPanels(nPanelID).Bottom), _
        mlRBColor

End Sub
```

7. The `Initialize` property creates the link between the calling form and the class. This property passes in the `PictureBox` as a parameter. It then initializes all the properties used for the status bar.

```
Public Property Set Initialize(picStatus As PictureBox)

' Initialize the status bar object

' Save local reference to the picture box
Set m_picStatus = picStatus
msCaption = ""

' Set the colors to be used for the borders
mlLTColor = vb3DShadow
```

```
mlRBColor = vb3DHighlight

' Compute the height of the status bar in
' twips (assumed to be the parent form default)
m_picStatus.Height = m_picStatus.TextHeight("ABC") _
        + ((PANEL_MARGIN + PANEL_BORDERSIZE) _
        * Screen.TwipsPerPixelY)

' Set the other status bar properties
m_picStatus.AutoRedraw = True
m_picStatus.Align = vbAlignBottom
m_picStatus.BorderStyle = 0          ' No border
m_picStatus.ScaleMode = vbPixels
m_picStatus.DrawWidth = 1
m_picStatus.BackColor = vb3DFace

' Now compute and store the height of the text
' and panels in pixels. Panel height accounts for
' the pixels used to draw the frames.
mnPanelHeight = m_picStatus.ScaleHeight - PANEL_BORDERSIZE
mnTextHeight = m_picStatus.TextHeight("ABC")

End Property
```

8. The next piece of code is a property **Let** procedure. This procedure enables the calling form to add or remove a date and time panel to the status bar. This routine uses bitwise operations to parse the **PANEL_DATE** and the **PANEL_TIME** value out of one parameter.

```
Public Property Let Panels(bitFlags As Integer)


miPanels = bitFlags

If (miPanels And PANEL_DATE) = PANEL_DATE Then
    mbDate = True
  Else
    mbDate = False
End If

If (miPanels And PANEL_TIME) = PANEL_TIME Then
    mbTime = True
  Else
    mbTime = False
End If

Me.Resize

End Property
```

9. Create the **Public Subroutine Resize** routine. This routine is called whenever the calling form is resized. It ensures that the status bar is always at the proper location on the calling form and that the width of the status bar fills the width of the calling form.

```
Public Sub Resize()

' The status bar is new or has been resized

m_picStatus.Cls
Call ComputeGeometry

' Draw the panels
Call DrawPanelFrame(1)
If mbDate = True Then
    Call DrawPanelFrame(2)
End If
If mbTime = True Then
    Call DrawPanelFrame(3)
End If

' Show the panel contents
Call DrawPanelText(msCaption, 1, TEXT_DRAW_FORMAT)
msDate = ""
mdtLast = 0
Me.Timer

End Sub
```

10. This property **Let** procedure gets called most of the time from the form. This procedure displays a status message in the status bar.

```
Public Property Let Caption(sCaption As String)

' Update the text displayed on the status bar
' in the first panel

msCaption = sCaption

Call DrawPanelText(msCaption, 1, TEXT_DRAW_FORMAT)

End Property
```

11. Add the **Timer** public subroutine to the class. This subroutine makes sure that the correct date and time are always being displayed. To cut down on processing overhead, it checks to make sure that at least one minute has elapsed since the last time the routine was called. If at least one minute has elapsed, it updates the date and time to the correct values.

```
Public Sub Timer()

' This is our timer callback event/method
```

```
' See if we are displaying either the date or time
If mbDate = True Or mbTime = True Then

    ' Now check to see if at least one minute has
    ' elapsed since the last time we were called
    If Abs(DateDiff("n", Now, mdtLast)) >= 1 Then

        If mbTime = True Then
            ' Update the time display
            Call DrawPanelText(Format$(Now, "Medium Time"), 3, _
                    DATE_DRAW_FORMAT)
        End If

        If mbDate = True And Format$(Now, "Short Date") <> msDate _
                Then
            ' Update the date display
            msDate = Format$(Now, "Short Date")
            Call DrawPanelText(msDate, 2, DATE_DRAW_FORMAT)
        End If

        mdtLast = Now              ' Save the current date/time

    End If
End If


End Sub
```

12. Add a property **Get** and a property **Let** procedure to control the visible state of the status bar. When the picture box is added to the calling form, its visible property defaults to **False**. After it is initialized, the visible property is set to **True**. This prevents a flicker of the status bar during form load while the correct geometry of the status bar is being calculated.

```
Public Property Let Visible(bVisible As Boolean)

mbVisible = bVisible
m_picStatus.Visible = mbVisible

End Property

Public Property Get Visible() As Boolean

Visible = mbVisible

End Property
```

13. Now that the class for the status bar is created, add the code to **frmMain** to demonstrate the status bar. Add the following code to the General Declarations section of **frmMain**. This section first creates an instance of the **clsStatusBar** and then sets the constants and variables that are used in the demonstration form.

```
Option Explicit

Dim clsMainStatusBar As New clsStatusBar
Dim miPanels As Integer
```

14. Add the following code to the `Click` event of `chkDateTime` check box. These check boxes are a control array. This enables you to keep common code together and prevents a lot of modules with very little code in them. When this code is executed, the variable `miPanels` is set. This variable contains that status for whether date or time panels are displayed in the status bar. Bitwise operations are performed here so that both statuses can be placed in one variable.

```
Private Sub chkDateTime_Click(Index As Integer)

    '-- Determine if the Date and Time should be displayed
    '   in the status bar

    Const CHK_DATE = 0
    Const CHK_TIME = 1

    If chkDateTime(CHK_DATE).Value = vbChecked And _
       chkDateTime(CHK_TIME).Value = vbChecked Then
        miPanels = PANEL_DATE Or PANEL_TIME

    ElseIf chkDateTime(CHK_DATE).Value = vbChecked And _
       chkDateTime(CHK_TIME).Value = vbUnchecked Then
        miPanels = PANEL_DATE

    ElseIf chkDateTime(CHK_DATE).Value = vbUnchecked And _
       chkDateTime(CHK_TIME).Value = vbChecked Then
        miPanels = PANEL_TIME

    Else
      '-- We do not want the date or the time displayed.
      miPanels = 0

    End If

    '-- Display the proper panels
    clsMainStatusBar.Panels = miPanels

End Sub
```

15. Add the following code to the `cmdLongProcedure CommandButton`. When this code is executed, it simulates a long procedure executing. Prior to the procedure starting, it displays a status message indicating that a long procedure is in progress. When the long procedure is completed, it displays a message indicating that the procedure has completed.

```
Private Sub cmdLongProcedure_Click()
  Dim sngStartTime          As Single
  Dim bWaitCompleted        As Boolean
  Const nInterval           As Integer = 5

  sngStartTime = Timer
  bWaitCompleted = False

  clsMainStatusBar.Caption = "Started long procedure"

  '-- This is a time delay to simulate a long procedure.
  Do
    If sngStartTime + nInterval < Timer Then
      bWaitCompleted = True
    End If
    DoEvents
  Loop Until bWaitCompleted = True

  clsMainStatusBar.Caption = "Completed long procedure"

End Sub
```

16. Add the following code to the `Click` event of the `cmdUpdateStatusBar` `CommandButton`. This code further demonstrates the status bar functionality. Whenever the following code is executed, the text in `txtStatusBar TextBox` is displayed in the status bar.

```
Private Sub cmdUpdateStatusBar_Click()

  clsMainStatusBar.Caption = txtStatusBar.Text

End Sub
```

17. The following code is placed in the `Form_Load` event of `frmMain`. This code initializes the status bar and then sets the proper panels. Finally, it sets the `Visible` property to `True`. The status bar is initially not displayed with time or date panels because `miPanels` is equal to zero at this point. The code is not required here, but it is displayed to demonstrate the proper place to initialize this value.

```
Private Sub Form_Load()

  picStatusBar.BackColor = frmMain.BackColor

  Set clsMainStatusBar.Initialize = picStatusBar

  clsMainStatusBar.Panels = miPanels

  clsMainStatusBar.Visible = True

End Sub
```

18. This next piece of code that is placed in the `Form_Resize` event of `frmMain` form ensures that the status bar is always at the bottom of the form and is the proper width.

```
Private Sub Form_Resize()

    Call clsMainStatusBar.Resize

End Sub
```

19. To finish off the demonstration form, add the following code to the `Timer` event of the `timStatusBarUpdate` timer. This code makes sure that the proper date and time are always displayed in the status bar by calling the `Timer` event of the status bar class.

```
Private Sub timStatusBarUpdate_Timer()

    Call clsMainStatusBar.Timer

End Sub
```

How It Works

The `clsStatusBar` that was created in the preceding steps is used in conjunction with a picture box that is placed on a form. The appearance and placement of the picture box is then manipulated by the `clsStatusBar` to take on the look and feel of a status bar. It can display the time, the date, or both in the status bar by simply setting the appropriate properties. By using a class to create this control, we have a powerful, light-weight control.

Comments

COMCTL32.OCX weighs in at 566KB; it includes the following controls: `TbStrip`, `Toolbar`, `ProgressBar`, `TreeView`, `ListView`, `ImageList`, `Slider`, and `StatusBar`. You do not have the option of selecting individual controls to include in your program. This type of design can greatly increase the size of your setup program. With more people wanting to place their programs on the Internet for download, the issue of program size becomes even more important. The `StatusBar` class in comparison is 9.41KB prior to compilation. By creating a container control using a class, you can have a status bar in your program without adding the heavier COMCTL32.OCX.

COMPLEXITY
INTERMEDIATE

3.5 How do I...
Understand and make use of apartment-threaded components?

COMPATIBILITY: VISUAL BASIC 6

Problem

I have several ActiveX components created in Visual Basic 5. I want to take advantage of performance optimizations that might be available in Visual Basic 6. I have heard of the Apartment Threaded Model, but I do not understand what it means. How do I understand and make use of the Apartment Threaded Model in Visual Basic components?

Technique

Threads are allocated to the process and not to the component. In Visual Basic, threading model properties are assigned to the project. If a project is an EXE, its process will be the owner of any thread or threads allocated by the Kernel. If a project is an in-process component, such as an ActiveX DLL or control, it will reside in the process space of the client EXE. Its objects will be attached to the thread or threads allocated to the process of the client EXE.

In the Apartment-Threaded Model, each thread within a process is given its own room or apartment. Each apartment has its own copy of the global data defined within the process. This means that a multithreaded component will have a separate instance of global data for each thread used by the process. Along with each thread having its own copy of global data, it will also have its own copy of data supplied by global objects, such as the **App** object. If a single thread is used, all objects will share the same global constants, global variables, and global object references.

To access the Threading Model properties of your project in Visual Basic, choose Project, Project Properties from the menu. The Project Properties dialog box appears. The Threading Model properties are located at the bottom-right of the General tab as illustrated in Figure 3.5.

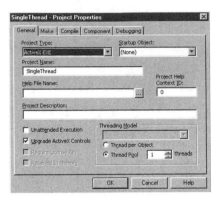

Figure 3.5 The Project Properties
window.

The Threading Model properties are different for each of the project types. Table 3.5 describes the Threading Model properties for each of the project types.

Table 3.5 Threading Model Properties for Each Project Type

PROJECT TYPE	PROPERTY	DESCRIPTION
Standard EXE	None	A Standard EXE project will have no Threading Model properties enabled, and will only utilize a single-threaded model.
ActiveX EXE	Thread Per Object	If you select Thread Per Object, every object of your component created by any client will be attached to its own thread, having its own apartment or global data. This model could degrade the overall performance of your system if your component provides many objects at any given time to its clients.
	Thread Pool of 1 Thread	If you select a Thread Pool of 1 Thread, you are utilizing the Single-Threaded Model. All objects of the component will share the same thread and global data.
	Thread Pool of 2 Threads	If you select a Thread Pool of 2 Threads, you are utilizing multithreading with the Apartment Threaded Model. ActiveX EXE Components that utilize this setting should strictly adhere to the reentrancy rules described in the paragraph following this table, to maintain thread safety.
ActiveX DLL	Single Threaded	Single Threaded forces your ActiveX DLL to use a single thread for all its objects, even if the client is multithreaded. If you use Single Threaded on a Multithreaded client, the performance of your application will be degraded due to cross-thread marshaling, which is discussed later in this section.

PROJECT TYPE	PROPERTY	DESCRIPTION
	Apartment Threaded	Selecting Apartment Threaded will not guarantee that your ActiveX DLL will use multiple threads. If the client application is single-threaded, then all objects of the ActiveX DLL will be attached to a single thread. If the client application is multithreaded, objects of the ActiveX DLL will be distributed and attached to multiple threads accordingly. Reentrancy rules should be strictly adhered to using this threading model with an ActiveX DLL.
ActiveX control	Single Threaded	The Single Threaded option is the same as with an ActiveX DLL, except that Single Threaded ActiveX controls cannot be used with multithreaded clients.
	Apartment Threaded	The Apartment Threaded option is the same as with an ActiveX DLL, except that an Apartment Threaded ActiveX control must be used with a multithreaded client.

Reentrancy occurs when a method or property procedure yields control of the processor before it has completed its task, and the same method or property procedure of the same object is called again, and the thread reenters the object's code a second time. If the thread changes module-level data that the first pass was using, the result can be unpredictable. You must fully serialize methods and property procedures for each object in your component to protect your component from reentrancy and make it fully thread safe. If your method or property procedure is coded in such a way that reentrancy would not affect it, then there might be no reason to guard against reentrancy. But if reentrancy could cause problems, then to guard against reentrancy, you should adhere to the following rules:

✔ Do not call `DoEvents` within any method or property procedure in your component.

✔ Do not invoke the properties or methods of objects on another thread.

✔ Do not raise an event that is handled by an object on another thread.

✔ Do not invoke a cross-thread or cross-process method from any method within your component.

✔ Do not show a modal form or `msgbox` from within your component.

✔ Do not include any code that would yield control of the processor to any other thread or process until after the completion of your method or property procedure.

A single-threaded ActiveX control can cause numerous problems in multithreaded clients. Therefore, Visual Basic prohibits the use of single-threaded controls in projects where the threading model is multithreaded or has been set to Apartment Threaded.

It is safe to use a single-threaded ActiveX DLL with a multithreaded client, but performance is extremely degraded due to cross-thread marshaling. The objects of a single-threaded component can only be attached to the primary thread of the client application. Cross-thread marshaling occurs within a process, when an object of a multithreaded component that resides on a non-primary thread makes a call to an object of the single-threaded component. Although cross-thread marshaling gives you more flexibility, if at all possible, you should obtain an apartment-threaded version of your ActiveX DLLs. This will allow your application to avoid the use of cross-thread marshaling. When accessing an apartment-threaded DLL, each object of the DLL created by your application will reside on the same thread as its client component. This will help to optimize the performance of your multithreaded application.

An MTS Component must be compiled as an in-process component. Therefore your only Threading Model choices are Single Threaded and Apartment Threaded. But for optimal performance as an MTS component, select Apartment Threaded. This will allow MTS to optimize the use of multithreading with your ActiveX DLL.

Steps

Now that you have been introduced to the Apartment Threaded Model, it is time to demonstrate the use of the various threading models available in Visual Basic. We will use four projects to demonstrate three different threading models: THREADTEST.VBP, SINGLETHREAD.VBP, TWOTHREAD.VBP, and PERTHREAD.VBP. The ThreadTest project is a Standard EXE that will be used to access each of the three other ActiveX EXE projects, which are configured for three different threading models: Single Threaded, Thread Per Object, and Thread Pool of 2 Threads. All three ActiveX EXE projects are using the Apartment Threading Model. Figure 3.6 demonstrates what the ThreadTest program should look like when it is running.

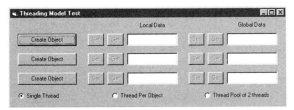

Figure 3.6 The ThreadTest program at runtime.

Complete the following steps to create these projects:

1. Create a new standard EXE project called THREADTEST.VBP.

2. Display Form1 and add two `Label` controls, five `CommandButton` controls, two `TextBox` controls, and three `OptionButton` controls to the form.

3. Display the properties of the form and its controls and change the properties that are listed in Table 3.6. Only those properties that need to be changed are listed. All other properties should be left at the default settings.

Table 3.6 `frmTest` Objects and Properties

OBJECT/CONTROL	PROPERTY	VALUE
Form	Name	frmTest
	Caption	Threading Model Test
	Height	2715
	StartUpPosition	2 - CenterScreen
	Width	8670
Label	Name	lblLocal
	Alignment	2 - Center
	Caption	Local Data
	Height	255
	Left	3600
	Top	120
	Width	1575
Label	Name	lblGlobal
	Alignment	2 - Center
	Caption	Global Data
	Height	255
	Left	6720
	Top	120
	Width	1575
CommandButton	Name	cmdCreateObj
	Caption	Create Object
	Height	375
	Left	240
	Top	480
	Width	1815

continued on next page

continued from previous page

OBJECT/CONTROL	PROPERTY	VALUE
CommandButton	Name	cmdSetLocal
	Caption	Set
	Enabled	False
	Height	375
	Left	2400
	Top	480
	Width	495
CommandButton	Name	cmdGetLocal
	Caption	Get
	Enabled	False
	Height	375
	Left	3000
	Top	480
	Width	495
TextBox	Name	txtLocal
	Enabled	False
	Height	375
	Left	3600
	Text	
	Top	480
	Width	1575
CommandButton	Name	cmdSetGlobal
	Caption	Set
	Enabled	False
	Height	375
	Left	5520
	Top	480
	Width	495
CommandButton	Name	cmdGetGlobal
	Caption	Get
	Enabled	False
	Height	375
	Left	6120
	Top	480
	Width	495

OBJECT/CONTROL	PROPERTY	VALUE
TextBox	Name	txtGlobal
	Enabled	False
	Height	375
	Left	6720
	Text	
	Top	480
	Width	1575
OptionButton	Name	optSingle
	Caption	Single Thread
	Height	255
	Left	240
	Top	2280
	Value	True
	Width	2295
OptionButton	Name	optPer
	Caption	Thread Per Object
	Height	255
	Left	3120
	Top	2280
	Width	2295
OptionButton	Name	optPool
	Caption	Thread Pool of 2 Threads
	Height	255
	Left	6000
	Top	2280
	Width	2295

4. Using the Pointer control of the toolbar, with the mouse cursor placed just at the top-left corner of the far left CommandButton on the form, click and drag to the bottom-right corner of the far right TextBox on the form. When you release your mouse button, the entire row of CommandButton and TextBox controls should be highlighted as shown in Figure 3.7.

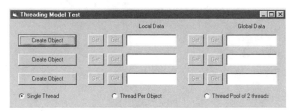

Figure 3.7 The ThreadTest form with row of controls highlighted.

Choose Edit, Copy from the menu. Make sure that the Form properties are displayed in the Properties window. Then choose Edit, Paste from the menu. You will be asked seven times whether you want to create an array of each control that is to be pasted. It is important that you select Yes for each of these dialog boxes. After the new row of controls appears on the form, choose Edit, Paste from the menu a second time for a third row of controls to be placed on the form.

5. Change the properties for all the additional pasted controls listed in Table 3.7, which makes the form look like Figure 3.8.

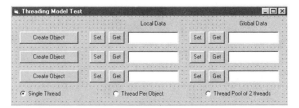

Figure 3.8 The completed form for the ThreadTest project.

Table 3.7 Additional Controls and Properties

CONTROL NAME	PROPERTY	VALUE
cmdCreateObj(1)	Left	240
	Top	1080
cmdSetLocal(1)	Left	2400
	Top	1080
cmdGetLocal(1)	Left	3000
	Top	1080
txtLocal(1)	Left	3600
	Top	1080

CONTROL NAME	PROPERTY	VALUE
cmdSetGlobal(1)	Left	5520
	Top	1080
cmdGetGlobal(1)	Left	6120
	Top	1080
txtGlobal(1)	Left	6720
	Top	1080
cmdCreateObj(2)	Left	240
	Top	1680
cmdSetLocal(2)	Left	2400
	Top	1680
cmdGetLocal(2)	Left	3000
	Top	1680
txtLocal(2)	Left	3600
	Top	1680
cmdSetGlobal(2)	Left	5520
	Top	1680
cmdGetGlobal(2)	Left	6120
	Top	1680
txtGlobal(2)	Left	6720
	Top	1680

6. Click the View Code option for the form. Because we will be creating three instances of the same object, we will need an array of object variables. We will also need a string to hold the name of the class of which we are creating an instance. Enter the following code into the General Declarations section of frmTest:

```
Dim objTest(0 To 2) As Object
Dim ThreadObject As String
```

7. Because the form is using control arrays, the code for each row of controls will only need to written one time. First, the code for the Create buttons should be as follows. Either double-click the CommandButton on the form, or select the appropriate procedure from the object list and procedure list at the top of the code editor.

```
Private Sub cmdCreateObj_Click(Index As Integer)

    'create the object for the specified index
    Set objTest(Index) = CreateObject(ThreadObject)

    'assign the local variable for this object
    objTest(Index).LocalVar = "LocalVar" & Str$(Index)

    'assign the global variable for this object
    objTest(Index).GlobalVar = "GlobalVar" & Str$(Index)

    'disable the Create Object button for this object
    cmdCreateObj(Index).Enabled = False

    'enable all Set and Get buttons for this object
    cmdSetLocal(Index).Enabled = True
    cmdGetLocal(Index).Enabled = True
    cmdSetGlobal(Index).Enabled = True
    cmdGetGlobal(Index).Enabled = True

    'enable all text boxes for this object
    txtLocal(Index).Enabled = True
    txtGlobal(Index).Enabled = True

End Sub
```

The code for the Set and Get buttons for each of the Local and Global Data variables should be as follows. When the local or global data variable is set, the **TextBox** should be cleared.

```
Private Sub cmdSetLocal_Click(Index As Integer)

    'set the local variable for this object
    objTest(Index).LocalVar = txtLocal(Index).Text

    'and clear the text box
    txtLocal(Index).Text = ""

End Sub

Private Sub cmdGetLocal_Click(Index As Integer)

    'get the local variable for this object
    txtLocal(Index).Text = objTest(Index).LocalVar

End Sub

Private Sub cmdSetGlobal_Click(Index As Integer)

    'set the global variable for this object
    objTest(Index).GlobalVar = txtGlobal(Index).Text

    'and clear the text box
    txtGlobal(Index).Text = ""
```

```
End Sub

Private Sub cmdGetGlobal_Click(Index As Integer)

    'get the global variable for this object
    txtGlobal(Index).Text = objTest(Index).GlobalVar

End Sub
```

8. Add the following code to the **Load** and **Unload** event procedures of the form. The **Load** event should set the default **ThreadObject,** and the **Unload** event should call the **DestroyAllObjects** method.

```
Private Sub Form_Load()

    'set the default test object
    ThreadObject = "SingleThread.clsTest"

End Sub

Private Sub Form_Unload(Cancel As Integer)

    DestroyAllObjects

End Sub
```

9. Put the following code into the **Click** event of each of the **OptionButtons** at the bottom of the form. Each **Click** event should first destroy any existing objects, reset the controls to startup defaults, and specify the selected **ThreadObject** class to be used by the form.

```
Private Sub optPer_Click()

    DestroyAllObjects
    ResetControls
    ThreadObject = "PerThread.clsTest"

End Sub

Private Sub optPool_Click()

    DestroyAllObjects
    ResetControls
    ThreadObject = "TwoThread.clsTest"

End Sub

Private Sub optSingle_Click()

    DestroyAllObjects
    ResetControls
    ThreadObject = "SingleThread.clsTest"

End Sub
```

10. Create the `DestroyAllObjects` and `ResetControls` subprocedures by entering the following code.

```
Private Sub DestroyAllObjects()

    Dim Ctr As Integer

    'destroy all objects before leaving
    For Ctr = 0 To 2
        Set objTest(Ctr) = Nothing
    Next

End Sub

Private Sub ResetControls()

    Dim Ctr As Integer

    'reset the form's controls to their defaults
    For Ctr = 0 To 2
        cmdCreateObj(Ctr).Enabled = True
        cmdSetLocal(Ctr).Enabled = False
        cmdGetLocal(Ctr).Enabled = False
        txtLocal(Ctr).Text = ""
        txtLocal(Ctr).Enabled = False
        cmdSetGlobal(Ctr).Enabled = False
        cmdGetGlobal(Ctr).Enabled = False
        txtGlobal(Ctr).Text = ""
        txtGlobal(Ctr).Enabled = False
    Next

End Sub
```

11. Save the `ThreadTest` project.

12. The next project is one of three ActiveX EXEs that will represent three different threading models. Choose File, New from the menu. Then choose ActiveX EXE. Choose Project, Project Properties from the menu. Change the Project Name to SingleThread. Make sure that the Threading Model is Thread Pool with one thread. Then click OK.

13. Change the name of the class module to `clsTest`. Make sure that the `Instancing` property for the class is set to `5 - MultiUse`.

14. Choose Project, Add Module from the menu. Choose New Module. Change the name of the module to `modGlobal`. Then add the following line of code in the General Declarations section of the module:

```
Global gData As String
```

15. Add the code for the `clsTest` class. The class should allow the client to access both the local and global data variables.

```
Public LocalVar As String        'define the local data variable

Public Property Let GlobalVar(vData As String)

    'assign the global string
    gData = vData

End Property

Public Property Get GlobalVar() As String

    'return the global string
    GlobalVar = gData

End Property
```

16. Save your project at this point. Then choose File, Make SingleThread.exe from the menu and save your project one last time.

17. Choose File, New Project from the menu. Then highlight ActiveX EXE and click OK. Choose Project, Add Class Module from the menu. Click the Existing Tab, select your clsTest.cls file, and click Open.

18. Then click the right mouse button over Class1 in the Project Explorer window. Select Remove Class1 from the drop-down menu. Do not save changes to Class1.

19. Now choose Project, Add Module from the menu. Click the Existing Tab, select your modGlobal.bas file, and click Open. Then choose Project, Project Properties from the menu. Change the Project Name to PerThread and select Thread Per Object as the Threading Model. Then click OK.

20. Now save your project. Then choose File, Make PerThread.exe from the menu. When the compile is finished, save your project one last time.

21. Follow steps 17 through 20 again, except that you should change the project name to TwoThread and select Thread Pool of 2 Threads as the Threading Model.

How It Works

After you have compiled the three ActiveX EXE projects, you are ready to run the ThreadTest project and demonstrate the three threading models available to Visual Basic programs. Compilation is necessary for each ActiveX EXE project to properly register the components. Load the ThreadTest project back into the Visual Basic environment. Then choose Run, Start from the menu.

First run the Single Thread test. If you click Create Object for each object in sequence, three instances of the test object will be created, each with its own local data, but all three will share the same global data. Because the Create Object initializes the local and global data for the object, the global data for all objects will contain the data assignment from the last object to be created, as illustrated in Figure 3.9. The reason this occurs in this manner is because of the Apartment-Threaded Model in Visual Basic. With a single-threaded component, all objects are created on the same thread. Since global data is allocated on a per-thread basis, all objects residing on the same thread share the same global data.

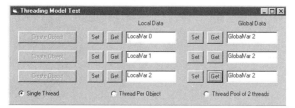

Figure 3.9 The ThreadTest project at runtime.

For the Thread Per Object test, when you select the Thread Per Object option button, the controls on the form are reset to their defaults, and the existing objects are destroyed. In this threading model, each instance of the test object will have its own apartment or copy of the global data. Because each object resides on its own thread, global data will not be shared between multiple instances of the test object.

In the final test using a Thread Pool of 2 Threads, the first two objects to be created will use separate apartments. The third object to be created will share its global data with the first object that was created. This is due to Visual Basic's Round-Robin Thread Pool. Each time a new instance of an object is created, Visual Basic creates that object on the next thread in sequence until it has created objects on all of the allocated threads. Then Visual Basic starts again with the first thread.

Comments

Using the Apartment-Threaded Model for your ActiveX DLLs and controls will ensure that your components are compatible with single-threaded and multithreaded clients. However, using the Apartment Model with ActiveX EXEs will give a different performance based on the specific Threading Model configuration and the environment in which the component is used.

Multithreading using a single processor machine optimizes the performance in applications where threads spend much of their allocated time slices blocked, either waiting for File I/O or some other shared resource. In most other situations, multithreading on a single processor will not optimize the performance, but more than likely degrade it.

COMPLEXITY
INTERMEDIATE

3.6 How do I...
Create a dependent object or collection within a class?

COMPATIBILITY: VISUAL BASIC 6

Problem

In the design of my ActiveX component, there are object-to-object relationships where one object of a particular class has ownership of another object of a different class. Or one object of a particular class encompasses an indeterminate number of dependent objects of a different class in a collection. I need to create an object model or structure within my component that can be used to maintain these relationships between objects. How do I create a dependent object or collection within a class?

Technique

Creating a dependent object or collection within a parent class is done by making references to the dependent object or collection only available to the client application through properties and methods of the parent object. A reference to the dependent object or collection is passed back to the client as either the return value of a property `get` procedure, or as the return value of a descriptive method, such as `GetDependent`.

```
Dim Parent as ParentClass
Dim Dependent As DependentClass

Set Parent = New ParentClass

Set Dependent = Parent.Dependent
```

or

```
Set Dependent = Parent.GetDependent
```

An object model is the structure of a set of objects and its hierarchical relationships. This approach of passing dependent object references is used to create an object model where hierarchical relationship rules are enforced. In other words, the client application must first create an instance of the parent class to access the dependent object or collection.

When creating a class that will be used as a dependent object, the `Instancing` property of the dependent class must be set to `PublicNotCreateable`. This will only allow the dependent object to be created by the parent object or by another object within the same component. After the dependent object is created, the dependent object reference can be passed to the client application.

If the `Instancing` property of the dependent class is set to `Private`, the dependent object reference cannot be returned to the client application. This object is considered to be internal and can only be referenced by other objects within the same component. The parent object, on the other hand, must be externally createable for the client application to gain access to its dependent objects or collections. The parent class will need to have the `Instancing` property set to any option other than `Private` or `PublicNotCreateable`.

Steps

Now that we have reviewed the technique of creating dependent objects and collections, let's illustrate the technique by making a simple object model and a small client application that will access the object model. To do so, complete the following steps:

1. Create a new ActiveX DLL project in Visual Basic by choosing File, New Project from the menu and highlighting ActiveX DLL; then click OK. We will use an ActiveX DLL project so that our client application can run in the same program group within the Visual Basic environment.

2. Change the Project Name in the Project Properties to ObjectModel.

3. Change the Class Name in the Class Properties to Parent.

4. Add another class to the project and name it Child.

5. Change the `Instancing` property of the `Child` class to `PublicNotCreateable`.

6. Highlight the `Child` class and choose View, Code from the menu. Enter the following lines of code into the General Declarations section of the `Child` class. This gives the `Child` class three distinct properties.

```
"child class properties
Public Name As String
Public Age As Integer
Public Grade as String
```

7. The `Parent` class will utilize property procedures to allow the client application to gain access to the `Child` objects. Add the private variable for the `Children` collection in the General Declarations section as follows:

```
'local copy of children collection
Private pChildren As Collection
```

8. Add three properties to the **Parent** class: the **Name** property referencing the present **Child** object; the **Child** property, which is used to maintain a reference to the present **Child** object; and the **Children** property, which is used to maintain a reference to the **Children** collection. The **Name** property will be a **Public** variable, whereas the **Child** and **Children** properties will be **Public Property Get** and **Set** procedures. Add the following code to the **Parent** class:

```
'Name used as key of Child object
Public Name As String

Public Property Get Child() As Child

    'get a member of the Child object
    Set Child = pChildren.Item(Name)

End Property

Public Property Set Child(pData As Child)

    'set a member of the Child object
    Set pChildren.Item(Name) = pData

End Property

Public Property Get Children() As Collection

    'get a member of the Children collection
    Set Children = pChildren

End Property

Public Property Set Children(pData As Collection)

    'set a member of the Children collection
    Set pChildren = pData

End Property
```

9. Add the **AddChild** method, which provides the service of creating a **Child** object and adding it to the **Children** collection using method parameters as the properties.

```
Public Sub AddChild(ByVal pName As String, ByVal pAge _
As Integer, ByVal pGrade As String)

    'create an instance of the Child class
    Dim pChild As New Child

    'assign the parameters to the properties
    pChild.Name = pName
```

continued on next page

continued from previous page

```
                pChild.Age = pAge
                pChild.Grade = pGrade

                'add the child object to the collection
                pChildren.Add pChild, pName

                'set the key to the Name of the Child
                Name = pName

                'destroy the local reference to the Child object
                Set pChild = Nothing

            End Sub
```

10. The **Initialize** event of the **Parent** object should instantiate the **Children** collection, whereas the **Terminate** event should eliminate it. Add the following code to the **Initialize** and **Terminate** events of the **Parent** class:

```
Private Sub Class_Initialize()

    'create new collection
    Set pChildren = New Collection

End Sub

Private Sub Class_Terminate()

    'set children collection to nothing when terminating
    Set pChildren = Nothing

End Sub
```

At this point, save the ObjectModel project.

11. While keeping the ActiveX DLL project open in the Visual Basic environment, choose File, Add Project from the menu. Highlight Standard EXE and click Open.

12. Choose Project, Project1 Properties from the menu. Change the Project Name to ModelTest and click OK.

13. Right-click ModelTest (ModelTest) in the Project Explorer window. When the drop-down menu appears, click Set as Start Up. This makes the Standard EXE project the starting program in the project group.

14. Display the form and drop the following controls onto the form: three **Labels**, one **ComboBox**, two **TextBoxes**, and two **CommandButtons**. Table 3.8 lists only those properties that need to be modified from the default settings after the controls are placed on the form, which should give the form the appearance of Figure 3.10.

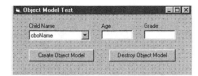

Figure 3.10 The frmModel
form in Visual Basic.

Table 3.8 frmModel Objects and Properties

OBJECT/CONTROL	PROPERTY	VALUE
Form	Name	frmModel
	Caption	Object Model Test
	Height	2250
	StartUpPosition	2 - CenterScreen
	Width	5655
Label	Name	lblName
	Caption	Child Name
	Height	255
	Left	480
	Top	240
	Width	1935
Label	Name	lblAge
	Caption	Age
	Height	255
	Left	2760
	Top	240
	Width	975
Label	Name	lblGrade
	Caption	Grade
	Height	255
	Left	4080
	Top	240
	Width	975

continued on next page

continued from previous page

OBJECT/CONTROL	PROPERTY	VALUE
ComboBox	Name	cboName
	Enabled	False
	Height	315
	Left	480
	Style	2 - Dropdown List
	Top	480
	Width	1935
TextBox	Name	txtAge
	Enabled	False
	Height	285
	Left	2760
	Text	
	Top	480
	Width	975
TextBox	Name	txtGrade
	Enabled	False
	Height	285
	Left	4080
	Text	
	Top	480
	Width	975
CommandButton	Name	cmdCreate
	Caption	Create Object Model
	Height	375
	Left	480
	Top	1080
	Width	2055
CommandButton	Name	cmdDestroy
	Caption	Destroy Object Model
	Enabled	False
	Height	375
	Left	3000
	Top	1080
	Width	2055

15. Choose Project, References from the menu. ObjectModel should be near the top of the Available References list. Make sure that a check is in the check box for ObjectModel; then click OK.

16. Select View, Code from the menu and add the following module-level object references to the General Declarations section.

```
'module-level object references
Private pParent As Parent
Private pChildren As Collection
Private pChild As Child
```

17. At this point, the event-handling code for our form needs to be added to the project. All the events in our application are user-driven.

When the user clicks on the Create Object Model button, several things need to take place. First, the Parent object should be instantiated. Then each **Child** object should be created and added to the **Children** collection. Then the appropriate controls on the form should be enabled, allowing the user to flow through the object model and make modifications to the **Age** and **Grade** properties of each **Child** object. Enter the following code in the **Click** event of the **cmdCreate** CommandButton:

```
Private Sub cmdCreate_Click()

    'create new Parent object, which will launch
    'the object model
    Set pParent = New Parent

    'add each Child to the Children collection
    pParent.AddChild "Anthony", 9, "A"
    pParent.AddChild "Andrew", 7, "A"
    pParent.AddChild "Michael", 4, "A"
    pParent.AddChild "Ahnna", 1, "A"

    'set a reference to the Children collection
    Set pChildren = pParent.Children

    'enable the text boxes
    txtAge.Enabled = True
    txtGrade.Enabled = True

    'enable and clear the dropdown list
    cboName.Enabled = True
    cboName.Clear

    'add each Child to the list
    For Each pChild In pChildren
```

continued on next page

continued from previous page

```
                cboName.AddItem pChild.Name
        Next

        'default to the first item in the list
        cboName.ListIndex = 0

        'set focus to the dropdown list and refresh it
        cboName.SetFocus
        cboName.Refresh

        'disable the Create button
        cmdCreate.Enabled = False

        'and enable the Destroy button
        cmdDestroy.Enabled = True

    End Sub
```

18. Add the following code to the **Click** event of the **cboName ComboBox** so that when the user selects a child name from the drop-down list, the Age and Grade text boxes should be updated with the data from the appropriate properties of the selected **Child** object.

```
Private Sub cboName_Click()

    'set a reference to the selected Child object
    Set pChild = pChildren.Item(cboName.Text)

    'display the Age and Grade of the Child object
    'in the appropriate text box
    txtAge.Text = Trim$(Str$(pChild.Age))
    txtGrade.Text = pChild.Grade

End Sub
```

19. Add the following code to the **txtGrade TextBox** so that when the user enters text into the **Grade TextBox**, all characters are forced to uppercase.

```
Private Sub txtGrade_KeyPress(KeyAscii As Integer)

    'force Grade to uppercase
    KeyAscii = Asc(UCase$(Chr$(KeyAscii)))

End Sub
```

20. Add the following code to the **Change** events of the two **TextBox**es so that when the user modifies the text in either of the **TextBox**es, the object model is updated to reflect the modifications.

```
Private Sub txtAge_LostFocus()

    'change the Child Age
    pChild.Age = Val(txtAge.Text)
```

```
End Sub

Private Sub txtGrade_LostFocus()

    'change the Child Grade
    pChild.Grade = txtGrade.Text

End Sub
```

21. Add the following code to the **Click** event of the **cmdDestroy CommandButton** so that when the user clicks on the Destroy Object Model button, all object references need to be destroyed, and the controls on the form reset to their startup defaults.

```
Private Sub cmdDestroy_Click()

    'clear and disable the dropdown list
    cboName.Clear
    cboName.Enabled = False

    'clear and disable the text boxes
    txtAge.Text = ""
    txtAge.Enabled = False
    txtGrade.Text = ""
    txtGrade.Enabled = False

    'destroy the references to the collection and objects
    Set pChild = Nothing
    Set pChildren = Nothing
    Set pParent = Nothing

    'enable the Create button
    cmdCreate.Enabled = True

    'and disable the Destroy button
    cmdDestroy.Enabled = False

End Sub
```

How It Works

Click the Create Object Model button. A Child Name, Age, and Grade should appear on the form. You should be able to modify the Age and Grade for the child, and the object model will reflect those changes.

Any changes made to the Age or Grade of any of the children are stored in the properties of the **Child** objects within the **Children** collection. As long as the object model exists, the changes are maintained within those properties.

The application could be extended to maintain multiple **Parent** objects, which in turn would manage each collection of **Child** objects.

Figure 3.11 The
ObjectModelTest project
group at runtime.

You could also add the ability to retrieve data from, and save changes to a database.

Comments

This technique combined with other techniques, design methods, and your own creative abilities, can be used to develop data and business object models that streamline your multitier applications.

Two-dimensional data structures, such as resultsets and arrays, are limited in their use, whereas object models can be used to create complex data structures that are related to multiple tables in a database.

Although you could take this technique and create your own virtual universe, the trade-off for using an object model as compared to a multidimensional array or recordset is in the fact that you will lose memory overhead and processor time to gain flexibility. But with the ever-increasing performance of the newer machines, this trade-off will soon become nebulous.

CHAPTER 4
OBJECT
FUNDAMENTALS

4

OBJECT FUNDAMENTALS

How do I...

4.1 Build a reusable About box dialog?

4.2 Create a busy dialog with animation or progress bars?

4.3 Enhance the VB Application Wizard splash screen?

4.4 Implement an application error log?

When building applications, you will discover a great deal of power in object-based development. Creating self-contained and reusable software components leverages the time and skills of software developers. This chapter introduces the fundamental concepts and terminology of object-oriented programming. These concepts are then applied to the development of some standard application dialogs. The final How-To in this chapter shows you how to integrate your own form-level components into the Visual Basic Application Wizard.

There is an extensive vocabulary of object-oriented programming terms that can be confusing, if not understood in the context of Visual Basic development. Refer to Appendix A, "Glossary," any time you come across a term you don't understand.

4.1 Build a Reusable About Box Dialog

This How-To demonstrates the design and implementation of a reusable About box dialog. This About box includes warning messages, a program-specific icon, information about the user, and a command button that launches the Microsoft system information application.

4.2 Create a Busy Dialog with Animation or Progress Bars

There are two types of extended processing, those of known and unknown duration. When you know how long a task takes, or how many steps or units it involves, you should use a progress bar to report status. When a process takes an unknown amount of time, using a simple animation is the best option. This How-To builds a form that displays both types of progress reporting and allows the user to cancel extended operations.

4.3 Enhance the VB Application Wizard Splash Screen

The Application Wizard supplied as part of the Visual Basic IDE is a powerful tool. You can add to and extend its capabilities by adding your own forms and dialogs to those already available. This How-To shows you how to supplement the wizard by adding features and visual appeal to the basic splash screen and how to integrate the result.

4.4 Implement an Application Error Log

The built-in error log features are limited and work only when programs are run as compiled executables. This How-To demonstrates the design and implementation of a reusable error log class. The class also provides call tracing, the ability to dump the call stack to the error log, and offers full customization of the log contents and format.

COMPLEXITY
INTERMEDIATE

4.1 How do I...
Build a reusable About box dialog?

COMPATIBILITY: VISUAL BASIC 5 AND 6

Problem

I want my applications to look like other standard Windows 95 and Windows NT programs. An About box is a common feature that I want to implement. However, I do not want to write a unique About box for each of my programs. How do I develop a self-contained About box dialog that includes application-specific information?

Technique

When building standard application components, start by looking at other programs that have the same feature. Examining other About boxes shows that there are several standard characteristics. The application icon, title, and description are included. There are also a few lines of legal information, such as copyright and trademark notices, and an infringement warning. The user and company names are generally displayed. Often there is also a command button that launches the Microsoft system information application.

This How-To builds a self-contained About box that has many of the standard features. It collects information about the version of your application and from the Windows Registry.

Steps

Open and run ABOUT BOX.VBP. The running program is shown in Figure 4.1. Choose About Dialog from the Help menu. Figure 4.2 shows the resulting About box dialog.

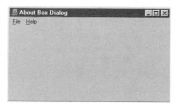

Figure 4.1 The main form at runtime.

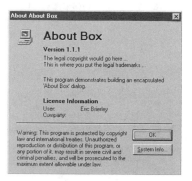

Figure 4.2 The About box dialog.

Follow these steps to complete this project:

1. Create a new project called ABOUT BOX.VBP.

2. Add a form to the project and set the objects and properties as they are listed in Table 4.1. Save the form as ABOUT MAIN.FRM. This form is used to test the About box dialog.

Table 4.1 The Project Form's Objects and Properties

OBJECT/CONTROL	PROPERTY	VALUE
Form	Name	frmMain
	Caption	About Box Dialog
	Icon	MYCOMP.ICO
Menu	Name	mnuFile
	Caption	&File
Menu	Name	mnuFileSel
	Caption	E&xit
	Index	0
Menu	Name	mnuHelp
	Caption	&Help
Menu	Name	mnuHelpSel
	Caption	&About Dialog
	Index	0

3. Place the following code segment in the form's **Load** event. These four statements get the form size and location directly from the Windows Registry. That data is used to restore the form to its previous size and location.

```
Private Sub Form_Load()

Me.Left = GetSetting("About Box Sample", _
            "Settings", _
            "MainLeft", _
            (Me.Left))

Me.Top = GetSetting("About Box Sample", _
            "Settings", _
            "MainTop", _
            (Me.Top))

Me.Width = GetSetting("About Box Sample", _
            "Settings", _
            "MainWidth", _
            (Me.Width))
```

```
Me.Height = GetSetting("About Box Sample", _
            "Settings", _
            "MainHeight", _
            (Me.Height))

End Sub
```

4. Add the following code to the form's `Unload` event. The code saves the current form size and location in the Windows Registry.

```
Private Sub Form_Unload(Cancel As Integer)

If Me.WindowState <> vbMinimized Then
    SaveSetting "About Box Sample", _
            "Settings", _
            "MainLeft", _
            Me.Left

    SaveSetting "About Box Sample", _
            "Settings", _
            "MainTop", _
            Me.Top

    SaveSetting "About Box Sample", _
            "Settings", _
            "MainWidth", _
            Me.Width

    SaveSetting "About Box Sample", _
            "Settings", _
            "MainHeight", _
            Me.Height

End If

End Sub
```

5. Add the program exit logic to the `Click` event of the `mnuFileSel` menu option. Even though there is only one element in this menu, a control array is used to facilitate adding more choices later.

```
Private Sub mnuFileSel_Click(Index As Integer)

Select Case Index
    Case 0              ' Exit
        Unload Me
        End

End Select

End Sub
```

6. Add the following code to the `mnuHelpSel` option's `Click` event. When the user chooses the About option from the Help menu, the About box form is loaded. Then the `Picture` property of the `picIcon` PictureBox on the About box is set to the icon from the main form of the application. Finally, the About box itself is shown as a modal dialog.

```
Private Sub mnuHelpSel_Click(Index As Integer)

Select Case Index
    Case 0                ' About...
        Load frmAbout
        frmAbout!picIcon.Picture = Me.Icon
        frmAbout.Show vbModal

End Select

End Sub
```

7. Add a second form to the project and set the objects and properties as they are listed in Table 4.2. Save the form as ABOUT BOX.FRM. This form is the actual About box dialog.

Table 4.2   The Project Form's Objects and Properties

OBJECT/CONTROL	PROPERTY	VALUE
Form	Name	frmAbout
	BorderStyle	3 - Fixed Dialog
	Caption	About Project1
	Icon	(None)
	MaxButton	0 - False
	MinButton	0 - False
	StartUpPosition	2 - CenterScreen
PictureBox	Name	picIcon
	AutoSize	True
	BackColor	&H00C0C0C0&
	BorderStyle	0 - None
	Picture	W95MBX02.ICO
CommandButton	Name	cmdAction
	Cancel	True
	Caption	OK
	Default	True
	Index	0

OBJECT/CONTROL	PROPERTY	VALUE
CommandButton	Name	cmdAction
	Caption	&System Info
	Enabled	0 - False
	Index	1
Label	Name	lblCopyright
	BackStyle	0 - Transparent
	Caption	Copyright and trademark notices
	ForeColor	&H00000000&
Line	Name	Line1
	BorderColor	&H80000014&
	Index	0
Line	Name	Line1
	BorderColor	&H80000015&
	BorderStyle	6 - Inside Solid
	Index	1
Label	Name	lblUserInfo
	BackStyle	0 - Transparent
	Caption	User information
	ForeColor	&H00000000&
Label	Name	lblUserLabels
	BackStyle	0 - Transparent
	Caption	User:
Label	Name	lblLicense
	BackStyle	0 - Transparent
	Caption	License Information
Label	Name	lblDescription
	BackStyle	0 - Transparent
	Caption	Descriptive text and comments
	ForeColor	&H00000000&
Label	Name	lblTitle
	BackStyle	0 - Transparent
	Caption	Application Title
	FontName	MS Sans Serif
	FontSize	18
	ForeColor	&H80000008&
	Index	0

continued on next page

continued from previous page

OBJECT/CONTROL	PROPERTY	VALUE
Label	Name	lblTitle
	BackStyle	0 - Transparent
	Caption	Application Title
	FontName	MS Sans Serif
	FontSize	18
	ForeColor	&H80000008&
	Index	1
Label	Name	lblVersion
	BackStyle	0 - Transparent
	Caption	Version
Label	Name	lblWarning
	BackStyle	0 - Transparent
	Caption	Warning: This program is protected by copyright law and international treaties. Unauthorized reproduction or distribution of this program, or any portion of it, may result in severe civil and criminal penalties, and will be prosecuted to the maximum extent allowable under law.
	ForeColor	&H00000000

8. Choose Project, Properties from the Visual Basic menu. When the Properties dialog appears, select the Make tab and set the Application Title to **About Box**. Also set the Version value to **1.1.1**. Optionally, you can fill in the text for the Copyright, Trademark, and Description fields.

9. Place the following code in the General Declarations section of the form. It defines a form scope variable that stores the path and filename of the system information program. Then the API constants and Registry functions are declared.

```
Option Explicit

Private msSysInfo        As String

' Reg Key ROOT Types...
Const HKEY_LOCAL_MACHINE = &H80000002
Const API_SUCCESS = 0
Const KEY_QUERY_VALUE = &H1
Const REG_SZ = 1

Private Declare Function RegOpenKeyEx Lib "advapi32" _
```

```
        Alias "RegOpenKeyExA" _
            (ByVal hKey As Long, _
            ByVal lpSubKey As String, _
            ByVal ulOptions As Long, _
            ByVal samDesired As Long, _
            ByRef phkResult As Long) As Long

Private Declare Function RegQueryValueEx Lib "advapi32" _
        Alias "RegQueryValueExA" _
            (ByVal hKey As Long, _
            ByVal lpValueName As String, _
            ByVal lpReserved As Long, _
            ByRef lpType As Long, _
            ByVal lpData As String, _
            ByRef lpcbData As Long) As Long

Private Declare Function RegCloseKey Lib "advapi32" _
        (ByVal hKey As Long) As Long
```

10. Several tasks are performed when the About box form is loaded. The icon is cleared from the form by loading a null picture into the **Icon** property. The Application Title is placed in the form caption and used to set the captions for two label controls. These label controls are offset from each other, one in black text and the other in white. This offset produces a recessed 3D look for the Application Title on the form.

Next the application Description, Copyright, Trademark, and Version number text are pulled from the version information and displayed in label control captions.

The two final steps involve pulling information from the Registry. The user name and company for the operating system's registered user are retrieved and displayed. Then the Registry is checked for the location of the system information program. If the program is found, the System Info command button is enabled.

```
Private Sub Form_Load()

Dim sTempStr            As String

' Clear the form icon
Me.Icon = LoadPicture()

' Set the title bar for the dialog box
Me.Caption = "About " & App.Title

' Get the program title
lblTitle(0).Caption = App.Title
lblTitle(1).Caption = App.Title

' Get the version information
If App.Revision = 0 Then
    lblVersion.Caption = "Version " & App.Major & _
                        "." & App.Minor
```

continued on next page

continued from previous page

```
      Else
        lblVersion.Caption = "Version " & App.Major & _
                             "." & App.Minor & _
                             "." & App.Revision
    End If

    ' Get the comments/description
    lblDescription.Caption = App.Comments

    ' Get the copyright and trademarks
    lblCopyright.Caption = App.LegalCopyright & vbCrLf & _
                           App.LegalTrademarks

    ' Load the license caption with the name of the registered
    ' user and company for this copy of the operating system

    ' Set the caption labels
    lblUserLabels.Caption = "User:" & vbCrLf & _
                            "Company:"

    ' Get the user name
    sTempStr = GetRegString(HKEY_LOCAL_MACHINE, _
            "SOFTWARE\Microsoft\Windows\CurrentVersion", _
            "RegisteredOwner")
    If Len(sTempStr) <> 0 Then
        lblUserInfo.Caption = sTempStr & vbCrLf
      Else
        lblUserInfo.Caption = "No user name available" & vbCrLf
    End If

    ' Get the company name
    sTempStr = GetRegString(HKEY_LOCAL_MACHINE, _
            "SOFTWARE\Microsoft\Windows\CurrentVersion", _
            "RegisteredOrganization")
    If Len(sTempStr) <> 0 Then
        lblUserInfo.Caption = lblUserInfo.Caption & _
                              vbCrLf & sTempStr
    End If

    ' Look for the system information program
    ' If it is found, enable the command button

    ' Try to get program and path name from the registry
    msSysInfo = GetRegString(HKEY_LOCAL_MACHINE, _
            "SOFTWARE\Microsoft\Shared Tools\MSInfo", _
            "PATH")
    If Len(msSysInfo) = 0 Then
        ' Did not find that, so ...
        ' Try to get path alone from the registry
        msSysInfo = GetRegString(HKEY_LOCAL_MACHINE, _
                "SOFTWARE\Microsoft\Shared Tools Location", _
                "MSINFO")
        If Len(msSysInfo) <> 0 Then
            ' We have a path so add the file name
            ' Look for the 32 bit version of the program
            msSysInfo = msSysInfo & "\MSINFO32.EXE"
        End If
```

```
End If

If Len(msSysInfo) <> 0 Then
    ' We have a reference to the system information program
    If (Dir(msSysInfo) <> "") Then
        ' The file exists so enable the button
        cmdAction(1).Enabled = True
    End If
End If

End Sub
```

11. Add the logic to handle the CommandButton `Click` event. When the user clicks the OK button, the form is unloaded. If the system information button is clicked, the information program gets launched. Note that the system information button is enabled only if the system information program was found in the Registry.

```
Private Sub cmdAction_Click(Index As Integer)

Dim lResult                 As Long

Select Case Index
    Case 0              ' OK
        Unload Me

    Case 1              ' System Information
        Call Shell(msSysInfo, vbNormalFocus)

End Select

End Sub
```

12. Add the following function to the form. This code encapsulates the API calls that get data items from the system Registry. Please refer to How-To 8.5 for more information on working with the Registry.

```
Private Function GetRegString _
            (lRegRoot As Long, _
            sRegKey As String, _
            sSubKey As String) As String

Dim hRegKey             As Long
Dim lResult             As Long
Dim lValueSize          As Long
Dim lValueType          As Long
Dim sTempStr            As String

Const REG_SZ = 1

GetRegString = ""

lResult = RegOpenKeyEx(lRegRoot, _
```

continued on next page

continued from previous page

```
                            sRegKey, _
                            0&, _
                            KEY_QUERY_VALUE, _
                            hRegKey)

            If lResult = API_SUCCESS Then
                ' Get the length of the value string
                lResult = RegQueryValueEx(hRegKey, _
                        sSubKey, _
                        0&, _
                        lValueType, _
                        ByVal 0&, _
                        lValueSize)

                ' Make sure it is a string value type
                If lValueType = REG_SZ Then
                    ' Initialize the variable to hold the string
                    sTempStr = String(lValueSize, " ")
                    ' Get the value from the registry
                    lResult = RegQueryValueEx(hRegKey, _
                        sSubKey, _
                        0&, 0&, _
                        ByVal sTempStr, _
                        lValueSize)

                    If lResult = API_SUCCESS Then
                        GetRegString = Left$(sTempStr, _
                                InStr(sTempStr, vbNullChar) - 1)
                    End If
                End If
                ' Close the registry key
                lResult = RegCloseKey(hRegKey)
            End If

        End Function
```

How It Works

The About box dialog is self-contained and encapsulated and customizes itself to the application that displays it. The only property of the form provided externally is the icon that is displayed. All information is retrieved from either the Registry or the main application.

Comments

You can consider adding other features to your own standard About box, which is a common place to put registration information for shareware applications. A number of programs also have a Credits button on the About box to display a list of the people who worked on the code and documentation.

COMPLEXITY
BEGINNING

4.2 How do I...
Create a busy dialog with animation or progress bars?

COMPATIBILITY: VISUAL BASIC 5 AND 6

Problem

I want to let users of my program know the progress of tasks my application is performing. Because there are two types of extended processing, those of known and unknown duration, I need to provide two styles of busy dialogs, one with animation and the other showing a progress bar. Also, I want to enable the user to halt a long process if it can be canceled. How do I develop an encapsulated Busy dialog box and offer animation or a progress bar that enables the user to cancel processing?

Technique

This How-To builds a form that provides both types of activity status by using animation or a progress bar. Public properties enable a program to load and customize the Busy dialog to specific needs. The Busy dialog also has an optional Cancel button. The program that displays the Busy dialog needs to be notified when the user clicks the Cancel button. This is done by supplying a public property set by the Busy dialog. When the property is set, the main program then stops processing.

This How-To does not use the Visual Basic animation control. Building portable components means avoiding the use of all but the basic controls. Using the animation control would require that the control be added to the project before the Busy dialog form can be included. Simple frame-based animation with icons is used in this project. Because the icons are smaller than an AVI file, there is the added advantage of keeping the size of the executable smaller.

Steps

Open and run BUSY DIALOG.VBP. An example of the running program is shown in Figure 4.3.

Click the Be Busy button for a sample of using animation, as shown in Figure 4.4. Cancel the Busy dialog box.

Figure 4.3 The main form at runtime.

Figure 4.4 The Busy dialog with animation.

Now select the Progress Bar option button, and then click the Be Busy button again. Figure 4.5 shows the result of these choices.

Figure 4.5 The Busy dialog with a progress bar.

Complete the following steps to create this project:

1. Create a new project called BUSY DIALOG.VBP. Add a form to the project and set the objects and properties listed in Table 4.3 for the form and save it as BUSY TEST.FRM. This form is used to test the Busy dialog.

Table 4.3 The Project Form's Objects and Properties

OBJECT/CONTROL	PROPERTY	VALUE
Form	Name	frmMain
	Caption	Busy Test
	Icon	PHONE02.ICO

OBJECT/CONTROL	PROPERTY	VALUE
OptionButton	Name	optStyle
	Caption	Animation
	Index	0
	Value	True
OptionButton	Name	optStyle
	Caption	Progress bar
	Index	1
	Value	0 - False
CheckBox	Name	chkAllowCancel
	Caption	Allow Cancel
	Value	1 - Checked
TextBox	Name	txtMessage
	MultiLine	True
	ScrollBars	2 - Vertical
	Text	We are now counting to ten very slowly...
CommandButton	Name	cmdAction
	Caption	Be Busy
	Index	0
CommandButton	Name	cmdAction
	Caption	E&xit
	Index	1
Label	Name	lblCaption
	Caption	Busy dialog style:
	Index	1

2. Put the following code into the General Declarations section of the form. The code defines the API call used to pause the program and establishes the form-scope variable used to store the current process cancellation status.

```
Option Explicit

Private Declare Sub Sleep Lib "kernel32" _
     (ByVal dwMilliseconds As Long)

Private mbBusyCancel          As Boolean
```

3. Add the following subroutine to the form. The routine is called when the user clicks the Be Busy command button. The code determines which style of Busy dialog is in use, and then counts to 10 one second at a time. After each second, the **BusyCancel** property is checked. If the property has been set, the function stops.

```
Private Sub DoSomething()

Dim nLoopCtr        As Integer
Dim nStyle          As Integer

nStyle = frmBusy.Style

' Count to ten slowly
For nLoopCtr = 1 To 10
    If nStyle = 1 Then
        ' Progress bar style busy dialog
        frmBusy.BarCaption = "Processing step " & _
                             Trim$(CStr(nLoopCtr)) & _
                             " of 10"
        frmBusy.BarPercent = nLoopCtr * 10
    End If
    DoEvents
    Sleep 1000
    If Me.BusyCancel = True Then Exit For
Next nLoopCtr

Unload frmBusy

End Sub
```

4. Place the following code in the **Click** event of the **cmdAction** command
button control array. If the first button is clicked by the user, the Busy
dialog is loaded, its properties are set based on the selections made by the
user, and the **DoSomething** subroutine is called. The second command
button exits the program.

```
Private Sub cmdAction_Click(Index As Integer)

Select Case Index
    Case 0            ' Be busy
        Me.BusyCancel = False
        Load frmBusy
        frmBusy.CallingForm = frmMain
        frmBusy.Message = txtMessage.Text
        If chkAllowCancel.Value = 1 Then
           frmBusy.AllowCancel = True
          Else
           frmBusy.AllowCancel = False
        End If
        If optStyle(0).Value = True Then
           frmBusy.Style = 0   ' Animated
          Else
           frmBusy.Style = 1   ' Progress bar
        End If

        frmBusy.Show

        Call DoSomething

    Case 1            ' Exit
        Unload frmMain
```

```
        End

    End Select

    End Sub
```

5. Add the following code for the **BusyCancel** property. This public property allows other forms and routines to set and query a Boolean value indicating whether the current program activity should be terminated.

```
Public Property Get BusyCancel() As Boolean

BusyCancel = mbBusyCancel

End Property


Public Property Let BusyCancel(ByVal bBusyCancel As Boolean)

mbBusyCancel = bBusyCancel

End Property
```

6. Insure that the Microsoft Common Controls 6.0 are added as a component of the project. Then add a second form to the project and set the objects and properties listed in Table 4.4 for the form. Save it as BUSY DIALOG.FRM. This form is the actual Busy box dialog. The following steps add code for the dialog's custom properties and features.

Table 4.4   The Busy Dialog's Objects and Properties

OBJECT/CONTROL	PROPERTY	VALUE
Form	Name	frmBusy
	Caption	Busy Dialog
	ControlBox	0 - False
	Icon	CLOCK03.ICO
	StartUpPosition	2 - CenterScreen
	MaxButton	0 - False
	MinButton	0 - False
Timer	Name	tmrBusy
	Enabled	0 - False
	Interval	500
CommandButton	Name	cmdAction
	Cancel	True
	Caption	Cancel

continued on next page

continued from previous page

OBJECT/CONTROL	PROPERTY	VALUE
ProgressBar	Name	ProgressBar1
	Visible	0 - False
	Appearance	1 - 3D
Label	Name	lblProgress
	Alignment	2 - Center
	Caption	Progress: 1 of 100
Image	Name	imgFrame
	Index	7
	Picture	MOON08.ICO
	Visible	0 - False
Image	Name	imgFrame
	Index	6
	Picture	MOON01.ICO
	Visible	0 - False
Image	Name	imgFrame
	Index	5
	Picture	MOON02.ICO
	Visible	0 - False
Image	Name	imgFrame
	Index	4
	Picture	MOON03.ICO
	Visible	0 - False
Image	Name	imgFrame
	Index	3
	Picture	MOON04.ICO
	Visible	0 - False
Image	Name	imgFrame
	Index	2
	Picture	MOON05.ICO
	Visible	0 - False
Image	Name	imgFrame
	Index	1
	Picture	MOON06.ICO
	Visible	0 - False
Image	Name	imgFrame
	Index	0
	Picture	MOON07.ICO
	Visible	0 - False

OBJECT/CONTROL	PROPERTY	VALUE
Image	Name	imgBusy
	Picture	MOON08.ICO
	Visible	0 - False
Label	Name	lblMessage
	Alignment	2 - Center
	Caption	We are busy now. Please wait...

7. Put the following code into the General Declarations section of the form. This code establishes the form-scope variables used to store local copies of the public properties. It also sets up a variable to store a frame reference for the animation.

```
Option Explicit

' Local property storage variables
Dim mnBarPercent    As Integer
Dim msMessage       As String
Dim msBarCaption    As String
Dim mnStyle         As Integer
Dim mbAllowCancel   As Boolean
Dim frmCalling      As Object

Dim mnFrame         As Integer
```

8. When the form loads, the default values for the properties are established. This is done by adding the following code to the form's **Load** event:

```
Private Sub Form_Load()

' Setup the defaults
mnFrame = 0          ' First frame
Me.Style = 0         ' Animation
Me.AllowCancel = True

End Sub
```

9. When the user clicks the Cancel button, this code sets the **BusyCancel** property of the form that loaded the Busy dialog box.

```
Private Sub cmdAction_Click()

frmCalling.BusyCancel = True

End Sub
```

10. The timer is activated only if the dialog style is set to animation. Add this code to the control's **Timer** event. The logic advances the frame reference and loads the current frame picture for display.

```
Private Sub tmrBusy_Timer()

' Advance to the next animation frame
mnFrame = mnFrame + 1

' Wrap around to the first frame if at the last one
If mnFrame > 7 Then mnFrame = 0

' Load the icon for the current frame
imgBusy.Picture = imgFrame(mnFrame).Picture

End Sub
```

11. Start adding the code to manage the public properties of the Busy dialog. This first property is used to set the percent complete for the progress bar. When the property is set, the value of the progress bar is updated.

```
Public Property Get BarPercent() As Integer

BarPercent = mnBarPercent

End Property


Public Property Let BarPercent(nBarPercent As Integer)

mnBarPercent = nBarPercent
ProgressBar1.Value = mnBarPercent

End Property
```

12. The next property determines whether the user is allowed to cancel the process. It is a Boolean property, also used directly to control the visibility of the Cancel command button. If the command button is not visible, then the height of the form is adjusted to remove the extra blank space at the bottom.

```
Public Property Get AllowCancel() As Boolean

AllowCancel = mbAllowCancel

End Property


Public Property Let AllowCancel(bAllowCancel As Boolean)

mbAllowCancel = bAllowCancel
cmdAction.Visible = mbAllowCancel

Select Case mbAllowCancel
    Case True
        frmBusy.Height = 2475

    Case False
        frmBusy.Height = 1995
```

```
End Select

End Property
```

13. The following property sets an object reference to the form that loaded the Busy dialog box. This reference is used to change the `BusyCancel` property of the calling form when the user clicks the Cancel button.

```
Public Property Get CallingForm() As Object

Set CallingForm = frmCalling

End Property


Public Property Let CallingForm(objCallingForm As Object)

Set frmCalling = objCallingForm

End Property
```

14. The following code supplies the `Get` and `Let` routines for the `Style` property. The style can be set to either `Animation` or `Progress bar`. The style determines which controls are visible on the form.

```
Public Property Get Style() As Integer

Style = mnStyle

End Property


Public Property Let Style(nStyle As Integer)

mnStyle = nStyle

' Check for legal property values
Select Case mnStyle
    Case 0           ' Animation
        imgBusy.Visible = True
        tmrBusy.Enabled = True
        lblProgress.Visible = False
        ProgressBar1.Visible = False

    Case 1           ' Progress bar
        imgBusy.Visible = False
        tmrBusy.Enabled = False
        lblProgress.Visible = True
        ProgressBar1.Visible = True
        ProgressBar1.Value = 1

End Select

End Property
```

15. When the progress bar is in use, a caption is displayed on the form. This code manages the `BarCaption` property for the dialog box.

```
Public Property Get BarCaption() As String

BarCaption = msBarCaption

End Property


Public Property Let BarCaption(sBarCaption As String)

msBarCaption = sBarCaption
lblProgress.Caption = msBarCaption

End Property
```

16. The final property for the form enables the calling program to set the message displayed at the top of the form.

```
Public Property Get Message() As String

Message = msMessage

End Property


Public Property Let Message(ByVal sMessage As String)

msMessage = sMessage
lblMessage.Caption = msMessage

End Property
```

How It Works

When a long process is started, the program loads the Busy dialog form and sets the property values. The properties of the form determine the appearance, behavior, and features of the Busy dialog box. If the user elects to cancel the process, a property of the calling form is set. The `BusyCancel` property of the main form is periodically checked during the processing. If it has been set to `True`, the processing terminates.

Comments

The `BusyCancel` property can also be implemented as a read-only property of the Busy dialog box; doing so results in looser coupling with the main form. Then when the process checks the `BusyCancel` state, it queries the property.

This How-To uses a different approach. The code shows how a program can invoke a method of another form without knowing the form's actual name.

COMPLEXITY
INTERMEDIATE

4.3 How do I...
Enhance the VB Application Wizard splash screen?

COMPATIBILITY: VISUAL BASIC 6

Problem

I want to produce a visually attractive splash screen for my application. The splash screen created by the Visual Basic Application Wizard is fairly plain and does not tailor itself to my program. How do I add features to the basic splash screen and integrate it with the Application Wizard?

Technique

The Application Wizard provided as part of the Visual Basic IDE is a powerful tool. This How-To builds a splash screen with additional graphics that stays on top of the main form and includes application-specific information. The new form is then integrated with the wizard. After integrating the new splash screen, the Application Wizard is used to create a simple SDI application that uses the new form.

Steps

Open and run SPLASH TEMPLATE.VBP. An example of the running program with the splash screen visible is shown in Figure 4.6.

To create this project, complete the following steps:

1. Create a new project called SPLASH TEMPLATE.VBP. Add a form to the project and set the form's properties as listed in Table 4.5. Save the form as SPLASH TEST.FRM.

Table 4.5 The Project Form's Properties

OBJECT/CONTROL	PROPERTY	VALUE
Form	Name	frmMain
	Caption	Splash Test
	Icon	LITENING.ICO
	StartUpPosition	2 - CenterScreen

Figure 4.6 The main form at runtime.

2. When the form loads, the splash screen is loaded, its properties are set, and then it is displayed. This is done by adding the following code to the **Load** event for the main test form.

```
Private Sub Form_Load()

' Load the splash screen
Load frmSplash

' Set splash screen properties
frmSplash.Delay = 15000
frmSplash.BackPicture = App.Path & _
                        "\STUCCO.GIF"
frmSplash.LogoPicture = App.Path & _
                        "\TYPEWRTR.GIF"

' Paint the splash screen
frmSplash.Show

End Sub
```

3. Even though the splash screen stays on top, after the main form is loaded, it is active and the user can click buttons and menus. If the user exits from the application while the splash screen is still displayed, the splash screen form must be unloaded before your program actually terminates. Put the following code in the form's **Unload** event to resolve this potential problem.

```
Private Sub Form_Unload(Cancel As Integer)

' If we are exiting and the splash screen
```

```
' is loaded, unload it
On Error Resume Next
Unload frmSplash
On Error GoTo 0

End Sub
```

4. Add a second form to the project and set the objects and properties of the form as listed in Table 4.6. Save the form as SPLASH TEMPLATE.FRM.

Table 4.6 The Splash Screen's Objects and Properties

OBJECT/CONTROL	PROPERTY	VALUE
Form	Name	frmSplash
	BorderStyle	3 - Fixed Dialog
	ControlBox	0 - False
	Icon	(None)
	MaxButton	0 - False
	MinButton	0 - False
	StartUpPosition	2 - CenterScreen
Timer	Name	tmrUnload
	Enabled	0 - False
	Interval	10000
Label	Name	lblCompany
	Alignment	1 - Right Justify
	BackStyle	0 - Transparent
	Caption	Company Name
	FontName	Arial
	FontSize	12
	FontItalic	True
	ForeColor	&H00000000&
Shape	Name	Shape1
	BorderColor	&H00808080&
	BorderWidth	2
	Index	1
Shape	Name	Shape1
	BorderColor	&H00FFFFFF&
	BorderWidth	2
	Index	0
Label	Name	lblCopyright
	BackStyle	0 'Transparent

continued on next page

continued from previous page

OBJECT/CONTROL	PROPERTY	VALUE
	Caption	This program is protected by US and international copyright laws as described in Help About.
	ForeColor	&H00000000&
Label	Name	lblUserInfo
	Alignment	1 - Right Justify
	BackStyle	0 'Transparent
	Caption	User information
	ForeColor	&H00000000&
Label	Name	lblLicense
	Alignment	1 - Right Justify
	BackStyle	0 - Transparent
	Caption	This product is licensed to:
	ForeColor	&H00000000&
Label	Name	lblTitle
	Alignment	2 - Center
	BackStyle	0 - Transparent
	Caption	Application Title
	FontName	Arial Black
	FontSize	27.75
	FontItalic	True
	ForeColor	&H00000000&
	Index	0
Label	Name	lblTitle
	Alignment	2 - Center
	BackStyle	0 - Transparent
	Caption	Application Title
	FontName	Arial Black
	FontSize	27.75
	FontItalic	True
	ForeColor	&H00FFFFFF&
	Index	1
Label	Name	lblVersion
	Alignment	2 - Center
	BackStyle	0 - 'Transparent
	Caption	Version
	ForeColor	&H00000000&
Image	Name	imgLogo

5. Place the following code in the General Declarations section of the form. It defines a form-scope variable that stores the number of milliseconds that the splash screen remains visible. Then the API constants and Registry functions are declared.

```
Option Explicit

' Private variables to store property values
Private mlDelay              As Long

Private Declare Function SetWindowPos Lib "user32" _
        (ByVal hwnd As Long, _
         ByVal hWndInsertAfter As Long, _
         ByVal x As Long, _
         ByVal y As Long, _
         ByVal cx As Long, _
         ByVal cy As Long, _
         ByVal wFlags As Long) As Long

' Reg Key ROOT Types...
Const HKEY_LOCAL_MACHINE = &H80000002
Const API_SUCCESS = 0
Const KEY_QUERY_VALUE = &H1
Const REG_SZ = 1

Private Declare Function RegOpenKeyEx Lib "advapi32" _
    Alias "RegOpenKeyExA" _
        (ByVal hKey As Long, _
         ByVal lpSubKey As String, _
         ByVal ulOptions As Long, _
         ByVal samDesired As Long, _
         ByRef phkResult As Long) As Long

Private Declare Function RegQueryValueEx Lib "advapi32" _
    Alias "RegQueryValueExA" _
        (ByVal hKey As Long, _
         ByVal lpValueName As String, _
         ByVal lpReserved As Long, _
         ByRef lpType As Long, _
         ByVal lpData As String, _
         ByRef lpcbData As Long) As Long

Private Declare Function RegCloseKey Lib "advapi32" _
        (ByVal hKey As Long) As Long
```

6. Several tasks are performed when the splash screen is loaded. Start by clearing the icon from the form by loading a null picture into the `Icon` property. The application title is used to set the captions for two label controls. These label controls are offset from each other, one in black text and the other in white. This produces a recessed 3D look for the application title on the form.

Next the application version numbers are displayed. The final step involves pulling information from the Registry. The user name and company for the registered user of the operating system are retrieved and displayed.

```
Private Sub Form_Load()

Dim tTempStr            As String

' Clear the splash form icon
Me.Icon = LoadPicture()

' Get the program title
lblTitle(0).Caption = App.Title
lblTitle(1).Caption = App.Title

' Get the company name
lblCompany.Caption = App.CompanyName

' Get the version information
If App.Revision = 0 Then
    lblVersion.Caption = "Version " & App.Major & _
                         "." & App.Minor
  Else
    lblVersion.Caption = "Version " & App.Major & _
                         "." & App.Minor & _
                         "." & App.Revision
End If

' Load the license caption with the name of the registered
' user and company for this copy of the operating system

' Get the user name
tTempStr = GetRegString(HKEY_LOCAL_MACHINE, _
        "SOFTWARE\Microsoft\Windows\CurrentVersion", _
        "RegisteredOwner")
If Len(tTempStr) <> 0 Then
    lblUserInfo.Caption = tTempStr & vbCrLf
  Else
    lblUserInfo.Caption = "No user name available" & vbCrLf
End If

' Get the company name
tTempStr = GetRegString(HKEY_LOCAL_MACHINE, _
        "SOFTWARE\Microsoft\Windows\CurrentVersion", _
        "RegisteredOrganization")
If Len(tTempStr) <> 0 Then
    lblUserInfo.Caption = lblUserInfo.Caption & tTempStr
End If

End Sub
```

7. Add the following function to the form. This code encapsulates the API calls that get data items from the system Registry. Please refer to How-To 8.5, "Create and Use Registry Entries," for more information on working with the Registry.

```vb
Private Function GetRegString _
                (lRegRoot As Long, _
                 sRegKey As String, _
                 sSubKey As String) As String

Dim hRegKey             As Long
Dim lResult             As Long
Dim lValueSize          As Long
Dim lValueType          As Long
Dim tTempStr            As String

Const REG_SZ = 1

GetRegString = ""

' Open the registry key we want to check
lResult = RegOpenKeyEx(lRegRoot, _
            sRegKey, _
            0&, _
            KEY_QUERY_VALUE, _
            hRegKey)

' Make sure we did not get an error
If lResult = API_SUCCESS Then
    ' Get the length of the value string
    lResult = RegQueryValueEx(hRegKey, _
            sSubKey, _
            0&, _
            lValueType, _
            ByVal 0&, _
            lValueSize)

    ' Make sure it is a string value type
    If lValueType = REG_SZ Then
        ' Initialize the variable to hold the string
        tTempStr = String(lValueSize, " ")
        ' Get the value from the registry
        lResult = RegQueryValueEx(hRegKey, _
            sSubKey, _
            0&, 0&, _
            ByVal tTempStr, _
            lValueSize)

        If lResult = API_SUCCESS Then
            GetRegString = Left$(tTempStr, _
                    InStr(tTempStr, vbNullChar) - 1)
        End If
    End If
    ' Close the registry key
    lResult = RegCloseKey(hRegKey)
End If

End Function
```

8. When the form **Paint** event fires, an API function is called to make the splash screen window stay on top of the other forms in the application. Then the delay timer is started.

```
Private Sub Form_Paint()

Dim lReturn                As Long

Const SWP_NOMOVE = 2
Const SWP_NOSIZE = 1
Const FLAGS = SWP_NOMOVE Or SWP_NOSIZE
Const HWND_TOPMOST = -1

' Set this form to stay on top of the other
' forms in the program
lReturn = SetWindowPos(frmSplash.hwnd, _
                HWND_TOPMOST, _
                0, 0, 0, 0, _
                FLAGS)

' Enable the timer now, so that it only starts
' counting down the time while the form is visible
If tmrUnload.Enabled = False Then
    tmrUnload.Enabled = True
End If

End Sub
```

9. When the **Timer** event is triggered, the splash screen is unloaded.

```
Private Sub tmrUnload_Timer()

Unload frmSplash

End Sub
```

10. Now start adding the following code to manage the public properties of the splash screen. This first property is used to set the time, in milliseconds, that the splash screen remains visible. The property value range is checked and must be between 1,000 and 60,000 milliseconds (1 to 60 seconds). The property value is then used to set the **Interval** property of the **Timer** control.

```
Public Property Get Delay() As Long

Delay = mlDelay

End Property


Public Property Let Delay(ByVal lDelay As Long)

' Save the property value
mlDelay = lDelay
```

```
' Perform a range check on the lower limit
If mlDelay < 1000 Then
    mlDelay = 1000
End If

' Perform a range check on the upper limit
If mlDelay > 60000 Then
    mlDelay = 60000
End If

' Set the timer interval from the property
tmrUnload.Interval = mlDelay

End Property
```

11. The next property is used to place a logo graphic on the splash screen. This property expects a filename passed as a string. The code ensures that the file exists and then loads it into the **Image** control.

```
Public Property Let LogoPicture(ByVal sLogoPicture As String)

' If the picture files exists, load it
If Dir$(sLogoPicture) <> "" Then
    imgLogo.Picture = LoadPicture(sLogoPicture)
End If

End Property
```

12. The final property is used to display a background image on the splash screen form itself. This property also expects a filename passed as a string. The logic checks to be sure the file exists and then loads it as the form's **Picture** property.

```
Public Property Let BackPicture(ByVal sBackPicture As String)

' If the picture files exists, load it
If Dir$(sBackPicture) <> "" Then
    frmSplash.Picture = LoadPicture(sBackPicture)
End If

End Property _
```

13. Give the user a way to close the splash screen without waiting for the timer to expire. To do this, add a call to the **Timer** control's **Timer** event routine in the form's **Click** event and each of its controls.

```
Private Sub Form_Click()

Call tmrUnload_Timer

End Sub


Private Sub imgLogo_Click()
```

continued on next page

continued from previous page

```
        Call tmrUnload_Timer

        End Sub


        Private Sub lblCompany_Click()

        Call tmrUnload_Timer

        End Sub


        Private Sub lblCopyright_Click()

        Call tmrUnload_Timer

        End Sub


        Private Sub lblLicense_Click()

        Call tmrUnload_Timer

        End Sub


        Private Sub lblTitle_Click(Index As Integer)

        Call tmrUnload_Timer

        End Sub


        Private Sub lblUserInfo_Click()

        Call tmrUnload_Timer

        End Sub


        Private Sub lblVersion_Click()

        Call tmrUnload_Timer

        End Sub
```

14. The new splash screen is now finished. After saving the project files, exit from Visual Basic. Copy the files SPLASH TEMPLATE.FRM and SPLASH TEMPLATE.FRX to the forms subdirectory of the Visual Basic templates directory. This makes the form available to the VB Application Wizard. The default location of the templates directory is C:\PROGRAM FILES\MICROSOFT VISUAL STUDIO\VB98\TEMPLATE. This location can be changed by choosing Tools, Options from the Visual Basic menu. The template location is set on the Environment tab.

15. Start Visual Basic and select VB Application Wizard from the available project types in the New tab, as shown in Figure 4.7. Click the Open button to continue.

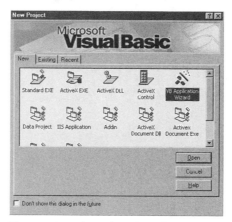

Figure 4.7 The Visual Basic New Project dialog.

16. The Application Wizard – Introduction screen is now displayed (see Figure 4.8). No changes are needed on this dialog, so click the Next button to proceed.

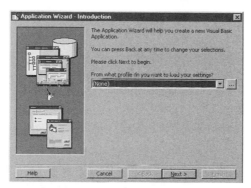

Figure 4.8 The Application Wizard – Introduction dialog.

17. When the Application Wizard – Interface Type dialog is displayed, select the Single Document Interface option. Enter `WizardTest` in the text box. The result is shown in Figure 4.9. Click the Next button to continue.

WARNING

Do not click the Finish command button until you have answered all the Application Wizard's questions. Doing so will complete the wizard dialogs and generate the code. This skips the steps needed to customize the wizard-generated application, and does not allow the selection of other template modules to include in the project.

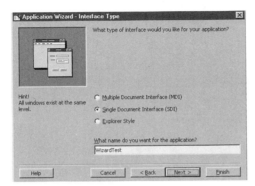

Figure 4.9 The Interface Type panel of the Application Wizard.

18. Next you will see the Menus panel of the wizard, as shown in Figure 4.10. Make any desired change to the default menu structure that is displayed. Click the Next button.

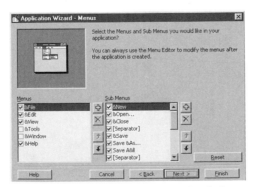

Figure 4.10 The Menus panel of the Application Wizard.

19. When the Application Wizard – Customize Toolbar dialog is displayed, the default toolbar buttons and sequence can be customized. The default for the dialog is shown in Figure 4.11. Click the Next button to proceed.

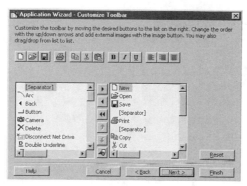

Figure 4.11 The Application Wizard – Customize Toolbar dialog.

20. The Resources panel of the wizard is now displayed (see Figure 4.12). Make sure the No option button is selected. Click the Next button.

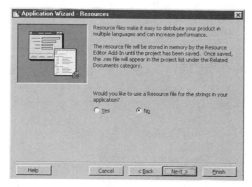

Figure 4.12 The Resources panel of the Application Wizard.

21. The Internet Connectivity panel of the wizard is now displayed, as shown in Figure 4.13. Make sure the No option button is selected to prevent including Internet controls and options in the program. Click the Next button.

Figure 4.13 The Internet Connectivity panel of the Application Wizard.

22. Now you will see the Standard Forms panel of the wizard, as shown in Figure 4.14. Select the Options Dialog for Custom Settings and About Box check boxes. Do not click the Next button.

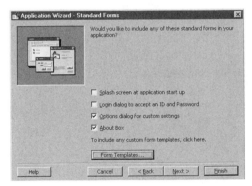

Figure 4.14 The Standard Forms panel of the Application Wizard.

23. Click the Form Templates command button to display the dialog. Select the Splash Template form from the list (see Figure 4.15). You might need to scroll down the list box to see all the choices. Click the OK button and then click the Next button when you get back to the Standard Forms panel of the wizard.

24. You will now see the Data Access Forms panel of the wizard, as shown in Figure 4.16. No action is required on this screen, so just click the Next button.

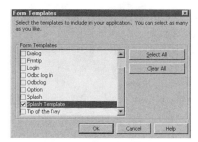

Figure 4.15 The Form Templates dialog of the Application Wizard.

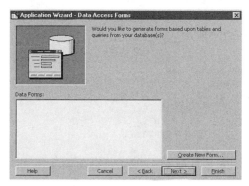

Figure 4.16 The Data Access Forms panel of the Application Wizard.

25. Next the wizard presents the Finished! panel, as shown in Figure 4.17. Click the Finish button and wait for the wizard to generate your application.

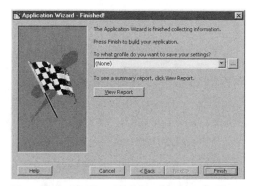

Figure 4.17 The Finished! panel of the Application Wizard.

26. Save the project files to the same directory where you stored the SPLASH TEST.VBP project files. You can use the default filenames for the forms and modules. Select MODULE1.BAS from the project window and view the code in Sub Main. You will see the following code listed:

```
Sub Main()
    Set fMainForm = New frmMain
    fMainForm.Show
End Sub
```

Modify the code by adding the splash screen control logic. This code loads the splash screen, sets the properties, and then displays the form. The new code lines are highlighted in boldface type.

```
Sub Main()

' Load the splash screen
Load frmSplash

' Set splash screen properties
frmSplash.Delay = 15000
frmSplash.BackPicture = App.Path & _
                        "\STUCCO.GIF"
frmSplash.LogoPicture = App.Path & _
                        "\TYPEWRTR.GIF"

' Paint the splash screen
frmSplash.Show

Set fMainForm = New frmMain
fMainForm.Show

End Sub
```

27. Choose Project, Properties from the Project menu. Go to the Make tab and modify the properties as shown in Figure 4.18. The key properties for this example are the version numbers, application title, and company name. These properties are used on the splash screen.

28. Run the finished project. The results with the new splash screen can be seen in Figure 4.19.

How It Works

You cannot directly modify the standard forms because they are built dynamically by the wizard. This How-To shows you how you can create your own version of one of the standard wizard forms and include it as a form template. The easiest way to ensure the quality of your add-on template forms is to develop them in a test environment. After they are debugged and working properly, move them to the template forms directory.

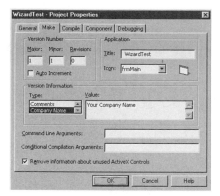

Figure 4.18 The Make tab of
the Project Properties dialog.

Figure 4.19 The Application Wizard results with the new
splash screen.

Comments

It is possible to build a form, move it to the template forms directory, and not
have it appear on the Form Templates dialog. If this happens to you, save the
form using a different filename. If the name you initially selected matches the
internal name of one of the standard wizard forms, it will not appear on the list.

Now that you understand the process, move some other standard forms into
the template directory. A couple of good candidates would be the About box and
Busy dialogs from How-Tos 4.1 and 4.2.

4.4 How do I...
Implement an application error log?

COMPATIBILITY: VISUAL BASIC 5 AND 6

Problem

The built-in error log does not allow the developer to control the format of the error log entries. In addition, the built-in error logging works only when programs are run as compiled executables. This makes it difficult to debug error log and trapping logic. When unexpected runtime errors do occur in a compiled executable, seeing the call stack would help isolate the code that generated the error. How do I implement a reusable error log that can be customized and also tracks the call stack?

Technique

Two projects are constructed in this How-To. The first one, used here for comparison purposes, implements an error log using the built-in logging features.

The second project builds a class module that offers full customization of the log contents and format. Class methods provide the ability to enable and disable logging. An array is used in the code to keep a call stack to supply call tracing. A form is also written that gives a visual test interface for the error log class module.

Steps

Open the project BUILT IN LOG.VBP. Make an executable file for the project and then run that executable. The program does not have a user interface. All it does is enable the built-in logging features and generate an error. A sample of the resulting error log is shown in Listing 4.1.

Listing 4.1   EXAMPLE1.LOG

```
Information Application D:\19980418.log: Thread ID: -730143 ,Logged: Built In Log
- Started at 4/18/98 5:27:38 PM
Error       Application D:\19980418.log: Thread ID: -730143 ,Logged: Test error
message
Warning     Application D:\19980418.log: Thread ID: -730143 ,Logged: Test warning
message
Information Application D:\19980418.log: Thread ID: -730143 ,Logged: Built In Log
- Stopped at 4/18/98 5:27:39 PM
```

Next, open and run ERROR LOG.VBP. The running program is shown in Figure 4.20. Select log and trace options and click the Make Calls and Generate the Error button. Listing 4.2 shows an example of a log file that includes call tracing and a call stack dump.

Figure 4.20 The main form at runtime.

Listing 4.2   EXAMPLE2.LOG

```
1998-04-20 11:40:24 Error Log (1.0.1), Info - Program started
1998-04-20 11:40:28 Error Log (1.0.1), Info - Enter: TestLevel1
1998-04-20 11:40:28 Error Log (1.0.1), Info - Enter: TestLevel2
1998-04-20 11:40:28 Error Log (1.0.1), Info - Enter: TestLevel3
1998-04-20 11:40:28 Error Log (1.0.1), Info - Enter: TestLevel4
1998-04-20 11:40:28 Error Log (1.0.1), Error - (62) Input past end of file
1998-04-20 11:40:28 Error Log (1.0.1), Info - Routine call stack:
1998-04-20 11:40:28 Error Log (1.0.1), Info -     TestLevel1
1998-04-20 11:40:28 Error Log (1.0.1), Info -     TestLevel2
1998-04-20 11:40:28 Error Log (1.0.1), Info -     TestLevel3
1998-04-20 11:40:28 Error Log (1.0.1), Info -     TestLevel4
1998-04-20 11:40:28 Error Log (1.0.1), Info - Exit:  TestLevel4
1998-04-20 11:40:28 Error Log (1.0.1), Info - Exit:  TestLevel3
1998-04-20 11:40:28 Error Log (1.0.1), Info - Exit:  TestLevel2
1998-04-20 11:40:28 Error Log (1.0.1), Info - Exit:  TestLevel1
1998-04-20 11:40:31 Error Log (1.0.1), Info - Program stopped
```

Complete the following steps to create this project:

1. Create a new project called BUILT IN LOG.VBP. This project uses the built-in log features.

2. Add a form to the project and set the objects and properties as listed in Table 4.7. Save the form as BUILT IN LOG.FRM. There are no visual elements or controls on this form. The code in the program establishes error logging, generates some test log messages, and then terminates the program.

Table 4.7   The Project Form's Objects and Properties

OBJECT/CONTROL	PROPERTY	VALUE
Form	Name	frmMain
	Caption	Built In Logging
	Icon	W95BX01.ICO

3. The following code is placed in the General Declarations section of the form. The single form scope variable is used to store an error log path and filename.

```
Option Explicit

Dim msLogFile          As String
```

4. Place this code segment in the form's **Load** event. The code defines the log filename, which is based on the application path and the current system date. Logging is then initiated. Notice that instead of accepting the default, logging is directed to a file. In Windows 95, the default logs messages to a file; in NT and NT Workstation, the defaults write to the system event log. Overriding the default produces the same results on all operating system platforms.

A call is made to a subroutine that encapsulates the message logging logic. An application startup message is written to the log, followed by two test messages. Finally, the code unloads the main form to initiate termination of the program.

```
Private Sub Form_Load()

' Define the log file name and path
msLogFile = App.Path & "\" & _
            Format$(Now, "yyyymmdd") & _
            ".log"

' Start the logging services
App.StartLogging msLogFile, vbLogToFile

' Log the application startup
LogEXEOnly App.Title & " - Started at " & Now, _
        vbLogEventTypeInformation

' Write two test messages to the log one error
' and one warning
LogEXEOnly "Test error message", _
        vbLogEventTypeError

LogEXEOnly "Test warning message", _
        vbLogEventTypeWarning

' Exit from the program
Unload Me

End Sub
```

5. Add the following code to the form's **Unload** event to log the application shutdown and turn off logging.

```
Private Sub Form_Unload(Cancel As Integer)

' Log the application shutdown
LogEXEOnly App.Title & " - Stopped at " & Now, _
vbLogEventTypeInformation

' Turn off logging
App.StartLogging msLogFile, vbLogOff

End Sub
```

6. Add the following subroutine to the form. This code invokes the method of the application object that writes a message to the log.

```
Private Sub LogEXEOnly(sLogText As String, _
                       nEventType As Integer)

' Record an event in the log file
App.LogEvent sLogText, nEventType

End Sub
```

7. Compile the project executable and run it. To view the results, you can use Notepad to open the generated log file.

8. Create a new Standard EXE project called ERROR LOG.VBP. Set the Startup Object property of the project to **Sub Main**. This project does not use the built-in error log.

9. Add a class module to the project and save it as CLSERRORLOG.CLS. Set the class name to **clsErrorLog**. Now, add the following code to the General Declarations section of the class. This code declares the private class variables and the local private variables used to store the class property values. A constant is also defined that is used to increase allocated stack storage space. When additional space is needed in the call stack array, a **ReDim Preserve** statement is used. It's an expensive operation because a new array is created in memory, all of the data is moved from the current array into the new one, and then Visual Basic releases the memory that contained the old version of the array. For this reason, extra space is included each time the array is redimensioned instead of adding array elements one at a time.

```
Option Explicit

' Routine call stack variables
Private msStack()        As String
Private mlPointer        As Long
Private mlEntries        As Long
```

continued on next page

continued from previous page

```
' Constant to define number of stack items
' to add each time the call stack is expanded
Private Const STACK_INCREMENT As Integer = 10

' Local variables to hold property values
Private msLogFileName      As String
Private msProgramName      As String
Private mbLogEnabled       As Boolean
Private mbTrace            As Boolean
```

10. When the class is first instantiated, the following code is executed. These statements allocate the initial call stack space, and then set the default values for the class properties.

```
Private Sub Class_Initialize()

' Initial the routine call stack array
ReDim msStack(STACK_INCREMENT) As String

' Set the call stack pointer to the first entry
mlPointer = 0

' Save the number of stack entries
mlEntries = UBound(msStack)

' Set the default property values
msLogFileName = "c:\" & _
                Format$(Now, "yyyymmdd") & _
                ".log"
msProgramName = "Unknown"
mbLogEnabled = False
mbTrace = False

End Sub
```

11. The following public method is called to start active logging. The class always performs passive logging when its methods are called so that the call stack is properly maintained. Disabling logging in the class just prevents the calls and messages from being written to the log file itself.

```
Public Sub StartLogging()

' Enable logging
mbLogEnabled = True

End Sub
```

12. Add the following method to disable active logging.

```
Public Sub StopLogging()

' Disable logging - All processing occurs but
' no information is written to the log file
mbLogEnabled = False

End Sub
```

13. The subroutine formats error log messages and writes them to the log file. This is the code that should be modified to make changes in the content and format of log file entries.

Please note that the log file is opened and closed each time a message is written to help ensure that the log file is current and prevent a program from terminating abnormally and leaving the log file with incomplete or missing entries.

```
Public Sub LogMessage(sText As String, _
                      nType As Integer)

Dim sLogText            As String
Dim nChannel            As String

' Build the log file text string starting
' with the current date and time
sLogText = Format$(Now, "yyyy-mm-dd HH:mm:ss ")

' Add the application name
sLogText = sLogText & msProgramName & ", "

' Add the message type as a string
Select Case nType
    Case vbLogEventTypeInformation
        sLogText = sLogText & "Info - "
    Case vbLogEventTypeWarning
        sLogText = sLogText & "Warning - "
    Case vbLogEventTypeError
        sLogText = sLogText & "Error - "
    Case Else
        sLogText = sLogText & "Unknown - "
End Select

' Finally add the message text itself
sLogText = sLogText & sText

' Get a channel number and open the log file
nChannel = FreeFile()
Open msLogFileName For Append As #nChannel

' Write the message to the log file
Print #nChannel, sLogText

' Close the log file
Close #nChannel

End Sub
```

14. Each time a new routine is entered in a program that uses this error log class, a call is made to the following method. The call stack pointer always references the next available stack entry location, so the code starts by adding the current routine name to the stack. If tracing is enabled, the class method is called to write the trace message to the log. Next the pointer to the next stack entry is incremented. Finally, the stack array is checked to see whether more space is needed. If so, the call stack array is redimensioned.

```
Public Sub RoutineEnter(sRoutineName As String)

Dim lNewSize            As Long

' Add a routine name to the call stack
msStack(mlPointer) = sRoutineName

' See if the class is tracing routines
If mbTrace = True Then
    ' Send a trace message to the log
    Me.LogMessage "Enter: " & sRoutineName, _
                vbLogEventTypeInformation

End If

' Increment the call stack pointer
mlPointer = mlPointer + 1

' Make sure there is space in the stack array
If mlPointer = mlEntries Then

    ' The call stack array is full so compute
    ' the new stack size
    lNewSize = UBound(msStack) + STACK_INCREMENT

    ' Expand the routine call stack array
    ReDim Preserve msStack(lNewSize) As String

    ' Save the current number of stack entries
    mlEntries = UBound(msStack)

End If

End Sub
```

15. When the programming using the logging class leaves a routine, the following method is called. Again, if tracing is enabled a trace message is written to the log file. Then the routine is removed from the call stack.

```
Public Sub RoutineExit(sRoutineName As String)

' See if the class is tracing routines
If mbTrace = True Then
    ' Send a trace message to the log
    Me.LogMessage "Exit:  " & sRoutineName, _
                vbLogEventTypeInformation

End If

' Decrement the call stack pointer
mlPointer = mlPointer - 1
```

```
' Remove a routine name from the call stack
msStack(mlPointer) = ""

End Sub
```

16. This next class method can be called at any time to write the entire call stack to the log file. The logic iterates through the call stack array and generates a log file message for each entry.

```
Public Sub LogStack()

Dim lLoopCtr                As Long

' Write the call stack to the log file
Me.LogMessage "Routine call stack:", _
              vbLogEventTypeInformation

For lLoopCtr = 0 To mlPointer - 1
    ' Write each stack entry to the log file
    Me.LogMessage "     " & msStack(lLoopCtr), _
                  vbLogEventTypeInformation

Next lLoopCtr

End Sub
```

17. The following routines allow setting and retrieving the class properties. The properties are **ProgramName** string, **LogFileName** string, and **Trace** as a Boolean.

```
Public Property Let ProgramName( _
              ByVal sProgramName As String)

msProgramName = sProgramName

End Property


Public Property Get ProgramName() As String

ProgramName = msProgramName

End Property


Public Property Let LogFileName( _
              ByVal sLogFileName As String)

msLogFileName = sLogFileName

End Property


Public Property Get LogFileName() As String
```

continued on next page

continued from previous page

```
LogFileName = msLogFileName

End Property


Public Property Get Trace() As Boolean

Trace = mbTrace

End Property


Public Property Let Trace(ByVal bTrace As Boolean)

mbTrace = bTrace

End Property
```

18. Add a code module to the project, and put the following code into the General Declarations section. Save the module as ERROR LOG.BAS.

```
Option Explicit

Public CErrorLog        As clsErrorLog
```

19. Insert a **Main** subroutine into the module. This code creates a project scope instance of the error log class and sets the class properties for the logging operations. Notice that the **ProgramName** property is set so that it includes both the program name and the version. This will help the debugging process if there is any chance that multiple versions of a program can be in simultaneous use. Next, error logging is started, and a program start message is logged. Finally, the main form is loaded and displayed.

```
Sub Main()

Dim sLogFile            As String
Dim sNameVer            As String

' Create an instance of the error log class
Set CErrorLog = New clsErrorLog

' Define the error log filename
sLogFile = App.Path & "\" & _
           Format$(Now, "yyyymmdd") & _
           ".log"

' Define the program name with the version
sNameVer = App.Title & " (" & _
           App.Major & "." & _
           App.Minor

' If revision is not 0, append it to the name
If App.Revision > 0 Then
```

```
        sNameVer = sNameVer & "." & _
                App.Revision
End If

' Add the trailing parenthesis to the name
sNameVer = sNameVer & ")"

' Initialize the class properties
CErrorLog.LogFileName = sLogFile
CErrorLog.ProgramName = sNameVer

' Activate error logging
CErrorLog.StartLogging

' Write the program startup info to the log
CErrorLog.LogMessage "Program started", _
                        vbLogEventTypeInformation

' Load and show the main application form
Load frmMain
frmMain.Show

End Sub
```

20. Whenever the program is stopped, this next subroutine needs to be called. This logic writes a program stop message to the log. Then logging is stopped and the error log class instance is destroyed.

```
Sub ProgramShutdown()

' Perform application shutdown tasks

' Write the program stop info to the log
CErrorLog.LogMessage "Program stopped", _
                        vbLogEventTypeInformation

' Deactivate error logging
CErrorLog.StopLogging

' Destroy the error log class instance
Set CErrorLog = Nothing

End Sub
```

21. Add a form to the project and set the objects and properties as listed in Table 4.8. Save the form as ERROR LOG.FRM.

Table 4.8 The Project Form's Objects and Properties

OBJECT/CONTROL	PROPERTY	VALUE
Form	Name	frmMain
	Caption	Error Log
	Icon	W95MBX01.ICO
CommandButton	Name	cmdAction
	Caption	Make Calls and Generate the Error
TextBox	Name	txtErrNum
	Text	62
CheckBox	Name	chkStackDump
	Caption	Dump Call Stack with Errors
CheckBox	Name	chkTrace
	Caption	Trace Calls in Log File
TextBox	Name	txtNameVer
	BackColor	&H00E0E0E0&
	Locked	True
TextBox	Name	txtLogFile
	BackColor	&H00E0E0E0&
	Locked	True
Label	Name	lblCaption
	Caption	Log File and Path:
	Index	0
Label	Name	lblCaption
	Caption	Program Name and Version:
	Index	1
Label	Name	lblCaption
	Caption	Error Number to Raise:
	Index	2

22. The following code is placed in the General Declarations section of the form. It defines a form scope variable used to determine whether the call stack should be dumped to the error log when a runtime error occurs.

```
Option Explicit

Public mbStackDump     As Boolean
```

23. When the form is loaded, the log file and program names are fetched from the error log class and displayed in locked text boxes.

```
Private Sub Form_Load()

' Get the error log class properties and
' display them on the form
txtLogFile.Text = CErrorLog.LogFileName
txtNameVer.Text = CErrorLog.ProgramName

End Sub
```

24. When the form is unloaded, a call is made to the program shutdown subroutine that was written in step 20.

```
Private Sub Form_Unload(Cancel As Integer)

Call ProgramShutdown

End Sub
```

25. These next two subroutines are added to the **Click** events of the two check boxes. The first one controls the local stack dump action by setting the form scope variable appropriately. The second routine sets the error log class property based on the state of the check box.

```
Private Sub chkStackDump_Click()

' Enable or disable stack dump logging
Select Case chkStackDump.Value
    Case vbChecked
        mbStackDump = True
    Case vbUnchecked
        mbStackDump = False
End Select

End Sub


Private Sub chkTrace_Click()

' Enable or disable log file tracing
Select Case chkTrace.Value
    Case vbChecked
        CErrorLog.Trace = True
    Case vbUnchecked
        CErrorLog.Trace = False
End Select

End Sub
```

26. Put the following code into the **Click** event of the **cmdAction** command button. The first subroutine in the test sequence is called. When the calls are completed, a message box is displayed to let the user know the series is finished.

```
Private Sub cmdAction_Click()

' Call the first subroutine in the tree
Call TestLevel1

' Pop up a message box indicating completion
MsgBox "Testing calls completed.", _
       vbOKOnly, "Finished"

End Sub
```

27. These next three subroutines are virtually identical. Each one invokes the **RoutineEnter** method of the error log class, calls the next subroutine in the test chain, and finishes by calling the **RoutineExit** method. Note the use of a local subroutine scope constant to store the routine names. This facilitates using cut-and-paste to replicate the logic that interacts with the error log class. Now the code itself does not have to be modified; only the contents of the local constant are edited.

```
Sub TestLevel1()

' Establish a constant for the routine name
Const ROUTINE_NAME = "TestLevel1"

' Log the routine entry
CErrorLog.RoutineEnter ROUTINE_NAME

Call TestLevel2

' Log the routine exit
CErrorLog.RoutineExit ROUTINE_NAME

End Sub


Sub TestLevel2()

' Establish a constant for the routine name
Const ROUTINE_NAME = "TestLevel2"

' Log the routine entry
CErrorLog.RoutineEnter ROUTINE_NAME

Call TestLevel3

' Log the routine exit
CErrorLog.RoutineExit ROUTINE_NAME

End Sub


Sub TestLevel3()
```

```
' Establish a constant for the routine name
Const ROUTINE_NAME = "TestLevel3"

' Log the routine entry
CErrorLog.RoutineEnter ROUTINE_NAME

Call TestLevel4

' Log the routine exit
CErrorLog.RoutineExit ROUTINE_NAME

End Sub
```

28. Add the last test subroutine. This code is the same as the previous three routines, except that it includes generating and trapping a user-specified testing error. After the routine entry method is called, local error trapping is enabled, and then an error is raised, using the value entered on the form. In the error-handling logic, the error is written to the log; if it is enabled, the error log class method is called to dump the call stack. After returning from the error-processing code, the **RoutineExit** method is invoked. This returns execution control back up the call chain to the **cmdAction Click** event, where the completion message box is displayed.

```
Sub TestLevel4()

' Establish a constant for the routine name
Const ROUTINE_NAME = "TestLevel4"

' Log the routine entry
CErrorLog.RoutineEnter ROUTINE_NAME

' Enable error trapping
On Error GoTo LocalErrorHandler

' Generate an error
Err.Raise Val(txtErrNum.Text)

' Turn off error trapping
On Error GoTo 0

' Log the routine exit
CErrorLog.RoutineExit ROUTINE_NAME

Exit Sub

LocalErrorHandler:

    ' Write the error info to the log
    CErrorLog.LogMessage "(" & Err.Number & _
                        ") " & Err.Description, _
                        vbLogEventTypeError
```

continued on next page

continued from previous page

```
If mbStackDump = True Then
    ' Tell the log class to dump the stack
    CErrorLog.LogStack
End If

Resume Next

End Sub
```

How It Works

The error log class is self-contained and encapsulated and can be customized by the developer. The class module is used to track all entries to and exits from routines in a program. It handles all the call stack management and interaction with the error log file. This is accomplished by adding the name of each entered routine to the stack array, and removing it when the **RoutineExit** method is called.

The class operates in two basic modes: active with logging enabled and passive with logging disabled. When class methods are called and logging is enabled, all messages are written to the log. If logging is inactive or disabled, no messages are written to the log files, but all call stack monitoring is performed. This allows an application developer to track the call stack history and write to the log file only when unplanned errors occur.

Comments

There are a few enhancements that can be added to the error log class. It can be integrated with the built-in error-logging features for use in an NT environment. This would allow debug and error messages to be written to the log file in the class, and system problems and code failures could be directed to the system event log. Because the system event log is often monitored in a production environment, these events could trigger action by support personnel to investigate the failures or outages.

Currently the class module does not contain any internal error checking. In a true production environment, this would be essential. Areas to cover would include monitoring available disk space on the drive that contains the log file, and error trapping for the log file open, write, and close statements.

Another enhancement would be adding generic error-handling logic to the class so the class itself could determine how to respond to the error and what to log.

CHAPTER 5
ACTIVEX CONTROLS

5

ACTIVEX CONTROLS

How do I...

Every time you take a button from Visual Basic's toolbox and place it on a form, you are using an ActiveX control. ActiveX controls are just that—controls residing on the toolbar that can be placed on a form and have properties, methods, and events you can use.

This chapter shows you how you can make your own ActiveX controls. You can define how they look, how they interact with the user, and what properties, methods, and events they will have.

Although this chapter focuses on the specifics of building the controls, you must not forget that ActiveX controls are not limited to the little gadgets you use to get a user's input. Some ActiveX controls are simple, such as the edit control, and others are very complex, such as a control for calculating the space shuttle trajectory by using data gathered from the NASA Web site. Even Microsoft's flagship Internet application, Internet Explorer, is nothing more than an ActiveX control with some menus and toolbars placed around it.

5.1 Create a Basic Control Project

Creating anything with Visual Basic starts with creating a new project. This How-To shows you how to create and set up a new ActiveX control project. Although creating it comes down to just a few clicks of the mouse, actually setting it up can sometimes be tricky.

5.2 Run the Control in Design Time Mode

After you create the control project, the control-to-be appears as an empty form. You can then either create some code that draws the control's contents on the form or place other controls on it so that the control you are building acts as a container for other controls.

5.3 Create the Properties of the Control

Each ActiveX control can have a set of properties, methods, and events that can be harnessed by the application using it. This How-To shows you how to add various properties to your control.

5.4 Define the Events for the Control

After users put your control on their form, they can catch the control's events as a kind of feedback from the control. This How-To teaches you to add the standard and custom events to the control you are building.

5.5 Add a Property Page to the Control with the Wizard

A properties toolbar that Visual Basic offers for tweaking any control's properties is fine if a control is a simple one, but for controls that require complex adjustments, nothing beats a custom, well-designed Properties dialog box. This How-To shows you how you can include those dialog boxes in your control.

5.6 Compile and Distribute the Control

After the control is finished, you will probably want to pack it up into an installation program or a .CAB file for Internet distribution. This How-To leads you through the process.

5.7 Convert a Simple Container Class to a Control

One of the advantages Visual Basic offers is portability between the desktop and the Internet. You can create a normal desktop application, and then seamlessly convert it into an ActiveX control to be used in Web pages.

5.1 How do I...
Create a basic control project?

COMPATIBILITY: VISUAL BASIC 5 AND 6

Problem

I want to create an ActiveX control that serves as a little calendar for use in my applications. The control should support three basic operations: programmatically setting the initial date, letting the user select another date, and reading the set date from my program.

Technique

Creating a new ActiveX control project is as easy as creating any other project—simply select the appropriate options from the menu and the new project is created. After a new control project is open, you need to set the name of the ActiveX control you are building and give it a brief description. When you are done, you should end up with a new control that appears as a simple, blank form.

Steps

1. Start Visual Basic 6, and if it doesn't immediately prompt you to create a new project, choose File, New Project from the menu; the New Project dialog appears, as shown in Figure 5.1.

2. Choose ActiveX Control from the list of project types offered, and then click Open. Visual Basic creates a new ActiveX control, as shown in Figure 5.2.

As you can see, the project consists of only one form, named **UserControl1**. That form represents your ActiveX control from now on. Every control you place on it appears on your ActiveX control. For all intents and purposes, that form—the **UserControl1**—is your ActiveX control.

3. Save the whole project. To save the project, you have to save both the actual project file and the **UserControl1** form. Choose File, Save Project from the menu, and two consecutive Save dialog boxes pop up, giving you a chance to save both these files. Because a proper naming convention is essential in programming, name the control CALENDAR.CTL and the project file CALENDAR.VBP.

Figure 5.1 Choose ActiveX Control
from a list of offered project types
in the New Project dialog box.

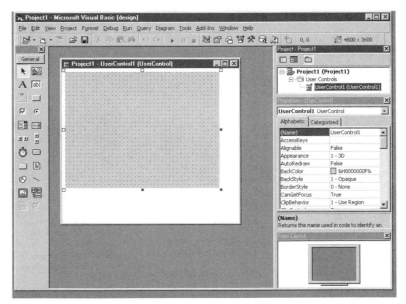

Figure 5.2 A new project is created, with an empty form on
which you can place controls.

By creating and saving the project, you have not defined any of the
fundamental control properties, such as description and other elements by
which the control is referenced from other programs. This is done in the
following steps.

4. Select the `UserControl1` user control in the Project Explorer toolbar, and then set its name to CalendarControl. From now on, this is the name by which your control is referenced. It's just like renaming a new form that Visual Basic has added to your project from `Form1` to `FindDialog`. It doesn't make any difference to Visual Basic, but it makes it easier for users of your control to know something about it when they add it to their projects.

5. Set the project's properties to uniquely identify the project. You saved it in a file that is uniquely named, but each control is also registered in the system Registry, along with a description of the control. To do this, choose Project, Project1 Properties from the menu. A dialog box, like the one shown in Figure 5.3, appears.

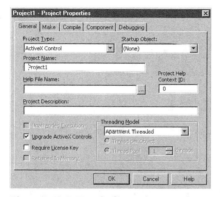

Figure 5.3 To define the project completely, you must also specify the name under which it is referenced in the Registry.

6. Click in the edit field labeled Project Name and type `CalendarProject` as a unique name that represents your project. Next, click in the Project Description edit box and type a description of the project that you are building, such as `Calendar control used to enter the dates`.

7. To see your control in action, you must first compile it to make the CALENDAR.OCX. Choose File, Make Calendar.ocx from the menu and select the destination directory when Visual Basic prompts you. The resulting OCX appears on your hard disk when Visual Basic is done compiling.

8. To test your control, choose File, Add Project from the menu. When the Add Project dialog box appears, select Standard EXE and then click the Open button. This adds a new Standard EXE project to your control project group and enables you to test and debug your control in the Visual Basic development environment.

9. After the new project is added, the standard empty form is topmost on the screen. Now try placing the Calendar control on this form. The tool palette contains an icon for the Calendar control, as shown in Figure 5.4; it has the generic Visual Basic 6 UserControl icon. Add it to the form.

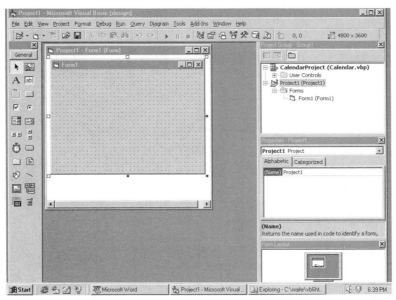

Figure 5.4 The Calendar control appears in the tool palette window, sporting the generic Visual Basic 6 UserControl icon.

After you add the control to the form, it's a bit of a disappointment because the control looks like a big empty rectangle that just sits there and does nothing. Don't worry—changing that is the next step.

TIP

To place the control as discussed in step 9 you must dismiss the controls menu. If the menu is still in designer mode, the control's representation on the toolbar will be grayed out and you will receive a warning when you try to select it.

How It Works

Each ActiveX control that is created actually exists in three different places. One is the Visual Basic project where the control is built. The other place is the resulting .OCX file the control is compiled into, just like a regular project is compiled into an .EXE file. And the third place is the system Registry, where a reference to the control is placed so that other programs on the computer know the control exists.

When reviewing the steps you've taken in this How-To, it is important to clearly separate each of these different aspects of your control, so that you know why you are doing what you're doing. In step 3, for example, when you saved the control project to CALENDAR.VBP, you were only giving a name to one of the source files, not setting the name under which the control appears to users.

Steps 1 and 2 covered the basic control creation. Simply choosing File, New Project from the menu is all it takes to create a new project and get an empty control. Step 3 was saving your project. Again, any names specified for the project files here have nothing to do with the actual control name that users see. Steps 4 and 5 covered setting the actual name by which users reference the control. This is done first in the project window by renaming the control from UserControl1 to a more identifiable name, and then in the Project Properties dialog box, where the actual project name to be written in the Registry is specified.

Comments

This How-To is only the tip of the iceberg. Yes, you have created your first control, but it is a control that does nothing—it simply appears to the users as a big gray rectangle that does nothing. To have your control start looking like a functional one, you have to place something on it, which is the topic of the next How-To.

COMPLEXITY
BEGINNING

5.2 How do I...
Run the control in design time mode?

COMPATIBILITY: VISUAL BASIC 5 AND 6

Problem

I've created a new control project, but it appears as an empty form. How do I add functionality?

Technique

To animate your ActiveX control, you can do one of two things. You can add code to its **Paint** event and draw some kind of custom figure right on the form, or you can place other controls on your form and have them do the work for you.

Drawing the control yourself is what you might do if you want to create a totally new control, such as a new button or a control that shows some graphics or animation. Or if, like me, you have no artistic talent and don't want to spend a lot of time fine-tuning the drawing algorithms, simply adding other controls to the form is much easier.

Steps

1. Start Visual Basic 6 and load the Calendar control project. Then draw a calendar, using other controls. The calendar should let you pick a month and a year and then show all the dates in that month. There are many ways to do that, but this How-To uses the standard paper calendar look. See Figure 5.5 for an example.

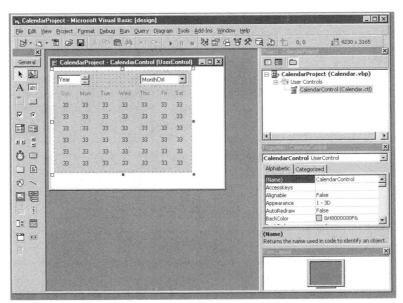

Figure 5.5 The Calendar control must contain the fields for setting the year, month, and day.

To create the form like the one shown in Figure 5.5, first add a text box control to the control and place it in the top-left corner. Set its **Name** property to **YearCtrl** because it is going to show the chosen year.

Next, choose Project, Components from the menu, and add the Microsoft Windows Common Controls 2 control library, which is the one that contains the Up-Down control. Add the Up-Down control and place it to the right of the text box control.

2. Click the Properties window and select the (Custom) property to display the Up-Down control's property page. On the second tab labeled Buddy, set the YearCtrl control as its buddy. Select Text from the Buddy Property drop-down list to associate the Up-Down control's value with the text box. This results in the property page looking like the one in Figure 5.6.

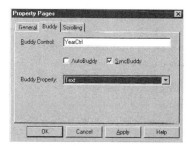

Figure 5.6 By setting the Buddy **property to some control, you ensure that the Up-Down control increases or decreases the value shown in that control.**

After you are done setting the Up-Down control's **Buddy** property, move to the third tab of the properties dialog box, Scrolling, and set the range for the Year control to **1980-2050**, with 1998 being a reasonable default.

3. Close the properties dialog box and add a combo box from the tool palette to the top-right corner of the control. Set its name to **MonthCtrl** because it is going to be used for picking months. Add the names of all 12 months to its **List** property. You can do this by clicking the drop-down next to the **List** property in the Properties window and typing the name of each month, followed by Ctrl+Enter.

4. Now comes the boring part. You have to create seven static text controls that will represent the day headings, and 42 (7 days × 6 rows = 42) static text controls that will represent the actual dates. So, first add seven static text controls to the form, giving them names like Sun, Mon, Tue, and so on. Next, select the static controls from Mon to Sat, and set their ForeColor property to blue. Then select the Sun control and set its ForeColor property to red to differentiate the Sunday column.

Next, add one label control and place it right under the Sun control. Set its name to DayCtrl. Copy and paste it back on the form; Visual Basic then asks if you want to create a control array. Click Yes because it is much easier to manipulate 42 day controls if they are in an array than if you have to reference each of them separately. Next, paste the control five more times until you form a row, and then copy the whole row and paste it back five more times, resulting in a 7×6 control matrix.

Talk about a tedious job! Fortunately, it is finished, and if you did it correctly, the form should resemble the one shown in Figure 5.5.

TIP

If you want to test what your control looks like when used in a project, close the UserControl window. The UserControl on your Standard EXE form is automatically updated with the changes you made to the control.

---

5. What you want to do now is to add some pizzazz to this control. To do that, you need to write the code that tracks the events that both the form and the various controls fire, and update the display. This generally breaks down to two separate jobs: first, tracking the YearCtrl and MonthCtrl controls and then updating the DayCtrl control array to show the appropriate date, and second, tracking clicks on any single DayCtrl and updating the display to reflect the user's selection.

To enter the code, double-click anywhere on the form. When the Code Editor pops up, type in the contents of Listing 5.1. An explanation of the listing follows.

Listing 5.1 This Code Brings Life to the Calendar Control

```
Dim shownDate As Date
Dim dayOfWeek As Integer
Dim monthLength As Integer


Private Sub ArrangeDates()
    Dim firstOfMonth As Date
```

```
    Dim firstOfNext As Date
    Dim i As Integer

    firstOfMonth = DateSerial(Year(shownDate), Month(shownDate), 1)

    If Month(firstOfMonth) = 12 Then
        firstOfNext = DateSerial(Year(firstOfMonth) + 1, 1, 1)
    Else
        firstOfNext = DateSerial(Year(firstOfMonth), _
                    Month(firstOfMonth) + 1, 1)
    End If

    monthLength = DateDiff("d", firstOfMonth, firstOfNext)
    dayOfWeek = WeekDay(firstOfMonth) - 1

    If Day(shownDate) > monthLength Then
        shownDate = DateSerial(Year(shownDate), Month(shownDate), monthLength)
    End If

    'Now lay out the dates
    For i = 0 To 41
        DayCtrl(i).BackColor = &H8000000F
        If i < dayOfWeek Then
            DayCtrl(i).Caption = ""
        ElseIf i < dayOfWeek + monthLength Then
            DayCtrl(i).Caption = Str(i - dayOfWeek + 1)
        Else
            DayCtrl(i).Caption = ""
        End If
    Next

    DayCtrl(Day(shownDate) + dayOfWeek - 1).BackColor = &H80000009
End Sub


Private Sub DayCtrl_Click(Index As Integer)
    If Index >= dayOfWeek And Index < dayOfWeek + monthLength Then
        DayCtrl(Day(shownDate) + dayOfWeek - 1).BackColor = &H8000000F
        shownDate = DateSerial(Year(shownDate), Month(shownDate), _
                Index - dayOfWeek + 1)
        DayCtrl(Index).BackColor = &H80000009
    End If
End Sub


Private Sub MonthCtrl_Click()
    shownDate = DateSerial(Year(shownDate), MonthCtrl.ListIndex + 1, _
            Day(shownDate))
    ArrangeDates
End Sub


Private Sub UpDown1_Change()
```

continued on next page

continued from previous page

```
    YearCtrl_LostFocus
End Sub

Private Sub UpDown1_DownClick()
    YearCtrl = Val(YearCtrl) - 1
End Sub

Private Sub UpDown1_UpClick()
    YearCtrl = Val(YearCtrl) + 1
End Sub

Private Sub UserControl_Initialize()
    shownDate = Now
    YearCtrl = Str(Year(shownDate))
    MonthCtrl.ListIndex = Month(shownDate) - 1
    ArrangeDates
End Sub


Private Sub YearCtrl_LostFocus()
    Dim y As Integer

    y = Val(Trim(YearCtrl.Text))
    If y < 1980 Or y > 2050 Then
        YearCtrl.Text = Trim(Str(Year(shownDate)))
    Else
        shownDate = DateSerial(y, Month(shownDate), Day(shownDate))
        ArrangeDates
    End If
End Sub
```

When analyzing an event-driven program like this, it is probably best to start with the form's initialization code, or, in this case, the `UserControl_Initialize()` subroutine.

This subroutine is called as soon as the control loads. The first thing it does is set the global `shownDate` variable to the current date, and then sets the YearCtrl and MonthCtrl controls to reflect that date. After those three lines of code are done, it calls the `ArrangeDates()` subroutine, which is responsible for the proper layout of the DayCtrl controls.

The `ArrangeDates()` subroutine first calculates the first day of the chosen month, and then the first day of the following month. The difference between those two dates is the month length. A call to Visual Basic's `WeekDay()` function retrieves the day of the week of the first day of the month, which is used for laying out the calendar.

Next, the `ArrangeDates()` subroutine traverses all 42 DayCtrl controls that represent the actual days, and sets each of their `Caption` properties to an empty string if they are not supposed to show any day, or to the actual number representing the day of the month.

Finally, the current day's control is changed so it has a white background, signaling that it is selected.

After the form is initialized and showing the proper date, the user can change it by typing in a new year, choosing a different month, or clicking any of the valid DayCtrl controls.

When the user changes the current year, all the code does in the `YearCtrl_LostFocus()` subroutine is change the year stored in the `shownDate` variable and call `ArrangeDates()` again. It's the same story for the MonthCtrl control; as soon as the user sets a new month, the `shownDate` global variable gets updated and the `ArrangeDates()` subroutine takes care of showing the new layout.

Clicking a new day of the month is even simpler. The `DayCtrl_Click()` subroutine simply makes the background of the previously selected control gray, and then sets the background of the new control to white to show the selection. In the process, it updates the `shownDate` global variable.

6. Save the project and then compile it. If there aren't any errors during the compile, your new control is ready to use. Close the UserControl window and run the standard EXE project; it should look similar to Figure 5.7. Click any day and see the display get updated.

Figure 5.7 The Calendar control at work.

How It Works

After you place the controls on a UserControl, they become an integrated part of your control. From that point on, your job is exactly the same as if you were dealing with a normal Visual Basic form with some controls on it.

The code in this How-To manipulates the controls on the form by making sure every change in the selected year or month is reflected on the day controls on the UserControl. It also tracks the user's selection and updates the global `shownDate` variable, which remembers the last date chosen.

The code in Listing 5.1, which is responsible for making all this happen, is best understood if you read it through in scenarios. The first code that is executed is when the UserControl is created, and the code that gets executed first is in the `UserControl_Initialize` subroutine. Then, assuming the initialization code has executed without any errors, you can see the events that get fired when the user changes the contents of any control on the form.

Comments

The control you are building is finally starting to look like a real control. It shows something, and it responds to the user's input. Unfortunately, you still can't read the date that the user has chosen, and you can't set the date, but that's coming in the next How-To, when you learn how to add properties to your control.

COMPLEXITY
BEGINNING

5.3 How do I...
Create the properties of the control?

COMPATIBILITY: VISUAL BASIC 5 AND 6

Problem

Okay, the control I've created works just fine, but the user choosing some date doesn't mean much to me if I can't read that date. What I need is a `SelectedDate` property that always returns the date that the calendar is showing. How do I implement that property?

Technique

Implementing properties in a control is a refreshing break from the usual Visual Basic routine. Instead of laying out the controls and writing code that coordinates the actions of those controls, there is a wizard that seamlessly adds any properties you need to your control. It's called the ActiveX Control Interface Wizard.

Steps

Before you begin working with the wizard, you must first make sure it is available from the Visual Basic environment. Run your copy of Visual Basic, if it is not already running, and open the Add-Ins menu. If you see an option saying ActiveX Control Interface Wizard there, then all is well and the wizard is available. If it is not there, select the Add-In Manager option from the same menu. When the dialog box appears, like the one shown in Figure 5.8, select VB 6 ActiveX Ctrl Interface Wizard from the Available Add-Ins list and put a check mark to the left of the Loaded/Unloaded and Load on Startup options. Click OK to close the dialog box. The wizard's option should appear on the Add-In menu.

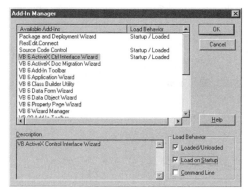

Figure 5.8 Make sure the Loaded/Unloaded and Load on Startup options are checked for the VB 6 ActiveX Ctrl Interface Wizard.

To add the properties, complete the following steps:

1. Run the wizard by choosing Add-Ins, ActiveX Control Interface Wizard from the menu. The Wizard pops up and displays a greeting page, as shown in Figure 5.9.

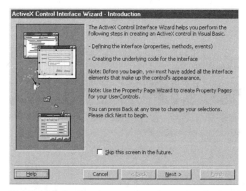

Figure 5.9 The greeting page of the Interface Wizard.

2. Click Next and the second page of the wizard, shown in Figure 5.10, appears. As you can see, the wizard is showing two list boxes, each sporting many properties, methods, and events, which is probably confusing the life out of you. Don't worry; it's not complicated. The lists are the properties, methods, and events that are fairly standard in most controls, and the wizard is simply offering to include them for your control. The list box on the left is showing the available names you can use and the one on the right is showing the list of the names the wizard thought you might want to use.

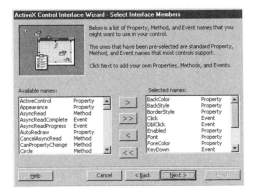

Figure 5.10 The wizard's second page offers a list of often used properties, methods, and events.

Because this is your first time using the wizard, you might want to go slowly and use the minimal number of interface elements necessary. Click the << button to clear the list of selected names, and then slowly go through the list of the names in the Available Names list box, and decide which ones you want to include for your control. In this case, I would suggest you include only the `BackColor` and `BorderStyle` properties to keep the clutter to a minimum.

YOU CAN ALWAYS CHANGE IT LATER...

Don't panic when the wizard offers you a multitude of choices. You can always run it later and change anything you don't like.

3. Click Next and you should be transferred to the third page of the wizard, shown in Figure 5.11. Here you can add any custom properties, methods, or events that you want. In the case of the Calendar control, the `SelectedDate` property you want to add is a good candidate.

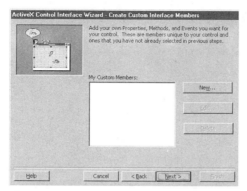

Figure 5.11 You can add any custom property you want to your control on the wizard's third page.

To add it, click the New button and a dialog box asking you for the interface element name and type should appear, as shown in Figure 5.12. Type `SelectedDate` for the name and select the Property radio button to tell it that you are adding a property. Then click OK, and the `SelectedDate` property is added to the list in the wizard.

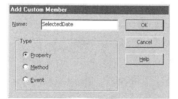

Figure 5.12 Type in any custom interface name and then set its type for it to be added to the control.

4. Click Next to move to page four of the wizard, shown in Figure 5.13. This page lets you delegate any properties of your control to the controls you have used in your project. For example, you have added the `BackColor` property to your control. If you want the `BackColor` property to be automatically synchronized with the `BackColor` property of your UserControl or one of its constituent controls, the wizard sets that relationship up for you here.

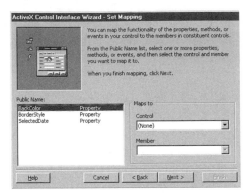

Figure 5.13 You can delegate your control's properties to the other controls you have used on your UserControl on page four of the wizard.

In the case of the Calendar control, it makes sense to delegate two out of three properties. The **BackColor** and the **BorderStyle** properties should probably be delegated to the UserControl that acts as a form because, in a sense, the UserControl is the actual control, and all the other controls are piggybacking on it.

So, select the **BackColor** property first, and then from the Control combo box, select the UserControl. Repeat the process for the **BorderStyle** property, and your job is finished.

5. Click Next and page five of the wizard pops up, as shown in Figure 5.14. This page asks you about any properties of your control that you didn't delegate to other controls, such as the **SelectedDate** property. You are supposed to declare its type and default value, as well as define how it behaves at both design time and runtime.

Because the **SelectedDate** property is a date, pick the type Date from the Data Type combo box and leave both the Design Time and Run Time combo boxes as Read/Write. There is nothing to be gained from restricting access to this particular property.

6. Click Next and the sixth page of the wizard, shown in Figure 5.15, appears; it's the last page of the wizard. Click Finish and the wizard does its magic, adding the properties **BackColor**, **BorderStyle**, and **SelectedDate** to your control.

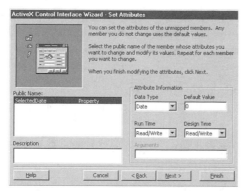

Figure 5.14 Specify the data types for any undefined properties on the fifth page of the wizard.

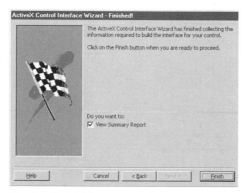

Figure 5.15 The wizard's last page informs you that you are done.

7. When the ActiveX Control Interface Wizard is finished, double-click the UserControl to open the code editor. If you examine the code, you can see that the wizard has made several additions to the code you have written.

First, at the top, there are two new declarations:

```
Const m_def_SelectedDate = 0
Dim m_SelectedDate As Date
```

These two lines of code represent the values used to store the `SelectedDate` property. The `m_SelectedDate` variable is used to hold the actual property value, and the `m_def_SelectedDate` constant defines the default value loaded into this variable when the control is created.

Moving down the code, there are also several subroutines added for manipulating these properties. You can see the interesting parts in Listing 5.2.

Listing 5.2 The Interface Wizard Has Added These Routines to Support the Three Added Properties

```
Public Property Get BackColor() As OLE_COLOR
    BackColor = UserControl.BackColor
End Property


Public Property Let BackColor(ByVal New_BackColor As OLE_COLOR)
    UserControl.BackColor() = New_BackColor
    PropertyChanged "BackColor"
End Property


Public Property Get BorderStyle() As Integer
    BorderStyle = UserControl.BorderStyle
End Property


Public Property Let BorderStyle(ByVal New_BorderStyle As Integer)
    UserControl.BorderStyle() = New_BorderStyle
    PropertyChanged "BorderStyle"
End Property


Public Property Get SelectedDate() As Date
    SelectedDate = m_SelectedDate
End Property


Public Property Let SelectedDate(ByVal New_SelectedDate As Date)
    m_SelectedDate = New_SelectedDate
    PropertyChanged "SelectedDate"
End Property

'Initialize Properties for User Control
Private Sub UserControl_InitProperties()
    m_SelectedDate = m_def_SelectedDate
End Sub


'Load property values from storage
Private Sub UserControl_ReadProperties(PropBag As PropertyBag)
```

```
    UserControl.BackColor = PropBag.ReadProperty("BackColor", &H8000000F)
    UserControl.BorderStyle = PropBag.ReadProperty("BorderStyle", 1)
    m_SelectedDate = PropBag.ReadProperty("SelectedDate", m_def_SelectedDate)
End Sub


'Write property values to storage
Private Sub UserControl_WriteProperties(PropBag As PropertyBag)

    Call PropBag.WriteProperty("BackColor", UserControl.BackColor, &H8000000F)
    Call PropBag.WriteProperty("BorderStyle", UserControl.BorderStyle, 1)
    Call PropBag.WriteProperty("SelectedDate", m_SelectedDate, _
                m_def_SelectedDate)
End Sub
```

8. The `SelectedDate` property has been added, but it still doesn't correspond to the actual date being shown on the calendar. What you need to do next is tweak the code so that the `SelectedDate` property corresponds to the `shownDate` global variable.

You can accomplish this in a lot of ways, but when your development environment is doing the lion's share of the work, it is often smarter to fit things into the code it writes than to change its code to suit you. So in this particular case, it would probably be wise to change the code you have written so that it uses the `m_SelectedDate` variable instead of the `shownDate` variable you have used until now.

To make this change, simply do a search-and-replace operation on your code, and replace every instance of the string `shownDate` with `m_SelectedDate`. Then, after the search-and-replace is finished, you need to tweak your code in one or two spots to synchronize the `SelectedDate` property with what is being displayed onscreen.

9. Find every place where you changed the `shownDate` variable, and add the following code right after it so your control knows the property has changed:

```
PropertyChanged "SelectedDate"
```

10. Remove the initialization of the `m_SelectedDate` variable in the `UserControl_Initialize()` subroutine because now all initialization is done in the `UserControl_InitProperties()` subroutine, and it would be sloppy to initialize the variables twice.

11. Find all the places in the code where the `SelectedDate` property is loaded or set, and add the code to update the calendar display at each place:

```
RaiseEvent Change(m_SelectedDate)
```

12. Move to the `UserControl_InitProperties()` subroutine, and change all occurrences of the variable `m_def_SelectedDate` to the function `Now()` so that the property is always initialized with the current date. Remove the declaration for the `m_def_SelectedDate` variable.

Listing 5.3 shows how your code should look after all these changes, with the bold type showing the lines that have changed.

Listing 5.3 Calendar Code That Works with the `SelectedDate` Property

```
Dim dayOfWeek As Integer
Dim monthLength As Integer
'Default Property Values:
Const m_def_SelectedDate = 0
'Property Variables:
Dim m_SelectedDate As Date


Private Sub ArrangeDates()
    Dim firstOfMonth As Date
    Dim firstOfNext As Date
    Dim i As Integer

    firstOfMonth = DateSerial(Year(m_SelectedDate), Month(m_SelectedDate), 1)

    If Month(firstOfMonth) = 12 Then
        firstOfNext = DateSerial(Year(firstOfMonth) + 1, 1, 1)
    Else
        firstOfNext = DateSerial(Year(firstOfMonth), _
                Month(firstOfMonth) + 1, 1)
    End If

    monthLength = DateDiff("d", firstOfMonth, firstOfNext)
    dayOfWeek = WeekDay(firstOfMonth) - 1

    If Day(m_SelectedDate) > monthLength Then
        m_SelectedDate = DateSerial(Year(m_SelectedDate), _
                    Month(m_SelectedDate), monthLength)
        PropertyChanged "SelectedDate"
    End If

    'Now lay out the dates
    For i = 0 To 41
        DayCtrl(i).BackColor = UserControl.BackColor
        If i < dayOfWeek Then
            DayCtrl(i).Caption = ""
        ElseIf i < dayOfWeek + monthLength Then
            DayCtrl(i).Caption = Str(i - dayOfWeek + 1)
        Else
            DayCtrl(i).Caption = ""
```

```
            End If
        Next

        DayCtrl(Day(m_SelectedDate) + dayOfWeek - 1).BackColor = &H80000009
    End Sub


    Private Sub DayCtrl_Click(Index As Integer)
        If Index >= dayOfWeek And Index < dayOfWeek + monthLength Then
            DayCtrl(Day(m_SelectedDate) + dayOfWeek - 1).BackColor = _
                    UserControl.BackColor
            m_SelectedDate = DateSerial(Year(m_SelectedDate), Month(m_SelectedDate), _
                    Index - dayOfWeek + 1)
            PropertyChanged "SelectedDate"
            DayCtrl(Index).BackColor = &H80000009
        End If
    End Sub


    Private Sub MonthCtrl_Click()
        m_SelectedDate = DateSerial(Year(m_SelectedDate), _
                    MonthCtrl.ListIndex + 1, Day(m_SelectedDate))
        PropertyChanged "SelectedDate"
        ArrangeDates
    End Sub


    Private Sub UpDown1_Change()
        YearCtrl_LostFocus
    End Sub

    Private Sub UserControl_Initialize()
        YearCtrl = Str(Year(m_SelectedDate))
        MonthCtrl.ListIndex = Month(m_SelectedDate) - 1
        ArrangeDates
    End Sub


    Private Sub YearCtrl_LostFocus()
        Dim y As Integer

        y = Val(Trim(YearCtrl.Text))
        If y < 1980 Or y > 2050 Then
            YearCtrl.Text = Trim(Str(Year(m_SelectedDate)))
        Else
            m_SelectedDate = DateSerial(y, Month(m_SelectedDate), _
                Day(m_SelectedDate))
            PropertyChanged "SelectedDate"
            ArrangeDates
        End If
    End Sub

Public Property Get BackColor() As OLE_COLOR
```

continued on next page

continued from previous page

```
    BackColor = UserControl.BackColor
End Property


Public Property Let BackColor(ByVal New_BackColor As OLE_COLOR)
    UserControl.BackColor() = New_BackColor
    PropertyChanged "BackColor"
End Property


Public Property Get BorderStyle() As Integer
    BorderStyle = UserControl.BorderStyle
End Property


Public Property Let BorderStyle(ByVal New_BorderStyle As Integer)
    UserControl.BorderStyle() = New_BorderStyle
    PropertyChanged "BorderStyle"
End Property


Public Property Get SelectedDate() As Date
    SelectedDate = m_SelectedDate
End Property


Public Property Let SelectedDate(ByVal New_SelectedDate As Date)
    m_SelectedDate = New_SelectedDate
    ArrangeDates
    YearCtrl = Str(Year(m_SelectedDate))
    MonthCtrl.ListIndex = Month(m_SelectedDate) - 1
    PropertyChanged "SelectedDate"
End Property


'Initialize Properties for User Control
Private Sub UserControl_InitProperties()
    m_SelectedDate = Now
    YearCtrl = Str(Year(m_SelectedDate))
    MonthCtrl.ListIndex = Month(m_SelectedDate) - 1
    ArrangeDates
End Sub

'Load property values from storage
Private Sub UserControl_ReadProperties(PropBag As PropertyBag)

    UserControl.BackColor = PropBag.ReadProperty("BackColor", &H8000000F)
    UserControl.BorderStyle = PropBag.ReadProperty("BorderStyle", 1)
    m_SelectedDate = PropBag.ReadProperty("SelectedDate", Now)
    YearCtrl = Str(Year(m_SelectedDate))
```

```
    MonthCtrl.ListIndex = Month(m_SelectedDate) - 1
    ArrangeDates
End Sub


'Write property values to storage
Private Sub UserControl_WriteProperties(PropBag As PropertyBag)

    Call PropBag.WriteProperty("BackColor", UserControl.BackColor, &H8000000F)
    Call PropBag.WriteProperty("BorderStyle", UserControl.BorderStyle, 1)
    Call PropBag.WriteProperty("SelectedDate", m_SelectedDate, Now)
End Sub
```

How It Works

After all these changes, the Calendar control finally looks and feels like a real
ActiveX control. You can place it on a form, set its properties, and then run a
program and have this control do some actual work in it. Adding properties to
the control is no big deal. In this How-To, the ActiveX Control Interface Wizard
was used to add properties. Some properties were mapped to other controls and
some were handled by code that was added to the control.

After the ActiveX Control Interface Wizard is finished, it inserts a variable in
your code for each of the unmapped properties. You can then use those variables
to perform whatever function those properties are supposed to have. Also, two
functions are created per each unmapped property: one for setting and one for
reading each property. Three other events also cover property initialization,
loading, and saving. Each of these functions is at your disposal—you can modify
them to do any job you want to do.

Comments

Adding properties using the ActiveX Control Interface Wizard is easy. As
demonstrated in the following How-To, events are added just as easily, using the
ActiveX Control Interface Wizard.

COMPLEXITY
BEGINNING

5.4 How do I...
Define the events for the control?

COMPATIBILITY: VISUAL BASIC 5 AND 6

Problem

The control works well and can be used in real-life programs, but what I really
need is for it to fire an event every time the date is changed. How do I do this?

Technique

Events are added to a control by using the same ActiveX Control Interface Wizard you have used to add properties. After the events are defined with the wizard, you can fire them any time you like with the `RaiseEvent` statement.

All this talk about events may seem confusing. Weren't events already used to track the user's selection of the year, month, and day? The answer is that those were events for the controls you've placed on your control. Those events are trapped in your control's source code. The topic of this How-To is the events that the UserControl fires and that the user of the control uses after it is compiled into an .OCX file.

Steps

1. Run Visual Basic and open the Calendar project if you haven't already done that.

2. Run the ActiveX Control Interface Wizard by choosing Add-Ins, ActiveX Control Interface Wizard from the menu. The wizard shows you the same greeting screen it did the last time you ran it, only now it remembers your past choices.

3. Click Next to move on to page two of the wizard, shown in Figure 5.16. This page offers you the standard set of properties, methods, and events that you can add or remove from your control. In the left pane is the list of all available interface elements, and the right pane holds a list of selected ones.

Currently the right pane holds only two lines—the `BackColor` property and the `BorderStyle` property. Because you want to fire an event when the contents of the calendar change, it would probably be wise to choose the standard `Change` event for that task, so scroll down in the left-hand list box and find the `Change` event. Double-click it to move it to the list on the right.

4. Click Next to move to the third page of the wizard, shown in Figure 5.17. You can see a list of custom interface elements for the control. Currently, only the `SelectedDate` property is on that list.

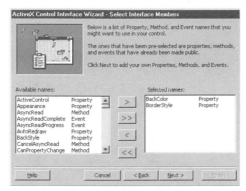

Figure 5.16 The wizard picks up where it left off, offering you only two standard properties that you have previously selected.

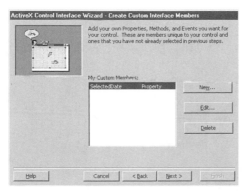

Figure 5.17 The custom interface elements page shows only the `SelectedDate` property.

5. Click Next to move to page four of the wizard, which lets you map any interface elements that you have defined to the controls you have placed on the UserControl and the UserControl itself. It is shown in Figure 5.18. The `BackColor` and the `BorderStyle` properties are mapped to the UserControl, but the `SelectedDate` property is unmapped because it is implemented in the code. You don't want to map the `Change` event to any of the events that the other controls fire.

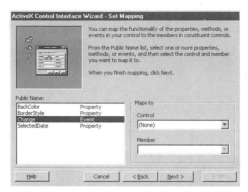

Figure 5.18 The fourth page lets you map the properties, methods, and events of your control to other controls, which are used to implement the `BackColor` and `BorderStyle` properties.

6. Click Next to move to the fifth page of the wizard, shown in Figure 5.19. You can finally define what the `Change` event looks like.

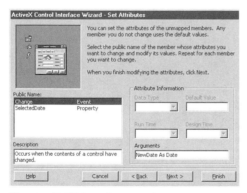

Figure 5.19 Implementing an event is as simple as defining its parameters on the wizard's fifth page.

7. Because events represent a one-way street from the control to the form where the control is placed, they don't return any values. All you have to do on this page is specify the parameters your event passes. If it passes no parameters, you simply leave the Arguments field empty. If you want the event to pass two integers, you write the arguments like this:

```
i1 As Integer, i2 As Integer
```

In the case of the Change event, it would probably be advantageous to pass the new date. So select the Change event, and then type in its argument:

```
NewDate As Date
```

Click Finish to officially define the Change event.

8. The Change event is now at your disposal. You can verify this by looking at your code editor. Near the top of your code, among the declarations, you should see the Change event declared in a line saying something like this:

```
Event Change(NewDate As Date)
```

Now, you can fire the event anytime you like by issuing a RaiseEvent statement, like this:

```
RaiseEvent Change (somedate)
```

In this particular case, you probably want to raise the Change event every time the SelectedDate property changes. The easiest way to do that is to simply go through your code, find every place where the PropertyChanged statement is used, and add the RaiseEvent statement immediately after it. For example, take the MonthCtrl_Click() subroutine. It uses the PropertyChanged statement to notify the container that one of its properties has changed:

```
Private Sub MonthCtrl_Click()
    m_SelectedDate = DateSerial(Year(m_SelectedDate), _
            MonthCtrl.ListIndex + 1, Day(m_SelectedDate))
    PropertyChanged "SelectedDate"
    ArrangeDates
End Sub
```

After the PropertyChanged statement, add a line with a call to RaiseEvent:

```
Private Sub MonthCtrl_Click()
    m_SelectedDate = DateSerial(Year(m_SelectedDate), _
            MonthCtrl.ListIndex + 1, Day(m_SelectedDate))
    PropertyChanged "SelectedDate"
    RaiseEvent Change (m_SelectedDate)
    ArrangeDates
End Sub
```

Repeat that procedure for all places where the PropertyChanged statement is executed, and you are finished with the events in this program.

9. Because the Calendar control is now firing events, you can test how that works. First, save the whole project by choosing File, Save Project from the menu; double-click the Calendar control on the form in your standard EXE project. The code editor pops up and lets you define your actions for the Calendar control's `Change` event, as you can see in Figure 5.20.

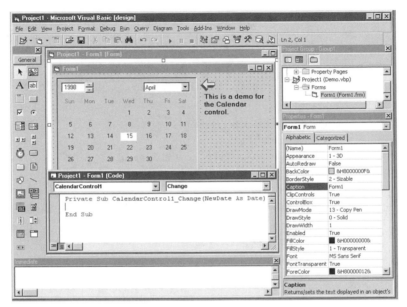

Figure 5.20 The `Change` event allows you to write code to handle that action.

10. To try the feature out, write some code for the event and see what happens. For example, pop up a message box showing the new date by typing in the following code:

```
Private Sub Calendar1_Change(NewDate As Date)
    MsgBox Str(NewDate)
End Sub
```

11. To try it out, simply run the program. If everything is correct, as soon as you change the date on the calendar, a message box pops up and tells you the new date. An example is shown in Figure 5.21.

That's it. The event has been added to the control and it works. If you want to add any more events, simply fire up the ActiveX Control Interface Wizard and then make as many `RaiseEvent` calls as you need.

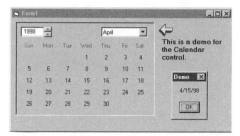

Figure 5.21 As soon as the date is changed, a message box pops up.

How It Works

The ActiveX Control Interface Wizard was used to define a new custom event. It took the event definition and added the appropriate variables and declarations to the UserControl project.

Most of the work that needs to be done comes down to the actual firing of events, something that you must do yourself by writing code. You pick the right spot and insert the `RaiseEvent` statement, and then whoever uses your control gets the events you sent them.

Comments

Never skimp on the events your control fires. The number one reason a control lacks value is limited events. Very often a control looks good, has all the properties you need, has all the methods necessary for it to work, and yet it lacks one or two crucial events necessary to make it truly valuable. Just one missing event is usually enough to make the whole control unusable.

The control you were building in these past four How-Tos is finished. Sure, it could be better, but in its current state, it is functional and can be used in other programs. If you got to this point, you can officially call yourself a control developer.

COMPLEXITY
INTERMEDIATE

5.5 How do I...
Add a property page to the control with the wizard?

COMPATIBILITY: VISUAL BASIC 5 AND 6

Problem

If a control has a lot of properties, it is often confusing to set them by using the Properties window. Is there a better way to set the control properties?

Technique

Each ActiveX control can have one or more property pages. If a control has a lot of properties that are complex to set, it is often better to be able to set these properties from a property page. This How-To leads you through creating a property page for the Calendar control.

Before you begin reading through the actual steps to create a property page, please note that I am talking about the property *pages*, not property *sheets*. A property *sheet* is what you would call a properties dialog box—one that contains several tabs you can click to show individual *pages*. When dealing with ActiveX controls, the control container supplies the actual property sheet—the dialog box—and a control supplies one or more property pages displayed inside that dialog box.

If this all sounds a bit confusing, you just have to remember that ActiveX controls, unlike desktop applications, don't execute on their own, but have to work with the container to give the user the illusion that they are a regular part of the system. So, users select one or more controls, and then choose Properties or some similar option from the menu. The container then pops up a properties dialog box, goes through the list of selected controls, and asks them to supply the property pages to be placed inside the dialog box. There are even some standard property pages that every control can use as its own—the ones for setting the `Font` property, a color selection property page for setting one of the color properties, and so on.

Steps

Just as with creating an interface for your control, there is a wizard that can help you create one or more property pages for your control. Open the Add-Ins menu in the Visual Basic environment. If you don't see an option for Property Page Wizard, choose Add-In Manager and add the VB 6 Property Page Wizard to the list of available add-ins.

Complete the following steps to create a property page:

1. Run Visual Basic and open the Calendar project if you haven't already done that.

2. Choose Add-Ins, Property Page Wizard from the menu. The intro screen of the wizard pops up, as shown in Figure 5.22.

3. Click Next to move to the second page of the wizard, shown in Figure 5.23. This page allows you to choose how many property pages you want your control to have. The wizard has detected that your control has a `BackColor` property, so it has already put the Standard Color dialog box on the list. It also lists all the other property pages in the project, so you can pick and choose which ones you want added to this control.

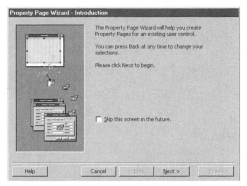

Figure 5.22 The Property Page Wizard lets you add one or more property pages to your control.

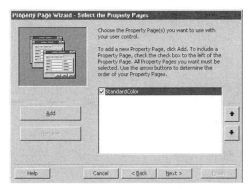

Figure 5.23 Adding a new property page is as easy as clicking Add on the second page of the wizard.

4. Because the purpose of this How-To is to show you how to create custom property pages, add one more page to the list. Click the Add button, and when the dialog box shown in Figure 5.24 pops up, type **SetDate** for the page name and click OK. This adds the SetDate page to the list of property pages your control supports.

5. Click Next to move to the third page of the wizard, shown in Figure 5.25. Using this page, you can decide what properties are manipulated on the Date property page you've just added. As you can see, you have at your disposal two lists—one on the left containing all the available properties, and one on the right listing all the properties that the **SetDate** property page can tweak.

Figure 5.24 Type in a new page name and click OK to add the page to the list of property pages your control supports.

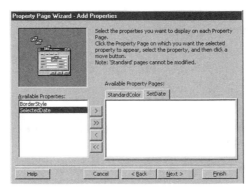

Figure 5.25 The wizard's third page lets you place one or more properties on the newly added property page.

6. Move the `SelectedDate` property from the left list to the right one by selecting it and clicking the > button. As soon as you do that, it disappears from the left list and appears in the right one.

7. Click Next to move to the last page of the wizard, shown in Figure 5.26. It is just a plain summary page.

8. Click Finish to have the wizard create your property page.

9. After the wizard is done, take a look at Project Explorer. As you can see in Figure 5.27, a new module has been added to the project, under the Property Pages folder.

10. What you want to do next is actually define what the Date property page looks like. To do this, double-click it in Project Explorer, and the newly added page pops up onscreen, as shown in Figure 5.28.

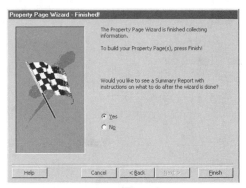

Figure 5.26 The last page of the wizard provides a summary.

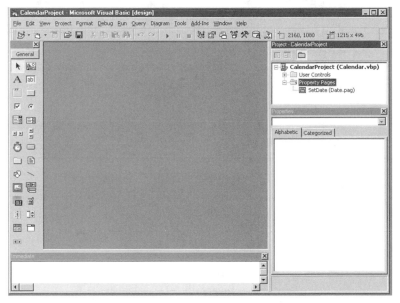

Figure 5.27 Project Explorer shows the newly added property page.

Pay attention, because now comes the more complicated part. The little text edit control that you see on the property page is the one in which the SelectedDate property appears. However, if you examine the control, look at its properties, and turn it up and down, you won't find any mention of the SelectedDate property. Just where does the link between the edit box and the actual ActiveX control property hide?

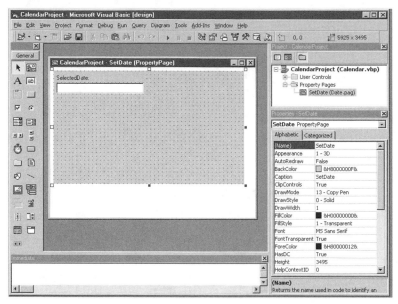

Figure 5.28 The newly added property page as the wizard has defined it.

A double-click on the property page reveals the secret. When the code editor pops up, you can see the following code:

```
Private Sub txtSelectedDate_Change()
    Changed = True
End Sub


Private Sub PropertyPage_ApplyChanges()
    SelectedControls(0).SelectedDate = txtSelectedDate.Text
End Sub


Private Sub PropertyPage_SelectionChanged()
    txtSelectedDate.Text = SelectedControls(0).SelectedDate
End Sub
```

The relationship is intricate. The property page has a property called **SelectedControls**, which is an array containing all the controls that are selected. It also has a **Change** property that it sets to **True** every time the user types something into the edit box.

As the code shows, there are three strategic functions you must examine to understand how the property page works. First, there is the

`PropertyPage_SelectionChanged()` subroutine, which gets called when the property page is loaded. This function is responsible for initializing the contents of the property page. The one line it executes is this:

`txtSelectedDate.Text = SelectedControls(0).SelectedDate`

This code fills the `txtSelectedDate` edit box with the contents of the `SelectedDate` property of the first selected control.

NOTE

Because a single property page can be brought up for multiple selected controls, the proper way to communicate with the controls would be to iterate through the `SelectedControls` array from 0 to `SelectedControls.Count - 1` and either read or write the values, as appropriate. In this How-To, only the first selected control is referenced using the `SelectedControls(0)` syntax to keep things simple.

The next subroutine of interest is the `txtSelectedDate_Change()` subroutine, which gets called every time the contents of the edit control change. It's not property page specific, but what it does is. The code in it changes the `Changed` property of the property page, in effect causing the Apply button on the Properties dialog box to become available, telling users, "Hey, you've made some changes and if you want to commit them, you must click OK or Apply."

Finally, there is the `PropertyPage_ApplyChanges()` subroutine, which takes care of taking the values from the property page and plugging them back into the controls for which the property page has been brought up.

The lesson here is clear. If you want the dates entered in some other way than by using a text edit control, simply remove the `txtSelectedDate` edit box and place the new control on the form. Then change the code so that it uses the new control instead of the old one, and that's all you have to do.

NOTE

When working with a property page, don't change its size. A property page has to fit into the Properties dialog box, and Microsoft has defined a standard size for them that you shouldn't deviate from, or your control's user interface will appear inconsistent.

11. To try out the new property page, simply save the project by choosing File, Save Project from the menu. Switch to the Standard EXE project, and then right-click on the Calendar control on the form in your Standard EXE project and select Properties from the shortcut menu. This brings up the new property page, as shown in Figure 5.29.

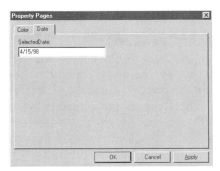

Figure 5.29 The property page is shown for the Calendar control.

You can now play with the property page. Use it to change the `BackColor` property or move to the Date tab and set the new date, and observe your selection being mirrored on the Calendar control.

> **NOTE**
>
> The technique for popping up the property page differs among the different environments. In Visual Basic, you do it from the (Custom) property in the Properties window or from the Properties shortcut menu. In Visual C++, you select it from a right-click context menu. In Microsoft's official ActiveX Control Test Container, you do it either from the context menu or from the regular menus. Consult your compiler's documentation for details.

How It Works

If your control needs a custom Properties dialog box, you don't need to create the whole dialog box. You create only the individual property pages, and the container takes care of creating the dialog box and inserting the pages into it.

You can create property pages by running the Property Page Wizard. It creates a new property page form and includes a number of subroutines in that form's code to support the property page's operations. The form's `SelectedControls` property is an array containing a list of controls that are selected while the property page is open.

> **WARNING**
>
> Property pages are non-modal, which means that the `SelectedControls` array can change while the dialog is open.

First of all, it includes a `Change` event handler for every element on the page and makes them all set the property page's `Changed` property to `True` when information changes. This is used to enable the Apply button on the Properties dialog box.

Second, it includes one routine called `PropertyPage_SelectionChanged()` that is responsible for form initialization. In it, the wizard includes some sample code that takes the values from the selected controls and plugs them into the controls on the form.

Third, it generates a routine called `PropertyPage_ApplyChanges()`, which does the reverse of initialization—it takes the values from the controls on the form and plugs them back into the selected controls. This subroutine is called when the user clicks the OK or Apply buttons.

Comments

You don't have to include a property page for every control you create just to enlarge its feature set. An unnecessary property page is is a burden—it complicates the code, makes the changes harder to make, and clutters the user's Properties window.

The rule of thumb when deciding whether to include a property page with your control is to see how complicated setting the control from a normal Properties window is. If it is easy and natural, then you probably don't need a property page. If, on the other hand, it requires setting some complex values that would be easier to set from a specially designed dialog box, then by all means include a property page.

For example, a simple text box doesn't need a property page. Its most essential property, `Text`, is readily accessible from the Properties window, and a property page only complicates things.

However, say you have designed an ActiveX control that works as a small photo editor. For such a control, a property page can greatly simplify the control's use. Just think about it—which is easier: selecting some special effect from the Visual Basic Properties window, or selecting it from a well-designed dialog box with a preview, bells, whistles, and all?

5.6 How do I...
Compile and distribute the control?

COMPATIBILITY: VISUAL BASIC 5 AND 6

Problem

Okay, the control is finished. Now I want to sell it to my clients so that they can use it in their programs. How do I move a control to another machine?

Technique

When a control is finished and compiled, you can't just take the control's .OCX file and place it on another machine. There are two reasons for this:

✔ Each control must be registered in the Registry

✔ Each control you build with Visual Basic requires a number of DLLs to work

Although you could copy the DLLs and make the Registry entries yourself, why not let Visual Basic do the job for you?

Steps

1. Run the Package and Deployment Wizard by choosing it from the Add-Ins menu. It appears on the screen looking just like a regular wizard, as shown in Figure 5.30.

2. Click the button labeled Package. This places you at the first information-gathering menu for this wizard, as shown in Figure 5.31.

3. First, there is Standard Setup Package option, which creates a normal, SETUP.EXE installation. Then there is the Internet Package option, which creates a .CAB file and a sample Web page that automatically downloads that .CAB file and installs it. And finally, there is a Dependency File function, which makes a file telling you what DLLs are needed for your control to work. For this How-To, select Standard Setup Package from the list because you want to make a standard desktop installation. Then click Next to move on to the next page.

4. Click Next to move to the third page of the wizard, which lets you pick a destination directory where the Setup files are placed. It's shown in Figure 5.32.

Figure 5.30 The Package and Deployment Wizard.

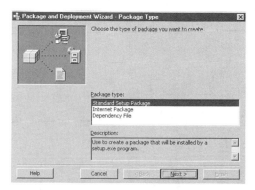

Figure 5.31 The Package Type page of the wizard.

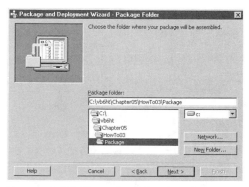

Figure 5.32 Choose a destination directory for the Setup files on this page.

5. The default is to create a package directory under your project. Accept the default location by clicking the Next button. The fourth page asks some seemingly complicated questions, so I'll spend some time explaining how it works. The page, shown in Figure 5.33, asks for any external files your control uses that are not a regular part of the Visual Basic environment. If your application uses an external program to process some information, or maybe a DLL's functions through `Declare` statements, you should list those files here.

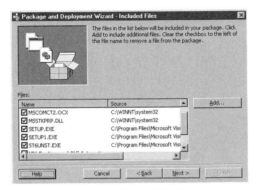

Figure 5.33 If your application uses some external files that the Setup couldn't detect, you should list them here.

For the Calendar control, no external files are needed. It runs no programs through the shell statement and it uses no DLLs through `Declare` statements.

6. Click Next to move to the fifth page of the wizard, shown in Figure 5.34. This page lets you decide which medium the Setup program should be partitioned for. You can choose to place the setup files in one CAB file or in multiple files for delivery by floppy disk.

Select the Single File option if you want to make a CD-ROM installation program, or maybe use the ZIP drive for carrying the files to another machine. Select the Multiple Files option if you want the setup to place files on your hard disk but plan to copy them to floppy disks later. When selecting this option, you can specify the size of the files so they fit your floppy disks. For this How-To, select Single File, as this is only an example, and the Setup program you are building will not be carried anywhere.

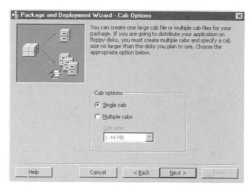

Figure 5.34 The Cab Options page of the wizard.

7. Click Next to move to page six of the wizard, which asks you to supply a name for the installation. This page is shown in Figure 5.35. The name provided will be used on the install wash screen.

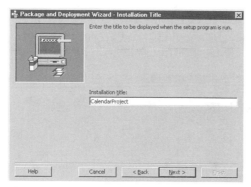

Figure 5.35 The Installation Title page of the wizard.

8. Click Next to move to the next page. The Start Menu Items page, shown in Figure 5.36, allows you to assign your deliverables to a program group. You can even split your items between program groups.

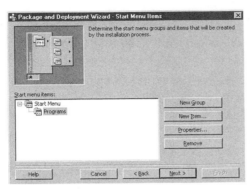

Figure 5.36 The Start Menu Items
page of the wizard.

9. Click Next to accept the defaults for Start menu groups and move to the next page. On the Install Locations menu shown in Figure 5.37, you can change where the files of the bundle will be delivered. You can change a location by selecting a file from the Files list and then selecting a new value from the Install Location pull-down list. For some of the predefined options, you can add your own paths. For instance, you might want to deliver a Help file that you would place at $(AppPath)\help.

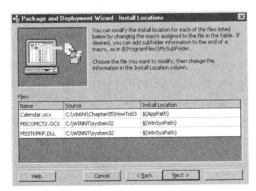

Figure 5.37 The Install Locations
page of the wizard.

10. Click Next to move on to the following page. If a file is expected to be used by more than one program, the file can be marked as shared. The file will not be removed by an Uninstall program until all the files that have registered its use are uninstalled. The Shared Files menu, shown in Figure 5.38, allows you to make flag files to be shared.

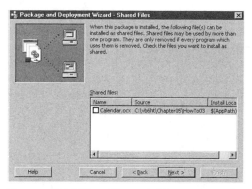

Figure 5.38 The Shared Files page of the wizard.

11. Click Next to accept the defaults for shared files and move to the last page of the wizard (see Figure 5.39), which allows you to save the information you have entered in the previous menus. This is especially useful if you added extra files to the bundle or changed default information.

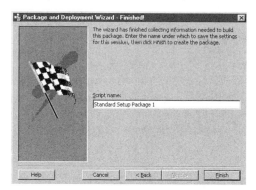

Figure 5.39 The wizard creates the files when you click the Finish button.

12. Click the Finish button to have the wizard gather the necessary files and create the Setup program. When the wizard is finished, a report menu is presented with information about the work just completed.

13. If you explore the directory where the wizard has stored the files, you find a program named SETUP.EXE there, as well as a file named CALENDAR.CAB. If you want to move the Calendar control to another computer, simply copy all these files, and then run SETUP.EXE.

14. To test your installation, run the setup you have created. The usual Setup screen, like the one shown in Figure 5.40, appears. Go through it to verify that everything is working.

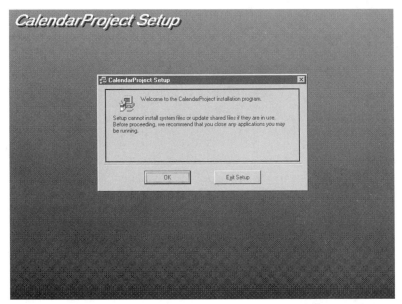

Figure 5.40 The Setup Wizard creates robust, professional-looking setups.

How It Works

Almost all the work you have to do when building a Setup program with the Application Setup Wizard comes down to deciding which files you need to include in your setup. As a general rule, you should explicitly add any files that you use in your code, but that you didn't add by using any of the Visual Basic wizards or dialog boxes.

As for removing files, most of the time you don't want to do that, unless you are absolutely sure that the destination computer has the same files as yours. And "same" means same—not only should the files have the same name, but they should also be the same version. Otherwise, you risk having your control not work because it uses some of the features found only in the latest version of some file.

Comments

Although the end of this How-To is not as dramatic as some, you have learned a lot about creating ActiveX controls. You know how to create them; how to add properties, methods, and events; how to create property changes; and how to create setups for installing the controls you create.

Now the best thing you can do to improve your knowledge of creating ActiveX controls is to actually create them.

COMPLEXITY
BEGINNING

5.7 How do I...
Convert a simple container class to a control?

COMPATIBILITY: VISUAL BASIC 5 AND 6

Problem

My boss is into this whole Internet craze, and he wants me to convert our applications so that they work on the Web. Can it be done?

Technique

Did you know that Internet Explorer, Microsoft's flagship application in Internet development, is only an ActiveX control, with a few kilobytes of menu and toolbar code around it?

Most of us think of controls as just little gadgets you put on a Visual Basic form, but ActiveX controls don't have to be small. In fact, they can contain a whole application, stored inside an .OCX file instead of an .EXE. To demonstrate this, this How-To leads you through taking a regular desktop application and converting it into an ActiveX control.

Steps

1. Create a new Standard EXE project, as shown in Figure 5.41. In this How-To, this project is converted into an ActiveX control.

2. Take a text box from the tool palette and place it on the form. Then take a button and place it to the right of the text box. When you are done, you should be looking at something similar to the form shown in Figure 5.42.

3. Now you want to animate the application you've just created. Double-click the button you've placed on the form, and when the code editor pops up, type in the following code:

```
Private Sub Command1_Click()
    MsgBox Text1.Text
End Sub
```

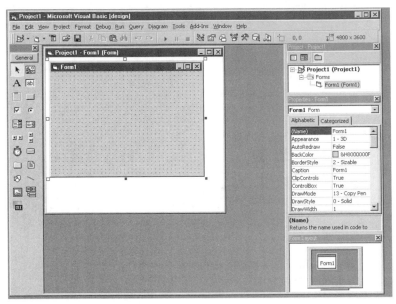

Figure 5.41 A new application that is used as an example.

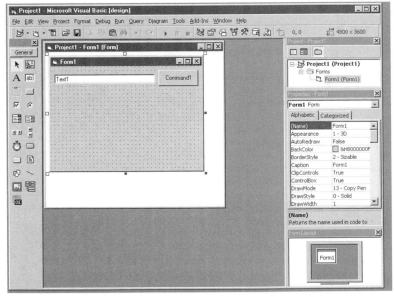

Figure 5.42 A text box and a button placed on the form.

Obviously, this code is supposed to pop up a message box with the contents of the text control when the user clicks the button.

4. Run the application to see if everything works correctly. You can see an example in Figure 5.43.

Figure 5.43 The desktop application at work.

The desktop application is finished. Now it's time to convert it to an ActiveX control.

5. Save the whole project. Save the project file as DESKTOP.VBP and the form as FORM1.FRM.

6. Choose File, New Project from the menu, and select ActiveX Control for the project type. Visual Basic opens up a new ActiveX control project, as shown in Figure 5.44.

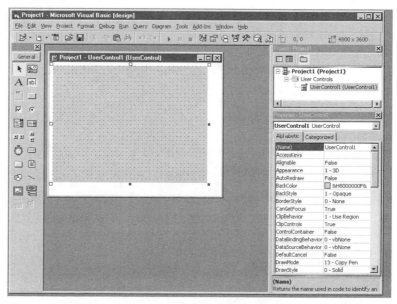

Figure 5.44 The new ActiveX control that is going to do the work of the desktop application created previously.

7. Choose Project, Project1 Properties from the menu, and then set the properties of the control you are building. Set the project name to `JavaKiller` and type `Desktop Application Incarnation` for the control description. Click OK to close the dialog box.

8. Now you need to import the desktop application forms, Form1 from the desktop project you've just completed. Choose Project, Add File from the menu. When the standard File Open dialog box pops up, navigate to the directory where the desktop project is saved. Add Form1 to the project. The Project Explorer toolbar now shows the newly added form.

9. Double-click Form1 in the Project Explorer toolbar, and when the form pops up, select all the controls on it by choosing Edit, Select All from the menu. Your screen should resemble the one shown in Figure 5.45.

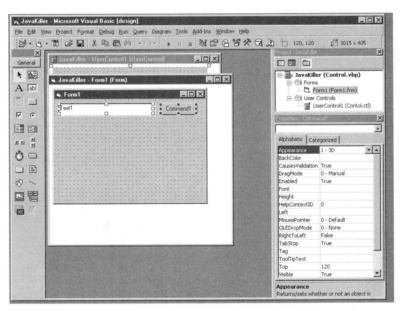

Figure 5.45 To migrate the controls from the form to the ActiveX control, first select all the controls on the form.

10. Choose Edit, Copy from the menu to copy all the controls to the Clipboard. Move to the ActiveX control form, and choose Edit, Paste from the menu. All the controls that were on Form1 now appear on the ActiveX control. The ActiveX control should now look just like Form1, as shown in Figure 5.46.

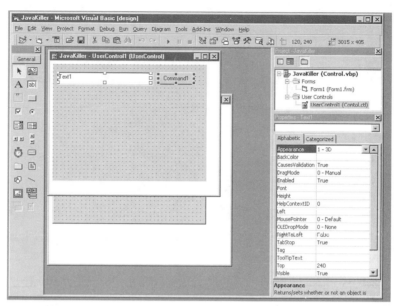

Figure 5.46 Paste the controls on the UserControl, and it should look just like the originating form.

11. Move again to the Form1 window, and double-click anywhere on the form to bring up the form editor. Choose Edit, Select All from the menu to select all the code, and then copy it to the Clipboard by choosing Edit, Copy. Move to the window showing the ActiveX control, double-click it, and then paste the code by choosing Edit, Paste. Now the ActiveX control has the same code that the form had.

12. Because you don't need Form1 any more, right-click it in the Project Explorer toolbar, and when the context menu comes up, choose the Remove Form1.frm option.

13. Select the ActiveX control again and change its **Name** property in the Properties window to **Form1**. That way, any references to Form1 in the code now go to your control.

14. The job is finished! Save the project, compile it, and then try it out in some test project. If everything is correct, it should work just like the original desktop application has. You can see a sample test application at work in Figure 5.47.

Figure 5.47 The same functionality as the desktop application, but now in an ActiveX control.

How It Works

Doing this kind of alchemy in Visual Basic is easy because it presents ActiveX controls just like normal forms on which you can place other controls.

However, you have to be careful if the original program uses many forms, instead of just one. In those cases, you usually convert only the main form to the ActiveX control and have it show the other forms, but you must be careful. If those other forms reference the main form, you have to change their code so that they reference the control instead.

There are other modality issues to think about when using forms in an ActiveX control that are not present when you build a standard executable. This is because ActiveX controls can be hosted in may different containers, but a Standard EXE project is completely self-contained in Visual Basic. Support for modal and non-modal forms varies from container to container, so if you intend to build a control for a specific host, make sure you check its documentation.

Comments

This whole "desktop-application-becomes-a-control" thing doesn't make any sense if you use the control in another desktop application. What you really want to do is plug the controls you build into a Web page, and make your applications accessible both from the intranet and the Internet, which is the topic of the next chapter.

CHAPTER 6

INTERNET INTEGRATION

6

INTERNET INTEGRATION

How do I...

During the past few years, the Internet has probably been the most talked-about computer topic. One of the most popular subtopics of that discussion has been the World Wide Web. The number of Web pages has exploded in recent years and continues to grow at an increasing pace. Microsoft Visual Basic has several features that make it easier for programmers to create applications that interact with the Internet and to create robust Web pages.

To run some of the How-Tos in this chapter, you need to have Microsoft Internet Explorer loaded. A copy of the browser should have been loaded when you installed Visual Basic. If not, or to get the latest version, you can download a copy from the Microsoft Web site at http://www.microsoft.com.

6.1 Create an ActiveX Document

This How-To examines creating a simple ActiveX document. Included in the example is how to store and retrieve information using a container's PropertyBag.

6.2 Build CAB Files to Distribute ActiveX Components

The Package and Deployment Wizard that comes with Visual Basic can be used to create distributable downloads for the Internet. This How-To shows how to use the wizard to create CAB files to distribute ActiveX components.

6.3 Include ActiveX Components on a Web Page

Now that you've built an ActiveX control or document, you may want to embed it in a Web page. This How-To covers the entries needed in an HTML file to cause the ActiveX component to be downloaded and registered.

6.4 Launch and Control a Web Browser

This How-To demonstrates techniques to invoke and control several aspects of the Microsoft Internet Explorer. The example uses OLE Automation to load several Web pages and show how to make use of the browser's own events to cause changes in your program to occur.

6.5 Use the WININET API to Transfer Files

Visual Basic 6 comes with a control called Microsoft Internet Transfer Control 6.0 that can be used to communicate with HTTP and FTP servers. These same actions can be accomplished directly by using the WININET API. This How-To uses the WININET API to implement a program to view directories on an FTP server and pull files to the local machine.

6.6 Create a DHTML Application

Visual Basic 6 has added the ability to create DHTML applications, which allow you to create programs that make use of Dynamic HTML to interact with the user and your desktop by using Visual Basic code. This How-To constructs a simple DHTML application to give you a starting point for creating exciting new Web applications.

COMPLEXITY
BEGINNING

6.1 How do I...
Create an ActiveX document?

COMPATIBILITY: VISUAL BASIC 5 AND 6

Problem

The users in my office are comfortable with Web browser interfaces, and we also need a way to provide updates to our in-house customers. Is there a way I can make use of the new ActiveX technology to accomplish these goals?

Technique

Microsoft Visual Basic enables the creation of ActiveX documents. These documents do not run as standalones, but are hosted by ActiveX containers. One such container is Microsoft Internet Explorer. This How-To uses Microsoft Internet Explorer as the container for a sample ActiveX document. Two other common containers are the Microsoft Office Binder and the Visual Basic Development Environment.

ActiveX documents are a hybrid. They exhibit some of the traits of ActiveX controls but can be fully functional Visual Basic programs. By using Visual Basic to create ActiveX documents, you can take advantage of Visual Basic strengths in menu design and ease of use to create robust applications that run from a Web browser.

Steps

Start Microsoft Internet Explorer and choose File, Open from the menu. Click the Browse button to find the file TOOLS.HTM located at \VB6HT\CHAPTER06. This ActiveX document does not have a digital signature. The default settings for Internet Explorer do not allow the document to be loaded. To run this example, you might need to lower the security settings for the browser. You can do this from the View, Internet Options menu in the Microsoft Internet Explorer browser.

After you load the file, the ActiveX document shown in Figure 6.1 is displayed. Select three tools from the Available Tools list and then click the >> button to copy those items to the text boxes. From the Internet Explorer pull-down menu, select the menu item ToolDoc. Select the subentry Entry 2, and then select Favorites on its submenu. This fills the text boxes with a set of preselected tools. Next, choose the ToolDoc menu item, then Entry 2, and finally Page 1. This menu item demonstrates using the Hyperlink ability of the container to jump to an HTML page. When you are through running this example, be sure to reset your security settings if you lowered them.

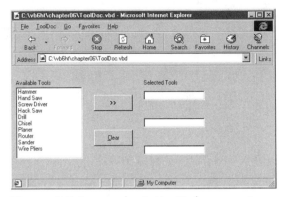

Figure 6.1 A sample ActiveX document.

Complete the following steps to create this project:

1. Use New Project to create an ActiveX Document EXE. Name the new project TOOLS.

2. Add the objects and properties listed in Table 6.1 to the user document. This is done the same way you would add controls and properties to a form in a standard Visual Basic program.

Table 6.1 Object and Properties for UserDocument

OBJECT	PROPERTY	SETTING
UserDocument	Name	ToolDoc
ListBox	Name	lbTools
	MultiSelect	1 - Simple
CommandButton	Name	cbCopy
	Caption	>>
CommandButton	Name	cbClear
	Caption	&Clear
TextBox	Name	tbTool1
	Text	" "
TextBox	Name	tbTool2
	Text	" "
TextBox	Name	tbTool3
	Text	" "
Label	Name	Label1
	Caption	Available Tools
Label	Name	Label2
	Caption	Selected Tools

3. Use the Menu Editor under the Tools pull-down menu to create the menu shown in Table 6.2. The NegotiatePosition field should be set to Left for the first entry (ToolDoc). When the ActiveX document is loaded, this menu integrates with the menu of the browser.

Table 6.2 Menu Specifications for UserDocument

CAPTION	NAME
&ToolDoc	mnuFile
-Entry 1	mnuToolDoc1
-Entry 2	mnuToolDoc2
-Page 1	mnuSub1
-Page 2	mnuSub2
-Favorites	mnuSub3
-Entry 3	mnuToolDoc3

4. Add the following line to the General Declarations section of UserDocument ToolDoc:

```
Option Explicit
```

5. Add the following code to the **Initialize** event of the UserDocument. The **AddItem** method of the ListBox is used to add a list of tool choices.

```
Private Sub UserDocument_Initialize()
    ' Load the Available Tools list
    lbTools.AddItem "Hammer"
    lbTools.AddItem "Hand Saw"
    lbTools.AddItem "Screw Driver"
    lbTools.AddItem "Hack Saw"
    lbTools.AddItem "Drill"
    lbTools.AddItem "Chisel"
    lbTools.AddItem "Planer"
    lbTools.AddItem "Router"
    lbTools.AddItem "Sander"
    lbTools.AddItem "Wire Pliers"
End Sub
```

6. Add the following code to the **ReadProperties** event of the UserDocument. The **ReadProperties** event is fired after the **Initialize** event and can be used to retrieve and load data that has been saved as part of the ActiveX object.

```
Private Sub UserDocument_ReadProperties(PropBag As PropertyBag)
    'Retrieve the values for the text boxes
    tbTool1 = PropBag.ReadProperty("Tool1", "")
    tbTool2 = PropBag.ReadProperty("Tool2", "")
    tbTool3 = PropBag.ReadProperty("Tool3", "")
End Sub
```

7. Add the following procedure, which is used to save properties to the PropertyBag of the ActiveX document. The container knows to call the WriteProperties event when the PropertyChanged method has been used.

```
Private Sub UserDocument_WriteProperties(PropBag As PropertyBag)
    'Save the values of the text boxes
    PropBag.WriteProperty "Tool1", tbTool1.Text, ""
    PropBag.WriteProperty "Tool2", tbTool2.Text, ""
    PropBag.WriteProperty "Tool3", tbTool3.Text, ""
End Sub
```

8. Use the following code to the cbClear_Click subroutine to clear out the selection boxes:

```
Private Sub cbClear_Click()
    ' Clear the Text Boxes
    tbTool1 = ""
    tbTool2 = ""
    tbTool3 = ""
End Sub
```

9. Use the following code to create the cbCopy_Click subroutine. The ListCount property is used to determine the number of objects in the ListBox. Each item in the ListBox is examined to see whether it has been selected. As selected items are encountered, they are copied to the next available TextBox. When three selected items have been copied, the For...Next loop is ended.

```
Private Sub cbCopy_Click()
    Dim lcv As Integer
    Dim toolscopied As Integer

    toolscopied = 0
    For lcv = 0 To lbTools.ListCount - 1
        ' Check to see if the list item is selected
        If lbTools.Selected(lcv) Then
            Select Case (toolscopied)
                Case 0
                    tbTool1 = lbTools.List(lcv)
                Case 1
                    tbTool2 = lbTools.List(lcv)
                Case 2
                    tbTool3 = lbTools.List(lcv)
            End Select
            toolscopied = toolscopied + 1
            If toolscopied = 3 Then Exit For
        End If
    Next lcv
End Sub
```

10. Add the following code to the subroutine mnuSub1_Click. The Hyperlink object can be used to request that an Internet-aware container jump to the specified URL. In this case, the Hyperlink object is used to jump to a local HTML file. If you loaded the sample files in a directory other than C:\VB6HT, then you need to change the NavigateTo locations in this step and the next one.

```
Private Sub mnuSub1_Click()
    ' Jump to another item
    Hyperlink.NavigateTo "c:\VB6HT\chapter06\page1.htm"
End Sub
```

11. Add the following code to the subroutine mnuSub2_Click:

```
Private Sub mnuSub2 Click()
    ' Jump to another item
    Hyperlink.NavigateTo "c:\VB6HT\chapter06\page2.htm"
End Sub
```

12. This subroutine adds a list of favorite tools to the selection boxes whenever the menu item mnuSub3 is chosen:

```
Private Sub mnuSub3_Click()
    ' Load the favorite tools
    tbTool1 = "Hammer"
    tbTool2 - "Screw Driver"
    tbTool3 = "Drill"
End Sub
```

13. Add the PropertyChanged method to the Change event to the three TextBox controls: tbTool1, tbTool2, and tbTool3. The PropertyChanged method notifies the container that a property value has been changed. This signals the container that the WriteProperties event needs to be fired.

```
Private Sub tbTool1_Change()
    'Indicate that something has changed that
    'needs to be saved.
    PropertyChanged
End Sub

Private Sub tbTool2_Change()
    'Indicate that something has changed that
    'needs to be saved.
    PropertyChanged
End Sub

Private Sub tbTool3_Change()
    'Indicate that something has changed that
    'needs to be saved.
    PropertyChanged
End Sub
```

How It Works

When you build your ActiveX document, the compiler also creates a VBD file that serves as an intermediate link between the container and the ActiveX document. When the VBD file is selected, the container loads the ActiveX document associated with it. The VBD is also used by some containers to store properties that are saved by using the `WriteProperties` event and the `WriteProperty` method.

Notice that the menu of the ActiveX document is merged with the menu of the browser. The Page 1 and Page 2 menu items demonstrate how the `HyperLink` object can be used in a hyperlink-aware container to navigate to specified URLs. The `NavigateTo` method of the `HyperLink` object can be used to jump to the following types of documents: HTML, Excel, Word, and ActiveX documents. If you have multiple ActiveX documents that work together, you can use the `HyperLink` object to move between the documents.

Comments

You should note that not all containers work exactly the same with an ActiveX document, so be sure to test your document with the containers you expect it to be used with. There are several restrictions you should keep in mind when preparing to create an ActiveX document. The first is that you cannot use the OLE Container control on an ActiveX document. Another thing to remember is that embedded objects, such as Word or Excel documents, cannot be used.

COMPLEXITY
BEGINNING

6.2 How do I...
Build CAB files to distribute ActiveX components?

COMPATIBILITY: VISUAL BASIC 5 AND 6

Problem

I've created some ActiveX controls and an ActiveX document. How do I bundle these objects so that they can be used on and distributed by Web pages?

Technique

The Package and Deployment Wizard enables you to select Internet Package as one of its options. This option creates a set of files that allow your programs to be delivered over the Internet and hosted on Web pages. By running this wizard on your project, it can determine which files are needed, bundle them together, and create sample HTML code to deliver and register your components. You should use this option to create Internet delivery mechanisms for your ActiveX components (controls, DLLs, EXEs, and documents) that you plan to use on Web pages. To run this wizard, you might need to add it to your menu by running the Add-In Manager.

Steps

1. Open the TSTCNT.VBP project.

2. Choose the Package and Deployment Wizard from the Add-Ins menu. A dialog box like the one shown in Figure 6.2 will be displayed.

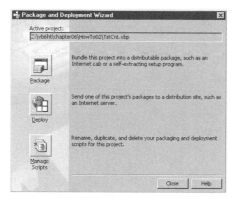

Figure 6.2 The Package and Deployment Wizard.

3. Click the Package button. The Package Type menu shown in Figure 6.3 will be displayed.

4. Select Internet Package for the type and click Next to move on to the Build Folder menu, as shown in Figure 6.4.

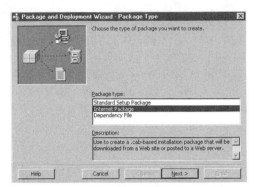

Figure 6.3 The Package Type dialog box of the wizard.

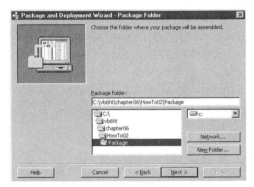

Figure 6.4 The Package Folder dialog box of the wizard.

5. On this menu, you select the location where the files created by the Package and Deployment Wizard will be located. This includes the CAB file and the files you need to re-create the CAB. The default location is a subdirectory to your project called Package. It is a good idea to leave this location as is. This keeps all the files needed to re-create the complete project together.

6. Click the Next button to continue to the Files menu, which is shown in Figure 6.5. This menu lists all the files that the wizard has determined need to be delivered as part of your component. If there are additional files you want to be delivered, you can click the Add button to include them.

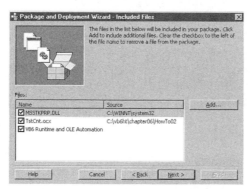

Figure 6.5 The Included Files dialog box of the wizard.

7. When you've finished adding files, click Next to continue on to the File Source dialog box shown in Figure 6.6. It is used to select where the files of this bundle will be delivered from. Each ActiveX control delivered with Microsoft Visual Basic has its Internet dependency information stored in a companion .DEP file. This information is used by the wizard when it creates the install.

If you select the MSVBVM60.DLL from the Dependencies list, you will see in the Runtime Components frame that this file will, by default, be delivered from a Microsoft Web site. This ensures that you are always using the latest component. If you prefer to deliver the file in your .CAB, select the Include in This Cab option. When the Download option is selected, you can enter an HTTP address or a UNC file path.

8. Click the Next button to move to the Safety Settings menu, which is used to indicate to the browser what type of operations your component might be capable of. This menu, as shown in Figure 6.7, enables you to mark components as being safe for initialization and safe for scripting. Marking components is covered in more detail later in this section.

Figure 6.6 The File Source dialog box of the wizard.

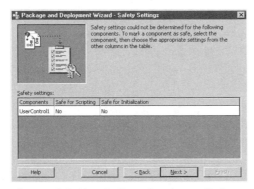

Figure 6.7 The Safety Settings dialog box of the wizard.

9. When you've finished adding files, click Next to continue. The Finished! panel, shown in Figure 6.8, can be used to save a copy of the work you've just done as a script. You can use the script the next time you want to build this package instead of having to redefine the elements. This is especially handy if you had to add elements along the way.

10. Click Finish to end the setup creation process. In the distribution location, you can now find two files created by the setup process: TSTCNT.CAB and TSTCNT.HTM. The cabinet file contains your OCX and its dependent files. The HTML file is an example of how to include this control in a Web page. For ActiveX documents, this directory also contains the .VBD file.

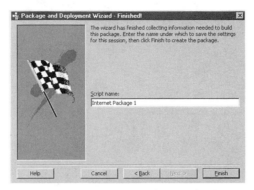

Figure 6.8 The Finished! panel of the
wizard.

In the subdirectory support, you find four more files: TSTCNT.BAT,
TSTCNT.OCX, TSTCNT.INF, and TSTCNT.DDF. The DDF file is the
control file for creating the cabinet file. The INF file contains the
information on how the control, TSTCNT.OCX, should be installed. The
files in the support directory can be used to re-create the CAB file. To
create a CAB file, use the MAKECAB program in the
\VB\Wizards\PDWizard directory; it takes the DDF file as an argument.
The TSTCCNT.BAT is a batch program that shows how to run the
MAKECAB program.

Marking Components Safe

By default, the security setting for Microsoft Internet Explorer does not enable
an ActiveX component to be instantiated in an HTML page unless it has been
marked as safe for initialization and scripting. Knowing how to mark a
component can be a tricky situation. This section just covers the highlights.

For more information on building controls that are safe for scripting and
initialization, you should read the following MSDN topics: Designing Controls
for Use With HTML, Building ActiveX Controls, and Creating ActiveX
Components.

Finally, most third-party ActiveX controls and the controls you develop in
VB6 require a license file to enable them to be used in a Web browser. (For more
information, read the MSDN article "Licensing ActiveX Controls.") "Safe for
scripting" means that the control cannot cause any damage when automated by
HTML script. Causing damage covers not only corrupting or deleting data, but

also retrieving unauthorized information from the system. Controls that are safe for scripting should not enable the following types of activities: creating named files, creating named Registry entries, retrieving named Registry entries, reading named files, deleting named files, and so on.

This list is not all-inclusive, but a pattern is beginning to emerge. Allowing the script to name items it will work with presents problems. If the control allows the script to provide file and Registry names for reading, creation, or deletion, the control can be used for malicious purposes.

"Safe for initialization" means that the control does not do anything bad despite the data used to initialize itself. This is a weaker level of safety than "safe for scripting," and most controls that are safe for scripting are safe for initialization unless there are specific parameters that can be set only during initialization. If a control is marked as safe for initialization, no data file or Registry entries should be modified as part of the initialization process.

Because a control is marked as safe for scripting and safe for initialization does not mean it is safe to use. The control could still perform malicious acts that have nothing to do with scripting or initialization. The idea behind marking a control as safe is to let the user know that other people cannot use the control to perform operations that could put their systems and data at risk. The assurance that the developer had no malicious intent is provided by the digital signature.

Digital Signing

By default, Microsoft Internet Explorer does not download components that have not been digitally signed. Therefore, if you are going to deliver your component outside your own intranet, you need to get a digital signature. Digital signatures are purchased from a certificate authority (CA). The CA verifies your identity and creates a digital certificate for you. This certificate gives the user a means to contact you in case something goes wrong. A digital signature supplies a level of accountability between your name and the components you deliver.

You can generate four types of files with Microsoft Visual Basic that you can digitally sign: .CAB, .DLL, .EXE, and .OCX. The software needed to digitally sign a component is not delivered with Visual Basic. Called Authenicode, it is part of the ActiveX SDK. For more information on the ActiveX SDK, check out the Microsoft Web site at `http://www.microsoft.com/intdev/sdk/`. The software and documentation are available for download from the Web site. You can also check out the MSDN article "Obtaining a Digital Signature."

How It Works

The Visual Basic Package and Deployment Wizard can create everything you need to deliver ActiveX components over the Internet. The wizard guides you through the information needed to construct an Internet-downloadable component.

After you have finished creating the downloadable component, you can use the sample HTML file created by the wizard to add the necessary HTML code to your Web pages. The Web browser is responsible for determining that an ActiveX component needs to be downloaded and takes care of all the details involved in installing the component.

Comments

If you plan on delivering ActiveX components over the Web, you need to familiarize yourself with marking components as safe for scripting and initialization. This topic was covered briefly in this How-To, but more information on the subject is available.

You also need to understand digital signing and the process of acquiring a certificate. People are hesitant to download controls and documents if they are not marked safe and do not have a certificate to authenticate the software. Both of these subjects are covered in more detail in MSDN and on the Microsoft Web page.

COMPLEXITY
BEGINNING

6.3 How do I...
Include ActiveX components on a Web page?

COMPATIBILITY: VISUAL BASIC 5 AND 6

Problem

How do I deliver and manipulate my ActiveX components on a Web page?

Technique

When you create a program, normally it is delivered to other users by means of a setup program the user runs on his or her machine. In the case of Internet components, the situation is handled differently. The browser takes care of recognizing that a component is needed, checking to see whether it is already loaded, and, if not, loading it.

In the previous section, you learned how to create a cabinet (.CAB) file. This file serves as a holding location for files that may need to be downloaded as part of your component. The cabinet file is identified in the HTML page that the component is part of. This section examines how to load and manipulate ActiveX components from an HTML page.

Steps

ActiveX components are added to HTML pages by using the HTML **OBJECT** tag. The **OBJECT** tag uses attributes to identify and download the control. The three most common attributes used when defining an ActiveX component are **CLASSID**, **CODEBASE**, and **ID**.

The **CLASSID** attribute is used to hold the component's Class ID that is stored in the Windows Registry. The **CODEBASE** attribute is used to point to the location where the .CAB file can be found, as well as specify a version for the component. The **ID** attribute is used to supply a name that can be used in scripting.

The Package and Deployment Wizard creates sample HTML files that show what HTML code is needed to add your components to a Web page. These sample files include the attributes just listed, along with the values they need. The following HTML code was created by the wizard when the test control was packaged for Internet delivery:

```
<HTML>
<OBJECT ID="UserControl1" WIDTH=328 HEIGHT=240
CLASSID="CLSID:134E6347-E2C7-11D0-913F-000000000000"
CODEBASE="TstCnt.CAB#version=1,0,0,0">
</OBJECT>
</HTML>
```

When the HTML page is loaded, the **OBJECT** tag causes the browser to check the Class ID defined in the **CLASSID** attribute to see whether the component is already loaded. If it is already loaded, it then checks the version to see whether the one on this Web page is newer. If the component is not found or the version is newer, the browser starts downloading any necessary files.

The sample HTML file for an ActiveX document has a similar **OBJECT** tag as well as VBScript code to initialize the document. In the following listing for the sample ActiveX document, you can see that the **OBJECT** declaration follows the same format as the one for the ActiveX control. The big difference is with VBScript code. The subroutine **Window_OnLoad** uses the **Document** reference to create an HTML frame to host the ActiveX document. The source of the frame is set to the VBD file created when the ActiveX document was compiled.

```
<HTML>
<OBJECT ID="ToolDoc"
CLASSID="CLSID:05B6638B-D877-11D0-9137-000000000000"
CODEBASE="tools.CAB#version=1,0,0,0">
</OBJECT>

<SCRIPT LANGUAGE="VBScript">
Sub Window_OnLoad
```

```
      Document.Open
      Document.Write "<FRAMESET>"
      Document.Write "<FRAME SRC=""ToolDoc.VBD"">"
      Document.Write "</FRAMESET>"
      Document.Close
End Sub
</SCRIPT>
</HTML>
```

Scripting ActiveX Components

You saw in the sample code for the ActiveX document that scripts were used to prepare the browser before loading the document. For most ActiveX components, you should use some form of scripting to control or enhance the component. In the following HTML code, two ActiveX components, CommandButton and ListBox, have been added to the Web page. A section of VBScript was added to catch the **Click** event of the button and to add items to the list box. By using ActiveX controls and VBScript, you can create robust Web pages by leveraging your Visual Basic skills.

```
<HTML>
<HEAD>
<TITLE>Scripting ActiveX Controls</TITLE>
</HEAD>
<BODY>
<H1>Scripting ActiveX Controls</H1><p>

You can use Visual Basic Script to control and provide additional
functionality to ActiveX Controls. The ActiveX button below
will add items to the list box by using VBScript to access the AddItem
method of the ActiveX ListBox.<p>

    <OBJECT ID="CommandButton1" WIDTH=96 HEIGHT=32
 CLASSID="CLSID:D7053240-CE69-11CD-A777-00DD01143C57">
    <PARAM NAME="Caption" VALUE="Select">
    <PARAM NAME="Size" VALUE="2540;847">
    <PARAM NAME="FontCharSet" VALUE="0">
    <PARAM NAME="FontPitchAndFamily" VALUE="2">
    <PARAM NAME="ParagraphAlign" VALUE="3">
</OBJECT><p>
    <OBJECT ID="ListBox1" WIDTH=96 HEIGHT=96
 CLASSID="CLSID:8BD21D20-EC42-11CE-9E0D-00AA006002F3">
    <PARAM NAME="ScrollBars" VALUE="3">
    <PARAM NAME="DisplayStyle" VALUE="2">
    <PARAM NAME="Size" VALUE="2540;2540">
    <PARAM NAME="MatchEntry" VALUE="0">
    <PARAM NAME="FontCharSet" VALUE="0">
    <PARAM NAME="FontPitchAndFamily" VALUE="2">
</OBJECT>

    <SCRIPT LANGUAGE="VBScript">
<!--
Sub CommandButton1_Click()
ListBox1.Additem "Item 1"
```

continued on next page

continued from previous page

```
ListBox1.Additem "Item 2"
ListBox1.Additem "Item 3"
end sub
-->
    </SCRIPT>
</BODY>
</HTML>
```

How It Works

When you use the Package and Deployment Wizard to generate an Internet download object, a sample HTML file is generated also. The sample file shows you what HTML constructs are needed to download and install your component. You can add these constructs to Web pages to enable the browser to download your components. The browser is responsible for checking to see whether the component is already loaded and, if so, whether the version numbers of the components are different. The browser is also responsible for distributing the files contained in the cabinet file according to the directions in the .INF (bundled inside the .CAB file).

Comments

Scripting plays an important part in most ActiveX Web-based projects. That is why How-To 6.2 discusses the importance of properly marking your components as safe for scripting and initialization.

The sample Web page presented in this chapter, SCRIPT.HTM, shows how Visual Basic Script can be used to interact with ActiveX controls. The controls in this sample are very simple but demonstrate how you would interact with any ActiveX component.

If you need help adding ActiveX controls to your Web pages, you can download the ActiveX Control Pad from the Microsoft Web site. The ActiveX Control Pad can be used to add ActiveX components and scripts to an HTML document. You can visually edit parameters for the components, and the proper HTML **OBJECT** statements are generated.

COMPLEXITY
BEGINNING

6.4 How do I...
Launch and control a Web browser?

COMPATIBILITY: VISUAL BASIC 5 AND 6

Problem

All my customers have Web browsers loaded on their systems. I would like to use a browser to point to software updates and information about our product.

Is there a way that I can control a browser from my application to accomplish this?

Technique

Two of the major browsers can be driven by OLE Automation to accomplish the problem described. Because Microsoft Internet Explorer is delivered on the Microsoft Visual Basic 6 CD-ROM, this How-To makes use of that browser to examine this problem. Before proceeding with this example, it is recommended that you load at least version 4.7x of Microsoft Internet Explorer. This software should have been installed when you loaded Visual Basic. It can also be found on the Microsoft Web page.

Steps

Load the project BROWSER.VBP. Be sure to change the HTML locations in the subroutines `Form_Load` and `cbNext_Click`. Then run the program. The form shown in Figure 6.9 appears, along with a copy of Internet Explorer.

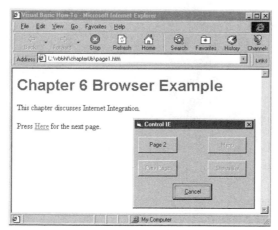

Figure 6.9 The control IE form.

Click the button labeled Page 2. Another HTML page is loaded. Then click the button labeled Prev Page to redisplay the first HTML page. The buttons Menu and Status Bar serve as toggles to switch the menus at the top of the browser and the status bar at the bottom of the browser on and off. Close the control IE form by clicking the Cancel button.

To create this project, complete the following steps:

1. Create a new project called BROWSER.VBP.

2. Use Form1 to create the objects and properties listed in Table 6.3.

Table 6.3 Object and Properties for IEBROWSER Form

OBJECT	PROPERTY	SETTING
Form	Name	IEBROWSE
	Caption	Control IE
CommandButton	Name	cbNext
	Caption	Page 2
CommandButton	Name	cbPrev
	Caption	Prev Page
	Enabled	False
CommandButton	Name	cbMenu
	Caption	Menu
	Enabled	False
CommandButton	Name	cbStatus
	Caption	Status Bar
	Enabled	False
CommandButton	Name	cbCancel
	Caption	Cancel

3. Save the form as IEBROWSE.FRM.

4. Add a reference to Microsoft Internet Controls by choosing the References menu item located under Project.

5. Add the following code to the General Declarations section of the IEBROWSE form. The **WithEvents** keyword makes the events of the **InternetExplorer** object available to this program.

```
Option Explicit

Public firstButton As Boolean

Public WithEvents ie As InternetExplorer
```

6. Add the following code to the **Load** event of the form IEBROWSE. Be sure to change the value of the argument passed to **Navigate** to the location of the page1.htm on your machine. The **Top** and **Left** properties of the form are set to **0** to move the form to the upper-left corner to make room for the Internet Explorer window.

After the **InternetExplorer** object is created, its **Visible** property is set to **True** because by default the value is **False**. The Internet Explorer window is then repositioned so that it lines up with the form for this program. Because the **Left**, **Top**, and **Width** properties of the **InternetExplorer** object take values in screen coordinates, a conversion is done to get proper numbers. The **Navigate** method is used to load the first HTML page.

```
Private Sub Form_Load()
    ' Position this form to upper-left corner
    Me.Top = 0
    Me.Left = 0
    Me.Show

    firstButton = False

    Set ie = New InternetExplorer

    'Make sure the browser is visible
    ie.Visible = True

    'Reposition and resize the browser
    ie.Left = Me.Width / 15
    ie.Top = 0
    ie.Width = (Screen.Width - Me.Width) / 15

    'Load the first page
    ie.Navigate ("c:\VBGht\chapter06\page1.htm")
End Sub
```

7. When the form unloads, make sure to unload Microsoft Internet Explorer by calling its **Quit** method:

```
Private Sub Form_Unload(Cancel As Integer)
    ' Unload the browser
    ie.Quit
End Sub
```

8. Add an **Unload** to the **Click** event of the **cbCancel** command button. This causes the form to unload.

```
Private Sub cbCancel_Click()
    Unload Me
End Sub
```

9. Add the following code to the **Click** event of the **cbNext** command button. Be sure to change the value of the argument passed to **Navigate** to the location of the page2.htm on your machine. This code uses the **Navigate** method of the **InternetExplorer** object to load a new HTML page. The argument could have been an HTTP address instead of a local file.

```
Private Sub cbNext_Click()
    ' Load the next page
    ie.Navigate ("c:\VB6ht\chapter06\page2.htm")
    firstButton = True
End Sub
```

10. Use the following code to create the **cbMenu_Click** and **cbStatus_Click** events. Each set of code toggles the state of its bar. The menu bar is located at the top of the browser window, and the status bar is at the bottom of the browser window.

```
Private Sub cbMenu_Click()
    ' Toggle the Menu Bar On/Off
    ie.MenuBar = Not ie.MenuBar
End Sub

Private Sub cbStatus_Click()
    ' Toggle the Status Bar On/Off
    ie.StatusBar = Not ie.StatusBar
End Sub
```

11. This procedure uses the **GoBack** method of the **InternetExplorer** object to reload the last page shown.

```
Private Sub cbPrev_Click()
    ' Go to the last loaded page
    ie.GoBack
End Sub
```

12. Add the following code to the **ie_DownloadComplete** event of the **InternetExplorer** object. Events for the **InternetExplorer** object are available to this program because of the **WithEvents** keyword that was used in the General Declarations section when defining the object **ie**. This code enables the other buttons after the second HTML page has been loaded.

```
Private Sub ie_DownloadComplete()
    If firstButton Then
        firstButton = False
        cbPrev.Enabled = True
        cbMenu.Enabled = True
        cbStatus.Enabled = True
    End If
End Sub
```

How It Works

Programs can invoke and control Microsoft Internet Explorer by adding a reference to the Microsoft Internet Controls to their project. If the local object is defined using the `WithEvents` keyword, then the events of the `InternetExplorer` object are available to the local program. These events can then be programmed just like the events of local controls. To see what properties, methods, and events exist for an object, you can use the Object Browser located under the View menu. The Object Browser is also available by pressing the F2 key.

Comments

This How-To gives only a brief example of using the events of the `InternetExplorer` objects with local code. The ability to program your own actions when these events fire gives the programmer a great deal of control over how Internet Explorer behaves and can be used. For instance, you might want to trap URLs that are not related to your company's site. You could use the `BeforeNavigate` event to check that any URLs are on your list of approved sites or pages.

COMPLEXITY
BEGINNING

6.5 How do I...

Use the WININET API to transfer files?

COMPATIBILITY: VISUAL BASIC 5 AND 6

Problem

My application needs to transfer files from a remote server. I know there is a control for Internet transfers, but I would prefer not to have to use another control if there is another way. Is there a way I can implement FTP transfers without using the control?

Technique

If you don't want to make use of the Microsoft Internet Transfer Control or if you find it difficult to use, you can go directly to the WININET API to perform the same functions. The API enables you to establish FTP, HTTP, and Gopher connections and perform the appropriate functions with each connection type.

The WININET.DLL is usually downloaded with Microsoft Internet Explorer, so you should have a copy of it available. If for some reason a copy did not get installed with Internet Explorer, you can download a copy as part of the ActiveX

SDK from the Microsoft Web site at http://www.microsoft.com. You can also find the documentation for the WININET functions on its Web site.

Steps

Load the project FTPAPI.VBP. To run this program, you must have an Internet connection and it must be active during program execution. Run the program. The form shown in Figure 6.10 is displayed.

Figure 6.10 The FTPLIST form.

Select a section from the drop-down list. Select one or more files from the Files list, and then click the Retrieve button. Make sure the directory displayed in the Download Directory box is the location where you want the files to be stored.

Complete the following steps to create this project:

1. Create a new project called FTPAPI.VBP.

2. Use Form1 to create the objects and properties listed in Table 6.4.

Table 6.4 Object and Properties for FTPLIST Form

OBJECT	PROPERTY	SETTING
Form	Name	FTPLIST
	Caption	Knowledge Base Files
	BorderStyle	3 - Fixed Dialog
	StartUpPosition	2 - CenterScreen
ComboBox	Name	cbKB
	Style	2 - Dropdown List

OBJECT	PROPERTY	SETTING
CommandButton	Name	cbRetrieve
	Caption	&Retrieve
ListBox	Name	lbFiles
	MultiSelect	1 - Simple
OptionButton	Name	opASCII
	Caption	ASCII
	Value	TRUE
OptionButton	Name	opBINARY
	Caption	Binary
TextBox	Name	tbCurDir
	Text	" "
Label	Name	Label1
	Caption	Section
Label	Name	Label2
	Caption	Files
Label	Name	Label3
	Caption	Download Directory
Label	Name	Label4
	Caption	Transfer Mode

3. Save the form as IEBROWSE.FRM.

4. Add a reference to Microsoft Internet Controls by using the References menu item located under Project.

5. Add the following code to the General Declarations section of the form FTPLIST.

```
Option Explicit

Private Declare Function InternetOpen Lib "wininet" Alias _
    "InternetOpenA" _
    (ByVal Agent As String, ByVal access As Long, ByVal proxy As _
    String, _
    ByVal bypass As String, ByVal flags As Long) As Long
Private Declare Function InternetOpen Lib "wininet" _
    Alias "InternetOpenA" (ByVal Agent As String, _
    ByVal access As Long, ByVal proxy As String, _
    ByVal bypass As String, ByVal flags As Long) As Long
```

continued on next page

continued from previous page

```
Private Declare Function InternetCloseHandle Lib "wininet" _
        (ByVal handle As Long) As Long

Const MAX_PATH = 260

Private Type FILETIME
        dwLowDateTime As Long
        dwHighDateTime As Long
End Type

Private Type WIN32_FIND_DATA
        dwFileAttributes As Long
        ftCreationTime As FILETIME
        ftLastAccessTime As FILETIME
        ftLastWriteTime As FILETIME
        nFileSizeHigh As Long
        nFileSizeLow As Long
        dwReserved0 As Long
        dwReserved1 As Long
        cFileName As String * MAX_PATH
        cAlternate As String * 14
End Type

Private Declare Function FtpFindFirstFile Lib "wininet" _
    Alias "FtpFindFirstFileA" (ByVal hFtpSession As Long, _
    ByVal lpszSearchFile As String, _
    lpFindFileData As WIN32_FIND_DATA, ByVal dwFlags As Long, _
    ByVal dwContext As Long) As Long
    lpFindFileData As WIN32_FIND_DATA, ByVal dwFlags As Long, _
                    ByVal dwContext As Long) As Long
Private Declare Function InternetFindNextFile Lib "wininet" _
    Alias "InternetFindNextFileA" (ByVal hFtpSession As Long, _
    lpFindFileData As WIN32_FIND_DATA) As Boolean
Private Declare Function FtpSetCurrentDirectory Lib "wininet" _
    Alias "FtpSetCurrentDirectoryA" (ByVal handle As Long, _
    ByVal directory As String) As Long
Private Declare Function FtpGetFile Lib "wininet" _
    Alias "FtpGetFileA" (ByVal handle As Long, _
    ByVal remotefile As String, _
    ByVal localfile As String, _
    ByVal ifexits As Long, ByVal attributes As Long, _
    ByVal flags As Long, ByVal context As Long) As Long

Const INTERNET_OPEN_TYPE_PRECONFIG As Long = 0
Const INTERNET_DEFAULT_PORT As Long = 21
Const INTERNET_INVALID_PORT_NUMBER As Long = 0
Const INTERNET_CONNECT_FLAG_PASSIVE As Long = &H80000000
Const INTERNET_SERVICE_FTP As Long = 1
Const FTP_TRANSFER_TYPE_ASCII As Long = 1
Const FTP_TRANSFER_TYPE_BINARY As Long = 2
Const FILE_ATTRIBUTE_NORMAL = &H80

Dim hNetConn As Long
Dim hFTPConn As Long
Dim sDir As String
```

6. Add the following code to the **Load** event of form FTPLIST. Add the Knowledge Base sections to the **cbKB** ComboBox. Use the function **InternetOpen** to establish a connection to the Internet. The handle **hNetConn** is used in other functions to open specific connections to the FTP server. The current directory is used as the location to download files.

The first argument of the **InternetOpen** function is a string that identifies the application. The second argument is the access type. This value should be one of the **INTERNET_OPEN_TYPE_*** constants defined in WININET.H. The value used here causes the proxy and direct configuration information to be read from the Registry. The third and fourth arguments are proxy name and proxy bypass, both of which are set to **vbNullString**. This setting causes the values to be read from the Registry. The last argument is a flag that affects the behavior of the function. This example takes the default behavior by using a **0** for the argument.

```
Private Sub Form_Load()
    ' Add Sections to ComboBox
    cbKB.AddItem "Microsoft Visual Basic"
    cbKB.AddItem "Microsoft Visual C++"
    cbKB.AddItem "Microsoft Access"
    cbKB.AddItem "Microsoft Excel"
    cbKB.AddItem "Microsoft Word"

    ' Initialize the WININET API
    hNetConn = InternetOpen("FTP Example", _
        INTERNET_OPEN_TYPE_PRECONFIG, _
        vbNullString, vbNullString, 0)

    ' Set the download directory
    tbCurDir = CurDir
End Sub
```

7. Add the following code to the **Click** event of **cbKB**. The **ListIndex** property of the ComboBox is used to select which directory on the server to look at. If an Internet connection has been established, then connect to the FTP server by using the **InternetConnect** function. If the connect succeeds, then use **FtpSetCurrentDirectory** to establish the directory that is used.

After setting the working directory, use **FtpFindFirstFile** to start the process of getting a list of files in that directory. The **FtpFindFirstFile** function returns the file data in a WIN32_FIND_DATA structure. Although this structure contains information, such as creation and modification dates, in this program only the name of the file is used. Clear the ListBox, **lbFiles**, before adding the new files to the list. The function **InternetFindNextFile** is used in a list to process all the files in the current directory. Before leaving the function, close the handle created to access the FTP server. This is necessary because **FtpFindFirstFile** can be called only once per handle.

The **InternetConnect** function takes eight arguments, the first of which is a handle returned by a call to **InternetOpen**. The second is the name or IP address of the server in which to connect. The third argument is the TCP/IP port number in which to connect on the server.

The value used in this subroutine causes the function to use the default port for the service. The next two arguments are user name and password. Because you are going to be using the FTP service, using **vbNullString** as the value for these arguments causes a UserName of anonymous and a password of the user's e-mail address to be sent. The sixth argument is the type of service to be started. The three types of services available are FTP, HTTP, and Gopher. The seventh argument is a flag defined for specific services. When the service type is FTP, use the value defined in WININET.H for **INTERNET_CONNECT_FLAG_PASSIVE**. The last argument is used to identify context for callbacks.

```
Private Sub cbkb_Click()
    Dim fConn As Long
    Dim fData As WIN32_FIND_DATA
    Dim fResult As Boolean
    Dim stat As Long

    ' Select a server directory
    Select Case cbKB.ListIndex
        Case 0
            sDir = "developr/vb/kb"
        Case 1
            sDir = "developr/visual_c/kb"
        Case 2
            sDir = "deskapps/access/kb"
        Case 3
            sDir = "deskapps/excel/kb"
        Case 4
            sDir = "deskapps/word/kb"
    End Select

    If hNetConn Then
        ' Set Mouse Pointer Busy
        Screen.MousePointer = 11
        ' Create FTP Server Connection
        hFTPConn = InternetConnect(hNetConn, "ftp.microsoft.com", _
            INTERNET_INVALID_PORT_NUMBER, vbNullString, _
                vbNullString, _
            INTERNET_SERVICE_FTP, INTERNET_CONNECT_FLAG_PASSIVE, 0)
        If hFTPConn Then
            If sDir <> "" Then
                stat = FtpSetCurrentDirectory(hFTPConn, sDir)
            End If
            fConn = FtpFindFirstFile(hFTPConn, "*.*", fData, 0, 0)
```

```
                    If fConn Then
                        fResult = True
                        ' Clear out the list box
                        lbFiles.Clear
                        Do While fResult
                            ' Add file name to list box
                            lbFiles.AddItem fData.cFileName
                            ' Get next file name
                            fResult = InternetFindNextFile(fConn, fData)
                        Loop
                    End If
                End If
                InternetCloseHandle (hFTPConn)
                ' Reset Mouse pointer
                Screen.MousePointer = 0
            End If
    End Sub
```

8. Add the following code to the subroutine **cbRetrieve_Click**. Check the value of **opASCII** to see whether the transfer is to use ASCII or binary mode. If an Internet connection has been established, then connect to the FTP server using the **InternetConnect** function. If the connection succeeds, then use **FtpSetCurrentDirectory** to establish the directory that is used. The contents of the list box are examined to determine which elements have been selected for retrieval. If an item has been selected in the list box, the **Selected** property is **True** for that item's index. The function **FtpGetFile** is used to retrieve the files from the FTP server.

The first argument for the **FtpGetFile** function is a handle to the FTP server connection opened with the **InternetConnect** function. The second and third arguments are the name of the remote file and the name of the file to be created locally. The fourth argument indicates what to do if the local file already exists. If the value is 1 and the local file already exists, then **FtpGetFile** fails. If the value is **0**, then **FtpGetFile** overwrites the local file.

The fifth argument specifies the attributes for the newly created file. These attributes are described by the **FILE_ATTRIBUTE_*** attributes defined in the Win32 SDK. The sixth argument indicates the file transfer mode to be used. In this example, **ASCII** and **BINARY** are the only options allowed. The last argument is used only if the application has called the **InternetSetStatusCallback** function to establish a callback function.

```
Private Sub cbRetrieve_Click()
    Dim i As Integer
    Dim stat As Long
    Dim transfer As Long

    ' Determine Transfer Mode
    If opASCII.Value Then
```

continued on next page

continued from previous page

```
                transfer = FTP_TRANSFER_TYPE_ASCII
        Else
                transfer = FTP_TRANSFER_TYPE_BINARY
        End If

        If hNetConn Then
            ' Set Mouse Pointer Busy
            Screen.MousePointer = 11
            ' Start FTP Server connection
            hFTPConn = InternetConnect(hNetConn, "ftp.microsoft.com", _
                INTERNET_DEFAULT_PORT, vbNullString, vbNullString, _
                INTERNET_SERVICE_FTP, INTERNET_FLAG_PASSIVE, 0)
            If hFTPConn Then
                If sDir <> "" Then
                    stat = FtpSetCurrentDirectory(hFTPConn, sDir)
                End If
            End If

            ' Check for selected files
            For i = 0 To lbFiles.ListCount - 1
                If lbFiles.Selected(i) Then
                    If hFTPConn Then
                        ' Retrieve file
                        stat = FtpGetFile(hFTPConn, lbFiles.List(i), _
                            tbCurDir.Text & "\" & lbFiles.List(i), 1, _
                            FILE_ATTRIBUTE_NORMAL, transfer, 0)
                    End If
                End If
            Next i

            InternetCloseHandle (hFTPConn)
            ' Reset Mouse Pointer
            Screen.MousePointer = 0
        End If
End Sub
```

9. Add the following code to the **lbFile_Click** subroutine. If files have been selected from the list box, enable the Retrieve button.

```
Private Sub lbFiles_Click()
    If lbFiles.SelCount > 0 Then
        cbRetrieve.Enabled = True
    Else
        cbRetrieve.Enabled = False
    End If
End Sub
```

10. Add the following code to the **Unload** event of form FTPLIST to close the Internet connection when the program terminates:

```
Private Sub Form_Unload(Cancel As Integer)
    InternetCloseHandle (hNetConn)
End Sub
```

How It Works

The `InternetOpen` function is used to initialize the WININET API and prepare the groundwork for connecting to servers. The `InternetConnect` function is then used to make the actual connection to a server. The connection can be to one of three types of servers: FTP, HTTP, or Gopher. The WININET API has functions defined to perform the task-specific features of each server type.

This How-To examines using the FTP functions to perform tasks with an FTP server. The program connects to the Microsoft FTP server to retrieve Knowledge Base articles. The pull-down list enables you to select a product area, and the `FtpSetCurrentDirectory` function is used to change to the proper product directory. The `FtpFindFirstFile` and `InternetFindNextFile` functions are then used to retrieve a list of the Knowledge Base articles for that product. The `FtpGetFile` function is used to retrieve those articles that have been selected from the list.

Comments

This How-To looks at using the WININET API to retrieve files from an FTP server. The same basic framework can be used to connect to HTTP and Gopher servers. The specifics of tasks for each server are different, but many functions in the WININET API can be used with all three servers. The WININET API makes it easier for you to add Internet transfer protocols to your programs. For example, you could use the HTTP functions to update HTML help files delivered with your program. The program could check your Web site for new or updated files and deliver them to the local machine.

 COMPLEXITY
INTERMEDIATE

6.6 How do I...
Create a DHTML application?

COMPATIBILITY: VISUAL BASIC 6

Problem

I've heard that Microsoft supports something called Dynamic HTML. Can I use Visual Basic to take advantage of that?

Technique

Microsoft Visual Basic 6 enables the creation of DHTML applications, which are combinations of Dynamic HTML and compiled Visual Basic. This combination allows the programmer to update the Web page without re-creating or reloading and interact with the browser and other desktop applications. Because much of the work in a DHTML application is done in Visual Basic code, you can leverage your knowledge of Visual Basic to create interesting Web deliverables.

Steps

Open the project BUGPROJ.VBP and run it. The Web page shown in Figure 6.11 is displayed. Use the select boxes to pick a product and a severity level of the problem. Click the Browse button to select a file to provide as a test case. Then enter a problem description and the name of the person logging the bug. Next, click the Submit button. The information entered is displayed in a message box.

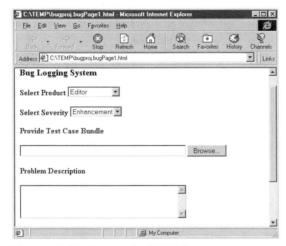

Figure 6.11 A sample DHTML page.

To create this project, complete the following steps:

1. Use New Project to create a DHTML application.

2. Name the new project BUGPROJ.

3. Add the objects and properties listed in Table 6.5 to the DHTML page. This is done the same way you would add controls and properties to a form in a standard Visual Basic program.

Table 6.5 Object and Properties

OBJECT	PROPERTY	SETTING
IDHTMLPageDesigner	Name	bugPage1
	BuildFile	bugproj.bugPage1.html
	id	DHTMLPage1

OBJECT	PROPERTY	SETTING
DispIHTMLSelectElement	(Id)	selProduct
	Name	Select1
DispIHTMLSelectElement	(Id)	selSeverity
	Name	Select2
DispIHTMLInputButton	Name	SubmitButton1
	(Id)	SubmitButton1
	Value	"Submit"
DispIHTMLInputButton	Name	ResetButton1
	(Id)	ResetButton1
	Value	"Reset"
DispIHTMLInputFileElement	(Id)	testPath
	Name	FileUpload1
	Value	""
DispIHTMLTextAreaElement	(Id)	probDesc
	Name	TextArea1
	Value	""
DispIHTMLInputTextElement	(Id)	opName
	Name	TextField1
	Value	""

4. Place the text shown in Figure 6.11 by placing the cursor in the appropriate place on the design portion of the DHTML page and typing in the strings at each location.

5. To add the selection choices to the select boxes, choose the custom button from the properties when a selection box is selected or use the properties item from the pop-up menu that appears when you right-click. The selection choices are added to the Options for SELECT Tag area. Add the entries in Table 6.6 to the **selProduct** selection box. Add the entries in Table 6.7 to the **selSeverity** selection box.

Table 6.6 Menu Selections for the Product Selection Box

TEXT	VALUE
Editor	Editor
Launcher	Launcher
Mail	Mail
Spread Sheet	Spread Sheet

Table 6.7 Menu Selections for the Severity Selection Box

TEXT	VALUE
Enhancement	Enhancement
Normal	Normal
Critical	Critical

6. Add the following code to the `ResetButton1_onclick` function in the `bugPage1` code. When the Reset button is clicked, the operator's name and problem description will be blanked out.

```
Private Function ResetButton1_onclick() As Boolean
    opName.Value = ""
    probDesc.Value = ""
End Function
```

7. To provide some feedback to the user, place the following code in the `SubmitButton1_onclick` function.

```
Private Function SubmitButton1_onclick() As Boolean
    Dim message As String

    message = "The following information has been logged : " + _
        vbLf + vbLf + _
        "Product : " + selProduct.Value + vbLf + _
        "Bug Severity : " + selSeverity.Value + vbLf + _
        "Test Case : " + testPath.Value + vbLf + _
        "Operator : " + opName.Value + vbLf + _
        "Description : " + probDesc.Value

    MsgBox message, vbInformation, "Bug Logging System"

End Function
```

How It Works

Building the project creates a DLL and an HTML page. The HTML page contains the hooks needed to load the DLL and take advantage of the Visual Basic code you have written to manipulate the Web page or other desktop applications. The following line was taken from an HTML page that was generated with the project for this How-To:

```
<object id="DHTMLPage1" classid="clsid:FF513A28-C38F-11D1-9182-000000000000"
width=0 height=0> </object>
```

This code is handled by the browser in the same way the objects in How-To 6.3 were described. The ID is for the DLL that was created along with the HTML file.

This How-To demonstrates a very elementary DHTML application. It is, however, enough to show you that you can combine Visual Basic code with HTML to create a more interesting Web interface.

Comments

In addition to creating the HTML file in the designer, you can import an HTML file. If you do so, be sure to assign each element you want to work with an ID. Only elements that have a unique ID can be programmed. You should also remember to use relative URLs. You can't be sure that the directory structure of your project will always be loaded in the same location, but the integrity of the structure should be maintained. By using relative paths, you can always find other files within your project structure.

This How-To covers only the basics of a DHTML application. See the MSDN article "Developing DHTML Applications" for more information on the subject.

CHAPTER 7
APPLICATION PERFORMANCE

7

APPLICATION PERFORMANCE

How do I...

This chapter uses various techniques to evaluate some of the factors that contribute to overall application performance. Aspects of computational, graphics, and object creation performance are explored. Understanding the characteristics and code factors that affect performance is only one part. Objective code and performance analysis are also very important.

Two general-purpose utilities are constructed in this chapter. The first, in How-To 7.3, analyzes some characteristics of the source code. The second tool, in How-To 7.4, provides routines to profile the execution of a program.

All the How-Tos in the chapter display the analysis results in a grid. The contents of these grids can be printed or saved to comma-separated value (CSV) files. The chapter concludes with a discussion of design and coding techniques that make it easier to analyze performance.

7.1 Measure Compute Performance

Some common approaches to improving compute performance include managing the size of variable data types, tuning a good algorithm, and finding faster algorithms. This How-To evaluates a few variations of two different computations. It enables an objective look at some of the factors that drive compute performance.

7.2 Evaluate Graphics Performance

Evaluation of graphics performance is sometimes difficult because there are so many possible causes of both good and bad performance. The code in this How-To enables the user to select various options for the graphics properties, run selected sets of tests, and see the performance results. The elusive set of property values and algorithms that yield optimum performance can be narrowed down to a few key characteristics.

7.3 Understand and Perform Static Code Analysis

This How-To builds a utility that performs simple static code analysis. The program counts code and comment lines, the ratio of comments to code, and a complexity value for each routine in the code. These simple metrics enable developers to target specific code for testing and to examine logic structures for possible simplification. The goal is to produce code that is understandable and easy to debug.

7.4 Instrument a Program for Code Profiling

Profiling a program's execution is a powerful tool to use when evaluating performance. It is important to know where a program spends its time so that the right routines can be tuned. This How-To provides a tool that manages creating and recording execution profile data. It tracks the routines that execute in a program, how often they run, and how long they run. During the testing process, code profiling helps to ensure that all parts of a program are tested.

7.5 Evaluate Object Creation Performance

Several factors affect the time it takes to create instances of objects. Objects can be created by using class modules that are part of the executable. They can also be created from external DLL modules. This How-To looks at the performance differences of these two object creation techniques.

7.6 Plan for Performance During Design and Construction

It is important to plan your code development to facilitate the performance analysis and debugging processes. This How-To discusses some coding techniques and styles that can make the task easier.

COMPLEXITY
BEGINNING

7.1 How do I...
Measure compute performance?

COMPATIBILITY: VISUAL BASIC 5 AND 6

Problem

The application I am writing performs many complex computations. There is some concern that the code will be too slow to meet its performance expectations. I know that some common approaches to improving compute performance are to use the smallest possible variable data types and to find a faster algorithm. How do I evaluate, document, and analyze a program's compute performance to find potential areas that can be improved?

Technique

To evaluate compute performance, the program uses two different computations. For the first one, the algorithm is changed; for the second computation, the variable types are changed. Each test records results on a grid to enable onscreen comparison of the performance.

Another feature of this How-To includes allowing the results to be printed and exported to a CSV file. The CSV file can be imported into a spreadsheet for further analysis.

Steps

Open and run COMPUTE PERFORMANCE.VBP. Select all five of the check boxes. The main form is shown in Figure 7.1.

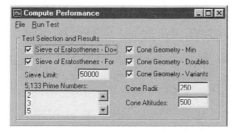

Figure 7.1 The main form at runtime.

Then, choose Test, Run Test from the menu. The test results are displayed in a grid on the test results form, as shown in Figure 7.2.

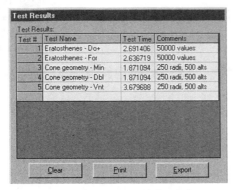

Figure 7.2 The test results form.

Complete the following steps to create this project:

1. Create a new project called COMPUTE PERFORMANCE.VBP.

2. Add a form to the project and set the objects and properties as they are listed in Table 7.1. Be sure to add the Microsoft FlexGrid control to the project. Save the form as TEST RESULTS.FRM.

Table 7.1 Test Results Form's Objects and Properties

OBJECT/CONTROL	PROPERTY	VALUE
Form	Name	frmResults
	Caption	Test Results
	ControlBox	0 ' False
	MaxButton	0 ' False
	MinButton	0 ' False
CommandButton	Name	cmdAction
	Caption	Clear
	Index	0
CommandButton	Name	cmdAction
	Caption	Print
	Index	1
CommandButton	Name	cmdAction
	Caption	Export
	Index	2
MSFlexGrid	Name	grdResults
	Cols	4
Label	lblCaption	Test Results:
	Caption	&Run Test

3. This next piece of code is placed in the general declarations section of the form. The code defines the variables used in the program. These variables track the start and end times of the performance tests and other test-specific information.

```
Option Explicit

' Pointer to the current row in the results grid
Dim mnCurrentRow            As Integer

' Start time of the current test
Dim mfStartTime             As Single

' Finish time of the current test
Dim mfEndTime               As Single

' The name of the current test
Dim msTestName              As String

'Comments related to the current test
Dim msComments              As String
```

4. The following code segment is placed in the form's **Load** event. The code sets the grid column titles and attributes. This grid is used to display the results of each performance test.

```
Private Sub Form_Load()

' Configure the results grid by setting the columns'
' captions and widths and alignment'
grdResults.Row = 0

' Set the properties for the first column
grdResults.Col = 0
grdResults.Text = "Test #"
grdResults.ColWidth(0) = 660
grdResults.FixedAlignment(0) = vbCenter

' Set the properties for the second column
grdResults.Col = 1
grdResults.Text = "Test Name"
grdResults.ColWidth(1) = 1935
grdResults.ColAlignment(1) = vbLeftJustify

' Set the properties for the third column
grdResults.Col = 2
grdResults.Text = "Test Time"
grdResults.ColWidth(2) = 840
grdResults.ColAlignment(2) = vbCenter

' Set the properties for the fourth column
grdResults.Col = 3
grdResults.Text = "Comments"
```

continued on next page

continued from previous page

```
grdResults.ColWidth(3) = 1605
grdResults.ColAlignment(3) = vbLeftJustify

' Initialize the variable that reference the current
' grid data row
mnCurrentRow = 1

End Sub
```

5. The following code, when added to the **Click** event of the **cmdAction** command button, dispatches the **Click** event to code that performs the action requested by the user. These actions are clear the test results grid, print the contents of the grid, or export the grid contents to a CSV file.

```
Private Sub cmdAction_Click(Index As Integer)

Select Case Index
    Case 0              ' Clear test results
        If (MsgBox("Are you sure you want to " & _
            "clear the results?", vbCritical + _
            vbYesNo)) = vbYes Then
                Call ResultsClear
        End If

    Case 1              ' Print test results
        Call ResultsPrint

    Case 2              ' Export test results
        Call ResultsExport

End Select

End Sub
```

6. Add the following subroutine to the form. This procedure takes the test results from the grid control and prints them. The current scale mode of the printer is saved and then changed to inches. Next, the column headings are retrieved from the grid and used to print the page and column headings. Then the code loops through each row of the grid and prints the results of each test. Finally, the printer is restored to its original scale mode.

```
Private Sub ResultsPrint()

Dim nLoopCtr            As Integer
Dim sOutput(4)          As String
Dim nScaleMode          As Integer

' Save the current printer scale mode and change it to inches
nScaleMode = Printer.ScaleMode
Printer.ScaleMode = vbInches

' Collect the data column headers from the grid
grdResults.Row = 0
```

```
grdResults.Col = 0
sOutput(0) = grdResults.Text
grdResults.Col = 1
sOutput(1) = grdResults.Text
grdResults.Col = 2
sOutput(2) = grdResults.Text
grdResults.Col = 3
sOutput(3) = grdResults.Text

' Print the page and column headers
PrintFont "Arial", 16, True, True, False
PrintText 0, 0, "Test Results - " & Me.Caption
PrintFont "Arial", 12, True, True, False
PrintText 0, 0.5, "Date: " & Date$
PrintFont "Arial", 12, True, False, True
PrintText 0, 1, sOutput(0)
PrintText 1, 1, sOutput(1)
PrintText 3, 1, sOutput(2)
PrintText 4, 1, sOutput(3)
PrintFont "Arial", 12, False, False, False

For nLoopCtr = 1 To mnCurrentRow - 1
    ' Collect the data from the grid
    grdResults.Row = nLoopCtr
    grdResults.Col = 0
    sOutput(0) = grdResults.Text
    grdResults.Col = 1
    sOutput(1) = grdResults.Text
    grdResults.Col = 2
    sOutput(2) = grdResults.Text
    grdResults.Col = 3
    sOutput(3) = grdResults.Text

    ' Print the row data
    PrintText 0, 1 + (nLoopCtr * 0.25), sOutput(0)
    PrintText 1, 1 + (nLoopCtr * 0.25), sOutput(1)
    PrintText 3, 1 + (nLoopCtr * 0.25), sOutput(2)
    PrintText 4, 1 + (nLoopCtr * 0.25), sOutput(3)
Next nLoopCtr

' Release the page to be printed
Printer.EndDoc

' Restore the scale mode
Printer.ScaleMode = nScaleMode

End Sub
```

7. Add the following subroutine to the form. This routine is used to clear all test results from the grid by reducing the number of grid rows to two and then clearing the remaining single row of data.

```
Private Sub ResultsClear()

' Resize the grid to just two rows
```

continued on next page

continued from previous page

```
mnCurrentRow = 1
grdResults.Rows = 2

' Clear the values from the remaining data row
grdResults.Row = mnCurrentRow
grdResults.Col = 1
grdResults.Text = ""
grdResults.Col = 2
grdResults.Text = ""
grdResults.Col = 3
grdResults.Text = ""
grdResults.Col = 0
grdResults.Text = ""

End Sub
```

8. To export the test results to a comma-separated value (CSV) file, add the following code to the form. The CSV file is opened in **Append** mode so that new results can be added to any existing results. The logic loops through each row of the grid and moves the data into a local string array. This array is then written to the file by using a **Write** statement. This language statement adds all the necessary CSV formatting to the output as it is being written.

```
Private Sub ResultsExport()

Dim nLoopRow             As Integer
Dim nLoopCol             As Integer
Dim nChannel             As Integer
Dim sOutput(4)           As String

' Get an available I/O channel number
nChannel = FreeFile

' Open a CSV file to store the grid contents
' Using append mode will add to the file if it exists
Open App.Path & "\" & App.EXEName & ".csv" _
               For Append As #nChannel

' Loop through the grid row by row
For nLoopRow = 1 To mnCurrentRow - 1

    ' Set the current grid row
    grdResults.Row = nLoopRow

    ' Loop through the grid columns
    For nLoopCol = 0 To 3

        ' Set the current column
        grdResults.Col = nLoopCol
        ' Save the column data to an array
        sOutput(nLoopCol) = grdResults.Text

    Next nLoopCol
```

```
' Write the array contents to the CSV file
Write #nChannel, sOutput(0), _
                 sOutput(1), _
                 sOutput(2), _
                 sOutput(3)

Next nLoopRow

' Close the results file
Close #nChannel

End Sub
```

9. Add the following public method to the form. This method is called to tell the form that a test is starting. The code records the test's start time.

```
Public Sub TestStart()

' Record the test start time
mfStartTime = Timer

End Sub
```

10. This next public method is called when a test is finished. The code records the test's end time and then adds the test details to the results grid.

```
Public Sub TestEnd()

' Record the test end time
mfEndTime = Timer

' Add the test results to the grid
grdResults.Row = mnCurrentRow
grdResults.Col = 1
grdResults.Text = msTestName
grdResults.Col = 2
grdResults.Text = Format$( _
    mfEndTime - mfStartTime, "##,###.000000")
grdResults.Col = 3
grdResults.Text = msComments
grdResults.Col = 0
grdResults.Text = mnCurrentRow

' Increment the pointer to reference the next available row
mnCurrentRow = mnCurrentRow + 1
' Be sure the row exists
If mnCurrentRow + 1 > grdResults.Rows Then
    ' It doesn't, so add it to the grid control
    grdResults.Rows = mnCurrentRow + 1
End If

grdResults.Refresh

End Sub
```

11. There are two custom public properties of the form. The following code provides the means to set the test's name and any test-specific comments. These properties are added to the results grid when the individual test is finished.

```
Public Property Let TestName(ByVal sTestName As String)

msTestName = sTestName

End Property


Public Property Let TestComments(ByVal sComments As String)

msComments = sComments

End Property
```

12. The next two subroutines provide simple interface wrappers for specific printing operations. This first one, **PrintFont**, sets all the font attributes of the printer object.

```
Private Sub PrintFont(sFontName As String, _
              nFontSize As Integer, _
              bFontBold As Boolean, _
              bFontItalic As Boolean, _
              bFontUnderline As Boolean)

' Encapsulate the property settings used to set the
' printer object font properties

Printer.FontName = sFontName
Printer.FontSize = nFontSize
Printer.FontBold = bFontBold
Printer.FontItalic = bFontItalic
Printer.FontUnderline = bFontUnderline

End Sub
```

13. Add the following subroutine, which prints text at a specified location on the current printer page. First the X and Y coordinates are set. Next, the text is stripped of carriage return and line feed characters. If these characters are not removed, they can adversely affect the formatting of the printed output. Finally, the text is printed to the page.

```
Private Sub PrintText(fXCoordinate As Single, _
              fYCoordinate As Single, _
              sText As String)

' Place text on the printer object at a specified location

Dim lStart          As Long
Dim lIndex          As Long
```

```
' Set the current coordinates as determined by the
' current ScaleMode of the printer
Printer.CurrentX = fXCoordinate
Printer.CurrentY = fYCoordinate

' Filter out carriage returns and line feeds. If this is
' not done, placement control is lost.
lStart = 1
' Scan the string to find return/line feed pairs
lIndex = InStr(lStart, sText, vbCrLf)
' If one was found, enter the loop
Do While lIndex <> 0
    ' Replace the character pair with spaces
    Mid$(sText, lIndex, 2) = "  "
    ' Adjust the scan start position
    lStart = lStart + lIndex
    ' Look for another return/line feed pair
    lIndex = InStr(lStart, sText, vbCrLf)
Loop

' Put the scrubbed text string on the printer page
Printer.Print sText

End Sub
```

14. Add a new form to the project and set the objects and properties as they are listed in Table 7.2. Save the form as COMPUTE PERFORMANCE.FRM.

Table 7.2 The Project Form's Objects and Properties

OBJECT/CONTROL	PROPERTY	VALUE
Form	Name	frmMain
	Caption	Compute Performance
Frame	Name	fraTest
	Caption	Test Selection and Results
TextBox	Name	txtLimit
	Text	50000
TextBox	Name	txtAltitudes
	Text	500
TextBox	Name	txtRadii
	Text	250
CheckBox	Name	chkTest
	Caption	Sieve of Eratosthenes - Do+
	Index	0

continued on next page

continued from previous page

OBJECT/CONTROL	PROPERTY	VALUE
CheckBox	Name	chkTest
	Caption	Sieve of Eratosthenes - For
	Index	1
CheckBox	Name	chkTest
	Caption	Cone Geometry - Min
	Index	2
CheckBox	Name	chkTest
	Caption	Cone Geometry - Doubles
	Index	3
CheckBox	Name	chkTest
	Caption	Cone Geometry - Variants
	Index	4
ListBox	Name	lstPrimes
Label	Name	lblCaption
	Caption	Sieve Limit:
	Index	4
Label	Name	lblCaption
	Caption	Cone Altitudes:
	Index	3
Label	Name	lblCaption
	Caption	Cone Radii:
	Index	2
Label	Name	lblCaption
	Caption	Prime Numbers:
	Index	0
Menu	Name	mnuFile
	Caption	&File
Menu	Name	mnuFileSel
	Caption	E&xit
	Index	0
Menu	Name	mnuTest
	Caption	&Run Test

15. Place this next piece of code in the general declarations section of the form that was just added to the project. A variable is declared to store a computed value for pi.

```
Option Explicit

' The value for this variable will be computed
' and then used as a constant
Dim PI                          As Double
```

16. Add the following code to the form's **Load** event. First, a value is computed for pi. The variable containing pi is used as a constant in the rest of the program. The code then loads and configures the form that stores and displays the test results.

```
Private Sub Form_Load()

' Compute a value for PI
PI = 4 * Atn(1)

' Load and position the test results form
Load frmResults
frmResults.Top = Me.Top + _
                Me.Height + 10
frmResults.Left = Me.Left
frmResults.Show

End Sub
```

17. Put the following code into the **Click** event of the File Exit menu to unload the form and exit from the application.

```
Private Sub mnuFileSel_Click(Index As Integer)

Select Case Index
    Case 0
        Unload Me

End Select

End Sub
```

18. Add the following code to the form's **Unload** event to unload the test results form and allow the program to exit gracefully.

```
Private Sub Form_Unload(Cancel As Integer)

' Unload the results form so the application can exit
On Error Resume Next
Unload frmResults
On Error GoTo 0

End Sub
```

19. The master control logic for the test executions is put into the **Click** event of the Run Test menu. First, the user-supplied test limit values are obtained from the text boxes on the form. The code then loops though the check boxes and performs the specific requested tests.

A number of common steps are performed for each test, and they are bracketed around the execution of each test. Initially, the caption of the current test check box is changed to red. Then the test start time is recorded. After each test, the end time is saved, causing the test results to be added to the grid, and the check box caption color is restored.

```vb
Private Sub mnuTest_Click()

Dim nLoopCtr            As Integer
Dim nRadii              As Integer
Dim nAltitudes          As Integer
Dim lLimit              As Long

' Set the mouse pointer to show that we are busy
Me.MousePointer = vbHourglass

' Get the data values and limits from the text boxes
lLimit = CLng(Val(txtLimit.Text))
nRadii = CInt(Val(txtRadii.Text))
nAltitudes = CInt(Val(txtAltitudes.Text))

' Loop through the check boxes to see which individual tests
' have been selected
For nLoopCtr = 0 To 4
    If chkTest(nLoopCtr).Value = vbChecked Then
        ' Highlight the selected to test to show it is being run
        chkTest(nLoopCtr).ForeColor = vbRed
        chkTest(nLoopCtr).Refresh

        ' Set the test name and comments for each test, then run
        ' it
        Select Case nLoopCtr
            Case 0
                ' Set test results properties
                frmResults.TestName = "Eratosthenes - Do+"
                frmResults.TestComments = lLimit & " values"
                ' Record the test start time
                frmResults.TestStart
                ' Perform the test
                Call Sieve1(lLimit)

            Case 1
                ' Set test results properties
                frmResults.TestName = "Eratosthenes - For"
                frmResults.TestComments = lLimit & " values"
                ' Record the test start time
                frmResults.TestStart
                ' Perform the test
                Call Sieve2(lLimit)

            Case 2
                ' Set test results properties
                frmResults.TestName = "Cone geometry - Min"
                frmResults.TestComments = nRadii & " radii, " & _
                            nAltitudes & " alts"
                ' Record the test start time
```

```
            frmResults.TestStart
            ' Perform the test
            Call ConeGeometryMin(nRadii, nAltitudes)

        Case 3
            ' Set test results properties
            frmResults.TestName = "Cone geometry - Dbl"
            frmResults.TestComments = nRadii & " radii, " & _
                        nAltitudes & " alts "
            ' Record the test start time
            frmResults.TestStart
            ' Perform the test
            Call ConeGeometryDbl(nRadii, nAltitudes)

        Case 4
            ' Set test results properties
            frmResults.TestName = "Cone geometry - Vnt"
            frmResults.TestComments = nRadii & " radii, " & _
                        nAltitudes & " alts "
            ' Record the test start time
            frmResults.TestStart
            ' Perform the test
            Call ConeGeometryVnt(nRadii, nAltitudes)

    End Select

    ' Record the test end time
    frmResults.TestEnd

    ' Remove the highlight from the current test
    chkTest(nLoopCtr).ForeColor = vbButtonText
    chkTest(nLoopCtr).Refresh

    End If

Next nLoopCtr

' Put the mouse pointer back to the default
Me.MousePointer = vbDefault

End Sub
```

20. The next three subroutines are all variations of the same process. Each one computes four attributes of solid cones with various heights and base diameters. Add this first subroutine, which performs all the computations using variables of the smallest possible data type that successfully gets the desired results.

```
Private Sub ConeGeometryMin _
            (nRadii As Integer, _
             nAltitudes As Integer)

' Compute cone geometry using the smallest possible
' variable data types
Dim nRadius                As Integer
```

continued on next page

continued from previous page

```
Dim nAltitude              As Integer
Dim sLateral               As Single
Dim sBaseArea              As Single
Dim sLateralArea           As Single
Dim sVolume                As Single

' Once through for each possible radius and altitude
For nRadius = 1 To nRadii
    For nAltitude = 1 To nAltitudes
        ' Determine the lateral height of the cone
        sLateral = Sqr(nAltitude ^ 2 + nRadius ^ 2)
        ' Calculate the area of the base
        sBaseArea = PI * (nRadius ^ 2)
        ' Compute the lateral surface area
        sLateralArea = PI * nRadius * sLateral
        ' Figure the total volume
        sVolume = (1 / 3) * PI * (nRadius ^ 2) * nAltitude
    Next nAltitude
Next nRadius

End Sub
```

21. Add the second cone geometry subroutine, which performs all the same computations, except it uses double precision variables.

```
Private Sub ConeGeometryDbl _
            (nRadii As Integer, _
            nAltitudes As Integer)

' Compute cone geometry using only double precision variables
Dim dRadius                As Double
Dim dAltitude              As Double
Dim dLateral               As Double
Dim dBaseArea              As Double
Dim dLateralArea           As Double
Dim dVolume                As Double

' Once through for each possible radius and altitude
For dRadius = 1 To nRadii
    For dAltitude = 1 To nAltitudes
        ' Determine the lateral height of the cone
        dLateral = Sqr(dAltitude ^ 2 + dRadius ^ 2)
        ' Calculate the area of the base
        dBaseArea = PI * (dRadius ^ 2)
        ' Compute the lateral surface area
        dLateralArea = PI * dRadius * dLateral
        ' Figure the total volume
        dVolume = (1 / 3) * PI * (dRadius ^ 2) * dAltitude
    Next dAltitude
Next dRadius

End Sub
```

22. Add the third cone geometry subroutine, which performs all the computations, but defines all the variables as variants.

```
Private Sub ConeGeometryVnt _
            (nRadii As Integer, _
             nAltitudes As Integer)

' Compute cone geometry using only variant variables
Dim vntRadius          As Variant
Dim vntAltitude        As Variant
Dim vntLateral         As Variant
Dim vntBaseArea        As Variant
Dim vntLateralArea     As Variant
Dim vntVolume          As Variant

' Once through for each possible radius and altitude
For vntRadius = 1 To nRadii
    For vntAltitude = 1 To nAltitudes
        ' Determine the lateral height of the cone
        vntLateral = Sqr(vntAltitude ^ 2 + vntRadius ^ 2)
        ' Calculate the area of the base
        vntBaseArea = PI * (vntRadius ^ 2)
        ' Compute the lateral surface area
        vntLateralArea = PI * vntRadius * vntLateral
        ' Figure the total volume
        vntVolume = (1 / 3) * PI * (vntRadius ^ 2) * vntAltitude
    Next vntAltitude
Next vntRadius

End Sub
```

23. The next two subroutines both determine sets of prime numbers using the Sieve of Eratosthenes with slightly different logic. This first routine is built around a **Do** loop.

The sieve operates on a fairly simple repetitive process. Start with a value of two and progress through a finite set of numbers, crossing out all multiples of two. Start back at the beginning of the set and find the next number that is not crossed out. This number is also prime. Go through the number set again and cross out all multiples of this new prime. Continue to repeat the process. All numbers that are not crossed out in the result set are primes.

```
Private Sub Sieve1(lLimit As Long)

Dim lLoopCtr          As Long
Dim lMultiCtr         As Long
Dim lPrimeCount       As Long

' Dimension the array of integer values
ReDim lValues(lLimit) As Long

' Clear the current list of primes
lstPrimes.Clear
```

continued on next page

continued from previous page

```
For lLoopCtr = 2 To lLimit
    lValues(lLoopCtr) = lLoopCtr
Next lLoopCtr

' Now run the array values through the sieve
lPrimeCount = 0
For lLoopCtr = 2 To lLimit
    If lValues(lLoopCtr) <> 0 Then
        ' The value is prime. Add it to the list
        lstPrimes.AddItem lLoopCtr
        ' ... and count it
        lPrimeCount = lPrimeCount + 1
        ' Clear all values that are multiples of
        ' this prime number
        lMultiCtr = lLoopCtr
        Do Until lMultiCtr > lLimit
            lValues(lMultiCtr) = 0
            lMultiCtr = lMultiCtr + lLoopCtr
        Loop
    End If
Next lLoopCtr

' Update the list box label
lblCaption(0).Caption = Format$(lPrimeCount, "##,###") & _
                        " Prime Numbers:"

End Sub
```

24. Add the following subroutine. This Sieve of Eratosthenes routine uses the same basic logic as the previous one, except it is built with a `For...Next` loop.

```
Private Sub Sieve2(lLimit As Long)

Dim lLoopCtr        As Long
Dim lMultiCtr       As Long
Dim lPrimeCount     As Long

' Dimension the array of integer values
ReDim lValues(lLimit) As Long

' Clear the current list of primes
lstPrimes.Clear

For lLoopCtr = 2 To lLimit
    lValues(lLoopCtr) = lLoopCtr
Next lLoopCtr

' Now run the array values through the sieve
lPrimeCount = 0
```

```
For lLoopCtr = 2 To lLimit
    If lValues(lLoopCtr) <> 0 Then
        ' The value is prime. Add it to the list
        lstPrimes.AddItem lLoopCtr
        ' ... and count it
        lPrimeCount = lPrimeCount + 1
        ' Clear all values that are multiples of
        ' this prime number
        For lMultiCtr = lLoopCtr To lLimit Step lLoopCtr
            lValues(lMultiCtr) = 0
        Next lMultiCtr
    End If
Next lLoopCtr

' Update the list box label
lblCaption(0).Caption = Format$(lPrimeCount, "##,###") & _
                    " Prime Numbers:"

End Sub
```

How It Works

The program performs two types of computations in a few different ways. There are two variations of the Sieve of Eratosthenes that use different algorithms. The three variations of the cone geometry calculations use different variable data types. As each test is run, the test performance is recorded and saved in a grid. These test results can then be printed or exported to a CSV file. The exported file can be imported into a spreadsheet program for further analysis.

The Limit, Altitudes, and Radii fields are all moved into Long Integer variables. Using larger and larger whole number values causes the program to run for incrementally longer periods of time.

Comments

The number of iterations for the tests in this program are very high, which indicates that the overall compute performance is fairly good. However, the results indicate that there are not any statistically significant differences between the sieve algorithms, or the variable data types. This leads to the conclusion that for these specific computations, the computer itself is the major performance factor.

When the COMPUTE PERFORMANCE project is run on different machines, the test results show significant variations. This shows that testing and performance evaluations that rely primarily on investigating code logic are not always conclusive.

7.2 How do I...
Evaluate graphics performance?

COMPATIBILITY: VISUAL BASIC 6

Problem

The application I am writing relies on some extensive manipulation of graphics and images, and there is some concern that the code will be too slow to meet its performance expectations. I am not sure how to determine the factors that influence graphics performance. How do I evaluate, document, and analyze the graphics performance of a program to find potential areas that can be improved, and understand which properties and techniques yield optimum performance?

Technique

To evaluate graphics performance, this How-To performs the same graphic manipulation three different ways. The user of the program is allowed to enable and disable the `AutoRedraw` and `Visible` properties to see the impact they have on performance. One other aspect of graphics activity that has a significant effect on performance is the type and size of graphic file involved in the operation. The user can browse and select a graphics file that is then used in the tiling operation. This project supports the following graphics file formats:

- ✔ ICO
- ✔ GIF
- ✔ BMP
- ✔ JPG

All the graphics operations take place in a separate target form. The test results are recorded in a grid. Another feature of this How-To lets the results be printed or exported to a CSV file, which can then be imported into a spreadsheet for further analysis.

This How-To uses the test results form that was written in How-To 7.1. Refer to the first 12 steps of that How-To for details on its implementation.

Steps

Open and run GRAPHICS PERFORMANCE.VBP. Select some of the test check boxes, as shown in Figure 7.3.

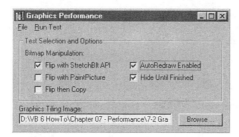

Figure 7.3 The main form at runtime.

Figure 7.4 shows sample results of a test using an ICO file.

Figure 7.4 The results of a test with an ICO file.

Select the Run Test menu. Make some other test selections and run the tests again. Figure 7.5 shows a series of results using different property values for each test.

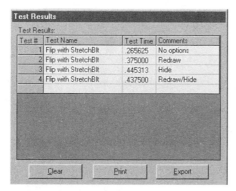

Figure 7.5 The results form for a test series.

To create this project, complete the following steps:

1. Create a new project called GRAPHICS PERFORMANCE.VBP.

2. Make a copy of the test results form, TEST RESULTS.FRM, from How-To 7.1 and add it to this project.

3. Add a form to the project and set the objects and properties as they are listed in Table 7.3. Be sure to add the Common Dialog control to the project. Save the form as GRAPHICS PERFORMANCE.FRM.

Table 7.3   The Main Form's Objects and Properties

OBJECT/CONTROL	PROPERTY	VALUE
Form	Name	frmMain
	Caption	Graphics Performance
Frame	Name	fraTest
	Caption	Test Selection and Options
CheckBox	Name	chkInvisible
	Caption	Hide Until Finished
CheckBox	Name	chkRedraw
	Caption	AutoRedraw Enabled
CheckBox	Name	chkTest
	Caption	Flip with StretchBlt API
	Index	0
CheckBox	Name	chkTest
	Caption	Flip with PaintPicture
	Index	1
CheckBox	Name	chkTest
	Caption	Flip then Copy
	Index	2
Label	Name	lblCaption
	Caption	Bitmap Manipulation:
	Index	0
Label	Name	lblCaption
	Caption	Graphics Tiling Image:
	Index	1
Menu	Name	mnuFile
	Caption	&File
Menu	Name	mnuFileSel
	Caption	E&xit
	Index	0

OBJECT/CONTROL	PROPERTY	VALUE
Menu	Name	mnuTest
	Caption	&Run Test
CommandButton	Name	cmdBrowse
	Caption	Browse ...
CommonDialog	Name	dlgCommon
TextBox	Name	txtTileFile
	Locked	-1 ' True

4. Place the following code segment in the form's **Load** event. This code loads and configures the form that stores and displays the test results.

```
Private Sub Form_Load()

' Set the default value of the tiling graphic
txtTileFile = App.Path & "\Arrow.bmp"

' Load and position the test results form
Load frmResults
frmResults.Top = Me.Top + _
                Me.Height + 10
frmResults.Left = Me.Left
frmResults.Show

End Sub
```

5. Add the following code to the **Unload** event of the form. It unloads the graphics target and test results forms in case they were not unloaded by the user.

```
Private Sub Form_Unload(Cancel As Integer)

' Unload the target and results forms
' so the application can exit
On Error Resume Next
Unload frmTarget
Unload frmResults
On Error GoTo 0

End Sub
```

6. Put the following code into the **Click** event of the File Exit menu to unload the form and exit from the application.

```
Private Sub mnuFileSel_Click(Index As Integer)

Select Case Index
    Case 0
        Unload Me
```

continued on next page

continued from previous page

```
        End Select

        End Sub
```

7. The master control logic for the test executions is in this next subroutine, which is put into the **Click** event of the Run Test menu. First, the user-supplied graphic properties are obtained from the check boxes on the form. The code then loops though the test selection check boxes and performs the requested tests.

A number of common steps are performed for each test, and they are bracketed around the execution of the tests themselves. Initially, the caption of the current test check box is changed to red. Then the graphics target form is unloaded and reloaded, and the test start time is recorded. After each test, the end time is saved, causing the test results to be added to the grid, and the check box caption color is restored.

```
Private Sub mnuTest_Click()

Dim nLoopCtr            As Integer
Dim sOptions            As String
Dim bRedraw             As Boolean
Dim bVisible            As Boolean
Dim sTileFile           As String

' Set the mouse pointer to show that we are busy
Me.MousePointer = vbHourglass

' Initialize the test variables
sOptions = ""
bRedraw = False
bVisible = True
sTileFile = txtTileFile.Text

' See if the tests are to be run with redraw on or off
If chkRedraw.Value = vbChecked Then
    bRedraw = True
    sOptions = "Redraw"
End If

' Find out if the test is run with controls and forms
' visible or not
If chkInvisible.Value = vbChecked Then
    bVisible = False
    If Len(sOptions) = 0 Then
        sOptions = "Hide"
      Else
        sOptions = sOptions & "/Hide"
    End If
End If

If Len(sOptions) = 0 Then
    sOptions = "No options"
End If
```

```vb
For nLoopCtr = 0 To 2
    If chkTest(nLoopCtr).Value = vbChecked Then
        ' Highlight the selected test to show it is being run
        chkTest(nLoopCtr).ForeColor = vbRed
        chkTest(nLoopCtr).Refresh

        ' Unload the target form if it is loaded
        On Error Resume Next
        frmTarget.picTile(0) = LoadPicture("")
        Unload frmTarget
        DoEvents
        On Error GoTo 0
        Load frmTarget
        ' Position the graphics target form
        frmTarget.Top = Me.Top
        frmTarget.Left = Me.Left + Me.Width
        ' Load the selected graphic image into the tiling picture
        ' box
        frmTarget.picTile(0) = LoadPicture(sTileFile)

        ' Set the test name and comments for each test then run it
        Select Case nLoopCtr
            Case 0
                ' Set test results properties
                frmResults.TestName = "Flip with StretchBlt"
                frmResults.TestComments = sOptions
                ' Configure the graphics target form
                frmTarget!lblCaption.Caption = "Flip with _
                StretchBlt:"
                frmTarget.Show
                ' Record the test start time
                frmResults.TestStart
                ' Perform the test
                Call frmTarget.TileBitmapAPI(bRedraw, bVisible)

            Case 1
                ' Set test results properties
                frmResults.TestName = "Flip with PaintPicture"
                frmResults.TestComments = sOptions
                ' Configure the graphics target form
                frmTarget!lblCaption.Caption = "Flip with _
                PaintPicture:"
                frmTarget.Show
                ' Record the test start time
                frmResults.TestStart
                ' Perform the test
                Call frmTarget.TileBitmapPaint(bRedraw, bVisible)

            Case 2
                ' Set test results properties
                frmResults.TestName = "Flip then Copy"
                frmResults.TestComments = sOptions
                ' Configure the graphics target form
                frmTarget!lblCaption.Caption = "Flip then Copy:"
                frmTarget.Show
                ' Record the test start time
```

continued on next page

continued from previous page

```
                              frmResults.TestStart
                              ' Perform the test
                              Call frmTarget.TileBitmapCopy(bRedraw, bVisible)

                     End Select

                     ' Record the test end time
                     frmResults.TestEnd

                     ' Remove the highlight from the current test
                     chkTest(nLoopCtr).ForeColor = vbButtonText
                     chkTest(nLoopCtr).Refresh

                End If

        Next nLoopCtr

        ' Put the mouse pointer back to the default
        Me.MousePointer = vbDefault

        End Sub
```

8. Place the following code in the **Click** event of the **cmdBrowse** command button. This code configures the common dialog control that is then used to select a graphics file for the tiling operations.

```
Private Sub cmdBrowse_Click()

' Configure the common dialog control
dlgCommon.DialogTitle = "Select a Tiling Graphic"
dlgCommon.Flags = cdlOFNFileMustExist + _
                     cdlOFNLongNames + _
                     cdlOFNPathMustExist
dlgCommon.Filter = "Graphics (*.bmp,*.gif,*.ico,*.jpg)|" & _
                     "*.bmp;*.gif;*.ico;*.jpg"
dlgCommon.FilterIndex = 1

' Show the file open dialog
dlgCommon.ShowOpen

txtTileFile = dlgCommon.FileName

End Sub
```

9. Add a third form to the project, and set the objects and properties as they are listed in Table 7.4. Save the form as GRAPHICS TARGET.FRM. This form is used as a target for the graphics operations being evaluated. The form also contains all the code that performs the graphics operations.

Table 7.4   The Target Form's Objects and Properties

OBJECT/CONTROL	PROPERTY	VALUE
Form	Name	frmTarget
	Caption	Graphics Target
PictureBox	Name	picCapture
PictureBox	Name	picTile
	Appearance	0 'Flat
	BorderStyle	0 'None
	Index	0
	Visible	0 'False
Label	Name	lblCaption
	Caption	Test Caption:

10. Add the following code to the General Declarations section of the form. It defines a form scope variable that stores the old scale mode of the graphics target controls. It also declares the API **StretchBlt** function and a constant needed in the code.

```
Private Declare Function StretchBlt Lib "gdi32" _
        (ByVal hdc As Long, _
        ByVal x As Long, ByVal y As Long, _
        ByVal nWidth As Long, ByVal nHeight As Long, _
        ByVal hSrcDC As Long, _
        ByVal xSrc As Long, ByVal ySrc As Long, _
        ByVal nSrcWidth As Long, ByVal nSrcHeight As Long, _
        ByVal dwRop As Long) As Long

Private Const SRCCOPY = &HCC0020     ' Destination equals source

Private mnPicTotal          As Integer
Private mnOldScale          As Integer
```

11. There is fairly extensive setup required for the bitmap tiling tests. The setup logic is contained in its own subroutine, as shown in the following code. It makes sure the form has been painted, saves the current scale mode, and changes the scale mode to pixels. Next the **Redraw** and **Visible** properties are set based on the user-selected options. Then it sets the properties for the picture box that contains the tiles and for the picture box that is tiled.

```
Private Sub ConfigPreTest _
        (bRedraw As Boolean, _
        bVisible As Boolean)

' Pretest configuration for the bitmap tile tests

' Ensure that the form is painted
```

continued on next page

continued from previous page

```
frmTarget.Show

' Save the current scale mode
mnOldScale = frmTarget.ScaleMode

' Set the scale mode to pixels
Me.ScaleMode = vbPixels

' Set the redraw state using the passed parameter
Me.AutoRedraw = bRedraw

' Set the properties for the primary target picture box
picCapture.Height = picTile(0).Height * 5
picCapture.Width = picTile(0).Width * 8
picCapture.AutoRedraw = bRedraw
picCapture.Visible = bVisible
picCapture.Picture = LoadPicture()

' Set the default properties for the first element of the
' tiling picture box control array
picTile(0).ScaleMode = vbPixels
picTile(0).AutoRedraw = True
picTile(0).Visible = bVisible
picTile(0).Top = 0
picTile(0).Left = 0

Me.Refresh

' Set the visible property using the input parameter
Me.Visible = bVisible

End Sub
```

12. Also, a number of post-test steps need to be performed for the tiling operations. First, all the controls are made visible. Then the scale mode is restored, and the target form is resized so that all the tiles can be seen. Add the following private subroutine to the form:

```
Private Sub ConfigPostTest _
            (bRedraw As Boolean, _
             bVisible As Boolean)

' Post-test configuration for the bitmap tile tests

Dim nLoopCtr            As Integer

' Restore visibility of the form and controls as needed
If bVisible = False Then
    ' There is some invisible stuff to fix
    Me.Visible = True
    picCapture.Visible = True
    ' Once for each tiled control
    For nLoopCtr = 0 To 39
        picTile(nLoopCtr).Visible = True
    Next nLoopCtr
End If
```

```
' Restore the old scale mode
Me.ScaleMode = mnOldScale

' Resize the form so the whole picture box shows
Me.Height = Me.Height - _
            Me.ScaleHeight + _
            picCapture.Top + _
            picCapture.Height

Me.Width = Me.Width - _
           Me.ScaleWidth + _
           picCapture.Left + _
           picCapture.Width

End Sub
```

13. The next three subroutines all tile bitmaps. All three of them use the same basic logic for the tiling, but each one uses a different technique to manipulate the bitmaps. This first routine uses the **StretchBlt** API to perform the actual graphic operations. Add them all to the form.

The logic starts by setting the **Caption** property of a label control to let the user know which graphic technique is being used. Then it calls the pretest configuration subroutine. Because embedded property references are time consuming, the code saves the height and width of the tiling bitmap in variables. These variables are then used in the rest of the routine, instead of using repeated references to the control properties.

The code then loops through by row and then by column, copying and flipping the bitmap tiles. When the tiling is finished, the post-test subroutine is called.

```
Public Sub TileBitmapAPI _
           (bRedraw As Boolean, _
            bVisible As Boolean)

Dim nLoopRow        As Integer
Dim nLoopCol        As Integer
Dim nPicCount       As Integer
Dim nPicWidth       As Integer
Dim nPicHeight      As Integer
Dim hDCSource       As Long
Dim hDCDest         As Long
Dim lResult         As Long

lblCaption.Caption = "Tiled using API:"

Call ConfigPreTest(bRedraw, bVisible)

' Save working reference copies of the tile picture box
' control array dimensions
nPicWidth = picTile(0).Width
nPicHeight = picTile(0).Height
```

continued on next page

continued from previous page

```vb
' Initialize the current control array element count
nPicCount = 1


' Flip each time with StretchBlt
For nLoopRow = 0 To 4
    If nLoopRow > 0 Then
        ' Load the first picture in the row
        ' Create a new picture box instance
        Load picTile(nPicCount)
        ' Redraw is required by the API function
        picTile(nPicCount).AutoRedraw = True
        ' Set visibility using the parameter
        picTile(nPicCount).Visible = bVisible
        ' Clear it out
        picTile(nPicCount).Picture = LoadPicture()
        ' Move it to the proper tiling location
        picTile(nPicCount).Left = 0
        picTile(nPicCount).Top = nPicHeight * nLoopRow
        ' Set the scale mode for the API call
        picTile(nPicCount).ScaleMode = vbPixels
        ' The first one is always a copy of element 0
        picTile(nPicCount).Picture = picTile(0).Picture
        ' Increment the control array pointer
        nPicCount = nPicCount + 1
    End If
    For nLoopCol = 1 To 7
        ' Load the remaining picture tiles in the row
        ' Create a new picture box instance
        Load picTile(nPicCount)
        ' Redraw is required by the API function
        picTile(nPicCount).AutoRedraw = True
        ' Set visibility using the parameter
        picTile(nPicCount).Visible = bVisible
        ' Clear it out
        picTile(nPicCount).Picture = LoadPicture()
        ' Move it to the proper tiling location
        picTile(nPicCount).Left = nPicWidth * nLoopCol
        picTile(nPicCount).Top = nPicHeight * nLoopRow
        ' Set the scale mode for the API call
        picTile(nPicCount).ScaleMode = vbPixels
        ' Get the source and destination device context handles
        hDCSource = picTile(nPicCount - 1).hdc
        hDCDest = picTile(nPicCount).hdc
        ' Copy and flip the image based on the column
        Select Case nLoopCol Mod 2
            Case 0              ' Flip on X axis
                lResult = StretchBlt(hDCDest, _
                        0&, nPicHeight - 1, _
                        nPicWidth, -nPicHeight, _
                        hDCSource, _
                        0&, 0&, _
                        nPicWidth, nPicHeight, _
                        SRCCOPY&)

            Case 1              ' Flip on Y axis
                lResult = StretchBlt(hDCDest, _
                        nPicWidth - 1, 0&, _
```

```
                                      -nPicWidth, nPicHeight, _
                                      hDCSource, _
                                      0&, 0&, _
                                      nPicWidth, nPicHeight, _
                                      SRCCOPY&)
              End Select
              ' Increment the control array pointer
              nPicCount = nPicCount + 1
         Next nLoopCol
    Next nLoopRow

    ' Save the number of picture boxes created
    mnPicTotal = nPicCount

    Call ConfigPostTest(bRedraw, bVisible)

    End Sub
```

14. Add this second tiling routine, which uses the **PaintPicture** method to perform the actual graphic operations. It uses the same logic as that described for the subroutine in step 13.

```
Public Sub TileBitmapPaint _
            (bRedraw As Boolean, _
             bVisible As Boolean)

Dim nLoopRow          As Integer
Dim nLoopCol          As Integer
Dim nPicCount         As Integer
Dim nPicWidth         As Integer
Dim nPicHeight        As Integer

lblCaption.Caption = "Tiled using PaintPicture:"

Call ConfigPreTest(bRedraw, bVisible)

' Save working reference copies of the tile picture box
' control array dimensions
nPicWidth = picTile(0).Width
nPicHeight = picTile(0).Height

' Initialize the current control array element count
nPicCount = 1

' Flip each time with PaintPicture
picCapture.Picture = LoadPicture()
For nLoopRow = 0 To 4
    If nLoopRow > 0 Then
         ' Load the first picture in the row
         ' Create a new picture box instance
         Load picTile(nPicCount)
         ' Redraw is required by PaintPicture
         picTile(nPicCount).AutoRedraw = True
         ' Set visibility using the parameter
         picTile(nPicCount).Visible = bVisible
         ' Clear it out
```

continued on next page

continued from previous page

```
                picTile(nPicCount).Picture = LoadPicture()
                ' Move it to the proper tiling location
                picTile(nPicCount).Left = 0
                picTile(nPicCount).Top = nPicHeight * nLoopRow
                ' Set the scale mode for PaintPicture
                picTile(nPicCount).ScaleMode = vbPixels
                ' The first one is always a copy of element 0
                picTile(nPicCount).Picture = picTile(0).Picture
                ' Increment the control array pointer
                nPicCount = nPicCount + 1
            End If
            For nLoopCol = 1 To 7
                ' Load the remaining picture tiles in the row
                ' Create a new picture box instance
                Load picTile(nPicCount)
                ' Redraw is required by the API function
                picTile(nPicCount).AutoRedraw = True
                ' Set visibility using the parameter
                picTile(nPicCount).Visible = bVisible
                ' Clear it out
                picTile(nPicCount).Picture = LoadPicture()
                ' Move it to the proper tiling location
                picTile(nPicCount).Left = nPicWidth * nLoopCol
                picTile(nPicCount).Top = nPicHeight * nLoopRow
                ' Set the scale mode for the API call
                picTile(nPicCount).ScaleMode = vbPixels
                Select Case nLoopCol Mod 2
                    Case 0              ' Flip on X axis
                        picTile(nPicCount).PaintPicture _
                                picTile(nPicCount - 1).Image, _
                                0, nPicHeight - 1, _
                                nPicWidth, -nPicHeight, _
                                0, 0, _
                                nPicWidth, nPicHeight, _
                                vbSrcCopy
                    Case 1              ' Flip on Y axis
                        picTile(nPicCount).PaintPicture _
                                picTile(nPicCount - 1).Image, _
                                nPicWidth - 1, 0, _
                                -nPicWidth, nPicHeight, _
                                0, 0, _
                                nPicWidth, nPicHeight, _
                                vbSrcCopy
                End Select
                ' Increment the control array pointer
                nPicCount = nPicCount + 1
            Next nLoopCol
        Next nLoopRow

        ' Save the number of picture boxes created
        mnPicTotal = nPicCount

        Call ConfigPostTest(bRedraw, bVisible)

End Sub
```

15. Add the third tiling routine, which uses the `PaintPicture` method to flip the tiles on the first row. Then it just copies the tile bitmaps for all the subsequent rows. The structural logic from the subroutine in step 13 is also used here.

```
Public Sub TileBitmapCopy _
              (bRedraw As Boolean, _
               bVisible As Boolean)

Dim nLoopRow          As Integer
Dim nLoopCol          As Integer
Dim nPicCount         As Integer
Dim nPicWidth         As Integer
Dim nPicHeight        As Integer

lblCaption.Caption = "Tiled using Flip and Copy"

Call ConfigPreTest(bRedraw, bVisible)

' Save working reference copies of the tile picture box
' control array dimensions
nPicWidth = picTile(0).Width
nPicHeight = picTile(0).Height

' Initialize the current control array element count
nPicCount = 1

' Fill in the first row of flipped images
nLoopRow = 0
For nLoopCol = 1 To 7
    ' Create a new picture box instance
    Load picTile(nPicCount)
    ' Redraw is required by PaintPicture
    picTile(nPicCount).AutoRedraw = True
    ' Set visibility using the parameter
    picTile(nPicCount).Visible = bVisible
    ' Clear it out
    picTile(nPicCount).Picture = LoadPicture()
        ' Move it to the proper tiling location
    picTile(nPicCount).Left = nPicWidth * nLoopCol
    picTile(nPicCount).Top = nPicHeight * nLoopRow
    ' Set the scale mode for the API call
    picTile(nPicCount).ScaleMode = vbPixels
    Select Case nLoopCol Mod 2
        Case 0          ' Flip on X axis
            picTile(nPicCount).PaintPicture _
                    picTile(nPicCount - 1).Image, _
                    0, nPicHeight - 1, _
                    nPicWidth, -nPicHeight, _
                    0, 0, _
                    nPicWidth, nPicHeight, _
                    vbSrcCopy
        Case 1          ' Flip on Y axis
            picTile(nPicCount).PaintPicture _
                    picTile(nPicCount - 1).Image, _
                    nPicWidth - 1, 0, _
```

continued on next page

continued from previous page

```
                        -nPicWidth, nPicHeight, _
                        0, 0, _
                        nPicWidth, nPicHeight, _
                        vbSrcCopy
        End Select
        ' Increment the control array pointer
        nPicCount = nPicCount + 1
    Next nLoopCol

    ' Load the tiles into the other rows
    For nLoopCol = 0 To 7
        For nLoopRow = 1 To 4
            Load picTile(nPicCount)
            ' Redraw is required by the API function
            picTile(nPicCount).AutoRedraw = bRedraw
            ' Set visibility using the parameter
            picTile(nPicCount).Visible = bVisible
            ' Clear it out
            picTile(nPicCount).Picture = LoadPicture()
            ' Move it to the proper tiling location
            picTile(nPicCount).Left = nPicWidth * nLoopCol
            picTile(nPicCount).Top = nPicHeight * nLoopRow
            ' *** Don't need to set scale mode this time
            'picTile(nPicCount).ScaleMode = vbPixels
            ' Copy the picture from the element at the top of the
            ' column
            picTile(nPicCount).Picture = picTile(nLoopCol).Image
            ' Increment the control array pointer
            nPicCount = nPicCount + 1
        Next nLoopRow
    Next nLoopCol

    ' Save the number of picture boxes created
    mnPicTotal = nPicCount

    Call ConfigPostTest(bRedraw, bVisible)

End Sub
```

16. Add the following code to the target form's Unload event. This code
unloads any tiling picture boxes and then sets the form itself equal to
Nothing. When the form is set to Nothing, all variable storage is released
and the form is completely removed from memory.

```
Private Sub Form_Unload(Cancel As Integer)

Dim nLoopCtr                As Integer

On Error Resume Next

' Unload all possible control instances
For nLoopCtr = mnPicTotal To 1 Step -1
    Unload picTile(nLoopCtr)
Next nLoopCtr
```

```
    On Error GoTo 0

    ' Make the form really go away
    Set frmTarget = Nothing

    End Sub
```

How It Works

The How-To examines the factors that affect the performance of graphics operations. The factors are the method used to perform the operation, the properties of the controls involved, and the type and size of the graphic that is manipulated. Three different algorithms are used to work with an image in a picture box, using different functions, methods, and techniques to get the same final result. As each test is run, the test performance is recorded and saved in a grid. These test results can then be printed or exported to a CSV file. The exported file can be imported into a spreadsheet program for further analysis.

Comments

There are statistically significant variations in the test results. The key factors in application-based graphics performance are the size of the images being manipulated and the state of the `AutoRedraw` and `Visible` properties. An important, but less significant, factor is to avoid manipulating an image that can be moved or copied. This is shown in the test results for the Flip then Copy test, which is fastest in all situations.

Hardware also plays a major role in graphics performance. You should test the graphics performance of your applications on the minimum configuration you intend to support. When checking graphics performance, it is also vital that the testing be done on identically configured machines.

COMPLEXITY
INTERMEDIATE

7.3 How do I...
Understand and perform static code analysis?

COMPATIBILITY: VISUAL BASIC 5 AND 6

Problem

I need a process to evaluate my code for planning and quality purposes. I want to make sure there is a good ratio of code to comments and that the code is not overly complex. A rating of code complexity can also allow me to target specific modules or routines for more extensive unit and system testing. How do I gather statistics on my code, determine its complexity, and decide whether it will be easy for others to understand?

Technique

This How-To demonstrates a technique for performing static analysis on a Visual Basic module. *Static analysis* is a passive statistical process that evaluates source code and does not involve execution of the program. The user selects a module to analyze, and the results of the analysis are presented in a grid. The analysis counts the total number of lines in each routine of the module. The number of comments provides a measure of understandability, so comments are also counted.

The evaluation of complexity involves more than just counting lines of code or comments. To do this, the program counts decision points in the code. Decision points are logical or conditional statements. The program uses a counting technique know as the McCabe Complexity Scale. This counting technique starts with one for each routine, adds one for each decision point, and adds another one for each **Case** statement in a **Select Case** structure.

Steps

Open and run STATIC ANALYSIS.VBP. The running program is shown in Figure 7.6.

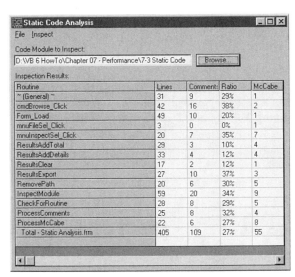

Routine	Lines	Comments	Ratio	McCabe
~ (General) ~	31	9	29%	1
cmdBrowse_Click	42	16	38%	2
Form_Load	49	10	20%	1
mnuFileSel_Click	3	0	0%	1
mnuInspectSel_Click	20	7	35%	7
ResultsAddTotal	29	3	10%	4
ResultsAddDetails	33	4	12%	4
ResultsClear	17	2	12%	1
ResultsExport	27	10	37%	3
RemovePath	20	6	30%	5
InspectModule	59	20	34%	9
CheckForRoutine	28	8	29%	5
ProcessComments	25	8	32%	4
ProcessMcCabe	22	6	27%	8
Total - Static Analysis.frm	405	109	27%	55

Figure 7.6 The main form at runtime.

Click the Browse command button to open the file dialog box shown in Figure 7.7.

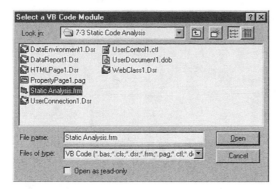

Figure 7.7 The module selection dialog box.

Complete the following steps to create this project:

1. Create a new project called STATIC ANALYSIS.VBP.

2. Add a form to the project and set the objects and properties as they are listed in Table 7.5. Make sure that the Microsoft FlexGrid control is added to the project. Save the form as STATIC ANALYSIS.FRM.

Table 7.5 The Project Form's Objects and Properties

OBJECT/CONTROL	PROPERTY	VALUE
Form	Name	frmMain
	Caption	Static Code Analysis
CommonDialog	Name	dlgCommon
CommandButton	Name	cmdBrowse
	Caption	Browse...
TextBox	Name	txtFile
	Locked	-1 'True
	TabStop	0 'False
MSFlexGrid	Name	grdResults
	AllowUserResizing	1 'ResizeColumns
	Appearance	0 'Flat
	Cols	5
	Rows	2
Label	Name	lblCaption
	Caption	Code Module to Inspect:
	Index	0

continued on next page

continued from previous page

OBJECT/CONTROL	PROPERTY	VALUE
Label	Name	lblCaption
	Caption	Inspection Results:
	Index	1
Menu	Name	mnuFile
	Caption	&File
Menu	Name	mnuFileSel
	Caption	E&xit
	Index	0
Menu	Name	mnuTest
	Caption	&Inspect
Menu	Name	mnuInspectSel
	Caption	&Inspect Module
	Enabled	0 'False
	Index	0
Menu	Name	mnuInspectSel
	Caption	-
	Index	1
Menu	Name	mnuInspectSel
	Caption	&Clear Results
	Index	2
Menu	Name	mnuInspectSel
	Caption	&Export Results
	Index	3

3. Put the following code in the General Declarations section of the form. The code defines the variables used in the program. These variables store variant arrays of parsing keywords, reference pointers for the analysis results grid, line count, total accumulators, and filenames and locations.

```
Option Explicit

' Define variants to hold keyword parsing arrays
Private msKeywords        As Variant
Private msRoutines        As Variant

' Pointer to the current row in the results grid
Private mnCurrentRow      As Integer

' Module scope variables to store incremental
' counters for routine level information
Private mlLines           As Long
Private mlComments        As Long
```

```
Private mlMcCabe              As Long

' Module scope variables to store incremental
' counters for module level totals
Private mlTotLines            As Long
Private mlTotComments         As Long
Private mlTotMcCabe           As Long

' Filename and extension of current code module
Private msMainName            As String

' Fully qualified path and filename of current module
Private msCurrentFile         As String

' Name of the current routine in the current module
Private msRoutineName         As String
```

4. Place the following code segment in the form's **Load** event. These statements set the grid column titles and attributes. This grid is used to display the results of the code analysis. Then the variant arrays are loaded with the code parsing keywords. There are two sets of keywords. The first contains the Visual Basic verbs and syntax statements that perform logical operations. These verbs represent decision points and are used to determine the McCabe complexity of each routine. The second set of syntax keywords is the group that starts new subroutines and functions.

```
Private Sub Form_Load()

' Configure the results grid

' Start with the first row
grdResults.Row = 0

' Set the width and caption of the first column
grdResults.Col = 0
grdResults.ColWidth(0) = 3500
grdResults.FixedAlignment(0) = vbLeftJustify
grdResults.Text = "Routine"

' Set the width and caption of the second column
grdResults.Col = 1
grdResults.ColWidth(1) - 800
grdResults.ColAlignment(1) = vbCenter
grdResults.FixedAlignment(1) = vbCenter
grdResults.Text = "Lines"

' Set the width and caption of the third column
grdResults.Col = 2
grdResults.ColWidth(2) = 800
grdResults.ColAlignment(2) = vbCenter
grdResults.FixedAlignment(2) = vbCenter
grdResults.Text = "Comments"
```

continued on next page

continued from previous page

```
' Set the width and caption of the fourth column
grdResults.Col = 3
grdResults.ColWidth(3) = 800
grdResults.ColAlignment(3) = vbCenter
grdResults.FixedAlignment(3) = vbCenter
grdResults.Text = "Ratio"

' Set the width and caption of the fifth column
grdResults.Col = 4
grdResults.Text = "McCabe"
grdResults.ColWidth(4) = 800
grdResults.FixedAlignment(4) = vbCenter
grdResults.ColAlignment(4) = vbCenter

' Set the variable that points to the first usable grid row
mnCurrentRow = 1

' Load the decision point keywords for McCabe complexity analysis
msKeywords = Array("SELECT CASE", "FOR", "DO", _
                "WHILE", "UNTIL", "IIF", "CHOOSE", _
                "SWITCH", "IF", "ELSEIF", "#IF", "#ELSEIF", _
                "CASE ", "AND ", "OR ")

' Load the routine start keyword array
msRoutines = Array("SUB ", "FUNCTION ", "PROPERTY ", "EVENT ", _
                "PUBLIC SUB ", "PUBLIC FUNCTION ", _
                "PUBLIC PROPERTY ", "PUBLIC EVENT ", _
                "PRIVATE SUB ", "PRIVATE FUNCTION ", _
                "PRIVATE PROPERTY ", "PRIVATE EVENT ", _
                "FRIEND SUB ", "FRIEND FUNCTION ", _
                "FRIEND PROPERTY ", "FRIEND EVENT ")

End Sub
```

5. The `Click` event of the `cmdBrowse` command button configures and
displays a common dialog box used to locate and select a code module for
analysis. If a code module is selected, the routine updates the read-only
text box with the module name and then enables the Inspect Module
menu item on the Inspect menu. If a code mode was not selected in the
dialog box, the text box is cleared, and the menu item is disabled.

```
Private Sub cmdBrowse_Click()

' Configure the common dialog control to select a module

' Set the dialog title
dlgCommon.DialogTitle = "Select a VB Code Module"

' Establish the file filter options
dlgCommon.Filter = "VB Code " & _
        "(*.bas;*.cls;*.dsr;*.frm;*.pag;*.ctl;*.dob)¦" & _
        "*.bas;*.cls;*.dsr;*.frm;*.pag;*.ctl;*.dob¦" & _
        "Class Modules (*.cls)¦*.cls¦" & _
        "Code Modules (*.bas)¦*.bas¦" & _
        "Designer Modules (*.dsr)¦*.dsr¦" & _
```

```
              "Form Modules (*.frm)¦*.frm¦" & _
              "Property Pages (*.pag)¦*.pag¦" & _
              "User Control (*.ctl)¦*.ctl¦" & _
              "User Document (*.dob)¦*.dob¦" & _
              "All Files (*.*)¦*.*"

       ' Set the current filter to the first one available
       dlgCommon.FilterIndex = 1

       ' Require that the path and file exist
       dlgCommon.Flags = cdlOFNFileMustExist + cdlOFNPathMustExist

       ' Now show the file open dialog
       dlgCommon.ShowOpen

       ' Get the fully qualified filename that the user selected
       msCurrentFile = dlgCommon.FileName

       ' See if we actually have a filename
       If Len(msCurrentFile) > 0 Then
           ' We have one so ...
           ' Show the selected file in the text box
           txtFile.Text = msCurrentFile

           ' Pull the file and extension and save them
           msMainName = RemovePath(msCurrentFile)

           ' Enable the "Inspect" menu choice
           mnuInspectSel(0).Enabled = True

       Else

           ' No file was selected so ...
           ' Clear the text box
           txtFile.Text = ""

           ' Clear the file and extension variable
           msMainName = ""

           ' Disable the "Inspect" menu choice
           mnuInspectSel(0).Enabled = False

       End If

       End Sub
```

6. Place the following code in the **Click** event of the File Exit menu to unload the form and exit from the application:

```
Private Sub mnuFileSel_Click(Index As Integer)

Unload Me

End Sub
```

7. Put the following code block into the **Click** event of the Inspect menu. This menu is set up as a menu control array, so a **Select Case** logic structure is used to dispatch the correct code for each menu choice. The code for each choice is located in individual subroutines. If the user has selected the Inspect Module menu item, the module-level accumulators are cleared before the analysis is performed.

```
Private Sub mnuInspectSel_Click(Index As Integer)

Select Case Index
    Case 0               ' Analyze the project/module
        ' Clear the module totals
        mlTotLines = 0
        mlTotComments = 0
        mlTotMcCabe = 0

        ' Perform the inspection
        InspectModule

    Case 1               ' Separator
        ' No code required here

    Case 2               ' Clear test results
        If (MsgBox("Are you sure you want to " & _
            "clear the results?", vbCritical + vbYesNo)) = vbYes _
            Then
                Call ResultsClear
        End If

    Case 3               ' Export test results
        Call ResultsExport

End Select

End Sub
```

8. Add the following subroutine, which adds individual routine analysis results to the grid. The results are added to the current row. The variable used to address the current row is then incremented, and another row is added to the grid if necessary. The routine analysis totals are then added to the module level accumulators, and the routine totals are cleared.

```
Private Sub ResultsAddDetails()

' Add inspection results to the grid
grdResults.Row = mnCurrentRow
grdResults.Col = 1
grdResults.Text = Format$(mlLines, "###,##0")
grdResults.Col = 2
grdResults.Text = Format$(mlComments, "###,##0")
grdResults.Col = 3

If mlComments = 0 Or _
    mlLines = 0 Then
```

```
        grdResults.Text = "0%"
    Else
      grdResults.Text = Format$((mlComments / _
          mlLines) * 100, "##0") & "%"
  End If

  grdResults.Col = 4
  grdResults.Text = Format$(mlMcCabe, "###,##0")
  grdResults.Col = 0
  grdResults.Text = msRoutineName

  ' Add another row to the grid
  mnCurrentRow = mnCurrentRow + 1
  If mnCurrentRow + 1 > grdResults.Rows Then
      grdResults.Rows = mnCurrentRow + 1
  End If

  grdResults.Refresh

  ' Update the cumulative totals
  mlTotLines = mlTotLines + mlLines
  mlTotComments = mlTotComments + mlComments
  mlTotMcCabe = mlTotMcCabe + mlMcCabe

  ' Clear the routine total counters
  mlLines = 0
  mlComments = 0
  mlMcCabe = 1

End Sub
```

9. Add the following subroutine. This subroutine is almost the same as the previous one, except that it adds the module-level totals to the results grid. The results are added to the current row. The variable used to address the current row is then incremented, and another row is added to the grid if necessary. The last task the routine performs is to clear the module analysis totals and refresh the grid.

```
Private Sub ResultsAddTotal()

  ' Add module totals to the grid
  grdResults.Row = mnCurrentRow
  grdResults.Col = 1
  grdResults.Text = Format$(mlTotLines, "###,##0")
  grdResults.Col = 2
  grdResults.Text = Format$(mlTotComments, "###,##0")
  grdResults.Col = 3

  If mlTotComments = 0 Or _
    mlTotLines = 0 Then
      grdResults.Text = "0%"
    Else
      grdResults.Text = Format$((mlTotComments / _
          mlTotLines) * 100, "##0") & "%"
  End If
```

continued on next page

continued from previous page

```
grdResults.Col = 4
grdResults.Text = Format$(mlTotMcCabe, "###,##0")
grdResults.Col = 0
grdResults.Text = "  Total - " & msMainName

' Add another row to the grid
mnCurrentRow = mnCurrentRow + 1
If mnCurrentRow + 1 > grdResults.Rows Then
    grdResults.Rows = mnCurrentRow + 1
End If

' Clear the module totals we just used
mlTotLines = 0
mlTotComments = 0
mlTotMcCabe = 0

grdResults.Refresh

End Sub
```

10. To export the test results to a comma-separated value (CSV) file, add the following code to the form. The CSV file is opened in **Append** mode so that new results can be added to any existing results. The logic loops through each row of the grid and moves the data into a local string array. This array is then written to the file by using a **Write** statement. This language statement adds all the necessary CSV formatting to the output as it is being written.

```
Private Sub ResultsExport()

Dim nLoopRow            As Integer
Dim nLoopCol            As Integer
Dim nChannel            As Integer
Dim sOutput(5)          As String

' Get an available I/O channel number
nChannel = FreeFile

' Open a CSV file to store the grid contents
' Using append mode will add to the file if it exists
Open App.Path & "\Inspection - " & msMainName & _
                ".csv" For Append As #nChannel

' Loop through the grid row by row
For nLoopRow = 1 To mnCurrentRow - 1
    ' Set the current grid row
    grdResults.Row = nLoopRow

    ' Loop through the grid columns
    For nLoopCol = 0 To 4
        ' Set the current column
        grdResults.Col = nLoopCol
```

```
                  ' Save the column data to an array
                  sOutput(nLoopCol) = grdResults.Text

             Next nLoopCol

             ' Write the array contents to the CSV file
             Write #nChannel, sOutput(0), _
                             sOutput(1), _
                             sOutput(2), _
                             sOutput(3), _
                             sOutput(4)

        Next nLoopRow

        ' Close the results file
        Close #nChannel

        End Sub
```

11. Add the following subroutine to clear all test results from the grid. This is accomplished by reducing the number of grid rows to two and then clearing the remaining row of data.

```
Private Sub ResultsClear()

' Reset the grid to have only the first two rows
mnCurrentRow = 1
grdResults.Rows = 2

' Clear first data row values
grdResults.Row = mnCurrentRow
grdResults.Col = 1
grdResults.Text = ""
grdResults.Col = 2
grdResults.Text = ""
grdResults.Col = 3
grdResults.Text = ""
grdResults.Col = 4
grdResults.Text = ""
grdResults.Col = 0
grdResults.Text = ""

End Sub
```

12. The RemovePath function extracts the filename and extension from a fully qualified path and filename. This is done by scanning backward though the path and filename string to find the last occurrence of the backslash (\) or colon (:) characters. These characters represent the directory and drive name delimiters, so finding one of them means that the pointer in the string is placed at the last character of the path name. It follows that the remainder of the string from that point, plus one character, to the end of the string is the filename and extension. That portion of the string is then extracted and passed back as the return value for the function.

```
Function RemovePath(sFullName As String) As String

Dim nLoopCtr            As Integer
Dim nTempInt            As Integer
Dim sTempStr            As String

' Scan backward through the input string to find the last
' directory qualifier "\" or the drive letter delimiter.
For nLoopCtr = Len(sFullName) To 1 Step -1

    Select Case Mid$(sFullName, nLoopCtr, 1)
        Case "\", ":"
            ' We have a drive or directory delimiter
            Exit For

        Case Else
            ' Build a return value that includes all characters
            ' that have been checked
            sTempStr = Mid$(sFullName, nLoopCtr)

    End Select

Next nLoopCtr

' Send back the results
RemovePath = sTempStr

End Function
```

13. Add the following subroutine to the form. This code drives the static analysis and code inspection process for an individual code module. It begins by resetting the routine-level counters. The initial routine name is set to "~ (General) ~" and the code Visual Basic source file is opened. The first line is read from the file. Next the code enters the primary control loop for the analysis.

The program does not analyze the control description code at the beginning of form modules. When a line is found that starts with the keyword BEGIN, all the code is ignored until a corresponding END is located.

To simplify parsing the code lines, the string containing the code is converted to all uppercase, and all leading and trailing white space characters are removed. Next, a routine is called to see whether a new routine has started. If a new routine was entered in the code, the called subroutine handles all the routine processing. Then the code line is checked for comments and rated for complexity. After all code has been processed, the file is closed, and the module totals are added to the results grid.

```
Private Sub InspectModule()

Dim nChannel            As Integer
```

```vb
Dim sCodeLine          As String
Dim bInControls        As Boolean
Dim sUpcaseCode        As String

' Reset the routine counters
mlLines = 0
mlComments = 0
mlMcCabe = 1

' Set the initial routine name
msRoutineName = "~ (General) ~"

' Get an available I/O channel number
nChannel = FreeFile

' Open the selected code module for analysis
Open msCurrentFile For Input As nChannel

' Read the first line of the module
Line Input #nChannel, sCodeLine

' Loop through the rest of the module line by line

Do

    ' Check for control descriptions in form modules
    If Left$(UCase$(sCodeLine), 5) = "BEGIN" Then
        bInControls = True
    End If

    ' See if we are now out of the control descriptions
    If bInControls = True Then
        If Left$(UCase$(sCodeLine), 3) = "END" Then
            bInControls = False
        End If
    End If

    ' Simplify parsing by upcasing the line and
    ' removing all leading and trailing spaces
    sCodeLine = Trim$(sCodeLine)
    sUpcaseCode = UCase$(sCodeLine)

    If bInControls = False Then

      Select Case Len(sCodeLine)
        Case 0
            ' This is a blank line so exclude it from
            ' the processing and statistics

        Case Else
            ' See if this is the end of a routine
            Call CheckForRoutine(sCodeLine)

            ' Count the code line
            mlLines = mlLines + 1
```

continued on next page

continued from previous page

```
                              ' Check for, strip out, and count comments
                              Call ProcessComments(sUpcaseCode)

                              ' Determine the McCabe complexity value
                              Call ProcessMcCabe(sUpcaseCode)

                  End Select

              End If

              ' Get the next line of code
              Line Input #nChannel, sCodeLine

      Loop Until EOF(nChannel)

      ' Close the code module file
      Close nChannel

      ' Add the totals for the final routine
      Call ResultsAddDetails

      ' Add the module totals to the results grid
      Call ResultsAddTotal

      End Sub
```

14. The `CheckForRoutine` subroutine determines whether a new routine has been entered during the code scan. Routines are considered to be subroutines, functions, and properties. The code line is checked to see if it starts with any one of the items in the variant array of routine keywords. If one of them is found, the code calls the subroutine to add the routine-level information to the grid. Then the logic parses the new routine name out of the code line.

```
Sub CheckForRoutine(sCodeLine As String)

Dim nLoopCtr            As Integer
Dim nPosition           As Integer

' Check for blank lines
If Len(sCodeLine) = 0 Then Exit Sub

' Look for statements that start new routines in the module
For nLoopCtr = 0 To UBound(msRoutines)

    If Left$(UCase$(sCodeLine), Len(msRoutines(nLoopCtr))) = _
       msRoutines(nLoopCtr) Then
        ' The keyword is at the start of the line
        ' so this is a routine
        Call ResultsAddDetails

        ' Get the new routine name
        nPosition = InStr(1, sCodeLine, "(")
```

```
        ' If the character was not found, assume the name
        ' is all alone
        If nPosition = 0 Then
            nPosition = Len(sCodeLine)
        End If

        ' Extract the routine name from the code line
        msRoutineName = Mid$(sCodeLine, _
                        Len(msRoutines(nLoopCtr)), _
                        nPosition - Len(msRoutines(nLoopCtr)))

        ' Clean up the routine name
        msRoutineName = Trim$(msRoutineName)
        Exit For

    End If

Next nLoopCtr

End Sub
```

15. Add the following subroutine, which looks for comments in a line of code. If the first character of the code line is a comment delimiter, the comments total is incremented by one. Because the line is just a comment, and there is no code logic on the line, the code line is blanked out. Blanking the code line prevents the comments from being analyzed for complexity.

If the entire line is not a comment, the subroutine looks for inline comments. This is accomplished by scanning backward, looking for a comment delimiter. If one is found, the comment count is incremented, and the comment is removed from the code line.

Note that even though the code lines are being changed by the program, the changes are not written back to the original source file.

```
Sub ProcessComments(sCodeLine As String)

Dim nLoopCtr            As Integer
Dim nTempInt            As Integer
Dim sTempStr            As String

' See the first character is a comment delimiter
If Left$(sCodeLine, 1) = Chr$(39) Then
    ' This is a comment line, so increment the count
    mlComments = mlComments + 1

    ' Clear out the entire code line
    sCodeLine = ""
    Exit Sub

End If

' See if there is a trailing comment
```

continued on next page

continued from previous page

```
       ' Scan backward through the code line to find the
       ' comment delimiter character
       For nLoopCtr = Len(sCodeLine) To 1 Step -1

           If Mid$(sCodeLine, nLoopCtr, 1) = Chr$(39) Then
               ' There is a comment on this line, so
               ' increment the count
               mlComments = mlComments + 1

               ' Remove the comment from the code line
               sCodeLine = Left$(sCodeLine, nLoopCtr)
               Exit Sub

           End If

       Next nLoopCtr

   End Sub
```

16. Add the `ProcessMcCabe` subroutine. This logic evaluates the complexity of a line of code by counting logic decision points. It is a simple parsing routine that does not handle very complex logic structures. It looks for logic verbs at the beginning of the code line and counts those it finds. After checking for the logic verbs, there are two code segments that look for the **AND** and **OR** conditional clauses.

```
   Sub ProcessMcCabe(sCodeLine As String)

   Dim nLoopCtr            As Integer
   Dim nStart              As Integer

   ' Check for blank lines
   If Len(sCodeLine) = 0 Then Exit Sub

   ' Look for conditional statements at the start of the line
   For nLoopCtr = 0 To UBound(msKeywords)

       If Left$(sCodeLine, Len(msKeywords(nLoopCtr))) = _
                   msKeywords(nLoopCtr) Then
           ' The keyword is at the start of the line
           mlMcCabe = mlMcCabe + 1
           Exit For
       End If

   Next nLoopCtr

   ' Check for conditional clauses in the code line
   If InStr(4, sCodeLine, " AND ") > 0 Then
       ' Found a logical condition clause
       mlMcCabe = mlMcCabe + 1
   End If
```

```
If InStr(4, sCodeLine, " OR ") > 0 Then
    ' Found a logical condition clause
    mlMcCabe = mlMcCabe + 1
End If

End Sub
```

How It Works

The user selects a code module to analyze. The code is checked for the number of lines of code, the number of comments, and a general complexity weighting. The ratio of comments to lines of code is computed. As the code is parsed and analyzed, the totals for each routine in the module are added to a grid. Totals for the entire module are maintained and then also added to the grid. The results can be exported to a CSV file for further analysis with a spreadsheet application.

Comments

This How-To provides a basis for some objective evaluation of code. The key items to notice are the ratio of comments compared to the complexity of a routine or module. A good general rule is that the more complex a piece of logic, the more comments it should have. Complexity also implies a need for thorough testing. Keep in mind that each decision point requires at least two different test cases to ensure that each logic branch is exercised. One other consideration is the length of each routine, or the number of lines of code in each routine. Longer routines are harder to understand and debug.

> **WARNING**
>
> Source code analysis is a powerful tool if used in the right way. Do not use static analysis to determine if code is good or bad. This type of analysis provides comparative data and should motivate good coding practices.

Several improvements can be made to this How-To. You can add logic to read and interpret a Visual Basic project file, which would enable a user to analyze an entire project without having to select each individual code module. The parsing routine is relatively simple and can be expanded to provide more comprehensive analysis.

COMPLEXITY
INTERMEDIATE

7.4 How do I...
Instrument a program for code profiling?

COMPATIBILITY: VISUAL BASIC 5 AND 6

Problem

I have a program that I want to tune for improved performance, but don't know where to start. I would like to know where my program spends most of its execution time. Also, during the testing process I want to ensure that all the code is run at least once. How do I record and analyze the execution profile of my program and find unused procedures?

Technique

To address the problem, a technique needs to be developed that tracks the routines that execute in a program, how often they run, and how long they run. Another important statistic is the percent of total execution time taken by the individual routines. Knowing the percent of time spent in a routine provides the information needed to focus performance-tuning efforts. The routine that uses the most execution time, or is executed the greatest number of times, is the one that should be well tuned. This How-To builds a code module that handles managing and recording the execution profile data and statistics.

Data is recorded for specific profile points. A profile point is any piece of code the developer wants to examine. It can be entire subroutines or functions, or fragments of code within a larger process.

The interface points into the profiling code are then added to an existing project at points of interest. Routines can then be identified that are never executed, are executed often but are very fast, and run frequently and are slow. This process helps to identify code to target for performance improvement. It also aids in understanding the dynamics of a program's execution profile. During the testing process, it is vital to ensure that all parts of a program get tested.

Steps

This How-To profiles the static analysis code from How-To 7.3. The user interface is identical. Open and run CP - STATIC ANALYSIS.VBP. The running program is shown in Figure 7.8.

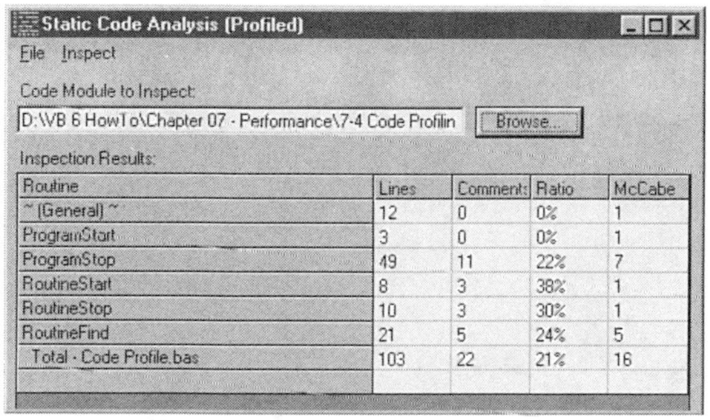

Figure 7.8 The main form at runtime.

Select and analyze a code module. The results of the profiling operation are not seen onscreen, but are saved to a comma-separated value (CSV) file. This CSV file is then opened with a spreadsheet program. An example of the resulting spreadsheet opened with Microsoft Excel is shown in Figure 7.9.

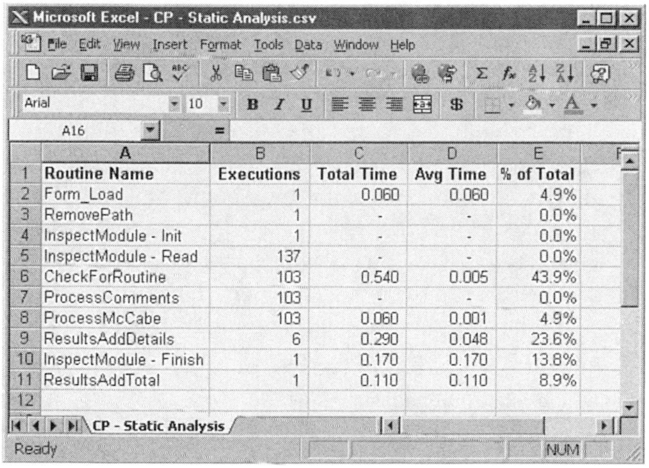

Figure 7.9 The execution profile results in Excel.

The spreadsheet you see in Figure 7.9 has had the column widths adjusted, data type formatting has been applied, and the first row has been set to bold for clarity. To create this project, complete the following steps:

1. Create a new project called CP - STATIC ANALYSIS.VBP.

2. Add a code module to the project and save it as CODE PROFILE.BAS.

3. Put the following code in the General Declarations section of the module. This code establishes a user-defined data type (UDT). An array is then declared of this UDT. The array is used to store profile point statistics.

```
Option Explicit

Type PROFILES
    sName           As String
    nExecutions     As Integer
    dDuration       As Double
    dAverage        As Double
    fPercent        As Single
    dLastStart      As Double
End Type

Private mData()     As PROFILES

Private mnID        As Integer
```

4. Add the following public subroutine to the module. This code preallocates 10 entries in the profile point array.

```
Public Sub ProgramStart()

ReDim mData(10) As PROFILES

End Sub
```

5. Add the following private subroutine. It is used to locate a profile point entry in the array storing the profile data. The code loops through the array elements looking for a specified profile name. If an unused array entry, identified by zero length data, is encountered, then it did not find the item. When the loop exits, the array pointer is located at the end of the array, at the next open array entry, or at the element associated with the name to be located. The array pointer is stored in a module-scope variable to make it available to the rest of the code in the profiling module. If the pointer is at the end of the array, 10 more elements are added. The profile point name is then saved in the array.

```
Private Sub RoutineFind(sName As String)

Dim sTempStr            As String

sTempStr = Trim$(sName)

For mnID = 0 To UBound(mData)
    If Len(Trim$(mData(mnID).sName)) = 0 Then
        ' Found a blank element so use this ID
        Exit For
    End If
    If mData(mnID).sName = sTempStr Then
        ' We found an entry for the routine
        Exit For
    End If
Next mnID

' If ID is greater than the UBound, add 10 more entries to
' the array
```

```
If mnID > UBound(mData) Then
    ReDim Preserve mData(UBound(mData) + 10) As PROFILES
End If

' Now store the routine name
mData(mnID).sName = sTempStr

End Sub
```

6. Add the following public routine, which is called when a new profile point starts or a specific routine is entered. The profile point name is passed to this subroutine by the calling program. A call is made to the RoutineFind subroutine written in step 3. The module scope variable mnID now references the array location where the data for this profile point is stored. The start time is recorded in the array, and the number of executions is incremented by one.

```
Public Sub RoutineStart(sName As String)

' Find the routine in the data array
Call RoutineFind(sName)

' Add the start time to the data
mData(mnID).dLastStart = Timer

' Increment the number of executions
mData(mnID).nExecutions = mData(mnID).nExecutions + 1

End Sub
```

7. Add the following public routine, which is called when a profile point starts or a specific routine is left. The profile point name is passed to this subroutine by the calling program. A call is made to the RoutineFind subroutine written in step 3 to point the module scope variable mnID to the array location where the data for this profile point is stored. This call is made again so that profile points can be nested. The elapsed execution time is then computed and recorded in the array.

```
Public Sub RoutineStop(sName As String)

Dim dExecTime          As Double

' Find the routine in the data array
Call RoutineFind(sName)

' Compute the execution time
dExecTime = Timer
dExecTime = dExecTime - mData(mnID).dLastStart

' Add the execution time to the total duration
mData(mnID).dDuration = mData(mnID).dDuration + dExecTime

End Sub
```

8. Add the following subroutine. It prepares the final data and writes it to the CSV file. The CSV output filename is passed to the subroutine. One pass is made through the profile data to compute the total execution times for all the profile points. A second pass is then made through the profile data array to compute the percent of the total execution time consumed by each profiled routine or logic section. Note that the percent of total values is skewed if the profile points are nested.

The code now is ready to export the profile results to the CSV file. The CSV file is opened in **Output** mode so that new data overwrites any existing results. The logic loops through each element of the array and saves the data to the file by using a **Write** statement. This language statement adds all the necessary CSV formatting to the output as it is being written.

```
Public Sub ProgramStop(sFileName As String)

Dim nLoopCtr         As Integer
Dim nChannel         As Integer
Dim dTotalTime       As Double

' Make pass through the data to compute the total execution time
dTotalTime = 0
For nLoopCtr = 0 To UBound(mData)
    If Len(Trim$(mData(nLoopCtr).sName)) <> 0 Then
        ' There is data so add it up
        dTotalTime = dTotalTime + mData(nLoopCtr).dDuration
    End If
Next nLoopCtr

' This second pass computes the percent of total
' time and average execution time for each routine
For nLoopCtr = 0 To UBound(mData)
    If Len(Trim$(mData(nLoopCtr).sName)) <> 0 Then
        ' There is data so compute the percentage
        mData(nLoopCtr).fPercent = mData(nLoopCtr).dDuration / _
                dTotalTime
        mData(nLoopCtr).dAverage = mData(nLoopCtr).dDuration / _
                mData(nLoopCtr).nExecutions
    End If
Next nLoopCtr

' Get an available I/O channel number
nChannel = FreeFile

' Open a CSV file for output to store the grid contents
Open App.Path & "\" & sFileName & ".csv" For Output As #nChannel

' Write out the column names
Write #nChannel, _
        "Routine Name", _
        "Executions", _
        "Total Time", _
        "Avg Time", _
        "% of Total"
```

```
        ' This final pass writes the data out to a CSV file
        For nLoopCtr = 0 To UBound(mData)
            If Len(Trim$(mData(nLoopCtr).sName)) <> 0 Then
                ' There is data so write it out
                Write #nChannel, _
                        Trim$(mData(nLoopCtr).sName), _
                        mData(nLoopCtr).nExecutions, _
                        mData(nLoopCtr).dDuration, _
                        mData(nLoopCtr).dAverage, _
                        mData(nLoopCtr).fPercent
            End If
        Next nLoopCtr

        ' Close the file
        Close #nChannel

End Sub
```

9. Add a form to the project and set the objects and properties as they are listed in Table 7.6. Add the Microsoft Common Dialog and FlexGrid controls to the project. Save the form as CP - STATIC ANALYSIS.FRM. This form is fundamentally identical to the STATIC ANALYSIS.FRM from How-To 7.3. The differences and changes are highlighted in bold in the table.

Table 7.6 The Project Form's Objects and Properties

OBJECT/CONTROL	PROPERTY	VALUE
Form	Name	frmMain
	Caption	Static Code Analysis (Profiled)
CommonDialog	Name	dlgCommon
CommandButton	Name	cmdBrowse
	Caption	Browse...
TextBox	Name	txtFile
	Locked	-1 'True
	TabStop	0 'False
MSFlexGrid	Name	grdResults
	AllowUserResizing	1 'ResizeColumns
	Appearance	0 'Flat
	Cols	5
	Rows	2
Label	Name	lblCaption
	Caption	Code Module to Inspect:
	Index	0

continued on next page

continued from previous page

OBJECT/CONTROL	PROPERTY	VALUE
Label	Name	lblCaption
	Caption	Inspection Results:
	Index	1
Menu	Name	mnuFile
	Caption	&File
Menu	Name	mnuFileSel
	Caption	E&xit
	Index	0
Menu	Name	mnuTest
	Caption	&Inspect
Menu	Name	mnuInspectSel
	Caption	&Inspect Module
	Enabled	0 'False
	Index	0
Menu	Name	mnuInspectSel
	Caption	-
	Index	1
Menu	Name	mnuInspectSel
	Caption	&Clear Results
	Index	2
Menu	Name	mnuInspectSel
	Caption	&Export Results
	Index	3

10. Add the following code to the form. It is identical to the code for this form in How-To 7.3. Explanations of the logic in the form are found in the previous How-To. The comments in the following steps relate only to the code added to the form to implement profiling. All profiling code that is added is highlighted in bold text in the remainder of the steps. There are no profiling statements that need to be added to the General Declarations section.

```
Option Explicit

' Define variants to hold keyword parsing arrays
Private msKeywords      As Variant
Private msRoutines      As Variant

' Pointer to the current row in the results grid
Private mnCurrentRow    As Integer
```

```
' Module scope variables to store incremental
' counters for routine level information
Private mlLines              As Long
Private mlComments           As Long
Private mlMcCabe             As Long

' Module scope variables to store incremental
' counters for module level totals
Private mlTotLines           As Long
Private mlTotComments        As Long
Private mlTotMcCabe          As Long

' Filename and extension of current code module
Private msMainName           As String

' Fully qualified path and filename of current module
Private msCurrentFile        As String

' Name of the current routine in the current module
Private msRoutineName        As String
```

11. When the form loads, profile subroutines are called to indicate the start of the program and the start of a routine. Notice that the routine name, or the name of a profiling point, is passed in the second subroutine call at the start of the event. If your program begins in a **Sub Main** routine, both of these initial calls need to be added there. The form **Load** event would then just have the second call.

A call is made at the end of the event logic to notify the profiling module that the routine is finished. Again, the routine name is passed in the call. The name must be identical to the one used at the beginning of the procedure.

```
Private Sub Form_Load()

Call ProgramStart
Call RoutineStart("Form_Load")

' Configure the results grid

' Start with the first row
grdResults.Row = 0

' Set the width and caption of the first column
grdResults.Col = 0
grdResults.ColWidth(0) = 3500
grdResults.FixedAlignment(0) = vbLeftJustify
grdResults.Text = "Routine"

' Set the width and caption of the second column
grdResults.Col = 1
grdResults.ColWidth(1) = 800
grdResults.ColAlignment(1) = vbCenter
```

continued on next page

continued from previous page

```vb
grdResults.FixedAlignment(1) = vbCenter
grdResults.Text = "Lines"

' Set the width and caption of the third column
grdResults.Col = 2
grdResults.ColWidth(2) = 800
grdResults.ColAlignment(2) = vbCenter
grdResults.FixedAlignment(2) = vbCenter
grdResults.Text = "Comments"

' Set the width and caption of the fourth column
grdResults.Col = 3
grdResults.ColWidth(3) = 800
grdResults.ColAlignment(3) = vbCenter
grdResults.FixedAlignment(3) = vbCenter
grdResults.Text = "Ratio"

' Set the width and caption of the fifth column
grdResults.Col = 4
grdResults.Text = "McCabe"
grdResults.ColWidth(4) = 800
grdResults.FixedAlignment(4) = vbCenter
grdResults.ColAlignment(4) = vbCenter

' Set the variable that points to the first usable grid row
mnCurrentRow = 1

' Load the decision point keywords for McCabe complexity analysis
msKeywords = Array("SELECT CASE", "FOR", "DO", _
                   "WHILE", "UNTIL", "IIF", "CHOOSE", _
                   "SWITCH", "IF", "ELSEIF", "#IF", "#ELSEIF", _
                   "CASE ", "AND ", "OR ")

' Load the routine start keyword array
msRoutines = Array("SUB ", "FUNCTION ", "PROPERTY ", "EVENT ", _
                   "PUBLIC SUB ", "PUBLIC FUNCTION ", _
                   "PUBLIC PROPERTY ", "PUBLIC EVENT ", _
                   "PRIVATE SUB ", "PRIVATE FUNCTION ", _
                   "PRIVATE PROPERTY ", "PRIVATE EVENT ", _
                   "FRIEND SUB ", "FRIEND FUNCTION ", _
                   "FRIEND PROPERTY ", "FRIEND EVENT ")
```

Call RoutineStop("Form_Load")

```vb
End Sub
```

12. Prepare the Click event for the Browse command button for profiling. A call is made to RoutineStart at the beginning of the event, and a call to RoutineStop is made at the end.

```vb
Private Sub cmdBrowse_Click()
```

Call RoutineStart("cmdBrowse_Click")

```vb
' Configure the common dialog control to select a module
```

```vb
' Set the dialog title
dlgCommon.DialogTitle = "Select a VB Code Module"

' Establish the file filter options
dlgCommon.Filter = "VB Code " & _
        "(*.bas;*.cls;*.dsr;*.frm;*.pag;*.ctl;*.dob)¦" & _
        "*.bas;*.cls;*.dsr;*.frm;*.pag;*.ctl;*.dob¦" & _
        "Class Modules (*.cls)¦*.cls¦" & _
        "Code Modules (*.bas)¦*.bas¦" & _
        "Designer Modules (*.dsr)¦*.dsr¦" & _
        "Form Modules (*.frm)¦*.frm¦" & _
        "Property Pages (*.pag)¦*.pag¦" & _
        "User Control (*.ctl)¦*.ctl¦" & _
        "User Document (*.dob)¦*.dob¦" & _
        "All Files (*.*)¦*.*"

' Set the current filter to the first one available
dlgCommon.FilterIndex = 1

' Require that the path and file exist
dlgCommon.Flags = cdlOFNFileMustExist + cdlOFNPathMustExist

' Now show the file open dialog
dlgCommon.ShowOpen

' Get the fully qualified filename that the user selected
msCurrentFile = dlgCommon.FileName

' See if we actually have a filename
If Len(msCurrentFile) > 0 Then
    ' We have one so ...
    ' Show the selected file in the text box
    txtFile.Text = msCurrentFile

    ' Pull the file and extension and save them
    msMainName = RemovePath(msCurrentFile)

    ' Enable the "Inspect" menu choice
    mnuInspectSel(0).Enabled = True

Else

    ' No file was selected so ...
    ' Clear the text box
    txtFile.Text = ""

    ' Clear the file and extension variable
    msMainName = ""

    ' Disable the "Inspect" menu choice
    mnuInspectSel(0).Enabled = False

End If

Call RoutineStop("cmdBrowse_Click")

End Sub
```

13. Before the program exits, a call is made to let the profiling module know
that it needs to perform its final calculations and save the profile data.

```
Private Sub mnuFileSel_Click(Index As Integer)

Call ProgramStop("CP - Static Analysis")

Unload Me

End Sub
```

14. Add the standard profiling hooks to the menu selection `Click` event. The
standard profile rigging makes a call to the `RoutineStart` and
`RoutineStop` subroutines at the beginning and end of each event,
subroutine, or function.

```
Private Sub mnuInspectSel_Click(Index As Integer)

Call RoutineStart("mnuInspectSel_Click")

Select Case Index
    Case 0                ' Analyze the project/module
        ' Clear the module totals
        mlTotLines = 0
        mlTotComments = 0
        mlTotMcCabe = 0

        ' Perform the inspection
        InspectModule

    Case 1                ' Separator
        ' No code required here

    Case 2                ' Clear test results
        If (MsgBox("Are you sure you want to " & _
            "clear the results?", vbCritical + vbYesNo)) = vbYes _
            Then
                Call ResultsClear
        End If

    Case 3                ' Export test results
        Call ResultsExport

End Select

Call RoutineStop("mnuInspectSel_Click")

End Sub
```

15. Insert the standard profile rigging into the `ResultsAddDetails`
subroutine.

```
Private Sub ResultsAddDetails()

Call RoutineStart("ResultsAddDetails")
```

```
' Add inspection results to the grid
grdResults.Row = mnCurrentRow
grdResults.Col = 1
grdResults.Text = Format$(mlLines, "###,##0")
grdResults.Col = 2
grdResults.Text = Format$(mlComments, "###,##0")
grdResults.Col = 3

If mlComments = 0 Or _
   mlLines = 0 Then
     grdResults.Text = "0%"
   Else
     grdResults.Text = Format$((mlComments / _
        mlLines) * 100, "##0") & "%"
End If

grdResults.Col = 4
grdResults.Text = Format$(mlMcCabe, "###,##0")
grdResults.Col = 0
grdResults.Text = msRoutineName

' Add another row to the grid
mnCurrentRow = mnCurrentRow + 1
If mnCurrentRow + 1 > grdResults.Rows Then
    grdResults.Rows = mnCurrentRow + 1
End If

grdResults.Refresh

' Update the cumulative totals
mlTotLines = mlTotLines + mlLines
mlTotComments = mlTotComments + mlComments
mlTotMcCabe = mlTotMcCabe + mlMcCabe

' Clear the routine total counters
mlLines = 0
mlComments = 0
mlMcCabe = 1

Call RoutineStop("ResultsAddDetails")

End Sub
```

16. Put the standard profile rigging in the `ResultsAddtotal` subroutine.

```
Private Sub ResultsAddTotal()

Call RoutineStart("ResultsAddTotal")

' Add module totals to the grid
grdResults.Row = mnCurrentRow
grdResults.Col = 1
grdResults.Text = Format$(mlTotLines, "###,##0")
grdResults.Col = 2
grdResults.Text = Format$(mlTotComments, "###,##0")
grdResults.Col = 3
```

continued on next page

continued from previous page

```
        If mlTotComments = 0 Or _
          mlTotLines = 0 Then
            grdResults.Text = "0%"
          Else
            grdResults.Text = Format$((mlTotComments / _
                mlTotLines) * 100, "##0") & "%"
        End If

        grdResults.Col = 4
        grdResults.Text = Format$(mlTotMcCabe, "###,##0")
        grdResults.Col = 0
        grdResults.Text = "  Total - " & msMainName

        ' Add another row to the grid
        mnCurrentRow = mnCurrentRow + 1
        If mnCurrentRow + 1 > grdResults.Rows Then
            grdResults.Rows = mnCurrentRow + 1
        End If

        ' Clear the module totals we just used
        mlTotLines = 0
        mlTotComments = 0
        mlTotMcCabe = 0

        grdResults.Refresh

        Call RoutineStop("ResultsAddTotal")

        End Sub
```

17. Add the standard profile rigging to the **ResultsExport** subroutine.

```
        Private Sub ResultsExport()

        Dim nLoopRow            As Integer
        Dim nLoopCol            As Integer
        Dim nChannel            As Integer
        Dim sOutput(5)          As String

        Call RoutineStart("ResultsExport")

        ' Get an available I/O channel number
        nChannel = FreeFile

        ' Open a CSV file to store the grid contents
        ' Using append mode will add to the file if it exists
        Open App.Path & "\Inspection - " & msMainName & ".csv" For Append _
        As #nChannel

        ' Loop through the grid row by row
        For nLoopRow = 1 To mnCurrentRow - 1
```

```
        ' Set the current grid row
        grdResults.Row = nLoopRow

        ' Loop through the grid columns
        For nLoopCol = 0 To 4
            ' Set the current column
            grdResults.Col = nLoopCol

            ' Save the column data to an array
            sOutput(nLoopCol) = grdResults.Text

        Next nLoopCol

        ' Write the array contents to the CSV file
        Write #nChannel, sOutput(0), sOutput(1), sOutput(2), _
        sOutput(3), sOutput(4)

    Next nLoopRow

    ' Close the results file
    Close #nChannel

    Call RoutineStop("ResultsExport")

End Sub
```

18. Insert the standard profile rigging into the `ResultsClear` subroutine.

```
Private Sub ResultsClear()

    Call RoutineStart("ResultsClear")

    ' Reset the grid to have only the first two rows
    mnCurrentRow = 1
    grdResults.Rows = 2

    ' Clear first data row values
    grdResults.Row = mnCurrentRow
    grdResults.Col = 1
    grdResults.Text = ""
    grdResults.Col = 2
    grdResults.Text = ""
    grdResults.Col = 3
    grdResults.Text = ""
    grdResults.Col = 4
    grdResults.Text = ""
    grdResults.Col = 0
    grdResults.Text = ""

    Call RoutineStop("ResultsClear")

End Sub
```

19. Modify the `RemovePath` subroutine to include the standard profile rigging.

```
Function RemovePath(sFullName As String) As String

Dim nLoopCtr              As Integer
Dim nTempInt              As Integer
Dim sTempStr              As String

Call RoutineStart("RemovePath")

' Scan backward through the input string to find the last
' directory
' qualifier "\" or the drive letter delimiter.
For nLoopCtr = Len(sFullName) To 1 Step -1

    Select Case Mid$(sFullName, nLoopCtr, 1)
        Case "\", ":"
            ' We have a drive or directory delimiter
            Exit For

        Case Else
            ' Build a return value that includes all characters
            ' that have been checked
            sTempStr = Mid$(sFullName, nLoopCtr)

    End Select

Next nLoopCtr

' Send back the results
RemovePath = sTempStr

Call RoutineStop("RemovePath")

End Function
```

20. Add the standard profile logic to the `InspectModule` subroutine.

```
Private Sub InspectModule()

Dim nChannel             As Integer
Dim sCodeLine            As String
Dim bInControls          As Boolean
Dim sUpcaseCode          As String

Call RoutineStart("InspectModule")

' Reset the routine counters
mlLines = 0
mlComments = 0
mlMcCabe = 1

' Set the initial routine name
msRoutineName = "~ (General) ~"
```

```
    ' Get an available I/O channel number
    nChannel = FreeFile

    ' Open the selected code module for analysis
    Open msCurrentFile For Input As nChannel

    ' Read the first line of the module
    Line Input #nChannel, sCodeLine

    ' Loop through the rest of the module line by line

    Do

        ' Check for control descriptions in form modules
        If Left$(UCase$(sCodeLine), 5) = "BEGIN" Then
            bInControls = True
        End If

        ' See if we are now out of the control descriptions
        If bInControls = True Then
            If Left$(UCase$(sCodeLine), 3) = "END" Then
                bInControls = False
            End If
        End If

        ' Simplify parsing by upcasing the line and
        ' removing all leading and trailing spaces
        sCodeLine = Trim$(sCodeLine)
        sUpcaseCode = UCase$(sCodeLine)

    If bInControls = False Then

        Select Case Len(sCodeLine)
          Case 0
              ' This is a blank line so exclude it from
              ' the processing and statistics

          Case Else
              ' See if this is the end of a routine
              Call CheckForRoutine(sCodeLine)

              ' Count the code line
              mlLines = mlLines + 1

              ' Check for, strip out, and count comments
              Call ProcessComments(sUpcaseCode)

              ' Determine the McCabe complexity value
              Call ProcessMcCabe(sUpcaseCode)

        End Select

    End If

        ' Get the next line of code
        Line Input #nChannel, sCodeLine
```

continued on next page

continued from previous page

```
Loop Until EOF(nChannel)

' Close the code module file
Close nChannel

' Add the totals for the final routine
Call ResultsAddDetails

' Add the module totals to the results grid
Call ResultsAddTotal

Call RoutineStop("InspectModule")

End Sub
```

21. Put the profile rigging code into the `CheckForRoutine` subroutine.

```
Sub CheckForRoutine(sCodeLine As String)

Dim nLoopCtr                As Integer
Dim nPosition               As Integer

Call RoutineStart("CheckForRoutine")

' Check for blank lines
If Len(sCodeLine) = 0 Then Exit Sub

' Look for statements that start new routines in the module
For nLoopCtr = 0 To UBound(msRoutines)

    If Left$(UCase$(sCodeLine), Len(msRoutines(nLoopCtr))) = _
        msRoutines(nLoopCtr) Then
        ' The keyword is at the start of the line
        ' so this is a routine
        Call ResultsAddDetails

        ' Get the new routine name
        nPosition = InStr(1, sCodeLine, "(")

        ' If the character was not found, assume the name
        ' is all alone
        If nPosition = 0 Then
            nPosition = Len(sCodeLine)
        End If

        ' Extract the routine name from the code line
        msRoutineName = Mid$(sCodeLine, _
                            Len(msRoutines(nLoopCtr)), _
                            nPosition - Len(msRoutines(nLoopCtr)))

        ' Clean up the routine name
        msRoutineName = Trim$(msRoutineName)
        Exit For

    End If

Next nLoopCtr
```

```
Call RoutineStop("CheckForRoutine")

End Sub
```

22. Insert the profile rigging code into **ProcessComments** subroutine.

```
Sub ProcessComments(sCodeLine As String)

Dim nLoopCtr              As Integer
Dim nTempInt              As Integer
Dim sTempStr              As String

Call RoutineStart("ProcessComments")

' See if the first character is a comment delimiter
If Left$(sCodeLine, 1) = Chr$(39) Then
    ' This is a comment line so increment the count
    mlComments = mlComments + 1

    ' Clear out the entire code line
    sCodeLine = ""
    Exit Sub

End If

' See if there is a trailing comment

' Scan backward through the code line to find the
' comment delimiter character
For nLoopCtr = Len(sCodeLine) To 1 Step -1

    If Mid$(sCodeLine, nLoopCtr, 1) = Chr$(39) Then
        ' There is a comment on this line, so
        ' increment the count
        mlComments = mlComments + 1

        ' Remove the comment from the code line
        sCodeLine = Left$(sCodeLine, nLoopCtr)
        Exit Sub

    End If

Next nLoopCtr

Call RoutineStop("ProcessComments")

End Sub
```

23. Place the profiling code hooks into the **ProcessMcCabe** subroutine.

```
Sub ProcessMcCabe(sCodeLine As String)

Dim nLoopCtr              As Integer
Dim nStart                As Integer

Call RoutineStart("ProcessMcCabe")
```

continued on next page

continued from previous page

```
    ' Check for blank lines
    If Len(sCodeLine) = 0 Then Exit Sub

    ' Look for conditional statements at the start of the line
    For nLoopCtr = 0 To UBound(msKeywords)

        If Left$(sCodeLine, Len(msKeywords(nLoopCtr))) = _
        msKeywords(nLoopCtr) Then
            ' The keyword is at the start of the line
            mlMcCabe = mlMcCabe + 1
            Exit For
        End If

    Next nLoopCtr

    ' Check for conditional clauses in the code line
    If InStr(4, sCodeLine, " AND ") > 0 Then
        ' Found a logical condition clause
        mlMcCabe = mlMcCabe + 1
    End If

    If InStr(4, sCodeLine, " OR ") > 0 Then
        ' Found a logical condition clause
        mlMcCabe = mlMcCabe + 1
    End If

    Call RoutineStop("ProcessMcCabe")

    End Sub
```

How It Works

This How-To instruments an existing program for code execution profiling. The profiling itself is isolated in a separate code module that can be added to any project. When the program being profiled starts, it calls a public subroutine in the code profiling module. As each function, subroutine, event, or property routine starts to execute, another public routine in the code profile module is called. This call records the entry into the routine, begins tracking the execution time, and maintains a count for the number of times the routine executes. As each routine completes, it calls a profiling routine to mark the end of the execution.

Comments

The granularity of the profiling points is important. As the code in the How-To is now rigged, the discreet tasks performed as part of the code analysis are all lumped into the InspectModule execution data. This aggregate profile point also encompasses the subroutines that check for entry into new routines, check for comments, and determine the code complexity.

The following copy of the primary code inspection subroutine has been modified to segment the individual portions of the analysis process. The original profiling calls have been commented out. New specific ones have been added for the initialization, for reading the code lines, and for the termination processing. Notice that the calls to analyze each code line are now excluded. This moves the profiling of those subroutines into their own profile entries.

```
Private Sub InspectModule()

Dim nChannel        As Integer
Dim sCodeLine       As String
Dim bInControls     As Boolean
Dim sUpcaseCode     As String

'Call RoutineStart("InspectModule")
Call RoutineStart("InspectModule - Init")

' Reset the routine counters
mlLines = 0
mlComments = 0
mlMcCabe = 1

' Set the initial routine name
msRoutineName = "~ (General) ~"

' Get an available I/O channel number
nChannel = FreeFile

' Open the selected code module for analysis
Open msCurrentFile For Input As nChannel

' Read the first line of the module
Line Input #nChannel, sCodeLine

Call RoutineStop("InspectModule - Init")

' Loop through the rest of the module line by line

Do

    Call RoutineStart("InspectModule - Read")

    ' Check for control descriptions in form modules
    If Left$(UCase$(sCodeLine), 5) = "BEGIN" Then
        bInControls = True
    End If

    ' See if we are now out of the control descriptions
    If bInControls = True Then
        If Left$(UCase$(sCodeLine), 3) = "END" Then
            bInControls = False
        End If
    End If
```

continued on next page

continued from previous page

```
        ' Simplify parsing by upcasing the line and
        ' removing all leading and trailing spaces
        sCodeLine = Trim$(sCodeLine)
        sUpcaseCode = UCase$(sCodeLine)

        Call RoutineStop("InspectModule - Read")

        If bInControls = False Then

            Select Case Len(sCodeLine)
              Case 0
                  ' This is a blank line, so exclude it from
                  ' the processing and statistics

              Case Else
                  ' See if this is the end of a routine
                  Call CheckForRoutine(sCodeLine)

                  ' Count the code line
                  mlLines = mlLines + 1

                  ' Check for, strip out, and count comments
                  Call ProcessComments(sUpcaseCode)

                  ' Determine the McCabe complexity value
                  Call ProcessMcCabe(sUpcaseCode)

            End Select

        End If

        ' Get the next line of code
        Line Input #nChannel, sCodeLine

Loop Until EOF(nChannel)

Call RoutineStart("InspectModule - Finish")

' Close the code module file
Close nChannel

' Add the totals for the final routine
Call ResultsAddDetails

' Add the module totals to the results grid
Call ResultsAddTotal

Call RoutineStop("InspectModule - Finish")
'Call RoutineStop("InspectModule")

End Sub
```

Some enhancements can be made to the code in this How-To. First, the profiling code can be moved into its own project. If it is then built as an object, it can be bound at runtime when needed. The code profile rigging can also be enclosed in conditional compile statements. This would enable the profiling to be activated during the development process and easily disabled when the final executable is built.

COMPLEXITY
INTERMEDIATE

7.5 How do I...
Evaluate object creation performance?

COMPATIBILITY: VISUAL BASIC 5 AND 6

Problem

I have heard there is a significant performance difference between the techniques used to create object instances. Dimensioning object variables by using the **New** syntax is supposedly slower. The alternative is to define the object variable without the **New** clause and then use the **Set** verb. Also, I would like to share binary code components, but I am concerned about the overhead involved when creating objects built as separate DLL modules. How do I evaluate and analyze the code differences used to create instances of objects and their effect on overall program performance?

Technique

Several factors affect the time it takes to create instances of objects. Objects can be created by using class modules that are part of the executable. They can also be created from external DLL modules. This How-To looks at the performance differences of these two object creation techniques.

In the following examples, the performance is evaluated for both techniques of object creation. Also, the code uses the created objects in two different loop structures to show the impact of code logic on performance. There are two versions of the program. One uses an integrated class module to define the object. The second one encapsulates the class in a DLL. The code uses a fairly simple class that accepts a long word value and splits it into high and low words.

This How-To uses the test results form written in How-To 7.1. Refer to the first 12 steps of that How-To for details on the implementation of the test results form.

Steps

Open and run OBJECT PERFORMANCE - INTERNAL.VBP. The main form appears, as shown in Figure 7.10.

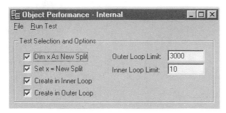

Figure 7.10 The internal object
main form at runtime.

Run the tests and examine the results. Sample results can be seen in
Figure 7.11.

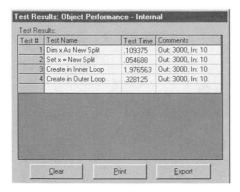

Figure 7.11 The results of the
internal object test.

Exit from the program. Next, open and run OBJECT PERFORMANCE -
EXTERNAL.VBP. Figure 7.12 shows the main form.

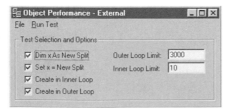

Figure 7.12 The external object
main form at runtime.

This program looks identical to the main form of the internal test program
because all the differences are in the code itself and are not visible through the
user interface. Run the tests in this program. The results can be seen in Figure
7.13.

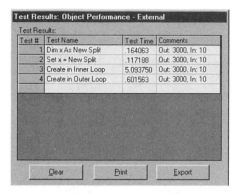

Figure 7.13 The results of the external object test.

Complete the following steps to create this project:

1. Create a new project called OBJECT PERFORMANCE - INTERNAL.VBP.

2. Make a copy of the test results form, TEST RESULTS.FRM, from How-To 7.1 and add it to this project.

3. Add a form to the project, and set the objects and properties as they are listed in Table 7.7. Save the form as OBJECT PERFORMANCE - INTERNAL.FRM.

Table 7.7 The Internal Object Form's Objects and Properties

OBJECT/CONTROL	PROPERTY	VALUE
Form	Name	frmMain
	Caption	Object Performance - Internal
Frame	Name	fraTest
	Caption	Test Selection and Options
TextBox	Name	txtOuter
	Text	10
TextBox	Name	txtInner
	Text	3000
CheckBox	Name	chkTest
	Caption	Dim x As New Split
	Index	0
CheckBox	Name	chkTest
	Caption	Set x = New Split
	Index	1

continued on next page

continued from previous page

OBJECT/CONTROL	PROPERTY	VALUE
CheckBox	Name	chkTest
	Caption	Create in Inner Loop
	Index	2
CheckBox	Name	chkTest
	Caption	Create in Outer Loop
	Index	3
Label	Name	lblCaption
	Caption	Outer Loop Limit:
	Index	0
Label	Name	lblCaption
	Caption	Inner Loop Limit:
	Index	1
Menu	Name	mnuFile
	Caption	&File
Menu	Name	mnuFileSel
	Caption	E&xit
	Index	0
Menu	Name	mnuTest
	Caption	&Run Test

4. Place the following code segment in the **Load** event of the form. This code loads and configures the form that stores and displays the test results.

```
Private Sub Form_Load()

' Load and position the test results form
Load frmResults
frmResults.Caption = frmResults.Caption & _
        ": " & Me.Caption
frmResults.Top = Me.Top + _
        Me.Height + 10
frmResults.Left = Me.Left
frmResults.Show

End Sub
```

5. This code, when added to the **Unload** event of the form, unloads all loaded forms, including the test results form, so that the application exits gracefully.

```
Private Sub Form_Unload(Cancel As Integer)

Dim nLoopCtr          As Integer
```

```
' Unload all loaded forms so the application can exit
On Error Resume Next
For nLoopCtr = Forms.Count - 1 To 1 Step -1
    Unload Forms(nLoopCtr)
Next nLoopCtr
On Error GoTo 0

End Sub
```

6. Put the following code into the **Click** event of the File Exit menu to unload the form and exit from the application:

```
Private Sub mnuFileSel_Click(Index As Integer)

Select Case Index
    Case 0
        Unload Me

End Select

End Sub
```

7. Add the following subroutine, which contains the master control logic for the test executions. This is put into the **Click** event of the Run Test menu. First, the user-supplied test parameters are obtained from the text boxes on the form. The code then loops though the test selection check boxes and performs the requested tests.

A number of common steps are performed for each test; they are bracketed around the execution of the tests themselves. Initially, the caption of the current test check box is changed to red. Then the graphics target form is unloaded and reloaded, and the test start time is recorded. After each test, the end time is saved, causing the test results to be added to the grid, and the check box caption color is restored.

```
Private Sub mnuTest_Click()

Dim nLoopCtr        As Integer
Dim sOptions        As String
Dim nOuter          As Integer
Dim nInner          As Integer

' Set the mouse pointer to show that we are busy
Me.MousePointer = vbHourglass

' Get the outer and inner loop values
nOuter = CInt(Val(txtOuter.Text))
nInner = CInt(Val(txtInner.Text))

' Build the test option string
sOptions = "Out: " & nOuter & _
            ", In: " & nInner
```

continued on next page

continued from previous page

```
For nLoopCtr = 0 To 3
    If chkTest(nLoopCtr).Value = vbChecked Then
        ' Highlight the selected to test to show it is being run
        chkTest(nLoopCtr).ForeColor = vbRed
        chkTest(nLoopCtr).Refresh

        ' Initialize random number generation to a known
        ' value. This ensures that the test sequences will
        ' be identical.
        Rnd 1

        ' Set the test name and comments for each test, then run
        ' it
        Select Case nLoopCtr
            Case 0
                ' Set test results properties
                frmResults.TestName = "Dim x As New Split"
                frmResults.TestComments = sOptions
                ' Record the test start time
                frmResults.TestStart
                ' Perform the test
                Call DimNew(nOuter, nInner)

            Case 1
                ' Set test results properties
                frmResults.TestName = "Set x = New Split"
                frmResults.TestComments = sOptions
                ' Record the test start time
                frmResults.TestStart
                ' Perform the test
                Call SetNew(nOuter, nInner)

            Case 2
                ' Set test results properties
                frmResults.TestName = "Create in Inner Loop"
                frmResults.TestComments = sOptions
                ' Record the test start time
                frmResults.TestStart
                ' Perform the test
                Call InsideLoop(nOuter, nInner)

            Case 3
                ' Set test results properties
                frmResults.TestName = "Create in Outer Loop"
                frmResults.TestComments = sOptions
                ' Record the test start time
                frmResults.TestStart
                ' Perform the test
                Call OutsideLoop(nOuter, nInner)

        End Select

        ' Record the test end time
        frmResults.TestEnd
```

```
            ' Remove the highlight from the current test
            chkTest(nLoopCtr).ForeColor = vbButtonText
            chkTest(nLoopCtr).Refresh

        End If

    Next nLoopCtr

    ' Put the mouse pointer back to the default
    Me.MousePointer = vbDefault

    End Sub
```

8. The next four subroutines all create instances of the class object being evaluated. All four of them perform the same basic task, but each one uses a different technique to create the object instances and varies the timing of the object creations. Add this first routine, which uses the `Dim...As New` syntax to create instances. All four subroutines are added to the form.

The outer and inner loop count limits are used to control nested loops. The random test value is established in the outer loop. This value is then used to set the long value property of the object and get the split word values in the inner loop. Notice that only one instance of the object is actually created and then referenced in the rest of the code.

```
Private Sub DimNew(nOuter As Integer, _
                   nInner As Integer)

Dim clsSplit          As New CSplitInt
Dim nLoopCtr          As Integer
Dim nInnerCtr         As Integer
Dim lTestVal          As Long
Dim nHighWord         As Integer
Dim nLowWord          As Integer

For nLoopCtr = 1 To nOuter
    lTestVal = CLng(Abs((2147483647 * Rnd) + 1))
    For nInnerCtr = 1 To nInner
        clsSplit.LongValue = lTestVal
        lTestVal = clsSplit.LongValue
        nHighWord = clsSplit.HighWord
        nLowWord = clsSplit.LowWord
    Next nInnerCtr
Next nLoopCtr

End Sub
```

9. Add the following code to the form. This version of the code omits the `New` clause from the `Dim` statement. The `Set` statement then creates a single instance of the object that is used inside the nested loops. With the exception of the lines in bold, this subroutine is identical to the `DimNew` procedure written previously.

```
Private Sub SetNew(nOuter As Integer, _
                   nInner As Integer)

Dim clsSplit          As CSplitInt
Dim nLoopCtr          As Integer
Dim nInnerCtr         As Integer
Dim lTestVal          As Long
Dim nHighWord         As Integer
Dim nLowWord          As Integer

Set clsSplit = New CSplitInt

For nLoopCtr = 1 To nOuter
    lTestVal = CLng(Abs((2147483647 * Rnd) + 1))
    For nInnerCtr = 1 To nInner
        clsSplit.LongValue = lTestVal
        lTestVal = clsSplit.LongValue
        nHighWord = clsSplit.HighWord
        nLowWord = clsSplit.LowWord
    Next nInnerCtr
Next nLoopCtr

Set clsSplit = Nothing

End Sub
```

10. Add the following subroutine to the form. This object creation test subroutine is the same as the previous one, except for the lines in bold. Notice that the creation and destruction of the object has been moved inside the inner loop.

```
Private Sub InsideLoop(nOuter As Integer, _
                       nInner As Integer)

Dim clsSplit          As CSplitInt
Dim nLoopCtr          As Integer
Dim nInnerCtr         As Integer
Dim lTestVal          As Long
Dim nHighWord         As Integer
Dim nLowWord          As Integer

For nLoopCtr = 1 To nOuter
    lTestVal = CLng(Abs((2147483647 * Rnd) + 1))
    For nInnerCtr = 1 To nInner
        Set clsSplit = New CSplitInt
        clsSplit.LongValue = lTestVal
        lTestVal = clsSplit.LongValue
        nHighWord = clsSplit.HighWord
        nLowWord = clsSplit.LowWord
        Set clsSplit = Nothing
    Next nInnerCtr
Next nLoopCtr

End Sub
```

11. Add the following code. Again, this code is identical to the preceding routine except for the lines in bold. In this subroutine, the object creation and destruction have been moved into the outer loop. Moving the object instantiation into the outer loop reduces the number of creation events dramatically.

```
Private Sub OutsideLoop(nOuter As Integer, _
                        nInner As Integer)

Dim clsSplit        As CSplitInt
Dim nLoopCtr        As Integer
Dim nInnerCtr       As Integer
Dim lTestVal        As Long
Dim nHighWord       As Integer
Dim nLowWord        As Integer

For nLoopCtr = 1 To nOuter
    Set clsSplit = New CSplitInt
    lTestVal = CLng(Abs((2147483647 * Rnd) + 1))
    For nInnerCtr = 1 To nInner
        clsSplit.LongValue = lTestVal
        lTestVal = clsSplit.LongValue
        nHighWord = clsSplit.HighWord
        nLowWord = clsSplit.LowWord
    Next nInnerCtr
    Set clsSplit = Nothing
Next nLoopCtr

End Sub
```

12. Add a class module to the project. Set the class **Name** property to **CSplitInt** and save it as CSPLITINT.CLS.

13. Add the following code to the General Declarations section of the class. This code defines the class scope variables that hold the property values.

```
Option Explicit

Private mlLongValue     As Long
Private mnHighWord      As Integer
Private mnLowWord       As Integer
```

14. Add a public property to the class. When this property is set, the code splits the long integer value into its respective high and low word values. These values are stored in the private class property variables.

```
Public Property Let LongValue(ByVal lLongValue As Long)

mlLongValue = lLongValue

' Split a long integer into high and low words.
```

continued on next page

continued from previous page

```
    If (mlLongValue And &H7FFFFFFF) <> mlLongValue Then
        ' Turn off the high bit
        mlLongValue = mlLongValue And &H7FFFFFFF
        ' Get the remaining bits of the high word
        mnHighWord = mlLongValue \ 65536
        ' Turn the high bit back on in the result
        mnHighWord = (mnHighWord And &H7FFF) + &H8000
        ' Restore the local property value
        mlLongValue = lLongValue
      Else
        mnHighWord = mlLongValue \ 65536
    End If

    If (mlLongValue And &HFFFF&) > &H7FFF Then
        mnLowWord = (mlLongValue And &HFFFF&) - &H10000
      Else
        mnLowWord = mlLongValue And &HFFFF&
    End If

End Property
```

15. These next three property routines are used to get the values of the three class properties.

```
Public Property Get LongValue() As Long

LongValue = mlLongValue

End Property


Public Property Get LowWord() As Integer

LowWord = mnLowWord

End Property


Public Property Get HighWord() As Integer

HighWord = mnHighWord

End Property
```

16. The test project for evaluating internal object creation is now complete. Create a second project called OBJECT PERFORMANCE - EXTERNAL.VBP.

17. Make a copy of the test results form, TEST RESULTS.FRM, from How-To 7.1 and add it to this project.

18. Add a form to the project and set the objects and properties as they are listed in Table 7.8. Save the form as OBJECT PERFORMANCE - EXTERNAL.FRM. This form and its code are virtually identical to the form and code used in the internal object test program, but there are a few notable exceptions. First, the caption of the main form has been changed. Next, there is no class module. A separate DLL is built later in the How-To. Finally, to avoid reference problems, the class name for the object has also been changed. The DLL is then used for object creation. Because the code is so similar, the explanatory comments have been condensed, and the differences are highlighted in bold.

Table 7.8 The External Object Form's Objects and Properties

OBJECT/CONTROL	PROPERTY	VALUE
Form	Name	frmMain
	Caption	Object Performance - External
Frame	Name	fraTest
	Caption	Test Selection and Options
TextBox	Name	txtOuter
	Text	10
TextBox	Name	txtInner
	Text	3000
CheckBox	Name	chkTest
	Caption	Dim x As New Split
	Index	0
CheckBox	Name	chkTest
	Caption	Set x = New Split
	Index	1
CheckBox	Name	chkTest
	Caption	Create in Inner Loop
	Index	2
CheckBox	Name	chkTest
	Caption	Create in Outer Loop
	Index	3
Label	Name	lblCaption
	Caption	Outer Loop Limit:
	Index	0
Label	Name	lblCaption
	Caption	Inner Loop Limit:
	Index	1
Menu	Name	mnuFile
	Caption	&File

continued on next page

continued from previous page

OBJECT/CONTROL	PROPERTY	VALUE
Menu	Name	mnuFileSel
	Caption	E&xit
	Index	0
Menu	Name	mnuTest
	Caption	&Run Test

19. Place the following code segment in the **Load** event of the form. This code loads and configures the form that stores and displays the test results:

```
Private Sub Form_Load()

' Load and position the test results form
Load frmResults
frmResults.Caption = frmResults.Caption & _
            ": " & Me.Caption
frmResults.Top = Me.Top + _
                Me.Height + 10
frmResults.Left = Me.Left
frmResults.Show

End Sub
```

20. Add this code for the form's **Unload** event:

```
Private Sub Form_Unload(Cancel As Integer)

Dim nLoopCtr            As Integer

' Unload all loaded forms so the application can exit
On Error Resume Next
For nLoopCtr = Forms.Count - 1 To 1 Step -1
    Unload Forms(nLoopCtr)
Next nLoopCtr
On Error GoTo 0

End Sub
```

21. Put the following code into the **Click** event of the File, Exit menu to unload the form and exit from the application:

```
Private Sub mnuFileSel_Click(Index As Integer)

Select Case Index
    Case 0
        Unload Me

End Select

End Sub
```

22. This is the code that drives the test process:

```
Private Sub mnuTest_Click()

Dim nLoopCtr          As Integer
Dim sOptions          As String
Dim nOuter            As Integer
Dim nInner            As Integer

' Set the mouse pointer to show that we are busy
Me.MousePointer = vbHourglass

' Get the outer and inner loop values
nOuter = CInt(Val(txtOuter.Text))
nInner = CInt(Val(txtInner.Text))

' Build the test option string
sOptions = "Out: " & nOuter & _
           ", In: " & nInner

For nLoopCtr = 0 To 3
    If chkTest(nLoopCtr).Value = vbChecked Then
        ' Highlight the selected to test to show it is being run
        chkTest(nLoopCtr).ForeColor = vbRed
        chkTest(nLoopCtr).Refresh

        ' Initialize random number generation to a known
        ' value. This ensures that the test sequences will
        ' be identical.
        Rnd 1

        ' Set the test name and comments for each test, then run
        ' it
        Select Case nLoopCtr
            Case 0
                ' Set test results properties
                frmResults.TestName = "Dim x As New Split"
                frmResults.TestComments = sOptions
                ' Record the test start time
                frmResults.TestStart
                ' Perform the test
                Call DimNew(nOuter, nInner)

            Case 1
                ' Set test results properties
                frmResults.TestName = "Set x = New Split"
                frmResults.TestComments = sOptions
                ' Record the test start time
                frmResults.TestStart
                ' Perform the test
                Call SetNew(nOuter, nInner)

            Case 2
                ' Set test results properties
                frmResults.TestName = "Create in Inner Loop"
                frmResults.TestComments = sOptions
```

continued on next page

continued from previous page

```
                                  ' Record the test start time
                                  frmResults.TestStart
                                  ' Perform the test
                                  Call InsideLoop(nOuter, nInner)

                        Case 3
                                  ' Set test results properties
                                  frmResults.TestName = "Create in Outer Loop"
                                  frmResults.TestComments = sOptions
                                  ' Record the test start time
                                  frmResults.TestStart
                                  ' Perform the test
                                  Call OutsideLoop(nOuter, nInner)

                  End Select

                  ' Record the test end time
                  frmResults.TestEnd

                  ' Remove the highlight from the current test
                  chkTest(nLoopCtr).ForeColor = vbButtonText
                  chkTest(nLoopCtr).Refresh

            End If

      Next nLoopCtr

      ' Put the mouse pointer back to the default
      Me.MousePointer = vbDefault

End Sub
```

23. Here is the first of the four object testing routines:

```
Private Sub DimNew(nOuter As Integer, _
                   nInner As Integer)

      Dim clsSplit         As New CSplitExt
      Dim nLoopCtr         As Integer
      Dim nInnerCtr        As Integer
      Dim lTestVal         As Long
      Dim nHighWord        As Integer
      Dim nLowWord         As Integer

      For nLoopCtr = 1 To nOuter
          lTestVal = CLng(Abs((2147483647 * Rnd) + 1))
          For nInnerCtr = 1 To nInner
              clsSplit.LongValue = lTestVal
              lTestVal = clsSplit.LongValue
              nHighWord = clsSplit.HighWord
              nLowWord = clsSplit.LowWord
          Next nInnerCtr
      Next nLoopCtr

End Sub
```

24. This is the second object creation test subroutine:

```
Private Sub SetNew(nOuter As Integer, _
                   nInner As Integer)

Dim clsSplit          As CSplitExt
Dim nLoopCtr          As Integer
Dim nInnerCtr         As Integer
Dim lTestVal          As Long
Dim nHighWord         As Integer
Dim nLowWord          As Integer

Set clsSplit = New CSplitExt

For nLoopCtr = 1 To nOuter
    lTestVal = CLng(Abs((2147483647 * Rnd) + 1))
    For nInnerCtr = 1 To nInner
        clsSplit.LongValue = lTestVal
        lTestVal = clsSplit.LongValue
        nHighWord = clsSplit.HighWord
        nLowWord - clsSplit.LowWord
    Next nInnerCtr
Next nLoopCtr

Set clsSplit = Nothing

End Sub
```

25. This is the code for the third test case:

```
Private Sub InsideLoop(nOuter As Integer, _
                       nInner As Integer)

Dim clsSplit          As CSplitExt
Dim nLoopCtr          As Integer
Dim nInnerCtr         As Integer
Dim lTestVal          As Long
Dim nHighWord         As Integer
Dim nLowWord          As Integer

For nLoopCtr = 1 To nOuter
    lTestVal = CLng(Abs((2147483647 * Rnd) + 1))
    For nInnerCtr = 1 To nInner
        Set clsSplit = New CSplitExt
        clsSplit.LongValue = lTestVal
        lTestVal = clsSplit.LongValue
        nHighWord = clsSplit.HighWord
        nLowWord = clsSplit.LowWord
        Set clsSplit = Nothing
    Next nInnerCtr
Next nLoopCtr

End Sub
```

26. Here is the code for the fourth object creation test to be added to the form:

```
Private Sub OutsideLoop(nOuter As Integer, _
                        nInner As Integer)

Dim clsSplit            As CSplitExt
Dim nLoopCtr            As Integer
Dim nInnerCtr           As Integer
Dim lTestVal            As Long
Dim nHighWord           As Integer
Dim nLowWord            As Integer

For nLoopCtr = 1 To nOuter
    Set clsSplit = New CSplitExt
    lTestVal = CLng(Abs((2147483647 * Rnd) + 1))
    For nInnerCtr = 1 To nInner
        clsSplit.LongValue = lTestVal
        lTestVal = clsSplit.LongValue
        nHighWord = clsSplit.HighWord
        nLowWord = clsSplit.LowWord
    Next nInnerCtr
    Set clsSplit = Nothing
Next nLoopCtr

End Sub
```

27. The second object creation project is now finished, but it cannot be run until the external DLL is created. After this DLL is created and built, add it as a reference in the external test program.

28. Create a new project and save it as CSPLITEXTDLL.VBP.

29. Add a class module to the project and set the **Name** property to **CSplitExt**. Save the class as CSPLITEXT.CLS.

30. Add the following code to the newly created class module. Notice that this is the same code used in the class module for the internal object test program.

```
Option Explicit

Private mlLongValue     As Long
Private mnHighWord      As Integer
Private mnLowWord       As Integer
```

31. Add the public property code to set the long integer value.

```
Public Property Let LongValue(ByVal lLongValue As Long)

mlLongValue = lLongValue

' Split a long integer into high and low words.

If (mlLongValue And &H7FFFFFFF) <> mlLongValue Then
    ' Turn off the high bit
```

```
      mlLongValue = mlLongValue And &H7FFFFFFF
      ' Get the remaining bits of the high word
      mnHighWord = mlLongValue \ 65536
      ' Turn the high bit back on in the result
      mnHighWord = (mnHighWord And &H7FFF) + &H8000
      ' Restore the local property value
      mlLongValue = lLongValue
   Else
      mnHighWord = mlLongValue \ 65536
End If

If (mlLongValue And &HFFFF&) > &H7FFF Then
   mnLowWord = (mlLongValue And &HFFFF&) - &H10000
  Else
   mnLowWord = mlLongValue And &HFFFF&
End If

End Property
```

32. Add the three property **Get** procedures and build the DLL.

```
Public Property Get LongValue() As Long

LongValue = mlLongValue

End Property


Public Property Get LowWord() As Integer

LowWord = mnLowWord

End Property


Public Property Get HighWord() As Integer

HighWord = mnHighWord

End Property
```

How It Works

The program uses two different techniques to create object instances and creates instances in two different areas of nested loops. As each test is run, the test performance is recorded and saved in a grid. These test results can then be printed or exported to a CSV file. The exported file can be imported into a spreadsheet program for further analysis.

Comments

Try running the tests with less iteration in the loops, and a pattern will develop. For small numbers of iterations, there is not a statistically significant difference between the `Dim x As New` syntax and the alternative without the `New` clause. Based on the number of iterations required to see a variation, use the code technique that works best for the logic in your code.

However, not all code can operate with a single instance of an object. When multiple instances are required, either simultaneously or over time, pay close attention to where the instances are created. It is easy to see from the sample results that more instances translate directly to increased time. Minimize instance creation whenever possible.

COMPLEXITY
INTERMEDIATE

7.6 How do I...
Plan for performance during design and construction?

COMPATIBILITY: VISUAL BASIC 5 AND 6

Problem

Now I know how to evaluate some of the aspects of performance and how to analyze the code objectively. I can also map the execution profile of my programs. How can I adapt my code and coding style to make these tasks easier?

Technique

It is important to plan your code development to facilitate the performance analysis and debugging processes. This How-To presents some options that may help. These options include coding techniques and styles.

Steps

1. Use good structured program techniques. This advice might sound odd for an event-driven language such as Visual Basic, but it is possible to write poor code in any language.

Two primary concepts of structured programming apply here. The first is coupling, and the second is cohesion. Coupling determines the strength of external reference and dependencies. Loose coupling is good. It implies that there are no external references, especially to project global variables. Loose coupling does not imply that you cannot call other routines and functions. Be sure not to rely on how the other routines perform their task, just on the results.

Cohesion defines the relatedness of code with a single routine to other code in the same routine. In the case of cohesion, tight is best. All the code in a subroutine or function should be related to the performance of a single task.

2. Keep it simple. Complex logic is hard to understand and even harder to debug. Most people can keep an average of seven things or topics in their active memory. Generally, if there are more than seven options, or seven nested logic layers, the code verges on being too complex. The McCabe Complexity scale, as discussed in How-To 7.3, is a good way to evaluate code complexity.

3. Comment, comment, and comment again. If there are no comments, the code is not finished. When the original developer, or the poor soul working behind him or her, goes back to tune or debug, a lack of comments makes the whole job much harder. Go back and look at some of your old code or someone else's code. Can you tell what is going on? Why or why not? Learn from what you see and, most important, what you don't see. The following listing is an example of a common code algorithm that uses single-character variable names and does not have any comments:

```
Public Function NoComments(n As Integer, _
                           v As Integer) As Integer

Dim x           As Integer
Dim l           As Integer
Dim r           As Integer
Dim s           As String * 4

Get #n, 1, s

r = Val(s) + 1
l = 2

Do
    x = (l + r) / 2
    Get #n, x, s
    If v < Val(s) Then
        r = x - 1
      Else
        l = x + 1
    End If
Loop Until (v = Val(s)) Or (l > r)

If v = Trim$(s) Then
    NoComments = x
  Else
    NoComments = 0
End If

End Function
```

The preceding code, a binary search function, is very hard to follow. Even having a function name would help. The next listing is a copy of the same code with the addition of meaningful variable names and comments. It is much easier to read and understand, thus improving its maintainability.

```
Public Function BinarySearch(nChannel As Integer, _
                        nKey As Integer) As Integer

Dim nCurRecord      As Integer
Dim nLeftEdge       As Integer
Dim nRightEdge      As Integer
Dim sDataStr        As String * 4

' The first record in the file is a control record
' and contains a count of the data records. Get this
' count and add one to it to use as the right edge
' of the search.
Get #nChannel, 1, sDataStr
nRightEdge = Val(sDataStr) + 1

' Set the left edge of the search to the first
' data record in the file exclusive of the
' control record
nLeftEdge = 2


Do          ' Primary loop for the binary search

    ' Compute a target record location, which is the
    ' midpoint between the current left and right edges
    nCurRecord = (nLeftEdge + nRightEdge) / 2

    ' Get the record at the computed location
    Get #nChannel, nCurRecord, sDataStr

    ' Compare the record value to the key we are seeking
    If nKey < Val(sDataStr) Then

        ' The key is less than the current value, so
        ' pull the right edge in
        nRightEdge = nCurRecord - 1

    Else

        ' The key is greater than the current value, so
        ' pull the left edge in
        nLeftEdge = nCurRecord + 1

    End If

' The loop will continue until the key matches the current data
' or the left edge has passed the right edge. If the latter
' condition occurs, it means the the key was not found in the
' data.
```

CHAPTER 8

USING THE WIN32 API

```
        Loop Until (nKey = Trim$(sDataStr)) Or (nLeftEdge > nRightEdge)

        ' Test to see if the key was located
        If nKey = Val(sDataStr) Then

            ' The key was found, so pass back its location
            BinarySearch = nCurRecord

        Else

            ' The key was not found, so pass back a zero
            BinarySearch = 0

        End If

        End Function
```

4. Know your tools. There are not a tremendous number of tools on the market to help write better, faster, or cheaper code. Find some that fill your needs and know them well. If you can't find them, write them and share with others.

5. Know yourself and your own limitations. All developers, even those who can't or won't admit it, have weaknesses. Peer code reviews are an excellent tool. Grab some friends and have them look at your code with you. Be sure they are honest and tell you what they find. Don't take what they say personally. Remember these are your friends and you are asking for their help.

6. Track your defects. Keep a personal list of the feedback from reviews of your code. Anytime you find or hear of a defect in your code, write it down. Before releasing new code, look it over yourself to see if any of the previous errors you made got into this new code. Most developers have at least one consistent blind spot. When you know where yours are, you can watch for them.

7. Never add new code to an existing and working program. Get the new or experimental code working on its own. Then check out the performance and try some alternatives. After it works, add it to the main program.

How It Works

Solid design and implementation facilitate the process of testing, performance analysis, and debugging. This explanatory How-To offered several items for consideration. Adapt these suggestions to your personal style and the tools you have available for testing and analysis.

Comments

Many of the suggestions made in this How-To sound like general programming practices, and they are. The better a developer is at writing solid and understandable code, the easier it is to analyze, tune, and support the program. This whole aspect of software development is the key to writing stable, well-performing, and verifiable code. It is also an area that is ignored by too many developers. There are a number of excellent references and books that present methods and ideas that help to improve the quality and professionalism of software developers, so keep reading.

8

USING THE WIN32 API

How do I...

This chapter explores several different aspects of using the Win32 Application Programmers Interface (API), a feature-rich set of functions and subroutines that you can use to extend and add features to your program. In addition, many of the API calls can supply information about the system that you cannot get any other way.

Two specific aspects of the API were previously not available to Visual Basic developers in the earliest versions of the language: callbacks and subclassing. Visual Basic now allows developers to call API functions that use callbacks and set hooks for subclassing. Examples of the use of both of these techniques are included.

8.1 Determine a Drive's Characteristics

In many situations, it is important to know details about the disk drives available to your program. This How-To demonstrates how to get information on the geometry of the system disks, including the amount of free space.

8.2 Use a Shared Resource File DLL

Visual Basic enables you to include a single resource file as part of your projects. This How-To describes how you can use multiple resource files that have been compiled into separate DLL modules. These DLL files can then be replaced or modified to change the appearance of your program without having to rebuild your EXE.

8.3 Accept Dropped Files Using Subclassing

Using third-party subclassing controls, it was possible to process files dropped from Explorer. This How-To shows how you can achieve the same result directly in Visual Basic, without any custom controls.

8.4 Interpret the Values in a Bit Mask

A number of API functions return information to programs in the form of bit masks, which are numeric values in which each bit in the number can represent unique data. This example shows how to parse the data from the binary value of a number and how to compare values and masks at the binary level.

8.5 Create and Use Registry Entries

Registry functions are built into the Visual Basic language. Those functions, however, always store your values in predefined locations in the Registry. This How-To provides code that enables you to read and write values into the Registry anywhere you want.

8.6 Enumerate Windows Using Callbacks

Callbacks are a powerful technique that enables one program to call a function in another program or module. This section shows how to implement a callback that lists all the windows that exist on the Windows desktop.

COMPLEXITY
BEGINNING

8.1 How do I...
Determine a drive's characteristics?

COMPATIBILITY: VISUAL BASIC 5 AND 6

Problem

I want to have my program check the amount of free disk space before adding to a database or writing a large amount of information to the drive. I would also like to know the minimum amount of space being allocated for each file that is created. How do I determine the physical profile and space characteristics of the drives on my system?

Technique

You don't want to list information for drive letters that are not in use, so the program starts by building a list of the valid local and networked drives. Then call an API function to get the drive characteristics. After you have all this information, you can compute the total size of the drive and the amount of free space.

Steps

Open and run DRIVE ATTRIBUTES.VBP, which is shown in Figure 8.1. When the program runs, it populates the drop-down list with the valid drive letters. It then displays the drive information for the first drive in the list. The steps for creating this program are as follows.

Figure 8.1 The main form at runtime.

1. Create a new project called DRIVE ATTRIBUTES.VBP. Add a form to the project, and set the objects and properties as listed in Table 8.1. Save the form as DRIVE ATTRIBUTES.FRM.

Table 8.1 The Project Form's Objects and Properties

OBJECT/CONTROL	PROPERTY	VALUE
Form	Name	frmMain
	Caption	"Drive Attributes"
	Icon	DRIVE01.ICO
	StartUpPosition	2 - CenterScreen

continued on next page

continued from previous page

OBJECT/CONTROL	PROPERTY	VALUE
ComboBox	Name	cboDrives
	Style	2 - Dropdown List
Label	Name	lblInfo
	Alignment	2 'Center
	BorderStyle	1 - Fixed Single
	Index	0
Label	Name	lblInfo
	Alignment	2 - Center
	BorderStyle	1 'Fixed Single
	Index	1
Label	Name	lblInfo
	Alignment	2 - Center
	BorderStyle	1 - Fixed Single
	Index	2
Label	Name	lblInfo
	Alignment	2 - Center
	BorderStyle	1 - Fixed Single
	Index	3
Label	Name	lblInfo
	Alignment	2 - Center
	BorderStyle	1 - Fixed Single
	Index	4
Label	Name	lblInfo
	Alignment	2 - Center
	BorderStyle	1 - Fixed Single
	Index	5
Label	Name	lblInfo
	Alignment	2 - Center
	BorderStyle	1 - Fixed Single
	Index	6
Label	Name	lblCaption
	Caption	"Available Drives:"
	Index	0
Label	Name	lblCaption
	Caption	"Drive Type:"
	Index	1

OBJECT/CONTROL	PROPERTY	VALUE
Label	Name	lblCaption
	Caption	"Sectors per Cluster:"
	Index	2
Label	Name	lblCaption
	Caption	"Bytes per Sector:"
	Index	3
Label	Name	lblCaption
	Caption	"Free Clusters:"
	Index	4
Label	Name	lblCaption
	Caption	"Total Clusters:"
	Index	5
Label	Name	lblCaption
	Caption	"Total Free Space:"
	Index	6
Label	Name	lblCaption
	Caption	"Total Drive Space:"
	Index	7

2. Add the following code to the General Declarations section of the form. These statements declare the function calls for the API routines that are used. They also define the constants used in the program.

```
Option Explicit

Private Declare Function GetDriveType Lib "kernel32" _
    Alias "GetDriveTypeA" _
        (ByVal nDrive As String) As Long

Private Declare Function GetDiskFreeSpace Lib "kernel32" _
    Alias "GetDiskFreeSpaceA" _
        (ByVal lpRootPathName As String, _
         lpSectorsPerCluster As Long, _
         lpBytesPerSector As Long, _
         lpNumberOfFreeClusters As Long, _
         lpTotalNumberOfClusters As Long) As Long

Private Declare Function GetLogicalDriveStrings Lib "kernel32" _
    Alias "GetLogicalDriveStringsA" _
        (ByVal nBufferLength As Long, _
         ByVal lpBuffer As String) As Long

Private Const DRIVE_UNKNOWN = 0
Private Const DRIVE_NOTEXIST = 1
Private Const DRIVE_REMOVABLE = 2
```

```
Private Const DRIVE_FIXED = 3
Private Const DRIVE_REMOTE = 4
Private Const DRIVE_RAMDISK = 6
Private Const DRIVE_CDROM = 5
```

3. Add the following code to the form's **Load** event. This code starts by getting a delimited list of the active drive letters for the system. The drive letters are three characters long. They are delimited by a null character and include the : and \ punctuation.

The delimiter drive letter string is parsed and the individual drive letters are added to the drop-down list. When all the drives have been added to the list, the first item in the list is selected.

```
Private Sub Form_Load()

Dim sDriveNames      As String
Dim lBuffer          As Long
Dim lReturn          As Long
Dim nLoopCtr         As Integer
Dim nOffset          As Integer
Dim sTempStr         As String

' Get the drive names

' Compute the string length
' 26 drive letters * Len("X:\" & Null) + final null
lBuffer = 26 * 4 + 1

' Allocate the return buffer space
sDriveNames = Space$(lBuffer)

' Make the API call
lReturn = GetLogicalDriveStrings(lBuffer, sDriveNames)

' Load the drive names into the drop-down list

' Initialize the parsing offset
nOffset = 1

Do
    ' Peel out the first drive string
    sTempStr = Mid$(sDriveNames, nOffset, 3)

    ' If the string starts with a null we are done
    If Left$(sTempStr, 1) = vbNullChar Then Exit Do

    ' Add the drive to the drop-down
    cboDrives.AddItem sTempStr

    ' Increase the offset to get the next drive
    nOffset = nOffset + 4

Loop
```

```
' Select the first drive in the list
cboDrives.ListIndex = 0

End Sub
```

4. Place the following code in the **Click** event of the **cboDrives** control. This code executes each time a selection is made from the drop-down list. The function begins by getting the drive letter from the list, and then passes the letter to an API function to determine the drive type. The display is then updated with a string that indicates the type of the selected drive.

Next, the **GetDiskFreeSpace** API function is called to get the drive's physical characteristics. The function does not return the free space directly; it must be computed from the data that is returned.

```
Private Sub cboDrives_Click()

Dim lSectorsPerCluster     As Long
Dim lBytesPerSector        As Long
Dim lFreeClusters          As Long
Dim lTotalClusters         As Long
Dim lReturn                As Long
Dim sDrive                 As String
Dim lMbFactor              As Long
Dim dByteSize              As Double
Dim dSpace                 As Double

' Get the currently selected drive root path
sDrive = cboDrives.List(cboDrives.ListIndex)

' Get the drive type using the API
lReturn = GetDriveType(sDrive)

' Evaluate the returned drive type
Select Case lReturn
    Case DRIVE_UNKNOWN
        lblInfo(0).Caption = "Unknown"
    Case DRIVE_NOTEXIST
        lblInfo(0).Caption = "Not Found"
    Case DRIVE_REMOVABLE
        lblInfo(0).Caption = "Removable"
    Case DRIVE_FIXED
        lblInfo(0).Caption = "Fixed"
    Case DRIVE_REMOTE
        lblInfo(0).Caption = "Remote"
    Case DRIVE_RAMDISK
        lblInfo(0).Caption = "Ram Disk"
    Case DRIVE_CDROM
        lblInfo(0).Caption = "CD-ROM"
End Select

' Get the drive geometry
lReturn = GetDiskFreeSpace(sDrive, _
            lSectorsPerCluster, _
```

```
                lBytesPerSector, _
                lFreeClusters, _
                lTotalClusters)

    ' Show the geometry information
    lblInfo(1).Caption = lSectorsPerCluster
    lblInfo(2).Caption = lBytesPerSector
    lblInfo(3).Caption = lFreeClusters
    lblInfo(4).Caption = lTotalClusters

    ' Compute a megabyte
    lMbFactor = 1024 ^ 2

    ' Compute and show the total free MB
    ' All values are cast to doubles to avoid
    ' overflow problems for large disks
    dByteSize = CDbl(lSectorsPerCluster) * _
            CDbl(lBytesPerSector) * _
            CDbl(lFreeClusters)
    lblInfo(5).Caption = Format$(dByteSize / lMbFactor, "###,##0")

    ' Compute and show the total drive MB
    ' All values are cast to doubles to avoid
    ' overflow problems for large disks
    dByteSize = CDbl(lSectorsPerCluster) * _
            CDbl(lBytesPerSector) * _
            CDbl(lTotalClusters)
    lblInfo(6).Caption = Format$(dByteSize / lMbFactor, "###,##0")

End Sub
```

How It Works

This program does not list all available drives in a table. In most cases, information about a specific drive is all that's required. The user chooses which drive to view information about by selecting it from the Available Drives drop-down list box.

TIP

To make a program that monitors drive characteristics proactive, add a Timer control that fires every minute or so. It can then recheck the free space and alert you if the space falls below a predefined limit.

Each time the user chooses a different drive from the Available Drives drop-down list box, the characteristics for that drive are retrieved. Then, information is placed into the appropriate labels. Some of the information must be calculated before it is placed into its label.

Comments

The logic in this code assumes that a megabyte of disk space is 1,024 bytes squared. When this program is run on different systems, however, with various drive types and geometries, some inconsistencies may occur. It seems that a megabyte is not always a megabyte, and even the information reported under drive properties with Explorer shows variations.

Do some math and see what a megabyte is for the drives on your system. If you check a dozen different drives, you might get that many different answers. The important thing to remember is to be conservative and consistent. Keep in mind that your mileage may vary.

COMPLEXITY
INTERMEDIATE

8.2 How do I...
Use a shared resource file DLL?

COMPATIBILITY: VISUAL BASIC 5 AND 6

Problem

I understand how to add a resource file to my program, but I would like to be able to change the resources that are used and not have to recompile my program to include the changes. I would also like to be able to change the resources used at runtime. What are the differences in how I use embedded and external resources, and how do I change resources at runtime?

Technique

Visual Basic enables you to include a single resource file as part of your projects and this How-To includes a simple example of this procedure. Next, the code is rewritten to use the same resources, but in the second version of the program, the resources are in an external DLL module. This section also demonstrates the construction of a second resource-only DLL and changes the DLL being used at runtime.

Steps

Open and run EMBEDDED RESOURCE.VBP. The running program is shown in Figure 8.2.

The same program rewritten to use a shared resource DLL is shown running in Figure 8.3. To see this second program, open and run SHARED RESOURCE. VBP.

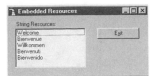

Figure 8.2 The
embedded resource
file at runtime.

Figure 8.3 Shared
resources with a
primary DLL.

Now, click the Change Resource command button. The results can be seen in Figure 8.4. Complete the following steps to create these programs.

Figure 8.4 Shared
resources with an
alternative DLL.

1. Use WordPad or Notepad to create a text file named RESVER1.RC, as shown in Listing 8.1. After the file is created, use the resource compiler, RC.EXE, to create an RES version of the file. You can find the compiler program in the \TOOLS\RESOURCE directory of the Visual Basic CD-ROM. This directory also includes a text file that explains the contents of resource files and the use of the resource compiler. Additional resource file and resource compiler information is available on the Microsoft Developer Network CD-ROM and online at the Microsoft Web site.

Listing 8.1 RESVER1.RC

```
// Resources template file

// String Tables

// English

#define ENG_WELCOME 1001

STRINGTABLE DISCARDABLE
BEGIN
    ENG_WELCOME "Welcome"
END

// French

#define FRA_WELCOME 2001

STRINGTABLE DISCARDABLE
BEGIN
    FRA_WELCOME "Bienvenue"
END

// German

#define GER_WELCOME 3001

STRINGTABLE DISCARDABLE
BEGIN
    GER_WELCOME "Willkommen"
END

// Italian

#define ITA_WELCOME 4001

STRINGTABLE DISCARDABLE
BEGIN
    ITA_WELCOME "Benvenuti"
END

// Spanish

#define SPA_WELCOME 5001

STRINGTABLE DISCARDABLE
BEGIN
    SPA_WELCOME "Bienvenido"
END
```

2. Create a new project called EMBEDDED RESOURCE.VBP. Add a form to the project, and set the objects and properties as listed in Table 8.2. Save the form as EMBEDDED RESOURCE.FRM.

Table 8.2 The Project Form's Objects and Properties

OBJECT/CONTROL	PROPERTY	VALUE
Form	Name	frmMain
	Caption	"Embedded Resources"
	Icon	"WATER.ICO"
CommandButton	Name	cmdAction
	Caption	"E&xit"
ListBox	Name	lstHello
Label	Name	lblCaption
	Caption	"String Resources:"

3. Add the following code to the form's **Load** and the command button's **Click** events. The **Form Load** code adds the string values from the resource file to the list box.

```
Private Sub Form_Load()

' Load the list box from the string resources
lstHello.AddItem LoadResString(1001)
lstHello.AddItem LoadResString(2001)
lstHello.AddItem LoadResString(3001)
lstHello.AddItem LoadResString(4001)
lstHello.AddItem LoadResString(5001)

End Sub

Private Sub cmdAction_Click()

Unload frmMain

End Sub
```

4. Add the resource file created in step 1, RESVER1.RES, to the project. This first project is now complete.

5. Use WordPad or Notepad to create a text file named RESVER2.RC, as shown in Listing 8.2. This file is almost identical to the first resource file you wrote. The only difference is that the language has been added to each resource string. After the file is created, use the resource compiler, RC.EXE, to create an RES version of the file. You can find the compiler program in the \TOOLS\RESOURCE directory of the Visual Basic CD-ROM.

Listing 8.2 RESVER2.RC

```
// Resources template file

// String Tables

// English

#define ENG_WELCOME 1001

STRINGTABLE DISCARDABLE
BEGIN
    ENG_WELCOME "Welcome (English)"
END

// French

#define FRA_WELCOME 2001

STRINGTABLE DISCARDABLE
BEGIN
    FRA_WELCOME "Bienvenue (French)"
END

// German

#define GER_WELCOME 3001

STRINGTABLE DISCARDABLE
BEGIN
    GER_WELCOME "Willkommen (German)"
END

// Italian

#define ITA_WELCOME 4001

STRINGTABLE DISCARDABLE
BEGIN
    ITA_WELCOME "Benvenuti (Italian)"
END

// Spanish

#define SPA_WELCOME 5001

STRINGTABLE DISCARDABLE
BEGIN
    SPA_WELCOME "Bienvenido (Spanish)"
END
```

6. Create a new ActiveX DLL project called RESVER1.VBP. Add the resource file created in step 1, RESVER1.RES, to the project. Choose Project, Project Properties from the menu. Go to the Compile Options tab and make sure the Compile to Native Code option button is selected. Compile the project into a DLL named RESVER1.DLL.

7. Create another new ActiveX DLL project called RESVER2.VBP. Add the resource file created in step 5, RESVER2.RES, to the project. Choose Project, Project Properties from the menu. Go to the Compile Options tab and make sure the Compile to Native Code option button is selected. Compile the project into a DLL named RESVER2.DLL.

8. Create a new Standard EXE project called SHARED RESOURCE.VBP. Add a class module to the project and save it as SHARED RESOURCE.CLS. Set the class name to **clsResource**, and the class description to **Resource DLL Management**. Now add the following code to the General Declarations section of the class. This code declares the public class variables, declares the local private variables to store the property values, defines the API functions that are used, and defines the API constants that are needed.

```
Option Explicit

' Public property values
Public Success            As Boolean
Public ErrorText          As String

' Local storage for public properties
Private msDLLName         As String
Private mlResourceID      As Long
Private mlResourceType    As Long
Private msStringValue     As String
' Class level variable to hold the library handle
Private mhLibHandle       As Long

' Load a named DLL library module into process memory
Private Declare Function LoadLibrary Lib "kernel32" _
    Alias "LoadLibraryA" _
        (ByVal lpLibFileName As String) As Long

' Unload a DLL library module from process memory
Private Declare Function FreeLibrary Lib "kernel32" _
        (ByVal hLibModule As Long) As Long

' Load a string resource from a loaded module
Private Declare Function LoadString Lib "user32" _
    Alias "LoadStringA" _
        (ByVal hInstance As Long, _
         ByVal wID As Long, _
         ByVal lpBuffer As String, _
         ByVal nBufferMax As Long) As Long

' Resource formats
Const RES_CURSOR = 1         ' cursor resource
```

```
Const RES_BITMAP = 2         ' Bitmap resource
Const RES_ICON = 3           ' Icon resource
Const RES_MENU = 4           ' Menu resource
Const RES_DIALOG = 5         ' Dialog box
Const RES_STRING = 6         ' String resource
Const RES_FONTDIR = 7        ' Font directory resource
Const RES_FONT = 8           ' Font resource
Const RES_ACCLTABLE = 9      ' Accelerator Table
Const RES_USERDEF = 10       ' User-defined resource
Const RES_GROUPCURSOR = 12   ' Group cursor
Const RES_GROUPICON = 14     ' Group Icon
```

9. The public properties for the class are listed in Table 8.3. The code that
follows the table supplies the Get and Let functions for the DLLName
property. The property Let function starts by checking whether the name
of the resource DLL file is actually being changed. If it is not, the function
exits because the DLL module is already loaded. If it is a new DLL name,
the code loads it as a library module, and then verifies that the load was
successful.

Table 8.3 Public Class Properties

PROPERTY	DATE TYPE	READ/WRITE
Success	Boolean	Read/Write
ErrorText	String	Read/Write
DLLName	String	Read/Write
ResourceType	Long	Read/Write
ResourceID	Long	Write
StringValue	String	Read

```
Public Property Get DLLName() As String

DLLName = msDLLName

End Property

Public Property Let DLLName(rsDLLName As String)

Dim lResult        As Long

Success = True          ' Assume success

' Only open the library if the name has changed
If msDLLName <> rsDLLName Then

    If Len(msDLLName) <> 0 Then
        ' There is an open and loaded DLL so close it
```

```
        lResult = FreeLibrary(mhLibHandle)
    End If

    msDLLName = rsDLLName
    mhLibHandle = LoadLibrary(msDLLName)

    ' Be sure the library was loaded by checking for
    ' a valid module handle
    If mhLibHandle = vbNull Then
        ' Unable to load the DLL
        msDLLName = ""              ' Clear the internal property
                                    ' value
        Success = False            ' Set the success and error
                                    ' properties
        ErrorText = "Unable to load the requested resource file: " & _
                            rsDLLName
    End If

End If

End Property
```

10. Add the code that implements **Get** and **Let** for the **ResourceType**
property. The **Let** procedure verifies that the selected resource type is one
supported by the class. In this How-To, only string resources are
supported. Refer to the Windows 32 SDK documentation for information
on extracting and using other resource types.

```
Public Property Get ResourceType() As Long

ResourceType = mlResourceType

End Property

Public Property Let ResourceType(rlResourceType As Long)

Dim lResult         As Long

Success = True          ' Assume success

' Validate the resource type
Select Case rlResourceType
    Case RES_STRING
        ' Type is supported by the class
        mlResourceType = rlResourceType

    Case Else
        ' Unsupported resource type
```

```
                    ' Clear the internal property value
                    rlResourceType = 0

                    ' Set the success and error property variables
                    Success = False
                    ErrorText = "Resource type '" & CStr(rlResourceType) & _
                                "' is not supported by the class."

            End Select

            End Property
```

11. Add the code to handle the **ResourceID** property. The routine starts by ensuring that all the required properties have values. If they do not, the code exits. If the properties have all been set, the specified resource is loaded from the DLL module. The resulting string is then saved in the **StringValue** property.

```
Public Property Let ResourceID(rlResourceID As Long)

    ' Get the resource from the DLL

    Dim lResult         As Long
    Dim sTempStr        As String

    ' Set the resource ID property
    mlResourceID = rlResourceID

    ' First check for all the required properties
    ' No error is flagged if the parameters have not been set
    If mlResourceID = 0 Or _
       mlResourceType = 0 Or _
       mhLibHandle = 0 Then Exit Property

    Select Case mlResourceType
        Case RES_STRING
            ' Clear the string value property
            msStringValue = ""

            ' Allocate the string space for the return value
            sTempStr = Space$(1024)

            ' Get the requested string resource
            lResult = LoadString(mhLibHandle, _
                                 mlResourceID, _
                                 sTempStr, _
                                 1024)

            ' See if a string was returned
            If lResult <> 0 Then
```

continued on next page

continued from previous page

```
                        ' Got a string so trim it down
                        msStringValue = Left$(sTempStr, lResult)

                        ' Release the temporary string space
                        sTempStr = ""

                        ' Set the success status property
                        Success = True

                    Else

                        ' Did not get a returned value
                        ' so indicate a failure
                        Success = False
                        ErrorText = "Unable to load the requested string _
                        resource."

                    End If

            Case Else
                ' *** Other resource types would be handled here

        End Select

        End Property
```

12. This next section of the class logic simply returns the text stored in the
StringValue property.

```
Public Property Get StringValue() As String

StringValue = msStringValue

End Property
```

13. The final piece of code for the class initializes the property values when a
class instance is created.

```
Private Sub Class_Initialize()

' Clear the class property values
msDLLName = ""
mlResourceID = 0
mlResourceType = 0
msStringValue = ""
ErrorText = ""
Success = True

End Sub
```

14. Add a form to the project and set the objects and properties listed in Table
8.4 for the form and save it as SHARED RESOURCE.FRM.

Table 8.4 The Project Form's Objects and Properties

OBJECT/CONTROL	PROPERTY	VALUE
Form	Name	frmMain
	Caption	"Shared Resources"
	Icon	"EARTH.ICO"
CommandButton	Name	cmdAction
	Caption	"Change Resource"
	Index	0
CommandButton	Name	cmdAction
	Caption	"E&xit"
	Index	1
ListBox	Name	lstHello
Label	Name	lblCaption
	Caption	"String Resources:"

15. Place the following code in the General Declarations section of the form. This code declares module-scope variables and constants.

```
Option Explicit

Dim cResource              As New clsResource

Dim mnCurrentResource      As Integer
Dim msResourceNames(2)     As String

Const RES_STRING = 6        ' String resource
```

16. The following code needs to be inserted in the form's **Load** event. The procedure starts by loading an array with the names of the DLL resource files. It then selects the first one and calls a form-level subroutine to load the resources.

```
Private Sub Form_Load()

' Load the array of resource filenames
msResourceNames(0) = App.Path & "\Resver1.dll"
msResourceNames(1) = App.Path & "\Resver2.dll"

' Set the current resource to the first one
mnCurrentResource = 0

' Call the routine to load the resources
Call LoadFromResourceFile

End Sub
```

17. This next subroutine clears any string resource values that may be displayed in the list box. Then it sets the class properties and gets the resulting string values. These values are then loaded into the list box.

```
Sub LoadFromResourceFile()

' Clear the list box
lstHello.Clear

' Set the resource class properties
cResource.DLLName = msResourceNames(mnCurrentResource)
cResource.ResourceType = RES_STRING

' Load the list box using the string resources
cResource.ResourceID = 1001
lstHello.AddItem cResource.StringValue
cResource.ResourceID = 2001
lstHello.AddItem cResource.StringValue
cResource.ResourceID = 3001
lstHello.AddItem cResource.StringValue
cResource.ResourceID = 4001
lstHello.AddItem cResource.StringValue
cResource.ResourceID = 5001
lstHello.AddItem cResource.StringValue

End Sub
```

18. The following code is associated with the `Click` event for the `cmdAction` command button control array. When the user selects the first button in the array to change the current resource file, the variable that references the current DLL name is changed. Then the subroutine written in step 17 is called to reload the list box using the new resources.

```
Private Sub cmdAction_Click(Index As Integer)

Select Case Index
    Case 0      ' Change Resource
        If mnCurrentResource = 0 Then
           mnCurrentResource = 1
        Else
           mnCurrentResource = 0
        End If

        ' Call the routine to load the resources
        Call LoadFromResourceFile

    Case 1      ' Exit
        Unload frmMain

End Select

End Sub
```

How It Works

The first program you wrote demonstrates the use of resources with the features and language syntax that are part of Visual Basic itself. The second program uses the two ActiveX DLLs you created to store the resources. These DLL modules are then loaded as they are needed, and the resources are extracted with the Win32 APIs for use in the program.

Comments

This How-To demonstrates the changing resources dynamically at runtime. Please note that you can also replace or modify the resource DLL at any time. If you do replace the DLL, be careful not to remove any of the resources being used by your program. You must also make sure not to change any of the internal resource ID numbers, or your program will not be able to find and load them.

COMPLEXITY
ADVANCED

8.3 How do I...
Accept dropped files using subclassing?

COMPATIBILITY: VISUAL BASIC 5 AND 6

Problem

I have a program that operates on one or more files. The program enables the user to select a file by using the common dialog boxes, but I would also like to make it possible for files to be dropped on the program from Windows Explorer. How do I allow my program to receive dropped files, and then detect when files are dropped and get the names of those files?

Technique

A file drop occurs when one or more files are selected in Windows Explorer and then dragged to another application and dropped. Accepting dropped files is a multiple-step process. You must first register your program as being able to accept dropped files. Then you need to subclass yourself by notifying the system that you want to process certain messages yourself, not have the operating system or Visual Basic handle them for you. The final step is to process the message delivered to your code when files are dropped.

Steps

Open and run DRAG AND DROP.VBP. Use Windows Explorer to select a group of files from a directory and drop them on the program. An example of the running program is shown in Figure 8.5. Use the following steps to complete this project.

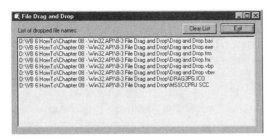

Figure 8.5 The main form at runtime.

1. Create a new project called DRAG AND DROP.VBP. Subclassing makes use of callbacks that require using the **AddressOf** statement. Functions referenced by **AddressOf** cannot be in a form and must exist in a code module or an active instance of a class module. Add a code module to the project, and put the following code into the General Declarations section. Save the module as DRAG AND DROP.BAS.

```
Option Explicit

Public Declare Function CallWindowProc Lib "user32" _
    Alias "CallWindowProcA" _
        (ByVal lPrevWndFunc As Long, _
         ByVal hWnd As Long, _
         ByVal Msg As Long, _
         ByVal wParam As Long, _
         ByVal lParam As Long) As Long

Public Declare Function SetWindowLong Lib "user32" _
    Alias "SetWindowLongA" _
        (ByVal hWnd As Long, _
         ByVal nIndex As Long, _
         ByVal dwNewLong As Long) As Long

Private lPrevWndProc    As Long
Private hHookWindow     As Long

Public Declare Sub DragAcceptFiles Lib "shell32.dll" _
```

```
             (ByVal hWnd As Long, _
              ByVal fAccept As Long)

Public Declare Sub DragFinish Lib "shell32.dll" _
        (ByVal hDrop As Long)

Public Declare Function DragQueryFile Lib "shell32.dll" _
      Alias "DragQueryFileA" _
          (ByVal hDrop As Long, _
           ByVal UINT As Long, _
           ByVal lpStr As String, _
           ByVal ch As Long) As Long

Public Const GWL_WNDPROC = -4
Public Const WM_DROPFILES = &H233
```

2. Add this subroutine to set the messaging hook. When called, it tells the operating system to pass all messages to this procedure. The third parameter of the **SetWindowLong** API call tells the system which function in the program handles the messages. The return value from the call is a pointer to the previous routine in the message-processing stack. This is needed later to clear the hook and restore the message call list to the previous state.

```
Public Sub SetHook(lHwnd As Long)

' Be sure the code is not already subclassing
If hHookWindow <> 0 Then Call Clearhook

' Save the handle of the calling window
hHookWindow = lHwnd

' Set the subclassing window message hook
lPrevWndProc = SetWindowLong(hHookWindow, _
                  GWL_WNDPROC, _
                  AddressOf HookCallback)

End Sub
```

3. The following subroutine is used to remove the subclassing message hook from the system. First it checks to make sure you have an active hook from this program. As long as you do, it then proceeds to remove the hook and restore the message call list to its previous state.

```
Public Sub Clearhook()

Dim lReturn        As Long

' Check to be sure that there is a hook active
If hHookWindow = 0 Then Exit Sub
```

continued on next page

continued from previous page

```
If IsEmpty(hHookWindow) = True Then Exit Sub
If IsNull(hHookWindow) = True Then Exit Sub

' Remove the hook from the system
lReturn = SetWindowLong(hHookWindow, _
            GWL_WNDPROC, _
            lPrevWndProc)

End Sub
```

4. This next subroutine is called by the operating system when there is a message for this program to process. If the message is for the main form of the application, the code calls a message-handling function in the main form itself. In all cases, you need to pass the message on to the next process in the message-handling stack.

```
Function HookCallback(ByVal hWnd As Long, _
            ByVal lMsg As Long, _
            ByVal wParam As Long, _
            ByVal lParam As Long) As Long

Select Case hWnd
    Case hHookWindow
        ' The message is for the window that is subclassed so ...
        ' Pass the message to the form for it to handle
        frmMain.MessageProc lMsg, wParam, lParam

    Case Else
        ' The message is for some other window so ...

End Select

' Pass the message through to the next message processor
HookCallback = CallWindowProc(lPrevWndProc, hWnd, lMsg, wParam, _
lParam)

End Function
```

5. Add a form to the project and set the objects and properties listed in Table 8.5 for the form; save it as DRAG AND DROP.FRM.

Table 8.5 The Project Form's Objects and Properties

OBJECT/CONTROL	PROPERTY	VALUE
Form	Name	frmMain
	Caption	"File Drag and Drop"
	Icon	"DRAG3PG.ICO"
ListBox	Name	lstFiles
CommandButton	Name	cmdAction
	Caption	"Clear List"
	Index	0

OBJECT/CONTROL	PROPERTY	VALUE
CommandButton	Name	cmdAction
	Caption	"E&xit"
	Index	1
Label	Name	lblCaption
	Caption	"List of dropped file names:"

6. Place the following code in the form's **Load** and **Terminate** events. The **Form Load** event code first calls the subroutine in the code module that sets the message hook. The program then notifies the operating system that it can now accept dropped files.

The **Form Terminate** event code removes this program from the message-processing stack.

```
Private Sub Form_Load()

' Establish the callback windows message hook
Call SetHook((Me.hWnd))

' Tell the OS this form accepts dropped files
Call DragAcceptFiles((Me.hWnd), True)

End Sub

Private Sub Form_Terminate()

Call Clearhook

End Sub
```

7. Add the code to process the dropped files message. The **Select Case** structure restricts the message processing to just the single message that relates to dropped files. Let the operating system handle all the other messages by not doing anything with them, even those such as mouse events that are directed to this form. The code uses the **DragQueryFile** API function to determine how many files were dropped on the form. Then it makes repeated calls to the function to get the specific filenames. Each filename is then added to the list box on the form. Because the subroutine is now finished processing the files, a call is made to release the internal dropped file event handle that was allocated by the operating system.

```
Public Sub MessageProc(lMsg As Long, _
              wParam As Long, _
              lParam As Long)

Dim nDropCount        As Integer
Dim nLoopCtr          As Integer
```

continued on next page

continued from previous page

```
        Dim lReturn              As Long
        Dim hDrop               As Long
        Dim sFileName           As String

        Select Case lMsg
            Case WM_DROPFILES
                ' Save the drop structure handle
                hDrop = wParam

                ' Allocate space for the return value
                sFileName = Space$(255)

                ' Get the number of filenames dropped
                nDropCount = DragQueryFile(hDrop, -1, sFileName, 254)

                ' Loop to get each dropped filename and
                ' add it to the list box

                For nLoopCtr = 0 To nDropCount - 1
                    ' Allocate space for the return value
                    sFileName = Space$(255)

                    ' Get a dropped filename
                    lReturn = DragQueryFile(hDrop, nLoopCtr, sFileName, 254)
                    lstFiles.AddItem Left$(sFileName, lReturn)

                Next nLoopCtr

                ' Release the drop structure from memory
                Call DragFinish(hDrop)

        End Select

    End Sub
```

8. Add code to handle the **Click** events for the **cmdAction** command button
control array. The first command button clears the list box and the second
command button ends the program.

```
Private Sub cmdAction_Click(Index As Integer)

Select Case Index
    Case 0          ' Clear List
        lstFiles.Clear

    Case 1          ' Exit
        Unload frmMain

End Select

End Sub
```

How It Works

The program inserts itself into the processing queue for system-generated messages. Most messages, such as mouse and keyboard events, are handled for you by Visual Basic. By establishing a message hook, this example subclasses the program and can be used to alter or extend standard Visual Basic message-handling behavior.

Comments

Subclassing is a powerful, but often dangerous, capability. Be careful to process only the specific messages that interest you, and only those messages directed to the particular program or window you are watching.

The operating system passes *all* messages to each hook procedure, and you have an obligation to pass on the messages not intended for you. If you forget to pass the messages on, you might find that other programs on your system stop responding. They cannot actually respond because you are keeping all the messages, so as far as other programs are concerned, nothing is happening.

COMPLEXITY
INTERMEDIATE

8.4 How do I...
Interpret the values in a bit mask?

COMPATIBILITY: VISUAL BASIC 5 AND 6

Problem

I know that there are many system functions that return results in the form of a bit mask (a set of bits). How do I extract data from this mask and tell whether one or more bits are set?

Technique

This How-To parses the data from the binary value of a number and sets values in arrays of check boxes to show which bits are on in a particular value. Bit mask comparisons are considered to be **True** if all the bits in the mask that are turned on are also turned on in the value being tested.

To provide sets of values and masks, the hex or decimal value entered in the program is split into high and low words. Each word is then split into high and low bytes. The resulting byte values are used as masks and test numbers.

Steps

Open and run BIT MASK.VBP. An example of the running program is shown in Figure 8.6. Complete the steps following Table 8.6 to create this program.

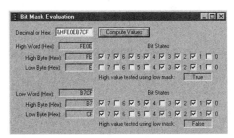

Figure 8.6 The main form at runtime.

In this example, a hex value has been entered and the bit values and mask testing results are shown. The use of hex values makes it easier to control and predict the resulting word, byte, and bit values. To have bits set for all four words in the example, you need to supply an eight-digit hex value. Refer to Table 8.6 for a list of hex digits and their respective binary bit values.

Table 8.6 Bit Values of Hex Digits

HEX DIGIT	BIT 3	BIT 2	BIT 1	BIT 0
0	0	0	0	0
1	0	0	0	1
2	0	0	1	0
3	0	0	1	1
4	0	1	0	0
5	0	1	0	1
6	0	1	1	0
7	0	1	1	1
8	1	0	0	0
9	1	0	0	1
A	1	0	1	0
B	1	0	1	1
C	1	1	0	0
D	1	1	0	1
E	1	1	1	0
F	1	1	1	1

1. Create a new project called BIT MASK.VBP. Add a code module to the project and add the following subroutine. This code uses integer division to split a word into its high and low bytes. Save the module as BIT MASK.BAS.

```
Public Sub SplitWord _
                (nWordIn As Integer, _
                 btByteHi As Byte, _
                 btByteLo As Byte)

' Split a word into high and low bytes.

If nWordIn < 0 Then
    ' Word value is negative so account for the
    ' make it positive and extract it
    btByteHi = (nWordIn + 65536) \ 256

  Else
    ' Extract the positive high byte
    btByteHi = nWordIn \ 256

End If

' Get the low byte from the word value
btByteLo = nWordIn And 255

End Sub
```

2. Add the following subroutine to the code module. This routine uses the logical **And** operator to determine whether all the bits in the mask are also on in the test value. If they are, then the results of the **And** operation will equal the value of the bit mask.

```
Public Function IsBitMaskSet _
                (lTestValue As Long, _
                 lBitMask As Long) As Boolean

' Determine if a set of bits in a value are all on.

Select Case lBitMask
Case 0
        ' No mask value available so it can't be tested
        IsBitMaskSet = False

    Case Else
        If (lTestValue And lBitMask) = lBitMask Then
            ' If logical AND of the two values equals the mask
            ' value, then the same bits are on in both values
            IsBitMaskSet = True

        Else
```

continued on next page

continued from previous page

```
                          ' All the same bits are not on in both values
                          IsBitMaskSet = False

              End If

      End Select

      End Function
```

3. The following Boolean function is used to determine whether a specific bit is on in the test value. Because each bit at the binary level is an increasing power of two, the code uses the power of two for the bit position in a single value mask. The same logic that was used for the **IsMaskSet** routine is then applied.

```
Public Function IsBitSet _
                (lTestValue As Long, _
                 nBitNumber As Integer) As Boolean

' Determine if a single bit in a value is set.

If (lTestValue And (2 ^ nBitNumber)) = (2 ^ nBitNumber) Then
    IsBitSet = True
  Else
    IsBitSet = False
End If

End Function
```

4. This next subroutine uses integer division to split a long word into its high and low integer word values.

```
Public Sub SplitLong _
                (ByVal lValue As Long, _
                 nWordHi As Integer, _
                 nWordLo As Integer)

' Split a long integer into high and low words.

' Get the high word value
If (lValue And &H7FFFFFFF) <> lValue Then
    ' Turn off the high bit
    lValue = lValue And &H7FFFFFFF

    ' Get the remaining bits of the high word
    nWordHi = lValue \ 65536

    ' Turn the high bit back on in the result
    nWordHi = (nWordHi And &H7FFF) + &H8000

  Else
```

```
        nWordHi = lValue \ 65536

    End If

    ' Get the low word value
    If (lValue And &HFFFF&) > &H7FFF Then
        nWordLo = (lValue And &HFFFF&) - &H10000
      Else
        nWordLo = lValue And &HFFFF&
    End If

    End Sub
```

5. Add a form to the project and set the objects and properties of the form as listed in Table 8.7. It is very important to set the index values of the check box control arrays correctly. Each of the four arrays must be numbered from left to right, starting with seven and decreasing to zero. Save the form as BIT MASK.FRM.

Table 8.7 The Project Form's Objects and Properties

OBJECT/CONTROL	PROPERTY	VALUE
Form	Name	frmMain
	Caption	"Bit Mask Evaluation"
	Icon	"TRFFC09.ICO"
CommandButton	Name	cmdCompute
	Caption	"Compute Values"
	Default	True
CheckBox	Name	chkLLBit
	Caption	"7"
	Index	7
CheckBox	Name	chkLLBit
	Caption	"6"
	Index	6
CheckBox	Name	chkLLBit
	Caption	"5"
	Index	5
CheckBox	Name	chkLLBit
	Caption	"4"
	Index	4
CheckBox	Name	chkLLBit
	Caption	"3"
	Index	3

continued on next page

continued from previous page

OBJECT/CONTROL	PROPERTY	VALUE
CheckBox	Name	chkLLBit
	Caption	"2"
	Index	2
CheckBox	Name	chkLLBit
	Caption	"1"
	Index	1
CheckBox	Name	chkLLBit
	Caption	"0"
	Index	0
CheckBox	Name	chkLHBit
	Caption	"7"
	Index	7
CheckBox	Name	chkLHBit
	Caption	"6"
	Index	6
CheckBox	Name	chkLHBit
	Caption	"5"
	Index	5
CheckBox	Name	chkLHBit
	Caption	"4"
	Index	4
CheckBox	Name	chkLHBit
	Caption	"3"
	Index	3
CheckBox	Name	chkLHBit
	Caption	"2"
	Index	2
CheckBox	Name	chkLHBit
	Caption	"1"
	Index	1
CheckBox	Name	chkLHBit
	Caption	"0"
	Index	0
CheckBox	Name	chkHLBit
	Caption	"7"
	Index	7

OBJECT/CONTROL	PROPERTY	VALUE
CheckBox	Name	chkHLBit
	Caption	"6"
	Index	6
CheckBox	Name	chkHLBit
	Caption	"5"
	Index	5
CheckBox	Name	chkHLBit
	Caption	"4"
	Index	4
CheckBox	Name	chkHLBit
	Caption	"3"
	Index	3
CheckBox	Name	chkHLBit
	Caption	"2"
	Index	2
CheckBox	Name	chkHLBit
	Caption	"1"
	Index	1
CheckBox	Name	chkHLBit
	Caption	"0"
	Index	0
CheckBox	Name	chkHHBit
	Caption	"7"
	Index	7
CheckBox	Name	chkHHBit
	Caption	"6"
	Index	6
CheckBox	Name	chkHHBit
	Caption	"5"
	Index	5
CheckBox	Name	chkHHBit
	Caption	"4"
	Index	4
CheckBox	Name	chkHHBit
	Caption	"3"
	Index	3

continued on next page

continued from previous page

OBJECT/CONTROL	PROPERTY	VALUE
CheckBox	Name	chkHHBit
	Caption	"2"
	Index	2
CheckBox	Name	chkHHBit
	Caption	"1"
	Index	1
CheckBox	Name	chkHHBit
	Caption	"0"
	Index	0
TextBox	Name	txtValue
	Alignment	1 - Right Justify
Label	Name	lblMask
	Alignment	2 - Center
	BorderStyle	1 - Fixed Single
	Index	1
Label	Name	lblMask
	Alignment	2 - Center
	BorderStyle	1 - Fixed Single
	Index	0
Label	Name	lblData
	Alignment	1 - Right Justify
	BorderStyle	1 - Fixed Single
	Index	5
Label	Name	lblData
	Alignment	1 - Right Justify
	BorderStyle	1 - Fixed Single
	Index	4
Label	Name	lblData
	Alignment	1 - Right Justify
	BorderStyle	1 - Fixed Single
	Index	3
Label	Name	lblData
	Alignment	1 - Right Justify
	BorderStyle	1 - Fixed Single
	Index	2

OBJECT/CONTROL	PROPERTY	VALUE
Label	Name	lblData
	Alignment	1 - Right Justify
	BorderStyle	1 - Fixed Single
	Index	1
Label	Name	lblData
	Alignment	1 - Right Justify
	BorderStyle	1 - Fixed Single
	Index	0
Label	Name	lblCaption
	Caption	"High value tested using low mask:"
	Index	10
Label	Name	lblCaption
	Caption	"High value tested using low mask:"
	Index	9
Label	Name	lblCaption
	Alignment	2 - Center
	Caption	"Bit States"
	Index	8
Label	Name	lblCaption
	Alignment	2 - Center
	Caption	"Bit States"
	Index	7
Label	Name	lblCaption
	Caption	"Low Byte (Hex):"
	Index	6
Label	Name	lblCaption
	Caption	"High Byte (Hex):"
	Index	5
Label	Name	lblCaption
	Caption	"Low Word (Hex):"
	Index	4
Label	Name	lblCaption
	Caption	"Low Byte (Hex):"
	Index	3

continued on next page

continued from previous page

OBJECT/CONTROL	PROPERTY	VALUE
Label	Name	lblCaption
	Caption	"High Byte (Hex):"
	Index	2
Label	Name	lblCaption
	Caption	"High Word (Hex):"
	Index	1
Label	Name	lblCaption
	Caption	"Decimal or Hex:"
	Index	0

6. Put the following code in the **Click** event of the **cmdCompute** command button. This code checks to be sure that the value entered in the text box is numeric. It then calls the two subroutines that split out the word and byte values, and sets the check boxes that correspond to the bits that are on.

```
Private Sub cmdCompute_Click()

Dim lValue          As Long

' Get the value entered by the user
If IsNumeric(txtValue.Text) = True Then
    ' The value is numeric
    lValue = CLng(txtValue.Text)

    ' Populate the form fields with the high word data
    Call FillHigh(lValue)

    ' Populate the form fields with the low word data
    Call FillLow(lValue)

Else
    ' The entered value is not numeric
    MsgBox "Enter a long integer or hex value. " & _
            "Hex values must start with '&H'."

End If
End Sub
```

7. Add the following subroutine, which populates the high word section of the form. It starts by splitting out the high word from the long value, and then splits that word into high and low bytes. Each byte value is then used to set the check box states for each bit in the byte. Finally, the low byte of this high word is used as a bit mask to test the high byte value.

```
Private Sub FillHigh(lValue As Long)

Dim bResult          As Boolean

Dim btHigh           As Byte
Dim btLow            As Byte
Dim btTest           As Byte

Dim nHigh            As Integer
Dim nLow             As Integer
Dim nTest            As Integer

Dim nLoopCtr         As Integer

' Split the passed value into words
Call SplitLong(lValue, nHigh, nLow)
lblData(0).Caption = Trim$(Hex$(nHigh))

' Split the high word value into bytes
Call SplitWord(nHigh, btHigh, btLow)
lblData(1).Caption = Trim$(Hex$(btHigh))
lblData(2).Caption = Trim$(Hex$(btLow))
' Show which bits are set in the two byte values

' Process the high byte value
For nLoopCtr = 0 To 7
    If IsBitSet(CLng(btHigh), nLoopCtr) = True Then
        ' The bit is on, so check the box
        chkHHBit(nLoopCtr).Value = vbChecked
    Else
        ' The bit is off, so clear the check box
        chkHHBit(nLoopCtr).Value = vbUnchecked
    End If
Next nLoopCtr

' Process the low byte value
For nLoopCtr = 0 To 7
    If IsBitSet(CLng(btLow), nLoopCtr) = True Then
        ' The bit is on, so check the box
        chkHLBit(nLoopCtr).Value = vbChecked
    Else
        ' The bit is off, so clear the check box
        chkHLBit(nLoopCtr).Value = vbUnchecked
    End If
Next nLoopCtr

' Compare the two byte values using the high as the
' test value and the low as the mask.
Select Case IsBitMaskSet(CLng(btHigh), CLng(btLow))
    Case True
        lblMask(0).Caption = "True"

    Case Else
        lblMask(0).Caption = "False"

End Select

End Sub
```

8. Add the following subroutine, which populates the low word section of the form. It starts by splitting out the low word from the long value, and then splitting that word into high and low bytes. As in the previous subroutine, each byte value is then used to set the check box states for each bit in the byte. Finally, the low byte of this low word is used as a bit mask to test the high byte value.

```vb
Private Sub FillLow(lValue As Long)

Dim bResult        As Boolean

Dim btHigh         As Byte
Dim btLow          As Byte
Dim btTest         As Byte

Dim nHigh          As Integer
Dim nLow           As Integer
Dim nTest          As Integer

Dim nLoopCtr       As Integer

' Split the passed value into words
Call SplitLong(lValue, nHigh, nLow)
lblData(3).Caption = Trim$(Hex$(nLow))

' Split the low word value into bytes
Call SplitWord(nLow, btHigh, btLow)
lblData(4).Caption = Trim$(Hex$(btHigh))
lblData(5).Caption = Trim$(Hex$(btLow))
' Show which bits are set in the two byte values

' Process the high byte value
For nLoopCtr = 0 To 7
    If IsBitSet(CLng(btHigh), nLoopCtr) = True Then
        ' The bit is on, so check the box
        chkLHBit(nLoopCtr).Value = vbChecked
      Else
        ' The bit is off, so clear the check box
        chkLHBit(nLoopCtr).Value = vbUnchecked
    End If
Next nLoopCtr

' Process the low byte value
For nLoopCtr = 0 To 7
    If IsBitSet(CLng(btLow), nLoopCtr) = True Then
        ' The bit is on, so check the box
        chkLLBit(nLoopCtr).Value = vbChecked
      Else
        ' The bit is off, so clear the check box
        chkLLBit(nLoopCtr).Value = vbUnchecked
```

```
        End If
Next nLoopCtr

' Compare the two byte values using the high as the
' test value and the low as the mask.
Select Case IsBitMaskSet(CLng(btHigh), CLng(btLow))
    Case True
        lblMask(1).Caption = "True"

    Case Else
        lblMask(1).Caption = "False"

End Select

End Sub
```

How It Works

This program takes advantage of the fact that binary and hex values are all powers of two. Working with hex values makes it easy to see how the test values and the bit masks relate to each other. Table 8.8 shows the results of a simple logical **And** operation on four bits of data with both **True** and **False** results. In the first case, all the bits in the mask are also on in the test value, so the results will equal the mask and the result is **True**. The second case yields **False** because not all the bits in the mask are on in the test value.

Table 8.8 Bitwise Logical And Results

	BIT 3	BIT 2	BIT 1	BIT 0
Test Value	1	1	1	1
Bit Mask	0	1	0	1
Results	0	1	0	1
Test Value	1	1	1	0
Bit Mask	0	1	0	1
Results	0	1	0	0

Comments

There are situations where you can make use of bit masks in your own code. If you have a series of Boolean values you want to record, consider putting them into a bit mask. Each Boolean variable is stored as a 2-byte (16-bit) value, and one Boolean value can be stored in each bit. Because long integers are 4 bytes, they can be used to store 32 Boolean values.

COMPLEXITY
INTERMEDIATE

8.5 How do I...
Create and use Registry entries?

COMPATIBILITY: VISUAL BASIC 5 AND 6

Problem

I know how to use the Registry functions that are part of the Visual Basic language, but I do not want all my entries stored in the HKEY_CURRENT _USER\Software\VB and VBA Program Settings section of the Registry. How do I create and manage Registry entries of my own?

Technique

The Registry stores information in an outline form. You can see this outline format by using the Registry editor, REGEDIT.EXE, found in your Windows directory. The display looks similar to Windows Explorer. Take a look at a sample outline, shown in Figure 8.7, and relate it back to the terms used by the Registry and the Registry API functions. Please note that the Registry does not use the letters and numbers; they have been added here for clarity.

I – Software
   A – ControlObjects
      1 – Gadgets
      2 – Gizmos
      3 – Widgets

Figure 8.7 A sample Registry outline.

WARNING

Please exercise extreme caution when using REGEDIT because it is possible to delete entries that prevent the proper operation of installed software applications, or it could even prevent the system from booting. Before performing any Registry manipulations, make a backup copy of the Registry itself.

The first item, I - Software, is regarded as a Registry *key*. Depending on their context, items at the next level into the outline are called either *keys* or *subkeys*. In this example, the A - ControlObjects item is a subkey of Software. When it is combined with its parent key, it is used to access its subkeys. Using Registry key notation, without the outline numbering and letters, this new key becomes \Software\ControlObjects and its subkeys are the numbered items 1 - Gadgets, 2 - Gizmos, and 3 - Widgets.

The following are the Registry's six predefined roots, used to organize and categorize data:

- ✔ HKEY_CLASSES_ROOT Defines and describes all document classes, by file types, and how they are handled and managed.

- ✔ HKEY_CURRENT_USER The configuration and preferences of the current user.

- ✔ HKEY_LOCAL_MACHINE Supplies information about this computer, including information about the physical hardware, software, network, and security.

- ✔ HKEY_USERS Lists all users who access this machine and their setup and configuration preferences.

- ✔ HKEY_CURRENT_CONFIG Provides local system display and printer configuration data.

- ✔ HKEY_DYN_DATA Provides dynamic data, including current performance statistics.

NOTE

It is recommended that you browse the Registry and find the place where your entries belong within the existing structure.

This How-To demonstrates creating a code module that encapsulates the Registry functions. The module provides subroutines and functions that can be used to manipulate keys and key values in the Registry. All Registry entries created and manipulated by this code are placed in the HKEY_LOCAL_MACHINE section of the Registry.

Steps

Open and run REGISTRY ENTRIES.VBP. The running program is shown in Figure 8.8. To create this program, complete the following steps.

Figure 8.8 The main form at runtime.

1. Create a new project called REGISTRY ENTRIES.VBP. Add a code module to the project and put the following code into the General Declarations section. These statements define the function prototypes for the API calls and declare the constants that are needed. Set the module name to **modRegistry** and save the module as REGISTRY ENTRIES.BAS.

```
Option Explicit

Const HKEY_CLASSES_ROOT = &H80000000
Const HKEY_CURRENT_USER = &H80000001
Const HKEY_LOCAL_MACHINE = &H80000002
Const HKEY_USERS = &H80000003
Const HKEY_DYN_DATA = &H80000004

Const REG_SZ = 1

' Registry API prototypes
Private Declare Function RegCreateKey Lib "advapi32.dll" _
  Alias "RegCreateKeyA" _
    (ByVal hkey As Long, _
     ByVal lpSubKey As String, _
     phkResult As Long) As Long

Private Declare Function RegDeleteKey Lib "advapi32.dll" _
  Alias "RegDeleteKeyA" _
    (ByVal hkey As Long, _
     ByVal lpSubKey As String) As Long

Private Declare Function RegDeleteValue Lib "advapi32.dll" _
  Alias "RegDeleteValueA" _
    (ByVal hkey As Long, _
     ByVal lpSubKey As String) As Long
Private Declare Function RegQueryValueEx Lib "advapi32.dll" _
  Alias "RegQueryValueExA" _
    (ByVal hkey As Long, _
     ByVal lpValueName As String, _
     ByVal lpReserved As Long, _
     lpType As Long, _
     lpData As Any, _
     lpcbData As Long) As Long

Private Declare Function RegSetValueEx Lib "advapi32.dll" _
  Alias "RegSetValueExA" _
```

```
    (ByVal hkey As Long, _
     ByVal lpValueName As String, _
     ByVal Reserved As Long, _
     ByVal dwType As Long, _
     lpData As Any, _
     ByVal cbData As Long) As Long


' Registry error constants
Const API_SUCCESS = 0&
Const ERROR_BADDB = 1009&
Const ERROR_BADKEY = 1010&
Const ERROR_CANTOPEN = 1011&
Const ERROR_CANTREAD = 1012&
Const ERROR_CANTWRITE = 1013&
Const ERROR_REGISTRY_RECOVERED = 1014&
Const ERROR_REGISTRY_CORRUPT = 1015&
Const ERROR_REGISTRY_IO_FAILED = 1016&
Const ERROR_NOT_REGISTRY_FILE = 1017&
Const ERROR_KEY_DELETED = 1018&
Const ERROR_NO_LOG_SPACE = 1019&
Const ERROR_KEY_HAS_CHILDREN = 1020&
Const ERROR_CHILD_MUST_BE_VOLATILE = 1021&
Const ERROR_RXACT_INVALID_STATE = 1369&
```

2. Add the following function to create new Registry keys. The code checks to make sure the key name is not blank, and then creates the key.

```
Public Function CreateRegKey(sRegistryKey As String) As Long

Dim lResult        As Long

CreateRegKey = 0           ' Assume success

' Make sure all parameters have values
If Len(sRegistryKey) = 0 Then
    ' The key property is not set, so flag an error
    CreateRegKey = ERROR_BADKEY
    Exit Function
End If

' Make the call to create the key
CreateRegKey = RegCreateKey(HKEY_LOCAL_MACHINE, _
                     sRegistryKey, lResult)

End Function
```

3. Add the following function to delete Registry keys. The code starts by making sure the two key name parameters are not blank. Then it opens the key to get the key ID, which is passed to the key delete API function. Notice throughout this code module that the key open function is never used; instead, the key creation function is used. This reduces some of the potential errors, and if the key already exists, the function does not create it, but returns the key ID.

```
Public Function DeleteRegKey _
            (sRegistryKey As String, _
            sSubKey As String) As Long

Dim lKeyId          As Long
Dim lResult         As Long

DeleteRegKey = 0            ' Assume success

' Make sure all parameters have values
If Len(sRegistryKey) = 0 Then
    ' The key parameter is not set
    DeleteRegKey = ERROR_BADKEY
    Exit Function
End If

If Len(sSubKey) = 0 Then
    ' The sub key parameter is not set
    DeleteRegKey = ERROR_BADKEY
    Exit Function
End If

' Open the key by attempting to create it. If it
' already exists, an ID is returned.
lResult = RegCreateKey(HKEY_LOCAL_MACHINE, sRegistryKey, lKeyId)

If lResult = 0 Then
    ' Got a key ID, so delete the entry
    DeleteRegKey = RegDeleteKey(lKeyId, ByVal sSubKey)
End If

End Function
```

4. Add the following function, which deletes the value of a key but leaves the key itself in the Registry. Again, it checks to be sure the parameter values are not blank, and then the value is cleared.

```
Public Function DeleteRegValue _
            (sRegistryKey As String, _
            sSubKey As String) As Long

Dim lKeyId          As Long
Dim lResult         As Long

DeleteRegValue = 0              ' Assume success

' Make sure all parameters have values
If Len(sRegistryKey) = 0 Then
    ' The key parameter is not set
    DeleteRegValue = ERROR_BADKEY
    Exit Function
End If

If Len(sSubKey) = 0 Then
    ' The sub key parameter is not set
    DeleteRegValue = ERROR_BADKEY
```

```
      Exit Function
End If
' Open the key by attempting to create it. If it
' already exists, an ID is returned.
lResult = RegCreateKey(HKEY_LOCAL_MACHINE, sRegistryKey, lKeyId)

If lResult = 0 Then
      ' Got a key ID, so delete the value
      DeleteRegValue = RegDeleteValue(lKeyId, ByVal sSubKey)
End If

End Function
```

5. The following code finds the current string value of a Registry key. After getting a key ID, a preliminary call is made to get the length of the key value string. After this length is known, space is allocated to hold the results and the API function is called to get the value.

```
Public Function GetRegValue _
            (sRegistryKey As String, _
            sSubKey As String, _
            sKeyValue As String) As Long

Dim lResult             As Long
Dim lKeyId              As Long
Dim lBufferSize         As Long

GetRegValue = 0                     ' Assume success

' Clear the return string parameter
sKeyValue = Empty

' Make sure all parameters have values
If Len(sRegistryKey) = 0 Then
    ' The key parameter is not set
    GetRegValue = ERROR_BADKEY
    Exit Function
End If

If Len(sSubKey) = 0 Then
    ' The sub key parameter is not set
    GetRegValue = ERROR_BADKEY
    Exit Function
End If

' Open the key by attempting to create it. If it
' already exists, an ID is returned.
lResult = RegCreateKey(HKEY_LOCAL_MACHINE, _
                sRegistryKey, lKeyId)

If lResult <> 0 Then
    ' Call failed; can't open the key, so exit
    GetRegValue = lResult
    Exit Function
```

continued on next page

continued from previous page

```
    End If
    ' Determine the size of the data in the Registry entry
    lResult = RegQueryValueEx(lKeyId, sSubKey, _
                0&, REG_SZ, 0&, lBufferSize)

    If lBufferSize < 2 Then
        ' No data value available
        Exit Function
    End If

    ' Allocate the needed space for the key data
    sKeyValue = String(lBufferSize + 1, " ")

    ' Get the value of the Registry entry
    lResult = RegQueryValueEx(lKeyId, sSubKey, _
                0&, REG_SZ, ByVal sKeyValue, lBufferSize)

    If lResult <> 0 Then
        ' Unexpected error, return the result
        GetRegValue = lResult

    Else

        ' Trim the null at the end of the returned value
        ' and send it back to the caller
        If InStr(sKeyValue, vbNullChar) > 0 Then
            sKeyValue = Left$(sKeyValue, lBufferSize - 1)
        End If

    End If

End Function
```

6. Add the following function, which sets Registry key values. After the key is opened, the value can be set. If the value that was passed to this function is blank, the key value in the Registry is cleared.

```
Public Function SetRegValue _
            (sRegistryKey As String, _
            sSubKey As String, _
            sKeyValue As String) As Long

Dim lKeyId              As Long
Dim lResult             As Long

SetRegValue = 0                     ' Assume success

' Make sure all parameters have values
If Len(sRegistryKey) = 0 Then
    ' The key parameter is not set
    SetRegValue = ERROR_BADKEY
    Exit Function
End If

If Len(sSubKey) = 0 Then
    ' The sub key parameter is not set
```

```
      SetRegValue = ERROR_BADKEY
      Exit Function
End If
' Open the key by attempting to create it. If it
' already exists, an ID is returned.
lResult = RegCreateKey(HKEY_LOCAL_MACHINE, _
               sRegistryKey, _
               lKeyId)


If lResult <> 0 Then
    ' Call failed; can't open the key, so exit
    SetRegValue = lResult
    Exit Function
End If


If Len(sKeyValue) = 0 Then
    ' No key value, so clear any existing entry
    SetRegValue = RegSetValueEx(lKeyId, _
            sSubKey, _
            0&, _
            REG_SZ, _
            0&, _
            0&)


  Else

    ' Set the Registry entry to the value
    SetRegValue = RegSetValueEx(lKeyId, _
            sSubKey, _
            0&, _
            REG_SZ, _
            ByVal sKeyValue, _
            Len(sKeyValue) + 1)


End If

End Function
```

7. This is the last function that goes in the code module. This routine returns a text string for each possible Registry function error value.

```
Public Function GetRegErrorText(lStatus As Long) As String

' Evaluate the status and return the error message text.

Select Case lStatus
  Case ERROR_BADDB
    GetRegErrorText = "The configuration registry database " & _
                      "is corrupt."

  Case ERROR_BADKEY
    GetRegErrorText = "The configuration registry key is " & _
                      "invalid."
```

continued on next page

continued from previous page

```
        Case ERROR_CANTOPEN
          GetRegErrorText = "The configuration registry key could " & _
                            "not be opened."

        Case ERROR_CANTREAD
          GetRegErrorText = "The configuration registry key could " & _
                            "not be read."

        Case ERROR_CANTWRITE
          GetRegErrorText = "The configuration registry key could " & _
                            "not be written."

        Case ERROR_REGISTRY_RECOVERED
          GetRegErrorText = "One of the files in the Registry " & _
                            "database had to be recovered " & _
                            "by use of a log or alternate copy. " & _
                            "The recovery was successful."

        Case ERROR_REGISTRY_CORRUPT
          GetRegErrorText = "The Registry is corrupt. The structure " & _
                            "of one of the files that contains " & _
                            "Registry data is corrupt, or the " & _
                            "system's image of the file in memory " & _
                            "is corrupt, or the file could not be " & _
                            "recovered because the alternate " & _
                            "copy or log was absent or corrupt."

        Case ERROR_REGISTRY_IO_FAILED
          GetRegErrorText = "An I/O operation initiated by the " & _
                            "Registry failed unrecoverably. " & _
                            "The Registry could not read in, or " & _
                            "write out, or flush, one of the files " & _
                            "that contain the system's image of " & _
                            "the Registry."

        Case ERROR_NOT_REGISTRY_FILE
          GetRegErrorText = "The system has attempted to load or " & _
                            "restore a file into the Registry, but the " & _
                            "specified file is not in a Registry " & _
                            "file format."

        Case ERROR_KEY_DELETED
          GetRegErrorText = "Illegal operation attempted on a " & _
                            "Registry key which has been marked " & _
                            "for deletion."

        Case ERROR_NO_LOG_SPACE
          GetRegErrorText = "System could not allocate the required " & _
                            "space in a Registry log."

        Case ERROR_KEY_HAS_CHILDREN
          GetRegErrorText = "Cannot create a symbolic link in a " & _
                            "Registry key that already " & _
                            "has subkeys or values."
```

```
Case ERROR_CHILD_MUST_BE_VOLATILE
    GetRegErrorText = "Cannot create a stable subkey under a " & _
                      "volatile parent key."

Case ERROR_RXACT_INVALID_STATE
    GetRegErrorText = "The transaction state of a Registry " & _
                      "subtree is incompatible with the " & _
                      "requested operation."

End Select

End Function
```

8. Add a new form to the project, and set the form objects and properties listed in Table 8.9 to the form and save the form as REGISTRY ENTRIES.FRM.

Table 8.9 The Project Form's Objects and Properties

OBJECT/CONTROL	PROPERTY	VALUE
Form	Name	frmMain
	Caption	"Registry Entries"
	Icon	"NOTE05.ICO"
ComboBox	Name	cboSubKey
	Style	2 - Dropdown List
CommandButton	Name	cmdAction
	Caption	"Create Registry Key"
	Index	0
CommandButton	Name	cmdAction
	Caption	"Get Key Value"
	Index	1
CommandButton	Name	cmdAction
	Caption	"Set Key Value"
	Index	2
CommandButton	Name	cmdAction
	Caption	"Delete Key Value"
	Index	3
CommandButton	Name	cmdAction
	Caption	"Exit"
	Index	4

continued on next page

continued from previous page

OBJECT/CONTROL	PROPERTY	VALUE
TextBox	Name	txtValue
TextBox	Name	txtRegistryKey
	Text	"\Software\Honey Bees\Species"
Label	Name	lblCaption
	Caption	"Value Contents:"
	Index	2
Label	Name	lblCaption
	Caption	"Value Name/Sub Key:"
	Index	1
Label	Name	lblCaption
	Caption	"Registry Key:"
	Index	0

9. Put the following code into the form's **Load** event. It populates the drop-down list with some sample key names, and then creates and sets values for those sample keys.

```
Private Sub Form_Load()

Dim sKey             As String
Dim lResult          As Long

' Load some test data into the combo and Registry
cboSubKey.AddItem "European (Western)"
cboSubKey.AddItem "Giant Tropical"
cboSubKey.AddItem "Asian (Eastern)"
cboSubKey.AddItem "Small Tropical"

sKey = "\Software\Honey Bees\Species"

lResult = SetRegValue(sKey, "European (Western)", _
                            "Apis mellifera")
lResult = SetRegValue(sKey, "Giant Tropical", _
                            "Apis dorsata")
lResult = SetRegValue(sKey, "Asian (Eastern)", _
                            "Apis cerana")
lResult = SetRegValue(sKey, "Small Tropical", _
                            "Apis florea")

End Sub
```

10. Because all good programmers clean up after themselves, stick the following code into the form's **QueryUnload** event. These few lines remove the sample keys and values that were created when the form loaded.

```
Private Sub Form_QueryUnload(Cancel As Integer, _
                             UnloadMode As Integer)

Dim lResult             As Long

' Remove the test data from the Registry
lResult = DeleteRegKey("\Software\Honey Bees", "Species")
lResult = DeleteRegKey("\Software", "Honey Bees")

End Sub
```

11. Set up the dispatch code for the command button clicks. Start by getting the key and subkey values that are being used. Then, based on the index value of the command button, the appropriate Registry functions are called in the code module.

```
Private Sub cmdAction_Click(Index As Integer)

Dim lResult             As Long
Dim sKey                As String
Dim sSubKey             As String
Dim sKeyValue           As String
Dim sError              As String

' Get the Registry keys from the contents
' of the text boxes.
sKey = txtRegistryKey.Text
sSubKey = cboSubKey.Text
' Get additional values, and then call the encapsulated
' Registry functions.
Select Case Index
    Case 0              ' Create key
        lResult = CreateRegKey(sKey)

    Case 1              ' Get value
        lResult = GetRegValue(sKey, sSubKey, sKeyValue)
        txtValue.Text = sKeyValue

    Case 2              ' Set value
        sKeyValue = txtValue.Text
        lResult = SetRegValue(sKey, sSubKey, sKeyValue)

    Case 3              ' Delete value
        lResult = DeleteRegValue(sKey, sSubKey)
        txtValue.Text = ""

    Case 4              ' Exit from program
        Unload frmMain
        End

End Select

' Check for error messages
If lResult <> 0 Then
```

continued on next page

continued from previous page

```
        sError = GetRegErrorText(lResult)
        MsgBox sError, vbExclamation + vbOKOnly, _
                                "Registry Entries Error"
    End If

    End Sub
```

How It Works

All the Registry values in this How-To are stored as strings. Other data types are supported by the API, but by using data type conversion when needed, strings provide access to the widest variety of data formats with a small amount of code. You can even define and use custom data type formats as long as they can be stored as strings.

Comments

It is possible to have an existing program that uses an INI file to automatically store its information in the Win32 Registry. To do this, you need to enable INI file mapping for the application by adding a specific entry to the Registry. These entries are made in the \Software\Microsoft\Windows\CurrentVersion\ IniFileMapping key under the HKEY_LOCAL_MACHINE section.

After the proper Registry entry has been made, any calls to the profile or private profile API functions store and retrieve data from the Registry. For example, if your program uses an INI file named MYAPP.INI, add the key \Software\Microsoft\Windows\CurrentVersion\IniFileMapping\MYAPP.INI. Any calls your application makes to that INI file in the future are redirected to the Registry.

COMPLEXITY
ADVANCED

8.6 How do I...
Enumerate windows using callbacks?

COMPATIBILITY: VISUAL BASIC 5 AND 6

Problem

I want to get a list of all the windows on the desktop so that I can find a specific one. When I know the window handle, I can then subclass that window and change some of its characteristics and behaviors. I have seen code that walks through the windows by using parent and child relationships. How do I write compact code that uses callbacks to enumerate all the available windows?

Technique

This How-To uses a window enumeration callback function to deliver window handles. The function receives the callback and populates a list box with the handles of the windows and the text associated with each window. In most cases, the window text is its caption. For controls such as command buttons, the window text is the button's caption.

Steps

Open and run WINDOW ENUMERATION.VBP. The running program is shown in Figure 8.9. Complete the following steps to create this program.

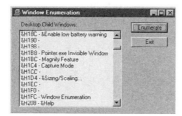

Figure 8.9 The main form at runtime.

1. Create a new project called WINDOW ENUMERATION.VBP. This program uses callbacks that make use of the **AddressOf** function. Functions referenced by **AddressOf** cannot be in a form; they must exist in a code module or an active instance of a class module. Add a code module to the project, and place the following code in the General Declarations section to define the API functions that are going to be called. Set the module name to **modWindowEmun** and save it as WINDOW ENUMERATION.BAS.

```
Option Explicit

' Local pointer to the main form list box
Private mListBox        As Control

Private Declare Function GetWindowText Lib "user32" _
    Alias "GetWindowTextA" _
        (ByVal hwnd As Long, _
         ByVal lpString As String, _
         ByVal cch As Long) As Long

Private Declare Function EnumChildWindows Lib "user32" _
        (ByVal hWndParent As Long, _
         ByVal lpEnumFunc As Long, _
         ByVal lParam As Long) As Boolean
```

2. Add the following subroutine to the module. This routine is called by the main program to get the list of windows. There are two parameters for this call. The first is an object reference to the **list box** on the main form. The second is the handle of the window where the children are listed. If this second parameter is an application window, all its children are listed. If the value is for the Windows desktop, all windows open in the system are listed.

```
Public Sub ListChildWindows _
            (ctlListBox As Control, _
            hwnd As Long)

Dim bResult        As Boolean

' Grab the pointer to the main form list box
Set mListBox = ctlListBox

' Clear the referenced list box
mListBox.Clear

' Make the call to start the callback series
bResult = EnumChildWindows(hwnd, _
            AddressOf ChildCallback, 0&)

End Sub
```

3. Add the following function (the callback target) to the module. It is called once for each window that needs to be enumerated. The first parameter is the handle of the enumerated window. The second parameter is a user-defined value that can be passed through from the **EnumChildWindows** function call. For each window handle received, an API call is made to get the text associated with the window. The handle and the text are then added to the list box on the main form.

```
Public Function ChildCallback _
            (ByVal hWndChild As Long, _
            lRaram As Long) As Boolean

Dim sTempStr       As String
Dim sListText      As String
Dim lResult        As Long

' Get the window text for the child window
sTempStr = String(255, " ")
lResult = GetWindowText(hWndChild, _
            ByVal sTempStr, 254&)

' Build a string containing the window text
If InStr(1, sTempStr, vbNullChar) > 0 Then
```

```
        sTempStr = Left$(sTempStr, Len(sTempStr) - 1)
    End If

    ' Concatenate the window handle and text
    sListText = "&H" & Trim$(Hex$(hWndChild)) & _
            " - " & sTempStr

    ' Add the item to the list box
    mListBox.AddItem sListText

    ' Set the return value to keep the callback going
    ChildCallback = True

End Function
```

4. Add a form to the project and set the objects and properties as listed in Table 8.10. Save the form as WINDOW ENUMERATION.FRM.

Table 8.10 The Project Form's Objects and Properties

OBJECT/CONTROL	PROPERTY	VALUE
Form	Name	frmMain
	Caption	"Window Enumeration"
	Icon	"MYCOMP.ICO"
CommandButton	Name	cmdAction
	Caption	"Enumerate"
	Index	0
CommandButton	Name	cmdAction
	Caption	"Exit"
	Index	1
ListBox	Name	lstWindows
	Sorted	True
Label	Name	lblCaption
	Caption	"Desktop Child Windows:"

5. Add the following code to the form's **Load** event. This code declares the function prototype for the API routine used to get the handle of the system desktop window.

```
Option Explicit

Private Declare Function GetDesktopWindow Lib "user32" () As Long
```

6. Add the following code to the **Click** event of the **cmdAction** command button control array. When the user clicks the first command button, the code gets the desktop window handle. It then passes the handle to the code module subroutine that gets the list of child windows. The second command button ends the program.

```
Private Sub cmdAction_Click(Index As Integer)

Dim hDesktop          As Long

Select Case Index
    Case 0                ' Enumerate
        hDesktop = GetDesktopWindow()
        Call ListChildWindows(lstWindows, hDesktop)

    Case 1                ' Exit
        Unload Me
        End

End Select

End Sub
```

How It Works

This How-To uses callbacks but does not set a message hook or use subclassing. One other point to make about this program is the use of variables that reference objects. In this case it is using a variable to reference a control on the calling form. Doing this lets you build general-purpose code modules that can be used in many projects. Because references to the control name are not hard-coded, there are no specific dependencies that would prevent general use of the module.

Comments

Callbacks are used by most of the API enumeration functions. In many cases, the same information is now available directly within Visual Basic in one of its built-in collections. For example, there are several API functions you could use to enumerate the list of available fonts or printers. You can get that information directly by using the **Font** and **Printer** collections.

WINDOWS SOCKET PROGRAMMING

9

WINDOWS SOCKET PROGRAMMING

How do I...

The How-To examples in this chapter all make use of Windows sockets on top of TCP/IP networking protocol. The use of sockets and TCP/IP enables non-Windows applications to connect to the services and participate in an enterprise-wide distributed application environment. To test and use these examples, networking must be installed on the system.

This chapter starts by building a simple socket-based task monitor. The initial How-To also establishes baseline code that is used as the foundation for the other examples. The second How-To constructs a simple time server used to synchronize the local system times of multiple systems.

Performance is often a key issue with shared and centralized service components. Management of performance dictates the ability to manage and control a pool of service resources. There are many ways to build pool management programs. The simplest is to use a fixed set of services and allocate clients to them by using a round-robin scheduling process. The final How-To demonstrates this by rebuilding the time server as a managed pool of services. The client application is then modified so that it can be redirected to any one of the pool of available time servers.

9.1 Use Sockets to Monitor Remote Object Status

This How-To uses Windows socket connections to monitor task status. The use of TCP/IP facilitates monitoring programs on any operating system that provides programmable interfaces to TCP/IP. Both active and passive monitoring are included in the example.

9.2 Keep the Time Synchronized for Accurate Time Stamps

Distributed applications often require that multiple systems have a consistent date and time. Some typical uses of date and time data in a distributed client-server environment include task synchronization, event time stamping, and database change logging. Windows sockets are used to offer centralized time services, supporting multiple concurrent connections. Network turnaround times are computed and factored into local time adjustments.

9.3 Manage a Pool of Objects and Services

This How-To constructs a simple pool manager for time services. When a client application requests a time service connection, the time service pool manager assigns the client to one of two time server engines. The client then connects directly to its assigned service.

9.4 Check for Messages in a Remote Mailbox

This How-To connects to a TCP/IP port and uses POP3 (Post Office Protocol) to communicate with an e-mail server and get message information. The program is small and fast and does not leave the port open after it has determined the number of waiting messages.

COMPLEXITY
INTERMEDIATE

9.1 How do I...
Use sockets to monitor remote object status?

COMPATIBILITY: VISUAL BASIC 5 AND 6

Problem

I have a distributed application with components on many machines. Some of the programs execute on computers that do not run Windows but do support TCP/IP. How do I actively and passively monitor the status of tasks running on different operating systems?

Technique

This How-To uses Windows socket connections to monitor task status. The monitoring program opens a port and then listens for remote tasks to connect. Each remote task is actively queried once a minute for simple status information.

The technique to determine when a remote task stops is known as a "dead-man" switch. As long as the task is alive, the switch stays open. After the task exits or dies, the switch closes. The operational status of each remote task is determined by the state of the TCP/IP port connection. When the connection is made, the task has started. If the connection closes, it indicates that the task has ended.

There are two programs in this How-To. The first is the program that monitors tasks. The second project is a program that starts multiple tasks that connect to the monitor and respond to status requests.

Steps

Open MONITOR.VBP and make an executable. Run the program and click the Listen command button (see Figure 9.1).

Figure 9.1 The monitor form at runtime.

Now, open and run REMOTE TASK.VBP, as shown in Figure 9.2.

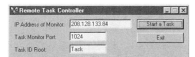

Figure 9.2 The remote task controller form at runtime.

Enter the TCP address of your system. Then click the Start a Task command button a couple of times to start some tasks. A sample of the form associated with each task is pictured in Figure 9.3. Exit from one of the tasks. The resulting connection status information is displayed on the monitor form.

Figure 9.3 The remote
task form at runtime.

Complete the following steps to create this project.

1. Create a new project called MONITOR.VBP.

2. Add a form to the project and set the objects and properties as they are
listed in Table 9.1. Be sure to add the Microsoft Winsock Control as a
component of the project. Save the form as MONITOR.FRM.

Table 9.1 The Monitor Form's Objects and Properties

OBJECT/CONTROL	PROPERTY	VALUE
Form	Name	frmMain
	Caption	Remote Task Monitor
	Icon	NET01.ICO
	StartUpPosition	2 'CenterScreen
CommandButton	Name	cmdAction
	Caption	Listen
	Index	0
CommandButton	Name	cmdAction
	Caption	Exit
	Index	1
Timer	Name	tmrUpdate
	Interval	5000
ListBox	Name	lstStatus
TextBox	Name	txtPort
	Text	1024
Winsock	Name	Winsock1
	Index	0
Label	Name	lblCaption
	Caption	Port Connection Status:
	Index	0

OBJECT/CONTROL	PROPERTY	VALUE
Label	Name	lblCaption
	Caption	Monitor Task Port:
	Index	1

3. Add the following code to the General Declarations section of the form. The code starts by declaring a constant used to limit the total number of lines displayed in the status list box. Then a number of module-scope variables are declared to track the tasks and task IDs. Finally, a variant is defined to store an array of socket connection status descriptions.

```
Option Explicit

' Constant used to limit the number of list
' box items before removing the oldest
Private Const MAX_LIST_ITEMS = 100

' Count the number of tasks being monitored
Private mnTaskCount            As Integer

' Count the number of socket control instances
Private mnSockets              As Integer

' Store the ID for each task being tracked
Private msTaskID()             As String

' Array of socket state descriptions
Private mvntSocketState        As Variant
```

4. Add the following code to the form's **Load** event. First the socket connection status array is loaded with state descriptions. Then the task ID array and reference counters are initialized.

```
Private Sub Form_Load()

' Load the variant array with socket states
mvntSocketState = Array("Closed", _
                        "Open", _
                        "Listening", _
                        "Connection Pending", _
                        "Resolving Host", _
                        "Host Resolved", _
                        "Connecting", _
                        "Connected", _
                        "Closing", _
                        "Error")

' Initialize the task ID array
ReDim msTaskID(10)

' The #1 element of the array is for the primary
```

continued on next page

continued from previous page

```
' listening socket
msTaskID(0) = "Reserved"

' Initialize the task count and socket count variables
mnTaskCount = 0
mnSockets = 0

End Sub
```

5. Place the following code in the **Click** event of the **cmdAction** command button control array. When the user selects the first button in the array to start listening, the text box values are checked. Then the command button itself is disabled to prevent an attempt to listen on the same port a second time. Next, the socket control properties are set. Then a subroutine is called to add the current socket status to the status list box.

The second command button in the array exits the program.

```
Private Sub cmdAction_Click(Index As Integer)

Dim nMonitorPort        As String

Select Case Index
    Case 0            ' Listen
        ' Get the value used for the connection
        nMonitorPort = CInt(txtPort.Text)
        If nMonitorPort = 0 Then
            MsgBox "Please enter the port to use " & _
                    "for monitoring."
            Exit Sub
        End If
        ' Disable this command button as the program
        ' can only be instructed to start listening once
        cmdAction(Index).Enabled = False
        ' Set the socket control port property
        If Winsock1(0).LocalPort <> nMonitorPort Then
            Winsock1(0).LocalPort = nMonitorPort
        End If
        ' Start listening
        Winsock1(0).Listen
        ' Update the connection status in the list box
        Call ShowSocketState(0)

    Case 1            ' Exit
        Unload Me

End Select

End Sub
```

6. Add the following subroutine. It is used to add the current socket state to the status list box. Because the socket control is an array, an index value is passed to this subroutine. First a text string is constructed containing the socket index number and the socket state description. This text is then added to the list box. A reference to the list location of the new item is obtained. This value is equivalent to the list count because the list box is not sorted. If the number of items in the list exceeds the constant value for the maximum number of entries, the list is trimmed down to size.

```
Private Sub ShowSocketState(Index As Integer)

Dim sTempStr            As String
Dim nListCount          As Integer
Dim nLoopCtr            As Integer

' Build a string containing the current socket state
sTempStr = "Socket " & Index & " State: " & vbTab & _
                mvntSocketState(Winsock1(Index).State)

' Add the string to the list box
lstStatus.AddItem sTempStr

' Get the index position where the item was added
nListCount = lstStatus.NewIndex

If nListCount > MAX_LIST_ITEMS Then
    ' Clean out old list entries
    For nLoopCtr = nListCount - MAX_LIST_ITEMS To 0 Step -1
        lstStatus.RemoveItem nLoopCtr
    Next nLoopCtr
    nListCount = lstStatus.ListCount - 1
End If

' Position at the last item on the list
lstStatus.ListIndex = nListCount

End Sub
```

7. Each time the timer control fires, the code queries every task. The tasks are sent a message asking for the length of time they have been running.

```
Private Sub tmrUpdate_Timer()

Dim nLoopCtr                As Integer

' Get the current uptime from each monitored task
For nLoopCtr = 1 To UBound(msTaskID)
    If Len(msTaskID(nLoopCtr)) > 0 Then
        ' This is a task so get its uptime
        Winsock1(nLoopCtr).SendData "Uptime"
        DoEvents
    End If
Next nLoopCtr

End Sub
```

8. When a connection request is received on the socket port, the following code is executed. The connection request details are added to the status list box. Then the index value of the socket control is checked. If the request was received on the primary control of the array, the connection is processed. The code looks for an available entry in the task ID array. If there are no open array slots, the array is extended. Also, if there is not a socket control associated with the task entry slot, another instance of the control is loaded.

The code then checks the state of the socket and closes it if it is not closed. The connection request is then accepted using the identified or created instance of the socket control. Calls are made to the socket status subroutine for the current instance and primary instances of the socket control. Finally, the task asking for a connection is asked to identify itself to report its uptime.

If the request came in on any element of the control array other than index 0, it is invalid. Ignoring the request is all that is needed to deny the connection.

```
Private Sub Winsock1_ConnectionRequest(Index As Integer, _
            ByVal requestID As Long)

Dim bFoundSlot              As Boolean
Dim nLoopCtr                As Integer
Dim nCurrentTask            As Integer

' Show the connection request ID
lstStatus.AddItem "Connect Request on Socket " & Index
lstStatus.AddItem "Connect Request:" & vbTab & _
            "ID " & requestID

If Index = 0 Then
    ' This was a primary listen request
    ' Find an available socket control
    bFoundSlot = False
    ' Loop through the array looking for a blank ID
    For nLoopCtr = 1 To UBound(msTaskID)
        If Len(msTaskID(nLoopCtr)) = 0 Then
            ' Set the flag indicating success
            bFoundSlot = True
            ' Save the a pointer into the array
            nCurrentTask = nLoopCtr
            Exit For
        End If
    Next nLoopCtr
    If bFoundSlot = False Then
        ' Increment the task counter
        mnTaskCount = mnTaskCount + 1
        ' See if the new count exceeds the array bounds
        If mnTaskCount > UBound(msTaskID) Then
            ' Need to increase the array size, so add 10 more
            ReDim Preserve msTaskID(UBound(msTaskID) + 10)
        End If
```

```
                ' Set the current task number to the total task count
                nCurrentTask = mnTaskCount
            End If
        Else
            ' The connect request arrived on an invalid socket
            Exit Sub
    End If

    ' See if a new socket control needs to be created
    If nCurrentTask > mnSockets Then
        ' Create a new instance of the control
        Load Winsock1(nCurrentTask)
        Winsock1(nCurrentTask).LocalPort = 0
        ' Increment the socket count
        mnSockets = mnSockets + 1
    End If

    ' If the response instance of the control is not closed,
    ' then close it
    If Winsock1(nCurrentTask).State <> sckClosed Then
        Winsock1(nCurrentTask).Close
        Call ShowSocketState(nCurrentTask)
    End If

    ' Accept the request using the requestID
    Winsock1(nCurrentTask).Accept requestID

    ' Update the connection status in the list box
    Call ShowSocketState(nCurrentTask)

    ' Update the primary connection status in the list box
    Call ShowSocketState(0)

    ' Ask the task for its task ID and uptime
    Winsock1(nCurrentTask).SendData "Identify"
    DoEvents
    Winsock1(nCurrentTask).SendData "Uptime"

End Sub
```

9. Successful connections always trigger the following event. The following code reports the new connection status by calling the status update subroutine.

```
Private Sub Winsock1_Connect(Index As Integer)

' Update the connection status in the list box
Call ShowSocketState(Index)

End Sub
```

10. The SendComplete event occurs each time the transmission of data is completed over the socket. The code in this event adds a transmission line to the status list box, and then calls the socket status update subroutine.

```
Private Sub Winsock1_SendComplete(Index As Integer)

' Show that the send was completed
lstStatus.AddItem "Send Complete"

' Update the connection status in the list box
Call ShowSocketState(Index)

End Sub
```

11. Incoming data is parsed by the following code that is added to the socket control's **DataArrival** event. This event fires to indicate that there is data available, so the code first gets the data from the socket. The data value and length are then added to the status list box.

Next the data is parsed. This form recognizes responses from requests for task IDs and task uptime reports. Task IDs are added to the task ID array. Recall that the **Index** value of the socket control corresponds directly to the task ID array element, so the task ID is updated using the socket control index.

```
Private Sub Winsock1_DataArrival(Index As Integer, _
            ByVal bytesTotal As Long)

Dim sData               As String
Dim sTempStr            As String

' Get the inbound data from the socket
Winsock1(Index).GetData sData, vbString, bytesTotal

' Show the data and its length in the list box
lstStatus.AddItem "Data Value:  " & vbTab & sData
lstStatus.AddItem "Data Length: " & vbTab & bytesTotal

' Parse the data and prepare the response to the request
' White space is removed, the string is uppercased, and only the
' two leftmost characters are examined to simplify parsing
Select Case Trim$(UCase$(Left$(sData, 2)))
    Case "UP"           ' How long has task been running
        sTempStr = msTaskID(Index) & " uptime:" & _
                    vbTab & Mid$(sData, Len("UPTIME: ") + 1)

    Case "ID"           ' Who is this task
        ' Extract and store the task ID
        msTaskID(Index) = Mid$(sData, Len("IDENTIFY: ") + 1)
        ' Clear the temporary string
        sTempStr = ""

    Case Else           ' Invalid request
        sTempStr = "Unknown data received"

End Select

' See if there is information for the list box
If Len(sTempStr) <> 0 Then
```

```
                          ' It is not blank, so add the data to the list box
                          lstStatus.AddItem sTempStr
                      End If

                      ' Update the connection status in the list box
                      Call ShowSocketState(Index)

                      End Sub
```

12. Add the following code. This event is probably incorrectly named. Its name should be **CloseRequest**. This event is fired to indicate that the other connected program is closing the port. The code here must close the port on this end of the connection.

The entry in the task ID array is cleared so it can be reused. The socket is then closed and the status list box is updated. If the primary listening port was closed, it is reset to continue listening.

```
Private Sub Winsock1_Close(Index As Integer)

' Update the connection status in the list box
Call ShowSocketState(Index)

If Winsock1(Index).State = sckClosing Then
    ' Clear the task ID entry in the array
    msTaskID(Index) = ""
    ' A close request was made, so close the port
    Winsock1(Index).Close
    ' Update the connection status in the list box
    Call ShowSocketState(Index)
    ' Start listening again if this is the primary port
    If Index = 0 Then
        Winsock1(Index).Listen
        ' Update the connection status in the list box
        Call ShowSocketState(Index)
    End If
End If

End Sub
```

13. Add the following code to the socket control's **Error** event. This code extracts details of the error and displays the data in the socket status list box.

```
Private Sub Winsock1_Error(Index As Integer, _
                ByVal Number As Integer, _
                Description As String, _
                ByVal Scode As Long, _
                ByVal Source As String, _
                ByVal HelpFile As String, _
                ByVal HelpContext As Long, _
                CancelDisplay As Boolean)
```

continued on next page

continued from previous page

```
' Show the error details
lstStatus.AddItem "Error on Socket " & Index
lstStatus.AddItem "Error Number: " & vbTab & Number
lstStatus.AddItem "Error Text:   " & vbTab & Description

' Update the connection status in the list box
Call ShowSocketState(Index)

End Sub
```

14. The first project of this How-To is now finished. Save the project and compile the program into an executable.

15. Create a new project called REMOTE TASK.VBP.

16. Add a form to the project and set the objects and properties as they are listed in Table 9.2. Save the form as REMOTE TASK CONTROLLER.FRM.

Table 9.2 The Remote Task Controller Form's Objects and Properties

OBJECT/CONTROL	PROPERTY	VALUE
Form	Name	frmMain
	BorderStyle	1 'Fixed Single
	Caption	Remote Task Controller
	Icon	NET02.ICO
	MaxButton	0 'False
	StartUpPosition	2 'CenterScreen
CommandButton	Name	cmdAction
	Caption	Start a Task
	Index	0
CommandButton	Name	cmdAction
	Caption	Exit
	Index	1
TextBox	Name	txtTaskRoot
	Text	Task
TextBox	Name	txtPort
	Text	1024
TextBox	Name	txtAddress
	Top	120
Label	Name	lblCaption
	Caption	IP Address of Monitor:
	Index	0
Label	Name	lblCaption
	Caption	Task Monitor Port:
	Index	1

OBJECT/CONTROL	PROPERTY	VALUE
Label	Name	lblCaption
	Caption	Task ID Root:
	Index	2

17. Add the following code to the General Declarations section of the form. The code declares a variable to store the number of active tasks.

```
Option Explicit

Private mnTaskCount    As Integer
```

18. Add the following code to the form's **Load** event. This line of code initializes the task counter. This is not really necessary as the variable is set to zero by default when Visual Basic creates the variables. This initialization step is performed for clarity, and is a good habit to help avoid uncertainty and ambiguity.

```
Private Sub Form_Load()

mnTaskCount = 0

End Sub
```

19. Add the following code. When the task controller form is unloaded, it must unload all the individual task forms. This code loops through the forms collection and unloads each form that is found.

```
Private Sub Form_Unload(Cancel As Integer)

Dim nLoopCtr          As Integer

' Unload all instances of the task forms
For nLoopCtr = Forms.Count - 1 To 0 Step -1
    ' Make sure the current form is not this one
    If Forms(nLoopCtr).hWnd <> Me.hWnd Then
        ' Unload the current form in the collection
        On Error Resume Next
        Unload Forms(nLoopCtr)
        On Error GoTo 0
    End If
Next nLoopCtr

End Sub
```

20. Place the following code in the **Click** event of the **cmdAction** command button control array. When the user selects the first button in the array to start a new task, the connection address and port number are obtained from the text boxes. A new instance of the task form is created and its custom properties are set. A custom method of the task form is then called to start up the task. Finally, the task reference counter is incremented.

The second command button in the array exits the program.

```
Private Sub cmdAction_Click(Index As Integer)

Dim sMonitorIP          As String
Dim nMonitorPort        As Integer
Dim sTaskRoot           As String
Dim oTaskForm           As Object

Select Case Index
    Case 0              ' Start a task
        ' Get the values used for the connections
        sMonitorIP = txtAddress.Text
        nMonitorPort = CInt(txtPort.Text)
        sTaskRoot = txtTaskRoot.Text
        ' Load an instance of the task form
        Set oTaskForm = New frmTask
        ' Set the task form properties
        oTaskForm.RemoteAddress = sMonitorIP
        oTaskForm.RemotePort = nMonitorPort
        oTaskForm.TaskID = sTaskRoot & _
                    Trim$(Str$(mnTaskCount))
        ' Start up the task
        oTaskForm.Start
        ' Increment the task counter
        mnTaskCount = mnTaskCount + 1

    Case 1              ' Exit
        Unload Me

End Select

End Sub
```

21. Add a second form to the project and set the objects and properties as they are listed in Table 9.3. Add the Microsoft Winsock Control as a component of the project. Save the form as REMOTE TASK.FRM. Instances of this form are created each time a new task is started.

Table 9.3 The Remote Task Form's Objects and Properties

OBJECT/CONTROL	PROPERTY	VALUE
Form	Name	frmTask
	BorderStyle	1 'Fixed Single
	Caption	Remote Task
	Icon	NET05.ICO
	MaxButton	0 'False
	StartUpPosition	2 'CenterScreen

OBJECT/CONTROL	PROPERTY	VALUE
ListBox	Name	lstStatus
CommandButton	Name	cmdAction
	Caption	Exit
	Default	-1 'True
TextBox	Name	txtTaskID
	Locked	-1 'True
Winsock	Name	Winsock1
Label	Name	lblCaption
	Caption	Port Connection Status:
	Index	0
Label	Name	lblCaption
	Caption	Task ID:
	Index	1

22. Add the following code to the General Declarations section of the form. The code starts by declaring a constant used to limit the total number of lines displayed in the status list box. Then some module-scope variables are declared to store connection references, a logical form status, and task start times. Finally, a variant is defined to store an array of socket connection status descriptions.

```
Option Explicit
Option Explicit

Private Const MAX_LIST_ITEMS = 100

' Define the custom properties of this form
Private msRemoteAddress     As String
Private mnRemotePort        As Integer
Private msTaskID            As String

' Form scope variable set when form is closing
Private mbClosing           As Boolean

' Set up a variable to record the task start time
Private mdtStartTime        As Double

' Array for socket state descriptions
Private mvntSocketState     As Variant
```

23. Add the following code to the form's **Load** event. First, the task start is recorded, and then the socket connection status array is loaded with state descriptions.

```
Private Sub Form_Load()
```

continued on next page

continued from previous page

```
' Record the task start time
mdtStartTime = Now

' Load the variant array with socket states
mvntSocketState = Array("Closed", _
                        "Open", _
                        "Listening", _
                        "Connection Pending", _
                        "Resolving Host", _
                        "Host Resolved", _
                        "Connecting", _
                        "Connected", _
                        "Closing", _
                        "Error")

' Set the form state flag to say it is active
mbClosing = False

End Sub
```

24. Add the following code to the form's **Unload** event. This code closes the socket connection if it is open, and then removes itself completely from memory.

```
Private Sub Form_Unload(Cancel As Integer)

' Close the socket if it is open
If Winsock1.State <> sckClosed And _
   Winsock1.State <> sckError Then
     ' Set the form state flag to say it is closing
     mbClosing = True
     Winsock1.Close
End If

' Completely remove all form references and
' structures from memory
Set frmTask = Nothing

End Sub
```

25. These next three routines provide the code used by other forms to set the custom properties of this instance of the task form. The properties set the remote connection port and address, and the task ID used by this form instance. Add the following code to the form.

```
Public Property Let RemoteAddress(ByVal sAddress As String)

' Save the property value
msRemoteAddress = sAddress

End Property
```

```
Public Property Let RemotePort(ByVal nPort As String)

' Save the property value
mnRemotePort = nPort

End Property


Public Property Let TaskID(ByVal sTaskID As String)

' Save the property value
msTaskID = sTaskID

' Update the read-only text box with the ID
txtTaskID.Text = msTaskID

End Property
```

26. Add the following code to the form. The custom **Start** method of the form begins by ensuring the task form is painted and visible. The remote port connection is then established. The socket state is then displayed by calling a subroutine that adds the status to the list box of the form.

```
Public Sub Start()

' Make sure the task form is visible
Me.Show

' Connect to the specified remote port
Winsock1.Connect msRemoteAddress, mnRemotePort

' Update the connection status in the list box
Call ShowSocketState

End Sub
```

27. Place the following code in the **Click** event of the **cmdAction** command button. The code closes the socket connection and then unloads the form.

```
Private Sub cmdAction_Click()

' Notify the monitor that this task is ending
If Winsock1.State <> sckClosed And _
   Winsock1.State <> sckError Then
     lstStatus.AddItem "Sending exit notification"
     Winsock1.SendData "Task done"
End If

' Close down the form
Unload Me

End Sub
```

28. Add the following code. This next subroutine is used to add the current socket state to the status list box. First, a text string is constructed containing the socket index number and the socket state description. This text is then added to the list box. A reference to the list location of the new item is obtained. This value is equivalent to the list count because the list box is not sorted. If the number of items in the list exceeds the constant value for the maximum number of entries, the list is trimmed down to size.

```
Private Sub ShowSocketState()

Dim sTempStr            As String
Dim nListCount          As Integer
Dim nLoopCtr            As Integer

' Build a string containing the current socket state
sTempStr = "Socket State: " & vbTab & _
                mvntSocketState(Winsock1.State)

' Add the string to the list box
lstStatus.AddItem sTempStr

' Get the index position where the item was added
nListCount = lstStatus.NewIndex

If nListCount > MAX_LIST_ITEMS Then
    ' Clean out old list entries
    For nLoopCtr = nListCount - MAX_LIST_ITEMS To 0 Step -1
        lstStatus.RemoveItem nLoopCtr
    Next nLoopCtr
    nListCount = lstStatus.ListCount - 1
End If

' Position at the last item on the list
lstStatus.ListIndex = nListCount

End Sub
```

29. When a connection request is received on the socket port, the following code is executed. This form does not accept connections, so an error message is added to the status list box.

No special action is required to deny the connection request. Ignoring it is all that is needed for denial.

```
Private Sub Winsock1_ConnectionRequest(ByVal requestID As Long)

' This event should never occur since this program
' does not listen on the port

' Show the connection request ID
lstStatus.AddItem "Unexpected Connection Request"
```

```
' The connection is refused by not accepting it

' Update the connection status in the list box
Call ShowSocketState

End Sub
```

30. Successful connections always trigger the following event. The following code reports the new connection status by calling the status update subroutine.

```
Private Sub Winsock1_Connect()

' Update the connection status in the list box
Call ShowSocketState

End Sub
```

31. The `SendComplete` event occurs each time the transmission of data is completed over the socket. The code in this event adds a transmission line to the status list box, and then calls the socket status update subroutine.

```
Private Sub Winsock1_SendComplete()

' Show that the send was completed
lstStatus.AddItem "Send Complete"

' Update the connection status in the list box
Call ShowSocketState

End Sub
```

32. Incoming data is parsed by the following code that is added to the `DataArrival` event of the socket control. This event fires to indicate that there is data available, so the code first gets the data from the socket. The data value and length are then added to the status list box.

Next the data is parsed. This form recognizes requests for task IDs and task uptime reports. The appropriate data is prepared and sent back over the socket port.

```
Private Sub Winsock1_DataArrival(ByVal bytesTotal As Long)

Dim sData              As String
Dim sReply             As String

' Get the inbound data from the socket
Winsock1.GetData sData, vbString, bytesTotal

' Show the data and its length in the list box
lstStatus.AddItem "Data Value:  " & vbTab & sData
lstStatus.AddItem "Data Length: " & vbTab & bytesTotal
```

continued on next page

continued from previous page

```
' Update the connection status in the list box
Call ShowSocketState

' Parse the data and prepare the response to the request
' White space is removed and the string is uppercased
' to make command parsing simpler
Select Case Trim$(UCase$(sData))
    Case "UPTIME"        ' How long has task been running
        sReply = "Uptime: " & Format$(Now - mdtStartTime, _
                 "h:mm:ss")

    Case "IDENTIFY"      ' Who is this task
        sReply = "Identify: " & msTaskID

    Case Else            ' Invalid request
        sReply = "Unknown request"

End Select

' Send the requested response data
If Len(sReply) <> 0 Then
    ' It is not blank, so send the reply
    Winsock1.SendData sReply
    ' Update the list box with the reply data
    lstStatus.AddItem "Data Sent:   " & vbTab & sReply
    ' Update the connection status in the list box
    Call ShowSocketState
End If

End Sub
```

33. This event is fired to indicate that the other connected program has closed the port. If this happens, the code reports an unexpected closure and notifies the user that monitoring has stopped.

```
Private Sub Winsock1_Close()

' The form is closing itself, so get out of here
If mbClosing = True Then Exit Sub

' Provide notification that the socket was closed
' unexpectedly, probably by the remote monitor
lstStatus.AddItem "Unexpected socket closure"
lstStatus.AddItem "Monitoring discontinued"

' Update the connection status in the list box
Call ShowSocketState

End Sub
```

34. Add the following code to the **Error** event of the socket control. This code extracts details of the error and displays the data in the socket status list box.

```
Private Sub Winsock1_Error(ByVal Number As Integer, _
                Description As String, _
                ByVal Scode As Long, _
                ByVal Source As String, _
                ByVal HelpFile As String, _
                ByVal HelpContext As Long, _
                CancelDisplay As Boolean)

' Show the error details
lstStatus.AddItem "Error Number: " & vbTab & Number
lstStatus.AddItem "Error Text:   " & vbTab & Description

' Update the connection status in the list box
Call ShowSocketState

End Sub
```

How It Works

The monitoring program opens a port and then listens. When a task starts, it connects to the monitor program. The monitor program asks the task for its ID and how long it has been running. At specific time intervals, the monitor program asks each task for an update of its runtime. When a task ends, the monitoring program is notified by the closure of the socket associated with each task.

Comments

Production applications would not show the connection status for the monitoring port to the user. The monitoring would occur in the background of the application. If the primary server fails, the client application should connect to a secondary server. This process is known as *failover*. Information about the address and port of the monitoring program, as well as possible failover locations, should be stored in the Registry.

An alternative to active status queries from the monitoring program to the tasks is to have the tasks send periodic status data. These task-initiated messages can be at regularly scheduled intervals or be generated only when the status changes. This second option is an effective method of reducing network traffic and still having current task status.

COMPLEXITY
INTERMEDIATE

9.2 How do I...
Keep the time synchronized for accurate time stamps?

COMPATIBILITY: VISUAL BASIC 5 AND 6

Problem

I have a distributed application that updates a database. The business rules for the program dictate that the date and time for all activities be recorded in the database. How do I ensure that the clocks on all the systems involved in the application are synchronized?

Technique

This How-To uses a Windows socket to offer centralized time services. Multiple connections are supported from any program on any operating system that supports TCP/IP. The code computes the network turnaround time and takes that into account when setting the local time by using server-supplied data.

There are two programs in this How-To. The first is the program that provides the current date and time in response to requests from client applications. The second project is a sample client application that requests the date and time from the server.

Steps

Open TIME SERVER.VBP and make an executable. Run the program and click the Listen command button (see Figure 9.4).

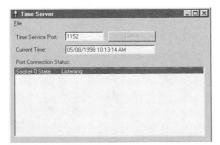

Figure 9.4 The time server form at runtime.

Now open and run TIME CLIENT.VBP, as shown in Figure 9.5. Enter the TCP address of your system. Click the Get Server Time command button to get the current date and time from the server program.

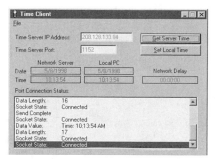

Figure 9.5 The time client form at runtime.

To create this project, complete the following steps.

1. Create a new project called TIME SERVER.VBP.

2. Add a form to the project and set the objects and properties as they are listed in Table 9.4. Also, add the Microsoft Winsock Control as a component of the project. Save the form as TIME SERVER.FRM.

Table 9.4 The Time Server Form's Objects and Properties

OBJECT/CONTROL	PROPERTY	VALUE
Form	Name	frmMain
	Caption	Time Server
	Icon	TIME.ICO
	StartUpPosition	2 'CenterScreen
TextBox	Name	txtTime
	Locked	-1 'True
Timer	Name	tmrUpdate
	Interval	60000
ListBox	Name	lstStatus
CommandButton	Name	cmdAction
	Caption	Listen
	Index	0
TextBox	Name	txtPort
	Text	1152

continued on next page

continued from previous page

OBJECT/CONTROL	PROPERTY	VALUE
Winsock	Name	Winsock1
	Index	0
Label	Name	lblCaption
	Caption	Current Time:
	Index	0
Label	Name	lblCaption
	Caption	Time Service Port:
	Index	1
Label	Name	lblCaption
	Caption	Port Connection Status:
	Index	2
Menu	Name	mnuFile
	Caption	&File
Menu	Name	mnuFileSel
	Caption	E&xit
	Index	0

3. Add the following code to the General Declarations section of the form. The code starts by declaring a constant used to limit the total number of lines displayed in the status list box. Then a number of module scope variables are declared to track the tasks and task IDs. Finally, a variant is defined to store an array of socket connection status descriptions.

```
Option Explicit

' Constant used to limit the number of list
' box items before removing the oldest
Private Const MAX_LIST_ITEMS = 100

' Count the number of tasks being served
Private mnTaskCount            As Integer

' Count the number of socket control instances
Private mnSockets              As Integer

' Store the ID for each task being served
' These will all be identical as the array
' is used strictly as a place holder
Private msTaskID()             As String

' Array of socket state descriptions
Private mvntSocketState        As Variant
```

4. Add the following code to the **Load** event of the form. First, the socket connection status array is loaded with state descriptions. Then the task ID array and reference counters are initialized. Finally, the timer control event routine is called to update the display of the current date and time.

```
Private Sub Form_Load()

' Load the variant array with socket states
mvntSocketState = Array("Closed", _
                        "Open", _
                        "Listening", _
                        "Connection Pending", _
                        "Resolving Host", _
                        "Host Resolved", _
                        "Connecting", _
                        "Connected", _
                        "Closing", _
                        "Error")

' Initialize the task ID array
ReDim msTaskID(10)

' The #1 element of the array is for the primary
' listening socket
msTaskID(0) = "Reserved"

' Initialize the task count and socket count variables
mnTaskCount = 0
mnSockets = 0

' Make an initial call to the timer event
' so that the current date and time show up
Call tmrUpdate_Timer

End Sub
```

5. The code in the **Timer** event displays the formatted date and time on the form.

```
Private Sub tmrUpdate_Timer()

' Get and display the current system time
txtTime.Text = Format$(Now, "mm/dd/yyyy") & " " & _
               Format$(Now, "Long Time")

End Sub
```

6. Place the following code in the **Click** event of the **cmdAction** command button control. First, the text box values are checked. Then the command button itself is disabled to prevent an attempt to listen on the same port a second time. Next, the socket control properties are set. Then a subroutine is called to add the current socket status to the status list box.

```
Private Sub cmdAction_Click(Index As Integer)

Dim nMonitorPort          As String
Select Case Index
    Case 0            ' Listen
        ' Get the value used for the connection
        nMonitorPort = CInt(txtPort.Text)
        If nMonitorPort = 0 Then
            MsgBox "Please enter the port to use " & _
                   "for monitoring."
            Exit Sub
        End If
        ' Disable this command button as the program
        ' can be instructed to start listening only once
        cmdAction(Index).Enabled = False
        ' Set the socket control port property
        If Winsock1(0).LocalPort <> nMonitorPort Then
            Winsock1(0).LocalPort = nMonitorPort
        End If
        ' Start listening
        Winsock1(0).Listen
        ' Update the connection status in the list box
        Call ShowSocketState(0)

End Select

End Sub
```

7. There is only one item on the File menu, and it is used to exit the program.

```
Private Sub mnuFileSel_Click(Index As Integer)

Select Case Index
    Case 0            ' Exit
        ' End the program when the user selects
        ' the File/Exit menu item
        Unload Me

End Select

End Sub
```

8. This next subroutine is used to add the current socket state to the status list box. Because the socket control is an array, an index value is passed to this subroutine. First, a text string is constructed containing the socket index number and the socket state description. This text is then added to the list box. A reference to the list location of the new item is obtained. This value is equivalent to the list count because the list box is not sorted. If the number of items in the list exceeds the constant value for the maximum number of entries, the list is trimmed down to size.

```
Private Sub ShowSocketState(Index As Integer)

Dim sTempStr            As String
Dim nListCount          As Integer
Dim nLoopCtr            As Integer

' Build a string containing the current socket state
sTempStr = "Socket " & Index & " State: " & vbTab & _
              mvntSocketState(Winsock1(Index).State)

' Add the string to the list box
lstStatus.AddItem sTempStr

' Get the index position where the item was added
nListCount = lstStatus.NewIndex

If nListCount > MAX_LIST_ITEMS Then
    ' Clean out old list entries
    For nLoopCtr = nListCount - MAX_LIST_ITEMS To 0 Step -1
        lstStatus.RemoveItem nLoopCtr
    Next nLoopCtr
    nListCount = lstStatus.ListCount - 1
End If

' Position at the last item on the list
lstStatus.ListIndex = nListCount

End Sub
```

9. When a connection request is received on the socket, the following code is
executed. The connection request details are added to the status list box.
Then the index value of the socket control is checked. If the request is
received on the primary control of the array, the connection is processed.
The code then looks for an available entry in the task ID array. If there are
no open array slots, the array is extended. Also, if there is not a socket
control associated with the task entry slot, another instance of the control
is loaded. The code then checks the state of the socket and closes it if it is
not closed. The connection request is then accepted using the identified or
created instance of the socket control. Calls are made to the socket status
subroutine for the current instance and primary instances of the socket
control.

If the request came in on any element of the control array other than index
0, it is invalid. Ignoring the request is all that is needed to deny the
connection.

```
Private Sub Winsock1_ConnectionRequest(Index As Integer, _
              ByVal requestID As Long)
```

continued on next page

continued from previous page

```
Dim bFoundSlot           As Boolean
Dim nLoopCtr             As Integer
Dim nCurrentTask         As Integer

' Show the connection request ID
lstStatus.AddItem "Connect Request on Socket " & Index
lstStatus.AddItem "Connect Request:" & vbTab & _
          "ID " & requestID

If Index = 0 Then
    ' This was a primary listen request
    ' Find an available socket control
    bFoundSlot = False
    ' Loop through the array looking for a blank ID
    For nLoopCtr = 1 To UBound(msTaskID)
        If Len(msTaskID(nLoopCtr)) = 0 Then
            ' Set the flag indicating success
            bFoundSlot = True
            ' Save the pointer into the array
            nCurrentTask = nLoopCtr
            Exit For
        End If
    Next nLoopCtr
    If bFoundSlot = False Then
        ' Increment the task counter
        mnTaskCount = mnTaskCount + 1
        ' See if the new count exceeds the array bounds
        If mnTaskCount > UBound(msTaskID) Then
            ' Need to increase the array size, so add 10 more
            ReDim Preserve msTaskID(UBound(msTaskID) + 10)
        End If
        ' Set the current task number to the total task count
        nCurrentTask = mnTaskCount
    End If
Else
    ' The connect request arrived on an invalid socket
    Exit Sub
End If

' See if a new socket control needs to be created
If nCurrentTask > mnSockets Then
    ' Create a new instance of the control
    Load Winsock1(nCurrentTask)
    Winsock1(nCurrentTask).LocalPort = 0
    ' Increment the socket count
    mnSockets = mnSockets + 1
End If

' If the response instance of the control is not closed,
' then close it
If Winsock1(nCurrentTask).State <> sckClosed Then
    Winsock1(nCurrentTask).Close
    Call ShowSocketState(nCurrentTask)
End If
```

```
' Accept the request using the requestID
Winsock1(nCurrentTask).Accept requestID

' Consume the entry in the task array
msTaskID(nCurrentTask) = "In use"

' Update the connection status in the list box
Call ShowSocketState(nCurrentTask)

' Update the primary connection status in the list box
Call ShowSocketState(0)

End Sub
```

10. Successful connections always trigger the following event. The following code reports the new connection status by calling the status update subroutine.

```
Private Sub Winsock1_Connect(Index As Integer)

' Update the connection status in the list box
Call ShowSocketState(Index)

End Sub
```

11. The SendComplete event occurs each time the transmission of data is completed over the socket. The code in this event adds a transmission line to the status list box and then calls the socket status update subroutine.

```
Private Sub Winsock1_SendComplete(Index As Integer)

' Show that the send was completed
lstStatus.AddItem "Send Complete"

' Update the connection status in the list box
Call ShowSocketState(Index)

End Sub
```

12. Incoming data is parsed by the following code that is added to the DataArrival event of the socket control. This event fires to indicate that there is data available so the code first gets the data from the socket. The data value and length are then added to the status list box.

Next, the data is parsed. This form recognizes requests for data loopback tests and transmission of the current local system date and time. The response data is prepared and sent back.

```
Private Sub Winsock1_DataArrival(Index As Integer, _
            ByVal bytesTotal As Long)

Dim sData           As String
Dim sTempStr        As String
Dim sReturn         As String
```

continued on next page

continued from previous page

```
' Get the inbound data from the socket
Winsock1(Index).GetData sData, vbString, bytesTotal

' Show the data and its length in the list box
lstStatus.AddItem "Data Value:  " & vbTab & sData
lstStatus.AddItem "Data Length: " & vbTab & bytesTotal

' Parse the data and prepare the response to the request
' White space is removed, the string is uppercased, and only the
' two leftmost characters are examined to simplify parsing
Select Case Trim$(UCase$(Left$(sData, 2)))
    Case "LO"             ' Loop back requested
        sTempStr = msTaskID(Index) & " loopback:" & _
                    vbTab & Mid$(sData, Len("LOOPBACK: ") + 1)
        ' Set the reply data
        sReturn = sData

    Case "DA"             ' Current date requested
        sTempStr = "Date request received"
        ' Set the reply data
        sReturn = "Date: " & Format$(Now, "mm/dd/yyyy")

    Case "TI"             ' Current time requested
        sTempStr = "Time request received"
        ' Set the reply data
        sReturn = "Time: " & Format$(Now, "Long Time")

    Case Else             ' Invalid request
        sTempStr = "Unknown data received"
        ' Set the reply data
        sReturn = "Error"

End Select

' Send any return data
If Len(sReturn) <> 0 Then
    ' Send the reply data
    Winsock1(Index).SendData sReturn
    DoEvents
End If

' See if there is information for the list box
If Len(sTempStr) <> 0 Then
    ' It is not blank, so add the data to the list box
    lstStatus.AddItem sTempStr
End If

' Update the connection status in the list box
Call ShowSocketState(Index)

End Sub
```

13. Add the following code. This event is probably incorrectly named. Its name should be `CloseRequest`. This event is fired to indicate that the other connected program is closing the port. The code here must close the port on this end of the connection.

The entry in the task ID array is cleared so it can be reused. The socket is then closed and the status list box is updated. If the primary listening port was closed, it is reset to continue listening.

```
Private Sub Winsock1_Close(Index As Integer)

' Update the connection status in the list box
Call ShowSocketState(Index)

If Winsock1(Index).State = sckClosing Then
    ' Clear the task ID entry in the array
    msTaskID(Index) = ""
    ' A close request was made so close the port
    Winsock1(Index).Close
    ' Update the connection status in the list box
    Call ShowSocketState(Index)
    ' Start listening again if this is the primary port
    If Index = 0 Then
        Winsock1(Index).Listen
        ' Update the connection status in the list box
        Call ShowSocketState(Index)
    End If
End If

End Sub
```

14. Add the following code to the `Error` event of the socket control. This code extracts details of the error and displays the data in the socket status list box.

```
Private Sub Winsock1_Error(Index As Integer, _
                ByVal Number As Integer, _
                Description As String, _
                ByVal Scode As Long, _
                ByVal Source As String, _
                ByVal HelpFile As String, _
                ByVal HelpContext As Long, _
                CancelDisplay As Boolean)

' Show the error details
lstStatus.AddItem "Error on Socket " & Index
lstStatus.AddItem "Error Number: " & vbTab & Number
lstStatus.AddItem "Error Text:   " & vbTab & Description

' Update the connection status in the list box
Call ShowSocketState(Index)

End Sub
```

15. The first project of this How-To is now finished. Save the project and compile the program into an executable.

16. Create a new project called TIME CLIENT.VBP.

17. Add a form to the project and set the objects and properties as they are listed in Table 9.5. Be sure to add the Microsoft Winsock Control to the project. Save the form as TIME CLIENT.FRM.

Table 9.5 The Time Client Form's Objects and Properties

OBJECT/CONTROL	PROPERTY	VALUE
Form	Name	frmMain
	BorderStyle	1 'Fixed Single
	Caption	Time Client
	Icon	TIME.ICO
	MaxButton	0 'False
	MinButton	-1 'True
	StartUpPosition	2 'CenterScreen
CommandButton	Name	cmdAction
	Caption	&Get Server Time
	Index	0
CommandButton	Name	cmdAction
	Caption	&Set Local Time
	Index	1
TextBox	Name	txtAddress
TextBox	Name	txtPort
	Text	1152
ListBox	Name	lstStatus
Winsock	Name	Winsock1
Label	Name	lblInfo
	Appearance	0 'Flat
	AutoSize	-1 'True
	Caption	Date
	Index	0
Label	Name	lblInfo
	Appearance	0 'Flat
	AutoSize	-1 'True
	Caption	Time
	Index	1

OBJECT/CONTROL	PROPERTY	VALUE
Label	Name	lblInfo
	Appearance	0 'Flat
	AutoSize	-1 'True
	Caption	Network Server
	Index	2
Label	Name	lblInfo
	Appearance	0 'Flat
	AutoSize	-1 'True
	Caption	Local PC
	Index	3
Label	Name	lblInfo
	Alignment	2 'Center
	Appearance	0 'Flat
	BorderStyle	1 'Fixed Single
	Index	4
Label	Name	lblNetTime
	Alignment	2 'Center
	Appearance	0 'Flat
	BorderStyle	1 'Fixed Single
Label	Name	lblPCTime
	Alignment	2 'Center
	Appearance	0 'Flat
	BorderStyle	1 'Fixed Single
Label	Name	lblNetDate
	Alignment	2 'Center
	Appearance	0 'Flat
	BorderStyle	1 'Fixed Single
Label	Name	lblPCDate
	Alignment	2 'Center
	Appearance	0 'Flat
	BorderStyle	1 'Fixed Single
Label	Name	lblDelay
	Alignment	2 'Center
	Appearance	0 'Flat
	BorderStyle	1 'Fixed Single

continued on next page

continued from previous page

OBJECT/CONTROL	PROPERTY	VALUE
Label	Name	lblCaption
	Caption	Time Server IP Address:
	Index	0
Label	Name	lblCaption
	Caption	Time Server Port:
	Index	1
Label	Name	lblCaption
	Caption	Port Connection Status:
	Index	2
Menu	Name	mnuFIle
	Caption	&File
Menu	Name	mnuFileSel
	Caption	E&xit"
	Index	0

18. Add the following code to the General Declarations section of the form. The code starts by declaring a constant used to limit the total number of lines displayed in the status list box. Then a number of module scope variables are declared to track the tasks and task IDs. Finally a variant is defined to store an array of socket connection status descriptions.

```
Option Explicit

Private Const MAX_LIST_ITEMS = 100

Private msRemoteAddress    As String
Private mnRemotePort       As Integer

' Variable used to compute network delay
Private mdtNetDelay        As Double

' Boolean used to control setting of local time
' If set to true, then local time is set when
' the server time is received
' If set to false, the local time is not adjusted
Private mbSetLocal         As Boolean

' Form scope variable set when form is closing
Private mbClosing          As Boolean

' Variable set when data is received
Private mbGotData          As Boolean

' Array for socket state descriptions
Private mvntSocketState    As Variant
```

19. Add the following code to the form's **Load** event. First, the socket connection status array is loaded with state descriptions. Then the form activity state flag is set to indicate that the form is not currently closing. This Boolean is used to prevent a control event loop when the program is closing down.

```
Private Sub Form_Load()

' Load the variant array with socket states
mvntSocketState = Array("Closed", _
                        "Open", _
                        "Listening", _
                        "Connection Pending", _
                        "Resolving Host", _
                        "Host Resolved", _
                        "Connecting", _
                        "Connected", _
                        "Closing", _
                        "Error")

' Set the form state flag to say it is active
mbClosing = False

End Sub
```

20. Add the following subroutine to the form. When the form is unloaded, close the socket if it is not closed, and then exit the program.

```
Private Sub Form_Unload(Cancel As Integer)

' Close the socket if it is open
If Winsock1.State <> sckClosed And _
   Winsock1.State <> sckError Then
     ' Set the form state flag to say it is closing
     mbClosing = True
     Winsock1.Close
End If

End

End Sub
```

21. There is only one item on the File menu, and it is used to exit the program.

```
Private Sub mnuFileSel_Click(Index As Integer)

Select Case Index
    Case 0
        ' Close down the form
        Unload Me

End Select

End Sub
```

22. Place the following code in the **Click** event of the **cmdAction** command button control array. When the user selects the first button in the array to get the time from the server, a flag is set to prevent using the server time to set the local time. A subroutine is then called to get the time from the server.

The second command button in the array gets the time from the server and then uses it to set the local system time. This is accomplished by setting the flag to enable setting the local time and calling the subroutine that gets the server time.

```
Private Sub cmdAction_Click(Index As Integer)

' Disable changes to the address and port
If txtAddress.Enabled = True Then
    txtAddress.Enabled = False
    txtPort.Enabled = False
End If

Select Case Index
    Case 0              ' Get time
        ' Get the server time but don't
        ' set the local time
        mbSetLocal = False
        Call GetServerTime

    Case 1              ' Set time
        ' Get the server time and use it to set
        ' the local time
        mbSetLocal = True
        Call GetServerTime

End Select

End Sub
```

23. This next subroutine is used to add the current socket state to the status list box. First, a text string is constructed containing the socket index number and the socket state description. This text is then added to the list box. A reference to the list location of the new item is obtained. This value is equivalent to the list count because the list box is not sorted. If the number of items in the list exceeds the constant value for the maximum number of entries, the list is trimmed down to size.

```
Private Sub ShowSocketState()

Dim sTempStr            As String
Dim nListCount          As Integer
Dim nLoopCtr            As Integer

' Build a string containing the current socket state
sTempStr = "Socket State: " & vbTab & _
                mvntSocketState(Winsock1.State)
```

```
' Add the string to the list box
lstStatus.AddItem sTempStr

' Get the index position where the item was added
nListCount = lstStatus.NewIndex

If nListCount > MAX_LIST_ITEMS Then
    ' Clean out old list entries
    For nLoopCtr = nListCount - MAX_LIST_ITEMS To 0 Step -1
        lstStatus.RemoveItem nLoopCtr
    Next nLoopCtr
    nListCount = lstStatus.ListCount - 1
End If

' Position at the last item on the list
lstStatus.ListIndex = nListCount

End Sub
```

24. When a connection request is received on the socket port, the following code is executed. This form does not accept connections, so an error message is added to the status list box.

No special action is required to deny the connection request. Ignoring it is all that is needed for denial.

```
Private Sub Winsock1_ConnectionRequest(ByVal requestID As Long)

' This event should never occur because this program
' does not listen on the port

' Show the connection request ID
lstStatus.AddItem "Unexpected Connection Request"

' The connection is refused by not accepting it

' Update the connection status in the list box
Call ShowSocketState

End Sub
```

25. Successful connections always trigger the following event. The following code reports the new connection status by calling the status update subroutine.

```
Private Sub Winsock1_Connect()

' Update the connection status in the list box
Call ShowSocketState

End Sub
```

26. The `SendComplete` event occurs each time the transmission of data is completed over the socket. The code in this event adds a transmission line to the status list box, and then calls the socket status update subroutine.

```
Private Sub Winsock1_SendComplete()

' Show that the send was completed
lstStatus.AddItem "Send Complete"

' Update the connection status in the list box
Call ShowSocketState

End Sub
```

27. Incoming data is parsed by the following code that is added to the `DataArrival` event of the socket control. This event fires to indicate that there is data available so the code first gets the data from the socket. The data value and length are then added to the status list box.

Next, the data is parsed. This form recognizes responses to requests for loopbacks, date, and time information. Dates and times are parsed out of the incoming data and used to update the display information on the form. If requested by the user, the local date and time are reset using the date and time obtained from the time server.

```
Private Sub Winsock1_DataArrival(ByVal bytesTotal As Long)

Dim sData           As String
Dim sReply          As String
Dim dtLocal         As Double      ' Local serial date/time
Dim dtServer        As Double      ' Server serial date/time
Dim sTempStr        As String

' Get the inbound data from the socket
Winsock1.GetData sData, vbString, bytesTotal

' Show the data and its length in the list box
lstStatus.AddItem "Data Value:  " & vbTab & sData
lstStatus.AddItem "Data Length: " & vbTab & bytesTotal

' Parse the data and prepare the response to the request
' White space is removed and the string is uppercased
' to make command parsing simpler
Select Case Left$(Trim$(UCase$(sData)), 2)
    Case "LO"           ' Loopback reply
        ' Compute the delay
        mdtNetDelay = (Now - mdtNetDelay) / 2
        ' Show the delay on the form
        lblDelay.Caption = Format$(mdtNetDelay, "hh:nn:ss")
        ' Let other code know we got the data
        mbGotData = True

    Case "DA"           ' Date response
        ' Extract the server date
```

```
            sTempStr = Mid$(sData, Len("TIME: ") + 1)
            dtServer = DateSerial(Year(sTempStr), _
                        Month(sTempStr), _
                        Day(sTempStr))
            ' Adjusted for the network delay
            dtLocal = Now + mdtNetDelay
            ' Change the local system date if requested, and then
            ' display the local date
            If mbSetLocal = True Then
                Date$ = Format$(dtServer + mdtNetDelay, "m/d/yyyy")
                lblPCDate.Caption = Format$(Now, "m/d/yyyy")
            Else
                lblPCDate.Caption = Format$(dtLocal, "m/d/yyyy")
            End If
            ' Display the server date
            lblNetDate.Caption = Format$(dtServer, "m/d/yyyy")
            ' Let other code know we got the data
            mbGotData = True

        Case "TI"              ' Time response
            ' Extract the server time
            sTempStr = Mid$(sData, Len("TIME: ") + 1)
            dtServer = TimeSerial(Hour(sTempStr), _
                        Minute(sTempStr), _
                        Second(sTempStr))
            ' Get the local time adjusted for the network delay
            dtLocal = Now + mdtNetDelay
            ' Change the local system time if requested, and then
            ' display the local time
            If mbSetLocal = True Then
                Time$ = Format$(dtServer + mdtNetDelay, "hh:nn:ss")
                lblPCTime.Caption = Format$(Now, "hh:nn:ss")
            Else
                lblPCTime.Caption = Format$(dtLocal, "hh:nn:ss")
            End If
            ' Display the server time
            lblNetTime.Caption = Format$(dtServer, "hh:nn:ss")
            ' Let other code know we got the data
            mbGotData = True

        Case Else              ' Invalid request
            ' Update the list box
            lstStatus.AddItem "Invalid data received"

    End Select

    ' Update the connection status in the list box
    Call ShowSocketState

End Sub
```

28. This event is fired to indicate that the other end of the port connection has closed. If that happens, the code reports an unexpected closure and notifies the user that time services are unavailable. To prevent accidental use of the services when the port is closed, the command buttons are all disabled.

```
Private Sub Winsock1_Close()

' The form is closing itself, so get out of here
If mbClosing = True Then Exit Sub

' Provide notification that the socket was closed
' unexpectedly, probably by the remote monitor
MsgBox "Unexpected socket closure. Time services no longer _
          available.", _
          vbCritical, "Connection Closed"

' Disable the command buttons
cmdAction(0).Enabled = False
cmdAction(1).Enabled = False

' Update the connection status in the list box
Call ShowSocketState

End Sub
```

29. Add the following code to the **Error** event of the socket control. This code extracts details of the error and displays the data in the socket status list box.

```
Private Sub Winsock1_Error(ByVal Number As Integer, _
              Description As String, _
              ByVal Scode As Long, _
              ByVal Source As String, _
              ByVal HelpFile As String, _
              ByVal HelpContext As Long, _
              CancelDisplay As Boolean)

' Show the error details
lstStatus.AddItem "Error Number: " & vbTab & Number
lstStatus.AddItem "Error Text:   " & vbTab & Description

' Update the connection status in the list box
Call ShowSocketState

End Sub
```

30. Add the following subroutine, which sends the requests to the time server to get the centralized date and time. The port and address are retrieved from the text boxes. If the socket is not open, the port connection is made. A loopback request is sent so the **DataArrival** can compute the roundtrip network delay time. Finally, the date and time are requested individually.

Socket data can be concatenated if it is not read on the receiving end of the connection before additional data is sent. For this reason, logic is needed to wait for data responses before sending subsequent requests. This is done several times in the following code by using the **mbGotData** variable. The variable is set to **False** and the data request is sent to the server. The code then goes into a tight **DoEvents** loop and waits for the flag to be set. When the reply is received in the **DataArrival** event of the socket control, the flag is set to **True**.

```
Private Sub GetServerTime()

Dim sRemoteAddress        As String
Dim nRemotePort           As Integer

' Get the server address and port
sRemoteAddress = txtAddress.Text
nRemotePort = CInt(txtPort.Text)

' Set the flag to wait for data
mbGotData = False

' If not connected, then connect to the remote port
If Winsock1.State <> sckConnected Then
    Winsock1.Connect sRemoteAddress, nRemotePort
    DoEvents
End If

' Save the current local time to compute delay
mdtNetDelay = Now

' Send a loopback request to compute the network delay
Winsock1.SendData "Loopback: Wise ones wait for the right time."

' Wait for the data to get here
Do Until mbGotData = True
    DoEvents
Loop

' Reset the flag to wait for data
mbGotData = False

' Send the server date request
Winsock1.SendData "Date"

' Wait for the data to get here
Do Until mbGotData = True
    DoEvents
Loop

' Reset the flag to wait for data
mbGotData = False

' Send the server time request
Winsock1.SendData "Time"

' Wait for the data to get here
Do Until mbGotData = True
    DoEvents
Loop

' Update the connection status in the list box
Call ShowSocketState

End Sub
```

How It Works

The time server supports simultaneous connections from multiple clients. This can be tested by starting several copies of the time client program. The server program responds to requests for data loopback and information about the current server date and time. The client program requests date and time data when the user requests an update.

Comments

Typically, time services such as this one occur in the background as a separate automated task. These types of services often appear as small icons in the system tray. The address and port of the time server program, and possible failover service locations, should be stored in the Registry. Instead of halting time services when the server disconnects, as is done in the example, backup time servers should be checked. If the backup services are unavailable, the program needs to keep trying to reconnect.

COMPLEXITY
INTERMEDIATE

9.3 How do I...
Manage a pool of objects and services?

COMPATIBILITY: VISUAL BASIC 5 AND 6

Problem

I am concerned about the ability of the centralized components in my application to support the anticipated workloads. I don't need an elaborate object broker or server, but I want to be able to manage a small pool of services and allocate the service loads. How do I manage a group of services and assign individual client applications to specific service tasks?

Technique

This How-To demonstrates simple pool management by rebuilding the time server as a managed pool of services. Round-robin allocation is used to assign clients to individual servers. The time client application is then modified so that it can be redirected to any one of the pool of available time servers.

There are three programs in this How-To. The first is the pool manager for the time services. The second program is the time service engine that offers time services to client applications. The final project is a sample client application that requests the date and time from the service manager. The management program directs the client to a time service engine.

Steps

Open TIME ENGINE.VBP and make an executable. Open TIME MANAGER.VBP and make an executable. Run TIME MANAGER.EXE and click the Listen command button, as shown in Figure 9.6.

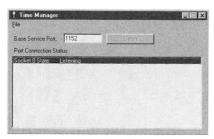

Figure 9.6 The time manager form at runtime.

The manager program starts two copies of the TIME ENGINE program. Figure 9.7 shows a sample.

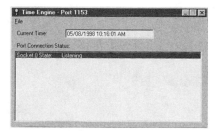

Figure 9.7 The time engine form at runtime.

Now, open and run TIME CLIENT REDIRECTED.VBP. The screen is shown in Figure 9.8. Enter the TCP address of your system. Click the Get Server Time command button to get the current date and time from the server program.

Complete the following steps to create this project.

1. Create a new project called TIME MANAGER.VBP.

2. Add a form to the project and set the objects and properties as they are listed in Table 9.6. Also, add the Microsoft Winsock Control to the project. Save the form as TIME MANAGER.FRM.

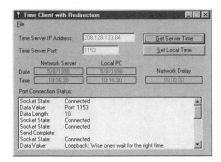

Figure 9.8 The time client form at runtime.

Table 9.6 The Time Manager Form's Objects and Properties

OBJECT/CONTROL	PROPERTY	VALUE
Form	Name	frmMain
	Caption	Time Manager
	Icon	TIME.ICO
	MaxButton	0 'False
	MinButton	-1 'True
	StartUpPosition	2 'CenterScreen
ListBox	Name	lstStatus
CommandButton	Name	cmdAction
	Caption	Listen
	Index	0
TextBox	Name	txtPort
	Text	1152
Winsock	Name	Winsock1
	Index	0
Label	Name	lblCaption
	Caption	Port Connection Status:
	Index	0
Label	Name	lblCaption
	Caption	Base Service Port:
	Index	1
Menu	Name	mnuFile
	Caption	&File
Menu	Name	mnuFileSel
	Caption	E&xit
	Index	0

3. Add the following code to the General Declarations section of the form. The code starts by declaring a constant used to limit the total number of lines displayed in the status list box. The next constant determines the number of time server engines that are launched and managed by the manager. The manager needs to assign and track the ports used by the time service engines, so an array is established to hold this reference data. Because the time services are allocated on a round-robin basis, the program uses the mnCurrentEngine variable to track which time server is next in the allocation rotation. Finally, a variant is defined to store an array of socket connection status descriptions.

```
Option Explicit

' Constant used to limit the number of list
' box items before removing the oldest
Private Const MAX_LIST_ITEMS = 100

' Constant used to limit the number of time
' engine tasks started
Private Const ENGINE_LIMIT = 2

' Engine port IDs
Private mnEnginePort(ENGINE_LIMIT + 1)      As Integer

' Reference to next engine to use
Private mnCurrentEngine          As Integer

' Array of socket state descriptions
Private mvntSocketState          As Variant
```

4. Add the following code to the **Load** event of the form. First, the socket connection status array is loaded with state descriptions, and then the round-robin engine pointer is initialized to reference the first engine.

```
Private Sub Form_Load()

' Load the variant array with socket states
mvntSocketState = Array("Closed", _
                        "Open", _
                        "Listening", _
                        "Connection Pending", _
                        "Resolving Host", _
                        "Host Resolved", _
                        "Connecting", _
                        "Connected", _
                        "Closing", _
                        "Error")

' Initialize the engine pointer to the first one
mnCurrentEngine = 1

End Sub
```

5. Place the following code in the Click event of the cmdAction command button. When the user clicks the button to start listening, the text box values are checked first. Then the command button itself is disabled to prevent an attempt to listen on the same port a second time. Next, the socket control properties are set. The time service engines are started and passed a port ID on the command line. Listening is then enabled for the time manager itself. Finally, a subroutine is called to add the current socket status to the status list box.

```
Private Sub cmdAction_Click(Index As Integer)

Dim nMonitorPort        As String
Dim lResult             As Long
Dim nLoopCtr            As Integer

Select Case Index
    Case 0              ' Listen
        ' Get the value used for the connection
        nMonitorPort = CInt(txtPort.Text)
        If nMonitorPort = 0 Then
            MsgBox "Please enter the port to use " & _
                    "for monitoring."
            Exit Sub
        End If
        ' Disable this command button as the program
        ' can be instructed to start listening only once
        cmdAction(Index).Enabled = False
        ' Set the socket control port property
        If Winsock1(0).LocalPort <> nMonitorPort Then
            Winsock1(0).LocalPort = nMonitorPort
        End If
        ' Start up the time engines
        For nLoopCtr = 1 To ENGINE_LIMIT
            ' Save the port reference for this engine
            mnEnginePort(nLoopCtr) = nMonitorPort + nLoopCtr
            ' Start the engine
            lResult = Shell(App.Path & "\Time Engine.exe /Port=" & _
                nMonitorPort + nLoopCtr)
        Next nLoopCtr
        ' Start listening
        Winsock1(0).Listen
        ' Update the connection status in the list box
        Call ShowSocketState(0)

End Select

End Sub
```

6. There is only one item on the File menu, used to exit the program.

```
Private Sub mnuFileSel_Click(Index As Integer)

Select Case Index
    Case 0              ' Exit
```

```
                   ' End the program when the user selects
                   ' the File/Exit menu item
                   Unload Me

           End Select

       End Sub
```

7. This next subroutine is used to add the current socket state to the status list box. Because the socket control is an array, an index value is passed to this subroutine. First, a text string is constructed containing the socket index number and the socket state description. This text is then added to the list box. A reference to the list location of the new item is obtained. This value is equivalent to the list count because the list box is not sorted. If the number of items in the list exceeds the constant value for the maximum number of entries, the list is trimmed down to size.

```
Private Sub ShowSocketState(Index As Integer)

Dim sTempStr            As String
Dim nListCount          As Integer
Dim nLoopCtr            As Integer

' Build a string containing the current socket state
sTempStr = "Socket " & Index & " State: " & vbTab & _
                mvntSocketState(Winsock1(Index).State)

' Add the string to the list box
lstStatus.AddItem sTempStr

' Get the index position where the item was added
nListCount = lstStatus.NewIndex

If nListCount > MAX_LIST_ITEMS Then
    ' Clean out old list entries
    For nLoopCtr = nListCount - MAX_LIST_ITEMS To 0 Step -1
        lstStatus.RemoveItem nLoopCtr
    Next nLoopCtr
    nListCount = lstStatus.ListCount - 1
End If

' Position at the last item on the list
lstStatus.ListIndex = nListCount

End Sub
```

8. When a connection request is received on the socket port, the following code is executed. The connection request details are added to the status list box and the index value of the socket control is checked. If the request was received on the primary control of the array, the connection is processed. The code looks for an available entry in the task ID array. If there are no open array slots, the array is extended. Also, if there is not a socket control associated with the task entry slot, another instance of the control is loaded. The code then checks the state of the socket and closes it if it is not closed. The connection request is then accepted, using the identified or created instance of the socket control. Calls are made to the socket status subroutine for the current instance and primary instances of the socket control.

If the request came in on any element of the control array other than index 0, it is invalid. Ignoring the request is all that is needed to deny the connection.

```
Private Sub Winsock1_ConnectionRequest(Index As Integer, _
            ByVal requestID As Long)

Dim bFoundSlot              As Boolean
Dim nLoopCtr                As Integer
Dim nCurrentTask            As Integer

' Show the connection request ID
lstStatus.AddItem "Connect Request on Socket " & Index
lstStatus.AddItem "Connect Request:" & vbTab & _
            "ID " & requestID

' Create a new instance of the control
nCurrentTask = Index + 1
Load Winsock1(nCurrentTask)
Winsock1(nCurrentTask).LocalPort = 0

' If the response instance of the control is not closed,
' then close it
If Winsock1(nCurrentTask).State <> sckClosed Then
    Winsock1(nCurrentTask).Close
    Call ShowSocketState(nCurrentTask)
End If

' Accept the request using the requestID
Winsock1(nCurrentTask).Accept requestID

' Send notification of the correct port to use
Winsock1(nCurrentTask).SendData "Port: " & _
            mnEnginePort(mnCurrentEngine)
DoEvents

' Increment the engine pointer
mnCurrentEngine = mnCurrentEngine + 1
If mnCurrentEngine > ENGINE_LIMIT Then
    ' Wrap the pointer around to the beginning
    mnCurrentEngine = 1
End If

' Close the socket
Winsock1(nCurrentTask).Close

' Remove the socket control instance
Unload Winsock1(nCurrentTask)
```

```
' Update the primary connection status in the list box
Call ShowSocketState(0)

End Sub
```

9. Successful connections always trigger the following event. The following code reports the new connection status by calling the status update subroutine.

```
Private Sub Winsock1_Connect(Index As Integer)

' Update the connection status in the list box
Call ShowSocketState(Index)

End Sub
```

10. The SendComplete event occurs each time the transmission of data is completed over the socket. The code in this event adds a transmission line to the status list box, and then calls the socket status update subroutine.

```
Private Sub Winsock1_SendComplete(Index As Integer)

' Show that the send was completed
lstStatus.AddItem "Send Complete"

' Update the connection status in the list box
Call ShowSocketState(Index)

End Sub
```

11. Incoming data is parsed by the following code that is added to the socket control's DataArrival event. This event fires to indicate that there is data available so the code first gets the data from the socket. The data value and length are then added to the status list box.

This form does not expect to receive data, so an error condition is indicated and reported to the status list box.

```
Private Sub Winsock1_DataArrival(Index As Integer, _
            ByVal bytesTotal As Long)

Dim sData           As String
Dim sTempStr        As String
Dim sReturn         As String

' Get the inbound data from the socket
Winsock1(Index).GetData sData, vbString, bytesTotal

' Show the data and its length in the list box
lstStatus.AddItem "Data Value:  " & vbTab & sData
lstStatus.AddItem "Data Length: " & vbTab & bytesTotal
```

continued on next page

continued from previous page

```
' Parse the data and prepare the response to the request
' White space is removed, the string is uppercased, and only the
' two leftmost characters are examined to simplify parsing
Select Case Trim$(UCase$(Left$(sData, 2)))
    Case Else              ' Invalid request
        sTempStr = "Unknown data:" & vbTab & sData
        ' Set the reply data
        sReturn = "Error"

End Select

' Send any return data
If Len(sReturn) <> 0 Then
    ' Send the reply data
    Winsock1(Index).SendData sReturn
    DoEvents
End If

' See if there is information for the list box
If Len(sTempStr) <> 0 Then
    ' It is not blank, so add the data to the list box
    lstStatus.AddItem sTempStr
End If

' Update the connection status in the list box
Call ShowSocketState(Index)

End Sub
```

12. This event is probably incorrectly named. Its name should be
CloseRequest. This event is fired to indicate that the other connected
program is closing the port. The code here must close the port on this end
of the connection. If the primary listening port was closed, it is reset to
continue listening.

```
Private Sub Winsock1_Close(Index As Integer)

' Update the connection status in the list box
Call ShowSocketState(Index)

If Winsock1(Index).State = sckClosing Then
    ' A close request was made, so close the port
    Winsock1(Index).Close
    ' Update the connection status in the list box
    Call ShowSocketState(Index)
    ' Start listening again if this is the primary port
    If Index = 0 Then
        Winsock1(Index).Listen
        ' Update the connection status in the list box
        Call ShowSocketState(Index)
    End If
End If

End Sub
```

13. Add the following code to the **Error** event of the socket control. This code extracts details of the error and displays the data in the socket status list box.

```
Private Sub Winsock1_Error(Index As Integer, _
                ByVal Number As Integer, _
                Description As String, _
                ByVal Scode As Long, _
                ByVal Source As String, _
                ByVal HelpFile As String, _
                ByVal HelpContext As Long, _
                CancelDisplay As Boolean)

' Show the error details
lstStatus.AddItem "Error on Socket " & Index
lstStatus.AddItem "Error Number: " & vbTab & Number
lstStatus.AddItem "Error Text:   " & vbTab & Description

' Update the connection status in the list box
Call ShowSocketState(Index)

End Sub
```

14. The first project of this How-To is now finished. Save the project and compile the program into an executable.

15. Create a new project called TIME ENGINE.VBP.

16. Add a form to the project and set the objects and properties as they are listed in Table 9.7. Add the Microsoft Winsock control to the project. Save the form as TIME ENGINE.FRM.

Table 9.7 The Time Engine Form's Objects and Properties

OBJECT/CONTROL	PROPERTY	VALUE
Form	Name	frmMain
	BorderStyle	1 'Fixed Single
	Caption	Time Engine
	Icon	TIME.ICO
	MaxButton	0 'False
	MinButton	-1 'True
	StartUpPosition	2 'CenterScreen
TextBox	Name	txtTime
	Locked	-1 'True
Timer	Name	tmrUpdate
	Interval	60000
ListBox	Name	lstStatus

continued on next page

continued from previous page

OBJECT/CONTROL	PROPERTY	VALUE
Winsock	Name	Winsock1
	Index	0
Label	Name	lblCaption
	Caption	Current Time:
	Index	0
Label	Name	lblCaption
	Caption	Port Connection Status:
	Index	1
Menu	Name	mnuFile
	Caption	&File
Menu	Name	mnuFileSel
	Caption	E&xit
	Index	0

17. Add the following code to the General Declarations section of the form. The code starts by declaring a constant used to limit the total number of lines displayed in the status list box. This program requires no user interaction to start listening, so a variable is created to store the connection port that is parsed out of the command line. Then a number of module-scope variables are declared to track the tasks and socket counts for multiple connection support. Finally, a variant is defined to store an array of socket connection status descriptions.

```
Option Explicit

' Constant used to limit the number of list
' box items before removing the oldest
Private Const MAX_LIST_ITEMS = 100

' This variable is from the command line
Private mnPort             As Integer

' Count the number of tasks being served
Private mnTaskCount        As Integer

' Count the number of socket control instances
Private mnSockets          As Integer

' Store the ID for each task being served
' These will all be identical as the array
' is used strictly as a place holder
Private msTaskID()         As String

' Array of socket state descriptions
Private mvntSocketState    As Variant
```

18. Add the following code. When the program starts, it gets the connection port number from the command line. If the port number is missing or invalid, the program exits. The socket connection status array is loaded with state descriptions, and then the task ID array and reference counters are initialized. Next, the timer control event routine is called to update the display of the current date and time. Finally, the socket control properties are set and the program begins listening for connections.

```
Private Sub Form_Load()

Dim sCommand             As String

' Parse the command line
sCommand = UCase$(Command$)
If InStr(1, sCommand, "/PORT=") = 0 Then
    ' Command missing
    MsgBox "Port number must be specified on the command line.", _
            vbCritical, "Bad command line"
    ' Exit from the program
    End
End If

' Get the port number from the command line
mnPort = CInt(Mid$(sCommand, InStr(1, sCommand, "=") + 1))

' Check for a valid port number
If mnPort = 0 Then
    ' Bad port number
    MsgBox "Port number must be greater than zero."
    ' Exit from the program
    End
End If

' Load the variant array with socket states
mvntSocketState = Array("Closed", _
                        "Open", _
                        "Listening", _
                        "Connection Pending", _
                        "Resolving Host", _
                        "Host Resolved", _
                        "Connecting", _
                        "Connected", _
                        "Closing", _
                        "Error")

' Initialize the task ID array
ReDim msTaskID(10)

' The #1 element of the array is for the primary
' listening socket
msTaskID(0) = "Reserved"

' Initialize the task count and socket count variables
mnTaskCount = 0
```

continued on next page

continued from previous page

```
mnSockets = 0

' Make an initial call to the timer event
' so that the current date and time show up
Call tmrUpdate_Timer

' Be sure the form is visible
Me.Show

' Set the socket control port property
If Winsock1(0).LocalPort <> mnPort Then
    Winsock1(0).LocalPort = mnPort
End If

' Update the form caption with the port number
Me.Caption = Me.Caption & " - Port " & mnPort

' Start listening
Winsock1(0).Listen

' Update the connection status in the list box
Call ShowSocketState(0)

End Sub
```

19. The code in the `Timer` event displays the formatted date and time on the form.

```
Private Sub tmrUpdate_Timer()

' Get and display the current system time
txtTime.Text = Format$(Now, "mm/dd/yyyy") & " " & _
               Format$(Now, "Long Time")

End Sub
```

20. Only one item is on the File menu, and it is used to exit the program.

```
Private Sub mnuFileSel_Click(Index As Integer)

Select Case Index
    Case 0          ' Exit
        ' End the program when the user selects
        ' the File/Exit menu item
        Unload Me

End Select

End Sub
```

21. Add the following subroutine to the form. This next subroutine is used to add the current socket state to the status list box. Because the socket control is an array, an index value is passed to this subroutine. A text string is first constructed containing the socket index number and the socket state description. This text is then added to the list box. A reference to the list location of the new item is obtained. This value is equivalent to the list count because the list box is not sorted. If the number of items in the list exceeds the constant value for the maximum number of entries, the list is trimmed down to size.

```vb
Private Sub ShowSocketState(Index As Integer)

Dim sTempStr          As String
Dim nListCount        As Integer
Dim nLoopCtr          As Integer

' Build a string containing the current socket state
sTempStr = "Socket " & Index & " State: " & vbTab & _
             mvntSocketState(Winsock1(Index).State)

' Add the string to the list box
lstStatus.AddItem sTempStr

' Get the index position where the item was added
nListCount = lstStatus.NewIndex

If nListCount > MAX_LIST_ITEMS Then
    ' Clean out old list entries
    For nLoopCtr = nListCount - MAX_LIST_ITEMS To 0 Step -1
        lstStatus.RemoveItem nLoopCtr
    Next nLoopCtr
    nListCount = lstStatus.ListCount - 1
End If

' Position at the last item on the list
lstStatus.ListIndex = nListCount

End Sub
```

22. Add the following code to the form. When a connection request is received on the socket port, the following code is executed. The connection request details are added to the status list box and then the index value of the socket control is checked. If the request was received on the primary control of the array, the connection is processed. The code looks for an available entry in the task ID array. If there are no open array slots, the array is extended. Also, if there is not a socket control associated with the task entry slot, another instance of the control is loaded. The code then checks the state of the socket and closes it if it is not closed. The connection request is then accepted, using the identified or created instance of the socket control. Calls are made to the socket status subroutine for the current instance and primary instances of the socket control.

If the request came in on any element of the control array other than index 0, it is invalid. Ignoring the request is all that is needed to deny the connection.

```vb
Private Sub Winsock1_ConnectionRequest(Index As Integer, _
            ByVal requestID As Long)

Dim bFoundSlot              As Boolean
Dim nLoopCtr                As Integer
Dim nCurrentTask            As Integer

' Show the connection request ID
lstStatus.AddItem "Connect Request on Socket " & Index
lstStatus.AddItem "Connect Request:" & vbTab & _
            "ID " & requestID

If Index = 0 Then
    ' This was a primary listen request
    ' Find an available socket control
    bFoundSlot = False
    ' Loop through the array looking for a blank ID
    For nLoopCtr = 1 To UBound(msTaskID)
        If Len(msTaskID(nLoopCtr)) = 0 Then
            ' Set the flag indicating success
            bFoundSlot = True
            ' Save the a pointer into the array
            nCurrentTask = nLoopCtr
            Exit For
        End If
    Next nLoopCtr
    If bFoundSlot = False Then
        ' Increment the task counter
        mnTaskCount = mnTaskCount + 1
        ' See if the new count exceeds the array bounds
        If mnTaskCount > UBound(msTaskID) Then
            ' Need to increase the array size, so add 10 more
            ReDim Preserve msTaskID(UBound(msTaskID) + 10)
        End If
        ' Set the current task number to the total task count
        nCurrentTask = mnTaskCount
    End If
Else
    ' The connect request arrived on an invalid socket
    Exit Sub
End If

' See if a new socket control needs to be created
If nCurrentTask > mnSockets Then
    ' Create a new instance of the control
    Load Winsock1(nCurrentTask)
    Winsock1(nCurrentTask).LocalPort = 0
    ' Increment the socket count
    mnSockets = mnSockets + 1
End If

' If the response instance of the control is not closed,
' then close it
If Winsock1(nCurrentTask).State <> sckClosed Then
    Winsock1(nCurrentTask).Close
    Call ShowSocketState(nCurrentTask)
End If
```

```
' Accept the request using the requestID
Winsock1(nCurrentTask).Accept requestID

' Consume the entry in the task array
msTaskID(nCurrentTask) = "In use"

' Update the connection status in the list box
Call ShowSocketState(nCurrentTask)

' Update the primary connection status in the list box
Call ShowSocketState(0)

End Sub
```

23. Successful connections always trigger the following event. The following code reports the new connection status by calling the status update subroutine.

```
Private Sub Winsock1_Connect(Index As Integer)

' Update the connection status in the list box
Call ShowSocketState(Index)

End Sub
```

24. The `SendComplete` event occurs each time the transmission of data is completed over the socket. The code in this event adds a transmission line to the status list box, then calls the socket status update subroutine.

```
Private Sub Winsock1_SendComplete(Index As Integer)

' Show that the send was completed
lstStatus.AddItem "Send Complete"

' Update the connection status in the list box
Call ShowSocketState(Index)

End Sub
```

25. Incoming data is parsed by the following code that is added to the socket control's `DataArrival` event. This event fires to indicate that there is data available so the code first gets the data from the socket. The data value and length are then added to the status list box.

Next, the data is parsed. This form recognizes requests for data loopback tests and transmission of the current local system date and time. The response data is prepared and sent back.

```
Private Sub Winsock1_DataArrival(Index As Integer, _
              ByVal bytesTotal As Long)

Dim sData                As String
Dim sTempStr             As String
```

continued on next page

continued from previous page

```
    Dim sReturn              As String

    ' Get the inbound data from the socket
    Winsock1(Index).GetData sData, vbString, bytesTotal

    ' Show the data and its length in the list box
    lstStatus.AddItem "Data Value:   " & vbTab & sData
    lstStatus.AddItem "Data Length: " & vbTab & bytesTotal

    ' Parse the data and prepare the response to the request
    ' White space is removed, the string is uppercased, and only the
    ' two leftmost characters are examined to simplify parsing
    Select Case Trim$(UCase$(Left$(sData, 2)))
        Case "LO"            ' Loop back requested
            sTempStr = msTaskID(Index) & " loopback:" & _
                        vbTab & Mid$(sData, Len("LOOPBACK: ") + 1)
            ' Set the reply data
            sReturn = sData

        Case "DA"            ' Current date requested
            sTempStr = "Date request received"
            ' Set the reply data
            sReturn = "Date: " & Format$(Now, "mm/dd/yyyy")

        Case "TI"            ' Current time requested
            sTempStr = "Time request received"
            ' Set the reply data
            sReturn = "Time: " & Format$(Now, "Long Time")

        Case Else            ' Invalid request
            sTempStr = "Unknown data received"
            ' Set the reply data
            sReturn = "Error"

    End Select

    ' Send any return data
    If Len(sReturn) <> 0 Then
        ' Send the reply data
        Winsock1(Index).SendData sReturn
        DoEvents
    End If

    ' See if there is information for the list box
    If Len(sTempStr) <> 0 Then
        ' It is not blank so add the data to the list box
        lstStatus.AddItem sTempStr
    End If

    ' Update the connection status in the list box
    Call ShowSocketState(Index)

End Sub
```

26. The following event is fired to indicate that the other connected program has closed the port. The code here must close the port on this end of the connection.

The entry in the task ID array is cleared so it can be reused. The socket is then closed and the status list box is updated. If the primary listening port is closed, it is reset to continue listening.

```
Private Sub Winsock1_Close(Index As Integer)

' Update the connection status in the list box
Call ShowSocketState(Index)

If Winsock1(Index).State = sckClosing Then
    ' Clear the task ID entry in the array
    msTaskID(Index) = ""
    ' A close request was made, so close the port
    Winsock1(Index).Close
    ' Update the connection status in the list box
    Call ShowSocketState(Index)
    ' Start listening again if this is the primary port
    If Index = 0 Then
        Winsock1(Index).Listen
        ' Update the connection status in the list box
        Call ShowSocketState(Index)
    End If
End If

End Sub
```

27. Add the following code to the **Error** event of the socket control. This code extracts details of the error and displays the data in the socket status list box.

```
Private Sub Winsock1_Error(Index As Integer, _
                ByVal Number As Integer, _
                Description As String, _
                ByVal Scode As Long, _
                ByVal Source As String, _
                ByVal HelpFile As String, _
                ByVal HelpContext As Long, _
                CancelDisplay As Boolean)

' Show the error details
lstStatus.AddItem "Error on Socket " & Index
lstStatus.AddItem "Error Number: " & vbTab & Number
lstStatus.AddItem "Error Text:   " & vbTab & Description

' Update the connection status in the list box
Call ShowSocketState(Index)

End Sub
```

28. The second project of this How-To is now finished. Save the project and compile the program into an executable.

29. Create a new project called TIME CLIENT REDIRECTED.VBP.

30. Add a form to the project and set the objects and properties as they are listed in Table 9.8. Also, add the Microsoft Winsock control as a component of the project. Save the form as TIME CLIENT REDIRECTED.FRM.

This project is essentially the same as the time client built in How-To 9.2. The only difference is the logic that has been added to support redirection of the time service requests to another port by the pool management program. For the benefit of readers who have come directly to this How-To, all the code is reproduced here. New and modified lines have been highlighted in boldface text.

Table 9.8 The Time Client Form's Objects and Properties

OBJECT/CONTROL	PROPERTY	VALUE
Form	Name	frmMain
	BorderStyle	1 'Fixed Single
	Caption	Time Client with Redirection
	Icon	TIME.ICO
	MaxButton	0 'False
	MinButton	-1 'True
	StartUpPosition	2 'CenterScreen
CommandButton	Name	cmdAction
	Caption	&Get Server Time
	Index	0
CommandButton	Name	cmdAction
	Caption	&Set Local Time
	Index	1
TextBox	Name	txtAddress
TextBox	Name	txtPort
	Text	1152
ListBox	Name	lstStatus
Winsock	Name	Winsock1
Label	Name	lblInfo
	Appearance	0 'Flat
	AutoSize	-1 'True
	Caption	Date
	Index	0

OBJECT/CONTROL	PROPERTY	VALUE
Label	Name	lblInfo
	Appearance	0 'Flat
	AutoSize	-1 'True
	Caption	Time
	Index	1
Label	Name	lblInfo
	Appearance	0 'Flat
	AutoSize	-1 'True
	Caption	Network Server
	Index	2
Label	Name	lblInfo
	Appearance	0 'Flat
	AutoSize	-1 'True
	Caption	Local PC
	Index	3
Label	Name	lblInfo
	Alignment	2 'Center
	Appearance	0 'Flat
	BorderStyle	1 'Fixed Single
	Index	4
Label	Name	lblNetTime
	Alignment	2 'Center
	Appearance	0 'Flat
	BorderStyle	1 'Fixed Single
Label	Name	lblPCTime
	Alignment	2 'Center
	Appearance	0 'Flat
	BorderStyle	1 'Fixed Single
Label	Name	lblNetDate
	Alignment	2 'Center
	Appearance	0 'Flat
	BorderStyle	1 'Fixed Single
Label	Name	lblPCDate
	Alignment	2 'Center
	Appearance	0 'Flat
	BorderStyle	1 'Fixed Single

continued on next page

continued from previous page

OBJECT/CONTROL	PROPERTY	VALUE
Label	Name	lblDelay
	Alignment	2 'Center
	Appearance	0 'Flat
	BorderStyle	1 'Fixed Single
Label	Name	lblCaption
	Caption	Time Server IP Address:
	Index	0
Label	Name	lblCaption
	Caption	Time Server Port:
	Index	1
Label	Name	lblCaption
	Caption	Port Connection Status:
	Index	2
Menu	Name	mnuFile
	Caption	&File
Menu	Name	mnuFileSel
	Caption	E&xit
	Index	0

31. Add the following code to the General Declarations section of the form. The code starts by declaring a constant used to limit the total number of lines displayed in the status list box. Then a number of module-scope variables are declared to track the tasks and task IDs. Finally, a variant is defined to store an array of socket connection status descriptions.

```
Option Explicit

Private Const MAX_LIST_ITEMS = 100

Private msRemoteAddress    As String
Private mnRemotePort       As Integer

' Variable used to compute network delay
Private mdtNetDelay        As Double

' Boolean used to control setting of local time
' If set to true, then local time is set when
' the server time is received
' If set to false, the local time is not adjusted
Private mbSetLocal         As Boolean

' Form scope variable set when form is closing
Private mbClosing          As Boolean

' Variable set when data is received
```

```
Private mbGotData          As Boolean

' Array for socket state descriptions
Private mvntSocketState    As Variant
```

32. Add the following code to the **Load** event of the form. First, the socket connection status array is loaded with state descriptions, and then the task ID array and reference counters are initialized.

```
Private Sub Form_Load()

' Load the variant array with socket states
mvntSocketState = Array("Closed", _
                        "Open", _
                        "Listening", _
                        "Connection Pending", _
                        "Resolving Host", _
                        "Host Resolved", _
                        "Connecting", _
                        "Connected", _
                        "Closing", _
                        "Error")

' Set the form state flag to say it is active
mbClosing = False

End Sub
```

33. When the form is unloaded, close the socket if it is not closed. Then exit the program.

```
Private Sub Form_Unload(Cancel As Integer)

' Close the socket if it is open
If Winsock1.State <> sckClosed And _
   Winsock1.State <> sckError Then
    ' Set the form state flag to say it is closing
    mbClosing = True
    Winsock1.Close
End If

End

End Sub
```

34. There is only one item on the File menu, used to exit the program.

```
Private Sub mnuFileSel_Click(Index As Integer)

Select Case Index
    Case 0
        ' Close down the form
        Unload Me

End Select

End Sub
```

35. Place the following code in the `Click` event of the `cmdAction` command button control array. When the user clicks the first button in the array to get the time from the server, a flag is set to prevent using the server time to set the local time. A subroutine is then called to get the time from the server.

The second command button in the array gets the time from the server and then uses it to set the local system time. This is accomplished by setting the flag to enable setting the local time and calling the subroutine that gets the server time.

```
Private Sub cmdAction_Click(Index As Integer)

' Disable changes to the address and port
If txtAddress.Enabled = True Then
    txtAddress.Enabled = False
    txtPort.Enabled = False
End If

Select Case Index
    Case 0            ' Get time
        ' Get the server time but don't
        ' set the local time
        mbSetLocal = False
        Call GetServerTime

    Case 1            ' Set time
        ' Get the server time and use it to set
        ' the local time
        mbSetLocal = True
        Call GetServerTime

End Select

End Sub
```

36. Add the following subroutine to the form. This next subroutine is used to add the current socket state to the status list box. A text string is constructed containing the socket index number and the socket state description. This text is then added to the list box. A reference to the list location of the new item is obtained. This value is equivalent to the list count because the list box is not sorted. If the number of items in the list exceeds the constant value for the maximum number of entries, the list is trimmed down to size.

```
Private Sub ShowSocketState()

Dim sTempStr          As String
Dim nListCount        As Integer
Dim nLoopCtr          As Integer

' Build a string containing the current socket state
sTempStr = "Socket State: " & vbTab & _
```

```
                    mvntSocketState(Winsock1.State)

    ' Add the string to the list box
    lstStatus.AddItem sTempStr

    ' Get the index position where the item was added
    nListCount = lstStatus.NewIndex

    If nListCount > MAX_LIST_ITEMS Then
        ' Clean out old list entries
        For nLoopCtr = nListCount - MAX_LIST_ITEMS To 0 Step -1
            lstStatus.RemoveItem nLoopCtr
        Next nLoopCtr
        nListCount = lstStatus.ListCount - 1
    End If

    ' Position at the last item on the list
    lstStatus.ListIndex = nListCount

End Sub
```

37. Add the following code. When a connection request is received on the socket port, the following code is executed. This form does not accept connections, so an error message is added to the status list box.

No special action is required to deny the connection request. Ignoring it is all that is needed for denial.

```
Private Sub Winsock1_ConnectionRequest(ByVal requestID As Long)

    ' This event should never occur because this program
    ' does not listen on the port

    ' Show the connection request ID
    lstStatus.AddItem "Unexpected Connection Request"

    ' The connection is refused by not accepting it

    ' Update the connection status in the list box
    Call ShowSocketState

End Sub
```

38. Successful connections always trigger the following event. The following code reports the new connection status by calling the status update subroutine.

```
Private Sub Winsock1_Connect()

    ' Update the connection status in the list box
    Call ShowSocketState

End Sub
```

39. The SendComplete event occurs each time the transmission of data is completed over the socket. The code in this event adds a transmission line to the status list box and then calls the socket status supdate subroutine.

```
Private Sub Winsock1_SendComplete()

' Show that the send was completed
lstStatus.AddItem "Send Complete"

' Update the connection status in the list box
Call ShowSocketState

End Sub
```

40. Incoming data is parsed by the following code that is added to the socket control's **DataArrival** event. This event fires to indicate that there is data available so the code first gets the data from the socket. The data value and length are then added to the status list box.

Next, the data is parsed. This form recognizes responses to requests for loopbacks, date, and time information. It also expects messages instructing it to communicate with a different port on the server to get its information. If port redirection data is received, four events occur: The form is updated with the new port, the current socket is closed, the socket control properties are modified using the new port, and the new port is opened.

Dates and times are parsed out of the incoming data and used to update the display information on the form. If requested by the user, the local date and time are reset using the date and time obtained from the time server.

```
Private Sub Winsock1_DataArrival(ByVal bytesTotal As Long)

Dim sData            As String
Dim sReply           As String
Dim dtLocal          As Double      ' Local serial date/time
Dim dtServer         As Double      ' Server serial date/time
Dim sTempStr         As String
Dim sRemoteAddress   As String
Dim nRemotePort      As Integer

' Get the inbound data from the socket
Winsock1.GetData sData, vbString, bytesTotal

' Show the data and its length in the list box
lstStatus.AddItem "Data Value:  " & vbTab & sData
lstStatus.AddItem "Data Length: " & vbTab & bytesTotal


' Parse the data and prepare the response to the request
' White space is removed and the string is uppercased
' to make command parsing simpler
Select Case Left$(Trim$(UCase$(sData)), 2)
    Case "PO"             ' New port specification reply
```

```
            ' Get the new target port
            sTempStr = Mid$(sData, Len("PORT: ") + 1)
            ' Show the new port on the form
            txtPort.Text = sTempStr
            ' Close the current port connection
            Winsock1.Close
            DoEvents
            ' Get the server address and port
            sRemoteAddress = txtAddress.Text
            nRemotePort = CInt(txtPort.Text)
            ' If not connected then connect to the remote port
            'If Winsock1.State <> sckConnected Then
                Winsock1.Connect sRemoteAddress, nRemotePort
                DoEvents
            'End If
            ' Let other code know we got the data
            mbGotData = True

    Case "LO"              ' Loopback reply
            ' Compute the delay
            mdtNetDelay = (Now - mdtNetDelay) / 2
            ' Show the delay on the form
            lblDelay.Caption = Format$(mdtNetDelay, "hh:nn:ss")
            ' Let other code know we got the data
            mbGotData = True

    Case "DA"              ' Date response
            ' Extract the server date
            sTempStr = Mid$(sData, Len("TIME: ") + 1)
            dtServer = DateSerial(Year(sTempStr), _
                        Month(sTempStr), _
                        Day(sTempStr))
            ' Adjusted for the network delay
            dtLocal = Now + mdtNetDelay
            ' Change the local system date if requested, then
            ' display the local date
            If mbSetLocal = True Then
                Date$ = Format$(dtServer + mdtNetDelay, "m/d/yyyy")
                lblPCDate.Caption = Format$(Now, "m/d/yyyy")
            Else
                lblPCDate.Caption = Format$(dtLocal, "m/d/yyyy")
            End If
            ' Display the server date
            lblNetDate.Caption = Format$(dtServer, "m/d/yyyy")
            ' Let other code know we got the data
            mbGotData = True

    Case "TI"              ' Time response
            ' Extract the server time
            sTempStr = Mid$(sData, Len("TIME: ") + 1)
            dtServer = TimeSerial(Hour(sTempStr), _
                        Minute(sTempStr), _
                        Second(sTempStr))
            ' Get the local time adjusted for the network delay
            dtLocal = Now + mdtNetDelay
```

continued on next page

continued from previous page

```
                        ' Change the local system time if requested, then
                        ' display the local time
                        If mbSetLocal = True Then
                            Time$ = Format$(dtServer + mdtNetDelay, "hh:nn:ss")
                            lblPCTime.Caption = Format$(Now, "hh:nn:ss")
                          Else
                            lblPCTime.Caption = Format$(dtLocal, "hh:nn:ss")
                        End If
                        ' Display the server time
                        lblNetTime.Caption = Format$(dtServer, "hh:nn:ss")
                        ' Let other code know we got the data
                        mbGotData = True

                Case Else            ' Invalid request
                        ' Update the list box
                        lstStatus.AddItem "Invalid data received"

            End Select

            ' Update the connection status in the list box
            Call ShowSocketState

            End Sub
```

41. This event is fired to indicate that the other end of the port connection has closed. If this happens, the code reports an unexpected closure and notifies the user that time services are unavailable. To prevent accidental use of the services when the port is closed, the command buttons are all disabled.

```
Private Sub Winsock1_Close()

' The form is closing itself, so get out of here
If mbClosing = True Then Exit Sub

' Provide notification that the socket was closed
' unexpectedly, probably by the remote monitor
MsgBox "Unexpected socket closure. Time services no longer _
            available.",
            vbCritical, "Connection Closed"

' Disable the command buttons
cmdAction(0).Enabled = False
cmdAction(1).Enabled = False

' Update the connection status in the list box
Call ShowSocketState

End Sub
```

42. Add the following code to the **Error** event of the socket control. This code extracts details of the error and displays the data in the socket status list box.

```
Private Sub Winsock1_Error(ByVal Number As Integer, _
              Description As String, _
              ByVal Scode As Long, _
              ByVal Source As String, _
              ByVal HelpFile As String, _
              ByVal HelpContext As Long, _
              CancelDisplay As Boolean)

' Show the error details
lstStatus.AddItem "Error Number: " & vbTab & Number
lstStatus.AddItem "Error Text:   " & vbTab & Description

' Update the connection status in the list box
Call ShowSocketState

End Sub
```

43. The following subroutine sends the requests to the time server to get the centralized date and time. The port and address are retrieved from the text boxes. If the socket is not open, the port connection is made. A loopback request is sent so the **DataArrival** can compute the roundtrip network delay time. Finally, the date and time are requested individually.

Socket data can be concatenated if it is not read on the receiving end of the connection before additional data is sent. For this reason, logic is needed to wait for data responses before sending subsequent requests. This is done several times in the following code by using the **mbGotData** variable. The variable is set to **False**, and the data request is sent to the server. The code then goes into a tight **DoEvents** loop and waits for the flag to be set. When the reply is received in the **DataArrival** event of the socket control, the flag is set to **True**.

```
Private Sub GetServerTime()

Dim sRemoteAddress          As String
Dim nRemotePort             As Integer

' Get the server address and port
sRemoteAddress = txtAddress.Text
nRemotePort = CInt(txtPort.Text)

' If not connected, then connect to the remote port
If Winsock1.State <> sckConnected Then
    ' Set the flag to wait for data
    mbGotData = False
    Winsock1.Connect sRemoteAddress, nRemotePort
    ' Wait for the port reassignment
    Do Until mbGotData = True
        DoEvents
    Loop
End If
```

continued on next page

continued from previous page

```
    ' Set the flag to wait for data
    mbGotData = False

    ' Save the current local time to compute delay
    mdtNetDelay = Now

    ' Send a loopback request to compute the network delay
    Winsock1.SendData "Loopback: Wise ones wait for the right time."

    ' Wait for the data to get here
    Do Until mbGotData = True
        DoEvents
    Loop

    ' Reset the flag to wait for data
    mbGotData = False

    ' Send the server date request
    Winsock1.SendData "Date"

    ' Wait for the data to get here
    Do Until mbGotData = True
        DoEvents
    Loop

    ' Reset the flag to wait for data
    mbGotData = False

    ' Send the server time request
    Winsock1.SendData "Time"

    ' Wait for the data to get here
    Do Until mbGotData = True
        DoEvents
    Loop

    ' Update the connection status in the list box
    Call ShowSocketState

End Sub
```

How It Works

The client and time server engine in this How-To are variations of client and server programs from How-To 9.2. A new program has been added to this How-To to launch and manage a pool of time servers. The pool manager handles connection requests from clients by directing the client application to the port assigned to an individual time server engine.

The time server itself has been rebuilt to operate without user interaction. This enables it to run unattended when launched by the time service manager.

Comments

Other techniques can be used to manage a pool of objects. The scheduling and server assignment logic can be expanded beyond the simple round-robin allocation used in this How-To. The pool manager can be modified to track the number of connections assigned to each server, which would enable dynamic load balancing for additional service requests. The load balancing would also require the use of a port for the manager and the services to talk to each other. The time service would need to tell the pool manager when connections were closed so the manager could accurately track service usage.

Visual Basic supplies sample pool manager code on the Enterprise Edition CD-ROM. That sample code uses an OLE server model, as opposed to the direct executable style used in this How-To. The Visual Basic sample pool manager is also intended to be a model for the implementation of your own pool manager.

The Microsoft Transaction Server (MTS) is more a full-feature object broker than a pool manager. MTS is a very powerful enterprise solution and does require an NT server. The automatic features of MTS are impressive and include thread allocation, dynamic load balancing, ODBC resource pooling, and object persistence for improved performance. Developers build single-user objects and drop them onto the MTS Explorer-style interface. MTS takes over from there and automates the use and sharing of the objects. You owe it to yourself to investigate this technology further.

COMPLEXITY
INTERMEDIATE

9.4 How do I...
Check for messages in a remote mailbox?

COMPATIBILITY: VISUAL BASIC 5 AND 6

Problem

I have e-mail accounts on multiple servers on both LAN and Internet-based systems. My e-mail client can be configured to get mail from all of them, but the program is large, so I do not like to leave it running on my desktop. How can I write a small, fast program that will check a mailbox for new messages?

Technique

The code in this How-To uses POP3 protocol messages to communicate with a mail server. The program allows the user to enter a server name, port number, user name (mailbox ID), and password. Except for the password, this information can usually be determined by breaking apart an e-mail address.

Everything in the address to the left of the @ character is the user name, and the string to the right is the domain. Generally, adding `mail.` to the domain provides the correct mail server address. For example, if the e-mail address is `frobozz@xyzzy.net`, the user name is `frobozz` and the mail server becomes `mail.xyzzy.net`. The standard port for POP3 servers is 110.

Table 9.9 provides descriptions of the POP3 commands that are used in this How-To. All command arguments are delimited in the syntax by using spaces. Every command that is sent must also be terminated with a CR/LF (carriage return/line feed) string pair.

Table 9.9 Abbreviated List of POP3 Server Commands

COMMAND	DESCRIPTION	ARGUMENTS	SERVER RESPONSES
USER	Identifies the target user mailbox to the server.	Mailbox ID (string)	+OK (the name is valid) - ERR (the name is unknown)
PASS	Used to send the user mailbox password to the server.	Mailbox Password (string)	+OK (the password is good) - ERR (the password is bad or the mailbox is in use)
STAT	Requests summary information on waiting messages.	None	+OK nn mm (nn = number of messages, mm = number of message bytes)
QUIT	Close the mailbox session with the server.	None	+OK (success)

For clarity, this program only checks one mailbox. Adding logic to check multiple mailboxes is left as an exercise for the reader. To facilitate the change, the logic to check a mailbox is not bound to a specific address.

Steps

Open and run MAIL CHECK.VBP. Complete the name of the e-mail server to be checked. Fill in a user name and password for a valid e-mail account. The sample shown in Figure 9.9 includes the results of two attempts to check mail.

The password was missing for the first attempt, as can be seen in the error message returned by the POP3 server. The second attempt, with a correct password, shows that there are two messages and a total of 5,344 bytes of message content. The user does not have to parse this information out of the POP3 reply string. When the MAIL CHECK program gets the data, it is parsed and displayed in a pop-up message box. To create this project, complete the following steps.

Figure 9.9 The main
form at runtime.

1. Create a new project called MAIL CHECK.VBP.

2. Add a form to the project and set the objects and properties as they are
listed in Table 9.10. Be sure to add the Microsoft Winsock control as a
component of the project. Save the form as MAIL CHECK.FRM.

Table 9.10 The Main Form's Objects and Properties

OBJECT/CONTROL	PROPERTY	VALUE
Form	Name	frmMain
	Caption	Mail Checker
	Icon	MAIL19B.ICO
	StartUpPosition	2 'CenterScreen
CommandButton	Name	cmdAction
	Caption	Check Mail
	Index	0
CommandButton	Name	cmdAction
	Caption	Exit
	Index	1
TextBox	Name	txtServer
	Text	mail.<your-domain>.net
TextBox	Name	txtPort
	Text	110
TextBox	Name	txtUser
	Text	<your-id>

continued on next page

continued from previous page

OBJECT/CONTROL	PROPERTY	VALUE
TextBox	Name	txtPassword
	PasswordChar	*
ListBox	Name	lstStatus
Winsock	Name	Winsock1
CheckBox	Name	chkLogStatus
	Caption	Log Port Status
Label	Name	lblCaption
	Caption	POP3 Server:
	Index	0
Label	Name	lblCaption
	Caption	POP3 Port:
	Index	1
Label	Name	lblCaption
	Caption	User Name:
	Index	2
Label	Name	lblCaption
	Caption	Password:
	Index	3
Label	Name	lblCaption
	Caption	Port Connection Status:
	Index	4

3. Add the following code to the General Declarations section of the form. The code starts by declaring a constant used to limit the total number of lines displayed in the status list box. Then a number of form-scope variables are declared to hold the POP3 server commands, the replies, and the message information. Finally, a variant is defined to store an array of socket connection status descriptions.

```
Option Explicit

' Constant used to limit the number of list
' box items before removing the oldest
Private Const MAX_LIST_ITEMS = 100

' Variables to store waiting message information
Private mnMessageCount        As Integer
Private mlMessageChars        As Long

' This variable holds the most recent command
' that was sent to the POP3 server
Private msCommand             As String
```

```
' State of the Log Port Status check box
Private mbLogStatus              As Boolean

' Variable to track state of socket data reception
Private mbGotData               As Boolean

' Array for socket state descriptions
Private mvntSocketState     As Variant
```

4. Add the following code to the **Load** event of the form. First, the socket connection status array is loaded with state descriptions. Then the Boolean variable used to control the logging of all socket events is set to its default value of **False**.

```
Private Sub Form_Load()

' Load the variant array with socket states
mvntSocketState = Array("Closed", _
                        "Open", _
                        "Listening", _
                        "Connection Pending", _
                        "Resolving Host", _
                        "Host Resolved", _
                        "Connecting", _
                        "Connected", _
                        "Closing", _
                        "Error")

' Initialize the log status state to false
mbLogStatus = False

End Sub
```

5. Insert the following code in the **Click** event of the **chkLogStatus** check box control. This code toggles the state of the Boolean that determines whether all IP port activity is written to the list box.

```
Private Sub chkLogStatus_Click()

' Update the state variable based on the
' value of the check box
If chkLogStatus.Value = vbChecked Then
    mbLogStatus = True
  Else
    mbLogStatus = False
End If

End Sub
```

6. Place the following code in the **Click** event of the **cmdAction** command button control array. When the user clicks the first button in the array to check for mail on the server, the code checks to ensure that a server name and port number have been supplied. Strictly for demonstration purposes, no similar checking is done for the user name and password text boxes.

This is intentional so that incorrect information can be passed to the POP3 server and the resulting errors can be seen. The command button itself is then disabled to prevent multiple mail checks from happening at the same time. Next, a subroutine is called to perform the server mail check. Finally, the command button is enabled.

The second command button exits from the program.

```
Private Sub cmdAction_Click(Index As Integer)

Dim nMonitorPort        As Integer
Dim sServer             As String

Select Case Index
    Case 0              ' Check for new mail
        ' Get the value used for the server name
        sServer = txtServer.Text
        If Len(sServer) = 0 Then
            MsgBox "Please enter the POP3 server name"
            Exit Sub
        End If

        ' Get the value used for the port connection
        nMonitorPort = CInt(txtPort.Text)
        If nMonitorPort = 0 Then
            MsgBox "Please enter the POP3 server " & _
                   "port (Default = 110)"
            Exit Sub
        End If

        ' Error checking for user name and password
        ' has been left out intentionally to show the
        ' error messages returned by the POP3 server.

        ' Disable this command button as the server
        ' should be treated as single-threaded for
        ' a specific user
        cmdAction(Index).Enabled = False

        ' Connect and get the message count
        Call POP3CheckMail

        ' Enable this command button
        cmdAction(Index).Enabled = True

    Case 1              ' Exit
        Unload Me

End Select

End Sub
```

7. Add the following subroutine. This subroutine is used to add the current socket state to the status list box. First, the socket status logging is checked. If logging is disabled, then the code exits from the subroutine.

Next, a text string is constructed containing the socket index number and the socket state description. This text is then added to the list box. A reference to the list location of the new item is obtained. This value is equivalent to the list count because the list box is not sorted. If the number of items in the list exceeds the constant value for the maximum number of entries, the list is trimmed down to size.

```
Private Sub ShowSocketState()

Dim sTempStr          As String
Dim nListCount        As Integer
Dim nLoopCtr          As Integer

' Check the state of port status logging
' If disabled, then exit from this sub
If mbLogStatus = False Then Exit Sub

' Build a string containing the current socket state
sTempStr = "Socket State: " & vbTab & _
                mvntSocketState(Winsock1.State)

' Add the string to the list box
lstStatus.AddItem sTempStr

' Get the index position where the item was added
nListCount = lstStatus.NewIndex

If nListCount > MAX_LIST_ITEMS Then
    ' Clean out old list entries
    For nLoopCtr = nListCount - MAX_LIST_ITEMS To 0 Step -1
        lstStatus.RemoveItem nLoopCtr
    Next nLoopCtr
    nListCount = lstStatus.ListCount - 1
End If

' Position at the last item on the list
lstStatus.ListIndex = nListCount

End Sub
```

8. When a connection request is received on the socket port, the following code is executed. This form does not accept connections, so an error message is added to the status list box.

No special action is required to deny the connection request. Ignoring it is all that is needed for denial.

```
Private Sub Winsock1_ConnectionRequest(ByVal requestID As Long)

' This event should never occur because this program
' does not listen on any ports

' Show the connection request ID
```

continued on next page

continued from previous page

```
If mbLogStatus = True Then
    lstStatus.AddItem "Unexpected Connection Request"
End If

' The connection is refused by not accepting it

' Update the connection status in the list box
Call ShowSocketState

End Sub
```

9. Successful connections always trigger the following event. The following
code reports the new connection status by calling the status update
subroutine.

```
Private Sub Winsock1_Connect()

' Update the connection status in the list box
Call ShowSocketState

End Sub
```

10. The **SendComplete** event occurs each time the transmission of data is
completed over the socket. If status logging is enabled, the code in this
event adds a transmission line to the status list box. Then it calls the
socket status update subroutine.

```
Private Sub Winsock1_SendComplete()

' Show that the send was completed
If mbLogStatus = True Then
    lstStatus.AddItem "Send Complete"
End If

' Update the connection status in the list box
Call ShowSocketState

End Sub
```

11. Incoming data is retrieved by the following code that is added to the
socket control's **DataArrival** event. This event fires to indicate that there
is data available so the code first gets the data from the socket. The data
value and length are then added to the status list box if logging is active.

POP3 protocol always puts a terminating CR and LF pair on each string
sent, so the code strips these two characters and moves the incoming
string to a form-scope variable. A global Boolean is then set to notify the
rest of the program that data is now available.

```
Private Sub Winsock1_DataArrival(ByVal bytesTotal As Long)

Dim sData              As String
```

```
' Get the inbound data from the socket
Winsock1.GetData sData, vbString, bytesTotal

' Show the data and its length in the list box
If mbLogStatus = True Then
    lstStatus.AddItem "Data Value:  " & vbTab & sData
    lstStatus.AddItem "Data Length: " & vbTab & bytesTotal
End If

' Move the data into the form scope command variable
msCommand = Left$(sData, bytesTotal - 2)

' Let other code know we got data
mbGotData = True

' Update the connection status in the list box
Call ShowSocketState

End Sub
```

12. Add the following event. This event is fired to indicate that the other end of the port connection has closed.

```
Private Sub Winsock1_Close()

' Update the connection status in the list box
Call ShowSocketState

End Sub
```

13. Add the following code to the **Error** event of the socket control. This code extracts details of the error and displays the data in the socket status list box. The state of the status-logging Boolean is ignored by this code so the user can be notified of the socket error.

```
Private Sub Winsock1_Error(ByVal Number As Integer, _
                Description As String, _
                ByVal Scode As Long, _
                ByVal Source As String, _
                ByVal HelpFile As String, _
                ByVal HelpContext As Long, _
                CancelDisplay As Boolean)

' Show the error details
lstStatus.AddItem "Error Number: " & vbTab & Number
lstStatus.AddItem "Error Text:   " & vbTab & Description

' Update the connection status in the list box
Call ShowSocketState

End Sub
```

14. Add the following subroutine. It drives the interaction with the POP3 mail server. The code starts by getting the server name, port, user name, and password from the text boxes. The code assumes failure and indicates this by setting the message count to a negative one (−1). When the connection is made to a POP3 port, the server replies with a success string that often provides optional data about the server itself. Because of this, the code sets the global flag indicating that it is waiting for data, connects to the port, and waits for the server reply to arrive. The logic then follows the same basic pattern to send the user name and password, request the mailbox status, and then quit from the POP3 session.

Whenever an error is detected, the code branches to the exit point of the subroutine, skipping over the intervening steps. If all the POP3 server interactions succeed, the code just falls through to the exit point. The exit point processing closes the socket that is connected to the server and then displays a message box telling the user what happened and how many messages were found.

```
Private Sub POP3CheckMail()

Dim sRemoteAddress          As String
Dim nRemotePort             As Integer
Dim sUserName               As String
Dim sPassword               As String
Dim bResult                 As Boolean

' Get the server address and port
sRemoteAddress = txtServer.Text
nRemotePort = CInt(txtPort.Text)

' Get the user name and password
sUserName = txtUser.Text
sPassword = txtPassword.Text

' Set the message count variable to indicate
' a failure to get the information. Also clear
' the variable holding message character length.
mnMessageCount = -1
mlMessageChars = 0

' Set the flag to wait for connection to open
' and the initial server reply to arrive
mbGotData = False

' If not connected, then connect to the remote port
If Winsock1.State <> sckConnected Then
    Winsock1.Connect sRemoteAddress, nRemotePort
End If

' Now wait for the server reply
Do Until mbGotData = True
    DoEvents
Loop

' Send user name
bResult = POP3SendString("USER " & sUserName)
' Check for errors
```

```
        If bResult = False Then GoTo CheckExitPoint

        ' Send the password
        bResult = POP3SendString("PASS " & sPassword)
        ' Check for errors
        If bResult = False Then GoTo CheckExitPoint

        ' Request the mailbox status
        bResult = POP3SendString("STAT")
        ' Check for errors
        If bResult = False Then GoTo CheckExitPoint

        ' Tell the POP 3 server we are done
        bResult = POP3SendString("QUIT")

CheckExitPoint:
        ' Close the port
        Winsock1.Close

        ' Display the message info or an error
        Select Case mnMessageCount
            Case 0
                MsgBox "There are no messages " & _
                        "waiting on the server."

            Case 1
                MsgBox "There is one message " & _
                        "waiting on the server. " & _
                        "It is " & mlMessageChars & _
                        " bytes is size."

            Case -1
                MsgBox "An error occurred getting " & _
                        "message data from the server."

            Case Else
                ' There is more than one message
                ' waiting so show the info
                MsgBox "There are " & mnMessageCount & _
                        " messages on the server. " & _
                        "They are " & mlMessageChars & _
                        " total bytes in size."

        End Select

    End Sub
```

15. Add the following subroutine. It is responsible for sending commands to and parsing the replies from the POP3 server. First, the function checks the outgoing command to be sure it is one of the four that are understood by this program. Information about valid commands gets added to the list box.

Before sending the command through the socket, the global flag is set indicating that the code is waiting for a reply from the server. The command string is now sent into the socket with the required terminating CR and LF string pair. A DoEvents loop is entered, waiting for the reply to be received. When the data returns, the DataArrival event of the socket control is fired and the global flag is set to True, and the DoEvents loop exits.

The data from the server is now parsed. There are two possible server replies: "+OK" indicating success, or "+ERR" meaning a failure of some kind. If there was a positive response, the reply is parsed based on the command that was sent to the server. The only reply that needs to be parsed is the response from the STAT command. This command reply contains the number of messages and bytes in the mailbox on the server.

```
Private Function POP3SendString( _
           sCommand As String) As Boolean

Dim sActiveCommand        As String
Dim sWorkStr              As String
Dim nCharLoc              As String

' This routine checks the command to ensure it is
' one the program is designed to parse
sActiveCommand = Left$(UCase(Trim$(sCommand)), 4)
Select Case sActiveCommand
    Case "USER", "PASS", "STAT", "QUIT"
        ' Valid command, so just display it
        If sActiveCommand = "PASS" Then
            ' Don't show the password itself
            lstStatus.AddItem "Server command: PASS ********"
        Else
            ' Otherwise, show the whole command
            lstStatus.AddItem "Server command: " & sCommand
        End If

    Case Else
        ' This is a command we are not set up to parse
        MsgBox "Unhandled POP3 command detected: " & _
            sCommand
        Exit Function

End Select

' Set the flag to wait for the data from the server
mbGotData = False

' Send the string to the POP3 server
Winsock1.SendData sCommand & vbCrLf

' Wait for the data to get here. Data is stored
' in the msCommand form-scope variable
Do Until mbGotData = True
    DoEvents
```

```
        Loop

        ' Parse the data in the reply from the server
        ' White space is removed and the string is uppercased
        ' to make command parsing simpler
        Select Case Left$(Trim$(UCase$(msCommand)), 3)
            Case "+OK"              ' Command accepted
                    ' Parse the command-specific replies
                    Select Case sActiveCommand
                        Case "USER"        ' Name is valid

                        Case "PASS"        ' Password is valid

                        Case "STAT"
                            ' Add the reply data to the list box
                            lstStatus.AddItem "Server reply: " & _
                                              msCommand
                            ' Parse out the message count and size
                            ' Start by removing the "+OK " string
                            sWorkStr = Right$(msCommand, _
                                            Len(msCommand) - 4)
                            ' Now find the space that delimits the
                            ' message count and bytes size data
                            nCharLoc = InStr(1, sWorkStr, " ")
                            ' Now extract the two values
                            mnMessageCount = CInt(Mid$(sWorkStr, _
                                                    1, _
                                                    nCharLoc - 1))
                            mlMessageChars = CLng(Mid$(sWorkStr, _
                                                    nCharLoc + 1))

                        Case "QUIT"        ' Now ready to disconnect

                    End Select

                    POP3SendString = True          ' Return success

            Case "-ER"               ' Got an error
                    ' Add the error information to the list box
                    lstStatus.AddItem "Error with command: " & _
                                      sActiveCommand
                    lstStatus.AddItem "Server reply: " & msCommand

                    POP3SendString = False         ' Return failure

            Case Else                ' Unexpected data from server
                    ' Update the list box
                    lstStatus.AddItem "Unexpected data from POP3 server"
                    lstStatus.AddItem "Data: " & msCommand

                    POP3SendString = False         ' Return failure

        End Select

        End Function
```

How It Works

This How-To opens a socket connection to a POP3 server. After the socket is opened, the commands are sent to log the application into the user mailbox on the server. The server is then asked to provide the mailbox status, which then tells the program how many messages are on the server and the total number of message bytes. The user session with the server is then terminated and the socket is closed.

Comments

This code example does not implement the entire POP3 prompt-and-reply protocol set. Full details of the protocol are documented in RFC1725 as published by The Internet Society. Copies of the protocol documents are widely available on the Internet. Please keep in mind that the full implementation of e-mail clients requires the use of two protocols. POP3 handles mail receipt and reading, and SMTP is used to send e-mail.

There are many areas where the code in this How-To can be expanded. First, the error handling can be added to check for user name and password. Two other suggestions for improvement are adding a timer to check for mail periodically and adding the ability to check multiple servers.

CHAPTER 10

FORMS

10

FORMS

How do I...

Most of the attention paid to Visual Basic applications and developing them is related to the controls that appear in the applications, such as buttons, list boxes, and so on. This isn't surprising because most applications are implemented using the controls provided. For example, a database application is implemented using the data control and some combination of controls used to navigate through records in the database or to display data from the database.

The Form control, however, is generally overlooked in terms of its flexibility and opportunities to implement. By programming the Form control, you can extend its functionality beyond that of serving as a container for your application's other controls. This chapter shows how you can build custom events and properties of the Form, as well as take advantage of some of the Form's flexibility to customize the Windows 95 and Windows NT desktop.

10.1 Add a Property to a Form

Most of the controls you use in VB applications contain exactly the properties you need to store and retrieve data about the control. For example, the text box control provides the properties that tell what text is in the control and the text's font, color, size, and more. The Form control, however, is limited in the flexibility available through its properties. By adding custom properties to the forms in your application, you can make your applications more powerful and easier to program and manage.

10.2 Add an Event to a Form

Visual Basic provides a number of standard events that occur on a form. As a Visual Basic developer, you can program what happens when these events occur. However, there may be occasions when you will need to build a custom event. Building an event procedure can be more efficient than trapping for numerous conditions in code.

10.3 Add an Icon to the Desktop Tray

The desktop tray in Windows 95 and Windows NT version 4.0 provides status information about certain programs running on your computer. For example, the current time is usually shown, but depending on the type of computer you're using and the applications and hardware installed, you might also see the status of your battery, the status of the fax/modem, and so on. You can add an icon to the tray for applications you build with VB. This chapter shows you how to display an icon for your application on the Windows desktop tray.

10.4 Animate an Icon on the Desktop Tray

In addition to displaying a static VB application icon on the Windows 95 and Windows NT desktop tray, you can also show an animated icon. This chapter shows you how to animate a Windows desktop tray icon.

COMPLEXITY
INTERMEDIATE

10.1 How do I...
Add a property to a form?

COMPATIBILITY: VISUAL BASIC 5 AND 6

Problem

Some applications use a number of forms, and at design time you don't always know how many instances of these forms are needed. For example, a data entry application might generate an instance of a certain data entry form every time a user needs to enter data into the application. There could be one user or 100 users executing this task. In addition, certain data might need to be associated with each instance of the form.

Technique

To solve this problem, the Form class is used to generate forms on-the-fly. For each form required by a user, a new instance of Form1 is created. Each new instance of the Form class also brings custom properties required by the application.

Steps

Open and run the FORMPROP.VBP project. Enter your name into the User Name box and then enter **PASSWORD** in the Password text box. Next, click the Generate Form button. Notice that a new instance of Form1 appears on the screen. It might seem as though the values you entered into the two text box controls have cleared, but drag the form just a bit, and you'll notice that a new version of the form is created.

Next, click the Generate Form button again on the form that still displays the values you entered. Another instance of the form is created. Drag this new instance so you can view all the buttons on all three instances of the form, as shown in Figure 10.1.

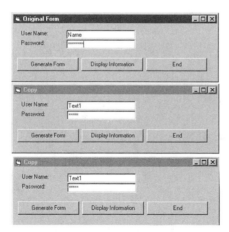

Figure 10.1 A new instance of the same form is created.

Click the Display Information button on each of the two new instances of the form. Notice that the user name you entered appears, and then the password and the time the form was created is also shown. To create this project, complete the following steps.

1. Create a new standard EXE project named FORMPROP.VBP.

2. Add the objects with the properties shown in Table 10.1 to Form1.

Table 10.1 Objects and Properties for Form1

OBJECT	PROPERTY	VALUE
Form	Name	Formprop
	Caption	Original
	Height	2160
	Left	3090
	Top	1815
	Width	6450
	LinkTopic	Form1
	ScaleHeight	2160
	ScaleWidth	6450
TextBox	Name	txtPassword
	Height	285
	Left	1680
	PasswordChar	*
	TabIndex	1
	Top	600
	Width	2175
TextBox	Name	txtUserName
	Height	285
	Left	1680
	TabIndex	0
	Top	240
	Width	2175
CommandButton	Name	cmbEnd
	Caption	End
	Height	495
	Left	4200
	TabIndex	5
	Top	1320
	Width	1935
CommandButton	Name	cmbDisplayInfor
	Caption	Display Information
	Height	495
	Left	2160
	TabIndex	3
	Top	1320
	Width	1935

OBJECT	PROPERTY	VALUE
CommandButton	Name	cmbGenForm
	Caption	Generate Form
	Height	495
	Left	120
	TabIndex	2
	Top	1320
	Width	1935
Label	Name	Label2
	Caption	Password:
	Height	375
	Left	240
	TabIndex	6
	Top	600
	Width	1215
Label	Name	Label1
	Caption	User Name:
	Height	255
	Left	240
	TabIndex	4
	Top	240

2. Add the code below to the Declarations section of **Formprop**. Each of these variables is a property for forms created in this project.

```
Public FormUser As String
Public FormUserPassword As String
Public LogonDateTime As Date
```

3. Add the following code to the **Click** event for the **cmbEnd** control. This code simply ends the project.

```
Private Sub cmbEnd_Click()
    End
End Sub
```

4. Add the following code to the **Click** event of the **cmbDisplayInfo** control. This code displays the value of each of the properties for the form you created in step 2.

```
Private Sub cmbDisplayInfor_Click()
    '
    MsgBox FormUser, , "User Id is: "
    MsgBox FormUserPassword, , "Password is: "
    '
End Sub
```

5. Add the following code to the **Click** event of the **cmbGenForm** control. This code first creates a new instance of the **Formprop** form. If you had called your form something other than **Formprop**, then you would need to supply that name instead. Because the **form** variable is declared with the **New** keyword, the form instance is not created until it is used in code for the first time, which happens on the second line of the event procedure. After the values you supplied in the text boxes on the form are assigned to the properties of the form, as well as the current date and time to the **LogonDateTime** property, the form is displayed.

```
Private Sub cmbGenForm_Click()
'
Dim NewForm As New Formprop
NewForm.FormUser = txtUserName.Text
NewForm.FormUserPassword = txtPassword.Text
NewForm.LogonDateTime = Now
NewForm.Caption = "Copy"
NewForm.Show
'
End Sub
```

How It Works

With each application, VB creates a global object variable for the **Formprop** class. This global object is hidden, and when you create additional instances of the form, you are creating additional instances of this global object. Keep in mind that the global object variable is not re-created for each instance of the form you create. The instance of the form lives only as long as it takes for VB to fire the **Show** method. Each additional form, then, is simply an instance of **Formprop**.

Now that you have an idea of what is working behind the scenes of **Formprop** (a global object variable), it becomes easy to understand how the object works. All the code for **Formprop**, in effect, represents a class module just for the form. Therefore, when you use the **Public** keyword to declare a variable in the Declaration section of the **Formprop** module, you are declaring properties for the **Formprop** class. Each instance of the class created also inherits those properties.

Comments

Two different techniques have been highlighted in this How-To. You have learned how to create new instances of **Formprop**, as well as how to create properties for a form. These techniques can easily be applied to any application that requires an indeterminate number of instances of the same form. By using the Forms collection, in which you can refer to individual forms by their index, you can track all the forms in your application and the properties for each, regardless of the number of forms in the application.

COMPLEXITY
INTERMEDIATE

10.2 How do I...
Add an event to a form?

COMPATIBILITY: VISUAL BASIC 5 AND 6

Problem

Almost all VB applications test for certain conditions, and most of these applications take some action when the condition is met. Sometimes, these conditions occur specific to a form rather than a specific control on the form. For instance, a series of actions on a form might trigger a certain condition. It would be helpful to manage code-writing efficiency to control the action triggered when certain events occur on a form with a real form event. This enables all the event handling to occur in one code location, compared to the extra conditional logic and switching that traditional solutions call for.

Technique

As you learned in the first How-To in this chapter, you can create an instance of a form. Extending this technique, you can create an instance of a form based on a class module that has the capability to capture and manage custom events that occur on the form. By using the `WithEvents` keyword, which gives you the capability to code custom events, you can build a solution that solves the problem described previously.

Steps

Open and run the FORMEVNT.VBP project. These steps simulate data entry, starting with values for key fields. Enter text in the Customer Number field, such as a site ID number. Next, enter some text in the Invoice Number field. Notice how a message appears immediately on the status bar informing you that values for key fields have been entered, as shown in Figure 10.2. The message appears as a result of an event being raised on the form, the event being the entry of values for each of the two key fields.

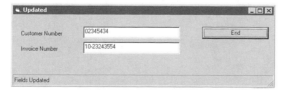

Figure 10.2 A message appears on the status bar as soon as values are entered for each of the key fields.

Complete the following steps to create this project.

1. Create a new standard EXE project named FORMEVNT.VBP.

2. Choose Projects, Components from the menu, and then select Microsoft Windows Common Controls 6.0 from the list box that appears under the Controls tab.

3. Add the objects with the properties shown in Table 10.2 to Form1.

Table 10.2 Objects and Properties for Form1

OBJECT	PROPERTY	VALUE
Form	Name	Form1
	Caption	Form1
	Height	2220
	Left	2115
	Top	1935
	Width	8085
	LinkTopic	Form1
	ScaleHeight	2220
	ScaleWidth	8085
StatusBar	Name	StatusBar1
	Align	2 'Align Bottom
	Height	375
	Left	0
	TabIndex	5
	Top	1845
	Width	8085
	_ExtentX	14261
	_ExtentY	661
	SimpleText	" "
	Style	1 - sbrSimple
	_Version	327680 Panels
		{0713E89E-850A-101B-AFC0-4210102A8DA7}
	NumPanels	1
CommandButton	Name	cmbEnd
	Caption	End
	Height	375
	Left	5880
	TabIndex	4

OBJECT	PROPERTY	VALUE
	Top	360
	Width	2055
TextBox	Name	txtInvoice
	Height	375
	Left	2160
	TabIndex	3
	Top	840
	Width	3015
TextBox	Name	txtCustNum
	Height	375
	Left	2160
	TabIndex	1
	Top	360
	Width	3015
Label	Name	Label2
	Caption	Invoice Number
	Height	375
	Left	240
	TabIndex	2
	Top	960
	Width	1695
Label	Name	Label1
	Caption	Customer Number
	Height	375
	Left	240
	TabIndex	0
	Top	480
	Width	1575

4. Add a new class module to the project. Change the name of the class module to `DataEntryForm`.

5. Add the following code to the new class module. The code provides the matching **Property Get** and **Property Set** procedures for the **Form** class that are being customized with the new event. Specifically, the code returns the form where the event is raised as a property of the **Form** class.

```
Public Property Get Form1() As Form1
    Set Form1 = mForm
End Property
```

continued on next page

continued from previous page

```
Public Property Set Form1(ByVal NewForm1 As Form1)
    Set mForm = NewForm1
End Property
```

6. Switch to Form1 and add the following code to the Declarations section. This code declares the custom event and an instance of the form object.

```
Event KeyFieldUpdated()
Private ThisForm As DataEntryForm
```

7. Switch to the class module and add the following code to the Declarations section of the module. This batch of code declares an instance of the form. Notice that the name of the form matches the form name used in the two Property procedures. More important, the `WithEvents` keyword is used, which signifies that the instance of the form, `mForm`, has custom events.

```
Private WithEvents mForm1 As Form1
```

8. Still in the class module, add the following code to the `KeyFieldUpdated` event for the `ThisForm` control. Notice now that `KeyFieldUpdated` appears in the procedure drop-down list for `ThisForm`. The code below updates the status bar on the instance of the form where the `KeyFieldUpdated` event is raised.

```
Private Sub mForm_KeyFieldUpdated()
mForm1.Caption = "Updated"
    mForm1.StatusBar1.SimpleText = "Fields Updated"
End Sub
```

9. Return to Form1, and add the following code to the `Load` event for the form. This code creates an instance of the form based on `DataEntryForm` where the new event handling is coded.

```
Private Sub Form_Load()
    Set ThisForm = New DataEntryForm
    Set ThisForm.Form1 = Me
End Sub
```

10. Add the following code to the `Change` event for the two text box controls. This code simply checks whether the user has changed the field by clearing its contents. If not, the other key field is checked and if that field passes inspection, the `KeyFieldUpdated` event is raised.

```
Private Sub txtCustNum_Change()
    If txtCustNum.Text <> "" Then
        If txtInvoice.Text <> "" Then
            RaiseEvent KeyFieldUpdated
        End If
    End If
```

```
End Sub
Private Sub txtInvoice_Change()
    If txtInvoice.Text <> "" Then
        If txtCustNum.Text <> "" Then
            RaiseEvent KeyFieldUpdated
        End If
    End If
End Sub
```

How It Works

Much of the techniques in this How-To are similar to those introduced in the first How-To in this chapter. A new instance of a form object is created, and through the use of the Me keyword, the instance of the form points to the current form. Also, the declaration of the form object in the class module uses the WithEvents keyword, which enables you to build custom events.

Comments

The WithEvents keyword is a powerful enabler. With it, you can access the events of other controls. For instance, if you place the Web browser control into a project, you can access the events that occur for actions that take place on the Web browser menus.

COMPLEXITY
INTERMEDIATE

10.3 How do I...
Add an icon to the desktop tray?

COMPATIBILITY: VISUAL BASIC 5 AND 6

Problem

Most applications that run in the background of Windows 95 or Windows NT provide an icon on the Windows desktop tray to signify to the user that a process is running. There is no out-of-the box functionality in VB that enables an icon for a VB-based process to appear on the Windows desktop tray.

Technique

A Windows API call helps solve this problem. Using a data structure that describes an icon, and then using a Windows API call to send that data to the tray, the icon associated with a VB form can appear on the Windows desktop tray.

Steps

Open and run the ICONTRAY.VBP project. Double-click each of the pictures provided. Notice how the picture you double-clicked appears on the Windows desktop tray, as shown in Figure 10.3.

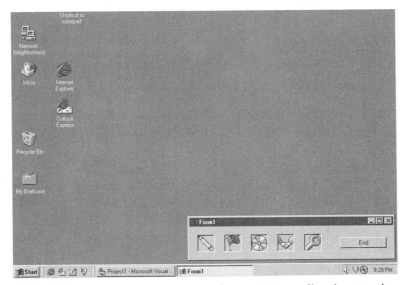

Figure 10.3 You can add an icon from a VB application to the Windows desktop tray.

To create this project, complete the following steps.

1. Create a new standard EXE project named ICONTRAY.VBP.

2. Add the objects with the properties shown in Table 10.3 to Form1.

Table 10.3 Objects and Properties for Form1

OBJECT	PROPERTY	VALUE
Form	Name	ICONTRAY
	Caption	Form1
	Height	1170
	Left	2835
	Top	2340
	Width	6465
	LinkTopic	Form1
	ScaleHeight	1170
	ScaleWidth	6465

OBJECT	PROPERTY	VALUE
PictureBox	Name	Picture5
	AutoSize	True
	Height	540
	Left	3480
	ScaleHeight	480
	ScaleWidth	480
	TabIndex	5
	Top	240
	Width	540
CommandButton	Name	cmbEnd
	Caption	End
	Height	495
	Left	4800
	TabIndex	4
	Top	240
	Width	1455
PictureBox	Name	Picture4
	AutoSize	True
	Height	540
	Left	2760
	ScaleHeight	480
	ScaleWidth	480
	TabIndex	3
	Top	240
	Width	540
PictureBox	Name	Picture3
	AutoSize	True
	Height	540
	Left	1920
	ScaleHeight	480
	ScaleWidth	480
	TabIndex	2
	Top	240
	Width	540
PictureBox	Name	Picture2
	AutoSize	True
	Height	540

continued on next page

continued from previous page

OBJECT	PROPERTY	VALUE
	Left	1080
	ScaleHeight	480
	ScaleWidth	480
	TabIndex	1
	Top	240
	Width	540
PictureBox	Name	Picture1
	AutoSize	True
	Height	540
	Left	240
	ScaleHeight	480
	ScaleWidth	480
	TabIndex	0
	Top	240
	Width	540

3. Add a module to the project.

4. Add the following code to the module. This code declares the **Shell_NotifyIcon** API function, whose job it is to place the icon on the Windows desktop tray. In addition, this code also declares the data structure that is used to pass information about the icon to the API. Six constants are also declared.

```
'Declare function
Declare Function Shell_NotifyIcon Lib "shell32.dll" (ByVal
dwMessage As Long, _
                lpData As NOTIFYICONDATA) As Long
'
'Define icon structure
Type NOTIFYICONDATA
        cbSize As Long
        hWnd As Long
        uID As Long
        uFlags As Long
        uCallbackMessage As Long
        hIcon As Long
        szTip As String * 64
End Type
'
'Used to pass message param to Shell_NotifyIcon
Global Const ADD_ICON = 0
Global Const MODIFY_ICON = 1
Global Const DELETE_ICON = 2
Global Const ICON_MESSAGE = 1
Global Const ICON_ICON = 2
Global Const ICON_TIP = 4
```

5. Add the following subroutine to the module. This function is called by the form to initialize the icon data structure. Because some of the fields in the structure are not used by VB, this function handles initializing those fields with the proper values. Fields not initialized by the following subroutine have their value passed in by the calling routine from the form, as shown later in this How-To.

```
Public Sub InitIconStruct(hWnd As Long, TheIcon As Long, sTip As _
String, _
            IconData As NOTIFYICONDATA)
    '
    IconData.cbSize = Len(IconData)
    IconData.hWnd = hWnd
    IconData.uID = vbNull
    IconData.uFlags = ICON_MESSAGE Or ICON_ICON Or ICON_TIP
    IconData.uCallbackMessage = vbNull
    IconData.hIcon = TheIcon
    IconData.szTip = sTip
    '
End Sub
```

6. Add the following code to the Declarations section of Form1. These constants point to the physical location of the icons used in the demonstration. Make sure the path for ICON_PATH is set to the proper location.

```
Const ICON_PATH = "c:\ VB6HT\Chapter10
Const ARROW = ICON_PATH + "\ POINT09.ICO"
Const COMM = ICON_PATH + "\ HANDSHAK.ICO"
Const COMPUTER = ICON_PATH + "\ CDROM01.ICO"
Const FLAG = ICON_PATH + "\ FLGUSA01.ICO"
Const WRENCH = ICON_PATH + "\ WRENCH.ICO"
```

7. To load the icons into the picture box's, place the following code in the Load event of Form1:

```
Private Sub Form_Load()
    Picture1.Picture = LoadPicture(ARROW)
    Picture2.Picture = LoadPicture(FLAG)
    Picture3.Picture = LoadPicture(COMPUTER)
    Picture4.Picture = LoadPicture(COMM)
    Picture5.Picture = LoadPicture(WRENCH)
End Sub
```

8. Add the following code to the double-click event for each of the five picture controls. The code calls the PostIcon subroutine, which wraps the Shell_NotifyIcon function.

```
Private Sub Picture1_DblClick()
    PostIcon (ARROW)
End Sub
```

continued on next page

continued from previous page

```
Private Sub Picture2_DblClick()
    PostIcon (FLAG)
End Sub
Private Sub Picture3_DblClick()
    PostIcon (COMPUTER)
End Sub
Private Sub Picture4_DblClick()
    PostIcon (COMM)
End Sub
Private Sub Picture5_DblClick()
    PostIcon (WRENCH)
End Sub
```

9. Add the following `PostIcon` subroutine to Form1. This subroutine manages the functionality involved in calling the Windows API. The first task is to create an icon data structure variable. Next, the picture passed to the function is assigned as the icon for the form. This is critical because the `Shell_NotifyIcon` function uses the icon associated with some form in the application, so you must first assign the icon you want to appear on the tray to the form. Next, the `InitIconData` function is called, which passes more information to the icon data structure. Lastly, the `Shell_Notifyicon` function is called, first to delete any icon that already appears on the tray, and second, to add the new icon to the tray.

```
Private Sub PostIcon(icoIcon As String)
    '
    Dim IconData As NOTIFYICONDATA
    ICONTRAY.Icon = LoadPicture(icoIcon)
    '
    InitIconStruct ICONTRAY.hWnd, ICONTRAY.Icon, _
        "This Icon Is Not Animated", IconData
    x = Shell_NotifyIcon(DELETE_ICON, IconData)
    x = Shell_NotifyIcon(ADD_ICON, IconData)
    '
End Sub
```

How It Works

This How-To makes use of the `Shell_NotifyIcon` function to add icons to the desktop tray. This function can be used to add, modify, or delete icons from the desktop tray. You can also assign tip text to the icons.

Comments

Visual Basic does not include built-in functions to access desktop items. The Windows API, however, has the functions necessary to access and manipulate these items. There are a wide range of "shell" functions that can be used in Visual Basic to greatly enhance your program's functionality.

COMPLEXITY
INTERMEDIATE

10.4 How do I...
Animate an icon on the desktop tray?

COMPATIBILITY: VISUAL BASIC 5 AND 6

Problem

In the previous How-To in this chapter, a problem was outlined about providing an icon on the Windows 95 and Windows NT desktop tray for a VB application. This icon is useful in alerting users when a process is underway. Placing a static icon on the desktop tray isn't too difficult, but there may be a requirement to animate that icon.

Technique

This technique, like the technique described in the previous How-To, also uses the Windows API to manage a data structure related to an icon. It also supplies the data structure to the Windows desktop tray so that the icon can appear there. Using the timer control, you can quickly update the icon appearing on the desktop tray, thereby creating an animation effect.

Steps

Open and run the ANIMICON.VBP project. Figure 10.4 shows the form for this project. Click the Boring button. Notice how the left arrow icon appears on the Windows tray. Now, click the Animated button. Notice how the arrow appears to spin on the Windows tray.

Figure 10.4 You can animate the icons that appear on the Windows desktop tray.

Complete the following steps to create this project.

1. Create a new standard EXE project named ANIMICON.VBP.

2. Add the objects with the properties shown in Table 10.4 to Form1.

Table 10.4 Objects and Properties for Form1

OBJECT	PROPERTY	VALUE
Form	Name	animicon
	Caption	Form1
	Height	1800
	Left	2835
	Top	2340
	Width	4275
	Icon	(None)
	LinkTopic	"Form1"
	ScaleHeight	1800
	ScaleWidth	4275
CommandButton	Name	cbEnd
	Cancel	True
	Caption	End
	Height	375
	Left	1560
	TabIndex	2
	Top	1200
	Width	1215
CommandButton	Name	cbAnimated
	Caption	Animated
	Height	495
	Left	2280
	TabIndex	1
	Top	240
	Width	1695
Timer	Name	Timer1
	Interval	100
	Left	360
	Top	1080
CommandButton	Name	cbStatic
	Caption	Boring
	Height	495
	Left	240
	TabIndex	0
	Top	240
	Width	1695

3. Add a module to the project.

4. Add the following code to the module. This code declares the
`Shell_NotifyIcon` API function, whose job it is to place the icon on the
Windows desktop tray. In addition, this code also declares the data
structure used to pass information about the icon to the API. Six constants
are also declared.

```
'Declare function
Declare Function Shell_NotifyIcon Lib "shell32.dll" (ByVal _
dwMessage As Long, _
                    lpData As NOTIFYICONDATA) As Long
'
'Define icon structure
Type NOTIFYICONDATA
        cbSize As Long
        hWnd As Long
        uID As Long
        uFlags As Long
        uCallbackMessage As Long
        hIcon As Long
        szTip As String * 64
End Type
'
'Used to pass message param to Shell_NotifyIcon
Global Const ADD_ICON = 0
Global Const MODIFY_ICON = 1
Global Const DELETE_ICON = 2
Global Const ICON_MESSAGE = 1
Global Const ICON_ICON = 2
Global Const ICON_TIP = 4
```

5. Add the following subroutine to the module. The form calls this function
to initialize the icon data structure. Because some of the fields in the
structure are not used by VB, this function handles initializing those fields
with the proper values. Fields not initialized by the following subroutine
have their value passed in by the calling routine from the form, as shown
later in this How-To.

```
Public Sub InitIconStruct(hWnd As Long, TheIcon As Long, sTip As _
String, _
                IconData As NOTIFYICONDATA)
        '
    IconData.cbSize = Len(IconData)
    IconData.hWnd = hWnd
    IconData.uID = vbNull
    IconData.uFlags = ICON_MESSAGE Or ICON_ICON Or ICON_TIP
    IconData.uCallbackMessage = vbNull
    IconData.hIcon = TheIcon
    IconData.szTip = sTip
        '
End Sub
```

6. Add the following code to the Declarations section of Form1. The constants declared in the code point to the physical location of the icons used in the demonstration. In addition, a number of module-level variables are declared that help manage the timer component of the application. Be sure the path for **ICON_PATH** is set correctly for your machine.

```
Dim m_intTimerStep As Integer
Dim flgStartTimer As Integer
Dim m_intRet As Integer
Dim m_IconData As NOTIFYICONDATA
Const ICON_PATH = "c:\VB6HT\Chapter10\"
Const LEFT_ICON = ICON_PATH + "arw02lt.ico"
Const RIGHT_ICON = ICON_PATH + "arw02rt.ico"
Const UP_ICON = ICON_PATH + "arw02up.ico"
Const DOWN_ICON = ICON_PATH + "arw02dn.ico"
```

7. Add the following code to the **Click** event of the **cbStatic** control. The code first loads the left arrow icon as the default icon for the form. Next, the **InitIconStruct** function is called, which supplies runtime information to the data structure for the icon. That data structure is then used by the Windows API function that posts the icon to the desktop tray. As you might recall, a number of elements of the structure unused by VB are supplied by the **InitIconStruct** function. Last, in the code, the **Shell_NotifyIcon** routine is called that does the actual work of placing the icon on the tray. The function requires the task the function should execute, **ADD_ICON**, in this case, as well as the icon data structure.

```
Private Sub cbStatic_Click()
    '
    animicon.Icon = LoadPicture(LEFT_ICON)
    '
    flgStartTimer = False
    InitIconStruct animicon.hWnd, animicon.Icon, _
        "This Icon Is Not Animated", m_IconData
    intRet = Shell_NotifyIcon(ADD_ICON, m_IconData)
    '
End Sub
```

8. Add the following code to the **Click** event of the **cbAnimated** button control. This code is executed when the user clicks the button with the Animated label. Slightly different from the preceding code, which is executed when the user clicks the Boring button, this event procedure also initializes the variable flags the Timer control uses.

```
Private Sub cbAnimated_Click()
    '
    flgStartTimer = True
    InitIconStruct animicon.hWnd, animicon.Icon, "Animated!", _
    m_IconData
    intRet = Shell_NotifyIcon(ADD_ICON, m_IconData)
    '
End Sub
```

9. Add the following code to the **Load** event for the Form control. This code sets the duration for the Timer control, as well as setting the default icon of the form and placement on the desktop tray.

```
Private Sub Form_Load()
    '
    m_intTimerStep = 1
    animicon.Icon = LoadPicture(LEFT_ICON)
    '
End Sub
```

10. Add the following code to the **Timer** event of the Timer1 control. The Timer control is used to manage the simulated animation of icons on the desktop tray. The icon used for display on the desktop tray changes every time the timer event changes. By managing what icon appears when, you can simulate animation on the tray. As you can see from the following code, the four different icons are cycled through the tray by calling the **Shell_NotifyIcon** every time the current icon for the form changes. The icon animation, however, occurs only when the **flgStartTimer** is set to **True**, which occurs only when the user clicks the Animate button.

```
Private Sub Timer1_Timer()
    '
    If Not (flgStartTimer) Then
        Exit Sub
    End If
    '
    Select Case m_intTimerStep
        Case 4
            animicon.Icon = LoadPicture(LEFT_ICON)
            '
        Case 3
            animicon.Icon = LoadPicture(UP_ICON)
            '
        Case 2
            animicon.Icon = LoadPicture(RIGHT_ICON)
            '
        Case 1
            animicon.Icon = LoadPicture(DOWN_ICON)
    End Select

    If m_intTimerStep <> 4 Then
        m_intTimerStep = m_intTimerStep + 1
    Else
        m_intTimerStep = 1
    End If
    '
    InitIconStruct animicon.hWnd, animicon.Icon, _
            "Animated!", m_IconData
    m_intRet = Shell_NotifyIcon(MODIFY_ICON, m_IconData)
    '
End Sub
```

11. Add the following code for the **Click** event to the **cmbEnd** control. This code deletes any icon on the desktop tray before ending the project.

```
Private Sub cbEnd_Click()
    '
    flgStartTimer = False
    m_intRet = Shell_NotifyIcon(DELETE_ICON, m_IconData)
    End
    '
End Sub
```

How It Works

Like most of the very powerful VB solutions presented in this book, the Windows API is used here. A data structure is used to collect and organize data about the icon used in a VB application, and this icon is passed to a Windows API function that posts the icon to the desktop tray. To achieve the animation effect, the code in this application cycles through a number of icons, updating the desktop tray icon every time the icon changes.

Comments

The shell32 library used in the following two How-Tos contains many functions that can enhance your Visual Basic programs. Included are functions to browse for directories (including network-based ones) and computers. There are also functions to get detailed information on files and directories or perform operations on files.

CHAPTER 11
DATABASES

11

DATABASES

How do I...

This chapter introduces some basic concepts behind using Visual Basic to work with databases. The native database for Visual Basic is the Microsoft Access database, which is accessed through the Jet engine. You can also access other types of databases using ISAM (Indexed Sequential Access Method) or ODBC (Open Database Connectivity) drivers. This chapter covers using the Jet engine in its default mode to access a native database as well as introduces you to using ISAM drivers to access other types of data.

The first three How-Tos demonstrate how to use a data control in conjunction with bound controls. The next two How-Tos (11.4 and 11.5) show how to use data access objects to accomplish database tasks. How-Tos 11.6 through 11.10 cover topics related to creating databases, discovering information about the database, and performing simple database maintenance. The next three How-Tos focus on using ISAM drivers to access data not in the native Jet engine format. The last How-To introduces the `DataRepeater` control.

11.1 Add and Delete Records Using Bound Controls

Most database applications need to add and delete records as well as edit them. This How-To covers editing, adding, and deleting records using the data control in conjunction with bound controls.

11.2 Use a List to Update Fields in a Recordset

Sometimes a field might need only a limited number of choices. Using a list to update these fields will keep users from entering inappropriate values. This How-To shows how to accomplish this with bound controls.

11.3 Handle Data Control Errors

Although error processing is an important part of any program, it can have special importance to a database program. This How-To covers some basics of error trapping.

11.4 Add and Delete Records Using Data Access Objects

Most database applications need to add and delete records as well as edit them. This How-To covers editing, adding, and deleting records using data access objects. The capability to undo changes is also covered.

11.5 Find Records Using Index Values with Data Access Objects

It is important in a database application to be able to quickly find the data the user needs; indexes are used to speed up queries. The Seek method can be used in conjunction with indexes to speed up search operations. This How-To demonstrates the use of index fields to quickly find data in table-type recordsets.

11.6 Create a New Database in Code

Visual Basic provides all the tools you need to create a database from scratch. You do not have to deliver empty database templates with your product. This How-To addresses the issue of creating a database from the ground up using just Visual Basic code. The topics of creating indexes and relations are covered as well.

11.7 Attach a Table from Another Database

In many cases your program will not work in a closed environment. Your program might have to use information from existing databases. This How-To covers how to attach a table from an external database to your local database for use in your program.

11.8 Compact and Repair a Database

Sometimes databases grow because of many deletions and additions. They might also experience problems due to index corruption or incomplete write events. This How-To covers how to compact a database to reduce its size and how to run the built-in repair mechanism.

11.9 Determine How Many Records Are in a Recordset

The `RecordCount` property of a recordset does not always return the total number of records. This How-To examines how you can get the total number of records for a given recordset.

11.10 Determine Other Information About a Table

The `TableDef` collection offers a tremendous amount of information about the tables of a database. Some information stored in a `TableDef` includes the number of records, the date the table was created, the date the table was last updated, the validation data, and other information. This How-To examines how to access some of the information stored in the `TableDef` collection.

11.11 Look Up dBASE, FoxPro, and Paradox Database Files with Data Access Objects

Visual Basic enables the use of databases other than Microsoft Access. Other databases are accessed either through OBDC or ISAM drivers. This How-To examines using data access objects with an ISAM driver to view, add, and delete records from a recordset.

11.12 Access Spreadsheet Files from a Visual Basic Application

You can access and display Excel worksheets from a Visual Basic application without having Excel loaded on the machine. This How-To uses the `MSFlexGrid` control to display data from an Excel file by using an ISAM driver to retrieve information from an Excel file.

11.13 Access Data in a Web (HTML) Page

Often data is represented on a Web page in the form of tables, but you can access tabular data from HTML files from inside your Visual Basic application. This How-To implements a tool that uses an ISAM driver to browse the tables of an HTML file and display the data of each.

11.14 Use the `DataRepeater` Control

This How-To discusses creating an ActiveX control and using that control with the `DataRepeater` control to view the contents of a database.

Data Controls

Visual Basic provides two data access methods: a data control and a data access object. The data control can be made to work with a minimal amount of code, whereas the data access object allows for more robust operations. The next two topics cover using the data control to perform basic database operations. The topic of data access objects is covered later in the chapter.

In How-Tos 11.1 and 11.2, all database operations use the Microsoft Jet database engine and operate on Microsoft Access databases. The Jet engine can be used to operate on other database types, and those topics are covered later in the chapter.

COMPLEXITY
BEGINNING

11.1 How do I...

Add and delete records using bound controls?

COMPATIBILITY: VISUAL BASIC 4, 5, AND 6

Problem

I know how to present existing records to my users for editing with bound controls, but how do I enable them to add new records or delete current records?

Technique

The mechanism for adding records to a data control's recordset is the `AddNew` method, which creates a new record in the recordset. This method initializes the fields with their default values (as determined by the table definition for the table being accessed). If no default values are defined, the fields are set to `NULL`.

The new record is not saved to the database until one of the following events happens: the current record pointer is moved to another record, another `AddNew` is performed, or the `Update` method is applied. If you don't call the `Update` method, moving to another record or calling `AddNew` again won't save it. The position of the new record in the recordset is determined by what type of recordset was defined. In dynaset recordsets, new records are added to the end of the recordset. In table recordsets, new records are added to their proper sort order if the `Index` property has been set. Otherwise, they are added to the end of the recordset.

Visual Basic updates preexisting records differently from newly created ones. If an existing record is modified and the form is then dismissed, the changes are saved. If the same thing is done with a record that was just created with **AddNew**, the data will not be saved. When a new record is added, the **Update** method must be called before the data will be saved.

The mechanism for deleting records from a data control's recordset is the **Delete** method, which removes the current record from the recordset. Even though the record is now inaccessible, it remains the current record; you must move the current record pointer to a valid record. After the record pointer has been moved to a valid record, the deleted record can no longer be made the current record. Trying to access a deleted record generates an error.

Steps

Load the project ADD_DEL.VBP. Be sure to change the **DatabaseName** property of the data control **Data1** to point to the copy of BIBLIO.MDB located in your Visual Basic directory. Now run the program, and the form shown in Figure 11.1 appears.

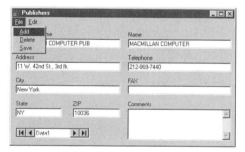

Figure 11.1 Publishers Add/Delete form.

Choose File, Add from the menu and enter appropriate values in the data fields. Select the last record button on the data control. Your record is displayed. Choose File, Delete from the menu. Answer Yes to the prompt, and your record is deleted. Complete the following steps to create this project.

1. Create a new project called ADD_DEL.VBP. Add the following line to the declarations section of **Form1**.

```
Public inDelete As Boolean
```

2. Use **Form1** to create the objects and properties listed in Table 11.1. Save the form as ADDDEL.FRM. Be sure to change the **DatabaseName** property of the data control **Data1** to point to the copy of BIBLIO.MDB located in your Visual Basic directory.

Table 11.1 Object and Properties for AddDel Form

OBJECT	PROPERTY	SETTING
Form	Name	AddDel
	Caption	Publishers
Data	Name	Data1
	Connect	ACCESS
	DatabaseName	C:\Program Files\Microsoft Visual Studio\VB6\BIBLIO.MDB
	RecordSetType	1 - Dynaset
	RecordSource	Publishers
TextBox	Name	Zip
	DataField	Zip
	DataSource	Data1
TextBox	Name	State
	DataField	State
	DataSource	Data1
TextBox	Name	City
	DataField	City
	DataSource	Data1
TextBox	Name	Address
	DataField	Address
	DataSource	Data1
TextBox	Name	Company
	DataField	Company Name
	DataSource	Data1
TextBox	Name	Cname
	DataField	Name
	DataSource	Data1
TextBox	Name	Comments
	DataField	Comments
	DataSource	Data1
	MultiLine	True
TextBox	Name	FAX
	DataField	Fax
	DataSource	Data1
TextBox	Name	Telephone
	DataField	Telephone
	DataSource	Data1

OBJECT	PROPERTY	SETTING
Label	Name	Label9
	Caption	Comments
Label	Name	Label8
	Caption	FAX
Label	Name	Label7
	Caption	Telephone
Label	Name	Label6
	Caption	Name
Label	Name	Label5
	Caption	ZIP
Label	Name	Label4
	Caption	State
Label	Name	Label3
	Caption	City
Label	Name	Label2
	Caption	Address
Label	Name	Label1
	Caption	Company

3. Use the Menu Editor (located under Tools) to create the entries listed in Table 11.2.

Table 11.2 Menu Specifications for AddDel.FRM

CAPTION	NAME
&File	File
-&Add	Add
-&Delete	Delete
-&Save	Save
&Edit	Edit
-&Undo	Undo

4. Add the following code to the **Data1_Validate** event. This code checks for two conditions: the company name is not blank, and the entry for state is two letters. The **CancelUpdate** variable is used to signal that something is wrong and the update to the recordset should not be allowed to proceed.

```
Private Sub Data1_Validate(Action As Integer, Save As Integer)
    Dim flen As Integer
```

continued on next page

continued from previous page

```
            Dim CancelUpdate As Boolean

            If not inDelete Then
                If Company.Text = "" Then
                    MsgBox "Please enter a Company Name"

                    'Indicates the data has not changed
                    Company.DataChanged = False

                    CancelUpdate = True
                End If
            End If

            If State.DataChanged Then
                flen = Len(State.Text)
                If flen <> 2 Then
                    MsgBox "Please Use the 2 Letter State Abbreviation"
                    'Indicates the data has not changed
                    State.DataChanged = False

                    'Set the focus to the offending field
                    State.SetFocus

                    'Override the new text
                    State.Text = Data1.Recordset.Fields("State")
                End If
            End If

            If CancelUpdate Then
                ' Cancel the changes
                Action = vbDataActionCancel
            End If
        End Sub
```

5. Add the following code to the `Add_Click` subroutine. One field of the Publisher table is not shown on the form, `PubID`. This field should always be a unique number so that the following code finds the largest ID currently in the table and adds one to it for use as the ID for the new record. After the `AddNew` method is called, the new ID is placed into the `PubID` field. The rest of the values for the table are entered using the edit fields on the form

```
Private Sub Add_Click()
    Dim NewID As Integer

    ' Determine the highest PubID and generate the next one
    Data1.Recordset.Sort = "PubID"
    Data1.Recordset.MoveLast
    NewID = Data1.Recordset.Fields("PubID") + 1

    ' Add a new record to the recordset
    ' AddNew sets the fields of the record to their default
    ' values or if no defaults exist - NULL
    Data1.Recordset.AddNew
    Data1.Recordset.Fields("PubID") = NewID
End Sub
```

6. Add the following code to the **Delete_Click** subroutine. The **MsgBox** presents the user with the option to continue or dismiss the delete operation. When a record is deleted, the current record pointer is undefined, so the current record pointer should be moved to a valid record. In this case, the **MovePrevious** method is used to move the record pointer. The code checks to make sure that the record that was just deleted was not the first record. If it was, the first record and then the **BOF** property will be **True**, and the **MoveFirst** method is used to reset the current record pointer to the new first record.

```
Private Sub Delete_Click()
    Dim question As String
    Dim answer As VbMsgBoxResult

    question = "Do you want to delete the entry for " + _
        Company.Text

    answer = MsgBox(question, vbQuestion & vbYesNo, _
            App.ProductName)
    If answer = vbYes Then
        inDelete = True
        ' The delete method deletes the current record
        Data1.Recordset.Delete

        'After a delete the current record is undefined.
        'Move to a valid record.
        Data1.Recordset.MovePrevious

        'If the first record was the one deleted reposition
        'the current record to the new first record
        If Data1.Recordset.BOF Then Data1.Recordset.MoveFirst
        Data1.Refresh
        inDelete = False
    End If
End Sub
```

7. Add the following code to the **Save_Click** subroutine. The **Update** method saves the current buffer to the recordset. The default mode of **Update** is to write the data to disk immediately, but the **Update** method, however, takes an argument that enables you to change when the data is saved. The **EditMode** property indicates the state of editing for the data control and may have one of three values: **dbEditAdd**, **dbEditInProgress**, or **dbEditNone**. The **EditMode** property is equal to **dbEditAdd** when the **AddNew** method has been used to create a new record that has not yet been saved.

```
Private Sub Save_Click()
    If Data1.EditMode = dbEditAdd Then
        ' Save the current record
        ' The default for update is no cache - write to disk now.
        Data1.Recordset.Update
    Else
```

continued on next page

continued from previous page

```
            Data1.Recordset.Move 0
        End If
    End Sub
```

8. Add the following code to the `Undo_Click` event. The `CancelUpdate` method discards changes made during `AddNew` or `Edit`. When an `AddNew` is canceled, the current record is undefined, and the current record pointer should be repositioned to a valid record.

```
Private Sub Undo_Click()
    If Data1.EditMode = dbEditAdd Then
        ' The CancelUpdate method discards changes resulting from
        ' AddNew or Edit
        Data1.Recordset.CancelUpdate

        'Move the current record to a valid entry
        Data1.Recordset.MoveFirst
    Else
        ' The UpdateControls method restores the values of bound
        ' controls to their original settings
        Data1.UpdateControls
    End If
End Sub
```

How It Works

The `AddNew` method of the `Data` control is used to create a new record buffer. The `Delete` method is used to remove an existing record from the recordset. When using these two methods, care must be taken to ensure that the current record is always valid.

The recordset has two special properties indicating that the record pointer has reached the beginning or end of the recordset. These properties are `BOF` (Beginning Of File) and `EOF` (End Of File). The `BOF` property is true when the record pointer has moved back past the first valid record. Similarly, the `EOF` property is true when the record pointer has moved past the last valid record. When the current record pointer becomes invalid, the record pointer needs to be set to a valid record. The `BOF` and `EOF` properties can help to make sure that the record you reposition to is also valid. If both `BOF` and `EOF` are `True`, then the recordset does not contain any records.

Comments

The `Data` control has two properties (`BOFAction` and `EOFAction`) that allow you to have some control over what happens when the record pointer reaches `BOF` or `EOF`. The `BOFAction` property can have two settings. The first setting is `vbBOFActionMoveFirst` and causes the first record to remain the current record; this mode is the default. The other setting is `vbBOFActionBOF`, which causes the `Validate` event to be invoked on the first record followed by a `Reposition` event. After these events, the Move Previous button is disabled.

The EOFAction property can have three settings. The first is vbEOFAction MoveLast and causes the last record to remain the current record; this is the default setting. The second setting is vbEOFActionEOF, which causes the Validate event to be invoked on the first record followed by a Reposition event. After these events, the Move Next button is disabled. The third setting, vbEOFActionAddNew, causes the Validation event to be invoked on the current record. This is followed by the AddNew method and a Reposition event to the new record.

COMPLEXITY
BEGINNING

11.2 How do I...
Use a list to update fields in a recordset?

COMPATIBILITY: VISUAL BASIC 4, 5, AND 6

Problem

Some fields of my database only allow for certain values. Instead of the user entering a bad value and catching it during the Validate event I want to provide the user with a list of the valid choices for those fields. How do I do this with bound controls?

Technique

The DBList and DBCombo controls are bound controls that can build up their lists from one data control and pass the selected information back to another data control. The DBList and DBCombo controls are normally used in conjunction with two data controls. One of the data controls is used to fill the list, whereas the other is used to update a field in the database. Table 11.3 lists some properties needed to implement this functionality.

Table 11.3 Important DBList/DBCombo Properties

PROPERTY	USE
DataSource	Data control that is updated when a selection is made
DataField	Name of the field in DataSource that is updated
RowSource	Data control that is used to fill the list
ListField	Name of the field in RowSource used to fill the list
BoundColumn	Field in RowSource to be passed back to DataSource
BoundText	The text value of BoundColumn

The properties in Table 11.3 can be set up so that when an item is selected from a **DBList/DBCombo** control, a value is passed back to the other data control (**DataSource**). This value is used to update a field (**DataField**) in that recordset. The value passed back does not have to be the value selected from the list (**ListField**). The field passed back is determined by **BoundColumn** and might be different from the field used to fill the list. In most cases, the data control used to fill the **DBList** or **DBCombo** controls list is not accessed by the user. Therefore, its **Visible** property can be set to **False**.

Steps

Load the project LIST.VBP. Be sure to change the **DatabaseName** property of the data control (**Data1**) to point to the copy of BIBLIO.MDB located in your Visual Basic directory. Run the program, and the form shown in Figure 11.2 appears.

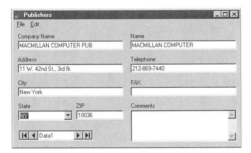

Figure 11.2 Publishers List Form.

Use the State combo box to change the location of the publisher. To create this project, complete the following steps.

1. Create a new project called LIST.VBP. Choose Projects, Components from the menu, and then choose Microsoft Data Bound List Controls 6.0.

2. Use **Form1** to create the objects and properties listed in Table 11.4. Save the form as LIST.FRM. Be sure to change the **DatabaseName** property of the data control **Data1** to point to the copy of BIBLIO.MDB located in your Visual Basic directory.

Table 11.4 Object and Properties for List Form

OBJECT	PROPERTY	SETTING
Form	Name	List
	Caption	Publishers

OBJECT	PROPERTY	SETTING
Data	Name	Data1
	Connect	ACCESS
	DatabaseName	C:\PROGRAM FILES\MICROSOFT VISUAL STUDIO\VB6\BIBLIO.MDB
	RecordSetType	1 - Dynaset
	RecordSource	Publishers
Data	Name	Data2
	Connect	ACCESS
	DatabaseName	C:\PROGRAM FILES\MICROSOFT VISUAL STUDIO\VB6\BIBLIO.MDB
	RecordSetType	1 - Dynaset
	Visible	False
DBCombo	Name	StateCombo
	BoundColumn	State
	DataSource	Data1
	ListField	State
	RowSource	Data2
TextBox	Name	Zip
	DataField	Zip
	DataSource	Data1
TextBox	Name	City
	DataField	City
	DataSource	Data1
TextBox	Name	Address
	DataField	Address
	DataSource	Data1
TextBox	Name	Company
	DataField	Company Name
	DataSource	Data1
TextBox	Name	Cname
	DataField	Name
	DataSource	Data1
TextBox	Name	Comments
	DataField	Comments
	DataSource	Data1
	MultiLine	True

continued on next page

continued from previous page

OBJECT	PROPERTY	SETTING
TextBox	Name	FAX
	DataField	Fax
	DataSource	Data1
TextBox	Name	Telephone
	DataField	Telephone
	DataSource	Data1
Label	Name	Label9
	Caption	Comments
Label	Name	Label8
	Caption	FAX
Label	Name	Label7
	Caption	Telephone
Label	Name	Label6
	Caption	Name
Label	Name	Label5
	Caption	ZIP
Label	Name	Label4
	Caption	State
Label	Name	Label3
	Caption	City
Label	Name	Label2
	Caption	Address
Label	Name	Label1
	Caption	Company

3. Use the Visual Basic Menu Editor to create the entries in Table 11.5.

Table 11.5 Menu Specifications for LIST.FRM

CAPTION	NAME
&File	File
-&Add	Add
-&Delete	Delete
-&Save	Save
&Edit	Edit
-&Undo	Undo

4. Add the following code to the **Form_Load** event. In the previous How-To, we assigned the **RecordSource** using the Properties menu. In this example, the **RecordSource** for data control **Data2** is set through code. This method is chosen because it allows for some fine-tuning of the recordset. In this case, we only want unique records with one field in our recordset.

```
Private Sub Form_Load()
    Data2.RecordSource = "Select Distinct State From Publishers"
    StateCombo.ListField = "State"
    StateCombo.DataField = "State"
    StateCombo.BoundColumn = "State"

    Data2.Refresh
End Sub
```

5. Add the following code to the **Data1_Validate** event. This code checks for two conditions: the company name is not blank, and the entry for the state is two letters. The **CancelUpdate** variable is used to signal that something is wrong and the update to the recordset should not be allowed to proceed.

```
Private Sub Data1_Validate(Action As Integer, Save As Integer)
    Dim flen As Integer
    Dim CancelUpdate As Boolean

    If Company.Text = "" Then
        MsgBox "Please enter a Company Name"

        'Indicates the data has not changed
        Company.DataChanged = False

        CancelUpdate = True
    End If

    If StateCombo.DataChanged Then
        flen = Len(StateCombo.Text)
        If flen <> 2 Then
            MsgBox "Please Use the 2 Letter State Abbreviation"
            'Indicates the data has not changed
            StateCombo.DataChanged = False

            'Set the focus to the offending field
            StateCombo.SetFocus

            'Override the new text
            StateCombo.Text = Data1.Recordset.Fields("State")
        End If
    End If

    If CancelUpdate Then
        ' Cancel the changes
        Action = vbDataActionCancel
    End If
End Sub
```

6. Add the following code to the **Add_Click** subroutine. One field of the Publisher table is not shown on the form, **PubID**. This field should always be a unique number so that the following code finds the largest ID currently in the table and adds one to it for use as the ID for the new record. After the **AddNew** method is called, the new ID is placed into the **PubID** field. The rest of the values for the table are entered using the edit fields on the form.

```
Private Sub Add_Click()
    Dim NewID As Integer

    ' Determine the highest PubID and generate the next one
    Data1.Recordset.Sort = "PubID"
    Data1.Recordset.MoveLast
    NewID = Data1.Recordset.Fields("PubID") + 1

    ' Add a new record to the recordset
    ' AddNew sets the fields of the record to their default
    ' values or if no defaults exist - NULL
    Data1.Recordset.AddNew
    Data1.Recordset.Fields("PubID") = NewID
End Sub
```

7. Add the following code to the **Delete_Click** subroutine. The **MsgBox** presents the user with the option to continue or dismiss the delete operation. When a record is deleted, the current record pointer is undefined, and the current record pointer should be moved to a valid record. The **MovePrevious** method is used to move the record pointer. The code checks to make sure that the record that was just deleted was not the first record. If it was the first record, then the **BOF** property is **True**, and the **MoveFirst** method is used to reset the current record pointer to the new first record.

```
Private Sub Delete_Click()
    On Error GoTo delErr

    Dim question As String
    Dim answer As VbMsgBoxResult

    question = "Do you want to delete the entry for " + _
        Company.Text

    answer = MsgBox(question, vbQuestion & vbYesNo, _
            App.ProductName)
    If answer = vbYes Then
        ' The delete method deletes the current record
        Data1.Recordset.Delete

        'After a delete the current record is undefined.
        'Move to a valid record.
        Data1.Recordset.MovePrevious

        'If the first record was the one deleted reposition
```

```
                     'the current record to the new first record
                     If Data1.Recordset.BOF Then Data1.Recordset.MoveFirst
                 End If
                 Exit Sub

             delErr:
                 MsgBox Err.Description, vbCritical, "Delete Error"
             End Sub
```

8. Add the following code to the **Save_Click** subroutine. The **Update** method saves the current buffer to the recordset. The default mode of **Update** is to write the data to disk immediately; however, the **Update** method takes an argument that enables you to change when the data is saved. The **EditMode** property indicates the state of editing for the data control and may have one of three values: **dbEditAdd**, **dbEditInProgress**, or **dbEditNone**. The **EditMode** property is equal to **dbEditAdd** when the **AddNew** method has been used to create a new record that has not yet been saved.

```
Private Sub Save_Click()
    If Data1.EditMode = dbEditAdd Then
        ' Save the current record
        ' The default for update is no cache - write to disk now.
        Data1.Recordset.Update
    Else
        Data1.Recordset.Move 0
    End If
End Sub
```

9. Add the following code to the **Undo_Click** subroutine. The **CancelUpdate** method discards changes made during **AddNew** or **Edit**. When an **AddNew** is canceled, the current record is undefined, and the current record pointer should be repositioned to a valid record.

```
Private Sub Undo_Click()
    If Data1.EditMode = dbEditAdd Then
        ' The CancelUpdate method discards changes resulting from
        ' AddNew or Edit
        Data1.Recordset.CancelUpdate

        'Move the current record to a valid entry
        Data1.Recordset.MoveFirst
    Else
        ' The UpdateControls method restores the values of bound
        ' controls to their original settings
        Data1.UpdateControls
    End If
End Sub
```

How It Works

This example introduced a second data control to the form. The new data control is used to construct a unique list of states from the Publishers table. The State field in the **Data2** recordset is used to fill the list of the **StateCombo** control. Note that **Data2** has its **Visible** property set to **False** because the user will not be interacting with it.

Each time an item is chosen from the **StateCombo** list, the value of **State** from **Data2** is sent to the **State** field in **Data1**. This transfer is controlled by the **BoundColumn** and **DataField** properties. The **BoundColumn** property of the **DBCombo** control indicates what field in the **RowSource** recordset is sent to a field in the **DataSource** recordset. The **DataField** property indicates what field in the **DataSource** recordset receives the incoming data.

Comments

The **DBCombo** and **DBList** controls are similar to their unbound counterparts. One thing they do not share is a **Sorted** property. If you want the data in a **DBCombo** or **DBList** control to be sorted, the sorting must be done in the recordset to which the control is bound. If the recordset represents a table, then an index can be set to specify a sort order. If the recordset is a dynaset or snapshot, then a SQL statement has to be used to specify an **Order By** clause to create a sort order.

COMPLEXITY
BEGINNING

11.3 How do I...
Handle data control errors?

COMPATIBILITY: VISUAL BASIC 4, 5, AND 6

Problem

When my program runs into an error condition, the program exits ungracefully. Is there a way that I can trap errors and report the problem to the user?

Technique

Visual Basic provides an **Err** object and an **On Error** statement that makes trapping errors in your program easy. The **Err** object has several properties that enable you to determine what error occurred and to provide a meaningful message to the user. The **On Error** statement sets up an error handling routine where program control is passed if an error occurs during the scope of that subroutine or function. If you do not set up error handling routines, an error causes the default Visual Basic error handling routine to be used. In the default routine, a message box is displayed with the error number and message and then the program terminates.

On Error

The **On Error** statement specifies or clears an error handling routine for a procedure. The **On Error** statement can take the following three forms:

- ✔ **On Error GoTo** *line*: enables the error handling routine located at *line*. The argument *line* is either a line number or a label. The *line* argument must point to a line number or label that is in the same procedure as the **On Error** statement.

- ✔ **On Error Resume Next**: passes to the statement following the statement that generated the error.

- ✔ **On Error GoTo 0**: disables any currently enabled error-handling routines in the procedure.

Error Handling Routines

Any runtime error that is not within the scope of an error handling routine causes a fatal error. The error handling routine is not a separate subroutine or function but is a section of the code within a subroutine or function that is marked with a label.

```
On Error Goto MyErrorHandlingRoutine
.
.
.
MyErrorHandlingRoutine:
.
.
    Resume Next
Exit Sub
```

Inside the error handling routine there needs to be code to process and then clear the error. You can use the **Err** object to determine what error has occurred. If the error is not serious (which you can determine by checking for specific error numbers), then the routine can just let it pass to the next statement by issuing a **Resume Next**. **Resume** is one of several statements that clear the **Err** object's properties. In serious cases, the error should be reported to the user or placed in a log file, or both.

Err Object

When a trappable error occurs, the properties of the **Err** object are filled with information specific to the error. This How-To uses the **Number** and **Description** properties of the **Err** object to report error conditions to the user. The **Number** property provides the error number associated with an error and can be used to detect specific conditions that you may want to trap. The **Description** property contains a string that describes the error and can be used to provide a user with more information about the problem.

After an error has occurred, the error handling routine should clear the `Err` object. The following statements perform this task, and one of them should be used at the end of the error handling routine: `Err.Clear`, `End`, `Resume`, `Resume line`, `Resume Next`, `Exit Function`, `Exit Property`, `Exit Sub`, or `On Error`.

Steps

Load the project ERRORS.VBP. Be sure to change the `DatabaseName` property of the data control `Data1` to point to the copy of BIBLIO.MDB located in your Visual Basic directory. Run the program, and the form shown in Figure 11.3 appears.

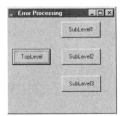

Figure 11.3 Error processing form.

Click the TopLevel button. A group of error messages is displayed (see Figure 11.4) as data access errors are generated in several different subroutines.

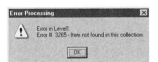

Figure 11.4 Error message.

Complete the following steps to create this project.

1. Create a new project called ERRORS.VBP.

2. Use `Form1` to create the objects and properties listed in Table 11.6. Save the form as ERROR.FRM. Also, be sure to change the `DatabaseName` property of the data control `Data1` to point to the copy of BIBLIO.MDB located in the Visual Basic directory.

Table 11.6 Objects and Properties of Error Form

OBJECT	PROPERTY	SETTING
Form	Name	Error
	Caption	Error Processing
Data	Name	Data1
	Connection	Access
	DatabaseName	C:\PROGRAM FILES\MICROSOFT VISUAL STUDIO\VB6\BIBLIO.MDB
	RecordSetType	1 - Dynaset
CommandButton	Name	Level1Button
	Caption	SubLevel1
CommandButton	Name	Level2Button
	Caption	SubLevel2
CommandButton	Name	Level3Button
	Caption	SubLevel3
CommandButton	Name	TopButton
	Caption	TopLevel

3. Add the following code to the **TopSub** subroutine. The **RecordSource** setting causes a 3078 error when the **Refresh** method is applied. Notice that there is an **Exit Sub** before the error handling routine. This is to keep the error handling routine from executing before the subroutine exits. If the **Exit Sub** is not there, the error handling routine, **toperr**, would run each time **TopSub** is called, regardless of whether any errors occurred. In fact, in this subroutine, **toperr** would run twice—once when the data control error happens and then again after the **Level1** subroutine finishes.

```
Sub TopSub()
    Dim msg As String
    On Error GoTo toperr

    'Table does not exist
    'When the Refresh method is used an error will occur
    Data1.RecordSource = "NewTable"
    Data1.Refresh

    Level1

    Exit Sub
toperr:
    ErrorMessage ("TopSub")
    Resume Next
End Sub
```

4. Add the following code to the **Level1** subroutine. Trying to access the nonexistent field generates error number 3265.

```
Sub Level1()
    Dim msg As String
    On Error GoTo lev1err

    Data1.RecordSource = "Publishers"
    Data1.Refresh

    ' Field does not exist in table
    msg = Data1.Recordset![Owner]

    Level2
    Level3

    Exit Sub
lev1err:
    ErrorMessage ("Level1")
    Resume Next
End Sub
```

5. Add the following code to the **Level2** subroutine. The assignment of a wrong datatype to a recordset generates error number 3421. Because there is no **On Error** statement, the subroutine has to pick up an error handling routine from the scope of another subroutine or the program terminates due to an untrapped error.

```
Sub Level2()

    Data1.RecordSource = "Publishers"
    Data1.Refresh

    ' Wrong DataType; PubID is an Integer
    Data1.Recordset![PubID] = "town"

    Level3
End Sub
```

6. Add the following code to the **Level3** subroutine. The illegal syntax of the **RecordSource** generates error number 3131.

```
Sub Level3()
    Dim msg As String
    On Error GoTo lev3err

    ' Syntax error; Order By is two words
    Data1.RecordSource = "Select PubID, [Company Name] From _
                    Publishers _
                    OrderBy PubID"
    Data1.Refresh

    Exit Sub
lev3err:
    ErrorMessage ("Level3")
    Resume Next
End Sub
```

7. Add the following code to the **ErrorMessage** subroutine. All the error handling routines in this program call this subroutine to construct an error message and display it.

```
Sub ErrorMessage(Location As String)
    Dim errMsg As String

    errMsg = "Error in " + Location + vbCr

    ' Give extra message if file error
    If Err.Number > 51 And Err.Number < 68 Then
        errMsg = errMsg + "File Error Detected" + vbCr
    End If

    errMsg = errMsg + "Error # " + _
        Str$(Err.Number) + " - " + Err.Description

    MsgBox errMsg, vbExclamation, "Error Processing"
End Sub
```

8. Add the following code to the **Level1Button_Click** subroutine.

```
Private Sub Level1Button_Click()
    Level1
End Sub
```

9. Add the following code to the **Level2Button_Click** subroutine. The **print** statement in this code generates error number 52 because no file has been opened.

```
Private Sub Level2Button_Click()
    On Error GoTo Button2

    Level2

    Print #1, "Test Message"

    Exit Sub
Button2:
    ErrorMessage ("Button2")
    Resume Next
End Sub
```

10. Add the following code to the **Level3Button_Click** subroutine.

```
Private Sub Level3Button_Click()
    Level3
End Sub
```

11. Add the following code to the **TopButton_Click** subroutine.

```
Private Sub TopButton_Click()
    TopSub
End Sub
```

How It Works

When an error handler is enabled, it has a scope of the procedure that it resides in. If a procedure with an error handler calls another procedure with an error handler, any error that happens in the second procedure is handled by the error handler of the second procedure. If the second procedure does not have an error handler, then the error handler of the first procedure picks up any errors from the second procedure.

The program for this How-To shows an example of both of these cases. Subroutine `TopSub` has an error handler called `toperr`. `TopSub` calls the subroutine `Level1`, which has its own error handler, `lev1err`. If an error occurs in subroutine `Level1`, the `lev1err` error handler deals with it.

Now for the second case. Subroutine `Level1` calls subroutine `Level2`. `Level2` does not have an error handler defined. If an error occurs in `Level2`, the error handler for `Level1` deals with it. If `Level2` is called from a procedure that does not have an error handler defined and an error occurs, the default error handling for Visual Basic takes over, issuing a message and terminating the program.

If the error has to pass back to a calling procedure, the error occurred. Take a look at the `Level1` subroutine. It calls subroutines `Level2` and `Level3`. `Level2` also calls `Level3`, so you might think that when `Level1` is invoked `Level3` is called twice.

Try selecting the button labeled `SubLevel1` on the program for this How-To. You only see one `Level3` message. This is because in `Level2` the error occurs before the `Level3` call is made. When the error in `Level2` occurs, control passes back to `Level1`, and the rest of the code in `Level2` is never executed. The `Resume Next` in `Level1` passes control to the `Level3` call because it is the next statement to follow the call to `Level2` where the error originated.

Comments

Error handling should be an important part of every program. A Visual Basic program should use the `Err` object to provide meaningful error messages to the user. If you believe that you will encounter specific types of error conditions, check for these error numbers in your error handling routines. This gives you an opportunity to provide additional information to a user about the number and description of the error.

Data Access Objects

In How-Tos 11.1, 11.2, and 11.3, the data control was examined. The data control is an easy-to-use method for accessing information in a database. The next two How-To topics examine how to use Data Access Objects (DAO) to access some of the same information. DAO is not really any harder to use than data controls, and it allows you to perform more robust operations. Each method has its pros and cons, and many applications can use both methods to access data.

When using a data control, much of the database access occurs in the background and is hidden from the user. Before getting into this topic, you need to take a quick look at what occurs in the background. In DAO, the Microsoft Jet database engine is represented by the **DBEngine** object. This object is available to you after adding one of the Microsoft DAO X.X Object Library references to your project. The **DBEngine** object consists of three collections as well as a set of properties and methods. The three collections are **Workspaces**, **Errors**, and **Properties**. The **Workspace** collection is the only **DBEngine** collection used in this chapter.

Each **Workspace** object is used to define a database session. The **Name**, **UserName**, and **Type** properties of the **Workspace** are used to establish a particular session. The scope of a session can contain the opening and closing of multiple databases as well as nested transactions. The default **Workspace** for the **DBEngine** object is **Workspace(0)**. This **Workspace** always exists and does not have to be created. The default properties for **Name** and **UserName** for **Workspace(0)** are "#Default Workspace#" and "Admin". To create a new **Workspace**, use the **CreateWorkspace** method of the **DBEngine** object.

To open a database, the **OpenDatabase** method of the **Workspace** is used. The **OpenDatabase** method requires at least one argument and can have as many as four. The first argument is the name of the database to be opened and is a required argument. The first argument to **OpenDatabase** is the only one used in this chapter. The three optional arguments control the privileges and access of the database. If you omit these arguments, the database is opened in shared mode with read/write access. One or more databases can be open for an existing **Workspace** object. Each database that is opened for a **Workspace** object is added to that **Workspace**'s **Database** collection.

After a database is opened with the **OpenDatabase** method, you can get to the records stored in the database. This is accomplished by opening a recordset. The **Database** object has a method called **OpenRecordset** that is used to perform this task. The **OpenRecordset** method allows five different types of recordsets to be created. The type of recordset created can be controlled by using the following Microsoft Visual Basic constants as an argument to **OpenRecordset**:

✔ *dbOpenTable*: Opens a table-type recordset. This type of recordset is used to open a single table in the database.

✔ *dbOpenDynamic*: Opens a dynamic-type recordset. This can only be used with **ODBCDirect** workspaces. This recordset is like the dynaset recordset, but data is dynamically updated as changes are made to the underlying tables.

✔ *dbOpenDynaset*: Opens a dynaset-type recordset. The dynaset-type recordset consists of fields from one or more tables and is updatable, allowing you to use it to manipulate the underlying table.

✔ *dbOpenSnapshot*: Opens a snapshot-type recordset. The snapshot-type recordset is a static set of records. If the underlying data is changed, the snapshot does not reflect it. Like the dynaset recordset, it can be made up of data from multiple tables.

✔ *dbOpenForwardOnly*: Opens a forward-only type recordset. The forward-only type recordset is just like the snapshot recordset except that you can only move forward through the resulting recordset. In situations where only one pass is to be made through the recordset, this method may improve performance.

If you don't specify one of the types in the list, the `OpenRecordset` creates a table-type recordset if possible. If you specify a query as the source to open, then the default is a dynaset-type recordset. The forward-only type of recordset is the default when working with `ODBCDirect` workspaces.

COMPLEXITY
BEGINNING

11.4 How do I...
Add and delete records using data access objects?

COMPATIBILITY: VISUAL BASIC 4, 5, AND 6

Problem

I know how to present existing records to my users for editing with bound controls, but how do I allow them to add new records or delete current records when using DAO?

Technique

The mechanism for adding records to a data access object's recordset is the `AddNew` method, which creates a new record in the recordset. The `AddNew` method initializes the fields with their default values, as determined by the table definition for the table being accessed. If no default values are defined, the fields are set to `Null`. The new record is not saved to the database until the `Update` method is called. The position of the new record in the recordset is determined by what type of `RecordSet` was defined. In dynaset recordsets, new records are added to the end of the recordset. In table recordsets, new records are added to their proper sort order if the `Index` property has been set. Otherwise, they are added to the end of the recordset.

The mechanism for deleting records from a data access object's recordset is the `Delete` method, which removes the current record from the recordset. Even though the record is now inaccessible, it remains the current record. You must move the current record pointer to a valid record. After the record pointer has been moved to a valid record, the deleted record is no longer capable of being made the current record. Trying to access a deleted record generates an error.

Steps

Load the project ADDDEL.VBP. Be sure to change the database name used in the OpenDatabase method to point to the copy of BIBLIO.MDB located in your Visual Basic directory. Run the program, and the form in Figure 11.5 appears.

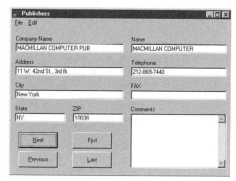

Figure 11.5 Browse form.

Choose File, Add from the menu. Enter appropriate values in the data fields. Click the Last button, and your record is displayed. Choose File, Delete from the menu. Click the Yes button on the confirmation dialog box, and your record is deleted.

To create this project, complete the following steps.

1. Create a new project called ADDDEL.VBP.

2. Add a reference to the Microsoft DAO 3.51 Object Library to your project. This library can be added by choosing Project, References from the menu.

3. Use Form1 to create the objects and properties listed in Table 11.7. Save the form as ADD_DEL.FRM.

Table 11.7 Object and Properties of Validate Form

OBJECT	PROPERTY	SETTING
Form	Name	Add_Del
	Caption	Publishers
CommandButton	Name	FirstRecord
	Caption	&First
CommandButton	Name	LastRecord
	Caption	&Last

continued on next page

continued from previous page

OBJECT	PROPERTY	SETTING
CommandButton	Name	NextRecord
	Caption	&Next
CommandButton	Name	PreviousRecord
	Caption	&Previous
TextBox	Name	Address
	Text	""
TextBox	Name	City
	Text	""
TextBox	Name	Comments
	MultiLine	True
	ScrollBars	2 - Vertical
TextBox	Name	Company
	Text	""
TextBox	Name	FAX
	Text	""
TextBox	Name	PubName
	Text	""
TextBox	Name	State
	Text	""
TextBox	Name	Telephone
	Text	""
TextBox	Name	ZIP
	Text	""
Label	Name	Label1
	Caption	Company Name
Label	Name	Label2
	Caption	Name
Label	Name	Label3
	Caption	Address
Label	Name	Label4
	Caption	City
Label	Name	Label5
	Caption	State
Label	Name	Label6
	Caption	ZIP
Label	Name	Label7
	Caption	Telephone

OBJECT	PROPERTY	SETTING
Label	Name	Label8
	Caption	FAX
Label	Name	Label9
	Caption	Comments

4. Use the Visual Basic Menu Editor to create the entries in Table 11.8.

Table 11.8 Menu Specifications for Add_Del.FRM

CAPTION	NAME
&File	File
·&Add	Add
-&Delete	Delete
-&Save	Save
&Edit	Edit
-&Undo	Undo

5. Add the following code to the General Declarations section of form Add_Del. The Option Explicit statement causes Visual Basic to require that all variables be explicitly defined. This helps eliminate errors because of misspelled variables. This section defines four variables that are used in several procedures.

```
Option Explicit

Dim db As Database
Dim pubTable As Recordset
Dim FieldsModified As Boolean
Dim AddingRecord As Boolean
```

6. Add the following code to the Load event of the Add_Del form. The Load event opens the database and a table-type recordset for the Publishers table. Be sure to change the database name used in the OpenDatabase method to point to the copy of BIBLIO.MDB located in your Visual Basic directory.

```
Private Sub Form_Load()
    On Error GoTo loadErr

    ' Open Database
    Set db = Workspaces(0).OpenDatabase("C:\PROGRAM _
                    FILES\MICROSOFT _
                    VISUAL STUDIO\VB6\BIBLIO.MDB")

    ' Open Table
```

continued on next page

continued from previous page

```
        Set pubTable = db.OpenRecordset("Publishers", dbOpenTable)

        ' If there are records in the table show the first one
        If Not pubTable.EOF Then UpdateFields

        Exit Sub

loadErr:
    ErrorMessage ("Load")
    Exit Sub
End Sub
```

7. Add the following code to the appropriate **Change** events for the text boxes. The **Change** event for a text box is invoked anytime the contents of the text box changes. The **FieldsModified** variable indicates that a field has been changed and a save might need to be performed on the record before moving to another one.

```
Private Sub Address_Change()
    ' The user has changed this field.
    FieldsModified = True
End Sub

Private Sub City_Change()
    ' The user has changed this field.
    FieldsModified = True
End Sub

Private Sub Comments_Change()
    ' The user has changed this field.
    FieldsModified = True
End Sub

Private Sub Company_Change()
    ' The user has changed this field.
    FieldsModified = True
End Sub

Private Sub FAX_Change()
    ' The user has changed this field.
    FieldsModified = True
End Sub

Private Sub PubName_Change()
    ' The user has changed this field.
    FieldsModified = True
End Sub

Private Sub State_Change()
    ' The user has changed this field.
    FieldsModified = True
End Sub

Private Sub Telephone_Change()
    ' The user has changed this field.
```

```
        FieldsModified = True
    End Sub

    Private Sub ZIP_Change()
        ' The user has changed this field.
        FieldsModified = True
    End Sub
```

8. Add the following code to the **Click** event of the **FirstRecord** button. This code emulates the first button on a data control by using the **MoveFirst** method. The **FieldsModified** variable is used to signal that data has changed and the user should be notified.

```
Private Sub FirstRecord_Click()
    On Error GoTo firstRec

    ' If any fields have been modified
    ' call this function to check on saving
    ' the changes
    If FieldsModified Then CheckToSave

    ' Move to the first record in the recordset
    pubTable.MoveFirst

    UpdateFields

    Exit Sub

firstRec:
    ErrorMessage ("Going To First Record")
    Exit Sub
End Sub
```

9. Add the following code to the **Click** event of the **LastRecord** button. This code emulates the last button on a data control by using the **MoveLast** method. The **FieldsModified** variable is used to signal that data has changed and the user should be notified.

```
Private Sub LastRecord_Click()
    On Error GoTo lastRec

    If FieldsModified Then CheckToSave

    'Move to the last record in the recordset
    pubTable.MoveLast

    UpdateFields

    Exit Sub

lastRec:
    ErrorMessage ("Going To Last Record")
    Exit Sub
End Sub
```

10. Add the following code to the **Click** event of the **NextRecord** button. This code emulates the third button on a data control by using the **MoveNext** method. If the current record is the last record, then the **MoveNext** method would try to move the record pointer past the last record. To keep this from happening, check the **EOF** property. If the **MoveNext** caused the record pointer to be past the end of the recordset, the **EOF** property is **True**, and you must use the **MoveLast** method to reposition the record pointer to the last record.

```
Private Sub NextRecord_Click()
    On Error GoTo nxtRec

    If FieldsModified Then CheckToSave

    ' Move to the next record in the recordset
    pubTable.MoveNext

    'If MoveNext move past the last record
    'set the pointer back to the last record
    If pubTable.EOF Then pubTable.MoveLast

    UpdateFields

    Exit Sub

nxtRec:
    ErrorMessage ("Going To Next Record")
    Exit Sub
End Sub
```

11. Add the following code to the **Click** event of the **PreviousRecord** button. This code emulates the second button on a data control by using the **MovePrevious** method. If the current record is the first record, then the **MovePrevious** tries to move the record pointer before the first record. To keep this from happening check the **BOF** property. If the **MovePrevious** caused the record pointer to move past the beginning of the recordset, the **BOF** property is **True**, and you must use the **MoveFirst** method to reposition the record pointer to the first record.

```
Private Sub PreviousRecord_Click()
    On Error GoTo prvRec

    If FieldsModified Then CheckToSave

    ' Move to the previous record in the recordset
    pubTable.MovePrevious

    'If MoveNext move past the first record
    'set the pointer back to the first record
    If pubTable.BOF Then pubTable.MoveFirst

    UpdateFields
```

```
        Exit Sub

prvRec:
    ErrorMessage ("Going To Previous Record")
    Exit Sub
End Sub
```

12. Create the `UpdateFields` subroutine using the following code. This code is used to change the values of the text boxes when a new record becomes current.

```
Sub UpdateFields()
    On Error GoTo fieldErr

If IsNull(pubTable![company Name]) Then
        Company = ""
    Else
        Company = pubTable![company Name]
    End If

    If IsNull(pubTable!Name) Then
        PubName = ""
    Else
        PubName = pubTable!Name
    End If

    If IsNull(pubTable!Address) Then
        Address = ""
    Else
        Address = pubTable!Address
    End If

    If IsNull(pubTable!City) Then
        City = ""
    Else
        City = pubTable!City
    End If

    If IsNull(pubTable!State) Then
        State = ""
    Else
        State = pubTable!State
    End If

    If IsNull(pubTable!ZIP) Then
        ZIP = ""
    Else
        ZIP = pubTable!ZIP
    End If

    If IsNull(pubTable!Telephone) Then
        Telephone = ""
    Else
        Telephone = pubTable!Telephone
    End If
```

continued on next page

continued from previous page

```
            If IsNull(pubTable!FAX) Then
                FAX = ""
            Else
                FAX = pubTable!FAX
            End If

            If IsNull(pubTable!Comments) Then
                Comments = ""
            Else
                Comments = pubTable!Comments
            End If

            FieldsModified = False

            Exit Sub

    fieldErr:
        ErrorMessage ("Updating Edit Boxes")
        Exit Sub
    End Sub
```

13. Add the following code to the **Unload** event of the **Add_Del** form. When the program is finished, close the database and the recordset.

```
Private Sub Form_Unload(Cancel As Integer)
    ' Close the Recordset
    pubTable.Close

    ' Close the database
    db.Close
End Sub
```

14. Create the **UpdateRecordset** subroutine using the following code. This subroutine checks to see whether the current operation is an **Add** record. If so, there is no need to use the **Edit** method to enable the record for changes. The fields of the record are then updated with the values from the text boxes. The **Update** method is used to save the data to the record. After the update, the **AddingRecord** and **FieldsModified** variables are reset.

```
Sub UpdateRecordSet()
    On Error GoTo updRec

    ' If the data does not check out don't update the recordset
    If Not DataOK Then Exit Sub

    ' Enable editing of the record if it already exists
    If Not AddingRecord Then pubTable.Edit

    'The fields of the Publisher table were not created to allow
    'zero length strings.
    If Company = "" Then pubTable![company Name] = Null Else _
                    pubTable! _
                    [company Name] = Company
    If PubName = "" Then pubTable!Name = Null Else pubTable!Name = _
                    PubName
```

```
        If Address = "" Then pubTable!Address = Null Else pubTable! _
                        Address = Address
        If City = "" Then pubTable!City = Null Else pubTable!City = _
                        City
        If State = "" Then pubTable!State = Null Else pubTable!State = _
                        State
        If ZIP = "" Then pubTable!ZIP = Null Else pubTable!ZIP = ZIP
        If Telephone = "" Then pubTable!Telephone = Null Else _
                        pubTable! _
                        Telephone = Telephone
        If FAX = "" Then pubTable!FAX = Null Else pubTable!FAX = FAX
        If Comments = "" Then pubTable!Comments = Null Else pubTable! _
                        Comments = Comments

        'Update the record
        pubTable.Update

        ' Reset Checks
        If AddingRecord Then AddingRecord = False
        If FieldsModified Then FieldsModified = False

        Exit Sub

updRec:
        ErrorMessage ("Updating Record")
        Exit Sub
End Sub
```

15. Create the **CheckToSave** subroutine using the following code. This subroutine presents the user with a message box to see whether he or she wants to save the current record.

```
Sub CheckToSave()

    Dim notice As String
    Dim answer As VbMsgBoxResult

    notice = "The current data has been changed. Do you wish to _
    save it?"

    answer = MsgBox(notice, vbYesNo, "Publisher")
    If answer = vbYes Then UpdateRecordSet

End Sub
```

16. Create the **DataOK** function using the following code. This function is used in this program to emulate the functionality of the **Validate** event in a data control. The function returns **True** if no problems are flagged and **False** if a problem is detected. This routine checks for two conditions: A value is supplied for company name, and the state entry is two characters in length.

```
Function DataOK() As Boolean
    On Error GoTo valErr
```

continued on next page

continued from previous page

```
            Dim flen As Integer

            If Company.Text = "" Then
                MsgBox "Please enter a Company Name"

                'Indicates that the data did not check out
                DataOK = False
            End If

            flen = Len(State.Text)
            If flen <> 2 Then
                MsgBox "Please Use the 2 Letter State Abbreviation"
                    'Indicates the data has not changed
                        State.DataChanged = False

                'Set the focus to the offending field
                State.SetFocus

                'Override the new text
                If IsNull(pubTable!State) Then State = " " Else State = _
                            pubTable!State
            End If

            Exit Function

    valErr:
        ErrorMessage ("Validating Data")
        Resume Next
    End Function
```

17. Add the following code to the **Add_Click** subroutine. The **AddNew** method is used to create a new record buffer. One field of the Publisher table is not shown on the form, **PubID**. This field should always be a unique number so that the code finds the largest ID currently in the table and adds one to it for use as the ID for the new record. The **AddingRecord** and **FieldsModified** flags are set to **True** so that other functions can tell what state the program is currently in.

```
Private Sub Add_Click()
    On Error GoTo addErr

    Dim idSql As String
    Dim idSet As Recordset
    Dim NewID As Integer

    pubTable.AddNew

    ' Reset the TextBoxes
    Company = ""
    PubName = ""
    Address = ""
    City = ""
    Address = ""
    State = ""
    ZIP = ""
    Telephone = ""
```

```
        FAX = ""
        Comments = ""

        idSql = "Select max(PubID) as MaxID from Publishers"
        Set idSet = db.OpenRecordset(idSql, dbOpenSnapshot)

        ' Determine the highest PubID and generate the next one
        If idSet.EOF Then NewID = 1 Else NewID = idSet!MaxID + 1
        pubTable!PubID = NewID

        AddingRecord = True
        FieldsModified = True

        Exit Sub
    addErr:
        ErrorMessage ("Adding Record")
        Exit Sub
    End Sub
```

18. Add the following code to the **Delete_Click** subroutine. If the **Delete** event is fired during the process of adding a record, then the fields on the form are blanked out, and the **AddNew** is canceled with the **CancelUpdate** method. If the user is not in the process of adding a record, then this code prompts him or her to find out whether the current record should be deleted. If so, the **Delete** method deletes the current record and then moves the current record pointer to another record.

```
Private Sub Delete_Click()
    On Error GoTo delErr

    Dim question As String
    Dim movePointer As Boolean
    Dim answer As VbMsgBoxResult

    movePointer = False

    ' If a new record has not been saved blank the fields
    ' and cancel the AddNew
    If AddingRecord Then
        Company = ""
        PubName = ""
        Address = ""
        City = ""
        Address = ""
        State = ""
        ZIP = ""
        Telephone = ""
        FAX = ""
        Comments = ""

        ' Cancel the AddNew
        pubTable.CancelUpdate

        ' No longer adding a new record
        AddingRecord = False
```

continued on next page

continued from previous page

```
            FieldsModified = False

            movePointer = True
        Else
            question = "Do you want to delete the entry for " + _
                Company.Text

            answer = MsgBox(question, vbQuestion & vbYesNo, _
                    "Publishers")
            If answer = vbYes Then
                ' The delete method deletes the current record
                ' Delete the record
                pubTable.Delete

                movePointer = True
            Else
                movePointer = False
            End If
        End If

        ' Move to a valid data entry
        If movePointer Then PreviousRecord_Click

        Exit Sub

    delErr:
        ErrorMessage ("Deleting Record")
        Exit Sub
    End Sub
```

19. Add the following code to the **Save_Click** subroutine. The
UpdateRecordset subroutine updates the current record with the data on
the form.

```
Private Sub Save_Click()
    ' Save any changes
    UpdateRecordSet
End Sub
```

20. Add the following code to the **Undo_Click** subroutine. If any changes have
been made, call the **UpdateFields** procedure to refresh the form's fields.

```
Private Sub Undo_Click()
    'If a change has been made refresh the fields
    If FieldsModified Then UpdateFields
End Sub
```

21. Create the **ErrorMessages** subroutine using the following code. This
procedure is used to present all the error messages to the user.

```
Sub ErrorMessage(Location As String)
    Dim errMsg As String

    errMsg = "Error in " + Location + vbCr
```

```
errMsg = errMsg + "Error # " + _
    Str$(Err.Number) + " - " + Err.Description

MsgBox errMsg, vbExclamation, "Error Processing"
End Sub
```

How It Works

Adding records to the recordset of a data access object is accomplished by using the `AddNew` method, which creates a new record buffer. After the user has entered the information into the controls on the dialog box, the information is transferred to the record buffer and then saved to the recordset by means of the `Update` method.

The recordset's `Delete` method is used to remove the current record from the recordset. If a current record is not defined, an error occurs when `Delete` is used. The `Delete` method leaves the current record undefined, so the program needs to move the current record pointer to a valid record.

Comments

If the user clicks the Add button and then exits this application before a save is done, the data for the new record is lost. Code could be added to the `QueryUnload` event of the form to check for such occurrences and prompt the user to save the record before the program exits.

COMPLEXITY
BEGINNING

11.5 How do I...
Find records using index values with data access objects?

COMPATIBILITY: VISUAL BASIC 4, 5, AND 6

Problem

I understand that using indexes can make searches faster. How do I use index fields to find data if I'm using DAO?

Technique

When a database is created, one or more fields in a table are usually indexed. An index on a field makes it easy and fast to find a matching entry in that field. If you open a table-type recordset, the `Seek` method can be used to find a record based on the current index. The current index is set by using the `Index` property. The combination of `Index` and `Seek` provides a fast way of finding records in indexed tables. Setting the `Index` property and using the `Seek` method to find a record only works on table-type recordsets.

Steps

Load the project USEINDEX.VBP. Be sure to change the database name used in the **OpenDatabase** method to point to the copy of BIBLIO.MDB located in your Visual Basic directory. Run the program, and the form in Figure 11.6 appears.

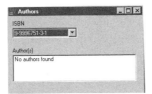

Figure 11.6 Index form.

Select an ISBN number from the combo box. The authors for that book appear in the list box. Complete the following steps to create this project.

1. Create a new project called USEINDEX.VBP.

2. Add a reference to the Microsoft DAO 3.51 Object Library to your project.

3. Use **Form1** to create the objects and properties listed in Table 11.9. Save the form as INDEX.FRM.

Table 11.9 Objects and Properties of Index Form

OBJECT	PROPERTY	SETTING
Form	Name	Index
	Caption	Authors
	StartUpPosition	2 - CenterScreen
ListBox	Name	authorList
ComboBox	Name	isbnList
	Style	2 - Dropdown List
Label	Name	Label1
	Caption	ISBN
Label	Name	Label2
	Caption	Author(s)

4. Add the following entries to the General Declarations section. The **Option Explicit** statement causes Visual Basic to require that all variables be explicitly defined. This helps eliminate errors due to variables that have been misspelled. The variables are used in several procedures.

```
Option Explicit
```

```
Dim db As Database
Dim tAuthor As Recordset
Dim author As Recordset
```

5. Place the following code in the **Load** event of the Index form. Be sure to change the database name used in the **OpenDatabase** method to point to the copy of BIBLIO.MDB located in your Visual Basic directory. After opening the database, three recordsets are opened. The first recordset is used to fill the combo box with a list of ISBN numbers taken from the Titles table. The next two recordsets are not directly used in this procedure but do have their **Index** property set for use in the next procedure.

```
Private Sub Form_Load()
    Dim title As Recordset

    On Error GoTo indexError

    ' Open the database
    Set db = Workspaces(0).OpenDatabase("C:\PROGRAM _
                        FILES\MICROSOFT _
                        VISUAL STUDIO\VB6\BIBLIO.MDB")

    ' Open the recordset
    Set title = db.OpenRecordset("Titles", dbOpenTable)

    ' Fill the combo box
    Do While Not title.EOF
        isbnList.AddItem title!ISBN
        title.MoveNext
    Loop

    ' Close the recordset
    title.Close

    ' Open the first recordset and set its index
    Set tAuthor = db.OpenRecordset("Title Author", dbOpenTable)
    tAuthor.index = "ISBN"

    ' Open the second recordset and set its index
    Set author = db.OpenRecordset("Authors", dbOpenTable)
    author.index = "PrimaryKey"

    Exit Sub
indexError:
    MsgBox Err.Description, vbExclamation, "Index"
    Exit Sub
End Sub
```

6. Fill in the details of the **Click** event for the control **isbnList** with the following code. When an ISBN number is selected from the list, it is used as an argument to the **Seek** method. If a match is found in the Title Author table, the author ID field, **Au_ID**, is used as an argument to another **Seek** to try to find the author in the Authors table. Because there might be more than one author, the author search needs to be performed in a loop. Notice that the result of the **Seek** operation is determined by examining the **NoMatch** property.

```
Private Sub isbnList_Click()
    On Error GoTo clkErr

    ' Clear the list
    authorList.Clear

    ' Search for the selected ISBN
    tAuthor.Seek "=", isbnList.Text

    If tAuthor.NoMatch Then
        ' Selected ISBN not found
        authorList.AddItem "No authors found"
    Else
        ' There may be more than one author for this book
        Do While Trim$(tAuthor!ISBN) = Trim$(isbnList.Text)
            ' Search for this Author
            author.Seek "=", tAuthor!Au_ID
            If Not author.No Match Then authorList.AddItem _
                            author!author

            ' See if there is another Author for this book
            tAuthor.MoveNext
            If tAuthor.EOF Then Exit Do
        Loop
    End If

    Exit Sub

clkErr:
    MsgBox Err.Description, vbExclamation, "Index"
    Exit Sub
End Sub
```

7. Add the following instructions to the **Unload** event of the Index form. Close the two recordsets and the database before exiting the program.

```
Private Sub Form_Unload(Cancel As Integer)
    ' Close the recordsets
    tAuthor.Close
    author.Close

    ' Close the database
    db.Close
End Sub
```

How It Works

The **Seek** method is used in this How-To to search in indexed fields. It works on the current index, so it is wise to use the **Index** property of the recordset before using the **Seek** method. The **Index** property and the **Seek** method work together to provide a fast mechanism for searching in indexed fields. This methodology can only be used on table-type recordsets.

The Seek method takes at least two arguments and can have as many as 14. The first argument is a string that defines the comparison operation to be used in the search. Examples of this argument include =, <, >, <=, and >=. Seek starts from different locations in the recordset depending on the comparison argument. If the argument is =, >, or >=, the operation starts from the beginning of the recordset as defined by the current index. If the argument is < or <=, then the operation starts from the end of the recordset as defined by the current index.

The second and following arguments are values for which you want to search. If the index is only made up of one field, then only one value is needed. If the index is a multifield index, then there can be one value for each field in the index. The value arguments must be of the same type as the fields in the recordset. For example, if the index is a single field index and the field is of type text, the value used with Seek must be a string.

The result of the Seek operation can be determined by checking the value of the NoMatch property. If a match is found, that record is made the current record, and the NoMatch property is set to False. If no match is found, the value of this property is set to True, and the current record is undetermined.

Comments

To perform searches on dynaset and snapshot recordsets, you can use the following four methods: FindFirst, FindLast, FindNext, and FindPrevious. These methods are similar to their Move counterparts except that they act within the scope of a criterion, which is provided as an argument for each of the Find methods. The FindFirst or FindLast methods should be used before using the FindNext or FindPrevious methods as the later two work off a position that has already been determined by the first two.

COMPLEXITY
INTERMEDIATE

11.6 How do I...
Create a new database in code?

COMPATIBILITY: VISUAL BASIC 4, 5, AND 6

Problem

I don't have a copy of Microsoft Access, and I want to be able to create new databases with my code so that the user can have different databases to store different items. I don't want to deliver a template database. Can I create a database just using Visual Basic code?

Technique

Visual Basic provides all the functionality you need to create a new database from code. The `CreateDatabase` method enables you to create the framework for a new database. After the database is created, the `CreateTableDef` method can be used to add tables to the database. Most tables have indexes on one or more fields. The `CreateIndex` method of a `TableDef` object enables you to create indexes for the fields defined in the table definition.

Another important function is creating relationships between tables. The `CreateRelation` method of the database object enables you to create relationships between the tables defined in the `TableDef` collection. A relationship can be used to maintain referential integrity between two tables. *Referential integrity* means that a key in the secondary (or foreign) table always refers to a valid record in the primary table. The attributes of a relation can be set up to provide for cascading updates or deletes. In the case of a cascading delete, if a record is deleted in the primary table, records in the secondary table that have a matching value in the linked field are also deleted. Table 11.10 shows some of the Microsoft Visual Basic constants that can be used to define the attributes the relation can have.

Table 11.10 Attributes for `CreateRelation` Method

CONSTANT	DESCRIPTION
dbRelationUnique	A one-to-one relationship exists.
dbRelationDontEnforce	Referential integrity is not enforced.
dbRelationUpdateCascade	Updates cascade to foreign table.
dbRelationDeleteCascade	Deletes cascade to foreign table.

Steps

Load the project CREATEDB.VBP and run the program. The form in Figure 11.7 will appear.

Figure 11.7 Create Database form.

Use the three buttons to create a database, create indexes for its tables, and establish a relationship between the two tables of the database. Complete the following steps to create this project.

1. Create a new project called CREATEDB.VBP.

2. Add a reference to the Microsoft DAO 3.51 Object Library to your project.

3. Use **Form1** to create the objects and properties listed in Table 11.11. Save the form as CREDB.FRM.

Table 11.11 Objects and Properties for Create Database Form

OBJECT	PROPERTY	SETTING
Form	Name	CREDB
	Caption	Create Database
	StartUpPositon	2 - Center Screen
CommandButton	Name	cbCreateDB
	Caption	Create Database
CommandButton	Name	cbCreateIndex
	Caption	Create Index
	Enabled	False
CommandButton	Name	CreateRelation
	Caption	Create Relationship
	Enabled	False
CommandButton	Name	cbExit
	Caption	Exit
	Enabled	False

4. Add the following code to the General Declarations section of form **CreDB**.

```
Option Explicit

Dim dbNewDB As Database
```

5. Add the following code to the **cbCreateDB_Click** event. The **CreateDatabase** method does not create a database if a file already exists with that same name. The **Dir** function can be used to check for that condition.

The **CreateDatabase** method can take three arguments; two are required, and one is optional. The two required arguments are the name of the database to be created (full path may be included) and the locale. The locale might be one of the Microsoft Visual Basic constants shown in Table 11.12. The locale sets the collating order. The optional third argument defines what version of database is created and whether it is encrypted. The default if no values are supplied is a version 3.0 database that is not encrypted. The Microsoft Visual Basic constants shown in Table 11.13 may be used for the third argument.

```
Private Sub cbCreateDB_Click()
    Dim msgans As VbMsgBoxResult
    Dim tdfNewTable As TableDef
    Dim fldNewField As Field

    On Error GoTo createErr

    ' If database already exists it must be deleted before a new
    ' database with the same name can be created.
    If Dir("members.mdb") <> "" Then
        msgans = MsgBox("Database - members.mdb - already exist. _
                            Delete?", _
                            vbYesNo, "Create Database")

        If msgans = vbYes Then
            Kill ("members.mdb")
        Else
            Exit Sub
        End If
    End If

    ' Create the new database
    Set dbNewDB = CreateDatabase("Members.mdb", dbLangGeneral)

    ' Create a new table called Members
    Set tdfNewTable = dbNewDB.CreateTableDef("Members")

    ' Add fields to the Members table
    With tdfNewTable
        .Fields.Append .CreateField("Last Name", dbText, 32)
        .Fields.Append .CreateField("First Name", dbText, 32)
        .Fields.Append .CreateField("Membership ID", dbInteger)
    End With

    ' Add the Members table to the database
    dbNewDB.TableDefs.Append tdfNewTable


    ' Create a new table called Dues
    Set tdfNewTable = dbNewDB.CreateTableDef("Dues")

    ' Add fields to the Dues table
    With tdfNewTable
        .Fields.Append .CreateField("Membership ID", dbInteger)
        .Fields.Append .CreateField("Dues Paid", dbBoolean)
        .Fields.Append .CreateField("Dues Due", dbDate)
    End With

    ' Add the Dues table to the database
    dbNewDB.TableDefs.Append tdfNewTable

    cbCreateIndex.Enabled = True
```

```
        cbExit.Enabled = True

        Exit Sub

    createErr:
        ErrorMessage ("Create Database")
        Exit Sub
End Sub
```

Table 11.12 Locale Constants for `CreateDatabase`

LOCALE CONSTANT	COLLATING ORDER
`dbLangGeneral`	English, German, French, Portuguese, Italian, Modern Spanish
`dbLangArabic`	Arabic
`dbLangChineseSimplified`	Chinese Simplified
`dbLangChineseTraditional`	Chinese Traditional
`dbLangCryillic`	Russian
`dbLangCzech`	Czech
`dbLangDutch`	Dutch
`dbLangGreek`	Greek
`dbLangHebrew`	Hebrew
`dbLangHungarian`	Hungarian
`dbLangIcelandic`	Icelandic
`dbLangJapanese`	Japanese
`dbLangKorean`	Korean
`dbLangNordic`	Nordic (Jet Engine 1.0 only)
`dbLangNorwDan`	Norwegian and Danish
`dbLangPolish`	Polish
`dbLangSlovenian`	Slovenian
`dbLangSpanish`	Traditional Spanish
`dbLangSwedFin`	Swedish and Finnish
`dbLangThai`	Thai
`dbLangTurkish`	Turkish

Table 11.13 Option Constants for `CreateDatabase`

CONSTANT	DESCRIPTION
`dbEncrypt`	Encrypt the database
`dbVersion10`	Create a 1.0 Jet database
`dbVersion11`	Create a 1.1 Jet database
`dbVersion20`	Create a 2.0 Jet database
`dbVersion30`	Create a 3.0 Jet database - (3.51) compatible

After the database is created, the `CreateTableDef` method of the database object can be used to add tables to the database. After the table definition is created, the `CreateField` method of the `TableDef` object can be used to add fields to the table definition.

The `CreateField` method takes two or three arguments depending on the type field being created. The first argument is the name of the field to create. The second argument is the type of field to create. For some field types, the size of the field must also be specified. Text is an example of a field for which size can be specified. After the new fields have been added to the table definition, the table can be added to the database by using `Append` method. Table 11.14 shows the Microsoft Visual Basic constants that can be used with the `CreateField` method.

Table 11.14 Type Constants for `CreateField`

CONSTANT	TYPE
dbBigInt	Big Integer
dbBinary	Binary
dbBoolean	Boolean
dbByte	Byte
dbChar	Char
dbCurrency	Currency
dbDate	Date/Time
dbDecimal	Decimal
dbDouble	Double
dbFloat	Float
dbGUID	GUID
dbInteger	Integer
dbLong	Long
dbLongBinary	Long Binary (OLE Object)
dbMemo	Memo
dbNumeric	Numeric
dbSingle	Single
dbText	Text
dbTime	Time
dbTimeStamp	Time Stamp
dbVarBinary	VarBinary

6. Add the following code to the `cbCreateIndex_Click` event. Indexes can be used to speed up many database operations. You can create indexes for your newly created table definitions by using the `CreateIndex` method of the `TableDef` object.

In the following code, `CreateIndex` is used to create an index object named `MembershipID`. The `CreateField` method of the `Index` object is used to add table fields to the index. The `MembershipID` index has only one field, but you can create multiple field indexes. The `Primary` property is set to `True` for the Membership ID field. A `Primary` index must uniquely identify all the records in the table. The `Primary` index may consist of more than one field as long as the combination of fields provides a unique identification.

Because a `Primary` index must be unique, the `Unique` property is also set to `True`. The `Unique` property indicates that every value in this field or combination of fields must be unique. For a single field index, that means for each entry in the table that field must have a different value than any other entry for that field in the table. For a multiple field index, the combination of the fields must be different from every other combination, whereas the individual fields may have duplicate values. When all the aspects of the index have been defined, the index is added to the database by using the `Append` method.

```
Private Sub cbCreateIndex_Click()
    Dim tdfTable As TableDef
    Dim idxNewIndex As Index
    Dim fldNewField As Field

    On Error GoTo indexErr

    'Create Indexes for Table Members
    Set tdfTable = dbNewDB!members

    ' Create Index MembershipID
    Set idxNewIndex = tdfTable.CreateIndex("MembershipID")

    'Use With structure to shorten notation
    With idxNewIndex
        .Fields.Append .CreateField("Membership ID")
        .Primary = True
        .Unique = True
    End With

    ' Add Index MembershipID to Table Definition
    tdfTable.Indexes.Append idxNewIndex
```

continued on next page

continued from previous page

```
' Create Index LastName
Set idxNewIndex = tdfTable.CreateIndex("LastName")
Set fldNewField = idxNewIndex.CreateField("Last Name")
idxNewIndex.Fields.Append fldNewField

' Add Index LastName to Table Definition
tdfTable.Indexes.Append idxNewIndex

' Create Index FirstName
Set idxNewIndex = tdfTable.CreateIndex("FirstName")
Set fldNewField = idxNewIndex.CreateField("First Name")
idxNewIndex.Fields.Append fldNewField

' Add Index FirstName to Table Definition
tdfTable.Indexes.Append idxNewIndex

' Create Indexes for Table Dues
Set tdfTable = dbNewDB!dues

Set idxNewIndex = tdfTable.CreateIndex("MembershipID")

With idxNewIndex
    .Fields.Append .CreateField("Membership ID")
    .Primary = True
    .Unique = True
End With

' Add Index MembershipID to Table Definition
tdfTable.Indexes.Append idxNewIndex

cbCreateRelation.Enabled = True

Exit Sub

indexErr:
    ErrorMessage ("Creating Indexes")
    Exit Sub
End Sub
```

7. Add the following code to the **cbCreateRelation_Click** event. Another important function is the creation of relationships between tables. The **CreateRelation** method of the database object can be used to create relationships between tables in your database.

The **CreateRelation** method takes four arguments. The first argument specifies the name of the relationship being created. The second argument is the name of the primary table. This is the table that drives any updates. The third argument is the name of the foreign table. This is the table that would be on the receiving end of any updates. The fourth argument is used to set up the type of relationship that exists between the two tables.

After the **Relation** object is created, the **CreateField** method of the **Relation** object is used to indicate what field in the primary table participates in the relationship. The **ForeignName** property of the newly created field is set to indicate what field in the foreign table participates in the relationship. After these parameters have been defined, the relationship is added to the database using the **Append** method of the **Relations** collection.

```
Private Sub cbCreateRelation_Click()
    Dim relNewRelation As Relation
    Dim fldField As Field

    On Error GoTo relationErr

    ' Create relationship MembershipID
    Set relNewRelation = dbNewDB.CreateRelation("ID", "Members", _
        "Dues", _
        dbRelationUnique + dbRelationDeleteCascade)

    ' Set Index names to be used in relationship
    Set fldField = relNewRelation.CreateField("Membership ID")
    fldField.ForeignName = "Membership ID"
    relNewRelation.Fields.Append fldField

    ' Add relationship to Database
    dbNewDB.Relations.Append relNewRelation

    Exit Sub

relationErr:
    ErrorMessage ("Creating Relation")
    Exit Sub
End Sub
```

8. Add the following code to the **cbExit_Click** event. This subroutine closes the database and unloads the form.

```
Private Sub cbExit_Click()
    dbNewDB.Close
    Unload Me
End Sub
```

9. Use the following code to create the **ErrorMessage** subroutine. This subroutine is used to provide error messages for the program.

```
Sub ErrorMessage(Location As String)
    Dim errMsg As String

    errMsg = "Error in " + Location + vbCr

    errMsg = errMsg + "Error # " + _
        Str$(Err.Number) + " - " + Err.Description

    MsgBox errMsg, vbExclamation, "Error Processing"
End Sub
```

How It Works

The `CreateDatabase` method creates the foundation from which you can build a database by creating a database object. `CreateDatabase` does not create a database if a file of the same name already exists. The `Dir` and `Kill` functions can be used to detect and delete an existing file. Be sure to ask the user before proceeding with deleting the file.

After the new database is created, the `CreateTableDef` and `CreateField` methods can be used to construct table definitions. These table definitions hold the data that is entered into the database.

Many database operations can be speeded up by the use of indexes. Indexes are usually created for the fields that are searched most often. Indexes can be created by use of the `CreateIndex` method. After the `Index` object has been created, the `CreateField` method can be used to add fields to the index. Indexes can contain one or more fields. If a single field index is defined as unique, then each record in that table must contain a different value for that field. If a multiple field index is defined as unique, the fields can have duplicate values, but the combinations of the fields must always produce a different value. If you attempt to add a new record that violates the uniqueness, an error occurs.

The `CreateRelation` method can be used to establish relationships between tables. Relationships can be used to help enforce referential integrity. Referential integrity means that a key in the secondary (or foreign) table always refers to a valid record in the primary table. The `CreateField` method of the `Relation` object is used to add the name of the field in the primary table that participates in the relation. The `ForeignName` property of the `Field` object is used to indicate the name of the field in the foreign table that participates in the relation. In the previous example, a relationship is defined between the Membership ID field of the two tables, Members and Dues. The attributes of this relation are defined as unique (`dbRelationUnique`) and with cascading delete enabled (`dbRelationDeleteCascade`). The unique relation means that there is a one-to-one relationship between the records in the two tables. The cascading delete means that if a record with a Membership ID of 10 is deleted in the Members table, then the corresponding record in the Dues table is also deleted.

Comments

The techniques of this How-To enable you to provide more flexibility in your database programs. If you need to make changes to the structure of a database, you can do so without delivering a new template database and a program to move the data from the original format to the new one. Creating a database from scratch also removes the worry that your template database might be deleted or corrupted.

COMPLEXITY
BEGINNING

11.7 How do I...
Attach a table from another database?

COMPATIBILITY: VISUAL BASIC 4, 5, AND 6

Problem

Another department has a database with a table that contains information I want to access from my program. Is there a way I can use this table's information with my program's database without having to do an `OpenDatabase` on the other database every time?

Technique

You can use the `CreateTableDef` method to attach an external table from another database to your own database. The attachment information is stored in your database, and the connection is re-established each time you open your database. Even though the data is visible each time you open your database, it is still stored in the external database.

Steps

Load the project ATTACH.VBP. Be sure to change the database names used in the `OpenDatabase` methods to point to the files located in your VB6HT\CHAPTER.11 directory. When you run the program, the form in Figure 11.8 appears.

The first two columns of data are from the attached table, whereas the second two columns represent data from the original database. To create this project, complete the following steps.

1. Create a new project called ATTACH.VBP. Choose Projects, Components from the menu, and then choose Microsoft Common Controls 6.0 from the list.

2. Add a reference to the Microsoft DAO 3.51 Object Library to your project.

3. Use `Form1` to create the objects and properties listed in Table 11.15. Save the form as AttTable.FRM.

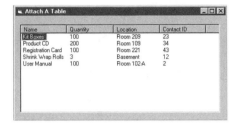

Figure 11.8 Attach form.

Table 11.15 Objects and Properties of Attach Form

OBJECT	PROPERTY	SETTING
Form	Name	AttTable
	Caption	Attach A Table
	StartUpPosition	2 - CenterScreen
ListView	Name	lvstorageList
	View	0 - lvwReport

4. Add the following code to the General Declarations section of form AttTable.

```
Option Explicit
```

5. Add the following code to the Form_Load event. Be sure to change the database names used in the OpenDatabase methods to point to the files located in your VB6HT\CHAPTER.11 directory.

The first thing to do is open the database to which you want to attach the table. The CreateTableDef method is then used to create a table definition. The name used here is used in the rest of the program to access the external data and does not have to be the same as the table name in the external database. The Connect property of the table definition is used to point to the location of the external database. The SourceTableName property is used to specify what table in the external database is to be attached to this database. After the table definition has been set up, it is added to the database with the Append method. After the table has been added to the database, it can be used in combination with the local tables. The following query pulls two fields from a local table and two fields from the external table.

```
Private Sub Form_Load()
    Dim db As Database
    Dim fpTab As TableDef
    Dim storeRs As Recordset
    Dim lstItem As ListItem
    Dim sqlStr As String
```

```
    ' Open Access database
    Set db = OpenDatabase("C:\VB6ht\chapter.11\storage.mdb")

    ' Create TableDef for Attached Table
    Set fpTab = db.CreateTableDef("BomTable")

    ' Set connection information for new table
    fpTab.Connect = ";DATABASE=c:\VB6ht\chapter.11\bom.mdb;"

    ' Table to attach from BOM database
    fpTab.SourceTableName = "INVENTORY"

    ' Add the table definition to the collection
    db.TableDefs.Append fpTab

    ' Create query to pull together the needed information
    ' from original table and new attached table
    sqlStr = "Select location.[Stock Location], " & _
        "location.[Contact ID], BomTable.Name, " & _
        "BomTable.Quantity From location, BomTable " & _
        "Where location.PARTID = BomTable.PARTID " & _
        "Order By BomTable.Name"

    ' Create headers for ListView control
    lvstorageList.ColumnHeaders.Add , , "Name"
    lvstorageList.ColumnHeaders.Add , , "Quantity"
    lvstorageList.ColumnHeaders.Add , , "Location"
    lvstorageList.ColumnHeaders.Add , , "Contact ID"

    ' Open the recordset as forward only
    Set storeRs = db.OpenRecordset(sqlStr, dbOpenForwardOnly)

    Do While Not storeRs.EOF
        ' Add a new row
        Set lstItem = lvstorageList.ListItems.Add(, , _
                    storeRs!Name)

        ' Add row items
        If Not IsNull(storeRs!quantity) Then
            lstItem.SubItems(1) = CStr(storeRs!quantity)
        End If
        If Not IsNull(storeRs![Stock Location]) Then
            lstItem.SubItems(2) = storeRs![Stock Location]
        End If
        If Not IsNull(storeRs![Contact ID]) Then
            lstItem.SubItems(3) = storeRs![Contact ID]
        End If

        storeRs.MoveNext
    Loop

    ' Remove the link to the Attached table
    db.TableDefs.Delete "BomTable"

    ' Close the database
    db.Close
End Sub
```

How It Works

External tables can be added to a local database by using the `CreateTableDef` method. The `Connect` and `SourceTableName` properties of the `TableDef` object are used to specify what external database and table are to be attached to the local database. You can access the external table as you would a local table with the following exception. You cannot open an external table as a table-type recordset. Trying to attach an external table that is already attached generates an error.

Comments

When you need to access information that someone else has already created, using an external table to work with the information may be a good solution. It is highly recommended that you use external tables to query ODBC databases because the response time is quicker than directly opening the database and performing the query.

COMPLEXITY
BEGINNING

11.8 How do I...
Compact and repair a database?

COMPATIBILITY: VISUAL BASIC 4, 5, AND 6

Problem

If the size of my database starts to grow large, not because of an increase in the number of records but because of deletions and additions, is there a way I can decrease its size? Also is there a way to repair a database that has had its indexes and fields corrupted due to things such as power outages?

Technique

Both of these situations are maintenance problems. Two utility functions provided with the Jet engine can be used to provide maintenance on a Jet database. Both are methods of the `DBEngine` object. The two methods are `CompactDatabase` and `RepairDatabase`.

When you delete a record from a Jet database, the record is marked as unavailable, but it is not removed from the physical database file. To remove the record and recover the disk space, the `CompactDatabase` method must be used. If your application is adding and deleting records on a regular basis, the size of your database can grow considerably. To recover the disk space, use the `CompactDatabase` method. The `CompactDatabase` method can only be used on Jet databases. Furthermore, any Jet database passed to the `CompactDatabase` method must not be currently opened. If the database is not a Jet database or the database is open, a runtime error is generated.

Sometimes elements of the database get corrupted. This could happen due to a failed read/write operation or a power failure. The `RepairDatabase` method can fix some of these problems but is not a cure for every problem. Be sure to make frequent backups of your database. The `RepairDatabase` method checks the system tables and all indexes. If the operation completes successfully, the database is flagged as safe and any data that could not be validated is discarded.

Steps

Load the project UTILITY.VBP and run the program. The form shown in Figure 11.9 appears.

Figure 11.9
Compact/Repair
form.

Click the Compact button and then use the common dialog box to select a database to compact. Enter the name of the compacted database to be created. Click the Repair button and use the common dialog box to select a database to repair.

Complete the following steps to create this project.

1. Create a new project called UTILITY.VBP.

2. Add a reference to the Microsoft DAO 3.51 Object Library to your project.

3. Add the Microsoft Common Dialog Control to your project by choosing Project, Components from the menu.

4. Use Form1 to create the objects and properties listed in Table 11.16. Save the form as AttTable.FRM.

Table 11.16 Objects and Properties of COMP_REP Form

OBJECT	PROPERTY	SETTING
Form	Name	COMP_REP
	Caption	Compact/Repair
	StartUpPosition	2 - CenterScreen

continued on next page

continued from previous page

OBJECT	PROPERTY	SETTING
CommandButton	Name	cbCompact
	Caption	Compact
CommandButton	Name	cbRepair
	Caption	Repair
CommonDialog	Name	cdOpenDB

5. Add the following code to the General Declarations section of form
Comp_Rep.

```
Option Explicit
```

6. Add the following code to the **cbCompact_Click** event. This subroutine
uses a common dialog box to prompt the user for the database names used
in the compact operation. It then checks to make sure that the user
entered two different names. If the names are the same, a warning is
issued. If the names are different, the **CompactDatabase** method is called
to compact the database.

```
Private Sub cbCompact_Click()
    Dim olddbname As String
    Dim newdbname As String

    On Error GoTo compErr

    ' Get Name of database to compact
    cdOpenDB.DialogTitle = "Select Database to Compact"
    cdOpenDB.CancelError = True
    cdOpenDB.Filter = "(*.mdb)¦*.mdb"
    cdOpenDB.ShowOpen

    olddbname = cdOpenDB.filename

    ' Get Name of new database
    cdOpenDB.DialogTitle = "New Database Name"
    cdOpenDB.CancelError = True
    cdOpenDB.Filter = "(*.mdb)¦*.mdb"
    cdOpenDB.ShowOpen

    newdbname = cdOpenDB.filename

    ' Check to make sure the new database name is different
    ' from the original name
    If StrComp(olddbname, newdbname, vbTextCompare) = 0 Then
        MsgBox _
           "The New Database name cannot be the same as the _
                              original Database Name.", _
           vbExclamation, "Compact Error"
        Exit Sub
    End If

    ' Compact the database
```

```
        Screen.MousePointer = 11 ' Set cursor to hourglass
        CompactDatabase olddbname, newdbname
        Screen.MousePointer = 0  ' Reset cursor

        Exit Sub

compErr:
    If Err.Number <> cdlCancel Then
        MsgBox Err.Description, vbExclamation, "Compact Error"
    End If
    Exit Sub
End Sub
```

7. Add the following code to the **cbRepair_Click** event. The same Common Dialog object used in the last subroutine is used in this one to prompt the user to enter the name of the database that needs to be repaired. Set the mouse pointer to indicate that the application is busy before calling the **RepairDatabase** method. Reset the mouse pointer when the repair is finished.

```
Private Sub cbRepair_Click()
    Dim dbname As String

    On Error GoTo repairErr

    ' Get Name of database to repair
    cdOpenDB.DialogTitle = "Select Database to Repair"
    cdOpenDB.CancelError = True
    cdOpenDB.Filter = "(*.mdb)¦*.mdb"
    cdOpenDB.ShowOpen

    dbname = cdOpenDB.filename

    ' Repair the database
    Screen.MousePointer = 11 ' Set cursor to hourglass
    RepairDatabase dbname
    Screen.MousePointer = 0  ' Reset cursor

    Exit Sub

repairErr:
    If Err.Number <> cdlCancel Then
        MsgBox Err.Description, vbExclamation, "Repair Error"
    End If
    Exit Sub
End Sub
```

How It Works

The **CompactDatabase** method removes records from the database that have been marked for deletion. In this How-To, only two arguments are used when using **CompactDatabase**: the database to compact and the name of a new compacted database.

> **WARNING**
>
> It is recommended that you always use a different name from the original when doing a compact. The reason is that the newly compacted database is deleted if the compact operation fails. If you use the same name for both the old and new database, then your data is lost. You can always rename the database to the original name if the operation is a success.

`CompactDatabase` takes two optional arguments not shown in this example. The two arguments are the same as the two optional arguments to `CreateDatabase`, locale and options. These arguments can be used to make the locale and options attributes of the new database different from the original.

The `RepairDatabase` method takes one argument, the name of the database on which to attempt a repair. Just like `CompactDatabase`, `RepairDatabase` only works on a database that is not open. The repair process may cause the database to increase in size due to items being found invalid. Any data that cannot be validated by the repair process is discarded. Therefore, it is a good idea to compact a database after the repair process is finished. If the repair operation cannot be completed, a trappable error is generated.

Comments

Even the best programs will have some mishaps. Many of them might even be out of your control (power failures, system crash, and so on). Therefore it is recommended that programs that use databases provide a set of utility functions. The two outlined in this How-To should be the minimum set. You might also want to provide a mechanism to back up the database.

COMPLEXITY
BEGINNING

11.9 How do I...
Determine how many records are in a recordset?

COMPATIBILITY: VISUAL BASIC 4, 5, AND 6

Problem

I'm having trouble determining how many records are in a recordset. How do I get an accurate count of the number of records?

Technique

The `Recordset` object has a property called `RecordCount` that returns the number of records, sort of. The value that `RecordCount` returns depends on the type of recordset that is open and how it has been used, if at all. If the recordset is a table-type recordset, then `RecordCount` returns the total number of records in the recordset. If the recordset is a dynaset, snapshot, or forward-only recordset, then the `RecordCount` property returns the number of records that have been accessed thus far. To force all of the records in the recordset to be accessed, the `MoveLast` method can be used.

Steps

Load the project RECORDCOUNT.VBP. Be sure to change the database name used in the `OpenDatabase` method to point to the copy of BIBLIO.MDB located in your Visual Basic directory. Run the program. The form shown in Figure 11.10 appears. The value of `RecordCount` is displayed for different types of recordsets and situations.

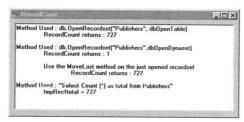

Figure 11.10 RecordCount form.

Complete the following steps to create this project.

1. Create a new project called RECORDCOUNT.VBP.

2. Add a reference to the Microsoft DAO 3.51 Object Library to your project.

3. Use `Form1` to create the objects and properties listed in Table 11.17. Save the form as COUNT.FRM.

Table 11.17 Objects and Properties for Count Form

OBJECT	PROPERTY	SETTING
Form	Name	Count
	Caption	RecordCount
TextBox	Name	RecInfo
	MultiLine	True

4. Add the following code to the **Load** event of the Count form. The
following code opens the Publishers table as both a table and dynaset-type
recordset to illustrate the differences in what the **Property RecordCount**
returns. A SQL statement is also demonstrated that determines the
number of records. Be sure to change the database name used in the
OpenDatabase method to point to the copy of BIBLIO.MDB located in
your Visual Basic directory.

```
Private Sub Form_Load()
    Dim db As Database
    Dim tmpRec As Recordset
    Dim info As String
    Dim sqlStr As String

    On Error GoTo cntError

    'Open Database
    Set db = Workspaces(0).OpenDatabase _
            ("c:\program files\devstudio\vb\biblio.mdb")

    ' Open a Table-Type Recordset
    Set tmpRec = db.OpenRecordset("Publishers", dbOpenTable)

    info = "Method Used : db.OpenRecordset(" & _
        Chr$(34) & "Publishers" & Chr$(34) & ", dbOpenTable)" & _
        vbCr & vbLf
    info = info & vbTab & "RecordCount returns : " & _
                tmpRec.RecordCount
    info = info & vbCr & vbLf & vbCr & vbLf
    tmpRec.Close

    ' Open a Dynaset-Type Recordset
    Set tmpRec = db.OpenRecordset("Publishers", dbOpenDynaset)

    info = info & "Method Used : db.OpenRecordset(" & _
        Chr$(34) & "Publishers" & Chr$(34) & ",dbOpenDynaset)" & _
        vbCr & vbLf
    info = info & vbTab & "RecordCount returns : " & _
                tmpRec.RecordCount
    info = info & vbCr & vbLf & vbCr & vbLf

    tmpRec.MoveLast
    info = info & vbTab & "Use the MoveLast method on the just _
                opened _
                        recordset" & vbCr & vbLf
    info = info & vbTab & vbTab & "RecordCount returns : " & _
                        tmpRec.RecordCount
    info = info & vbCr & vbLf & vbCr & vbLf

    tmpRec.Close

    ' Use a SQL statement with a Dynaset-type Recordset
    sqlStr = "Select Count(*) as total from Publishers"
    Set tmpRec = db.OpenRecordset(sqlStr, dbOpenDynaset)
```

```
        info = info & "Method Used : " & _
            Chr$(34) & "Select Count (*) as total from Publishers" & _
            Chr$(34) & _
            vbCr & vbLf
        info = info & vbTab & "tmpRec!total = " & tmpRec!total

        RecInfo = info

        tmpRec.Close
        db.Close

        Exit Sub
cntError:
        MsgBox Err.Description, vbExclamation, "Count"
        Exit Sub
End Sub
```

How It Works

For a table-type recordset, the documentation indicates that `RecordCount` returns an accurate count of the number of records. Some programmers take issue with its accuracy, so judge for yourself. For the other types of recordsets, `RecordCount` returns the number of records that have been accessed thus far. To make sure that all the records have been accessed, use the `MoveLast` method of the recordset. Checking the `RecordCount` property after using the `MoveLast` method ensures that all the records are reported. Another method of determining the number of records is to use the `Count` function in a SQL statement. When using the wildcard argument "*", `Count` returns the total number of records.

Comments

If you are looking for the number of records to set up a loop counter, there is an easier way. For instance if you are trying to get the number of records to do this:

```
For I = 1 to myrecset.RecordCount
.
.
    myrecset.MoveNext
Next I
```

you could use the following loop instead. It processes through the recordset until the last record has been accessed. The `While` condition is then `False`, and the loop execution ends.

```
Do While Not myrecset.EOF
.
.
    myrecset.MoveNext
Loop
```

11.10 How do I...
Determine other information about a table?

COMPATIBILITY: VISUAL BASIC 4, 5, AND 6

Problem

I want to obtain information about tables in my database. Can I find out how many records exist or when the table was created or last updated?

Technique

To find out information about tables in a database, you should check the **TableDefs** collection. This collection contains all the table definitions for a Jet database. This includes systems tables, which usually are named Msys*.

Because the structure of these tables is not documented and is not guaranteed not to change from one version of Microsoft Access to the next, it is recommended that you do not try to access them directly in your programs. In most cases, all the information you need to obtain about your tables is contained in the **TableDef** object for that table.

Steps

Load the project TABLEINFO.VBP. Run the program and use the common dialog box to select a database (see Figure 11.11).

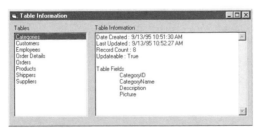

Figure 11.11 Table Information.

Select one of the table names from the Tables list. Information about the table is displayed in the text box on the right.

Complete the following steps to create this project.

1. Create a new project called TABLEINFO.VBP.

2. Add a reference to the Microsoft DAO 3.51 Object Library to your project.

3. Add the Microsoft Common Dialog control to your project.

4. Use Form1 to create the objects and properties listed in Table 11.18. Save the form as TABLE.FRM.

Table 11.18 Objects and Properties for Table Form

OBJECT	PROPERTY	SETTING
Form	Name	Table
	Caption	Table Information
	StartUpPosition	2 - CenterScreen
CommonDialog	Name	cdOpenDB
ListBox	Name	lbTableList
TextBox	Name	tbTableInfo
	Locked	True
	MultiLine	True
	ScrollBars	2 - Vertical

5. Add the following code to the General Declarations section of form Table.

```
Option Explicit
Public db As Database
```

6. Add the following code to the Load event of the Table form. This subroutine uses a common dialog box to prompt the user for the name of the database to be used. After the database is selected and opened, the TableDefs collection is traversed. The Attributes property of the TableDef object is used to make sure that no System tables are added to the lbTableList list box.

```
Private Sub Form_Load()
    Dim tabdef As TableDef

    On Error GoTo ldErr

    ' Get Name of database
    cdOpenDB.DialogTitle = "Select Database"
    cdOpenDB.CancelError = True
    cdOpenDB.Filter = "(*.mdb)|*.mdb"
    cdOpenDB.ShowOpen

    Set db = OpenDatabase(cdOpenDB.filename)

    For Each tabdef In db.TableDefs
```

continued on next page

continued from previous page

```
                    ' If it's a system table don't add it to the tree
                    If (tabdef.Attributes And dbSystemObject) = 0 Then
                        If tabdef.Attributes <> dbAttachedTable Then
                            ' Add the table to the tree.
                            lbTableList.AddItem tabdef.Name
                        End If
                    End If
            Next

            Exit Sub
        ldErr:
            ' If the error was not caused by selecting cancel on the
            ' common dialog box, display an error message and end
            ' the program.
            If Err.Number <> cdlCancel Then
                MsgBox Err.Description, vbExclamation, "Table Error"
            End If
            End
        End Sub
```

7. Add the following code to the **Unload** event of form Table. It is good
practice to close any databases that are opened during the execution of
your program.

```
Private Sub Form_Unload(Cancel As Integer)
    ' Close the database
    db.Close
End Sub
```

8. Use the following code to create the **lbTableList_Click** event. This
subroutine takes the name of the table selected in the **lbTableList** box
and uses it to access the **TableDef** collection to get the **TableDef** object
for that table. A **TableDef** object contains a lot of interesting information
about a table. Four of those properties are placed into the text box in this
procedure.

The **TableDef** object also has a **Fields** collection. The **Fields** collection
can be traversed to get the names of all the fields in the table. The field
names are added to the **tbTableInfo** text box along with the information
from the **TableDef** object.

```
Private Sub lbTableList_Click()
    Dim tdTable As TableDef
    Dim fdTabField As Field
    Dim sFields As String

    ' Get the table definition for the selected table
    Set tdTable = db.TableDefs(lbTableList)

    ' Add information from the Table Definition to the text box
    tbTableInfo = "Date Created : " + Trim$(tdTable.DateCreated) + _
                                        vbCr + vbLf + _
```

```
            "Last Updated : " + Trim$(tdTable.LastUpdated) + vbCr + _
            vbLf + _
            "Record Count : " + Trim$(tdTable.RecordCount) + vbCr + _
            vbLf + _
            "Updateable : " + Trim$(tdTable.Updatable) + vbCr + vbLf

        ' Get the names of the fields in this table
        sFields = vbCr + vbLf + "Table Fields" + vbCr + vbLf
        For Each fdTabField In tdTable.Fields
            sFields = sFields + vbTab + fdTabField.Name + vbCr + vbLf
        Next

        tbTableInfo = tbTableInfo + sFields
    End Sub
```

How It Works

A `Database` object contains a `TableDef` collection, which holds information about the tables that make up the database. This collection contains both user-defined tables and system tables used by the Jet engine. Avoid basing your program on system tables because they could change from release to release of Microsoft Access. The `TableDef` object provides you with a wealth of information about a table, so accessing system tables really isn't necessary.

The `TableDef` object has two collections, `Fields` and `Indexes`. The `Fields` collection provides a list of all the fields that make up a table. A `Field` object contains such properties as `Name`, `Type`, `Size`, and `Required` to mention just a few. The `Indexes` collection contains a list of all the indexes defined for the table. The `Index` object has properties such as `Name`, `Primary`, and `Unique`, among others.

Comments

This How-To only presents a few of the properties that exist for the `TableDef` object. Many other properties can be useful when developing your applications; see the Visual Basic help file for a complete listing.

ISAM Databases

The Microsoft Jet database engine provides for two ways to access data that is stored in an external format. The Jet engine considers the Microsoft Access database format its native format, so any other formats are considered external. The two methods for accessing external formats are ODBC and ISAM. The next three sections cover how to use ISAM drivers to access data not stored in Microsoft Access databases. Visual Basic delivers ISAM drivers for the external data sources listed in Table 11.19.

Table 11.19 ISAM Drivers Delivered with Microsoft Visual Basic

SOURCE	VERSIONS
Microsoft FoxPro	2.0, 2.5, 2.6, 3.0, and DBC
dBASE	III, IV, and 5.0
Paradox	3.X, 4.X, and 5.X
Microsoft Excel Worksheets	3.0, 4.0, 5.0, 7.0, and 8.0
Lotus Spreadsheets	WKS, WK1, WK3, and WK4
ASCII Text Files	Tabular format
HTML	Tabular data

Before you can use one of the drivers listed in Table 11.19 to access an ISAM database, you have load the driver for that database. The ISAM drivers delivered with Visual Basic are selectable during the install process. The ISAM drivers are a subset of the Data Access choice during setup. Clicking the Change Option button while Data Access is selected displays the options available. One of the options is ISAM Drivers. Clicking the Change Option button while ISAM Drivers is selected displays the list of ISAM drivers available. Make sure that the check box is selected on those drivers that you need. Table 11.20 lists the DLLs that implement the ISAM drivers listed in Table 11.19.

Table 11.20 ISAM DLLs

SOURCE	DLL NAME
Microsoft FoxPro	MSXBSE35.DLL
dBASE	MSXBSE35.DLL
Paradox	MSPDOX35.DLL
Microsoft Excel Worksheets	MSEXCL35.DLL
Lotus Spreadsheets	MSLTUS35.DLL
ASCII Text Files	MSTEXT35.DLL
HTML	MSTEXT35.DLL

Accessing External Data

The Jet engine knows about its native format but does not know anything about the formats of external data. This is why extra DLLs are needed to provide a layer with which the Jet engine can access data in other formats. You also have to provide some additional information to the data controls or DAO.

This additional information is provided by means of the **Connect** argument or property. The **Connect** string is made up of a database type and a list of optional parameters that might be needed by a particular ISAM driver. The **Connect** string is used as the last argument to the `OpenDatabase` method or with the `Connect` property on objects such as `TableDef` and data controls. Table 11.21 shows a list of properties that can be used as the database type portion of the `Connect` string. For example, if you wanted to open an Excel 5.0 worksheet, you could use the following statement:

```
Set db = OpenDatabase("c:\quarter4\sales.xls", False, False, "Excel 5.0;")
```

Table 11.21 Database Types for the `Connect` Property

DATABASE TYPE	CONNECT PROPERTY
dBASE III	dBASE III;
dBASE IV	dBASE IV;
dBASE 5	dBASE 5.0;
Excel 3.0	Excel 3.0;
Excel 4.0	Excel 4.0;
Excel 5.0 or Excel 95	Excel 5.0;
Excel 97	Excel 97;
FoxPro 2.0	FoxPro 2.0;
FoxPro 2.5	FoxPro 2.5;
FoxPro 2.6	FoxPro 2.6;
FoxPro 3.0	FoxPro 3.0;
HTML	HTML Export;
	HTML Import;
Lotus WKS	Lotus WK1;
Lotus WK1	Lotus WK1;
Lotus WK3	Lotus WK3;
Lotus WK4	Lotus WK4;
Paradox 3.X	Paradox 3.X;
Paradox 4.X	Paradox 4.X;
Paradox 5.X	Paradox 5.X;
Text	Text;

Unsupported Objects and Methods

Not all Jet functions are available to you when using ISAM drivers. Table 11.22 lists the actions you cannot perform on these types of databases. With `CreateField`, you can use this method on new tables, but you can't use it to expand tables with existing fields.

Table 11.22 Microsoft Jet Objects and Methods not Supported by ISAM Drivers

MICROSOFT JET SPECIFIC ITEMS	TYPE
CompactDatabase	Method
Container	Object
CreateDatabase	Method
CreateField	Method
CreateQueryDef	Method
Document	Object
QueryDef	Object
Relation	Object
RepairDatabase	Method

FoxPro, dBASE, and Paradox Databases

Microsoft Access databases are represented by a single file. The xBase type databases, FoxPro and dBASE, use a directory structure format. Paradox, although based on a different internal system, is structured in the same way for the purposes of the Jet engine. In these systems, you can think of the directory as the database name and the files in the directory as the tables. For instance, if you wanted to use a Data control named **dcMyData** to access a table called MEMBERS in a FoxPro database, you would use the following settings. The location of the file MEMBERS.DBF would be used as the **DatabaseName** property. The value of the **RecordSource** property would be set to the name of the actual file.

```
dcMyData.Connect = "FoxPro 2.6;"
dcMyData.DatabaseName = "C:\Club"
dcMyData.RecordSource = "MEMBERS"
```

If you needed to access another table called OFFICERS, you would change the **RecordSource** property. The same methodology works for accessing dBASE and Paradox files.

Registering the ISAM Drivers

In previous versions of Microsoft Visual Basic, the configuration information for ISAM drivers was stored in INI files, specifically in the VB.INI file or the applications INI file.

In Microsoft Visual Basic 6, this information is located in the Windows Registry. The default or shadow settings are stored in the Registry at HKEY_LOCAL_MACHINE\SOFTWARE\Microsoft\Jet\3.5\Engines. The ISAM format information for a specific driver is now stored at HKEY_LOCAL_MACHINE\SOFTWARE\Microsoft\Jet\3.5\ISAM Formats. This information is created automatically when you load Visual Basic if you elected to load the ISAM portion of Data Access. If you use the Setup Wizard provided with Visual Basic, you can specify which ISAM drivers your program uses. This causes the appropriate Registry entries to be made on the target machine when your application is installed.

COMPLEXITY
BEGINNING

11.11 How do I...
Look up dBASE, FoxPro, and Paradox database files with data access objects?

COMPATIBILITY: VISUAL BASIC 5 AND 6

Problem

A customer wants us to convert one of our programs to use a FoxPro database that she already has. Can I convert my program to use ISAM drivers?

Technique

Most of the things available to you when accessing a Microsoft Access database are also available when using an ISAM database (see Table 11.22 for a list of exceptions). In this How-To, an ISAM driver is used in conjunction with a DAO object to open a FoxPro database. The program enables the user to browse, add, and delete records from the database. The same techniques used in this How-To also apply to dBASE and Paradox files.

Steps

Load the project DAOBJECT.VBP. Be sure to change the directory specified in **OpenDatabase** to the VB6HT directory before proceeding. Run the program, and the form shown in Figure 11.12 appears.

Figure 11.12
Inventory form.

Use the buttons to scroll through the records. From the Edit pull-down menu, you can add and delete records. To create this project, complete the following steps.

1. Create a new project called DAOBJECT.VBP.

2. Add a reference to the Microsoft DAO 3.51 Object Library to your project.

3. Use Form1 to create the objects and properties listed in Table 11.23. Save the form as INVENTORY.FRM.

Table 11.23 Objects and Properties for INVENTORY

OBJECT	PROPERTY	SETTING
Form	Name	Inventory
	Caption	Inventory
	StartUpPosition	2 - CenterScreen
TextBox	Name	PID
	DataField	PARTID
	DataSource	INVENTORY
	Text	" "
TextBox	Name	PartName
	DataField	NAME
	DataSource	INVENTORY
	Text	" "
TextBox	Name	PartQuantity
	DataField	QUANTITY
	DataSource	INVENTORY
	Text	" "
CommandButton	Name	FirstRec
	Caption	&First
CommandButton	Name	LastRec
	Caption	&Last
CommandButton	Name	NextRec
	Caption	&Next
CommandButton	Name	PreviousRec
	Caption	&Previous
Label	Name	Label1
	Caption	Part ID
Label	Name	Label2
	Caption	Name
Label	Name	Label3
	Caption	Quantity

4. Use the entries in Table 11.24 and the Menu Editor to create a menu for form Inventory.

Table 11.24 Menu Items for INVENTORY

CAPTION	NAME
&Edit	Edit
-&Add	Add
-&Delete	Delcte
-	Sep
-&Exit	Exit

5. Add the following lines to General Declarations. The variables will be used in various procedures in this form.

```
Option Explicit

Dim db As Database
Dim bomRs As Recordset
Dim FieldsModified As Boolean
Dim AddingRecord As Boolean
```

6. Add the following code to the **Load** event of the form. Be sure to change the location of the directory in **OpenDatabase** to match the location of the VB6HT directory on your machine. After opening the database, use the **OpenRecordset** method to open the **BOM** table. If the recordset is not empty, call **UpdateFields** to add data from the first record in the form's edit fields.

```
Private Sub Form_Load()
    ' Set the directory for the FoxPro database
    Set db = OpenDatabase("c:\VB6HT\Chapter.11", False, _
                False, "FoxPro 2.6")

    ' Open the recordset
    Set bomRs = db.OpenRecordset("BOM", dbOpenTable)

    ' If there is at least one record update the
    ' fields of the form.
    If Not bomRs.EOF Then UpdateFields
End Sub
```

7. Add the following code to the form's **Unload** event. Close the recordset and the database before the program ends.

```
Private Sub Form_Unload(Cancel As Integer)
    ' Close the recordset
    bomRs.Close

    ' Close the database
    db.Close
End Sub
```

8. Create `Change` events for the text boxes based on the following code. The `Change` event for a text box is invoked anytime the contents of the text box change. The `FieldsModified` variable indicates whether a field has been changed and a save might need to be performed on the record before moving to another one.

```
Private Sub PartName_Change()
    FieldsModified = True
End Sub

Private Sub PartQuantity_Change()
    FieldsModified = True
End Sub

Private Sub PID_Change()
    FieldsModified = True
End Sub
```

9. Add the following code to the `Click` event of the `FirstRec` command button. This code emulates the first button on a data control by using the `MoveFirst` method. The `FieldsModified` variable is used to signal that data has changed and the user should be notified. After the current record pointer has been moved, the `UpdateFields` subroutine refreshes the form.

```
Private Sub FirstRec_Click()
    On Error GoTo FirstRec

    ' If any fields have been modified
    ' call this function to check on saving
    ' the changes
    If FieldsModified Then CheckToSave

    ' Move to the first record in the recordset
    bomRs.MoveFirst

    UpdateFields

    Exit Sub

FirstRec:
    ErrorMessage ("Going To First Record")
    Exit Sub
End Sub
```

10. Add the following code to the `Click` event of the `LastRec` command button. This code emulates the last button on a data control by using the `MoveLast` method. The `FieldsModified` variable is used to signal that data has changed and the user should be notified.

```
Private Sub LastRec_Click()
    On Error GoTo LastRec

    If FieldsModified Then CheckToSave
```

```
        'Move to the last record in the recordset
        bomRs.MoveLast

        UpdateFields

        Exit Sub

LastRec:
        ErrorMessage ("Going To Last Record")
        Exit Sub
End Sub
```

11. Add the following code to the **Click** event of the **NextRec** command button. This code emulates the third button on a data control by using the **MoveNext** method. If the current record is the last record, then the **MoveNext** tries to move the record pointer past the last record. To keep this from happening, check the **EOF** property. If the **MoveNext** caused the record pointer to be at the end of the recordset, use the **MoveLast** method to reposition the record pointer to the last record.

```
Private Sub NextRec_Click()
        On Error GoTo nxtRec

        If FieldsModified Then CheckToSave

        ' Move to the next record in the recordset
        bomRs.MoveNext

        'If MoveNext move past the last record
        'set the pointer back to the last record
        If bomRs.EOF Then bomRs.MoveLast

        UpdateFields

        Exit Sub

nxtRec:
        ErrorMessage ("Going To Next Record")
        Exit Sub
End Sub
```

12. Add the following code to the **Click** event of the **PreviousRec** command button. This code emulates the second button on a data control by using the **MovePrevious** method. If the current record is the first record, then the **MovePrevious** tries to move the record pointer past the first record. To keep this from happening, check the **BOF** property. If the **MovePrevious** caused the record pointer to be at the beginning of the recordset, use the **MoveFirst** method to reposition the record pointer to the first record.

```
Private Sub PreviousRec_Click()
        On Error GoTo prvRec

        If FieldsModified Then CheckToSave
```

continued on next page

continued from previous page

```
        ' Move to the previous record in the recordset
        bomRs.MovePrevious

        'If MoveNext move past the first record
        'set the pointer back to the first record
        If bomRs.BOF Then bomRs.MoveFirst

        UpdateFields

        Exit Sub

prvRec:
        ErrorMessage ("Going To Previous Record")
        Exit Sub
End Sub
```

13. Add the following code to the **Click** event of the Add menu item. The **AddNew** method is used to create a new record buffer. The **PARTID** field of this table should always be a unique number so that the code finds the largest ID currently in the table and adds one to it for use as the ID for the new record. The **AddingRecord** and **FieldsModified** flags are set to **True** so that other functions can tell what state the program is in currently.

```
Private Sub Add_Click()
        Dim newid As Integer
        Dim idsql As String
        Dim idset As Recordset

        On Error GoTo adderr

        ' Create new record
        bomRs.AddNew

        ' Blank the form fields
        PID = ""
        PartName = ""
        PartQuantity = ""

        ' Determine the highest PartID and generate the next one
        idsql = "Select max(PARTID) as MaxID from BOM"
        Set idset = db.OpenRecordset(idsql, dbOpenSnapshot)

        ' Determine the highest PubID and generate the next one
        If idset.EOF Then newid = 1 Else newid = idset!MaxID + 1

        bomRs!PartID = newid
        PID = Trim$(newid)

        FieldsModified = True
        AddingRecord = True

        Exit Sub

adderr:
```

```
            ErrorMessage ("Adding Record")
            Exit Sub
    End Sub
```

14. Add the following code to the **Click** event of the Delete menu item. If the **Delete** event is fired during the process of adding a record, then the fields on the form are just blanked out and the **AddNew** is canceled with the **CancelUpdate** method. If the user was not in the process of adding a record, then the code prompts him or her to see whether the current record should be deleted. If so, use the **Delete** method to delete the current record and then move the current record pointer to another record.

```
Private Sub Delete_Click()
    On Error GoTo delErr

    Dim question As String
    Dim movePointer As Boolean
    Dim answer As VbMsgBoxResult

    movePointer = False

    ' If a new record has not been saved blank the fields
    ' and cancel the AddNew
    If AddingRecord Then
        PID = ""
        PartName = ""
        PartQuantity = ""

        ' Cancel the AddNew
        bomRs.CancelUpdate

        ' No longer adding a new record
        AddingRecord = False
        FieldsModified = False

        movePointer = True
    Else
        question = "Do you want to delete the entry for " + _
            PartName.Text

        answer = MsgBox(question, vbQuestion & vbYesNo, _
                "Inventory")
        If answer = vbYes Then
            ' The delete method deletes the current record
            ' Delete the record
            bomRs.Delete

            movePointer = True
        Else
            movePointer = False
        End If
    End If
```

continued on next page

continued from previous page

```
    ' Move to a valid data entry
    If movePointer Then PreviousRec_Click

    Exit Sub

delErr:
    ErrorMessage ("Deleting Record")
    Exit Sub
End Sub
```

15. Add the following code to the **Click** event of the Exit menu item to dismiss the program. The **Unload** statement causes the form's **Unload** event to be triggered.

```
Private Sub Exit_Click()
    Unload Me
End Sub
```

16. Use the following code to create the **UpdateFields** subroutine. This code is used to change the values of the text boxes when a new record becomes current. Because assigning a **Null** value to a text box causes a runtime error, this function tests for **Null** values and assigns a space to the edit fields instead of a **Null**.

```
Sub UpdateFields()
    ' If field is not NULL load data
    If IsNull(bomRs!PartID) Then
        PID = ""
    Else
        PID = bomRs!PartID
    End If

    If IsNull(bomRs!Name) Then
        PartName = ""
    Else
        PartName = bomRs!Name
    End If

    If IsNull(bomRs!Quantity) Then
        PartQuantity = ""
    Else
        PartQuantity = bomRs!Quantity
    End If

    FieldsModified = False
End Sub
```

17. Create the **CheckToSave** subroutine based on the following code. This subroutine presents the user with a message box to see whether he or she wants to save the current record.

```
Sub CheckToSave()
```

```
Dim notice As String
Dim answer As VbMsgBoxResult

notice = "The current data has been changed. Do you wish to _
          save it?"

answer = MsgBox(notice, vbYesNo, "Publisher")
If answer = vbYes Then UpdateRecordSet

End Sub
```

18. Use the following code to create the **UpdateRecordSet** procedure. This subroutine checks to see whether the current operation is an Add by checking the **AddingRecord** variable. If it is an add operation, there is no need to use the **Edit** method to enable the record for changes. The fields of the record are updated with the values from the text boxes. The **Update** method is used to save the data to the record. After the update, the **AddingRecord** and **FieldsModified** variables are reset.

```
Sub UpdateRecordSet()
    On Error GoTo updRec

    ' Enable editing of the record if it already exists
    If Not AddingRecord Then bomRs.Edit

    If PID = "" Then bomRs!PartID = Null Else bomRs!PartID = PID
    If PartName = "" Then bomRs!Name = Null Else bomRs!Name = _
                  PartName
    If PartQuantity = "" Then bomRs!Quantity = Null Else _
                  bomRs!Quantity = PartQuantity

    'Update the record
    bomRs.Update

    ' Reset Checks
    If AddingRecord Then AddingRecord = False
    If FieldsModified Then FieldsModified = False

    Exit Sub

updRec:
    ErrorMessage ("Updating Record")
    Exit Sub
End Sub
```

19. Use the following code to create the **ErrorMessage** subroutine. This procedure is used to present all the error messages to the user.

```
Sub ErrorMessage(Location As String)
    Dim errMsg As String

    errMsg = "Error in " + Location + vbCr

    errMsg = errMsg + "Error # " + _
```

continued on next page

continued from previous page

```
            Str$(Err.Number) + " - " + Err.Description

        MsgBox errMsg, vbExclamation, "Error Processing"
    End Sub
```

How It Works

Adding records to the recordset of a DAO object is accomplished by using the **AddNew** method, which creates a new record buffer. After the user has entered the information into the controls on the dialog box, the information is transferred to the record buffer and then saved to the recordset by means of the **Update** method.

The recordset's **Delete** method is used to remove the current record from the recordset. If a current record is not defined, an error occurs when **Delete** is used. The **Delete** method leaves the current record undefined, so the program needs to move the current record pointer to a valid record.

Comments

If the user invokes the **Add** method and then exits this application before a save is done, the data for the new record is lost. Code could be added to the **QueryUnload** event of the form to check for such occurrences and prompt the user to save the record before the program exits.

COMPLEXITY
BEGINNING

11.12 How do I...
Access spreadsheet files from a Visual Basic application?

COMPATIBILITY: VISUAL BASIC 5 AND 6

Problem

Another department generates a set of data that I want to display in our application. The data is stored in Excel format. How can I display this data in my Visual Basic application without having Excel loaded on every machine?

Technique

Visual Basic includes an ISAM driver for accessing Excel files. The driver supports Excel versions 3.0, 4.0, 5.0, 7.0, and 8.0. The example in this section uses this driver to open an Excel 5.0 file and display data from its worksheets.

Restrictions

There are a few restrictions when working with the Microsoft Excel ISAM driver. The following restrictions apply to both worksheets and workbooks:

✔ Encrypted data cannot be read.

✔ Rows cannot be deleted.

✔ Indexes cannot be created.

✔ Cells that contain formulas cannot be cleared or modified.

Excel 8.0 allows for the creation of files that can be opened in either Excel 8.0 or Excel 7.0. Any Excel file saved in this manner is only available for opening in a read-only mode.

Options

Several options available when opening an Excel spreadsheet are not shown in this example but are worth mentioning. The first is the HDR parameter used as part of the `Connect` argument to `OpenDatabase`. This argument indicates whether the first row of the spreadsheet is to be treated as a row of data or as column headers. The default value is `YES`. In default mode, the first row of data is treated as header columns. If the parameter is supplied and a value of `NO` is used, the first row is treated as data. The following is an example of how you set this value when opening the spreadsheet:

```
Set dbs = OpenDatabase("C:\Sample.xls", False, False, "Excel 5.0;HDR=NO;")
```

After the spreadsheet has been opened, options can be used on individual worksheets. One option is to use named ranges that have been saved in the workbook when opening a worksheet. This allows for subsets of the data to be viewed. The following example shows the opening of a named range:

```
Set rst = dbs.OpenRecordset("Range1")
```

Another option is to provide a range of cells to use when the worksheet is opened. This method provides a slightly more flexible approach than the named range method. The following example demonstrates opening a range of a worksheet:

```
Set rst = dbs.OpenRecordset("Sheet1$B2:H6")
```

Steps

Open and run the file XLS.VBP. A common dialog box asks you to select an Excel 5.0 file. Select the file SALES.XLS in the VB6HT\Chapter.11 directory. The list box displays the name of the worksheets available. The first sheet is already selected and the data associated with it displayed in the grid labeled Sheet Data (see Figure 11.13).

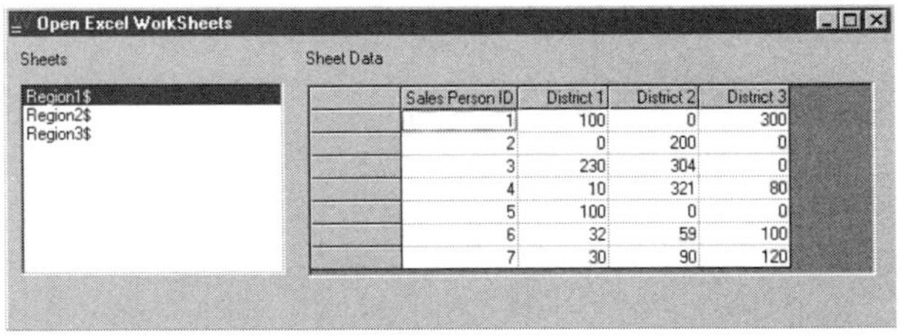

Figure 11.13 The XLS form.

Select another sheet from the list, and the data from that sheet is now displayed in the grid. Choose Close from the menu's control icon to end the program.

Complete the following steps to create this project.

1. Create a new project called XLS.VBP.

2. Add a reference to the Microsoft DAO 3.51 Object Library to your project.

3. Add the Microsoft Common Dialog control and the Microsoft FlexGrid control to your project.

4. Use Form1 to create the objects and properties listed in Table 11.25 and save them as EXCEL.FRM.

Table 11.25 Objects and Properties for the Excel Form

OBJECT	PROPERTY	SETTING
Form	Name	Excel
	Caption	Open Excel Worksheets
Data	Name	Data1
	Visible	False
CommonDialog	Name	cmDlg
ListBox	Name	SheetList
Label	Name	lblTables
	Caption	Sheets
Label	Name	lblTableData
	Caption	Sheet Data

OBJECT	PROPERTY	SETTING
MSFlexGrid	Name	SheetData
	AllowUserResizing	1 - flexResizeColumns
	DataSource	Data1

5. Add the following code to the General Declarations section of Excel. The variable **db** will be used in various procedures in this form.

```
Option Explicit
Dim db As Database
```

6. Enter the following code into the **Load** event of the Excel form. This code uses a common dialog box to get the name of the Excel file to open. After the name is known, the file is opened, and the names of any worksheets are extracted and displayed. If no worksheets are available, an error message is displayed. If worksheets are available, the first one will be made active.

```
Private Sub Form_Load()
    Dim tblDef As TableDef

    On Error GoTo XLSError

    'Select Excel 5.0 File to open
    With cmDlg
        cmDlg.DialogTitle = "Select Excel 5.0 File"
        cmDlg.Filter = "Excel 5.0¦*.xls"
        cmDlg.CancelError = True
        cmDlg.ShowOpen
    End With

    'Open the Excel Spreadsheet
    Set db = DBEngine.Workspaces(0).OpenDatabase(cmDlg.filename, _
        False, False, "Excel 5.0;")

    'Add the names of the worksheets to the list
    For Each tblDef In db.TableDefs
        SheetList.AddItem tblDef.Name
    Next

    If SheetList.ListCount > 0 Then
        'Select the first item in the list.  This will cause the
        'grid to be filled.  See SheetList_Click for details.
        SheetList.ListIndex = 0
    Else
        MsgBox "No Sheets Available.", vbInformation, _
        "Information"
    End If
Exit Sub

XLSError:
```

continued on next page

continued from previous page

```
        MsgBox Error$, vbExclamation, "Error Message"
        End
End Sub
```

7. Enter the following code into the **SheetList_Click** event of the Excel form. This code checks to make sure an item has been selected from the list. If an item has been selected, that name is used to try and open a recordset. The data control has its recordset set to the newly opened worksheet. The data control is then refreshed so that the new data shows up in the grid.

```
Private Sub SheetList_Click()
    Dim newData As Recordset

    ' Check to make sure an item in the list has been selected.
    If SheetList.ListIndex <> -1 Then
        'Open the Sheet as a Table and set the DataControl's
        'Recordset
        Set newData = db.OpenRecordset(SheetList.Text, _
        dbOpenTable)
        Set Data1.Recordset = newData
        Data1.Refresh
    End If
End Sub
```

How It Works

When the form loads, it uses a common dialog box to ask for the name of an Excel file to open. The Excel spreadsheet is opened as a database, and the **TableDefs** collection is used to get the name of all the worksheets. The names of the worksheets are added to a list box, and the first name from the list is selected. This selection causes the **Click** event for the list box to be executed. In this subroutine, a recordset is opened for the worksheet selected. The data control's recordset is updated, and the data control refreshed.

The grid **SheetData** is bound to the data control. Anytime the recordset of the data control is changed, the data in the grid changes to reflect that. Therefore anytime a new worksheet is selected from the list, the **SheetList_Click** event causes the data control to be updated, which in turn updates the grid.

Comments

This application could be enhanced in several ways. One way would be to allow ranges to be used. Other enhancements would be to allow the user to select the version of the Excel file to be opened or provide a switch to determine how the first row is processed. In addition to opening an Excel file as a database, you could attach a worksheet to another database. See How-To 11.7 for an example of how to attach tables to a Microsoft Access database.

COMPLEXITY
BEGINNING

11.13 How do I...
Access data in a Web (HTML) page?

COMPATIBILITY: VISUAL BASIC 5 AND 6

Problem

Another company generates a set of sales information that I want to display in my application. The data exists as tables in an HTML file. How can I access this data from my program?

Technique

Visual Basic includes an ISAM driver for accessing HTML files. You can use this driver to open HTML files and access the data stored in any HTML <TABLE> constructs that exist in the file.

How the HTML Driver Interprets Data

By default the HTML driver interprets the contents of cells for a table and assigns a data type based on the data it finds. The data type is assigned on a majority rules basis. If the majority of values for a particular column are numeric, then either **Long** or **Double** is assigned. This determination is also made based on whether more integer or floating point values are present in the column. If a column contains multiple data types, some of the data might be lost. If the table has a column that has 15 integers and 5 strings, a field of type **Long** is created for that column. When the table is opened, the former string fields contain a **NULL** value.

There is a way around having the HTML driver make its own determination of data types. A file called SCHEMA.INI can be used to force columns of data to take on a particular data type. This file must exist in the same directory as the HTML file from which the data is being imported. The following is an example of what this file might look like.

```
[Sales]
ColNameHeader=False
Format=FixedLength
MaxScanRows=20
CharacterSet=OEM
Col1=columnname Char Width 20
Col2=columnname2 Date Width 12
Col3=columnname4 Integer Width 8
```

The HTML specification defines a table header tag `<TH>`. The HTML driver does not process these tags as field names. All data between the `<TH>/<\TH>` tags is treated as normal data. This is because `<TH>` tags can be used anywhere in the table, not just on the first row.

Table names are taken from the table caption if one exists. If captions don't exist for the tables, they are named after the `<TITLE>` of the HTML file. If more than one table exists, numbers are appended to the name. If you want to access a table that does not have a caption, you can reference the tables sequentially using Table1, Table2, and on up. The driver interprets this to mean first unnamed table, second unnamed table, and so on.

Options

A couple of options available when opening an HTML file are not shown in this example but are worth mentioning. The first is the `HDR` parameter, which can be used as part of the `Connect` argument to `OpenDatabase`. This argument indicates whether the first row of the table is to be treated as a row of data or as field names. The default value is `YES`. In default mode, the first row of data is treated as field names. If the parameter is supplied and a value of `NO` is used, the first row is treated as data. The following is an example of how you would set this value during the opening of the spreadsheet:

```
Set dbs = OpenDatabase("C:\SALES.HTM", False, False, "HTML Import;HDR=NO;")
```

The application in this How-To accesses an HTML file that resides locally on the machine. The file does not have to be on the local machine, which is where the real power of this driver comes in. The first argument to `OpenDatabase` can be in the form of an HTTP address.

```
Set dbs = OpenDatabase("HTTP://www.myserver.edu/enrollment/byclass.html", False, _
False, "HTML Import;")
```

Steps

Open and run the file HTM.VBP. A common dialog box will ask you to select an HTML file. Select the file SALES.HTM in the VB6HT\Chapter.11 directory. The list box displays the name of the tables available. The first table is already selected and the data associated with it displayed in the grid labeled Table Data (see Figure 11.14).

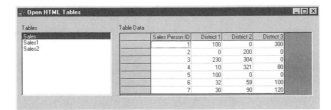

Figure 11.14 The HTML form.

Select another table from the list. The data from that table is now displayed in the grid. Choose Close from the menu's control icon to end the program.

To create this project, complete the following steps.

1. Create a new project called HTM.VBP.

2. Add a reference to the Microsoft DAO 3.51 Object Library to your project.

3. Add the Microsoft Common Dialog control and the Microsoft FlexGrid control to your project.

4. Use Form1 to create the objects and properties listed in Table 11.26 and save them as HTML.FRM.

Table 11.26 Objects and Properties for the HTML Form

OBJECT	PROPERTY	SETTING
Form	Name	Excel
	Caption	Open HTML Tables
Data	Name	Data1
	Visible	False
CommonDialog	Name	cmDlg
ListBox	Name	TableList
Label	Name	lblTables
	Caption	Tables
Label	Name	lblTableData
	Caption	Table Data
MSFlexGrid	Name	TableData
	AllowUserResizing	1 - flexResizeColumns
	DataSource	Data1

5. Add the following code to the declarations section of HTML.FRM. The variable **db** will be used in various procedures in this form.

```
Option Explicit
Dim db As Database
```

6. Enter the following code into the Load event of the HTML form. This code uses a common dialog box to get the name of the Excel file to open. After the name is known, the file is opened and the names of any tables are extracted and displayed. If no tables are available, an error message is displayed. The names are determined by stepping through the **TableDefs** collection. If tables are available, the first one is made active.

```
Private Sub Form_Load()
    Dim tblDef As TableDef
```

continued on next page

continued from previous page

```
        On Error GoTo HTMError

        'Select HTML File to open
        With cmDlg
            cmDlg.DialogTitle = "Select HTML File"
            cmDlg.Filter = "HTM¦*.htm¦HTML¦*.html"
            cmDlg.CancelError = True
            cmDlg.ShowOpen
        End With

        'Open the HTML File
        Set db = DBEngine.Workspaces(0).OpenDatabase(cmDlg.filename, _
                            False, _
                            False, "HTML Import;")

        'Add the names of the tables to the list
        For Each tblDef In db.TableDefs
            TableList.AddItem tblDef.Name
        Next

        If TableList.ListCount > 0 Then
            'Select the first item in the list.  This will cause the
            'grid to be filled.  See TableList_Click for details.
            TableList.ListIndex = 0
        Else
            MsgBox "No Tables Available.", vbInformation, _
            "Information"
        End If
    Exit Sub

HTMError:
    MsgBox Error$, vbExclamation, "Error Message"
    End
End Sub
```

7. Enter the following code into the **TableList_Click** event of the HTML form. This code checks to make sure an item has been selected from the list. If an item has been selected, that name is used to try and open a recordset. The data control has its recordset set to the newly opened table. The data control is then refreshed so that the new data shows up in the grid.

```
Private Sub TableList_Click()
    Dim newData As Recordset

    ' Check to make sure an item in the list has been selected.
    If TableList.ListIndex <> -1 Then
        'Open the Table and set the DataControl's Recordset
        Set newData = db.OpenRecordset(TableList.Text, _
        dbOpenTable)
        Set Data1.Recordset = newData
        Data1.Refresh
    End If
End Sub
```

How It Works

When the form loads, it uses a common dialog box to ask for the name of an HTML file to open. The HTML file is opened as a database, and the `TableDefs` collection is used to get the name of all the tables. The names of the tables are added to a list box, and the first name from the list is selected. This selection causes the `Click` event for the list box to be executed. In this subroutine, a recordset is opened for the worksheet selected. The data control's recordset is updated, and the data control refreshed.

The grid TableData is bound to the data control. Anytime the recordset of the data control is changed, the data in the grid changes to reflect that. Therefore, anytime a new worksheet is selected from the list, the `TableList_Click` event causes the data control to be updated, which in turn updates the grid.

Comments

Web pages are becoming more popular to store information on company intranets. The techniques outlined in this How-To enable you to retrieve information that other departments or companies have made available on their Web pages. Even within the same company, the department from which you need to get information might be located on the other side of the world. The only thing you might be able to see at the other site is what the department's Web server makes available to you. With the example presented here, you can retrieve tabular data from the Web site for use in your own programs and reports.

COMPLEXITY
BEGINNING

11.14 How do I...
Use the DataRepeater control?

COMPATIBILITY: VISUAL BASIC 6

Problem

I like the look of the new `DataRepeater` control, but I'm not sure how to go about using it. Do I have to do some up-front work before I can take advantage of it?

Technique

This edition of Visual Basic introduced a new control named the `DataRepeater`. The `DataRepeater` control allows you to create a view of your data similar to the Continuous Forms option in Microsoft Access forms. The `DataRepeater` control does not work alone, however. You need a bound control to work with it. This How-To examines creating your own data bound control to use with the `DataRepeater` control.

Steps

Open and compile the file INVCNT.VBP located in the INVCNT directory. This will build a fresh copy of the bound control and make sure that it is registered on your system. Load the project file DATAREPEAT.VBP located in the NewInv directory. Be sure to change the Source location in the **Connect** string property of the active data control **Adodc1** to point to the copy of BOM.MDB located in your VB6\Chapter.11 directory. Now run the program, and the form shown in Figure 11.15 appears.

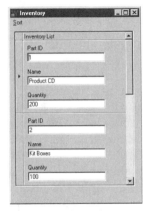

Figure 11.15 The Inventory form.

Select the different sort options on the Sort pull-down menu to see the data ordered in the chosen way. Complete the following steps to create this project.

1. Create a new ActiveX control project called INVCNT.VBP.

2. Use **UserControl1** to create the objects and properties listed in Table 11.27 and save them as INVENT.CTL.

Table 11.27 Objects and Properties for the INVCNT Form

OBJECT	PROPERTY	SETTING
UserControl	Name	Invent
TextBox	Name	tPartId
	Text	" "
TextBox	Name	tName
	Text	" "
TextBox	Name	tQuantity
	Text	" "

OBJECT	PROPERTY	SETTING
Label	Name	lblPartID
	Caption	Part ID
Label	Name	lblName
	Caption	Name
Label	Name	lblQuantity
	Caption	Quantity

3. Add the following code to the declarations section of INVENT.CTL.

```
Option Explicit
```

4. Enter the following code to create **Get** events for each of the text boxes.

```
Public Property Get PartID() As String
    PartID = tPartId.Text
End Property

Public Property Get PartName() As String
    PartName = tName.Text
End Property

Public Property Get PartQuantity() As String
    PartQuantity = tQuantity.Text
End Property
```

5. Enter the following **Let** events for each of the text boxes.

```
Public Property Let PartID(ByVal newPartID As String)
    tPartId.Text = newPartID
End Property

Public Property Let PartName(ByVal newPartName As String)
    tName.Text = newPartName
End Property

Public Property Let PartQuantity(ByVal newQuantity As String)
    tQuantity.Text = newQuantity
End Property
```

6. Enter the following code into the **Change** events for each of the text boxes.

```
Private Sub tName_Change()
    PropertyChanged "PartName"
End Sub

Private Sub tPartId_Change()
    PropertyChanged "PartID"
End Sub

Private Sub tQuantity_Change()
    PropertyChanged "PartQuantity"
End Sub
```

7. Choose Tools, Property Attributes from the main menu. On the Procedure Attributes dialog box, select the button labeled Advanced, as shown in Figure 11.16.

Figure 11.16 The Procedure Attributes menu.

Select each of the three properties from the Name drop-down list. The property names match the names on the **Let** and **Get** function created earlier. For each of the properties, make sure that both the Property Is Data Bound and Show in DataBindings Collection at Design Time check boxes are selected. When all the properties have these settings, click the OK button to exit the menu.

8. Save the project and compile the OCX.

9. Create a new project called DATAREPEAT.VBP.

10. Add a reference to the Microsoft ActiveX Data Objects 2.0 Library to the project and don't forget to change the source location in the **Connection** string property.

11. Use **Form1** to create the objects and properties listed in Table 11.28 and save them as INVENTORY.FRM.

Table 11.28 Objects and Properties for the INVENTORY Form

OBJECT	PROPERTY	SETTING
Form	Name	Inventory
	StartUpPosition	2 - CenterScreen

OBJECT	PROPERTY	SETTING
AdoDC	Name	Adodc1
	Connection String	Provider=Microsoft.Jet.OLEDB.3.51;Data Source=c:\vb6ht\chapter.11\bom.mdb
	CursorLocation	3 - adUseClient
	RecordSource	SELECT * from Inventory order by partid
	Visible	False
DataRepeater	Name	InvList
	Caption	Inventory List
	DataSource	Adodc1
	RepeatedControlName	InvCnt.invent

12. Use the Menu Editor to create the entries in Table 11.29.

Table 11.29 Menu Specifications for INVENTORY.FRM

CAPTION	NAME
&Sort	Sort
-Sort By &Part ID	SortPartID
-Sort By &Name	SortName
-Sort By &Quantity	SortQuantity
-	Sep1
-&Exit	Exit

13. Select the **Custom** property from the DataRepeaters property list or use the right mouse button to select DataRepeater Properties.

Select the Repeater Bindings tab on the Property Pages menu (see Figure 11.17). Use the Property Name drop-down list to select the **PartID** property. Use the **DataField** drop-down list to select the **PARTID** field. This selection binds the **PartID** property to the **PARTID** data field in the BOM database. Click the Add button to add this relationship to the control. Repeat this process for the other two properties. When all three properties have been mapped, click the OK button to dismiss the Property Page menu.

14. Add the following code to the **Form_Load** event.

```
Private Sub Form_Load()
    SortPartID.Checked = True
End Sub
```

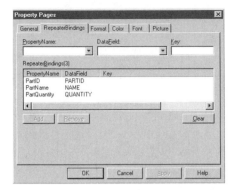

Figure 11.17 The DataRepeaters
Property Page menu.

15. Add the following code to appropriate `Click` events of the Sort menu
items. These functions will sort the recordset of the data control and flag
the appropriate menu item.

```
Private Sub SortName_Click()
    SortPartID.Checked = False
    SortName.Checked = True
    SortQuantity.Checked = False
    Adodc1.RecordSource = "Select * from Inventory order by name"
    Adodc1.Refresh
    InvList.Refresh
End Sub

Private Sub SortPartID_Click()
    SortPartID.Checked = True
    SortName.Checked = False
    SortQuantity.Checked = False
    Adodc1.RecordSource = "Select * from Inventory order by _
            partid"
    Adodc1.Refresh
    InvList.Refresh
End Sub

Private Sub SortQuantity_Click()
    SortPartID.Checked = False
    SortName.Checked = False
    SortQuantity.Checked = True
    Adodc1.RecordSource = "Select * from Inventory order by _
    quantity"
    Adodc1.Refresh
    InvList.Refresh
End Sub
```

16. Add the following code to the `Click` event of the Exit menu item.

```
Private Sub Exit_Click()
    Unload Me
End Sub
```

How It Works

The `DataRepeater` control works in relationship with other controls. In this How-To, an ActiveX control needed to be created before we could create the program that was actually using the `DataRepeater` control. In the ActiveX control, `Property` functions were added to provide a way to exchange information between the control and any program using it. These properties were used in the `DataRepeater`'s Repeater Bindings tab to bind the control properties to data fields in the Inventory table of the BOM database.

The actions on the Sort pull-down menu use the `RecordSource` property of the data control to reorder the contents of the data control's recordset. The `Checked` property of the menu items is used to indicate which `Sort` method is currently being used.

Comments

The `DataRepeater` provides a view of data that is similar to the Continuous Forms view that can be used when creating forms in Microsoft Access. In this How-To, a custom control was created for use with the `DataRepeater` control. You might not have to create your own control for use with `DataRepeater`. The `RepeatedControlName` property of the `DataRepeater` control lists the registered controls that you can use.

Beware that just because a control is listed does not mean that it is suitable for use with the `DataRepeater` control. The `RepeatedControlName` property drop-down list will contain controls that have nothing to do with data access. Be sure to choose one that is related to data access for use with the `DataRepeater` control.

CHAPTER 12

LOGO-COMPLIANT APPLICATIONS

12

LOGO-COMPLIANT APPLICATIONS

How do I...

12.1 Build a compliant user interface?

12.2 Implement drag-and-drop support with Registry entries?

12.3 Meet other miscellaneous requirements?

12.4 Create Install and Uninstall programs?

Many developers seek to have their applications certified to carry the Designed for Microsoft Windows NT and Windows 95 logo. Building compliant applications is still desirable even if the certification is not sought or obtained. Building compliant applications ensures that the programs behave in a manner consistent with user expectations.

An existing program, the Static Code Analysis utility from How-To 7.3, is used as the starting point for the How-Tos in this chapter. Beginning with that program, each How-To modifies and adds logic to make the application logo compliant. The full code of the application is not shown in each of the following How-Tos. Only routines that are modified or added to the project are listed.

This chapter is not exhaustive in its coverage of the logo certification requirements. The requirements have evolved and might well change again. The information in this chapter is based on version 3.0b of the *Applications Logo Handbook for Software Applications*, a 50-plus page document from Microsoft.

The handbook itemizes required and recommended application features. There are also a number of exceptions, exemptions, and miscellaneous requirements and recommendations. Monitor the Microsoft Web site for the latest information on both the certification process, testing fees, and specific requirements. Updated criteria covering Windows 98 should also be available soon. The site address is `http://www.microsoft.com/windows/thirdparty/winlogo.htm`.

The certification process itself contains a number of steps. Read the *Logo Handbook for Software Applications*, which outlines several tests that can be performed before submitting the application. These include interface reviews, a pretest installation verifier, and descriptions of some of the tests that are run on the application. There is a vendor questionnaire that must be completed and submitted with your install disks and some signed agreements for testing to start.

12.1 Build a Compliant User Interface

There are a relatively small number of user interface requirements. The program must operate well without a mouse, and all the functions need to be accessible from the keyboard. Many interface requirements deal with color. Primarily, the application must use the system color scheme selected by the user from the Control Panel and work under high contrast color schemes. This How-To shows techniques to enable keyboard access, and how to check to ensure that programs comply with the color requirements.

12.2 Implement Drag-and-Drop Support with Registry Entries

Drag-and-drop file access is a key feature for many programs. This How-To explains how to add drag-and-drop capability for a custom file type supported by the program. It builds file import and export dialog boxes to support the new file type and makes the necessary Registry entries to enable the Windows Explorer file open operations to launch the application.

To support the needs of the installation and application removal programs, the application is also made into a self-registering executable.

12.3 Meet Other Miscellaneous Requirements

There are a number of secondary requirements and recommendations for logo-compliant applications. This How-To summarizes these assorted criteria and provides brief discussions of how to address them in applications.

12.4 Create Install and Uninstall Programs

The installation kits built by the Application Setup Wizard are fairly complete. This How-To explains the requirements of compliant Install and Uninstall programs.

12.1 How do I...
Build a compliant user interface?

COMPATIBILITY: VISUAL BASIC 5 AND 6

Problem

My program has a user interface that looks good to me, but I am not sure whether it adheres to all the appropriate interface standards and guidelines. What are the interface criteria for the logo program, and how do I make my program compliant?

Technique

There are just a handful of user interface requirements. Because the program must be operational without a mouse, each control and function of the program needs to be accessible from the keyboard. This implies the use of accelerators and keyboard shortcuts. All shortcuts, other than visible accelerators, must be documented.

The next major requirement deals with color. The application must use the system color scheme selected by the user from the Control Panel. Use the default colors of the controls when they are added to the project; the color should not be changed unless there is good cause. A few controls, including MSFlexGrid, don't use the system color constants for all their color properties. The other color-related requirement is that the program must function in high contrast modes. This is checked by using the Control Panel to select the high contrast color schemes and running the program. Checking the execution of a program in the high contrast modes highlights any problems with the use of nonsystem color values.

Applications are also required to provide notification to the system about which control has focus. Visual Basic does this so that individual programs do not have to implement any code to meet this requirement.

Steps

Open and run STATIC ANALYSIS.VBP. The existing noncompliant interface is shown in Figure 12.1. The user interface needs to legible, and the program must be functional when the system is operating in high contrast display modes.

The program as it appears under the High Contrast Black settings is shown in Figure 12.2 and under High Contrast White in Figure 12.3. Notice that in High Contrast Black mode some of the grid lines are not visible. The GridColor property uses a fixed, medium-gray color that is not always rendered well in high contrast modes.

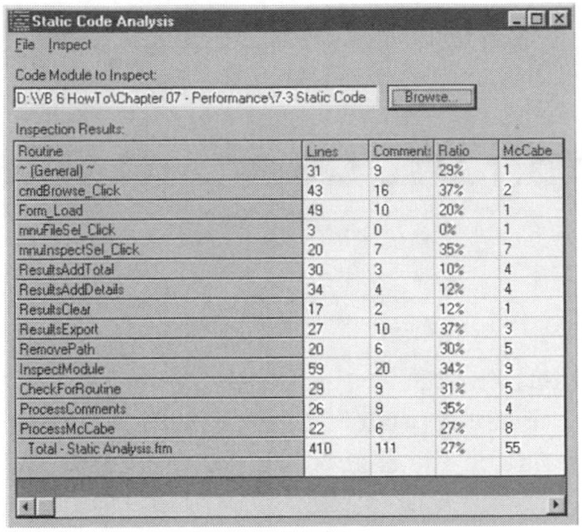

Figure 12.1 The main form at runtime.

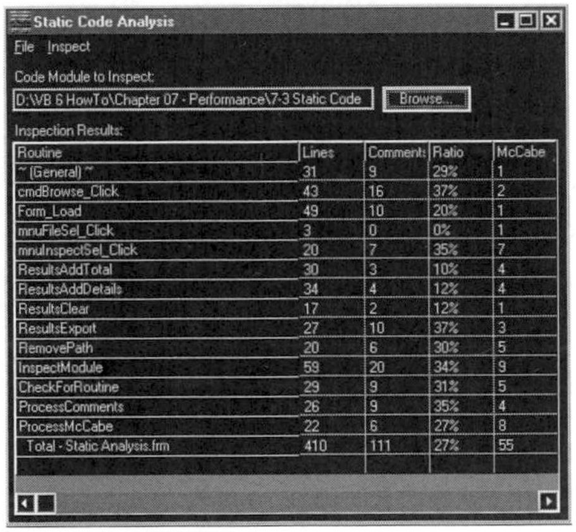

Figure 12.2 The main form in High Contrast Black.

The modified version of the program is seen in Figure 12.4. The visible differences are the addition of a program icon and keyboard shortcuts for all menu items and controls.

To create the logo-compliant user interface, complete the following steps:

1. Open the existing project STATIC ANALYSIS.VBP from How-To 7.3 and save a new copy in a different directory.

2. Modify the form and control properties as they are listed in Table 12.1. The new and modified property settings are highlighted in bold. Most of the changes are made to the control captions to add keyboard shortcuts or accelerators.

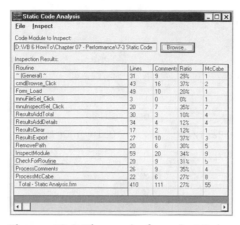

Figure 12.3 The main form in High Contrast White.

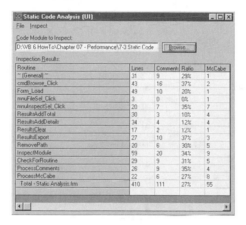

Figure 12.4 The main form with a corrected user interface.

Table 12.1 Project Form's Objects and Properties

OBJECT/CONTROL	PROPERTY	VALUE
Form	Name	frmMain
	Caption	Static Code Analysis (UI)
	Icon	GRAPH01.ICO
CommonDialog	Name	CommonDialog1
CommandButton	Name	cmdBrowse
	Caption	&Browse...
	TabIndex	2

continued on next page

continued from previous page

OBJECT/CONTROL	PROPERTY	VALUE
TextBox	Name	txtFile
	Locked	-1 'True
	TabStop	0 'False
	TabIndex	1
MSFlexGrid	Name	grdResults
	AllowUserResizing	1 'ColumnsOnly
	Appearance	0 'Flat
	Cols	5
	Rows	2
	TabIndex	4
Label	Name	lblCaption
	Caption	&Code Module to Inspect:
	Index	0
	TabIndex	0
Label	Name	lblCaption
	Caption	Inspection &Results:
	Index	1
	TabIndex	3
Menu	Name	mnuFile
	Caption	&File
Menu	Name	mnuFileSel
	Caption	E&xit
	Index	0
Menu	Name	mnuTest
	Caption	&Inspect
Menu	Name	mnuInspectSel
	Caption	&Inspect Module
	Enabled	0 'False
	Index	0
Menu	Name	mnuInspectSel
	Caption	-
	Index	1
Menu	Name	mnuInspectSel
	Caption	&Clear Results
	Index	2
Menu	Name	mnuInspectSel
	Caption	&Export Results
	Index	3

3. Modify the **Load** event of the form by adding the code highlighted in bold. Well-behaved applications need to save and restore the window position when the user changes it. The code added here calls a subroutine to get the settings that were saved from the previous execution of the program.

```
Private Sub Form_Load()

' *** Get the previous form settings
Call GetAppSettings

' Configure the results grid

' Start with the first row
grdResults.Row = 0

' Set the width and caption of the first column
grdResults.Col = 0
grdResults.ColWidth(0) = 3500
grdResults.FixedAlignment(0) = vbLeftJustify
grdResults.Text = "Routine"

' Set the width and caption of the second column
grdResults.Col = 1
grdResults.ColWidth(1) = 800
grdResults.ColAlignment(1) = vbCenter
grdResults.FixedAlignment(1) = vbCenter
grdResults.Text = "Lines"

' Set the width and caption of the third column
grdResults.Col = 2
grdResults.ColWidth(2) = 800
grdResults.ColAlignment(2) = vbCenter
grdResults.FixedAlignment(2) = vbCenter
grdResults.Text = "Comments"

' Set the width and caption of the fourth column
grdResults.Col = 3
grdResults.ColWidth(3) = 800
grdResults.ColAlignment(3) = vbCenter
grdResults.FixedAlignment(3) = vbCenter
grdResults.Text = "Ratio"

' Set the width and caption of the fifth column
grdResults.Col = 4
grdResults.Text = "McCabe"
grdResults.ColWidth(4) = 800
grdResults.FixedAlignment(4) = vbCenter
grdResults.ColAlignment(4) = vbCenter

' Set the variable that points to the first usable grid row
mnCurrentRow = 1

' Load the decision point keywords for McCabe complexity analysis
msKeywords = Array("SELECT CASE", "FOR", "DO", _
```

continued on next page

continued from previous page

```
                                "WHILE", "UNTIL", "IIF", "CHOOSE", _
                                "SWITCH", "IF", "ELSEIF", "#IF", "#ELSEIF", _
                                "CASE ", "AND ", "OR ")

    ' Load the routine start keyword array
    msRoutines = Array("SUB ", "FUNCTION ", "PROPERTY ", "EVENT ", _
                                "PUBLIC SUB ", "PUBLIC FUNCTION ", _
                                "PUBLIC PROPERTY ", "PUBLIC EVENT ", _
                                "PRIVATE SUB ", "PRIVATE FUNCTION ", _
                                "PRIVATE PROPERTY ", "PRIVATE EVENT ")

End Sub
```

4. Add the highlighted code to the **Unload** event of the form. This code
executes when the application exits, and it calls a subroutine to save the
current settings for the application.

```
Private Sub Form_Unload(Cancel As Integer)

' *** Save the current form settings
Call SaveAppSettings

End Sub
```

5. The following subroutine is used to retrieve the previous form position
and then it moves the form to the specified location.

```
Private Sub GetAppSettings()

Dim nLeft            As Integer
Dim nTop             As Integer

' Get the previous left position of the form
nLeft = GetSetting(App.Title, "General", "Left", 0)

' Get the previous top position of the form
nTop = GetSetting(App.Title, "General", "Top", 0)

' Now reposition the form
Me.Move nLeft, nTop

End Sub
```

6. To save the current form location, add this final subroutine to the form.

```
Private Sub SaveAppSettings()

' Save the current form position and dimensions
SaveSetting App.Title, "General", "Left", Me.Left
SaveSetting App.Title, "General", "Top", Me.Top

End Sub
```

How It Works

There were not many changes necessary to make the user interface compliant. The two most common items that need attention are the keyboard shortcuts and the color properties. To make the program compliant, the control captions are changed. Also, the color properties for each control are checked to ensure that system color constant values are always used.

Comments

A word of caution is in order. Pay close attention to the accelerator keys that you use. It is not unusual to find an application that uses the same shortcut key more than once. Be sure to test your program using only the keyboard and keep a list of the accelerators that you have already assigned to the controls on each form.

COMPLEXITY
ADVANCED

12.2 How do I...
Implement drag-and-drop support with Registry entries?

COMPATIBILITY: VISUAL BASIC 5 AND 6

Problem

The Static Analysis program exports data to comma-separated value (CSV) files. I want to save data to a file that is specific to the code analysis process and then be able to import this file into the application. I also want to register the file type so that users can open the file from the Windows Explorer and have the program launch and import the file. Users should also be able to drop the files on the Static Analysis program and have the file opened and imported. How do I establish a custom file type, provide custom import and export, and allow the files to be dropped on the program?

Technique

The problems addressed by this How-To are not all direct requirements for logo certification for a utility program such as Static Analysis. Program support for these characteristics, however, is strongly recommended. Three areas are addressed in this How-To. First, dialog boxes are added to support the import and export functions. The export dialog box enables data to be saved as a CSV file or as a new custom file type. This new file type will be Static Analysis Data files with an extension of .SAD. The Inspect menu is changed to support the two new dialog boxes.

File drag-and-drop capabilities are added as well. This feature allows .SAD files to be dropped on the application. They are then imported, and the data they contain is added to the results grid. This logic depends on the subclassing of the main form and implementing a message callback handling routine. Additional information on subclassing, windows hooks, and callbacks is available in Chapter 8, "Using the Win32 API."

The third major new feature makes the program a self-registering executable. This logic is required to enable the program to meet installation and application removal requirements. The installation program runs the application and instructs it to register itself. At that time, entries are added to the Registry to establish shell support of the new .SAD file type.

Steps

Open and run STATIC ANALYSIS.VBP. Click the Browse command button and select the file DRAGDROP.BAS. Have the program perform the inspection. The program with the revised Inspect menu displaying the analysis results is shown in Figure 12.5.

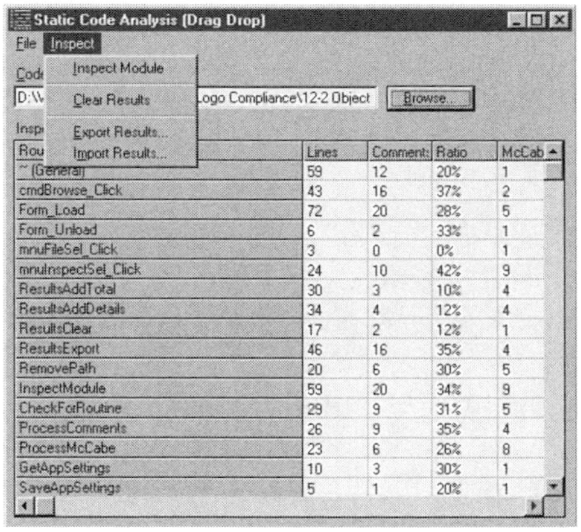

Figure 12.5 The main form at runtime with the new menu.

Choose the Export Results menu option. An example of the export dialog box is shown in Figure 12.6.

The corresponding import dialog box is shown in Figure 12.7. Complete the following steps to drag and drop support Registry entries for the Static Analysis program:

1. Open the existing STATIC ANALYSIS.VBP project with the modified user interface from the previous How-To and save a new copy in a different directory.

Figure 12.6 The new export
dialog box.

Figure 12.7 The new import
dialog box.

2. Modify the form and control properties as they are listed in Table 12.2. The new and modified property settings are highlighted in bold. The changes all relate to the new menu items.

Table 12.2 Project Form's Objects and Properties

OBJECT/CONTROL	PROPERTY	VALUE
Form	Name	frmMain
	Caption	Static Code Analysis (Drag Drop)
	Icon	GRAPH01.ICO

continued on next page

continued from previous page

OBJECT/CONTROL	PROPERTY	VALUE
CommonDialog	Name	CommonDialog1
CommandButton	Name	cmdBrowse
	Caption	&Browse...
TextBox	Name	txtFile
	Locked	-1 'True
	TabStop	0 'False
MSFlexGrid	Name	grdResults
	AllowUserResizing	1 'ColumnsOnly
	Appearance	0 'Flat
	Cols	5
	Rows	2
Label	Name	lblCaption
	Caption	&Code Module to Inspect:
	Index	0
Label	Name	lblCaption
	Caption	Inspection &Results:
	Index	1
Menu	Name	mnuFile
	Caption	&File
Menu	Name	mnuFileSel
	Caption	E&xit
	Index	0
Menu	Name	mnuTest
	Caption	&Inspect
Menu	Name	mnuInspectSel
	Caption	&Inspect Module
	Enabled	0 'False
	Index	0
Menu	Name	mnuInspectSel
	Caption	-
	Index	1
Menu	Name	mnuInspectSel
	Caption	&Clear Results
	Index	2
Menu	Name	mnuInspectSel
	Caption	-
	Index	3

OBJECT/CONTROL	PROPERTY	VALUE
Menu	Name	mnuInspectSel
	Caption	&Export Results...
	Index	4
Menu	Name	mnuInspectSel
	Caption	I&mport Results...
	Index	5

3. Add the highlighted code to the General Declarations section of the form. This new code provides the API constant declarations and also declares the API function prototypes for the Registry functions used later in the program.

```
Option Explicit

' Define variants to hold keyword parsing arrays
Private msKeywords        As Variant
Private msRoutines        As Variant

' Pointer to the current row in the results grid
Private mnCurrentRow      As Integer

' Module scope variables to store incremental
' counters for routine level information
Private mlLines           As Long
Private mlComments        As Long
Private mlMcCabe          As Long

' Module scope variables to store incremental
' counters for module level totals
Private mlTotLines        As Long
Private mlTotComments     As Long
Private mlTotMcCabe       As Long

' Filename and extension of current code module
Private msMainName        As String

' Fully qualified path and filename of current module
Private msCurrentFile     As String

' Name of the current routine in the current module
Private msRoutineName     As String

' *** Establish constants for the registry functions
Const HKEY_CLASSES_ROOT = &H80000000
Const HKEY_CURRENT_USER = &H80000001
Const HKEY_LOCAL_MACHINE = &H80000002
Const HKEY_USERS = &H80000003
Const HKEY_DYN_DATA = &H80000004

Const REG_SZ = 1
```

continued on next page

continued from previous page

```
' Registry error constants
Const ERROR_SUCCESS = 0&
Const ERROR_BADKEY = 1010&

' Registry API prototypes
Private Declare Function RegCreateKey Lib "advapi32.dll" _
  Alias "RegCreateKeyA" _
    (ByVal hkey As Long, _
     ByVal lpSubKey As String, _
     phkResult As Long) As Long

Private Declare Function RegSetValueEx Lib "advapi32.dll" _
  Alias "RegSetValueExA" _
    (ByVal hkey As Long, _
     ByVal lpValueName As String, _
     ByVal Reserved As Long, _
     ByVal dwType As Long, _
     lpData As Any, _
     ByVal cbData As Long) As Long

Private Declare Function RegDeleteKey Lib "advapi32.dll" _
  Alias "RegDeleteKeyA" _
    (ByVal hkey As Long, _
     ByVal lpSubKey As String) As Long
```

4. Modify the **Load** event of the form by adding the code highlighted in bold.
The new code at the beginning of the event parses the command line used
to start the program. It looks for the switch delimiter /. If this character is
found, the program was asked to perform a self-registration task, either to
add or remove its Registry data. The command line is passed to a
subroutine that performs those two tasks.

The new code added to the end of the **Load** event calls a subroutine to
notify the operating system that this program accepts dropped files. It then
parses filenames out of the command line. When the application-specific
file extension is registered and the user opens a file from the Windows
Explorer, the operating system runs the program and passes the filename
to it on the command line. If a filename is found, the file is imported.

```
Private Sub Form_Load()

Dim sCommandLine            As String

' *** Make a local copy of the command line
sCommandLine = Command()

' *** Check for registration commands
If Len(sCommandLine) <> 0 And _
   InStr(1, sCommandLine, "/") <> 0 Then
     ' There are command line arguments with switches
     ' indicating the possibility of registry actions
     Call SelfRegister(sCommandLine)
End If
```

```
' Get the previous form settings
Call GetAppSettings

' Configure the results grid

' Start with the first row
grdResults.Row = 0

' Set the width and caption of the first column
grdResults.Col = 0
grdResults.ColWidth(0) = 3500
grdResults.FixedAlignment(0) = vbLeftJustify
grdResults.Text = "Routine"

' Set the width and caption of the second column
grdResults.Col = 1
grdResults.ColWidth(1) = 800
grdResults.ColAlignment(1) = vbCenter
grdResults.FixedAlignment(1) = vbCenter
grdResults.Text = "Lines"

' Set the width and caption of the third column
grdResults.Col = 2
grdResults.ColWidth(2) = 800
grdResults.ColAlignment(2) = vbCenter
grdResults.FixedAlignment(2) = vbCenter
grdResults.Text = "Comments"

' Set the width and caption of the fourth column
grdResults.Col = 3
grdResults.ColWidth(3) = 800
grdResults.ColAlignment(3) = vbCenter
grdResults.FixedAlignment(3) = vbCenter
grdResults.Text = "Ratio"

' Set the width and caption of the fifth column
grdResults.Col = 4
grdResults.Text = "McCabe"
grdResults.ColWidth(4) = 800
grdResults.FixedAlignment(4) = vbCenter
grdResults.ColAlignment(4) = vbCenter

' Set the variable that points to the first usable grid row
mnCurrentRow = 1

' Load the decision point keywords for McCabe complexity analysis
msKeywords = Array("SELECT CASE", "FOR", "DO", _
                "WHILE", "UNTIL", "IIF", "CHOOSE", _
                "SWITCH", "IF", "ELSEIF", "#IF", "#ELSEIF", _
                "CASE ", "AND ", "OR ")

' Load the routine start keyword array
msRoutines = Array("SUB ", "FUNCTION ", "PROPERTY ", "EVENT ", _
                "PUBLIC SUB ", "PUBLIC FUNCTION ", _
                "PUBLIC PROPERTY ", "PUBLIC EVENT ", _
```

continued on next page

continued from previous page

```
                              "PRIVATE SUB ", "PRIVATE FUNCTION ", _
                              "PRIVATE PROPERTY ", "PRIVATE EVENT ")

    ' *** Tell the OS that the form accepts file drops
    Call EnableFileDrops(frmMain)

    ' *** Check for a non-registration command line with a
    ' file to import
    If Len(sCommandLine) <> 0 Then
        ' Make sure it is a SAD format file
        If UCase$(Right$(sCommandLine, 4)) = ".SAD" Then
            ' It is the correct file type so import it
            Call ResultsImportFile(sCommandLine)
        End If
    End If

    End Sub
```

5. The following code, when added to the Unload event of the form, calls a subroutine to notify the operating system that this program no longer accepts dropped files.

```
Private Sub Form_Unload(Cancel As Integer)

    ' *** Clear the file drop windows hook
    Call DisableFileDrops

    ' Save the current form settings
    Call SaveAppSettings

    End Sub
```

6. Modify the mnuInspectSel Click event procedure to handle the revised Inspect menu choices. The export and import menu items each call a subroutine that performs the respective tasks.

```
Private Sub mnuInspectSel_Click(Index As Integer)

Select Case Index
    Case 0                  ' Analyze the project/module
        ' Clear the module totals
        mlTotLines = 0
        mlTotComments = 0
        mlTotMcCabe = 0
        ' Perform the inspection
        InspectModule

    Case 1                  ' Separator
        ' No code required here

    Case 2                  ' Clear test results
        If (MsgBox("Are you sure you want to " & _
            "clear the results?", vbCritical + vbYesNo)) = vbYes _
        Then
                Call ResultsClear
```

```
                    End If

            Case 3               ' Separator
               ' No code required here

            Case 4               ' Export test results
               Call ResultsExport

            Case 5               ' Import previous results
               Call ResultsImportDialog

      End Select

      End Sub
```

7. The ResultsExport subroutine is modified so that it displays the new export dialog box before exporting the data. The dialog box is displayed as a modal form. When the user is finished with the dialog box, the selected information is pulled into local variables, and the export dialog box form is unloaded. If the user cancels out of the dialog box, the code exits from the subroutine. The next block of code is unchanged except that the open statement now uses the filename chosen by the user.

```
Private Sub ResultsExport()

Dim nLoopRow            As Integer
Dim nLoopCol            As Integer
Dim nChannel            As Integer
Dim sOutput(5)          As String

Dim sExportFile         As String
Dim nExportFormat       As String
Dim bExportCancel       As String

' *** Show the export dialog form
frmExport.Show vbModal

' Get the properties from the dialog
sExportFile = frmExport.FileName
nExportFormat = frmExport.ExportFormat
bExportCancel = frmExport.CancelDialog

' Unload the export dialog form
Unload frmExport

' Check to see if the user canceled the export
If bExportCancel = True Then Exit Sub

' Get an available I/O channel number
nChannel = FreeFile

' For this program there is no functional difference
' between the two output formats. The CSV and SAD formats
' are identical.
```

continued on next page

continued from previous page

```
' Open the output to store the grid contents
Open sExportFile For Output As #nChannel

' Loop through the grid row by row
For nLoopRow = 1 To mnCurrentRow - 1
    ' Set the current grid row
    grdResults.Row = nLoopRow
    ' Loop through the grid columns
    For nLoopCol = 0 To 4
        ' Set the current column
        grdResults.Col = nLoopCol
        ' Save the column data to an array
        sOutput(nLoopCol) = grdResults.Text
    Next nLoopCol
    ' Write the array contents to the file
Write #nChannel, sOutput(0), _
                 sOutput(1), _
                 sOutput(2), _
                 sOutput(3), _
                 sOutput(4)
Next nLoopRow

' Close the results file
Close #nChannel

End Sub
```

8. Add the following new subroutine to the form. This code configures the common dialog box control to display the file import dialog box. After the user selects a file, a subroutine is called to perform the import.

```
Private Sub ResultsImportDialog()

Dim sImportFIle             As String

' *** Configure the common dialog control to select an export file

' Only SAD files can be imported

' Set the dialog title
CommonDialog1.DialogTitle = "Open SAD File for Import"

' Establish the file filter options
CommonDialog1.Filter = "Static Analysis Data (*.sad)¦" & "*.sad"

' Set the current filter to the first one available
CommonDialog1.FilterIndex = 1

' Require that the path and file exist
CommonDialog1.Flags = cdlOFNPathMustExist + _
                      cdlOFNFileMustExist + _
                      cdlOFNHideReadOnly + _
                      cdlOFNLongNames

' Set the initial path used in the dialog
CommonDialog1.InitDir = App.Path
```

```
' Clear the dialog filename
CommonDialog1.FileName = ""

' Tell the control to raise an error on cancel
CommonDialog1.CancelError = True

' Now show the file save dialog
On Error GoTo ResultsImportDialog_CancelError
CommonDialog1.ShowOpen
On Error GoTo 0

' Get the fully qualified file name that the user selected
sImportFIle = CommonDialog1.FileName

' Call the subroutine to import the results file
Call ResultsImportFile(sImportFIle)

ResultsImportDialog_Exit:
' Exit from the subroutine
Exit Sub

ResultsImportDialog_CancelError:
' Resume to the subroutine exit point
Resume ResultsImportDialog_Exit

End Sub
```

9. This next new subroutine physically imports a file of the correct file type. It opens the file passed in as a parameter. Then it reads each line in the file and adds the data to the grid on the main form.

```
Private Sub ResultsImportFile(sFileName)

Dim nLoopRow            As Integer
Dim nLoopCol            As Integer
Dim nChannel            As Integer
Dim sInput(5)           As String

' *** Get an available I/O channel number
nChannel = FreeFile

' Open the input to fetch data to add to the grid
Open sFileName For Input As #nChannel

' Read through the file adding data to the grid row by row
Do Until EOF(nChannel) = True
    ' Read the array contents from the SAD file
    ' This file is in standard CSV format
    Input #nChannel, sInput(0), _
                     sInput(1), _
                     sInput(2), _
                     sInput(3), _
                     sInput(4)
    ' Move the data into the grid
    grdResults.Row = mnCurrentRow
    grdResults.Col = 1
```

continued on next page

continued from previous page

```
            grdResults.Text = sInput(1)
            grdResults.Col = 2
            grdResults.Text = sInput(2)
            grdResults.Col = 3
            grdResults.Text = sInput(3)
            grdResults.Col = 4
            grdResults.Text = sInput(4)
            grdResults.Col = 0
            grdResults.Text = sInput(0)
            ' Add another row to the grid
            mnCurrentRow = mnCurrentRow + 1
            If mnCurrentRow + 1 > grdResults.Rows Then
                grdResults.Rows = mnCurrentRow + 1
            End If
    Loop

    ' Close the input file
    Close #nChannel

    End Sub
```

10. When files are dropped on the form, a message is sent to the program by the operating system. A code module that has not yet been added to the project handles the message itself. When the file drop message is processed, this custom public method of the form is called, and a list of the dropped files is passed in a variant array. This array is read and each filename is passed to the file import subroutine written in the previous step.

```
Public Sub DroppedFiles(vFileList As Variant)

Dim nLoopCtr            As Integer
Dim sFileName           As String

' *** Loop through the variant array to process
' each dropped file
For nLoopCtr = 0 To UBound(vFileList)
    ' Get the current filename from the array
    sFileName = vFileList(nLoopCtr)
    ' Make sure it is a SAD format file
    If UCase$(Right$(sFileName, 4)) = ".SAD" Then
        ' It is the correct file type so import it
        Call ResultsImportFile(sFileName)
    End If
Next nLoopCtr

End Sub
```

11. The following new subroutine handles all the self-registration tasks. Two commands are passed to a self-registering executable by the Install and Uninstall programs. No interaction can occur with the user installing or removing the program, and the code must terminate as soon as it completes the Registry tasks.

The first command invoked by the Install program is /RegServer, and it instructs the program to register itself and make any other Registry entries that it needs. Four Registry entries are needed to establish a custom file type. They are all placed in the HKEY_CLASSES_ROOT section of the Registry. The first key defines the file type, in this case .SAD, which represents Static Analysis Data. This key points to the next section, which defines the file handling parameters. The second key created provides the name used to describe files of the registered type. There are then two subkeys for the second entry. The first subkey provides a reference to the icon that is associated with the file type. The second subkey provides the command used to open the file.

The second command is used by the Uninstall program and is called /UnRegServer. It tells the program to remove all its entries from the Registry. In addition to removing the Registry entries created during the self-registration process, the program also removes any application settings created.

```
Private Sub SelfRegister(sCommandLine As String)

Dim lResult               As Long

' Check to see if the code needs to establish registry settings
If InStr(1, UCase$(sCommandLine), "/REGSERVER") <> 0 Then
    ' Create the file type entries

    ' Register the file extension
    lResult = SetRegValue(HKEY_CLASSES_ROOT, _
                ".sad", _
                "", _
                "StaticAnalysisData")

    ' Register the extension shell handling
    lResult = SetRegValue(HKEY_CLASSES_ROOT, _
                "StaticAnalysisData", _
                "", _
                "Static Code Analysis Export File")
    lResult = SetRegValue(HKEY_CLASSES_ROOT, _
                "StaticAnalysisData\DefaultIcon", _
                "", _
                App.Path & "\" & App.EXEName & ",0")
    lResult = SetRegValue(HKEY_CLASSES_ROOT, _
                "StaticAnalysisData\Shell\open\Command", _
                "", _
                App.Path & "\" & App.EXEName & " " & _
                    Chr$(34) & "%1" & Chr$(34))

    ' Exit from the program
    End

End If
```

continued on next page

continued from previous page

```
' Check to see if the code needs to remove registry settings
If InStr(1, UCase$(sCommandLine), "/UNREGSERVER") <> 0 Then
    ' Delete the form and application settings

    ' The error trapping is in case the application
    ' specific entries do not exist
    On Error Resume Next
    DeleteSetting App.Title, "General"
    DeleteSetting App.Title
    On Error GoTo 0

    ' Delete the file type entries
    lResult = DeleteRegKey(HKEY_CLASSES_ROOT, _
                ".sad", _
                "")
    lResult = DeleteRegKey(HKEY_CLASSES_ROOT, _
                "StaticAnalysisData", _
                "")

    ' Exit from the program
    End

End If

' If the program gets here there were no self-registration
' tasks to perform, so go back to form load

End Sub
```

12. This next function is used to set Registry key values. Notice that throughout the Registry manipulation code module that the key open function is not used. Instead, the code uses the key creation function. If the key does not exist, it is created and then opened. This reduces some potential errors, and if the key already exists, the function does not create it but opens it and returns the key ID. After the key is opened, the value can be set. If the value passed to this function is blank, the key value in the Registry is cleared.

```
Private Function SetRegValue _
            (lKeyRoot As Long, _
             tRegistryKey As String, _
             tSubKey As String, _
             tKeyValue As String) As Long

Dim lKeyId              As Long
Dim lResult             As Long

SetRegValue = 0                     ' Assume success

If Len(tRegistryKey) = 0 Then
    ' The key parameter is not set
    SetRegValue = ERROR_BADKEY
    Exit Function
End If
```

```
' Open the key by attempting to create it. If it
' already exists we get back an ID.
lResult = RegCreateKey(lKeyRoot, _
                tRegistryKey, _
                lKeyId)

If lResult <> 0 Then
    ' Call failed, can't open the key so exit
    SetRegValue = lResult
    Exit Function
End If

If Len(tKeyValue) = 0 Then
    ' No key value, so clear any existing entry
    SetRegValue = RegSetValueEx(lKeyId, _
            tSubKey, _
            0&, _
            REG_SZ, _
            0&, _
            0&)
  Else
    ' Set the registry entry to the value
    SetRegValue = RegSetValueEx(lKeyId, _
            tSubKey, _
            0&, _
            REG_SZ, _
            ByVal tKeyValue, _
            Len(tKeyValue) + 1)
End If

End Function
```

13. Add the following function to delete Registry keys. The code starts by making sure that the key name parameter is not blank. Then it opens the key to get the key ID. This ID is then passed to the key delete API function.

```
Private Function DeleteRegKey _
        (lKeyRoot As Long, _
        tRegistryKey As String, _
        tSubKey As String) As Long

Dim lKeyId          As Long
Dim lResult         As Long

DeleteRegKey = 0            ' Assume success

If Len(tRegistryKey) = 0 Then
    ' The key parameter is not set
    DeleteRegKey = ERROR_BADKEY
    Exit Function
End If

' Open the key by attempting to create it. If it
' already exists we get back an ID.
lResult = RegCreateKey(lKeyRoot, tRegistryKey, lKeyId)
```

continued on next page

continued from previous page

```
If lResult = 0 Then
    ' We got a key ID so we can delete the entry
    DeleteRegKey = RegDeleteKey(lKeyId, ByVal tSubKey)
End If

End Function
```

14. Add a new code module and save it as DRAGDROP.BAS. Place the following code in the General Declarations section of the module. This code declares the API functions used to hook operating system messages and manage the receipt and handling of dropped files. A few module-scope variables are established to track window handles and an object reference to the main form of the application.

```
Option Explicit

Private Declare Function CallWindowProc Lib "user32" _
    Alias "CallWindowProcA" _
        (ByVal lpPrevWndFunc As Long, _
        ByVal hWnd As Long, _
        ByVal Msg As Long, _
        ByVal wParam As Long, _
        ByVal lParam As Long) As Long

Private Declare Function SetWindowLong Lib "user32" _
    Alias "SetWindowLongA" _
        (ByVal hWnd As Long, _
        ByVal nIndex As Long, _
        ByVal dwNewLong As Long) As Long

Private mlPrevWndProc       As Long
Private mhHookWindow        As Long
Private moDropForm          As Object

Private Declare Sub DragAcceptFiles Lib "shell32.dll" _
        (ByVal hWnd As Long, _
        ByVal fAccept As Long)

Private Declare Sub DragFinish Lib "shell32.dll" _
        (ByVal hDrop As Long)

Private Declare Function DragQueryFile Lib "shell32.dll" _
    Alias "DragQueryFileA" _
        (ByVal hDrop As Long, _
        ByVal UINT As Long, _
        ByVal lpStr As String, _
        ByVal ch As Long) As Long

Private Const GWL_WNDPROC = -4
Private Const WM_DROPFILES = &H233
```

15. Add the following public subroutine to the module. The code begins by making sure that messages are not already being hooked. If they are, a call is made to disable the current hooks before settings new ones. Next, the object reference to the main form is stored, and its window handle is obtained. Now the code can set the message-processing hook and notify the operating system that the main form will accept dropped files.

```
Public Sub EnableFileDrops(oDropTarget As Form)

' Be sure we are not already subclassing drops
If mhHookWindow <> 0 Then Call DisableFileDrops

' Save the handle and object reference
' of the calling window
Set moDropForm = oDropTarget
mhHookWindow = moDropForm.hWnd

' Set the subclassing window message hook
mlPrevWndProc = SetWindowLong(mhHookWindow, _
                GWL_WNDPROC, _
                AddressOf HookCallback)

' Tell the OS that the specified window accepts
' dropped files
Call DragAcceptFiles(mhHookWindow, True)

End Sub
```

16. Add the following public subroutine to the module. This subroutine clears the message hook and notifies the operating system that the form no longer accepts dropped files.

```
Public Sub DisableFileDrops()

Dim lReturn        As Long

' Check to be sure that there is a hook active
If mhHookWindow = 0 Then Exit Sub
If IsEmpty(mhHookWindow) = True Then Exit Sub
If IsNull(mhHookWindow) = True Then Exit Sub

' Tell the OS that the specified window no longer
' accepts dropped files
Call DragAcceptFiles(mhHookWindow, False)

' Remove our hook from the system
lReturn = SetWindowLong(mhHookWindow, _
                GWL_WNDPROC, _
                mlPrevWndProc)

' Clear the window handles and references
mhHookWindow = 0
mlPrevWndProc = 0
Set moDropForm = Nothing

End Subthat
```

17. Add the following subroutine, which the operating system calls when it has messages for this program. The code checks to see whether the message is for the main form's window and then looks at the message type to see whether the message is a file drop notification. If the message is the result of a file drop operation, a subroutine is called to get the files of dropped filenames. In all cases, the message is passed on to the next window in the message-processing stack.

```
Function HookCallback(ByVal hWnd As Long, _
            ByVal lMsg As Long, _
            ByVal wParam As Long, _
            ByVal lParam As Long) As Long

Select Case hWnd
    Case mhHookWindow
        ' The message is for the window we subclassed so ...
        ' See if this is a file drop message
        If lMsg = WM_DROPFILES Then
            ' Get the list of dropped files from the OS
            Call GetDropFileList(wParam, lParam)
        End If

    Case Else
        ' The message is for some other window

End Select

' Pass the message through to the next message processor
HookCallback = CallWindowProc(mlPrevWndProc, _
                            hWnd, _
                            lMsg, _
                            wParam, _
                            lParam)

End Function
```

18. Add the following subroutine, which makes repeated API function calls to obtain the list of dropped files. These filenames are put into a variant array, which is then passed to a custom public method of the main form for further processing.

```
Private Sub GetDropFileList(wParam As Long, _
                    lParam As Long)

Dim nDropCount      As Integer
Dim nLoopCtr        As Integer
Dim lReturn         As Long
Dim hDrop           As Long
Dim sFileName       As String
Dim vFileNames      As Variant

' Save the drop structure handle
hDrop = wParam
```

```
' Allocate space for the return value
sFileName = Space$(255)

' Get the number of file names dropped
nDropCount = DragQueryFile(hDrop, -1, sFileName, 254)

' Allocate variant array elements to store the
' dropped file names
vFileNames = Array(" ")
ReDim vFileNames(nDropCount - 1) As String

' Loop to get each dropped file name and
' add it to the variant array
For nLoopCtr = 0 To nDropCount - 1
    ' Allocate space for the return value
    sFileName = Space$(255)
    ' Get a dropped filename

    lReturn = DragQueryFile(hDrop, nLoopCtr, sFileName, 254)
    vFileNames(nLoopCtr) = Left$(sFilcName, lReturn)
Next nLoopCtr

' Release the drop structure from memory
Call DragFinish(hDrop)

' Call the form method to pass the list of dropped files
Call moDropForm.DroppedFiles(vFileNames)

End Sub
```

19. Add a form to the project and set the objects and properties as they are
listed in Table 12.3. Save the form as STATIC ANALYSIS EXPORT.FRM.

Table 12.3   Project Form's Objects and Properties

OBJECT/CONTROL	PROPERTY	VALUE
Form	Name	frmExport
	Caption	Export
	Icon	(None)
CommandButton	Name	cmdAction
	Caption	OK
	Default	-1 'True
	Index	0
CommandButton	Name	cmdAction
	Cancel	-1 'True
	Caption	Cancel
	Index	1

continued on next page

continued from previous page

OBJECT/CONTROL	PROPERTY	VALUE
TextBox	Name	txtFileName
	Locked	-1 'True
	TabStop	0 'False
CommandButton	Name	cmdBrowse
	Caption	&Browse...
OptionButton	Name	optFormat
	Caption	&Comma Separated Value (CSV) File
	Index	0
	Value	-1 'True
OptionButton	Name	optFormat
	Caption	&Static Analysis Data (SAD) Format
	Index	1
CommonDialog	Name	CommonDialog1
Label	Name	lblCaption
	Caption	Select the output format for the data:
	Index	0
Label	Name	lblCaption
	Caption	Select the &output file:
	Index	1

20. Put the following code into the General Declarations section of the form. This code sets up the form scope variables used to store custom properties of the form.

```
Option Explicit

' Define variable to hold the custom form properties

' The user selected filename for the export file
Private msFileName        As String

' The user selected export file format
Private mnExportFormat        As Integer

' Internal logical value used to indicate that the
' user has canceled the dialog
Private mbCancelDialog        As Boolean
```

21. Add the following code to the **Load** event of the form. This logic centers the export dialog box over the main form and sets the default value for the export file type.

```
Private Sub Form_Load()

Dim nLeft        As Integer
```

```
Dim nTop              As Integer

' Center the export form over the main form
nLeft = frmMain.Left + _
        ((frmMain.Width - Me.Width) / 2)
nTop = frmMain.Top + _
        ((frmMain.Height - Me.Height) / 2)
Me.Move nLeft, nTop

' Set the export format to the default
optFormat(0).Value = True

End Sub
```

22. When the user clicks the Browse command button, the following code is executed. This subroutine configures a common dialog box control to enable the user to select an export file. Based on the values of the file type option buttons, the common dialog box is set up to look for either .CSV or .SAD file types. After the user makes a selection, the form and control properties are updated.

```
Private Sub cmdBrowse_Click()

' Configure the common dialog control to select an export file

' Set the dialog title
CommonDialog1.DialogTitle = "Save Export File As"

' Establish the file filter options
Select Case mnExportFormat
    Case 0              ' CSV
        CommonDialog1.Filter = "Comma Separated Value (*.csv)¦" & _
                               "*.csv"

    Case 1              ' SAD
        CommonDialog1.Filter = "Static Analysis Data (*.sad)¦" & _
                               "*.sad"

End Select

' Set the current filter to the first one available
CommonDialog1.FilterIndex = 1

' Require that the path and file exist
CommonDialog1.Flags = cdlOFNPathMustExist + _
                      cdlOFNHideReadOnly + _
                      cdlOFNLongNames + _
                      cdlOFNOverwritePrompt

' Set the initial path used in the dialog
CommonDialog1.InitDir = App.Path

' Tell the control to raise an error on cancel
CommonDialog1.CancelError = True
```

continued on next page

continued from previous page

```
' Now show the file save dialog
On Error GoTo cmdBrowse_CancelError
CommonDialog1.ShowOpen
On Error GoTo 0

' Get the fully qualified filename that the user selected
' and store it as the filename property value
msFileName = CommonDialog1.FileName

' Update the text box contents with the property value
txtFileName.Text = msFileName

cmdBrowse_Exit:
' Exit from the subroutine
Exit Sub

cmdBrowse_CancelError:
' The user clicked the dialog cancel button
' Clear the filename property value
msFileName = ""

' Resume to the subroutine exit point
Resume cmdBrowse_Exit

End Sub
```

23. When a specific file type is selected, the option button values are used to update the custom file type property of the form.

```
Private Sub optFormat_Click(Index As Integer)

' Get the user selected export file type
If optFormat(0).Value = True Then
    mnExportFormat = 0       ' CSV
  Else
    mnExportFormat = 1       ' SAD
End If

End Sub
```

24. The user can either accept the selection or cancel the export dialog box. If the dialog box is canceled, the custom form property is set. The dialog box was displayed as a modal form, so in both cases the form is hidden. Hiding the form enables the code in the main program to continue and fetch the properties from the dialog box.

```
Private Sub cmdAction_Click(Index As Integer)

Select Case Index
    Case 0          ' OK

    Case 1          ' Cancel
        ' Set the cancel property
        mbCancelDialog = True
```

```
End Select

' The code still needs to get property value so do not
' unload the form, just hide it
Me.Hide

End Sub
```

25. All three of the custom form properties are read-only, so only property **Get** procedures are provided. This first routine returns the value of the **FileName** property.

```
Public Property Get FileName() As String

' This is a read-only property!

' Return the property value
FileName = msFileName

End Property
```

26. This second property procedure returns the value of the export format, or file type, that the user selected.

```
Public Property Get ExportFormat() As Integer

' This is a read-only property!

' Return the property value
ExportFormat = mnExportFormat

End Property
```

27. The final property sends back the Boolean value that tells the main program whether the user canceled the export dialog box.

```
Public Property Get CancelDialog() As Boolean

' This is a read-only property!

' Return the property value
CancelDialog = mbCancelDialog

End Property
```

28. When the export dialog box form is unloaded by the main program, this code completely removes the form and all its structures from memory.

```
Private Sub Form_Unload(Cancel As Integer)

' Clear all form references and structures from memory
Set frmExport = Nothing

End Sub
```

How It Works

Window hooks and message callbacks are used to implement file drop handling. The program also now provides dialog boxes that support both imports and exports. The same import logic is used to provide the final processing during file drop operations. Logic has also been added to perform the required self-registration tasks.

Comments

The capability to drop files onto the main form is available as soon as the code is completed. To test the custom file type handling, however, modify the project properties, set the command-line value to /RegServer, and run the project. Use the REGEDIT program to check the Registry keys and values. Then change the command-line property to /UnRegServer and run the project again to clear the Registry settings.

To verify full operation of the self-registration code, the program needs to be installed.

COMPLEXITY
BEGINNING

12.3 How do I...
Meet other miscellaneous requirements?

COMPATIBILITY: VISUAL BASIC 5 AND 6

Problem

There are a significant number of general requirements for logo certification, and many recommendations might become requirements. What are these requirements and recommendations, and do I need to take them into account in my code, or during the certification process?

Technique

This How-To lists many of the general requirements and recommendations in the following steps. Each item is covered in a single step.

Steps

1. The program must be a 32-bit executable or be an add-on for a 32-bit application. If the program is not a compiled executable, it must use a 32-bit runtime library. Visual Basic programs comply with this requirement.

2. The code must be stable and not disrupt or impact the stability of the operating systems. Visual Basic itself meets this requirement, but it is possible to write programs with Visual Basic that won't. Be especially careful and thorough in the testing of programs that heavily use API functions.

WARNING

It is your responsibility to ensure that any third-party controls included in your program comply with the stability requirement. Remember that the certification testing process checks everything installed and used by your code, even if you are not the one who wrote it. If a third-party control endangers your chances of passing the testing process, you have three choices:

✔ Get the vendor to fix its control

✔ Use an alternate control

✔ Don't use the control

3. Multitasking support is required. The program must deal correctly with Alt+Tab or Ctrl+Esc. Visual Basic programs already do this.

4. Because Windows NT supports more than one hardware platform, if your program offers versions for more than one platform, all versions must be part of the same installation kit.

5. The application must run correctly on both Windows 95 and Windows NT.

6. It is strongly recommended that the installations do not require reboots of the system. Also, they should not copy files to the \SYSTEM32 directory.

7. Plan for the future and try to ensure that your program runs on and can be installed from a network.

8. Take advantage of administrator-driven policy management features available with Windows NT and Windows 95. Zero Administration Windows is a significant Microsoft initiative. Remote-user profiles are now supported by Windows 95 and Windows NT. Learn all you can about these topics and plan for them to become requirements soon. Many specific recommendations for policy and user management are in the *Logo Handbook for Software Applications*.

9. Applications should be capable of telling when the operating system is upgraded from Windows 95 to Windows NT. Code and information on detecting the version and type of operating system can be found online at the Microsoft Web site in the MSDN Online area. When the OS changes, adapt your program without requiring user interaction. This is currently only a logo-compliance recommendation.

10. There are a number of recommendations for the support of Microsoft Active Accessibility. These recommendations make it easier for people with motor-skill and visual disabilities to use the applications. The operating system supports most of these services within the standard window and control classes. Some specific recommendations are to adjust fonts and window sizes based on system settings, avoid fonts smaller than 10 points, and avoid nonstandard keyboard and mouse behaviors. Handbooks and white papers are available online that provide suggestions and guidelines for developers regarding accessibility features.

11. It is required that ActiveX controls be digitally signed. It is recommended that ActiveX controls offer automatic Internet download and install, provide help as HTML, and produce browser viewable documents. Refer to Chapters 5 and 6 of this book for information on control creation and distribution.

12. There are a number of specific OLE and COM requirements for document-centric applications. These requirements address the features and functions of OLE containers and servers. Non-file based, or data-centric, applications, utility programs, and Java and multimedia applications are exempt from these requirements in most cases. Refer to the *Logo Handbook for Software Applications* for specific details on the requirements and allowable exemptions.

13. Programs must support Universal Naming Convention and long filenames. These attributes must work on Windows NT FAT, NTFS, and compressed NTFS. Specific requirements include filenames of up to 255 characters, support for all legal filenames supported by the Windows Explorer, use of long filenames whenever filenames are shown in the user interface, and leading and trailing spaces stripping from user-entered filenames. The standard Visual Basic controls and dialog boxes meet these requirements. If the program provides alternative ways for users to enter filenames, care must be taken to ensure these requirements are addressed.

14. There are a number of requirements for TAPI, ACPI/OnNow, and multimonitor support. If your application uses these features, refer to the details in the *Logo Handbook for Software Applications*.

How It Works

Attempt to conform the user interface of new applications to the look and feel of Windows 95 and Windows NT 4. Generally, this positions the program for minor adjustments to make it logo-compliant.

Comments

Always check the Microsoft and third-party testing sites for current information on the logo certification requirements and process. These requirements have changed several times, and the current edition of the handbook states that new requirements are forthcoming. Changes are especially likely when upgrades of the Windows operating systems are released.

COMPLEXITY
INTERMEDIATE

12.4 How do I...
Create customized Install and Uninstall programs?

COMPATIBILITY: VISUAL BASIC 6

Problem

Now that the program itself is ready for logo testing, I need to build compliant installation and uninstallation programs. I want to provide some additional sample files during the install and have them added to the same startup group as the application. The program also needs to perform the self-registration tasks. How do I modify the installation kit built by the Package and Deployment Wizard, and get the program to register itself during the install?

Technique

Many requirements exist for logo-compliant Install and Uninstall programs. The standard installation kit built by the Package and Deployment Wizard already covers many of them. For reference purposes, the following summarizes the install and uninstall requirements:

✔ The Install program must be a 32-bit graphical application. The Install programs produced by the Package and Deployment Wizard meet this requirement.

✔ The program must lead the user through the install process step-by-step. A good example of this is a wizard-style interface. Again, this requirement is already met.

✔ The install code must detect the version and type of 32-bit Windows operating system, such as Windows 95 or Windows NT, and install the correct version of the program and all supporting components. The Package and Deployment Wizard produces an Install program that does this.

✔ All Start menu shortcuts must work. Build the installation kit and test it to be sure.

✔ If your application is distributed on CD, it must support Autoplay.

✔ The Install and Uninstall programs must be capable of being started by the user from the Add/Remove Application section of the Control Panel. Install kits built with the Package and Deployment Wizard support this capability.

✔ All programs need to default their installation location to a subdirectory of \PROGRAM FILES. The Package and Deployment Wizard can be instructed to use this default. This setting is placed in the SETUP.LST file. Just don't change it.

✔ Do not put any application-specific DLLs in the system root directory. This is also the default in SETUP.LST. Resist the temptation to change it.

✔ Before starting any specific install task, make sure that there are adequate resources to complete it. For example, check the amount of free disk space before copying files. The wizard-generated install kit performs these checks.

✔ Register all shared components that the Install program loads but do not increment their reference counts. During application removals, do not decrement the counts. This happens automatically when the Package and Deployment Wizard is used to build the kits.

✔ Version check all components being installed. Again, the wizard-created code does this.

✔ Perform the appropriate DLL, executable, and shared component registration functions. The Setup Wizard kit supports this requirement but only performs the task for system components. If the kit includes a nonsystem self-registering program, the install kit must be modified to tell the Install program to register the program.

✔ The Uninstall program is required to remove all files and folders created during installation, Registry entries created to launch the uninstaller, and all Start menu and desktop shortcuts for the application, and is required decrement application-specific reference counts in the Registry. If a self-registering program was installed, it must be invoked to unregister itself.

✔ The Uninstall program must remove itself from the system when finished.

✔ If the application being installed creates non-user initiated files, the Uninstall program also needs to remove them. If these files are not deleted, the Uninstall program cannot delete the program directory. A common example of this situation is the creation of GID files by the help engine.

To have the Uninstall program remove these types of files, include a file with the same name with zero length as part of the install kit.

There are currently defects in the Package and Deployment Wizard that impact its ability to build functional and compliant installation programs. Also, the Uninstall program provided with the wizard always reports errors when it is run. Details on the defects and some workarounds are listed in the following sections.

How It Works

There are a number of significant defects in the Package and Deployment Wizard as it currently exists. These include the following:

✔ Start menu shortcuts are not created incorrectly for any menu items that reference long filenames containing spaces. To avoid this problem, rebuild all executables so there are no spaces in their filenames. You will also have to rename all files that will be used as Start menu items.

✔ Self-registering executables are not run by the installation program. There is no effective workaround to this problem other than patching the source code of the SETUP1 program to correct the defect.

✔ The Uninstall program always reports a serious failure, even when the application removal is a success. There is no workaround for this defect.

Comments

Until the defects in the Package and Deployment Wizard are addressed by Microsoft, you should use an alternate tool. The InstallShield program is an alternative solution that produces compliant Install and Uninstall programs.

Please monitor the MCP Web site at www.mcp.com for an update to this How-To. When the defects in the Package and Deployment Wizard are corrected, this How-To will be republished with steps and examples.

EXTENDING VB AND MANAGING DEVELOPMENT

13

EXTENDING VB AND MANAGING DEVELOPMENT

How do I...

13.1 Use the repository?

13.2 Use Visual SourceSafe?

13.3 Build an add-in?

13.4 Create a wizard?

Since its inception, Visual Basic has been an extensible language. In fact, its ability to be extended was one of the driving forces behind its success. The Visual Basic Extension (VBX) format has since been replaced by the ActiveX specification (renamed from OCX controls during Microsoft's Internet thrust). One area where Visual Basic was not particularly strong in the past, however, was in extending the development environment and providing integration with version control systems. Third-party tools, such as VBAssist, filled many of the gaps in earlier versions of Visual Basic, and Visual Basic 4 provided limited add-in support, primarily to integrate Visual SourceSafe.

With the release of Visual Basic 5, Microsoft shipped a powerful new extensibility object model. It enabled manipulation of form objects, user interface objects, code objects, project and component objects, and add-in management objects, as well as providing the capability to respond to events in the integrated development environment (IDE), such as project saves. Also included was the new repository, which is used by tools such as the Visual Component Manager to offer significant object storage and manipulation capabilities.

Starting with Visual Basic 5 and continuing with version 6, the language has arrived regarding extensibility and the capabilities required to manage enterprise development. In this chapter, you will see how you can use these new and improved tools to manage team development, enhance code reuse, and simplify advanced tasks such as code generation.

13.1 Use the Repository

Based on Microsoft's repository, the Visual Component Manager (VCM) enables you to store and manage Visual Basic components (in the broadest sense of the term, including forms, code, classes, controls, and so on). This How-To focuses on repository basics and using the VCM from an individual developer's perspective or for team coding in a networked environment.

13.2 Use Visual SourceSafe

First bundled with the Enterprise Edition of Visual Basic 4, Visual SourceSafe found a receptive audience with Visual Basic corporate developers. Visual Basic 6 Enterprise Edition also includes the version control software. The fundamentals necessary to deploy and integrate Visual SourceSafe into your development practices are covered in this How-To.

13.3 Build an Add-In

Add-in capability first appeared in Visual Basic 4, but the later releases have shown dramatic improvements to the Add-In model. This How-To covers the creation of simple add-ins, illustrating the nearly limitless possibilities available to the developer extending the IDE.

13.4 Create a Wizard

Wizard add-in capability offers many exciting possibilities for automating complex tasks. This How-To covers the creation of a message box wizard that illustrates the fundamentals of wizard-style add-ins.

COMPLEXITY
INTERMEDIATE

13.1 How do I...
Use the repository?

COMPATIBILITY: VISUAL BASIC 5 AND 6

Problem

I need a way to extend Visual Basic to store, organize, and share reusable components. I've tried using Visual SourceSafe as well as simple file sharing over a network but have found both to be less than adequate solutions to the problem of managing Visual Basic resources in an enterprise environment. Is there a way I can take advantage of features available in Visual Basic to implement good component management?

Technique

Visual Basic 6 is packaged with a wealth of tools aimed at strengthening and securing its place in enterprise development. One of the least known, the repository, is perhaps one of the most powerful. As you will see, the repository is an enabling technology that serves as a foundation for tools designed to significantly extend the functionality of Visual Basic. With a working knowledge of the repository, you can create or implement your own component management solutions.

Introducing the Repository

The repository is designed to dynamically store, organize, and share information as objects, allowing the developer the ability to catalogue and reuse all types of Visual Basic components, including projects, forms, and code. Among other things, Microsoft developed the repository to improve the support of object reuse, tracking of object dependencies, visualization of application structure, data resource management, and team development. Although the repository can be used to store object information pertaining to just about anything, this How-To focuses on its usefulness as an extension to the Visual Basic IDE.

At its core, the repository is an engine exposing methods that read and write object-oriented data to a relational database, such as Access or SQL Server, to create and manage data, tool descriptions, and object instances. You may find it beneficial to think of the repository as a toolset composed of the engine, information models, tools, and data.

There are essentially two ways you can use the repository to extend Visual Basic. The first is to install a Microsoft or third-party tool that uses the repository, such as the Visual Component Manager (which is discussed shortly), or you can manipulate the repository directly with Visual Basic. In either case, you will find a good working understanding of repository fundamentals to be useful.

Repository Fundamentals

The repository can use either JET or SQL Server to store data, but the Repository Add-In does require that Data Access Objects (DAO) be present. Because Visual Basic installs DAO by default, this shouldn't be a problem unless you have removed DAO. Even though the repository uses databases familiar to most Visual Basic developers, to be safe, you should never write directly to the database; instead, use the repository's data manipulation methods. The Repository Engine contains both ActiveX and DCOM interfaces to manage the repository and its data.

The Type Information Model is the special model used by the repository to understand all Tool Information Models (TIMs). A *TIM* is a model that describes the objects and relationships for a particular repository-based tool. Visual Basic 6, for example, has a TIM named `MdoTypeLib` that details all the objects and relationships that make up a Visual Basic project.

The Microsoft Development Objects Model (MDO model) is an extensible information model for storing and manipulating Visual Basic project data. If you develop a tool to use the repository, you can create your own TIM, use MDO, or extend MDO.

The Visual Basic Repository Add-In uses MDO and provides automatic updating of Visual Basic project data in the repository. The add-in ships with the Professional and Enterprise editions of Visual Basic. It is not, however, activated during installation and you cannot enable it by using Visual Basic's Add-In Manager. You can manually register the add-in, but in most cases you would not want to activate the add-in yourself. Once activated, the add-in automatically populates the repository database with information about your Visual Basic projects, and your only means of using this information is by directly manipulating the repository. Therefore, there is little point in incurring the overhead of running the add-in without a tool to use the data automatically being written to the repository.

The Repository Browser, however, can be used to view repository data and information models, and it is very useful if you are developing a repository tool, but it wouldn't be of much help in actually using the data written by the add-in. The browser was developed by Crescent Software, and it can be found in OS\MSAPPS\REPOSTRY\REPBROWS.EXE on the Visual Basic CD-ROM. What use is the add-in then? Well, it can be activated and used by third-party tools designed to extend Visual Basic, or you can use it yourself if you intend to develop your own tools that use the repository to extend Visual Basic.

If you intend to programmatically manipulate the repository, review the MSDN article "The Microsoft Repository—An Overview." The article contains a pointer to a sample application. The samples include a simple Repository

Browser that is a useful example of repository programming. It also includes an MDO.BAS module, as well as a module containing declarations for variables that represent object identifiers for Type Information Model objects. The other sample included is a custom TIM with two interfaces designed to illustrate the finer details of repository programming.

The Visual Component Manager (VCM)

The repository can be put to good use by Visual Basic without using the add-in and programming it yourself, as evidenced by the Visual Component Manager (VCM). VCM comes with the Enterprise edition of Visual Basic. The Visual Component Manager appears under the Enterprise Tools selection on the setup menus. VCM uses the repository to manage and store reusable project components.

VCM has many features that are useful to the enterprise developer as well as the garage programmer. You can use it to store and search for ActiveX controls, database connections, documents, projects, and templates, including forms, classes, and code. Because VCM databases can be accessed over a network, you can easily publish and share common components with a group of developers.

If you have installed VCM, you will find a Visual Component Manager item under the View menu and on the toolbar. The first time you run VCM it automatically creates a local repository database containing all the components it finds on your system.

VCM uses an Explorer-style interface to display your components. Because it is preloaded with all the components supplied by Visual Basic, you can do a lot of exploring before adding your own elements. Figure 13.1 displays the VCM interface.

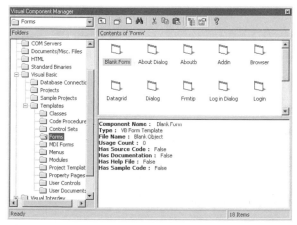

Figure 13.1 The Visual Component Manager main interface.

The hierarchy used by VCM is as follows:

Databases ▶ Groups ▶ Items

The following descriptions apply to the different levels of this hierarchy:

✔ Repository Databases can be either JET or SQL Server, local or remote.

✔ Groups exist for each type of data that can be kept in the database. Group folders can also contain other groups.

✔ Items are the basic elements that VCM stores, such as forms and code.

The following are the available group types:

✔ ActiveX Controls

✔ ActiveX Designers

✔ ActiveX Servers

✔ Class Templates

✔ Code Procedure Templates

✔ ControlSet Templates

✔ Database Connections

✔ Documents/Files

✔ Form Templates

✔ MDI Form Templates

✔ Menu Templates

✔ Module Templates

✔ Projects

✔ Project Templates

✔ Property Page Templates

✔ Samples

✔ Shortcuts

✔ Templates

✔ User Control Templates

✔ User Document Templates

✔ Wizards

Learn How VCM Stores Items

When you add items, it is important to note how VCM behaves if the item is changed in Visual Basic. For example, if you have a form named `frmTest` (filename frmTest.frm) and you add it as an item to the Form Templates group, subsequent changes have the following consequences:

Action: Using VCM, `frmTest` is added to a new project; the form is then changed and you save the project.

Result: You are prompted for the file path to use when saving `frmTest`. Remember, unless your intention is to change the form template itself, you should save to a new location that is specific to the project you are working on.

Action: `frmTest` is deleted from VCM.

Result: The disk file, frmTest.frm, is unchanged.

Action: The frmTest.frm file is deleted or moved and using VCM you attempt to add `frmTest` to a project.

Result: A Template Failed to Load Correctly, File Not Found error occurs. In this case, even though the item's underlying file has been deleted, VCM does not remove the item automatically. In fact, you can right-click the item and choose the Change Location Reference menu to point the item at another form file.

Create or Open a VCM Repository Database

Right-click the VCM icon in the left pane (most things in VCM are initiated by right-clicking). Choose the Repository Database menu item and then select from the Open Database or Create New Database items. The VCM menu is shown in Figure 13.2.

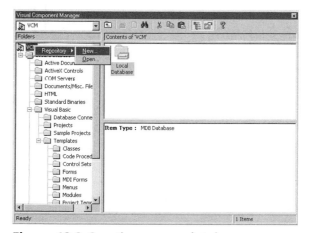

Figure 13.2 Creating a new database in VCM.

The default local database is stored in your Windows directory under \MSAPPS\REPOSTRY\REPOSTRY.MDB. You might want to create a new database to store your own components or your department's components separately from the default local database. When you create a new database, it has the same groups as the default database, but it contains no items—it's up to you to add new items and groups.

Add an Item to Your Project

Double-click the item in the contents pane or right-click the item and select the Add to my Project menu. In some cases, the menu may be Add to Toolbar, Add Reference to My Project, and so on, depending on what type of item you are adding.

Add a New Group

Right-click the parent group that you want to contain the new group. If the parent group is a database, such as the local database, then you can make the group any type you would like. Otherwise, the new group's type is dictated by the parent group's type. For example, if you create a group under Projects, the new group is of type Project.

Add a New Item

Select the group that you want to place the item into, then right-click the contents pane and select New from the menu. You should see a submenu of the appropriate type; select it and use the file requester to locate the item's file.

Delete a Group or Item

Right-click the group or item to remove and then select the Delete menu. You can also use the Delete key to remove selected groups and items.

Manage a Shared Network Repository Database

Publishing Visual Basic components on a network for a group of developers goes a long way toward promoting code reuse as well as providing a mechanism to keep your components properly versioned. When publishing a component, the primary consideration is whether the developer needs to make a local copy of the component.

If you want to retrieve a project or class from a shared network database, the VCM help file instructs you to drag the component from the shared database to the appropriate group in your local database, and then use Windows Explorer to copy the physical component to your system. The component's path property must then be edited to reflect the file location on your local machine. Finally, select Install on My System to insert the component into your project.

Another option, in some cases, is to publish the component so that the files are read-only, and the component properties reflect the UNC file path (\\SERVER\SHARE\FILENAME). This eliminates the step of editing the component's properties, and because the file is read-only, the user can't save over the original template. When the developer saves the project, a new local file path has to be specified anyway. This way the developer does not keep a local version of the component template itself, which can minimize version problems.

If the component is an ActiveX control then it needs to be copied to the local machine. The component can be copied by dragging it from the shared database to a local database. At this point, the OCX file itself has not been copied and the path to it in VCM is wrong because it is referencing the location of the file in relation to the server where it was originally installed (for example, C:\WINDOWS\SYSTEM\AGRID.OCX). To fix the path, right-click the component in your local database and then choose Edit Properties and enter the UNC path (for example, \\SATURN\ACCTSHARE\WINDOWS\SYSTEM\AGRID.OCX).

Next, right-click the component in the local database and choose Add to Project. This method actually copies the OCX, registers it with your local system, and inserts it into your current project. This is a slick way to distribute ActiveX controls to developers, but controls with support DLLs will not work properly, so they still must be installed by using a setup program. The component installation menu is shown in Figure 13.3.

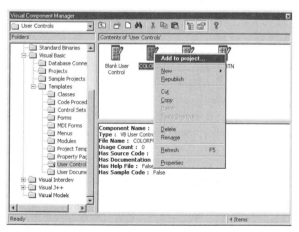

Figure 13.3 Install a component on the local machine.

How It Works

The repository is a flexible technology that offers a powerful way to extend Visual Basic. As you have seen, the repository can be best thought of as a toolset composed of the database engine, information models, tools, and data. You can use the Visual Component Manager (VCM), a repository-based tool, to add strong component management and reuse capabilities to Visual Basic.

Comments

A thorough discussion of repository programming is beyond the scope of this book, but you have seen the usefulness of readily available repository-based tools, such as the Visual Component Manager. VCM can be used in a variety of ways to solve problems related to organizing and sharing reusable components for yourself, for a team, or for the enterprise.

COMPLEXITY
INTERMEDIATE

13.2 How do I...
Use Visual SourceSafe?

COMPATIBILITY: VISUAL BASIC 4, 5, AND 6

Problem

My development team needs a way to manage shared Visual Basic projects so that we can minimize version problems and keep track of project changes without a lot of administrative overhead. Would Visual SourceSafe do all of this?

Technique

Visual SourceSafe is the version control management system that ships with the Enterprise edition of Visual Basic 6, and although it offers broad functionality, it remains easy to set up, use, and administer. If you have ever worked in a team-coding environment then you are probably painfully aware of the need for a source code management system in such a situation. Change management is difficult enough in a single-programmer situation, but problems increase exponentially with team development.

Visual SourceSafe (VSS) can work with many kinds of data, but it is particularly well suited to use with Visual Basic because it is integrated into the development environment as an add-in. A large part of effective version control and source code management involves the standards and practices that are put into place. Each team member must follow the same check-in and check-out procedures as well as agreed-upon standards.

You should probably anticipate that VSS, or any version control software for that matter, will likely result in a significant cultural change at your site. Some programmers can be protective of their work and are reluctant to have it readily available to other team members. Others are concerned that their work will be excessively scrutinized, and some simply don't like to share their code. These attitudes are unproductive. Quality work can withstand scrutiny, and good team development requires code sharing. This point can't be overemphasized, so plan for some difficulties if you have a large shop, and try to emphasize the positive aspects of source code control.

Guidelines for Setting Up Visual SourceSafe

VSS enables a standalone or network installation. The administrator needs to determine how clients access VSS. Clients can run VSS directly over the network, but it can be slow and restrict bandwidth. A full network install enables clients to be set up from the network (by running NSETUP), which is convenient because developers can handle the client installation themselves.

One of the more advantageous features that VSS sports is its tight integration with Visual Basic's IDE. If Visual Basic was already installed when you installed VSS, you will find that VSS is not available in the IDE. To get VSS to appear in the IDE, run the VSS Setup from your hard drive. Select Add/Remove and then click Enable SourceSafe Integration. The next time you run Visual Basic, a SourceSafe item appears under the Tools menu.

Setting up VSS appropriately from the beginning is a critical factor in successfully using the product. For example, you could be in an environment that includes several ongoing projects that are being developed by both in-house staff and contractors. Because the code might be relatively sensitive corporate data that needs to be safeguarded, it is important that a contractor who might have been hired for a one-month stint on a small project be prevented from walking off with all the corporate code. VSS handles these problems easily because it makes the assignment of user, project, and folder rights quite straightforward. If the source code is maintained on one of the network servers, backup copies can be made during the nightly backup.

After installation, you must set the Admin password, create the user list and user passwords, create projects, and set access rights. The Admin password must be set up; otherwise, any user can run VSS Administrator. User list creation is straightforward; you simply enter a name and password. A user can also be set to have read-only status at this time. If project security is enabled, the user's rights are set to whatever default has been set in the VSS Administrator. The Admin password dialog is shown in Figure 13.4.

Figure 13.4 Set the Admin
password.

A typical security concern is preventing users such as testers from being able
to change project code. The easiest way to handle such a situation is to assign
read-only rights at the user level. User-level rights are set to either read-only or
read-write (the default).

In most cases, however, there are developers who need read-write access to
some projects, but not to all projects. Furthermore, finer control is often needed
than that provided by the read-only/read-write user-level rights. This can easily
be accomplished by using project security. Project security is not enabled by
default, so it must be activated by using the Visual SourceSafe Administrator.
After activation, you can access project security by using the Tools menu, where
rights can be seen by project, assignments for users, and copy user rights listed.
User rights are shown in Figure 13.5.

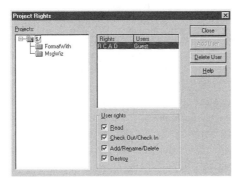

Figure 13.5 Setting rights.

Rights are assigned in VSS using combinations of RCAD:

✔ Read

✔ Check Out/Check In

✔ Add/Rename/Delete

✔ Destroy

It is a simple matter to associate rights for each person by project or for each project by person; use whatever is most convenient.

Copy user rights lets you set up a new user by copying the settings from an existing user. After copying, changes made to either user's settings do not affect the other's rights.

Another critical issue that must be considered by the administrator is whether to allow multiple checkouts. The default is to not permit multiple checkouts, so a project can be checked out only by a single user at a time. If you have projects where two or more developers need to be working on the same code at the same time, then multiple checkouts can be very useful. It can also be fraught with peril because at check-in the programmer is basically merging a branch, and careful thought must go into each decision on which code to keep and which to overwrite. The multiple checkout property is shown in Figure 13.6.

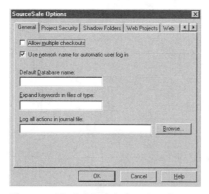

Figure 13.6 Multiple checkout property.

How you organize your projects is, to some degree, a matter of personal preference, but just as with file directories, a well-thought-out hierarchy pays off in the long run. Subprojects can make code much easier to manage, so try to break large projects into smaller pieces.

Maintain VSS

The VSS database is stored in the DATA directory and it must be accessible to all users. The data is stored as database files shared across several directories, so any attempt to view those native files is futile.

The DATA folder contains all the project data for your team, so it should be regularly backed up. If users are in VSS when you make the backup, RIGHTS.DAT is not copied, so it is best to make a separate backup of it. The central database can become corrupt, as can any database, so you need to run the VSS Analyze program from the command prompt to make repairs.

VSS Basics

The VSS Explorer is the easiest way to interact with the product, but command line access is also available and can be useful to an administrator needing to run batch jobs. The Explorer is styled after Windows Explorer, and as such it is easy to use. Because of the tight integration with the Visual Basic IDE basic VSS features can be managed from within Visual Basic. The VSS menu is shown in Figure 13.7.

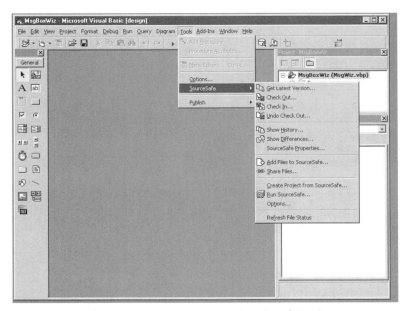

Figure 13.7 The VSS menu structure in Visual Basic.

Each project has an associated working directory that is the local directory to which files are copied when a file is checked out. As changes are made to the project, only the local copy in the working directory is affected until the project is checked back in. After they're checked in, the files in the local directory are posted to the VSS database. If you load a checked-in project from your working directory, you will find that Visual Basic marks the files as read-only. This is a handy reminder that the project should be checked out before you edit it.

The most elemental tasks a developer performs in VSS include checking code in and out. VSS uses a reverse Delta scheme, so that the latest version is stored in full and all previous versions are stored as differences from the current version. This provides a permanent history of all changes made to the project, as well as allows you to revert to previously saved versions.

One powerful feature of the history function is visual differences (diff'ing), in which changes, additions, and deletions can easily be compared across different versions of your code. The visual differences interface is shown in Figure 13.8.

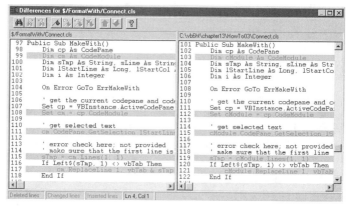

Figure 13.8 Visual differences.

Checking files in and out is easy enough—you can even do it from Visual Basic's IDE—but developers must check in at least daily, if not more frequently. Turning on the Leave Checked Out property is usually not a good idea because it limits your ability to use history and to track project changes. In most cases, you don't want to include executables in VSS either, because diff'ing binary files is pointless. When a product is shipped, however, it is a good idea to save the entire release, including executables, so that you can better manage version and release control.

Another way to retrieve project files, other than by checking them out, is to use the Get Latest Version command. Doing so places a read-only copy of the project in the working directory. This can be useful if you want to compile the project or to review its status.

As you populate the VSS database, you will likely encounter situations where you have files that are common to more than one project, such as a .BAS file. VSS accommodates this situation by allowing files to be shared across projects. The database stores a single copy of the file, so any changes made to the file from any project are replicated across all projects that share the file. This powerful feature ensures that all projects are using the latest version of the code. On the other hand, developers need to be aware that any changes they make to shared files propagate to all projects that share the code. A developer who inserts changes to shared code for the purposes of testing, for example, would not want to check the project in because it appears in all projects using the file.

As projects are checked in, VSS developers are given the opportunity to apply a version label. Projects should be appropriately labeled in VSS to simplify version management. Consistent project labeling is another practice that developers must be strongly encouraged to follow.

Become Familiar with Advanced VSS Features

Cloaking is useful when you need to perform an action on a group of projects and you want to omit select subprojects. For example, if you wanted to get the latest version of all files under the Klingon project except documentation, you would simply cloak the documentation subproject.

If you need to make sure your project always has a particular version of a shared file, you can *pin* the file. Pinning a file, in effect, freezes it at a specific version. Even if other developers make subsequent changes to the shared file, the project that has pinned the file always uses the pinned version.

Branching and merging are among VSS's most powerful and complex features. They require a heightened vigilance on the developer's part because many decisions may be required concerning which code to keep. A *branched file* is a shared file that been separated into two distinct development paths. This may be done to accommodate a new version while maintenance changes are being made to the current version or to keep separate code based on client customizations. Whatever your reasons, it is important to remember that changes to a branched file do not propagate as they do with a basic shared file.

Branched files can later be merged to restore a single development path. If the Visual Merge option is set, VSS displays a visual dialog box when merging. This feature is a convenient way to manage conflicts resulting from merging.

How It Works

SourceSafe was an established product when Microsoft purchased it and reworked it into what is now Visual SourceSafe. Visual Basic developers who have not used version control management systems will find that the minimal time required to set up and administer VSS is well worth the effort. Very few tools can offer the excellent return on investment that VSS can offer the Visual Basic development shop.

Comments

Visual SourceSafe is an intuitive, mature tool that can easily serve as the cornerstone of a corporate configuration management system. The extensive hooks into Visual Basic's IDE make using SourceSafe very convenient, and although it is not as full-featured as its main rival PVCS, it is easier to set up and use.

COMPLEXITY
INTERMEDIATE

13.3 How do I...
Build an Add-In?

COMPATIBILITY: VISUAL BASIC 5 AND 6

Problem

I need a way to customize Visual Basic's development environment to automate some of the repetitive tasks that my team performs every day.

Technique

Almost any task that can be accomplished in the Visual Basic IDE can be automated with an add-in. Add-ins can operate on multiple projects, manipulate code, and dock their interface window to the Visual Basic IDE windows. Menus and toolbars can be customized and your add in menu items can be inserted directly into Visual Basic's IDE. User actions (events) can be trapped, allowing detailed control over a programming session. Visual Basic 6 supports four add-in types:

- ✔ *Add-Ins.* This is the basic add-in type, the one discussed in this section, that can be used to interact with the IDE or to respond to IDE events.

- ✔ *Wizards.* You have undoubtedly encountered Microsoft Wizards at some point. Wizards are typically used to automate a complex task by guiding the user through a series of steps while collecting information. Wizard construction is examined in detail later in this chapter (see How-To 13.4).

- ✔ *Utilities.* Utilities do not require Visual Basic to run (they can be IDE add-ins, however), so they must be compiled as ActiveX executables.

- ✔ *Builders.* Builders are used to display control properties and typically are used to change properties values for a group of controls.

The easiest way to build an add-in is to use the Add-In template provided with Visual Basic 6. When creating a new project, you have the opportunity to select the Add-In template, as shown in Figure 13.9.

The Add-In template creates a project named MyAddIn that includes a form named frmAddIn, a module named AddIn, and a class named Connect. The AddIn module contains an AddToINI subroutine that writes the required entry to VBAddIn.ini to register the add-in. The Connect class contains event handling for the add-in. The form is intended as a starting point for your add-in's interface.

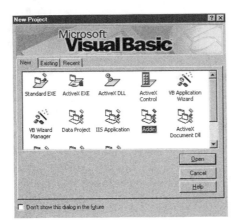

Figure 13.9 Project templates.

The Extensibility Object model is programmed when developing an add-in. VBIDE.VBE is the root object that contains all other objects and collections represented in the Visual Basic Environment. Use the Object Browser to view the details of the object model (see Figure 13.10).

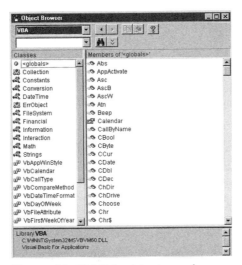

Figure 13.10 VBA objects and collections.

VBIDE also contains an interface named `IDTExtensibility` that, when implemented, lets you manipulate VBIDE.VBE objects. The `Connect` class provided by the Add-In template includes a declaration to implement

`IDTExtensibility`. Note that if you were to create an add-in without using the template, you would be required to manually include a reference to the Microsoft Visual Basic 6.0 Extensibility Object Library as well as the Microsoft Office 8.0 Object Library (needed for CommandBar controls).

After selecting the Add-In template, to get a simple add-in working all that is required is to compile the project as an ActiveX DLL or ActiveX EXE; then in the Immediate window, enter `AddToIni`. Note that the Add-In template defaults to the ActiveX EXE compilation setting. Next, use the File menu to select a new Standard EXE project. Finally, from the Add-Ins menu, choose Add-In Manager and select your new add-in. This add-in doesn't do anything useful, but from this basic shell, you can construct very powerful add-ins.

One important decision that must be made concerning add-ins is whether to compile them as ActiveX DLLs or ActiveX EXEs. DLLs are in-process and, as such, are much faster than EXEs, so in most cases add-ins should be compiled to a DLL. If the add-in needs to run standalone, then it must be compiled as an EXE.

The Add-In template can be used as a starting point for a demonstration project that does something a little more useful than just popping up a message box on connection. It is not uncommon to have code, often imported from Visual Basic 3, that does not take advantage of the `With` statement available in later versions of Visual Basic. It can be quite tedious to manually convert a block of code, such as the following

```
FrmTest.Left = 100
FrmTest.Top = 100
FrmTest.Height = 2000
FrmTest.Width = 2000
```

To this

```
With frmTest
  .Left = 100
  .Top = 100
  .Height = 2000
  .Width = 2000
End With
```

Steps

This is a good candidate for an add-in. The simplest design would be to insert an item on the Visual Basic menu that when clicked converts the selected code to the `With`/`End With` format. To accomplish this, the add-in needs to do the following:

✔ Add a menu item to the IDE.

✔ Identify the active control (containing the code).

✔ Retrieve the contents of the selection.

✔ Validate the format of the selection.

✔ Parse and reformat the selection.

✔ Paste the modified code back into the code module.

Complete the following steps to create this project.

1. The sample code for the **FormatWith** project is included on the CD-ROM. Compile and run **AddToIni** in break mode, as described previously, to prepare the add-in.

2. Use the Add-In Manager to start the add-in (see Figure 13.11). The form provided by the Add-In template was removed because the only interface required for the project was the IDE menu item.

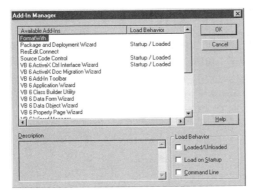

Figure 13.11 The Add-In Manager.

3. Add a menu item to the IDE. The Add-In template supplies a routine named **AddToAddInCommandBar** that can be used to add a menu item to the IDE under Add-Ins (see Listing 13.1).

Listing 13.1 Insert Menu Item into IDE

```
Function AddToAddInCommandBar(sCaption As String) As Office.CommandBarControl
    Dim cbMenuCommandBar As Office.CommandBarControl   'command bar object
    Dim cbMenu As Object

    On Error GoTo AddToAddInCommandBarErr
    'see if we can find the Add-Ins menu
    Set cbMenu = VBInstance.CommandBars("Add-Ins")

    If cbMenu Is Nothing Then
        'not available so we fail
```

```
        Exit Function
    End If

    'add it to the command bar
    Set cbMenuCommandBar = cbMenu.Controls.Add(1)
    'set the caption
    cbMenuCommandBar.Caption = sCaption
    Set AddToAddInCommandBar = cbMenuCommandBar
    Exit Function
AddToAddInCommandBarErr:
End Function
```

Also provided by the Add-In template is a `MenuHandler` routine that can be used to detect a click on any menu items you might insert into the IDE. This part of the project is quite simple; the template handles most of the details.

4. Identify the active control. CodePanes let you access the code contained in a form, module, or class. The CodeModule enables direct manipulation of the code. When these objects are combined, they permit total programmatic control over code contained in a project. In the FormatWith project, you can determine the active object—that is, the window in which the developer is coding—by using the ActiveCodePane property (see Listing 13.2).

Listing 13.2 Using `CodePane` and `CodeModule`

```
Public Sub MakeWith()
    Dim cp As CodePane
    Dim cm As CodeModule
    Dim sTmp As String, sLine As String, sObj As String
    Dim lStartLine As Long, lStartCol As Long, lEndLine As Long, _
                    lEndCol As Long
    Dim i As Integer

    On Error GoTo ErrMakeWith

    ' get the current codepane and codemodule
    Set cp = VBInstance.ActiveCodePane
    Set cm = cp.CodeModule

    ' get selected text
    cm.CodePane.GetSelection lStartLine, lStartCol, lEndLine, lEndCol

    ' error check here; not provided
    ' make sure that the first line is pre-pended with a tab
    ' or we'll crash
    sTmp = cm.Lines(1, 1)
    If Left$(sTmp, 1) <> vbTab Then
        cm.ReplaceLine 1, vbTab & sTmp
```

continued on next page

continued from previous page

```
    End If

    ' modify text and insert into the codemodule
    For i = lStartLine To lEndLine
        sLine = cm.Lines(i, 1)
        sTmp = Right$(sLine, Len(sLine) - InStr(sLine, ".") + 1)
        sTmp = vbTab & sTmp

        ' replace the original line with the modified line
        cm.ReplaceLine i, sTmp
    Next 'l

    ' insert the with/end with statements
    ' NOTE: sLine can be used because it still contains the object name
    sObj = Left$(sLine, InStr(sLine, ".") - 1)
    ' insert the End With 1st
    cm.InsertLines lEndLine + 1, "End With"

    ' insert the With
    cm.InsertLines lStartLine, "With " & sObj

    ' error handler - basically we just eat the error
    Exit Sub
ErrMakeWith:
    MsgBox "The Code Could Not Be Formatted", vbInformation, _
                "Format With Error"
End Sub
```

5. Retrieve the contents of the selection. The code selection area in a Visual Basic window can now include partial lines, not just whole lines, as Visual Basic 3 required. To reformat code for this project, however, partial lines are treated as whole lines. The `GetSelection` method of the `CodePane` object returns the starting and ending rows and columns for the selected text (code). After the row and column information has been collected, it is a simple matter to read and manipulate the selected code. In the `FormatWith` sample, the `Lines` property of the `CodeModule` is used to retrieve each line of code, one at a time.

6. Validate the format of the selection. This exercise has been left up to the reader, for the most part. In such a project, you normally want to perform some sort of validation to ensure that the selected code is appropriate for processing. `FormatWith` handles formatting errors by providing a simple error trap to discard any errors and terminate formatting.

7. Parse and reformat the selection. `FormatWith` first extracts the control name, such as `frmTest`. You can find the control name by reading the code up to the first period (using `InStr` and `Left$`). Each line is then processed and reformatted by stripping out the control name.

8. Paste the modified code back into the code module. After each line is read and reformatted, it is then re-inserted back into the **CodeModule**. After all lines have been reformatted, the **With** and **End With** statements are inserted.

How It Works

The Extensibility Object Model now provided for use with Visual Basic is extremely powerful and remarkably easy to use. The quickest way to get started building an add-in is to use the Add-In template and modify it to suit your needs. The **IDTExtensibility** interface greatly simplifies the details of connecting and disconnecting add-ins, so it is now much easier to develop add-ins than it was in previous releases.

Comments

FormatWith is a simple example of an add-in. Typically, an entire add-in would not be devoted to a single reformatting task, but **FormatWith** could easily be enhanced to provide a series of handy code manipulations. Additionally, more robust error trapping would improve its usefulness.

The ability to extend the IDE has never been this expansive. Myriad possible add-ins that have yet to be conceived of will, no doubt, start popping up on the Web and as commercial products. Add-ins clearly are offering a new level of Visual Basic extensibility.

COMPLEXITY

INTERMEDIATE

13.4 How do I...
Create a wizard?

COMPATIBILITY: VISUAL BASIC 5 AND 6

Problem

How can I make an easy-to-use front-end to simplify complex step-by-step Visual Basic development tasks?

Technique

As discussed in 13.3, add-ins provide a powerful way to automate tasks by programmatically controlling the IDE. One type of add-in, the wizard, is especially useful for tasks that are step oriented.

Wizards dictate a particular, step-by-step style that Microsoft has been successfully using in their applications for some time now. A well constructed wizard can simplify very involved tasks and can be used to solve a wide variety of development problems.

In Visual Basic the Wizard Manager can be used to keep track of the steps included in a wizard while it is being developed. It lets you add, change, and delete steps from the wizard and it provides an initial framework for a wizard-style add-in.

The Wizard Manager is not required to create a wizard, but it greatly simplifies the task. The Wizard Manger supplies the following tools:

✔ *Move Step.* Moves the currently visible step off the screen.

✔ *Add New Step.* Adds a new step to the end of the list before the Finished step.

✔ *Insert Step.* Inserts a new step before the currently selected step.

✔ *Move Step Up.* Moves the currently selected step forward one position in the list.

✔ *Move Step Down.* Moves the currently selected step backward one position in the list.

✔ *Refresh Step List.* Updates the list of steps to reflect any changes that might have been made.

If you haven't done so yet, read How-To 13.3, "Build an Add-In." Wizards are a type of add-in, so the information covered in 13.3 is necessary to understand wizard creation. Issues related to installing and connecting the add-in are not covered again.

To illustrate the creation of a basic wizard using the Wizard Manager, a simple message box wizard is developed. The code for the wizard is included on the CD-ROM. To set up the wizard, follow the instructions for installing an add-in in How-To 13.3. The wizard helps the developer create a message box, including automating the selection of the prompt, buttons, and title. Admittedly, most experienced developers do not consider the creation of a message box a complex task, but it serves as a good example of a basic wizard construction.

Steps

1. Choose Add-Ins, Add-In Manager from the menu.

2. Check the Visual Basic Wizard Manager box.

3. Open the Wizard Manager from the Add-Ins menu. It first comes up with a message box informing you that no wizard form was found and asking if you would like to create a new wizard project. Answering No to this prompt results in the Wizard Manager popping up empty. If you let the

Wizard Manager construct a new wizard project, however, the manager interface is populated with several items, including an introduction step, four sample steps, and a finished step. Figure 13.12 shows the Wizard Manager.

Figure 13.12 The
Wizard Manager.

The entire wizard is composed of a single form that uses an image and label control array. You can add additional controls, and the Wizard Manager toggles their visibility based on what step is displayed.

4. Start your wizard by creating all the steps that you think are needed to accomplish the task. If you do happen to forget a step, it is still quite easy to add steps later. The wizard label control named lblStep is a control array that the Wizard Manager keeps track of for you.

At first, it appears that you can use the Property Manager to set the lblStep's caption, just as you would for any label. Because each label is a member of the control array, you can edit any of the label's properties and they are displayed only on the currently selected step. In design mode everything appears to work, but if captions are changed via the Property Manager, the changes do not persist at runtime. The Wizard Manager loads strings at runtime from a resource file, however, so any captions you change in design mode are overwritten at runtime.

5. To set control captions, edit the Wizard.rc string-table file and recompile the resource file, or use a tool such as the Resource Editor add-in.

The sample MsgBox wizard includes the following steps:

✔ Introduction

✔ Prompt

✔ Title

✔ Buttons

✔ Finished

6. After the basic steps have been added with the Wizard Manager, you can then place controls on each step. The Introduction and Finished steps did not require additional controls, but the other steps needed text boxes to collect the prompt and title and a list box to display button options.

How It Works

The wizard is somewhat convoluted in that the prompt and title have their own steps. A real-world wizard would typically collect much more information and require the user to make more decisions in each step. The Buttons step does require the user to pick a button and icon style by using an extended-selection style list box. It is this step that is useful because, unlike creating a message box in code, it doesn't require the user to remember specific styles, style numbers, or Visual Basic style constants. It also lets the user preview the message box to make sure the right settings have been selected before finishing. After completing the message box, clicking Finished pastes the code for the message box into the code window at the current caret position. The Message Box Wizard is pictured in Figure 13.13.

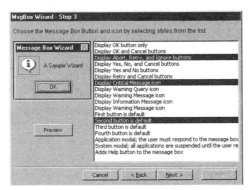

Figure 13.13 The Message Box Wizard.

Comments

The Wizard Manager is an add-in designed to simplify wizard creation by supplying a framework on which a standard Microsoft-style wizard can be built. It uses a single form and a control array of frames to manage wizard steps. Controls and code can be added as needed to make the wizard collect and respond to information from the user.

Wizard development is greatly simplified by using the Wizard Manager, but it is no substitute for careful planning and good interface design. The Message Box Wizard is a simple example of wizard programming, but it doesn't go very far in simulating a real-world wizard. Typically, a wizard deals with a more complex problem. A well-designed wizard can, however, make a complicated task seem much easier because the task is broken into smaller steps, which is what good programming is all about, anyway.

CHAPTER 14
ADVANCED DATA OBJECTS

14.

ADVANCED DATA OBJECTS

How do I...

14.1 **Compare ADO to DAO and RDO?**

14.2 **Include ADO as part of my project?**

14.3 **Access recordsets using ADO?**

14.4 **Manage data structures returned as variant arrays?**

14.5 **Create a simple database front-end using the ADO data control?**

ActiveX Data Objects, commonly referred to as ADO, were initially designed to be used with Active Server Pages as a server-side data access interface. ADO's lightweight, fast performance, and its ease-of-use make it an ideal component for developing Web-based database applications.

Since ADO's first release to the public, many developers have discovered its rich capabilities with client/server and distributed applications. Considering that ADO is an ActiveX component, it is easy to include it as part of a standard application.

This chapter presents several practical How-Tos that will introduce you to ActiveX Data Objects and demonstrate its use in several applications.

14.1 Compare ADO to DAO and RDO

What are the differences between the various data access interfaces? Which interface is best for my application? This How-To compares ADO (ActiveX Data Objects) to DAO (Data Access Objects) and RDO (Remote Data Objects). This section helps you gain an understanding of the features and benefits that each data access interface has to offer. This section also gives you an idea of when it is most appropriate to use ActiveX Data Objects in your applications.

14.2 Include ADO as Part of My Project

Before you can start adding ADO data logic into your project, you need to reference the ADO object library. This topic demonstrates how to include ADO as part of your project and how to access the ADO object model.

14.3 Access Recordsets Using ADO

The capability to access recordsets is essential to any reliable data access interface. This How-To presents two techniques for accessing recordsets using ADO: a connectionless static cursor method and a dynamic cursor method that maintains a connection to the data source.

14.4 Manage Data Structures Returned as Variant Arrays

One feature of ADO is its capability to return a recordset as a variant array. This How-To discusses the various reasons why you might want to return data structures in variant arrays and some techniques used to make variant arrays easier to manage.

14.5 Create a Simple Database Front-End Using the ADO Data Control

One of the newest features of ADO 2.0 is the ADO data control. The ADO data control provides the capability to bind controls to a local or remote data source without writing code. This How-To demonstrates the use of the ADO data control with the new Visual Basic 6 `DataGrid` control.

14.1 How do I...
Compare ADO to DAO and RDO?

COMPATIBILITY: VISUAL BASIC 5 AND 6

Problem

I am not sure which data access interface will provide the best performance for my application. The necessity to understand the differences between ADO, DAO, and RDO is essential in determining which data access interface is best suited for any application. How do I compare ADO to DAO and RDO?

Technique

Look at the ADO object model. Compare its object model, hierarchy and interface layers to that of DAO and RDO. Look also at the features and benefits of ADO and compare them to DAO and RDO. Know the value and the benefits of each data access interface so that you will can determine which one would be ideal for any application.

Data Access Objects/Jet

Let's first look at DAO (Data Access Objects) for Microsoft Jet databases, otherwise known as DAO/Jet. DAO/Jet is the interface to the Jet database engine and was specifically designed to access native Jet and ISAM databases such as Access, Btrieve, dBASE, FoxPro, and Paradox. DAO/Jet is an ideal solution when accessing local data. But when it comes to working with remote databases, although DAO/Jet is capable of accessing ODBC data sources, its performance leaves somewhat to be desired. Additionally, its remote database functionality is limited when compared to direct API interfaces and Remote Data Objects.

Data Access Objects/ODBCDirect

Starting with DAO 3.5, ODBCDirect has provided an interface to Remote Data Objects without the necessary licensing requirements, such as is provided with Visual Basic Enterprise Edition. Because ODBCDirect does not use the resource-consuming Jet database engine, it outperforms DAO/Jet when accessing remote data sources. Figure 14.1 illustrates the object model for DAO ODBCDirect. The database security features that are in DAO/Jet database engine are not in ODBCDirect.

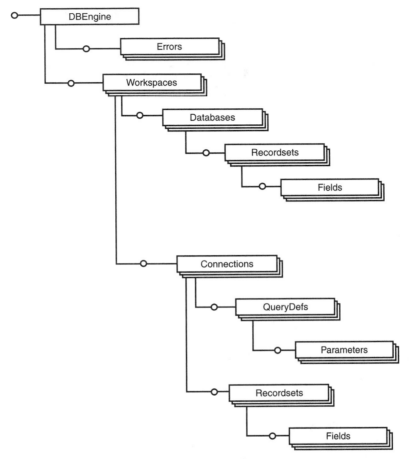

Figure 14.1 This is the object model for Data Access Objects/ODBCDirect.

The structure of the DAO object model for ODBCDirect is less complex than that of the Microsoft Jet database engine. Although ODBCDirect does not perform as well as RDO, it does allow you to utilize RDO's remote data access features through an object model similar to DAO.

Remote Data Objects

For several years now, RDO (Remote Data Objects) has been the best performer of all the COM-based data access interfaces used with Visual Basic. RDO was especially designed for use with remote ODBC data sources. Figure 14.2 illustrates the object model for RDO.

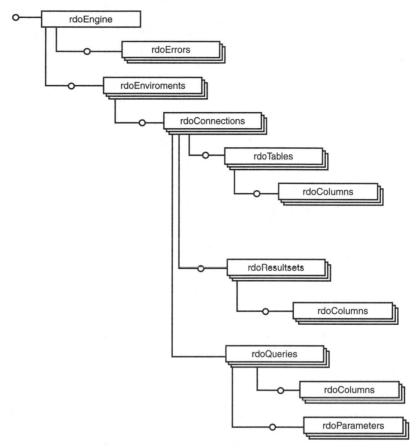

Figure 14.2 This is the object model for Remote Data Objects.

Although RDO does not support certain DAO/Jet features, such as table-based interfaces or DDL (Data Definition Language), RDO does support robust enterprise-level functionality. Until know this functionality has made it the primary solution when working with any relational database accessed through an ODBC driver, such as Oracle and SQL Server.

ActiveX Data Objects

Now that you have reviewed DAO and RDO, let's look at ADO (ActiveX Data Objects). Since its inception, ADO has evolved from being the data access interface designed especially for use with Active Server Pages into the complete solution for just about all your data access needs. ADO's object model is the least complex of all other data access interface object models.

ADO is the COM interface to OLE DB, Microsoft's latest all-encompassing heterogeneous interface to data in general. Figure 14.3 illustrates the object model for ADO. Notice how simple the ADO object model is compared to DAO and RDO.

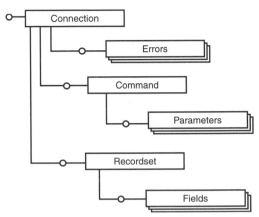

Figure 14.3 This is the object model for ActiveX Data Objects.

With DAO, a connection to a data source must first be established and maintained before a recordset can be created. This not only means more lines of code but also more object references that would need to be managed, therefore more overhead in your Visual Basic application.

With ADO, the `Recordset` object is the main interface to the database. A minimal amount of code can be used to access a table or recordset. That means that with ADO there are fewer lines of code and less overhead needed to generate a recordset. With the new ADO recordset model (Microsoft ActiveX Data Objects Recordset 2.0 Library— a smaller, limited version of ADO), even fewer resources are necessary to access recordsets and update the database.

DAO, RDO, and ADO Interface Layers

DAO/Jet interfaces to the Jet database engine, a thick layer of resource-consuming functionality, which can either access Jet and ISAM databases directly, or access other relational databases through an interface to the ODBC API. DAO/Jet gives its best performance when accessing local Jet and ISAM databases.

Using DAO/ODBCDirect, DAO interfaces to the ODBCDirect layer, which interfaces to RDO, which in turn interfaces to remote data sources through the ODBC API. Although there are two more layers with ODBCDirect than with Jet, the layers are very thin, and ODBCDirect gives much better performance accessing remote data sources than DAO/Jet.

RDO is basically a thin wrapper around the ODBC API. Until now, it has given the highest performance of all data access layers accessing remote data sources. Figure 14.4 illustrates the data access layers that exist from the application down to the data source.

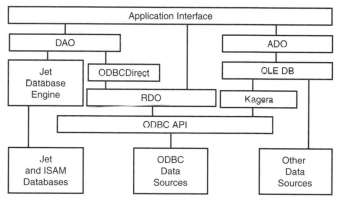

Figure 14.4 These are the interface layers for DAO, RDO, and ADO.

OLE DB is Microsoft's latest data access tool designed to provide access to an infinite variety of data sources. OLE DB cannot be accessed directly from Visual Basic but is accessible through the COM interface called ActiveX Data Objects. ADO is available for use with a variety of programming languages, including scripting languages such as VBScript and Active Server Pages.

By understanding the differences between ADO, RDO, and DAO, you can better decide which data access interface is most appropriate for your application.

Comments

As ADO is upgraded and improved, it will replace all other data access interfaces. One interface that ADO might not replace as easily is DAO because of its hearty Jet database support.

COMPLEXITY
BEGINNING

14.2 How do I...
Include ADO as part of my project?

COMPATIBILITY: VISUAL BASIC 5 AND 6

Problem

I want to access the ADO object model within my project and use early binding to improve performance. I also want to take full advantage of Visual Basic's active code editing features and use the Object Browser to obtain a visual overview of the ADO object model. How do I include ADO as part of my project?

Technique

Because ADO is an ActiveX component and utilizes COM interfaces, you can include it in your project just like any other ActiveX component. This How-To demonstrates how to include ADO as part of your project as well as explores what benefits you have within the Visual Basic development environment when referencing the ADO object model.

Steps

Complete the following steps to create this project:

1. Create a new ActiveX DLL project.

2. Choose Project, Project1 Properties from the menu and change the Project Name to **DataAccess**. Also display the properties of the **Class1** module and change the **Name** property to **ADOAccess**.

3. Add a reference to the Microsoft ActiveX Data Objects 2.0 Library to your project.

USE THE OBJECT BROWSER TO LEARN THE ADO OBJECT MODEL

Press the F2 key to open the Object Browser. Click the drop-down arrow of the Project/Library list at the top left of the Object Browser. (The type library name for the ADO Object Model is ADODB.) Select ADODB from the list. A list of classes, enumerations, and other modules appears in the left column of the Object Browser, whereas members of the selected class will appear in the right column of the Object Browser.

If you select the Connection class in the left column, then all the members (properties, methods, and events) of the Connection class will appear in the right column. Then when you select a member, a detailed description of the selected member will appear in the bottom section of the Object Browser. The Object Browser is a useful tool in learning the details of the ADO object model.

4. Now that you have a reference within your project to the ADO object model, enter the following line of code into the General Declarations section of the ADOAccess module:

```
Dim ADOConn As ADODB.Connection
```

5. Enter the following code, which tests a connection string, into your ADOAccess class module:

```
Public Function TestConnection(ConnStr As String) As Long

    'Handle any error locally
    On Error Goto TestConnection_Err

    'Create a new Connection object.
    Set ADOConn = New ADODB.Connection

    'Attempt to establish a connection using the specified
    'connection string.
    ADOConn.Open ConnStr
    'Check to see if an error has occurred.
    If ADOConn.Errors.Count > 0 Then
        'If so, then return the error number
        TestConnection = ADOConn.Errors(1).Number
    End If

    'Close the connection before leaving. This
    'was only a test.
    ADOConn.Close

    'Destroy the Connection object
    Set ADOConn = Nothing

TestConnection_Cont:
    'All done.
    Exit Function

TestConnection_Err:
    'An error occurred attempting to establish a connection
    'using the specified connection string. Return the
    'error number and resume to exit function.
    TestConnection = Err
    Resume TestConnection_Cont

End Function
```

Save the **DataAccess** project. Now you know how to reference the ADO object model within your project and how to utilize features within Visual Basic to learn more about ActiveX Data Objects.

How It Works

The **TestConnection** method provides you with the ability to verify that a connection string—with its data source name, database name, user identification, and password—is valid. The **TestConnection** method of your **ADOAccess** class comes in handy later in this chapter. But for now, you can use this project to familiarize yourself with ADO using the Object Browser.

Comments

Even though the ADO object model is much simpler than that of DAO and RDO, there are some properties, methods, and events that you will need to become familiar with.

COMPLEXITY
BEGINNING

14.3 How do I...
Access recordsets using ADO?

COMPATIBILITY: VISUAL BASIC 5 AND 6

Problem

I need to provide numerous recordsets to business objects from various ODBC data sources based on specific requests. I am looking for a generic solution that will use the latest technology. How do I access recordsets using ADO?

Technique

A unique feature of ActiveX Data Objects is its capability to access a recordset without first having to make a connection or open a database in Visual Basic. ADO is much easier to use than DAO or RDO when it comes to providing recordsets or resultsets to client/server applications or business objects. This reduces the amount of resources required by your data logic and the amount of code you need to write to access a recordset.

This How-To demonstrates two techniques of accessing a recordset using ADO. The first technique accesses a recordset using a dynamic cursor maintaining the connection to the database. The second accesses a recordset using a static cursor with connectionless access.

Steps

To create this project, complete the following steps:

1. Open the 32bit ODBC Data Source Administrator in the Control Panel and click the System DSN tab. Click the Add button, select the Microsoft Access Driver, and click the Finish button. Specify "Biblio" as the Data Source Name and then click the Select button. Locate the Biblio.mdb file and click the OK button. A copy of the file should be in the directory C:\Program Files\DevStudio\VB. After you have clicked OK, Biblio should then appear in the list of System DSNs, as shown in Figure 14.5.

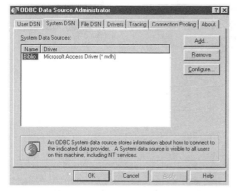

Figure 14.5 This is how the Biblio data source appears in the ODBC Data Source Administrator.

2. Open up the DataAccess project you created in How-To 14.2. The DataAccess project is used and modified throughout this chapter.

3. Enter the following code into the **ADOAccess** class module to create the GetDynamicRecordset method:

```
Public Function GetDynamicRecordset(SQLStr As String, _
ConnStr As String)
'This function will return a Recordset using a dynamic
'cursor and allow the calling procedure to maintain a
'direct connection to the database. We will use a variant
'as the return variable so that we'll have the ability
'to return a Recordset object, as well as return
'an error number if the Open function fails.

    'Handle any error locally.
    On Error GoTo GetDynamicRecordset_Err

    'Create a new Recordset object.
    Dim ADORecordset As ADODB.Recordset
```

continued on next page

continued from previous page

```
        Set ADORecordset = New ADODB.Recordset
        'Open the Recordset specified by the SQL statement
        'and connection string using a dynamic cursor.
        ADORecordset.Open SQLStr, ConnStr, adOpenDynamic

        'Return the reference to the Recordset
        Set GetDynamicRecordset = ADORecordset

        'Destroy the local reference to the Recordset.
        Set ADORecordset = Nothing

        'All done.
        Exit Function

GetDynamicRecordset_Err:
        'An error occurred in either the SQL statement or the
        'connection object. Return the error number and resume
        'to the next statement and exit function.
        GetDynamicRecordset = Err
        Resume Next

End Function
```

4. Create the GetRows method of our ADOAccess class by adding the
following code to the class module:

```
Public Function GetRows(SQLStr As String, ConnStr As _
String)
'This function will return a variant array containing the
'rows of the Recordset returned by the Open function. We
'will close our connection once we have retrieved the data
'in order to eliminate the connection.

        'Handle any error locally.
        On Error GoTo GetRows_Err

        'Create a new Recordset object.
        Dim ADORecordset As ADODB.Recordset
        Set ADORecordset = New ADODB.Recordset
        'Return the Recordset specified by the SQL statement
        'and connection string using a dynamic cursor.
        ADORecordset.Open SQLStr, ConnStr, adOpenStatic

        'Return a variant array of our recordset.
        GetRows = ADORecordset.GetRows

        'Close the recordset and connection.
        ADORecordset.Close

GetRows_Cont:
        'Destroy the local reference to the Recordset.
        Set ADORecordset = Nothing
```

```
        'All done.
        Exit Function

GetRows_Err:
        'An error occurred in either the SQL statement or the
        'connection object. Return the error number and resume
        'to the next statement and exit function.
        GetRows = Err
        Resume GetRows_Cont

End Function
```

Now that you have created the methods needed for our **ADOAccess** class to access recordsets, you must create a simple project that uses those methods to retrieve recordsets and also use the **TestConnection** method that you created in section 14.2.

5. Keep the **ADOAccess** project loaded and create a new Standard EXE project.

6. Right-click Project1 in the Project Explorer window and select Set as Start Up.

7. Choose Project, Project1 Properties from the Menu. Change the Project Name to ADOTest1 and click the OK button.

8. Add a reference to DataAccess to the new project. DataAccess should be the first unchecked reference in the Available References list.

9. Modify the form so that its objects and properties match those listed in Table 14.1.

Table 14.1 ADOTest1 Form and Control Properties

OBJECT/CONTROL	PROPERTY	VALUE
Form	Name	frmADOTest1
	Caption	ADO Connection and Recordset Test
	Height	3540
	StartUpPosition	2 - CenterScreen
	Width	4725
CommandButton	Name	cmdTestConn
	Caption	Test Connection
	Height	375
	Left	240
	Top	240
	Width	4095

continued on next page

continued from previous page

OBJECT/CONTROL	PROPERTY	VALUE
CommandButton	Name	cmdTestDyna
	Caption	Test GetDynamicRecordset
	Height	375
	Left	240
	Top	1200
	Width	4095
CommandButton	Name	cmdTestRows
	Caption	Test GetRows
	Height	375
	Left	240
	Top	2160
	Width	4095
TextBox	Name	txtTestConn
	Height	405
	Left	240
	Text	
	Top	600
	Width	4095
TextBox	Name	txtTestDyna
	Height	375
	Left	240
	Text	
	Top	1560
	Width	4095
TextBox	Name	txtTestRows
	Height	375
	Left	240
	Text	
	Top	2520
	Width	4095

10. Double-click the cmdTestConn CommandButton. Enter the following code into the Click event procedure of the cmdTestConn control.

```
Private Sub cmdTestConn_Click()

    'Dimension local variables.
    Dim Status As Long
    Dim ConnStr As String

    'Create a new ADOAccess object.
    Dim ADO As New ADOAccess

    'We will access the Biblio ODBC DataSource.
    ConnStr = "DSN=Biblio"

    'Execute the TestConnection method to see if we
    'can connect to the Biblio datasource.
    Status = ADO.TestConnection(ConnStr)

    If Status = 0 Then
        'If no error, then display successful message.
        txtTestConn.Text = "Test Connection Successful."
    Else
        'Otherwise display the error number.
        txtTestConn.Text = "Error" & Str$(Status)
    End If

End Sub
```

11. Enter the following code into the **Click** event procedure of the
cmdTestDyna CommandButton.

```
Private Sub cmdTestDyna_Click()

    'Dimension local variables.
    Dim RecSet As Object
    Dim SQLStr As String
    Dim ConnStr As String
    Dim NumberOfRows As Long
    Dim Status As Long

    'Create a new ADOAccess object.
    Dim ADO As New ADOAccess

    'Select all rows from the Publishers table in the
    'Biblio database.
    SQLStr = "SELECT * FROM Publishers;"
    ConnStr = "DSN=Biblio"

    'Retrieve the specified Recordset
    Set RecSet = ADO.GetDynamicRecordset(SQLStr, _
    ConnStr, Status)

    If Status = 0 Then
        'Successful. Display number of rows retrieved.
```

continued on next page

continued from previous page

```
                    'RecordCount may not always retrieve the number
                    'of rows in the recordset. If our RecordCount is
                    'is less than one, then we will use a loop until
                    'EOF is true.

                    'Check to see how many records
                    RecSet.MoveLast          'Move to the last record and
                    RecSet.MoveFirst         'and then back to the first.
                    NumberOfRows = RecSet.RecordCount

                    txtTestDyna.Text = "Test Successful. Retrieved " _
                    & Trim$(Str$(NumberOfRows)) & " Records."
                Else
                    'Otherwise display the error number.
                    txtTestDyna.Text = "Error " + Trim$(Str$(Status))
                End If

                'Destroy all objects before leaving
                Set RecSet = Nothing
                Set ADO = Nothing

            End Sub
```

12. Enter the following code into the `Click` event procedure of the `cmdTestRows` CommandButton.

```
Private Sub cmdTestRows_Click()

        'Dimension local variables.
        Dim RecSet
        Dim SQLStr As String
        Dim ConnStr As String
        Dim NumberOfRows As Long

        'Create a new ADOAccess object.
        Dim ADO As New ADOAccess

        'Select all rows from the Publishers table in the
        'Biblio database.
        SQLStr = "SELECT * FROM Publishers;"
        ConnStr = "DSN=Biblio"

        'Retrieve the specified rows as a variant array
        RecSet = ADO.GetRows(SQLStr, ConnStr)

        If IsArray(RecSet) Then
            'If the result is an array then it was successful.
            'Display the number of rows returned.
            NumberOfRows = UBound(RecSet, 2) + 1
```

```
        txtTestRows.Text = "Test Successful. Retrieved " _
        & Trim$(Str$(NumberOfRows)) & " Records."
    Else
        'Otherwise display the error number.
        txtTestRows.Text = "Error " + Trim$(Str$(RecSet))
    End If

    'Destroy all objects before leaving
    Set ADO = Nothing

End Sub
```

13. Save your project group and press F5 to start the ADOTest1 project.

How It Works

When the form appears at runtime, as illustrated in Figure 14.6, click the Test Connection button to confirm that ADO can make a connection to the ODBC data source as specified. Then click the Test GetDynamicRecordset button to confirm that the dynamic recordset is retrieved. The number of records retrieved should be displayed in the text box. This test application confirms that you have created several procedures for your **ADOAccess** class that can be used by your applications to access recordsets from ODBC data sources.

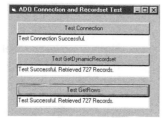

Figure 14.6 This is the ADOTest1 project as it appears at runtime.

Comments

Creating recordsets is a fundamental task which is required for most database applications. ADO can provide this function using a single object—the **Recordset** object.

14.4 How do I...
Manage data structures returned as variant arrays?

COMPATIBILITY: VISUAL BASIC 6

Problem

I need to provide recordsets to the client that can be marshaled across our network from the server. Because of the limitations of marshaling objects across the network in Visual Basic, I will need to use the `GetRows` method of the `Recordset` object to convert the `Recordset` to a variant array. Although an object cannot be marshaled across a network using Visual Basic, a variant array can. How do I manage recordsets that are passed as variant arrays?

Technique

Using a variant array as a returned data structure actually gives you some flexibility in handling the data at the user interface. Although information about the serialized data structure must be maintained on the client side, you could use a client-side object to convert the variant array into an object model or user-defined type that would be more appropriate for the user interface to manage. This conversion could be separate from the user interface so that you can maintain the three-tier architectural model without compromising data integrity.

Visual Basic 6 introduces the capability to define Public user-defined types within publicly creatable class modules. You can also store copies of Public user-defined types within a collection.

Now with the conversion from the serialized data structure of a variant array to an object model or collection of user-defined types within an object, the data could then be accessed from the user interface using properties and methods. This would help to manage the data so that when new fields are added or existing fields are modified, the properties of the object model would still be the same. Only the client-side object would need to know of structural changes to the variant array returned from a server-side object or data source. This would help to minimize application maintenance.

This How-To demonstrates the conversion of a variant array into a collection of user-defined types. The collection will then be exposed to the user interface through properties and methods of the local object.

Steps

Complete the following steps to create this project. The local class module is created first. Then the user interface is created.

1. Open up the DataAccess project that you created in How-To 14.2 and 14.3.

2. Add an ActiveX DLL project.

3. Choose Project, Project1 Properties from the menu and change the Project Name to Biblio. Then change the Class1 Name to Publishers.

4. Enter the following code into the General Declarations section of the **Publishers** class module.

```
Option Explicit

'Our type must be public in order to use it in a
'collection. Structure the type to match the requested
'columns from the Publishers table.
Public Type PubType
    PubID As Long
    Name As String
    CompanyName As String
    Address As String
    City As String
    State As String
    Zip As String
    Telephone As String
    Fax As String
    Comments As String
End Type

'We need a working copy of the type.
Private Pub As PubType

'Module level enumeration of the data structure for use in
'our Properties property.
Private Enum PropertiesIndex
    ePubID
    eName
    eCompanyName
    eAddress
    eCity
    eState
    eZip
    eTelephone
    eFax
    eComments
End Enum
'Reference to our collection of rows
Private Pubs As Collection
```

5. Enter the following property procedures into the **Publishers** class module. These enable the user interface to access the data.

```
Private Property Let Properties(Index As Integer, vData)
'This property allows this class to enumerate through
'assigning the columns in a row.

    On Error GoTo LetProperties_Err

    Select Case Index
        Case PropertiesIndex.ePubID
            Pub.PubID = vData

        Case PropertiesIndex.eName
            Pub.Name = vData

        Case PropertiesIndex.eCompanyName
            Pub.CompanyName = vData

        Case PropertiesIndex.eAddress
            Pub.Address = vData

        Case PropertiesIndex.eCity
            Pub.City = vData

        Case PropertiesIndex.eState
            Pub.State = vData

        Case PropertiesIndex.eZip
            Pub.Zip = vData

        Case PropertiesIndex.eTelephone
            Pub.Telephone = vData

        Case PropertiesIndex.eFax
            Pub.Fax = vData

        Case PropertiesIndex.eComments
            Pub.Comments = vData

    End Select

    Exit Property

LetProperties_Err:
    Resume Next

End Property

Public Property Get Properties(Index As Integer)
'This property allows the application to enumerate through
'retrieving the columns in a row.
```

```
        Select Case Index
            Case PropertiesIndex.ePubID
                Properties = Pub.PubID

            Case PropertiesIndex.eName
                Properties = Pub.Name

            Case PropertiesIndex.eCompanyName
                Properties = Pub.CompanyName

            Case PropertiesIndex.eAddress
                Properties = Pub.Address

            Case PropertiesIndex.eCity
                Properties = Pub.City

            Case PropertiesIndex.eState
                Properties = Pub.State

            Case PropertiesIndex.eZip
                Properties = Pub.Zip

            Case PropertiesIndex.eTelephone
                Properties = Pub.Telephone

            Case PropertiesIndex.eFax
                Properties = Pub.Fax

            Case PropertiesIndex.eComments
                Properties = Pub.Comments

        End Select

    End Property
```

6. You need to have access to the row count of the returned recordset, and you need to clear the local copy of the user-defined type each time you create an item for the collection. To accomplish this, enter the following code into the **Publishers** class module.

```
Public Property Get RowCount()

    'Return the number of items in the collection.
    RowCount = Pubs.Count

End Property

Private Sub ClearPub()
'Used to clear the Pub type.

    Pub.PubID = 0
    Pub.Name = ""
    Pub.CompanyName = ""
```

continued on next page

continued from previous page

```
            Pub.Address = ""
            Pub.City = ""
            Pub.State = ""
            Pub.Zip = ""
            Pub.Telephone = ""
            Pub.Fax = ""
            Pub.Comments = ""

      End Sub
```

7. Enter the following code into the **Publishers** class module to create the **GetAllPubs** method, which retrieves the entire Publishers table. This method uses the Biblio data source created in How-To 14.2.

```
Public Sub GetAllPubs()
'This is the method that will retrieve the entire
'Publishers table in a specified structure as a variant
'array and convert it to a collection of types.

      'Dimension local variables.
      Dim SQLStr As String
      Dim ConnStr As String
      Dim TempData
      Dim Row As Long, Col As Integer

      'Create the ADOAccess object.
      Dim ADO As New ADOAccess

      'Specify the SELECT statement.
      SQLStr = "SELECT PubID,Name,[Company Name]," & _
      "Address,City,State,Zip,Telephone,Fax,Comments " & _
      "FROM Publishers ORDER BY PubID;"

      'Specify the data source.
      ConnStr = "DSN=Biblio"

      'Retrieve the variant array of rows.
      TempData = ADO.GetRows(SQLStr, ConnStr)

      'Start with a new collection.
      Set Pubs = New Collection

      'If the returned value is an array,
      If IsArray(TempData) Then
          'then enumerate through the rows and columns creating
          'the collection of User-Defined Types.
          For Row = LBound(TempData, 2) To UBound(TempData, 2)
              ClearPub
              For Col = 0 To 9
                  Properties(Col) = TempData(Col, Row)
              Next
              Pubs.Add Pub, Trim$(Str$(Pub.PubID))
```

```
        Next
    End If

    'Destroy the ADOAccess object.
    Set ADO = Nothing

End Sub
```

8. Enter the following code into the **Publishers** class module to provide the capability to navigate through the collection either by selecting a specific index number or by selecting the Publisher ID.

```
Public Sub MoveTo(Pointer As Long)

    'Make sure that the pointer stays within the
    'acceptable range.
    If Pointer > Pubs.Count Then
        Pointer = Pubs.Count
    ElseIf Pointer < 1 Then
        Pointer = 1
    End If

    'Retrieve the specified type from the collection.
    Pub = Pubs.Item(Pointer)

End Sub

Public Function SearchForPubID(Item As String) As Boolean

    'Handle errors locally.
    On Error GoTo SearchForPubID_Err

    'Retrieve the specified item from the collection.
    Pub = Pubs.Item(Item)

    'Report the success.
    SearchForPubID = True

SearchForPubID_Cont:
    'All done.
    Exit Function

SearchForPubID_Err:
    'Report the failure.
    SearchForPubID = False

    'Get out of here.
    Resume SearchForPubID_Cont

End Function
```

Save the Biblio project at this time.

9. Add a new Standard EXE project.

10. Choose Project, Project1 Properties from the menu and change the Project Name to ADOTest2.

11. Right-click the ADOTest2 project in the Project Explorer and select Set as Start Up when the shortcut menu appears.

12. Modify the ADOTest2 form so that it has the objects and properties listed in Table 14.2. Note that all the TextBox controls are contained in a control array, except for the Search text box. The Search text box and command button should be placed within the frame placed on this form.

Table 14.2 The ADOTest2 Form and Control Properties

OBJECT/CONTROL	PROPERTY	VALUE
Form	Name	frmADOTest2
	Caption	Publishers Table
	Height	6240
	StartUpPosition	2 - CenterScreen
	Width	6990
Frame	Name	fraSearch
	Caption	Search by Publisher ID
	Height	855
	Left	240
	Top	4800
	Width	6375
TextBox: txtPub(0)	Height	285
	Left	240
	Locked	True
	Text	
	Top	360
	Width	1335
TextBox: txtPub(1)	Height	285
	Left	1800
	Locked	True
	Text	
	Top	360
	Width	4335

OBJECT/CONTROL	PROPERTY	VALUE
TextBox: txtPub(2)	Height	285
	Left	240
	Locked	True
	Text	
	Top	960
	Width	5895
TextBox: txtPub(3)	Height	285
	Left	240
	Locked	True
	Text	
	Top	1560
	Width	5895
TextBox: txtPub(4)	Height	285
	Left	240
	Locked	True
	Text	
	Top	2160
	Width	3015
TextBox: txtPub(5)	Height	285
	Left	3480
	Locked	True
	Text	
	Top	2160
	Width	735
TextBox: txtPub(6)	Height	285
	Left	4440
	Locked	True
	Text	
	Top	2160
	Width	1695
TextBox: txtPub(7)	Height	285
	Left	240
	Locked	True
	Text	
	Top	2760
	Width	2775

continued on next page

continued from previous page

OBJECT/CONTROL	PROPERTY	VALUE
TextBox: txtPub(8)	Height	285
	Left	3360
	Locked	True
	Text	
	Top	2760
	Width	2775
TextBox: txtPub(9)	Height	765
	Left	240
	Locked	True
	MultiLine	True
	ScrollBars	2 - Vertical
	Text	
	Top	3360
	Width	5895
TextBox	Name	txtSearch
	Height	285
	Left	840
	Text	
	Top	360
	Width	2895
Label	Name	lblPubID
	Caption	Publisher ID
	Height	255
	Left	240
	Top	120
	Width	1335
Label	Name	lblName
	Caption	Name
	Height	255
	Left	1800
	Top	120
	Width	4335
Label	Name	lblCompany
	Caption	Company Name
	Height	255
	Left	240
	Top	720
	Width	5895

OBJECT/CONTROL	PROPERTY	VALUE
Label	Name	lblAddress
	Caption	Address
	Height	255
	Left	240
	Top	1320
	Width	5895
Label	Name	lblCity
	Caption	City
	Height	255
	Left	240
	Top	1920
	Width	3015
Label	Name	lblState
	Caption	State
	Height	255
	Left	3480
	Top	1920
	Width	735
Label	Name	lblZip
	Caption	Zip Code
	Height	255
	Left	4440
	Top	1920
	Width	1695
Label	Name	lblTelephone
	Caption	Telephone Number
	Height	255
	Left	240
	Top	2520
	Width	2775
Label	Name	lblFax
	Caption	Fax Number
	Height	255
	Left	3360
	Top	2520
	Width	2775

continued on next page

continued from previous page

OBJECT/CONTROL	PROPERTY	VALUE
Label	Name	lblComments
	Caption	Comments
	Height	255
	Left	240
	Top	3120
	Width	5895
VScrollBar	Name	VScroll1
	Enabled	False
	Height	3975
	Left	6360
	Top	120
	Width	255
CommandButton	Name	cmdGetArray
	Caption	Get the Publishers Table
	Height	375
	Left	240
	Top	4320
	Width	6375
CommandButton	Name	cmdSearch
	Caption	Search
	Enabled	False
	Height	255
	Left	3960
	Top	360
	Width	1335

After you have completed the property modifications as listed Table 14.2, your form should appear in the Visual Basic environment as illustrated in Figure 14.7.

13. Insert the following code into the General Declarations section of the form module.

```
Option Explicit

'Maintain a module-level reference to the Publishers
'object.
Dim Pubs As Biblio.Publishers
```

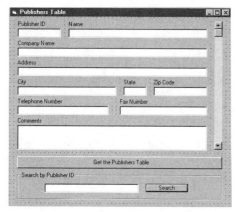

Figure 14.7 This is the frmADOTest2 Form as it appears in the Visual Basic development environment.

14. Insert the following code into the **Click** event procedure of the **cmdGetArray** object.

```vb
Private Sub cmdGetArray_Click()

    'Disable the GetArray button after use.
    cmdGetArray.Enabled = False

    'Create a new Publishers object.
    Set Pubs = New Biblio.Publishers

    'Retrieve the Publishers table.
    Pubs.GetAllPubs

    'Enable and initialize the vertical scrollbar.
    VScroll1.Enabled = True
    VScroll1.Min = 1                 'start at 1
    VScroll1.Max = Pubs.RowCount     'end at rowcount
    VScroll1.SmallChange = 1         'step 1
    VScroll1.LargeChange = 10        'or step 10
    VScroll1.Value = 1               'start at one

    'Allow the user to search by PubID.
    cmdSearch.Enabled = True

End Sub
```

15. Insert the following code into the **Click** event procedure of the **cmdSearch** object.

```
Private Sub cmdSearch_Click()

    'Only search if something in the textbox.
    If Len(txtSearch.Text) > 0 Then
        If Pubs.SearchForPubID(txtSearch.Text) Then
            'If success, clear the search textbox
            txtSearch.Text = ""
            'and update the field textboxes.
            UpdateControls
        Else
            'Otherwise, specify not found in the search
            'textbox.
            txtSearch.Text = "Item not found."
        End If
    End If

    'Set focus to the search textbox.
    txtSearch.SetFocus

End Sub
```

16. Insert the following code into the **Change** event procedure of the **VScroll1** object.

```
Private Sub VScroll1_Change()

    'When the vertical scrollbar changes, adjust the
    'pointer for the collection.
    Pubs.MoveTo VScroll1.Value

    'Update the field textboxes.
    UpdateControls

End Sub
```

17. Add an **UpdateControls** procedure to the form module as follows.

```
Private Sub UpdateControls()

    'Dimension local counter.
    Dim Ctr As Integer

    'Enumerate through the columns assigning the data to
    'the textbox control array on the form.
    For Ctr = 0 To 9
        txtPub(Ctr).Text = Pubs.Properties(Ctr)
    Next

End Sub
```

How It Works

When you run the ADOTest2 project, the form appears in the center of the screen as illustrated in Figure 14.8. Click the Get the Publishers Table button to retrieve the recordset and create the collection. When you click the button, the `GetAllPubs` method of the `Publisher` object is executed, which in turn executes the `GetRows` method of the `ADOAccess` object using the proper SQL statement. The `GetRows` method returns the variant array to the GetAllPubs method, which populates the collection using a user-defined type. Once the collection is populated, navigating through the collection is as simple as navigating through a static recordset. Although there are many ways to manage data, a collection of user-defined types is one of the newer techniques that are available using Visual Basic 6.

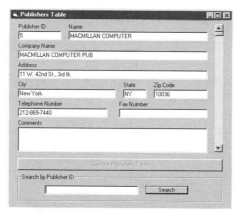

Figure 14.8 This is the ADOTest2 project as it appears at runtime.

After the collection is created and the first record appears in the textboxes, use the scrollbar and search feature to navigate through the collection.
Make sure you have properly defined a data source named Biblio which is attached to the biblio.mdb Access database. Otherwise, errors will occur in your program when you click the Get the Publishers Table button.

Comments

If you develop your external objects with similar techniques, your user interface will have flexible access to data with a minimal amount of code. And with this type of architecture, it is easy to make modifications.

COMPLEXITY
BEGINNING

14.5 How do I...
Create a simple database front-end using the ADO data control?

COMPATIBILITY: VISUAL BASIC 6

Problem

I have an OBDC data source that I want to display recordsets from in a simple flexible front-end. I understand that there is now a way to access an ODBC data source using ADO without having to write a lot of code in Visual Basic 6. How do I create a simple database front-end using the new ADO data control?

Technique

One of the newest components included with Visual Basic 6 is the ADO Data Control. The ADO Data Control allows you to use OLE DB to access a local or remote data source and bind it to other controls on a form without having to write much code.

This How-To creates a simple front-end using the ADO Data Control and the `DataGrid` control. It is not necessary to write any code for this project.

Steps

To create this project, complete the following steps:

1. Create a new Standard EXE project and name it ADOTest3.

2. Add the Microsoft ADO Data Control 6.0 and Microsoft DataGrid Control 6.0 to the project.

3. Drop an ADO data control and a `DataGrid` control onto the form.

4. Set the properties of this project as listed in Table 14.3.

Table 14.3 Form and Object Properties for ADOTest3

OBJECT/CONTROL	PROPERTY	VALUE
Form	Name	frmPublishers
	Caption	ADO Simple Database Front-end
	Height	5415
	StartUpPosition	2 - CenterScreen
	Width	6975

OBJECT/CONTROL	PROPERTY	VALUE
ADO Data Control	Name	dcPublishers
	Caption	Publishers Table
	CommandType	1 - adCmdText
	ConnectString	DSN=Biblio
	CursorType	2 - adOpenDynamic
	Height	330
	Left	240
	RecordSource	SELECT * FROM Publishers;
	Top	4440
	Width	6375
DataGrid	Name	dgPublishers
	AllowAddNew	True
	AllowDelete	True
	AllowUpdate	True
	Caption	Publishers Table
	DataSource	dcPublishers
	Height	3975
	Left	240
	Top	240
	Width	6375

5. Right-click over the **DataGrid** control and select Retrieve Fields from the pop-up menu that appears. A message box appears asking you whether you want to replace existing grid layout with new field definitions. Click the Yes button. This automatically assigns the field definitions of the recordset being accessed by the ADO data control to the **DataGrid** control.

6. Right-click over the **DataGrid** control again. This time select Properties from the shortcut menu. Click the Layout tab and select columns using the Column drop-down list. Assign the layout properties for each column as listed in Table 14.4.

Table 14.4 DataGrid Property Page Layout Properties

COLUMN	PROPERTY	VALUE
Column 0	Width	600
Column 1	Width	4000
Column 2	Width	4000
Column 3	Width	4000

continued on next page

continued from previous page

OBJECT/CONTROL	PROPERTY	VALUE
Column 4	Width	1500
Column 5	Width	600
Column 6	Width	1200
Column 7	Width	1500
Column 8	Width	1500
Column 9	Width	6000
	WrapText	Checked

7. Save and run the project, as shown in Figure 14.9.

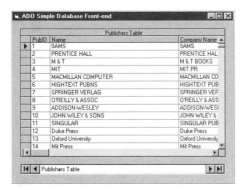

Figure 14.9 This is the ADOTest3 project as it appears at runtime.

How It Works

Using a `DataGrid` control and binding it to an ADO Data Control, allows you to quickly create a database front-end for viewing multiple records, making changes, and even adding or deleting records.

Comments

This technique of binding to the ADO Data Control is applied best when creating administrative utilities that allow users to make changes directly to a data source. When complicated business rules need to be applied or multiple tables need to be accessed, then you might want to avoid using this technique and apply a more sophisticated method of managing data, presenting it to the user, and updating the data source.

CHAPTER 15

BUILDING MULTITIER WEB-BASED APPLICATIONS

BUILDING MULTITIER WEB-BASED APPLICATIONS

How do I...

15.1 Design component-based applications?

15.2 Build a reusable data access component?

15.3 Create business objects?

15.4 Create an application that accesses remote business objects?

15.5 Build an MTS-enabled component?

For many years, Visual Basic enterprise applications have been developed using a two-tier application model composed of a client layer and a server layer. The client provides the complete Visual Basic application with all its process-oriented functionality—which, although may be located on the server's hard disk, is executed solely in the client's memory space—and the servers provide the ODBC data sources. This model requires as many ODBC connections to the database as there are active clients. Most companies pay an annual fee to maintain a certain number of active connections to their database.

Recently, Microsoft has developed a new design structure for developing applications, which is called the Microsoft Solutions Framework (MSF) application model. This new architecture utilizes a services-based paradigm. With the introduction of Component Object Model (COM) and Distributed COM, this application model is being put to good use in developing the next generation of high-performance enterprise-level applications. These applications can now share resources that in the old model were normally confined to each occurrence of the application. With the new model, reusable business components reside on servers and have the capability to interact with each other to optimize the use of resources, as well as optimize the overall performance and maintenance of application systems. This architecture immensely reduces the number of concurrent data source connections necessary to deliver data to the applications.

This chapter introduces this architecture and provides you with the capability to design and develop your own distributed component-based applications.

15.1 Design Component-Based Applications

This How-To demonstrates techniques used in component-based application design that help you to isolate and generalize specific functionality. You should then be able to use these design methods to segregate the various services required by your applications and create independent objects that can become shared resources.

15.2 Build a Reusable Data Access Component

This How-to presents a technique for creating reusable data access components that provide data services to the business objects in your applications.

15.3 Create Business Objects

With the use of ActiveX and object-oriented programming, this How-To demonstrates creating several business objects that encompass the `ProductBase` object model that was designed in How-To 15.2.

15.4 Create an Application That Accesses Remote Business Objects

In this How-To, you learn about what it takes to access remote business objects from a client application. You create an application that accesses the `ProductBase` object model that you created in the previous How-To.

15.5 Build an MTS-Enabled Component

Microsoft Transaction Server (MTS) is presently the best solution for managing remote objects. This How-To demonstrates the implementation of MTS into your server-based components. This section shows you how to add several lines of code to your remote components that help them to work directly with MTS to optimize the performance of your application.

Understanding Multitier Architecture?

Multitier architecture is derived from the MSF application model. MSF is defined by Microsoft as "a suite of concepts and reference models that help organizations build and deploy enterprise systems."

This section introduces the MSF application model. In the process, it will help you to understand the delineation and the scope of each of the three layers structured into the application model's archetype.

The term "application" must no longer be understood as "a set of executables and a database," but should be redefined as "a network of services needed to provide the solution to a business problem." To clearly define those services being provided for a solution and delineate the various types of services available to applications, Microsoft has developed the MSF application model. The application model consists of three distinct layers or categories of services: user services, business services, and data services.

The user services consist of the user interface and any localized functionality or logic related to the input and display of information for the user. This would also include any visual components utilized in the user interface.

User services are the consumers of business services. A user service might need to provide information to a business component to utilize the business service that is provided. The business services are composed of any functionality that interacts between the user interface and the data services, or any functionality or business logic related to specific rules that encompass the process of converting the characteristics of data from one state to another, as requested by a user service or another business component. Other business or data components may be called to perform these processes.

The data services are isolated to any functionality that either encapsulates a data source or acts as a data source to provide information to the business services. A data service may also act as a generic data access interface to any number of data sources.

In the old world of client/server applications, the application usually runs solely on the client computer while accessing data sources residing on servers or through mainframe gateways. This architecture demands many resources from the servers because a connection is usually maintained for each client actively running an application.

With the new architecture, data source connections are now maintained by middleware running on the servers rather than the client, enabling the server to use fewer concurrent connections to provide data services to the applications.

To maintain hierarchical integrity, a user service should never be the direct consumer of a data service but should utilize a business service to request information from a data source.

The application model is a logical model and not a physical model. Some business logic could reside on the client, and some business and data logic could reside on multiple servers.

The application model doesn't specifically apply to Visual Basic or Visual C++ applications. This model can apply to any type of application on varying platforms. In the case of an Internet application, the user services could be provided by various scripted languages and browser-based controls through a Web browser, and the business and data services could be provided by server-side scripting and other back office technologies. Visual Basic may provide the business objects, whereas Internet Explorer is the container for the user interface.

As to how multitier architecture works, it can be easily understood using this real-world analogy.

You need to arrange a trip to Acapulco, Mexico. To streamline the process, you want to use the services of your local travel agency. You, of course, are the user. The telephone is the user interface. The local travel agency is the business service provider. The airline, hotel, and car rental reservation administrators provide the data services, and a seat on a flight, the hotel suite, and a rental car are the finished product of the business services. You do not have to directly interface to the data services to receive the requested product, but you only need to provide specific parameters to the business service: the destination and time of stay. The business service will then perform all the necessary business logic to return the results of a seat on a flight to and from the destination, a hotel suite during your stay, and a rental car for local transportation.

In the preceding analogy, the protocol used to communicate from the user to the travel agency did not include passing the phone numbers of the airline, hotel, and rental car company, but only a simple where and when. It is the responsibility of the travel agency to obtain the necessary phone numbers and compile specific information required by the airline, hotel, and rental car company to produce the results requested by the user. In the same manner, a user service should never have to know the protocol necessary to interface with a data service or data source. This is business logic.

Isolating the technical details of data service protocols and business logic from the user services allows several different user interfaces on varying platforms to access the same business objects. The user interface could be created using Visual Basic, Java, HTML, VBScript, Microsoft Access, Active Server Pages, and others. The list goes on. Each application could have different types of user interfaces that use the same business objects.

With two-tier architecture, the client computer normally performs all the application functionality including execution of data access interfaces and ODBC drivers. The performance of these client/server applications depends mostly on the speed of the client processor.

With multitier architecture, the majority of the functionality is shared among servers. In most cases, these servers are latest-technology high-performance processors and multiprocessors and can perform the services and return the results to the client faster than ever before. This factor combined with fewer concurrent data source connections, provides for a more scalable application using fewer resources.

As you proceed through this chapter, you will see many examples of this architecture and how it is applied using Visual Basic.

COMPLEXITY
BEGINNING

15.1 How do I...
Design component-based applications?

COMPATIBILITY: VISUAL BASIC 4, 5, AND 6

Problem

I have never designed or developed distributed component-based applications. I have spent the last several years developing process-based client/server applications. How do I design component-based applications?

Technique

Although the capability to create distributed component-based applications in Visual Basic has been available since Visual Basic 4, remote automation with Visual Basic 4 OLE components was rarely used in enterprise applications due to performance and scalability issues. Objects running on the server needed to be better managed.

To take full advantage of component-based development, object-oriented design should be applied from the start. Designing component-based applications was seen mostly in C++ shops where object-oriented development was in full use.

When Visual Basic 5 and DCOM (Distributed Component Object Model) were introduced, users were given the capability to create high-performance component-based distributed applications. This concept has been taken a step further in Visual Basic 6 where newer features relating to MTS have been introduced. MTS is discussed in greater detail in How-To 15.5.

Steps

Complete the following steps to design a component-based application. These steps use a fictitious inventory management application to illustrate the techniques for designing component-based applications.

1. Identify the Warehouse Inventory Management Problem. For you to design a component-based application, you need to first identify a business problem so that you can provide a solution.

In this scenario, you are contracted to develop a system of applications for an office supplies wholesale distributor. The system will be used to manage the inventory in the warehouse at their distribution center. The problem is that they only have a system of paperwork and spreadsheets. When shipments of products arrive at the receiving dock, the receiving clerk manually checks the manifest and verifies the quantity received against the quantity ordered. Then the forklift operator takes the palletized product, places it in an available location in the warehouse, and notes it on a clipboard. If the product is not on a pallet, it is the forklift operator's responsibility to palletize the product. The clipboard is then brought to the clerk's office where the data is keyed into a spreadsheet and sorted for reports. Sometimes data is lost in the process, and a lost product is not located until the quarterly physical inventory.

The company wants you to create a new system of applications that will help to streamline inventory management.

2. Define the solution to the problem. One of the main objectives of the new Warehouse Inventory Management System is to track the location and quantities of all products stored in the warehouse. This begins when the product is received at the receiving dock and ends when the product is loaded onto a shipment at the shipping dock. The system should maintain a location for all products stored in the warehouse at all times.

Because you are with one of the top consulting firms in the country, you will propose some of the latest technology. Because all products entering the warehouse are marked with a bar code, you recommend that the clerks and forklift operators use radio frequency bar code scanners. You also recommend that the clerks and administrators have access to the applications at their desktops, and you recommend that several terminals be disbursed around the warehouse in various locations for warehouse personnel to have random access to the applications.

3. Understand the foundation of distributed application design. Just as paper and pencil are necessary to draw a picture, here are a few basic elements necessary to design your component-based applications.

One basic element of distributed application design is the service provider. The service provider is the object that the consumer or user component must interface with to request a service or group of services. A service provider is implemented within the application design as an object interface or component.

Another basic element of distributed application design is the service. A service is simply a process or logical unit of work—add product, receive quantity, ship quantity, or delete product—that can be performed by a service provider. These services should be performed without the consumer needing to possess the knowledge required to render the service.

The specific protocol used to request a logical unit of work is the interface. The request protocol for all services rendered by a specific service provider is integrated into the service provider's interface. This interface is implemented within the application design as one or more properties or methods of an object.

With these basic elements, along with others that you will discover along the way, you will continue the task of designing your first component-based application.

4. Create an object model. To begin your design, you need to identify the objects of the warehouse and the functions of those objects. Then, you must form the hierarchy of the objects into an object model.

The first object is the **ProductBase** object. The product base is the substance of the inventory itself. Without a product base, there is no inventory. The **ProductBase** object will contain several methods that relate directly to products stored in the warehouse and the vendors that provide those products.

The **Vendor** object is the next object to identify. The **Vendor** object will provide product-related services and vendor-specific information. Each product is supplied by a vendor.

The **Product** object is the last object in the **ProductBase** object model or hierarchy. The **Product** object will provide product-specific information.

The **Inventory** object is the start of another object model. The **Inventory** object will provide location-related services to the client.

The next object in the model is the **Location** object. The location is basically a fixed holding facility for a pallet or stack of pallets. There are many locations in the warehouse where pallets of products are stored. The **Location** object will provide pallet-related services and location-specific information.

The next object in the model is the **Pallet** object. The pallet may contain one or more items of varying quantities. The **Pallet** object will provide item-related services and pallet-specific information.

The last object in this hierarchy is the **Item** object. The item is identified by the pallet and the product. The **Item** object will provide item-specific information.

This completes our example warehouse object model. In a real-world system of applications, many more objects could be identified. In fact, the object model would more than likely be different for different warehouses, depending on the type of inventory stored and the structure of the facility. The complexity of an application of this nature would go beyond the scope of this book. So we will try to keep it simple.

Look at the simple object model you have created. Figure 15.1 illustrates your warehouse object model with the objects that you have identified.

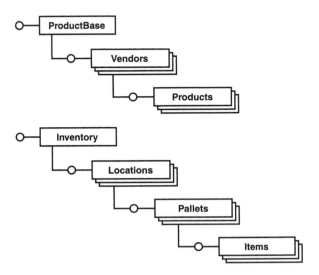

Figure 15.1 This is an illustration of the hierarchical relationships of the warehouse object model that was created.

5. Identify the characteristics of the objects. The characteristics of an object differentiate one object from another of the same type or class. The characteristics are implemented as properties of an object.

Because you are creating a simple application, you will only include the primary characteristics of each object. In the real world, there would be many more. Table 15.1 lists the characteristics of each object.

Table 15.1 Object Characteristics

OBJECT	CHARACTERISTIC
ProductBase	Vendors
Vendor	VendorID
	VendorName
	Products
Product	ProductID
	Description
	VendorID
	VendorName

OBJECT	CHARACTERISTIC
	ReorderQuantity
	MinimumQuantity
Inventory	Locations
Location	LocationID
	Description
	Pallets
Pallet	PalletID
	LocationID
	Items
Item	PalletID
	ProductID
	Description
	Quantity

6. Identify the services to be provided. You need to identify the services to be provided by each of the objects in the object model. The services are implemented as methods of an object.

The following are some of the services that should be provided by the objects:

- ✔ NewProduct
- ✔ UpdateProduct
- ✔ RemoveProduct
- ✔ UpdateVendor
- ✔ MovePallet
- ✔ NewItem
- ✔ MoveItem
- ✔ RemoveItem
- ✔ AdjustQuantity
- ✔ MoveQuantity

How It Works

By identifying the objects, object characteristics, and the services to be provided by each of the objects, you can design an object model or set of objects that could be used as the core functionality for your applications.

Comments

In order to provide optimal component-based solutions to business problems, the skill of identifying objects, object characteristics, and object services will need to be mastered. It would be a good idea to practice these concepts by looking at other business problem scenarios that may be found in various commercial and industrial environments.

COMPLEXITY
BEGINNING

15.2 How do I...
Build a reusable data access component?

COMPATIBILITY: VISUAL BASIC 4, 5, AND 6

Problem

I want to be able to create a data access component that will be generic enough that I could use it for all my warehouse applications. How do I build a reusable data access component?

Technique

In this case, you use a single data source for storing and retrieving data to and from the Warehouse database. But whether you are using a single data source or you have several data sources, it is simple enough to generalize the process so that only the business objects have any knowledge of the access protocol or data source parameters.

There are basically two data services you need to save and retrieve data. The **GetRows** service retrieves resultsets, whereas the **Execute** service performs nonresult SQL statements.

Steps

To create this project, complete the following steps:

1. Open the Control Panel and run the 32-bit ODBC Administrator.

2. Click the System DSN tab of the ODBC dialog box, and then click the Add button. Select Microsoft Access Driver (*.mdb) from the list. Then click the Finish button. Now enter the Data Source Name as **Warehouse** and click the Select button. Locate Warehouse.mdb from the CD-ROM included with the book and click OK. Click the next OK button, and the Warehouse DSN should appear in the list of System Data Sources, as shown in Figure 15.2.

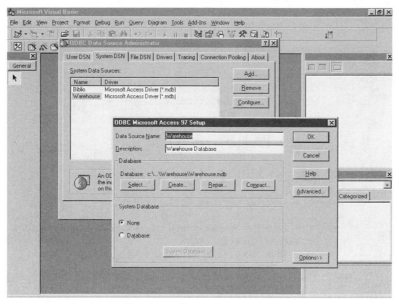

Figure 15.2 This is the Warehouse Data Source as it appears in the ODBC Administrator and Setup dialog boxes.

3. Create a new ActiveX DLL project and name it WIMData. Also, change the name of the `ClassModule` to `WarehouseData`.

4. Add a reference to the Microsoft ActiveX Data Objects 2.0 Library to the project.

5. Create a new standard module named `modErrorMgt`. This module is used throughout this chapter.

6. Add the following error-related functions to the `modErrorMgt` module:

```
Option Explicit

Function NoError()
    'Define local ErrorType.
    Dim pError(2)

    'Assign no error.
    pError(0) = 0
    pError(1) = ""
    pError(2) = ""

    'Return the ErrorType.
    NoError = pError

End Function

Function SetError(ErrNumber As Long, ErrDescription As _
String, ErrSource As String)
```

continued on next page

continued from previous page

```
'This function will return a variant array of three elements
'set to the passed parameters.
    'Define local ErrorType.
    Dim pError(2)

    'Assign no error.
    pError(0) = ErrNumber
    pError(1) = ErrDescription
    pError(2) = ErrSource

    'Return the ErrorType.
    SetError = pError

End Function

Function ErrTrue(Status) As Boolean

    'First check to make sure Status is an array.
    If IsArray(Status) Then
        'Then make sure first element is numeric.
        If IsNumeric(Status(0)) Then
            'Then if it is not zero
            If Status(0) <> 0 Then
                'an error occurred.
                ErrTrue = True
            End If
        End If
    End If

End Function
```

7. Create the `GetRows` method for retrieving resultsets. `GetRows` returns resultsets as a variant array so that you can pass the resultsets across the network. Enter the following code into the `WarehouseData` class module:

```
Public Function GetRows(ByVal SQLStr As String)

    'handle all errors locally
    On Error GoTo GetRows_Err

    'dimension local variables
    Dim Status
    Dim ConnStr As String

    'create an ADO Recordset object
    Dim ADO As ADODB.Recordset
    Dim ADOConn As ADODB.Connection

    Set ADO = New ADODB.Recordset
    Status = NoError

    'access our Warehouse data source
    ConnStr = "DSN=Warehouse"
```

```
            'open a static Recordset specified by SQLStr
            ADO.Open SQLStr, ConnStr, adOpenStatic
            GoSub GetRows_CheckStatus
            'if no errors then
            If Status(0) <> 0 Then
                GetRows = Status
            ElseIf ADO.RecordCount <> 0 Then
                'retrieve the rows as a variant array
                GetRows = ADO.GetRows
                GoSub GetRows_CheckStatus
            Else
                GetRows = SetError(3021, "Record Not Found", _
                "WarehouseData")
            End If

            'close the Recordset
            ADO.Close
            'and destroy the Recordset object
            Set ADO = Nothing

    GetRows_Cont:
        'all done
        Exit Function

    GetRows_Err:
        'pass it back
        With Err
            GetRows = SetError(.Number, .Description, .Source)
        End With

        'all done
        Resume GetRows_Cont

    GetRows_CheckStatus:
        'check the ADO Errors collection for any error
        'greater than zero
        Set ADOConn = ADO.ActiveConnection
        If ADOConn.Errors.Count > 0 Then
            With ADOConn.Errors(0)
                If .Number > 0 Then
                    'assign error information
                    Status = SetError(.Number, .Description, _
                    .Source)
                End If
                'pass it back
                GetRows = Status
            End With
        End If

        'done checking
        Set ADOConn = Nothing

        Return

End Function
```

8. Enter the following code, which passes nonresult SQL commands to the database server, into your `WarehouseData` class module:

```
Public Function Execute(ByVal SQLStr As String)

        'handle all errors locally
        On Error GoTo Execute_Err

        'dimension our local variables
        Dim Status
        Dim ConnStr As String
        Status = NoError
        Execute = NoError

        'create an ADO Connection object
        Dim ADO As ADODB.Connection
        Set ADO = New ADODB.Connection

        'specify our warehouse data source
        ConnStr = "DSN=Warehouse"

        'open the connection
        ADO.Open ConnStr
        GoSub Execute_CheckStatus
        If Status(0) = 0 Then
            'execute the command
            ADO.Execute SQLStr
            GoSub Execute_CheckStatus
        End If

        'close the connection
        ADO.Close

        'and destroy the Connection object
        Set ADO = Nothing

Execute_Cont:
    Execute = Status

        'all done
        Exit Function

Execute_Err:
    'pass it back
    With Err
        Execute = SetError(.Number, .Description, .Source)
    End With

    'all done
    Resume Execute_Cont

Execute_CheckStatus:
    'check the ADO Errors collection for any error
    'greater than zero
    If ADO.Errors.Count > 0 Then
        With ADO.Errors(0)
```

```
                    If .Number > 0 Then
                        Status = SetError(.Number, .Description, _
                        .Source)
                    End If
                End With
            End If

            'done checking
            Return

        End Function
```

9. Save the project and choose File, Make WIMData.dll from the menu. If all is well syntactically, the project will compile and register.

How It Works

The GetRows method of the WIMData component encapsulates the creation of an ADO Recordset object, and then uses the GetRows method of the Recordset object to return a variant array of the data contained in the Recordset. The Execute method of the WIMData component encapsulates the Execute method of the ADO Connection object exclusively for processing non-result SQL statements.

The WIMData component with the GetRows and Execute methods provides our business objects with the capability to access the Warehouse database—a simple and straightforward task that is easily generalized into a shared component.

Comments

The fact that the GetRows method of the WIMData component returns a variant array allows you to marshal resultsets across a network using DCOM or Remote Automation, without maintaining an instance of the ADO Recordset object on the server.

The WIMData component is used throughout this chapter. Make sure that you have successfully compiled the project before continuing on to the next section.

COMPLEXITY
BEGINNING

15.3 How do I...
Create business objects?

COMPATIBILITY: VISUAL BASIC 5 AND 6

Problem

I have read the first three How-Tos in this chapter and have created the data component in the previous section that is used to access the Warehouse database. I am really interested in taking the concepts and the object model design created in How-To 15.2 and turning it into actual objects that I can use in a practical application. How do I create business objects?

Technique

Taking the design of an object model and an application concept and putting it into code is the most exciting part of all this because you get to see your design become substance.

Several issues need to be considered when creating remote business objects that will be accessed by client applications. Most of those issues relate to server performance. If asynchronous methods are not feasible—which is the case with most enterprise applications—then synchronous business objects should be developed in such a way that the client can perform the following:

- ✔ Create the object.

- ✔ Access the specific service or services needed, without holding the reference to the server-side object during any client-side processing.

- ✔ Destroy the object.

No connection between the client and server should be idle for any period of time. Client to server access should be an open and shut case.

To optimize server performance, you should have the client applications make as few trips as possible to the server. Accessing multiple properties of a server object means multiple trips back and forth to and from the server for each property accessed. A single property or method should be used to pass rows of data or large blocks of data from server-side objects. Multiple parameters of a method may be used to pass data to the business object because all a method's parameters are passed in one trip. If you are passing a set of updates to a business object as a transaction, then you should pass it as a variant array.

Return values of server-side functions and properties to be accessed by the client should only be defined as types that can be passed by value. User-defined types and objects cannot be passed by value but are only passed by reference. Therefore, avoid the use of user-defined types and object references as parameters or return values of remote object members. If an object reference is passed back from a server, then every time the client accesses that reference, the request is marshaled across the network, and the members of the object are executed on the server.

Steps

The following steps create the business objects related to the `ProductBase` portion of the object model designed in section 15.2 and create a test application to access the `ProductBase`, `Vendor`, and `Product` objects.

1. Create a new ActiveX DLL project named WIM. Change the name of the class module to **ProductBase**. You will use a DLL initially so that you can test your business objects using a project group.

2. Add two class modules to the project; name them **Vendor** and **Product**.

3. Add a new standard module named **modWIM** to the project and add the **modErrorMgt** module (created in How-To 15.3) using the Existing tab of the New Module dialog box.

4. When the variant return value is passed back from the **GetRows** method of the **WarehouseData** object, it is a variant array. If the variant array has two dimensions, then it is a resultset. Otherwise, the variant array has only one dimension, and an error has occurred either within the **WarehouseData** object or possibly in ADO or ODBC. Therefore, you need a function that can determine the number of dimensions in a variant array. At this point, no intrinsic function in Visual Basic provides this service. Therefore, enter the following code into the **modWIM** module:

```
Option Explicit

Function Dimensions(VariantArray) As Integer
'Determine the number of dimensions for a variant array

    'Handle all errors locally.
    On Error GoTo Dimensions_Err

    'Define local variables.
    Dim Ctr As Integer
    Dim TestVal As Long

    Do
        'Loop and increment counter.
        Ctr = Ctr + 1
        'Test the upper bound of the dimension.
        TestVal = UBound(VariantArray, Ctr)
    Loop

Dimensions_Cont:
    'All done.
    Exit Function

Dimensions_Err:
    'When an error occurs we have exceeded the number of
    'dimensions in our variant array by one. The true number
    'of dimensions is the counter less one.
    Dimensions = Ctr - 1

    'Reset the Err object and exit the function.
    Resume Dimensions_Cont

End Function
```

5. To streamline the building of SQL statements within our business objects, it would be nice to have a few simple functions that would convert numeric variables to strings with or without a trailing comma, and that would take a string and surround it with quotes with or without a trailing comma. These functions will help make our code easier to read. Add the following lines of code to the modWIM module:

```
Function SQLVal(InputValue) As String
'Trim and convert a value to a string for a SQL statement.

    SQLVal = Trim$(Str$(InputValue))

End Function

Function SQLValC(InputValue) As String
'Trim and convert a value to a string for a SQL statement
'and place a comma at the end.

    SQLValC = SQLVal(InputValue) & ","

End Function

Function SQLText(StringData As String) As String
'Surround a text string with single quotes for a SQL
'statement.

    SQLText = "'" & StringData & "'"

End Function

Function SQLTextC(StringData As String) As String
'Surround a text string with single quotes for a SQL
'statement and place a comma at the end.

    SQLTextC = SQLText(StringData) & ","

End Function
```

6. Because the client application should make as few trips to the server as possible, all properties are local to the component so that only objects in the object model can have direct access to the properties. All client access to the properties is by both parameters and return values of methods, or by returning a single variant array containing all the properties. This helps optimize the server performance and maintain a stateless interface to our object model. Define all properties as private to the class, but expose those properties to the other objects in our component by using Friend Property procedures. Enter the following code into the **Product** class:

```
'Define the local properties.
Private pProductID As String
Private pDescription As String
Private pVendorID As String
Private pVendorName As String
```

```
        Private pReorderQuantity As Long
        Private pMinimumQuantity As Long

        Friend Property Get ProductID() As String
        'Define component-level properties.

            'Return the ProductID
            ProductID = pProductID

        End Property

        Friend Property Let ProductID(pData As String)

            'Assign the ProductID
            pProductID = pData

        End Property

        Friend Property Get Description() As String

            'Return the Description
            Description = pDescription

        End Property

        Friend Property Let Description(pData As String)

            'Assign the Description
            pDescription = pData

        End Property

        Friend Property Get VendorID() As String

            'Return the VendorID
            VendorID = pVendorID

        End Property

        Friend Property Let VendorID(pData As String)

            'Assign the VendorID
            pVendorID = pData

        End Property

        Friend Property Get VendorName() As String

            'Return the VendorName
            VendorName = pVendorName

        End Property

        Friend Property Let VendorName(pData As String)
```

continued on next page

continued from previous page

```
        'Assign the VendorName
        pVendorName = pData

End Property

Friend Property Get ReorderQuantity() As Long

        'Return the ReorderQuantity
        ReorderQuantity = pReorderQuantity

End Property

Friend Property Let ReorderQuantity(pData As Long)

        'Assign the ReorderQuantity
        pReorderQuantity = pData

End Property

Friend Property Get MinimumQuantity() As Long

        'Return the MinimumQuantity
        MinimumQuantity = pMinimumQuantity

End Property

Friend Property Let MinimumQuantity(pData As Long)

        'Assign the MinimumQuantity
        pMinimumQuantity = pData

End Property

Public Property Get Properties()
'Return the Properties variant array.

        'Define a temporary variant array.
        Dim TempVar(5)

        'Assign the private properties to the array.
        TempVar(0) = pProductID
        TempVar(1) = pDescription
        TempVar(2) = pVendorID
        TempVar(3) = pVendorName
        TempVar(4) = pReorderQuantity
        TempVar(5) = pMinimumQuantity

        'Return the variant array.
        Properties = TempVar

End Property
```

7. Enter the following lines of code into the **Vendor** class module:

```
Option Explicit
'Define the local properties.
```

```
Private pVendorID As String
Private pVendorName As String

'Define the Product object reference.
Public Product As Product

Friend Property Get VendorID() As String
'Define component-level properties.

    'Return the VendorID.
    VendorID = pVendorID

End Property

Friend Property Let VendorID(pData As String)

    'Assign the VendorID.
    pVendorID = pData

End Property

Friend Property Get VendorName() As String

    'Return the VendorName.
    VendorName = pVendorName

End Property

Friend Property Let VendorName(pData As String)

    'Assign the VendorName.
    pVendorName = pData

End Property

Public Property Get Properties()
'Define the public Properties variant array.

    'Define a temporary variant array.
    Dim VendorVar(1)

    'Assign the properties.
    VendorVar(0) = pVendorID
    VendorVar(1) = pVendorName

    'Return the variant array.
    Properties = VendorVar

End Property
```

8. The **Product** and **Vendor** objects must provide the standard Retrieve, Insert, Update, and Delete services to other business objects in the object model. These methods should be defined as **Friend** functions, accessible only to other objects within the component. Enter the following lines of code into the **Product** class module:

```
Friend Function Insert()

    'Handle all errors locally.
    On Error GoTo Insert_Err

    'Define the SQL string
    Dim SQLStr As String

    'Create the Warehouse data object.
    Dim WD As New WIMData.WarehouseData

    'Build the SQL statement used to insert a new Product
    'row into the Products table.
    SQLStr = "INSERT INTO Products (ProductID," & _
    "Description,VendorID,ReorderQty,MinimumQty) " & _
    "VALUES (" & SQLTextC(pProductID) & _
    SQLTextC(pDescription) & SQLTextC(pVendorID) & _
    SQLValC(pReorderQuantity) & SQLVal(pMinimumQuantity) _
    & ")"

    'Insert the row.
    Insert = WD.Execute(SQLStr)

Insert_Cont:
    'Destroy the data object.
    Set WD = Nothing

    'All done.
    Exit Function

Insert_Err:
    'If an error occurs then pass back the error variant.
    With Err
        Insert = SetError(.Number, .Description, .Source)
    End With

    'Reset the Err object and exit the function.
    Resume Insert_Cont

End Function

Friend Function Retrieve()

    'Handle all errors locally.
    On Error GoTo Retrieve_Err

    'Define local variables.
    Dim Results    'The variant resultset.
    Dim SQLStr As String    'The SQL string

    'Create the Warehouse data object.
    Dim WD As New WIMData.WarehouseData

    'Build the SQL statement used to select a specific
    'Product row from the Products table.
    SQLStr = "SELECT Products.ProductID," & _
```

```
                "Products.Description,Products.VendorID," & _
                "Vendors.VendorName,Products.ReorderQty," & _
                "Products.MinimumQty FROM Products,Vendors " & _
                "WHERE Products.ProductID=" & SQLText(pProductID) & _
                " AND Vendors.VendorID=Products.VendorID;"

            'Retrieve the row.
            Results = WD.GetRows(SQLStr)

            'If the result is 2-dimensional, then it is a
            'variant resultset.
            If Dimensions(Results) = 2 Then
                'Assign the properties.
                pProductID = Results(0, 0)
                pDescription = Results(1, 0)
                pVendorID = Results(2, 0)
                pVendorName = Results(3, 0)
                pReorderQuantity = Results(4, 0)
                pMinimumQuantity = Results(5, 0)

                'And return the NoError variant.
                Retrieve = NoError
            Else
                'Otherwise it is an error variant.
                Retrieve = Results
            End If

    Retrieve_Cont:
            'Destroy the data object.
            Set WD = Nothing

            'All done.
            Exit Function

    Retrieve_Err:
            'If an error occurs then pass back the error variant.
            With Err
                Retrieve = SetError(.Number, .Description, .Source)
            End With

            'Reset the Err object and exit the function.
            Resume Retrieve_Cont

    End Function

    Friend Function Update()

            'Handle all errors locally.
            On Error GoTo Update_Err

            'Define the SQL string
            Dim SQLStr As String

            'Create the Warehouse data object.
            Dim WD As New WIMData.WarehouseData
```

continued on next page

continued from previous page

```
                    'Build the SQL statement used to update the specific
                    'Product row in the Products table.
                    SQLStr = "UPDATE Products SET " & _
                    "Description=" & SQLTextC(pDescription) & _
                    "VendorID=" & SQLTextC(pVendorID) & _
                    "ReorderQty=" & SQLValC(pReorderQuantity) & _
                    "MinimumQty=" & SQLVal(pMinimumQuantity) & _
                    " WHERE ProductID=" & SQLText(pProductID)

                    'Update the row.
                    Update = WD.Execute(SQLStr)

            Update_Cont:
                    'Destroy the data object.
                    Set WD = Nothing

                    'All done.
                    Exit Function

            Update_Err:
                    'If an error occurs then pass back the error variant.
                    With Err
                        Update = SetError(.Number, .Description, .Source)
                    End With

                    'Reset the Err object and exit the function.
                    Resume Update_Cont

            End Function

            Friend Function Delete()

                    'Handle all errors locally.
                    On Error GoTo Delete_Err

                    'Define the SQL string
                    Dim SQLStr As String

                    'Create the Warehouse data object.
                    Dim WD As New WIMData.WarehouseData

                    'Build the SQL statement used to delete the specific
                    'Product row from the Products table.
                    SQLStr = "DELETE FROM Products WHERE ProductID=" & _
                    SQLText(pProductID)

                    'Delete the row.
                    Delete = WD.Execute(SQLStr)

            Delete_Cont:
                    'Destroy the data object.
                    Set WD = Nothing

                    'All done.
                    Exit Function

            Delete_Err:
```

```
'If an error occurs then pass back the error variant.
With Err
    Delete = SetError(.Number, .Description, .Source)
End With

'Reset the Err object and exit the function.
Resume Delete_Cont

End Function
```

9. Enter the following lines of code into the Vendor class module:

```
Friend Function Insert()

    'Handle all errors locally.
    On Error GoTo Insert_Err

    'Define the SQL string variable.
    Dim SQLStr As String

    'Create the Warehouse data object.
    Dim WD As New WIMData.WarehouseData

    'Build the SQL statement that will Insert a new Vendor
    'row into the Vendors table.
    SQLStr = "INSERT INTO Vendors (VendorID,VendorName) " & _
    "VALUES (" & SQLTextC(pVendorID) & SQLText(pVendorName) _
    & ")"

    'Insert the row.
    Insert = WD.Execute(SQLStr)

    'Destroy the data object.
    Set WD = Nothing

Insert_Cont:
    'All done.
    Exit Function

Insert_Err:
    'If an error occurs then pass back the error variant.
    With Err
        Insert = SetError(.Number, .Description, .Source)
    End With

    'Reset the Err object and exit the function.
    Resume Insert_Cont

End Function

Friend Function Retrieve()

    'Handle all errors locally.
    On Error GoTo Retrieve_Err

    'Define the resultset variant.
```

continued on next page

continued from previous page

```
        Dim Results

        'Define the SQL string variable.
        Dim SQLStr As String

        'Create the Warehouse data object.
        Dim WD As New WIMData.WarehouseData

        'Build the SQL statement that will retrieve the
        'specified Vendor row from the Vendors table.
        SQLStr = "SELECT VendorID,VendorName FROM Vendors " & _
        "WHERE VendorID=" & SQLText(pVendorID)

        'Get the row.
        Results = WD.GetRows(SQLStr)

        'If dimensions are 2, then it is a resultset.
        If Dimensions(Results) = 2 Then
            'Store the fields into the Vendor properties.
            pVendorID = Results(0, 0)
            pVendorName = Results(1, 0)

            'Pass back the NoError variant.
            Retrieve = NoError
        Else
            'Otherwise, it is an error variant.
            Retrieve = Results
        End If

        'Destroy the data object.
        Set WD = Nothing

Retrieve_Cont:
        'All done.
        Exit Function

Retrieve_Err:
        'If an error occurs then pass back the error variant.
        With Err
            Retrieve = SetError(.Number, .Description, .Source)
        End With

        'Reset the Err object and exit the function.
        Resume Retrieve_Cont

End Function

Friend Function Update()

        'Handle all errors locally.
        On Error GoTo Update_Err

        'Define the SQL string variable.
        Dim SQLStr As String

        'Create the Warehouse data object.
        Dim WD As New WIMData.WarehouseData
```

```
        'Build the SQL statement that will update the
        'specified Vendor row in the Vendors table.
        SQLStr = "UPDATE Vendors SET VendorName=" & _
        SQLText(pVendorName) & " WHERE VendorID=" & _
        SQLText(pVendorID)

        'Update the row.
        Update = WD.Execute(SQLStr)

        'Destroy the data object.
        Set WD = Nothing

Update_Cont:
        'All done.
        Exit Function

Update_Err:
        'If an error occurs then pass back the error variant.
        With Err
            Update = SetError(.Number, .Description, .Source)
        End With

        'Reset the Err object and exit the function.
        Resume Update_Cont

End Function

Friend Function Delete()

        'Handle all errors locally.
        On Error GoTo Delete_Err

        'Define the SQL string variable.
        Dim SQLStr As String

        'Create the Warehouse data object.
        Dim WD As New WIMData.WarehouseData

        'Build the SQL statement that will delete the
        'specified Vendor row from the Vendors table.
        SQLStr = "DELETE FROM Vendors WHERE VendorID=" & _
        SQLText(pVendorID)

        'Delete the row.
        Delete = WD.Execute(SQLStr)

        'Destroy the data object.
        Set WD = Nothing

Delete_Cont:
        'All done.
        Exit Function

Delete_Err:
        'If an error occurs then pass back the error variant.
        With Err
```

continued on next page

continued from previous page

```
            Delete = SetError(.Number, .Description, .Source)
        End With

        'Reset the Err object and exit the function.
        Resume Delete_Cont

End Function
```

10. To maintain the hierarchical structure of the object model, public or client access to certain services should be provided by the parent object. This includes creating a new **Product** or deleting an existing **Vendor**. Only accessing the object itself should provide the existing properties of the **Product** or **Vendor**. Now you need to provide the vendor-related services of the **ProductBase** object. Enter the following code into the **ProductBase** class module:

```
Option Explicit

'Define the Vendor object reference.
Public Vendor As Vendor

Private Sub SetNewVendor()
'If the Vendor object is nothing then create a new instance.

    If Vendor Is Nothing Then
        Set Vendor = New Vendor
    End If

End Sub

Public Function NewVendor(ByVal pVendorID As String, ByVal _
pVendorName As String)
'Add a new Vendor to the database.

    'Handle all errors locally.
    On Error GoTo NewVendor_Err

    'Make sure Vendor object exists
    SetNewVendor

    With Vendor
        'Assign all properties
        .VendorID = pVendorID
        .VendorName = pVendorName

        'Insert the new record
        NewVendor = .Insert
    End With

NewVendor_Cont:
    'All done.
    Exit Function

NewVendor_Err:
    'If an error occurs then pass back the error variant.
```

```
        With Err
            NewVendor = SetError(.Number, .Description, .Source)
        End With

        'Reset the Err object and exit the function.
        Resume NewVendor_Cont

End Function

Public Function OpenVendor(ByVal pVendorID As String) As _
Variant
'Retrieve the specified Vendor and store in the Vendor
'object.

        'Handle all errors locally.
        On Error GoTo OpenVendor_Err

        'Make sure Vendor object exists
        SetNewVendor
        With Vendor
            'Assign the unique property
            .VendorID = pVendorID

            'Retrieve the specified row
            OpenVendor = .Retrieve
        End With

OpenVendor_Cont:
        'All done.
        Exit Function

OpenVendor_Err:
        'If an error occurs then pass back the error variant.
        With Err
            OpenVendor = SetError(.Number, .Description, .Source)
        End With

        'Reset the Err object and exit the function.
        Resume OpenVendor_Cont

End Function

Public Function UpdateVendor(ByVal pVendorID As String, _
ByVal pVendorName As String)
'Update the specified Vendor in the database.

        'Handle all errors locally.
        On Error GoTo UpdateVendor_Err

        'Make sure Vendor object exists.
        SetNewVendor
        With Vendor
            'Assign all properties.
            .VendorID = pVendorID
            .VendorName = pVendorName
```

continued on next page

continued from previous page

```
                        'Update the specified row.
                        UpdateVendor = .Update
                End With

        UpdateVendor_Cont:
                'All done.
                Exit Function

        UpdateVendor_Err:
                'If an error occurs then pass back the error variant.
                With Err
                        UpdateVendor = SetError(.Number, .Description, _
                        .Source)
                End With

                'Reset the Err object and exit the function.
                Resume UpdateVendor_Cont

        End Function

        Public Sub CloseVendor()
        'Destroy the Vendor object.

                Set Vendor = Nothing

        End Sub

        Public Function RemoveVendor(ByVal pVendorID As String) As _
        Variant
        'Remove the specified Vendor from the database.

                'Handle all errors locally.
                On Error GoTo RemoveVendor_Err

                'Make sure Vendor object exists.
                SetNewVendor
                With Vendor
                        'Assign the unique property.
                        .VendorID = pVendorID

                        'Delete the specified row.
                        RemoveVendor = .Delete
                End With

        RemoveVendor_Cont:
                'All done.
                Exit Function

        RemoveVendor_Err:
                'If an error occurs then pass back the error variant.
                With Err
                        RemoveVendor = SetError(.Number, .Description, _
                        .Source)
                End With

                'Reset the Err object and exit the function.
```

```
        Resume RemoveVendor_Cont

End Function
```

11. In the same manner that vendor-related services are to be provided by the **ProductBase** object, product-related services are to be provided by the **Vendor** object. Enter the following code into the **Vendor** class module:

```
Private Sub SetNewProduct()
'If the Product object is nothing then create a new instance.

    If Product Is Nothing Then
        Set Product = New Product
    End If

End Sub

Public Function NewProduct(ByVal pProductID As String, _
ByVal pDescription As String, ByVal pReorderQuantity As _
Long, ByVal pMinimumQuantity As Long)

    'Handle all errors locally.
    On Error GoTo NewProduct_Err

    'Make sure Product object is created.
    SetNewProduct
    With Product
        .ProductID = pProductID
        .Description = pDescription
        .VendorID = pVendorID
        .VendorName = pVendorName
        .ReorderQuantity = pReorderQuantity
        .MinimumQuantity = pMinimumQuantity

        NewProduct = .Insert
    End With

NewProduct_Cont:
    'All done.
    Exit Function

NewProduct_Err:
    'If an error occurs then pass back the error variant.
    With Err
        NewProduct = SetError(.Number, .Description, .Source)
    End With

    'Reset the Err object and exit the function.
    Resume NewProduct_Cont

End Function

Public Function OpenProduct(ByVal pProductID As String) As _
Variant

    'Handle all errors locally.
```

continued on next page

continued from previous page

```
        On Error GoTo OpenProduct_Err

        'Make sure Product object is created.
        SetNewProduct
        With Product
            'Assign the unique Product property.
            .ProductID = pProductID

            'Retrieve the specified Product row.
            OpenProduct = .Retrieve

            'Assign the Product's Vendor properties.
            pVendorID = .VendorID
            pVendorName = .VendorName
        End With

OpenProduct_Cont:
        'All done.
        Exit Function

OpenProduct_Err:
        'If an error occurs then pass back the error variant.
        With Err
            OpenProduct = SetError(.Number, .Description, _
            .Source)
        End With

        'Reset the Err object and exit the function.
        Resume OpenProduct_Cont

End Function

Public Function UpdateProduct(ByVal pProductID As String, _
ByVal pDescription As String, ByVal pReorderQty As Long, _
ByVal pMinimumQty As Long)

        'Handle all errors locally.
        On Error GoTo UpdateProduct_Err

        'Define local error variant.
        Dim Status

        'Make sure Product object is created.
        SetNewProduct
        With Product
            'Assign all Product properties.
            .ProductID = pProductID
            .Description = pDescription
            .VendorID = VendorID
            .VendorName = VendorName
            .ReorderQuantity = pReorderQty
            .MinimumQuantity = pMinimumQty

            'Update the Product.
            UpdateProduct = .Update
        End With
```

```
UpdateProduct_Cont:
    'All done.
    Exit Function

UpdateProduct_Err:
    'If an error occurs then pass back the error variant.
    With Err
        UpdateProduct = SetError(.Number, .Description, .Source)
    End With

    'Reset the Err object and exit the function.
    Resume UpdateProduct_Cont

End Function

Public Sub CloseProduct()
'Destroy any Product object.

    Set Product = Nothing

End Sub

Public Function RemoveProduct(ByVal ProductID As String) As _
Variant

    'Handle all errors locally.
    On Error GoTo RemoveProduct_Err

    'Make sure Product object is created.
    SetNewProduct
    With Product
        'Assign the unique Product property.
        .ProductID = ProductID

        'Delete the specified Product from the database.
        RemoveProduct = .Delete
    End With

RemoveProduct_Cont:
    'All done.
    Exit Function

RemoveProduct_Err:
    'If an error occurs then pass back the error variant.
    With Err
        RemoveProduct = SetError(.Number, .Description, _
        .Source)
    End With

    'Reset the Err object and exit the function.
    Resume RemoveProduct_Cont

End Function
```

12. Normally, you would first open a specific **Vendor** object and then open a
Product object related to the **Vendor**. But in this object model, you

provide the capability to access a Product without first accessing its Vendor. Because the ProductID is unique without the VendorID, it is possible to access a Product without first accessing a Vendor. The Product-related services of the ProductBase object provide the Vendor object to the client related to the Product. The Product-related services of the ProductBase object subclass the Product-related services of the Vendor object. To provide Product-related services without first opening a Vendor object, you need to create the following methods in the ProductBase class module:

```
Public Function NewProduct(ByVal pProductID As String, _
ByVal pDescription As String, ByVal pVendorID As String, _
ByVal pReorderQty As Long, ByVal pMinimumQty As Long) As _
Variant
'Add the specified Product to the database.

    'Handle all errors locally.
    On Error GoTo NewProduct_Err

    'Define local error variant.
    Dim Status

    'Make sure Vendor object exists.
    SetNewVendor
    With Vendor
        'Assign the unique property of the Vendor.
        .VendorID = pVendorID

        'Retrieve the specified Vendor row.
        Status = .Retrieve
        If Status(0) = 0 Then
            'If successful, execute the NewProduct method
            'of the Vendor object.
            NewProduct = .NewProduct(pProductID, _
            pDescription, pReorderQty, pMinimumQty)
        Else
            'Otherwise return the error variant.
            NewProduct = Status
        End If
    End With

    'destroy the Vendor object
    CloseVendor

NewProduct_Cont:
    'All done.
    Exit Function

NewProduct_Err:
    'If an error occurs then pass back the error variant.
    With Err
        NewProduct = SetError(.Number, .Description, .Source)
    End With

    'Reset the Err object and exit the function.
```

```
        Resume NewProduct_Cont

End Function

Public Function OpenProduct(ByVal ProductID As String) As _
Variant
'Retrieve the specified Product and store in the Product
'object.

    'Handle all errors locally.
    On Error GoTo OpenProduct_Err

    'Make sure Vendor object exists.
    SetNewVendor

    'Execute the OpenProduct method of the Vendor object.
    OpenProduct = Vendor.OpenProduct(ProductID)

OpenProduct_Cont:
    'All done.
    Exit Function

OpenProduct_Err:
    'If an error occurs then pass back the error variant.
    With Err
        OpenProduct = SetError(.Number, .Description, _
        .Source)
    End With

    'Reset the Err object and exit the function.
    Resume OpenProduct_Cont

End Function

Public Sub CloseProduct()
'Destroy the Product object.

    'If the Vendor object exists,
    If Not Vendor Is Nothing Then
        'then execute the CloseProduct method.
        Vendor.CloseProduct
    End If

End Sub

Public Function UpdateProduct(ByVal pProductID As String, _
ByVal pDescription As String, ByVal pVendorID As String, _
ByVal pReorderQty As Long, ByVal pMinimumQty As Long) As _
Variant
'Update the specified Product in the database.

    'Handle all errors locally.
    On Error GoTo UpdateProduct_Err

    'Define local error variant.
    Dim Status
```

continued on next page

continued from previous page

```
        'Make sure Vendor object exists.
        SetNewVendor
        With Vendor
            'Assign the unique Vendor property.
            .VendorID = pVendorID

            'Retrieve the specified Vendor row.
            Status = .Retrieve

            'If the Vendor exists,
            If Status(0) = 0 Then
                'then update the Product row.
                UpdateProduct = .UpdateProduct(pProductID, _
                pDescription, pReorderQty, pMinimumQty)
            Else
                'Otherwise, return the error variant.
                UpdateProduct = Status
            End If
        End With

UpdateProduct_Cont:
        'All done.
        Exit Function

UpdateProduct_Err:
        'If an error occurs then pass back the error variant.
        With Err
            UpdateProduct = SetError(.Number, .Description, _
            .Source)
        End With

        'Reset the Err object and exit the function.
        Resume UpdateProduct_Cont

End Function

Public Function RemoveProduct(ByVal ProductID As String) As _
Variant
'Remove the specified product from the database.

        'Handle all errors locally.
        On Error GoTo RemoveProduct_Err

        'Make sure Vendor object exists.
        SetNewVendor

        'Remove the specified Product row.
        RemoveProduct = Vendor.RemoveProduct(ProductID)

RemoveProduct_Cont:
        'All done.
        Exit Function

RemoveProduct_Err:
        'If an error occurs then pass back the error variant.
        With Err
            RemoveProduct = SetError(.Number, .Description, _
```

```
          .Source)
     End With

     'Reset the Err object and exit the function.
     Resume RemoveProduct_Cont

End Function
```

13. The last of the Vendor-related and Product-related services that the
ProductBase object model should provide are Vendor and Product lists.
Although our test application won't be accessing the list services, go ahead
and write the code for the **Public Property Get** procedures. Enter the
following **Property** procedure into the **Vendor** class module:

```
Public Property Get Products()
'Return a product list of all products for the present
'VendorID as a variant array.

     'Handle all errors locally.
     On Error GoTo Products_Err

     'Define the SQL string variable.
     Dim SQLStr As String

     'Create the Warehouse data object.
     Dim WD As New WIMData.WarehouseData

     'Build the SQL statement that will retrieve the products
     'list for the present Vendor.
     SQLStr = "SELECT Products.ProductID," & _
     "Products.Description,Products.VendorID," & _
     "Vendors.VendorName,Products.ReorderQty," & _
     "Products.MinimumQty FROM Products,Vendors WHERE " & _
     "Products.VendorID=" & SQLText(pVendorID) & _
     " AND Vendors.VendorID=Products.VendorID;"

     'Retrieve the rows.
     Products = WD.GetRows(SQLStr)

     'Destory the data object reference.
     Set WD = Nothing

Products_Cont:
     'All done.
     Exit Property

Products_Err:
     'If an error occurs then pass back the error variant.
     With Err
          Products = SetError(.Number, .Description, .Source)
     End With

     'Reset the Err object and exit the function.
     Resume Products_Cont

End Property
```

14. Enter the following `Property` procedures into the `ProductBase` class module:

```
Public Property Get Vendors()
'Return a vendor list as a variant array.

    'Handle all errors locally.
    On Error GoTo Vendors_Err

    'Define local variables.
    Dim SQLStr As String
    Dim TempVar

    'Create the WarehouseData object.
    Dim WD As New WIMData.WarehouseData

    'Build SQL statement. The SELECT fields must be
    'synchronized with the structure of the VendorType.
    SQLStr = "SELECT VendorID,VendorName FROM Vendors"

    'Retrieve all Vendor records.
    Vendors = WD.GetRows(SQLStr)

    'Destroy WarehouseData object.
    Set WD = Nothing

Vendors_Cont:
    'All done.
    Exit Function

Vendors_Err:
    'An error occurred in our Property procedure. Return
    'theerror variant to the parent.
    With Err
        Vendors = SetError(.Number, .Description, .Source)
    End With

    'Resume to exit the function.
    Resume Vendors_Cont

End Property

Public Property Get Products()
'Return a complete product list as a variant array.

    'Handle all errors locally.
    On Error GoTo Products_Err

    'Define local variables.
    Dim SQLStr As String
    Dim TempVar

    'Create WarehouseData object.
    Dim WD As New WIMData.WarehouseData

    'Build SQL statement. The SELECT fields must be
    'synchronized with the structure of the ProductType.
```

```
        SQLStr = "SELECT Products.ProductID," & _
        "Products.Description,Products.VendorID," & _
        "Vendors.VendorName,Products.ReorderQty," & _
        "Products.MinimumQty FROM Products,Vendors " & _
        "WHERE Vendors.VendorID=Products.VendorID"

        'Retrieve all Product records.
        Products = WD.GetRows(SQLStr)

        'Destroy WarehouseData object.
        Set WD = Nothing

    Products_Cont:
        'All done.
        Exit Function

    Products_Err:
        'An error occurred in our Property procedure.
        'Return theerror variant to the parent.
        With Err
            Products = SetError(.Number, .Description, .Source)
        End With

        'Resume to exit the function.
        Resume Products_Cont

    End Property
```

15. Save the project and compile it.

How It Works

The WIM.dll component provides the services necessary for a client application to access the **ProductBase** object and add, update, and delete **Vendors** and **Products** in the Warehouse database.

Since the hierarchy of the business object model is enforced, the **Vendor** and **Product** objects are only accessible through the **ProductBase** object. Though the **Product** object is subordinate to the **Vendor** object in the object model, the **Product** object may be accessed either through the **Vendor** object, or directly through the **ProductBase** object. Although a product will always be supplied by a vendor, each product has its own unique identifier, which allows it to be identified without a vendor.

Comments

When creating business objects for distributed applications, it is best to maintain binary compatibility for the life of the business object. Maintaining binary compatibility requires that you adhere to the following rules:

✔ Never add new parameters to an existing public property or method.

✔ Never change the type of an existing public property or method.

✔ Never change the type of a parameter of an existing public property or method.

✔ Never delete an existing public property or method.

If you think you need to break the rules in order to resolve an issue, there are alternatives. You can add new public properties or methods to augment an existing interface without losing binary compatibility.

If you need to add another parameter to an existing public method, you can do so by creating a new public method which subclasses the old method and contains the new parameters and functionality. Or you could create a new public method which provides only the extended services.

If you need to change the type of a public property or method, including the need to change the type of a parameter, it is good to create a new public property or method without deleting the old. There are preventive techniques that you could use when establishing types at the design phase. You could use the variant type whenever possible to give yourself more flexibility.

If a public property or method is no longer used, you could delete the code contained in the property or method, but leave the `Public` function or `Sub` structure intact.

A new feature of Visual Basic 6 gives you the power to override the loss of binary compatibility. But that leaves the responsibility of maintaining true compatibility in your hands. If you delete a public property or method that is still in use, an error will occur when that property or method is called.

COMPLEXITY
BEGINNING

15.4 How do I...
Create an application that accesses remote business objects?

COMPATIBILITY: VISUAL BASIC 5 AND 6

Problem

I have completed the first three How-Tos in this chapter and have created the `WIMData` component and the `WIM` component from the two previous sections. I want to know how to access remote objects through a Visual Basic application. I also want to test the `ProductBase` object model and see that the services are fully functional. How do I create an application that accesses remote business objects?

Technique

To create an object, whether locally or remotely, a process called binding must be performed on the object reference. *Binding* enables an application to access the properties, methods, and events that are members of an object. There are two different types of binding: early binding and late binding. If an object reference in an application is declared as a specific class, then early binding is used.

```
Dim MyObject As MyClass
```

If an object reference is declared as `Object`, then late binding is used.

```
Dim MyObject As Object
```

When early binding is used, Visual Basic resolves the reference to the class at compile time. Globally Unique Identifiers (GUID), which are created when the class is compiled, are used to identify the component and its interfaces. These GUIDs along with information from the component's type library, are stored with the compiled application. If changes are made to the existing interface of the class and binary compatibility is not maintained for the component of the class, new GUIDs are created when the class is recompiled. If the GUIDs are changed for any reason, the application using the class must also be recompiled to be compatible. For this reason, early binding is not a viable solution for enterprisewide distributed applications.

When late binding is used, the reference to the class is resolved during runtime using the Windows Registry. This means that if any of the GUIDs or the type library is changed for whatever reason, the application does not need to be recompiled. Only the Windows Registry needs to be updated if the GUIDs are modified. Although late binding might be slower than early binding, it is the only feasible solution for distributed applications where the business objects reside on servers.

To access remote business objects on a server, you need to use the VBA function `CreateObject` with a `Set` statement on a variable defined as `Object`. The `CreateObject` function provides a service similar to the `New` keyword used with the `Dim` or `Set` statements, except that a reference to the type library is not required in your project to implement the object into your application.

```
Dim MyObject As Object
Set MyObject = CreateObject("MyComponent.MyClass")
```

In this How-To, you actually access the `WIM` component locally so that a server is not required, but you use late binding and the `CreateObject` function to simulate a distributed application. Use the following lines of code to access the `ProductBase` object model.

```
Dim PB As Object
Set PB = CreateObject("WIM.ProductBase")
```

Steps

Complete the following steps to create an application that allows the user to access **Vendors** and **Products** in the **ProductBase** using the existing business objects of the **ProductBase** object model. There is no need to set a reference to the WIM.dll file or type library for this project.

1. Create a new Standard EXE project named **Products**.

2. Add objects to the form and set the properties of the form and the objects it contains so that they match Table 15.2. The frame on the lower half of the form should contain a set of four labels, text boxes, and command buttons.

Table 15.2 Objects and Properties of `frmProducts`

OBJECT/CONTROL	PROPERTY	VALUE
Form	Name	frmProducts
	Caption	Products
	Height	4590
	StartUpPosition	2 - CenterScreen
	Width	6495
Frame	Name	fraProductInfo
	Caption	Product Information
	Height	2295
	Left	120
	Top	2160
	Width	6255
Label	Name	lblVendorID
	Caption	Vendor ID
	Height	255
	Left	240
	Top	240
	Width	1815
Label	Name	lblVendorName
	Caption	Vendor Name
	Height	255
	Left	240
	Top	840
	Width	6015
Label	Name	lblProductID
	Caption	Product ID
	Height	255
	Left	240
	Top	360
	Width	1695

OBJECT/CONTROL	PROPERTY	VALUE
Label	Name	lblDescription
	Caption	Description
	Height	255
	Left	2280
	Top	360
	Width	3615
Label	Name	lblReorderQty
	Caption	Reorder Quantity
	Height	255
	Left	240
	Top	960
	Width	1695
Label	Name	lblMinimumQty
	Caption	Minimum Quantity
	Height	255
	Left	2280
	Top	960
	Width	1815
Text	Name	txtVendorID
	Height	285
	Left	240
	Text	
	Top	480
	Width	1815
Text	Name	txtVendorName
	Height	285
	Left	240
	Text	
	Top	1080
	Width	6015
Text	Name	txtProductID
	Height	285
	Left	240
	Text	
	Top	600
	Width	1695

continued on next page

continued from previous page

OBJECT/CONTROL	PROPERTY	VALUE
Text	Name	txtDescription
	Height	285
	Left	2280
	Text	
	Top	600
	Width	3615
Text	Name	txtReorderQty
	Height	285
	Left	240
	Text	
	Top	1200
	Width	1695
Text	Name	txtMinimumQty
	Height	285
	Left	2280
	Text	
	Top	1200
	Width	1815
CommandButton	Name	cmdNewVendor
	Caption	New Vendor
	Height	375
	Left	240
	Top	1560
	Width	1335
CommandButton	Name	cmdOpenVendor
	Caption	Open Vendor
	Height	375
	Left	240
	Top	1560
	Width	1335
CommandButton	Name	cmdUpdateVendor
	Caption	Update Vendor
	Height	375
	Left	3360
	Top	1560
	Width	1335

OBJECT/CONTROL	PROPERTY	VALUE
CommandButton	Name	cmdRemoveVendor
	Caption	Remove Vendor
	Height	375
	Left	4920
	Top	1560
	Width	1335
CommandButton	Name	cmdNewProduct
	Caption	New Product
	Height	375
	Left	120
	Top	1680
	Width	1335
CommandButton	Name	cmdOpenProduct
	Caption	Open Product
	Height	375
	Left	1680
	Top	1680
	Width	1335
CommandButton	Name	cmdUpdateProduct
	Caption	Update Product
	Height	375
	Left	3240
	Top	1680
	Width	1335
CommandButton	Name	cmdRemoveProduct
	Caption	Remove Product
	Height	375
	Left	4800
	Top	1680
	Width	1335

After you have completed the property modifications, the form should appear as shown in Figure 15.3.

3. Add the modErrorMgt.bas module created in How-To 15.2 to the project by choosing Project, Add Module from the menu and selecting the module on the Existing page of the Add Module dialog box.

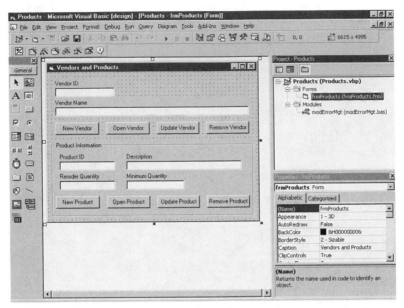

Figure 15.3 The is the `frmProducts` form as it appears in the Visual Basic development environment.

4. Add a new module to the project and name it `modErrorMsg`.

5. Create a generic routine in the new module that displays an error message using the **Status** variant array created by the modErrorMgt.bas module by adding the following code:

```
Option Explicit

Sub ErrMsg(Status, CaptionText As String)
'The Status parameter should be passed as a variant array
'of 3 elements as listed:
'    0 - Error Number
'    1 - Error Description
'    2 - Error Source

    'Define local variables
    Dim ErrStr As String

    'Build the error information.
    ErrStr = "Error " & Trim$(Str$(Status(0))) & " In " & _
    Status(2) & ": " & Status(1)

    'Display the error information
    MsgBox ErrStr, vbExclamation, CaptionText

End Sub
```

6. The first procedures of the Form module should be those that resolve internal references in the Form's control events. Two subprocedures are used to clear **TextBoxes** in your application.

Enter the following code into the General section of the **frmProducts** module:

```
Option Explicit

Sub ClearVendor()

    'Clear the Vendor textboxes.
    txtVendorID = ""
    txtVendorName = ""

End Sub

Sub ClearProduct()

    'Clear the Product textboxes.
    txtProductID = ""
    txtDescription = ""
    txtReorderQty = ""
    txtMinimumQty = ""

End Sub
```

7. When the user clicks the **cmdNewVendor CommandButton**, the **txtVendorID** and **txtVendorName TextBoxes** should contain the **VendorID** and **VendorName** for a **Vendor** that does not exist in the Vendors table. The **Vendor** properties should be passed to the **NewVendor** method of the **ProductBase** object. Then the **Status** variable should be checked for errors.

Enter the following code into the **Click** event of the **cmdNewVendor CommandButton**:

```
Private Sub cmdNewVendor_Click()

    'Handle all errors locally
    On Error GoTo cmdNewVendor_Err

    'Define local variables
    Dim Status      'The local error variant.
    Dim PB As Object        'The ProductBase object reference.

    'Create the ProductBase object.
    Set PB = CreateObject("WIM.ProductBase")

    'Execute the NewVendor method.
    Status = PB.NewVendor(txtVendorID, txtVendorName)

    'Destroy the ProductBase object.
    Set PB = Nothing
```

continued on next page

continued from previous page

```
        'If an error occurred then
        If ErrTrue(Status) Then
            'display the error information.
            ErrMsg Status, Caption
        Else
            'Otherwise clear the Vendor textboxes.
            ClearVendor
        End If

    cmdNewVendor_Cont:
        'All done.
        Exit Sub

    cmdNewVendor_Err:
        'Display the error information.
        With Err
            ErrMsg SetError(.Number, .Description, .Source), _
            Caption
        End With

        'Reset the Err object and exit the procedure.
        Resume cmdNewVendor_Cont

End Sub
```

8. When the user clicks on the `cmdOpenVendor CommandButton`, the data contained in the `txtVendorID TextBox` should be used to access the specified `Vendor`. The `VendorID` should be passed as the parameter of the `OpenVendor` method of the `ProductBase` object. The `OpenVendor` method should return the `Status` variant array. Check to make sure there are no errors. Then download the `Vendor` properties using the `Properties` property of the `Vendor` object. Both the `VendorID` and `VendorName` will be returned in a variant array. Before parsing the properties returned, destroy any references to the `ProductBase` object model to optimize server resources.

Enter the following code into the `Click` event of the `cmdOpenVendor CommandButton`:

```
Private Sub cmdOpenVendor_Click()

    'Handle all errors locally
    On Error GoTo cmdOpenVendor_Err

    'Define local variables
    Dim VendorVar     'The local variant resultset.
    Dim Status        'The local error variant.
    Dim PB As Object        'The ProductBase object reference.

    'Create the ProductBase object.
    Set PB = CreateObject("WIM.ProductBase")

    'Execute the OpenVendor method.
    Status = PB.OpenVendor(txtVendorID)
```

```
        'If no error then
        If Not ErrTrue(Status) Then
            'retrieve the Vendor Properties variant array.
            VendorVar = PB.Vendor.Properties
        End If

        'Destroy the Vendor object.
        PB.CloseVendor

        'Destroy the ProductBase object.
        Set PB = Nothing

        'If an error occurred then
        If ErrTrue(Status) Then
            'display the error information.
            ErrMsg Status, Caption
        Else
            'Otherwise assign the Vendor text fields.
            txtVendorID = VendorVar(0)
            txtVendorName = VendorVar(1)
        End If

cmdOpenVendor_Cont:
        'All done.
        Exit Sub

cmdOpenVendor_Err:
        'Display the error information.
        With Err
            ErrMsg SetError(.Number, .Description, .Source), _
            Caption
        End With

        'Reset the Err object and exit the procedure.
        Resume cmdOpenVendor_Cont

End Sub
```

9. When the user clicks on the `cmdUpdateVendor` CommandButton, the data contained in the `txtVendorName` TextBox should be updated for the Vendor ID specified in the `txtVendorID` TextBox. All you need to do is pass the `VendorID` and `VendorName` as parameters to the `UpdateVendor` method of the `ProductBase` object. Then check the returned status variant array for errors.

Enter the following code into the `Click` event of the `cmdUpdateVendor` CommandButton:

```
Private Sub cmdUpdateVendor_Click()

    'Handle all errors locally
    On Error GoTo cmdUpdateVendor_Err

    'Define local variables
    Dim Status    'The local error variant.
```

continued on next page

continued from previous page

```
        Dim PB As Object            'The ProductBase object reference.

        'Create the ProductBase object.
        Set PB = CreateObject("WIM.ProductBase")

        'Execute the UpdateVendor method.
        Status = PB.UpdateVendor(txtVendorID, txtVendorName)

        'Destroy the ProductBase object.
        Set PB = Nothing

        'If an error occurred then
        If ErrTrue(Status) Then
            'display the error information.
            ErrMsg Status, Caption
        Else
            'Otherwise clear the Vendor textboxes.
            ClearVendor
        End If

cmdUpdateVendor_Cont:
    'All done.
    Exit Sub

cmdUpdateVendor_Err:
    'Display the error information.
    With Err
        ErrMsg SetError(.Number, .Description, .Source), _
        Caption
    End With

    'Reset the Err object and exit the procedure.
    Resume cmdUpdateVendor_Cont

End Sub
```

10. The last `Vendor`-related `CommandButton` is the `cmdRemoveVendor`. When the user clicks this `CommandButton`, the `VendorID` specified in the `txtVendorID TextBox` references the `Vendor` record that should be removed from the database. `txtVendorID` should be passed as a parameter to the `RemoveVendor` method of the `ProductBase` object. Then the `Status` variable should be checked for errors.

Enter the following code into the `Click` event of the `cmdRemoveVendor CommandButton`:

```
Private Sub cmdRemoveVendor_Click()

    'Handle all errors locally
    On Error GoTo cmdRemoveVendor_Err

    'Define local variables
    Dim Status     'The local error variant.
    Dim PB As Object          'The ProductBase object reference.
```

```
    'Create the ProductBase object.
    Set PB = CreateObject("WIM.ProductBase")

    'Execute the RemoveVendor method.
    Status = PB.RemoveVendor(txtVendorID)

    'Destroy the ProductBase object.
    Set PB = Nothing

    'If an error occurs then
    If ErrTrue(Status) Then
        'display the error information.
        ErrMsg Status, Caption
    Else
        'Otherwise clear the Vendor textboxes.
        ClearVendor
    End If

cmdRemoveVendor_Cont:
    'All done.
    Exit Sub

cmdRemoveVendor_Err:
    'Display the error information.
    With Err
        ErrMsg SetError(.Number, .Description, .Source), _
        Caption
    End With

    'Reset the Err object and exit the procedure.
    Resume cmdRemoveVendor_Cont

End Sub
```

11. The code for the **Click** events of the **Product**-related **CommandButton**s is similar to that of the **Vendor**-related **CommandButton**s.

Enter the following code into the **Click** events of the **Product**-related **CommandButton**s within the **Frame** control on the Form:

```
Private Sub cmdNewProduct_Click()

    'Handle all errors locally
    On Error GoTo cmdNewProduct_Err

    'Define local variables
    Dim Status      'The local error variant.
    Dim PB As Object        'The ProductBase object reference.

    'Create the ProductBase object.
    Set PB = CreateObject("WIM.ProductBase")

    'Execute the NewProduct method.
    Status = PB.NewProduct(txtProductID, txtDescription, _
    txtVendorID, txtReorderQty, txtMinimumQty)
```

continued on next page

continued from previous page

```
            'Destroy the ProductBase object.
            Set PB = Nothing

            'If an error occurred then
            If ErrTrue(Status) Then
                'display the error information.
                ErrMsg Status, Caption
            Else
                'Otherwise clear the Product textboxes.
                ClearProduct
            End If

    cmdNewProduct_Cont:
        'All done.
        Exit Sub

    cmdNewProduct_Err:
        'Display the error information.
        With Err
            ErrMsg SetError(.Number, .Description, .Source), _
            Caption
        End With

        'Reset the Err object and exit the procedure.
        Resume cmdNewProduct_Cont

    End Sub

    Private Sub cmdOpenProduct_Click()

        'Handle all errors locally
        On Error GoTo cmdOpenProduct_Err

        'Define local variables
        Dim ProductVar      'The local variant resultset.
        Dim Status          'The local error variant.
        Dim PB As Object        'The ProductBase object reference.

        'Create the ProductBase object.
        Set PB = CreateObject("WIM.ProductBase")

        'Execute the OpenProduct method.
        Status = PB.OpenProduct(txtProductID)

        'If no error then
        If Not ErrTrue(Status) Then
            ProductVar = PB.Vendor.Product.Properties
        End If

        'Destroy the ProductBase object.
        Set PB = Nothing

        'If no error then
        If ErrTrue(Status) Then
            'Otherwise display the error information.
            ErrMsg Status, Caption
        Else
```

```
          'assign the text fields.
          txtProductID = ProductVar(0)
          txtDescription = ProductVar(1)
          txtVendorID = ProductVar(2)
          txtVendorName = ProductVar(3)
          txtReorderQty = Trim$(Str$(ProductVar(4)))
          txtMinimumQty = Trim$(Str$(ProductVar(5)))
     End If

cmdOpenProduct_Cont:
     'All done.
     Exit Sub

cmdOpenProduct_Err:
     'Display the error information.
     With Err
          ErrMsg SetError(.Number, .Description, .Source), _
          Caption
     End With

     'Reset the Err object and exit the procedure.
     Resume cmdOpenProduct_Cont

End Sub

Private Sub cmdUpdateProduct_Click()

     'Handle all errors locally
     On Error GoTo cmdUpdateProduct_Err

     'Define local variables
     Dim Status                'The local error variant.
     Dim PB As Object          'The ProductBase object reference.

     'Create the ProductBase object.
     Set PB = CreateObject("WIM.ProductBase")

     'Execute the UpdateProduct method.
     Status = PB.UpdateProduct(txtProductID, txtDescription, _
     txtVendorID, Val(txtReorderQty), Val(txtMinimumQty))

     'Destroy the ProductBase object.
     Set PB = Nothing

     'If an error occurs then
     If ErrTrue(Status) Then
          'Clear the Product textboxes.
          ClearProduct
     Else
          'Otherwise display the error information.
          ErrMsg Status, Caption
     End If

cmdUpdateProduct_Cont:
     'All done.
     Exit Sub
```

continued on next page

continued from previous page

```
cmdUpdateProduct_Err:
    'Display the error information.
    With Err
        ErrMsg SetError(.Number, .Description, .Source), _
        Caption
    End With

    'Reset the Err object and exit the procedure.
    Resume cmdUpdateProduct_Cont

End Sub

Private Sub cmdRemoveProduct_Click()

    'Handle all errors locally
    On Error GoTo cmdRemoveProduct_Err

    'Define local variables
    Dim Status      'The local error variant.
    Dim PB As Object        'The ProductBase object reference.

    'Create the ProductBase object.
    Set PB = CreateObject("WIM.ProductBase")

    'Execute the RemoveProduct method.
    Status = PB.RemoveProduct(txtProductID)

    'Destroy the ProductBase object.
    Set PB = Nothing

    'If an error occured then
    If ErrTrue(Status) Then
        'display the error information.
        ErrMsg Status
    Else
        'Otherwise clear the Product textboxes.
        ClearProduct
    End If

cmdRemoveProduct_Cont:
    'All done.
    Exit Sub

cmdRemoveProduct_Err:
    'Display the error information.
    With Err
        ErrMsg SetError(.Number, .Description, .Source), _
        Caption
    End With

    'Reset the Err object and exit the procedure.
    Resume cmdRemoveProduct_Cont

End Sub
```

12. If the user begins to change the `VendorID` or `ProductID`, then the related `TextBoxes` should automatically be cleared.

Enter the following code into the `Change` events of `txtVendorID` and `txtProductID` TextBoxes:

```
Private Sub txtVendorID_Change()

    'Clear the VendorName textbox.
    If txtVendorName <> "" Then txtVendorName = ""

End Sub

Private Sub txtProductID_Change()

    'Clear the other property textboxes.
    If txtDescription <> "" Then txtDescription = ""
    If txtReorderQty <> "" Then txtReorderQty = ""
    If txtMinimumQLy <> "" Ihen txtMinimumQty = ""

End Sub
```

How It Works

The `Vendors` and `Products` client application allows the user to add, update, and delete `Vendors` and `Products` to and from the Warehouse database. It also allows the user to access specific `Vendor` and `Product` information. This client application accesses the `ProductBase` business object model to access the Warehouse database. If you have completed How-Tos 15.1 through 15.4, then you have taken part in the design and development of a distributed application using multitier architecture. Figure 15.4 shows how all the components from the first five sections of this chapter are integrated.

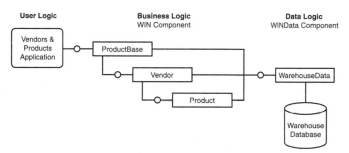

Figure 15.4 This figure illustrates the Vendor & Products distributed application architecture.

Comments

Congratulations on your first distributed application. After you grasp the concept of component-based design and development, you won't want to go back to the old way of developing applications. If you're like me, you will start to look back on some of your previous designs and see how this architecture would not only improve the performance but also the development time and the maintenance.

COMPLEXITY
ADVANCED

15.5 How do I...
Build an MTS-enabled component?

COMPATIBILITY: VISUAL BASIC 6

Problem

I have completed sections 15.1 through 15.4, and I now have an understanding of distributed application design and development. I want to scale my applications and optimize their performance using MTS. How do I build an MTS-enabled component?

Technique

MTS provides a type library that allows you to implement **Context** and **Control** objects into your components to integrate your component into the MTS environment. The name of the type library is MTxAS.dll. This library should be installed with MTS on your NT server. If you are connected to your NT server, make sure that you have direct access to the type library from your development computer. You may also copy the file from your NT server to your development computer. You need to create a reference in Visual Basic to the type library.

It is important that your component maintain a reference to the object **MTxAS.ContextObject** when a method of the MTS object is accessed. If your MTS object is part of an object hierarchy, then a local reference to the **ContextObject** should be maintained for each object within the hierarchy. Do not use a global variable to maintain the reference because this could cause apartment threading conflicts in MTS.

When a client creates an MTS object, MTS creates an **ObjectContext** for that specific object. Two flags are maintained through the **ObjectContext**: The **Done** flag and the **Consistent** flag. When an MTS object method is returned to the client, these flags signify to MTS the current state of the object and its transaction, if a transaction is used.

The `Consistent` flag is used to signify the current state of the transaction being maintained by the object. This flag is set to `True` by default. When the transaction is complete, this flag informs MTS to either commit or roll back the updates of the transaction. If no transaction is used, then this flag is insignificant.

The `Done` flag is used to signify the current state of the object itself. When the method returns to the client, if the `Done` flag is set to `False`, then MTS will retain the `ObjectContext` for the object, allowing the object to maintain its state for the client. If the `Done` flag is set to `True`, then MTS will deactivate the object. If a transaction is used by the object, then if the `Consistent` flag is set to `True`, the transaction updates will be committed.

There are several `ContextObject` methods that you need to use within your MTS objects for MTS to properly manage the state of your object and its transactions:

- ✔ `CreateInstance`

- ✔ `DisableCommit`

- ✔ `EnableCommit`

- ✔ `SetAbort`

- ✔ `SetComplete`

The `CreateInstance` method should be used instead of Visual Basic's intrinsic function `CreateObject` to create other MTS objects from within your MTS object. This ensures that the MTS object created is managed within the existing context.

The `DisableCommit` and `EnableCommit` methods are used in situations where multiple methods of an object are executed within the same context of a transaction. The `DisableCommmit` method sets both the `Done` flag and the `Consistent` flag to `False`. This in turn will inform MTS that the transactional updates under the present context are inconsistent or that an unrecoverable error has occurred, but also informs MTS to continue to maintain the state of the object and its transaction for the client. The `EnableCommit` method sets the `Done` flag to `False`, but sets the `Consistent` flag to `True`. This informs MTS that there are no errors or inconsistencies in the transactional updates thus far but also tells MTS to continue to maintain the state of the object and its transaction.

The `SetAbort` and `SetComplete` methods are used to inform MTS that the overall task of an object is complete and the present object can now be deactivated. The `SetAbort` method sets the `Done` flag to `True` but sets the `Consistent` flag to `False`. This informs MTS that the transactional updates under the present context are inconsistent or there has been an unrecoverable error. MTS then rolls back the updates of the transaction and deactivates the object. The `SetComplete` method sets both the `Done` flag and `Consistent` flag to `True`. This informs MTS that all transactional updates were successful and there were no errors. MTS then commits the updates of the transaction and deactivates the object.

Steps

Using the `ContextObject` within your objects, you not only make your object MTS-enabled, but you also make MTS aware of the state of your object and its transactions. Complete the following steps to create the `Inventory` object model using the `ContextObject` to properly create the object hierarchy and manage transactions. This creates a component called WIM2_MTS.

1. Create a new ActiveX DLL project named `WIM2_MTS`.

2. Add a reference to the Microsoft Transaction Server Type Library to the project. (If the item does not exist on the list, click the Browse button and locate the file MTxAS.dll.) You may use the Object Browser to familiarize yourself with `MTxAS` objects and interfaces. For this topic, you will be using the `ObjectContext` object within your component.

3. Add three class modules to the project—for a total of four class modules. Change the name and `MTSTransactionMode` property of the class module so that they match Table 15.3.

Table 15.3 WIM2_MTS Project Class Modules

CLASS MODULE	MTSTRANSACTIONMODE
Inventory	4 – RequiresNewTransaction
Item	3 – UsesTransaction
Pallet	3 – UsesTransaction
Location	3 – UsesTransaction

4. Add the modErrorMgt.bas (How-To 15.2) and modWIM.bas (How-To 15.3) class modules to the project.

5. The Warehouse Inventory Management object model design from How-To 15.1 manages a specific product on a pallet as an item while managing any number of pallets stored in a specific location within the warehouse. A pallet could have multiple items, and a location could have multiple pallets.

First, create the code for your `Item` class. Notice the use of the `MTxAS.ObjectContext` object within the class. Because the `Item` class is not a top-level object, then the `SetAbort` and `SetComplete` methods of the `ObjectContext` should not be used. Use the `DisableCommit` and `EnableCommit` methods instead. Start by creating all the properties and property procedures related to the `Item` object. The only `Public Property` that needs to be created is the `Properties` property, which returns all the properties in a variant array. Enter the following code into the `Item` class module:

```
Option Explicit

'private properties
Private pProductID As String
Private pDescription As String
Private pPalletID As String
Private pQuantity As Long

'Local reference to the MTS ObjectContext
Private ObjContext As MTxAS.ObjectContext

Friend Property Get ProductID() As String
'Define component-level properties.

    'Return the ProductID.
    ProductID = pProductID

End Property

Friend Property Let ProductID(pData As String)

    'Assign the ProductID.
    pProductID = pData

End Property

Friend Property Get Description() As String

    'Return the Description.
    Description = pDescription

End Property

Friend Property Let Description(pData As String)

    'Assign the Description.
    pDescription = pData

End Property

Friend Property Get PalletID() As String

    'Return the PalletID.
    PalletID = pPalletID

End Property

Friend Property Let PalletID(pData As String)

    'Assign the PalletID.
    pPalletID = pData

End Property

Friend Property Get Quantity() As Long
```

continued on next page

continued from previous page

```
                'Return the ProductID.
                Quantity = pQuantity

        End Property

        Friend Property Let Quantity(pData As Long)

                'Assign the ProductID.
                pQuantity = pData

        End Property

        Public Property Get Properties()
        'Return the Properties variant array.

                'Define a temporary variant array.
                Dim TempVar(3)

                'Assign the private properties to the array.
                TempVar(0) = pProductID
                TempVar(1) = pDescription
                TempVar(2) = pPalletID
                TempVar(3) = pQuantity

                'Return the variant array.
                Properties = TempVar

        End Property
```

6. Create the standard database I/O routines `Insert`, `Update`, `Delete`, and
`Retrieve`. These methods will only be used by objects within your
component, therefore define these functions as `Friend` and not as `Public`.
Remember to use the `CreateInstance` method of the `ObjectContext`
object to create any other MTS objects. Append the following code to the
`Item` class module:

```
Friend Function Insert()

        'Set the MTS ObjectContext reference
        Set ObjContext = MTxAS.GetObjectContext

        'Handle all errors locally.
        On Error GoTo Insert_Err

        'Define the SQL string
        Dim SQLStr As String
        Dim WD As Object

        'Create the Warehouse data object.
        Set WD = ObjContext.CreateInstance( _
        "WIMData.WarehouseData")

        'Build the SQL statement used to insert a new Item
        'row into the Items table.
        SQLStr = "INSERT INTO Items (ProductID,PalletID," & _
```

```
            "Quantity) VALUES (" & SQLTextC(pProductID) & _
        SQLTextC(pPalletID) & SQLVal(pQuantity) & ")"

        'Insert the row.
        Insert = WD.Execute(SQLStr)

Insert_Cont:
    'Destroy the data object.
    Set WD = Nothing

    'All done.
    Exit Function

Insert_Err:
    'If an error occurs then pass back the error variant.
    With Err
        Insert = SetError(.Number, .Description, .Source)
    End With

    'prepare to roll back any transaction
    ObjContext.DisableCommit

    'Reset the Err object and exit the function.
    Resume Insert_Cont

End Function

Friend Function Retrieve()

    'Set the MTS ObjectContext reference
    Set ObjContext = MTxAS.GetObjectContext

    'Handle all errors locally.
    On Error GoTo Retrieve_Err

    'Define local variables.
    Dim Results 'The variant resultset.
    Dim SQLStr As String    'The SQL string
    Dim WD As Object

    'Create the Warehouse data object.
    Set WD = ObjContext.CreateInstance( _
    "WIMData.WarehouseData")

    'Build the SQL statement used to select a specific
    'Item row from the Items table.
    SQLStr = "SELECT Item.ProductID,Products.Description," & _
    "Item.PalletID,Items.Quantity FROM Items,Products " & _
    "WHERE Items.ProductID=" & SQLText(pProductID) & _
    " AND Items.PalletID=" & SQLText(pPalletID) & _
    " AND Products.ProductID=Items.ProductID"

    'Retrieve the row.
    Results = WD.GetRows(SQLStr)
```

continued on next page

continued from previous page

```
        'If the result is 2-dimensional, then it is a
        'variant resultset.
        If Dimensions(Results) = 2 Then
            'Assign the properties.
            pProductID = Results(0, 0)
            pDescription = Results(1, 0)
            pPalletID = Results(2, 0)
            pQuantity = Results(3, 0)

            'And return the NoError variant.
            Retrieve = NoError
        Else
            'Otherwise it is an error variant.
            Retrieve = Results
        End If

Retrieve_Cont:
    'Destroy the data object.
    Set WD = Nothing

    'All done.
    Exit Function

Retrieve_Err:
    'If an error occurs then pass back the error variant.
    With Err
        Retrieve = SetError(.Number, .Description, .Source)
    End With

    'Reset the Err object and exit the function.
    Resume Retrieve_Cont

End Function

Friend Function Update()

    'Set the MTS ObjectContext reference
    Set ObjContext = MTxAS.GetObjectContext

    'Handle all errors locally.
    On Error GoTo Update_Err

    'Define the SQL string
    Dim SQLStr As String
    Dim WD As Object

    'Create the Warehouse data object.
    Set WD = ObjContext.CreateInstance( _
    "WIMData.WarehouseData")

    'Build the SQL statement used to update the specific
    'Item row in the Items table.
    SQLStr = "UPDATE Items SET Quantity=" & _
    SQLVal(pQuantity) & " WHERE ProductID=" & _
    SQLText(pProductID) & " AND PalletID=" & _
    SQLText(pPalletID)
```

```
            'Update the row.
            Update = WD.Execute(SQLStr)

    Update_Cont:
            'Destroy the data object.
            Set WD = Nothing

            'All done.
            Exit Function

    Update_Err:
            'If an error occurs then pass back the error variant.
            With Err
                Update = SetError(.Number, .Description, .Source)
            End With

            'prepare to roll back any transaction
            ObjContext.DisableCommit

            'Reset the Err object and exit the function.
            Resume Update_Cont

    End Function

    Friend Function Delete()

            'Set the MTS ObjectContext reference
            Set ObjContext = MTxAS.GetObjectContext

            'Handle all errors locally.
            On Error GoTo Delete_Err

            'Define the SQL string
            Dim SQLStr As String
            Dim WD As Object

            'Create the Warehouse data object.
            Set WD =  ObjContext.CreateInstance( _
            "WIMData.WarehouseData")

            'Build the SQL statement used to delete the specific
            'Item row from the Items table.
            SQLStr = "DELETE FROM Items WHERE ProductID=" & _
            SQLText(pProductID) & " AND PalletID=" & _
            SQLText(pPalletID)

            'Delete the row.
            Delete = WD.Execute(SQLStr)

    Delete_Cont:
            'Destroy the data object.
            Set WD = Nothing

            'All done.
            Exit Function
```

continued on next page

continued from previous page

```
Delete_Err:
    'If an error occurs then pass back the error variant.
    With Err
        Delete = SetError(.Number, .Description, .Source)
    End With

    'prepare to roll back any transaction
ObjContext.DisableCommit

    'Reset the Err object and exit the function.
    Resume Delete_Cont

End Function
```

7. After you have completed the component-level functions, you need to create two public functions that will be accessed by the client. The `AdjustQuantity` method adjusts the quantity level of the present `Item` object by the specified amount. If an error occurs in this function, the `DisableCommit` method should be executed to inform MTS that the present transaction should be rolled back and not committed.

```
Public Function AdjustQuantity(pQty As Long)

    'Set the MTS ObjectContext reference
    Set ObjContext = MTxAS.GetObjectContext

    On Error GoTo AdjustQuantity_Err

    'adjust existing quantity
    pQuantity = pQuantity + pQty

    'update the item
    AdjustQuantity = Update

AdjustQuantity_Cont:
    Exit Function

AdjustQuantity_Err:
    'If an error occurs then pass back the error variant.
    With Err
        AdjustQuantity = SetError(.Number, .Description, _
        .Source)
    End With

    'prepare to roll back any transaction
    ObjContext.DisableCommit

    'Reset the Err object and exit the function.
    Resume AdjustQuantity_Cont

End Function
```

8. The `MoveQuantity` method is used by the client to move the specified quantity of the present `Item` to another pallet. If the item already exists on the target pallet, the quantity of that item is appropriately adjusted; otherwise, a new item is added for the target pallet with the specified quantity. If an error occurs within this function, the `DisableCommit` method of the `ObjectContext` is executed as in the previous function.

```
Public Function MoveQuantity(pQty As Long, pNewPalletID As _
String)

    'Set the MTS ObjectContext reference
    Set ObjContext = MTxAS.GetObjectContext

    On Error GoTo MoveQuantity_Err

    Dim Status
    Dim OldPalletID As String

    'first reduce quantity of item on source pallet
    pQuantity = pQuantity - pQty

    'update source pallet
    Status = Update
    If ErrTrue(Status) Then
        'prepare to rollback any transaction
        ObjContext.DisableCommit
    Else
        'then check for item existence on target pallet
        OldPalletID = pPalletID
        pPalletID = pNewPalletID

        'attempt retrieve
        Status = Retrieve
        If ErrTrue(Status) Then
            'if not exist then set quantity
            pQuantity = pQty

            'and insert new item on pallet
            Status = Insert
            If ErrTrue(Status) Then
                'prepare to roll back any transaction
                ObjContext.DisableCommit
            End If
        Else
            'if exist already, then add to existing qty
            pQuantity = pQuantity + pQty

            'and update item on pallet
            Status = Update
            If ErrTrue(Status) Then
                'prepare to roll back any transaction
                ObjContext.DisableCommit
            End If
        End If
    End If

MoveQuantity_Cont:
    Exit Function
```

continued on next page

continued from previous page

```
MoveQuantity_Err:
    'If an error occurs then pass back the error variant.
    With Err
        MoveQuantity = SetError(.Number, .Description, .Source)
    End With

    'prepare to roll back any transaction
    ObjContext.DisableCommit

    'Reset the Err object and exit the function.
    Resume MoveQuantity_Cont

End Function
```

9. Create the properties and property procedures for the `Pallet` class. The public properties needed for the `Pallet` object are the reference to the `Item` object, the `Properties` property, and the `Items` property. The `Items` property provides a list of `Items` attached to the present `Pallet` as a variant array.

```
Option Explicit

'public reference to Item object
Public Item As Item

'private properties
Private pPalletID As String
Private pLocationID As String

'Local reference to the MTS ObjectContext
Private ObjContext As MTxAS.ObjectContext

Friend Property Get PalletID() As String
'Define component-level properties.

    'Return the PalletID
    PalletID = pPalletID

End Property

Friend Property Let PalletID(pData As String)

    'Assign the PalletID
    pPalletID = pData

End Property

Friend Property Get LocationID() As String

    'Return the LocationID
    LocationID = pLocationID

End Property

Friend Property Let LocationID(pData As String)
```

```
        'Assign the LocationID
        pLocationID = pData

End Property

Public Property Get Properties()
'Return the Properties variant array.

        'Define a temporary variant array.
        Dim TempVar(1)

        'Assign the private properties to the array.
        TempVar(0) = pPalletID
        TempVar(1) = pLocationID

        'Return the variant array.
        Properties = TempVar

End Property

Public Property Get Items()
'Return an item list of all items for the present
'PalletID as a variant array.

        'Set the MTS ObjectContext reference
        Set ObjContext = MTxAS.GetObjectContext

        'Handle all errors locally.
        On Error GoTo Items_Err

        'Define the SQL string variable.
        Dim SQLStr As String
        Dim WD As Object

        'Create the Warehouse data object.
        Set WD = ObjContext.CreateInstance( _
        "WIMData.WarehouseData")

        'Build the SQL statement that will retrieve the items
        'list for the present Pallet.
        SQLStr = "SELECT Items.ProductID,Products.Description " & _
        "FROM Items,Products WHERE Items.PalletID=" & _
        SQLText(pPalletID) & " AND Products.ProductID=" & _
        "Items.ProductID"

        'Retrieve the rows.
        Items = WD.GetRows(SQLStr)

        'Destroy the data object reference.
        Set WD = Nothing

Items_Cont:
        'All done.
        Exit Property
```

continued on next page

continued from previous page

```
Items_Err:
    'If an error occurs then pass back the error variant.
    With Err
        Items = SetError(.Number, .Description, .Source)
    End With

    'Reset the Err object and exit the function.
    Resume Items_Cont

End Property
```

10. To isolate the creation of the **Item** object to a single procedure, create a
private subprocedure called **SetNewItem** that is used within your **Pallet**
object to create a new instance of the **Item** object—if the **Item** object does
not yet exist. This procedure implements the **CreateInstance** method of
ObjectContext to create the **Item** object within the present MTS context.

```
Private Sub SetNewItem()
'If the Item object is nothing then create a new instance.

    If Item Is Nothing Then
        'create the object using MTS
        Set Item = ObjContext.CreateInstance("WIM.Item")
    End If

End Sub
```

11. As in the **Item** class, you need to create the standard database I/O methods
as **Friend** functions. But only **Retrieve** and **Update** methods are
necessary for the **Pallet** object. **Insert**s and **Delete**s of **Pallet** records
are managed outside the scope of this application. Remember to use the
CreateInstance method of the **ObjectContext** object to create any other
MTS objects. Append the following code to the **Pallet** class module:

```
Friend Function Retrieve()

    'Set the MTS ObjectContext reference
    Set ObjContext = MTxAS.GetObjectContext

    'Handle all errors locally.
    On Error GoTo Retrieve_Err

    'Define local variables.
    Dim Results              'The variant resultset.
    Dim SQLStr As String     'The SQL string
    Dim WD As Object

    'Create the Warehouse data object.
    Set WD = ObjContext.CreateInstance( _
    "WIMData.WarehouseData")

    'Build the SQL statement used to select a specific
    'Pallet row from the Pallets table.
    SQLStr = "SELECT PalletID,LocationID FROM Pallets " & _
```

```
        "WHERE PalletID=" & SQLText(pPalletID)

        'Retrieve the row.
        Results = WD.GetRows(SQLStr)

        'If the result is 2-dimensional, then it is a
        'variant resultset.
        If Dimensions(Results) = 2 Then
            'Assign the properties.
            pPalletID = Results(0, 0)
            pLocationID = Results(1, 0)

            'And return the NoError variant.
            Retrieve = NoError
        Else
            'Otherwise it is an error variant.
            Retrieve = Results
        End If

Retrieve_Cont:
    'Destory the data object.
    Set WD = Nothing

    'All done.
    Exit Function

Retrieve_Err:
    'If an error occurs then pass back the error variant.
    With Err
        Retrieve = SetError(.Number, .Description, .Source)
    End With

    'Reset the Err object and exit the function.
    Resume Retrieve_Cont

End Function

Friend Function Update()

    'Set the MTS ObjectContext reference
    Set ObjContext = MTxAS.GetObjectContext

    'Handle all errors locally.
    On Error GoTo Update_Err

    'Define the SQL string
    Dim SQLStr As String
    Dim WD As Object

    'Create the Warehouse data object.
    Set WD = ObjContext.CreateInstance( _
    "WIMData.WarehouseData")

    'Build the SQL statement used to update the specific
    'Pallet row in the Pallets table.
    SQLStr = "UPDATE Pallets SET LocationID=" & _
```

continued on next page

continued from previous page

```
            SQLText(pLocationID) & " WHERE PalletID=" & _
            SQLText(pPalletID)

            'Update the row.
            Update = WD.Execute(SQLStr)

    Update_Cont:
            'Destroy the data object.
            Set WD = Nothing

            'All done.
            Exit Function

    Update_Err:
            'If an error occurs then pass back the error variant.
            With Err
                Update = SetError(.Number, .Description, .Source)
            End With

            'prepare to roll back any transaction
            ObjContext.DisableCommit

            'Reset the Err object and exit the function.
            Resume Update_Cont

    End Function
```

12. The `Pallet` object provides the following `Item`-related services as `Public` methods: `NewItem`, `OpenItem`, `MoveItem`, `CloseItem`, and `RemoveItem`. As with the `Item` object, the `Pallet` object is not a top-level object, and therefore should use the `DisableCommit` and `EnableCommit` methods to manage the state of the present transaction. Append the following code to the `Pallet` class module:

```
Public Function NewItem(pProductID As String, pQuantity As _
Long)

    'Set the MTS ObjectContext reference
    Set ObjContext = MTxAS.GetObjectContext

    'Handle all errors locally.
    On Error GoTo NewItem_Err

    'Make sure Item object is created.
    SetNewItem
    With Item
        'assign the necessary properties
        .ProductID = pProductID
        .PalletID = pPalletID
        .Quantity = pQuantity

        'insert new item
        NewItem = .Insert
    End With
```

```
NewItem_Cont:
    'All done.
    Exit Function

NewItem_Err:
    'If an error occurs then pass back the error variant.
    With Err
        NewItem = SetError(.Number, .Description, .Source)
    End With

    'prepare to roll back any transaction
    ObjContext.DisableCommit

    'Reset the Err object and exit the function.
    Resume NewItem_Cont

End Function

Public Function OpenItem(pProduotID A3 String)

    'Set the MTS ObjectContext reference
    Set ObjContext = MTxAS.GetObjectContext

    'Handle all errors locally.
    On Error GoTo OpenItem_Err

    'Make sure Item object is created.
    SetNewItem
    With Item
        'Assign the unique Item properties.
        .ProductID = pProductID
        .PalletID = pPalletID

        'Retrieve the specified Item row.
        OpenItem = .Retrieve
    End With

OpenItem_Cont:
    'All done.
    Exit Function

OpenItem_Err:
    'If an error occurs then pass back the error variant.
    With Err
        OpenItem = SetError(.Number, .Description, _
        .Source)
    End With

    'prepare to roll back any transaction
    ObjContext.DisableCommit

    'Reset the Err object and exit the function.
    Resume OpenItem_Cont

End Function
```

continued on next page

continued from previous page

```
Public Function MoveItem(pProductID As String, pNewPalletID _
As String)

    'Set the MTS ObjectContext reference
    Set ObjContext = MTxAS.GetObjectContext

    'Handle all errors locally.
    On Error GoTo MoveItem_Err

    Dim Status        'need local Status

    'start with noerror
    Status = NoError

    'Make sure Item object is created.
    SetNewItem
    With Item
        'Assign the unique properties.
        .ProductID = pProductID
        .PalletID = pPalletID

        'Retrieve the existing entry for Item.
        Status = .Retrieve
        If ErrTrue(Status) Then
            'prepare to roll back any transaction
            ObjContext.DisableCommit
        Else
            'insert new entry for item
            .PalletID = pNewPalletID

            Status = .Insert
            If ErrTrue(Status) Then
                'prepare to roll back any transaction
                ObjContext.DisableCommit
            Else
                'delete old entry for item
                .PalletID = pPalletID

                Status = .Delete
                If ErrTrue(Status) Then
                    'prepare to roll back any transaction
                    ObjContext.DisableCommit
                End If
            End If
        End If
    End With

    'return status
    MoveItem = Status

MoveItem_Cont:
    'All done.
    Exit Function

MoveItem_Err:
    'If an error occurs then pass back the error variant.
    With Err
```

```vb
            MoveItem = SetError(.Number, .Description, _
            .Source)
        End With

        'prepare to roll back any transaction
        ObjContext.DisableCommit

        'Reset the Err object and exit the function.
        Resume MoveItem_Cont

End Function

Public Sub CloseItem()

        'Destroy the Item object
        Set Item = Nothing

End Sub

Public Function RemoveItem(pProductID As String)

        'Set the MTS ObjectContext reference
        Set ObjContext = MTxAS.GetObjectContext

        'Handle all errors locally.
        On Error GoTo RemoveItem_Err

        'Make sure Item object is created.
        SetNewItem
        With Item
            'Assign the unique Item properties.
            .ProductID = pProductID
            .PalletID = pPalletID

            'Delete the specified Item from the database.
            RemoveItem = .Delete
        End With

RemoveItem_Cont:
        'All done.
        Exit Function

RemoveItem_Err:
        'If an error occurs then pass back the error variant.
        With Err
            RemoveItem = SetError(.Number, .Description, _
            .Source)
        End With

        'prepare to roll back any transaction
        ObjContext.DisableCommit

        'Reset the Err object and exit the function.
        Resume RemoveItem_Cont

End Function
```

13. Create the properties and property procedures for the **Location** class. The public properties needed for the **Location** object are the reference to the **Pallet** object, the **Properties** property, and the **Pallets** property. The **Pallets** property will provide a list of **Pallets** stored in the present **Location** as a variant array.

```
Option Explicit

'public reference to Pallet object
Public Pallet As Pallet

'private properties
Private pLocationID As String
Private pDescription As String

'Local reference to the MTS ObjectContext
Private ObjContext As MTxAS.ObjectContext

Friend Property Get LocationID() As String
'Define component-level properties.

    'Return the LocationID
    LocationID = pLocationID

End Property

Friend Property Let LocationID(pData As String)

    'Assign the LocationID
    pLocationID = pData

End Property

Friend Property Get Description() As String

    'Return the Description
    Description = pDescription

End Property

Friend Property Let Description(pData As String)

    'Assign the Description
    pDescription = pData

End Property

Public Property Get Properties()
'Return the Properties variant array.

    'Define a temporary variant array.
    Dim TempVar(1)
```

```
          'Assign the private properties to the array.
          TempVar(0) = pLocationID
          TempVar(1) = pDescription

          'Return the variant array.
          Properties = TempVar

End Property

Public Property Get Pallets()
'Return a pallet list of all pallets for the present
'LocationID as a variant array.

          'Set the MTS ObjectContext reference
          Set ObjContext = MTxAS.GetObjectContext

          'Handle all errors locally.
          On Error GoTo Pallets_Err

          'Define the SQL string variable.
          Dim SQLStr As String
          Dim WD As Object

          'Create the Warehouse data object.
          Set WD = ObjContext.CreateInstance( _
          "WIMData.WarehouseData")

          'Build the SQL statement that will retrieve the Pallets
          'list for the present Location.
          SQLStr = "SELECT PalletID FROM Pallets WHERE " & _
          "LocationID=" & SQLText(pLocationID)

          'Retrieve the rows.
          Pallets = WD.GetRows(SQLStr)

          'Destroy the data object reference.
          Set WD = Nothing

Pallets_Cont:
          'All done.
          Exit Property

Pallets_Err:
          'If an error occurs then pass back the error variant.
          With Err
              Pallets = SetError(.Number, .Description, .Source)
          End With

          'Reset the Err object and exit the function.
          Resume Pallets_Cont

End Property
```

14. Similar to the private subprocedure `SetNewItem` in the `Pallet` class, create a private subprocedure called `SetNewPallet` that is used within your `Location` object to create a new instance of the `Pallet` object—if the `Pallet` object does not yet exist. Append the following code to the `Location` class module:

```
Private Sub SetNewPallet()
'If the Pallet object is nothing then create a new instance.

    If Pallet Is Nothing Then
        'Create the object using MTS
        Set Pallet = ObjContext.CreateInstance("WIM.Pallet")
    End If

End Sub
```

15. For database I/O, only a `Retrieve` function is necessary for the `Location` object. Location table management falls outside the scope of the application. Append the following code to the `Location` class module:

```
Friend Function Retrieve()

    'Set the MTS ObjectContext reference
    Set ObjContext = MTxAS.GetObjectContext

    'Handle all errors locally.
    On Error GoTo Retrieve_Err

    'Define local variables.
    Dim Results            'The variant resultset.
    Dim SQLStr As String   'The SQL string
    Dim WD As Object

    'Create the Warehouse data object.
    Set WD = ObjContext.CreateInstance( _
    "WIMData.WarehouseData")

    'Build the SQL statement used to select a specific
    'Location row from the Locations table.
    SQLStr = "SELECT LocationID,Description FROM " & _
    "Locations WHERE LocationID=" & SQLText(pLocationID)

    'Retrieve the row.
    Results = WD.GetRows(SQLStr)

    'If the result is 2-dimensional, then it is a
    'variant resultset.
    If Dimensions(Results) = 2 Then
        'Assign the properties.
        pLocationID = Results(0, 0)
        pDescription = Results(1, 0)

        'And return the NoError variant.
        Retrieve = NoError
    Else
```

```
                    'Otherwise it is an error variant.
                    Retrieve = Results
            End If

    Retrieve_Cont:
            'Destroy the data object.
            Set WD = Nothing

            'All done.
            Exit Function

    Retrieve_Err:
            'If an error occurs then pass back the error variant.
            With Err
                    Retrieve = SetError(.Number, .Description, .Source)
            End With

            'Reset the Err object and exit the function.
            Resume Retrieve_Cont

    End Function
```

16. The `Location` object provides the following `Pallet`-related services as
`Public` methods: `OpenPallet`, `MovePallet`, and `ClosePallet`. As with the
`Pallet` object, the `Location` object is not a top-level object, and therefore
should use the `DisableCommit` and `EnableCommit` methods to manage the
state of the present transaction. Append the following code to the
`Location` class module:

```
Public Function OpenPallet(pPalletID As String)

        'Set the MTS ObjectContext reference
        Set ObjContext = MTxAS.GetObjectContext

        'Handle all errors locally.
        On Error GoTo OpenPallet_Err

        'Make sure Item object is created.
        SetNewPallet
        With Pallet
            'Assign the unique Item properties.
            .PalletID = pPalletID

            'Retrieve the specified Item row.
            OpenPallet = .Retrieve
        End With

OpenPallet_Cont:
        'All done.
        Exit Function

OpenPallet_Err:
        'If an error occurs then pass back the error variant.
        With Err
            OpenPallet = SetError(.Number, .Description, _
```

continued on next page

continued from previous page

```
                .Source)
        End With

        'prepare to roll back any transaction
        ObjContext.DisableCommit

        'Reset the Err object and exit the function.
        Resume OpenPallet_Cont

End Function

Public Function MovePallet(pPalletID As String, _
pNewLocationID As String)

        'Set the MTS ObjectContext reference
        Set ObjContext = MTxAS.GetObjectContext

        'Handle all errors locally.
        On Error GoTo MovePallet_Err

        Dim Status        'need local Status

        'start with noerror
        Status = NoError

        'Make sure Item object is created.
        SetNewPallet
        With Pallet
            'Assign the unique properties.
            .PalletID = pPalletID

            'Retrieve the existing entry for Item.
            Status = .Retrieve
            If ErrTrue(Status) Then
                'prepare to roll back any transaction
                ObjContext.DisableCommit
            Else
                'insert new entry for item
                .LocationID = pNewLocationID

                Status = .Update
                If ErrTrue(Status) Then
                    'prepare to roll back any transaction
ObjContext.DisableCommit
                End If
            End If
        End With

        'return status
        MovePallet = Status

MovePallet_Cont:
        'All done.
        Exit Function
```

```
MovePallet_Err:
    'If an error occurs then pass back the error variant.
    With Err
        MovePallet = SetError(.Number, .Description, _
        .Source)
    End With

    'prepare to rollback any transaction
    ObjContext.DisableCommit

    'Reset the Err object and exit the function.
    Resume MovePallet_Cont

End Function

Public Sub ClosePallet()

    'Destroy the Pallet object.
    Set Pallet = Nothing

End Sub
```

17. Create the properties for the `Inventory` class. The only public property needed for the `Inventory` object is the reference to the `Location` object. Also, create the private subprocedure `SetNewLocation`.

```
Option Explicit

'Define the Location object reference.
Public Location As Location

'Local reference to the MTS ObjectContext
Private ObjContext As MTxAS.ObjectContext

Private Sub SetNewLocation()
'If the Location object is nothing then create a new instance.

    If Location Is Nothing Then
        Set Location = ObjContext.CreateInstance( _
        "WIM.Location")
    End If

End Sub
```

18. The `Inventory` object provides the `OpenLocation` and `CloseLocation` services as `Public` methods. The `Inventory` object is the top-level object of the object model. Therefore, you need to use the `SetAbort` and `SetComplete` methods of the `ObjectContext` to manage the present transaction. Append the following code to the `Inventory` class module:

```
Public Function OpenLocation(ByVal pLocationID As String)

    'start of new context
    Set ObjContext = MTxAS.GetObjectContext
```

continued on next page

continued from previous page

```
        'Handle all errors locally.
        On Error GoTo OpenLocation_Err

        'Make sure Item object is created.
        SetNewLocation
        With Location
            'Assign the unique Item properties.
            .LocationID = pLocationID

            'Retrieve the specified Item row.
            OpenLocation = .Retrieve
        End With

    OpenLocation_Cont:
        'All done.
        Exit Function

    OpenLocation_Err:
        'If an error occurs then pass back the error variant.
        With Err
            OpenLocation = SetError(.Number, .Description, _
            .Source)
        End With

        'prepare to roll back any transaction
        ObjContext.SetAbort

        'Reset the Err object and exit the function.
        Resume OpenLocation_Cont

End Function

Public Sub CloseLocation()

    'destroy Location object
    Set Location = Nothing

    'deactivate object
    ObjContext.SetComplete

End Sub
```

How It Works

The WIM2_MTS component provides a client application with inventory-related services from an MTS-based scalable component. The services can be used for several distributed applications to maintain the inventory in the warehouse. The WIM2_MTS component runs only in the MTS 2.0 environment. Figure 15.5 shows the Inventory object model provided by the WIM2_MTS component along with its interfaces.

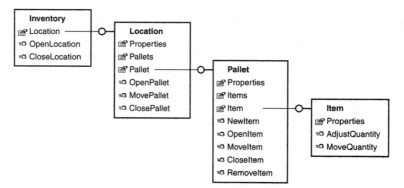

Figure 15.5 This figure illustrates the inventory object model with its properties and methods.

Comments

In the process of completing this chapter, you have not only developed a component-based distributed application but have also reused existing components, created MTS-enabled business objects, and worked with all three layers of the MSF application model.

With this knowledge and experience developing a distributed application using Visual Basic, you should be able to design and develop your own distributed applications and even upgrade some of your existing client/server applications.

CHAPTER 16

MISCELLANEOUS TOPICS

MISCELLANEOUS TOPICS

How do I...

16.1 Expose an object to multiple applications in Visual Basic?

16.2 Request information from a Web server in an ActiveX document or control?

16.3 Use the Class Builder utility to create an object model?

This chapter contains three How-Tos of varying concepts that could be used to streamline design and development within your systems and applications.

16.1 Expose an Object to Multiple Applications in Visual Basic

In this How-To, you learn one technique used to expose an object to multiple applications in Visual Basic. This technique uses the Apartment Threading model to expose a global object within a component to multiple applications outside the component. This exposure allows you to access a common object that could be used to pass or share information between applications.

16.2 Request Information from a Web Server in an ActiveX Document or Control

This How-To demonstrates a simple technique of requesting data from a Web server running Internet Information Server with Active Server Pages and parsing the data after it is received within an ActiveX Document or control running in Internet Explorer.

16.3 Use the Class Builder Utility to Create an Object Model

The Class Builder utility provides you with the ability to graphically create and modify classes within a single project. This section demonstrates the use of the Class Builder utility in constructing a complex object model for a component.

COMPLEXITY
ADVANCED

16.1 How do I...
Expose an object to multiple applications in Visual Basic?

COMPATIBILITY: VISUAL BASIC 5 AND VISUAL BASIC 6

Problem

I would like to create a Visual Basic application that can expose a global object to other applications. I need the ability to maintain localized client information during runtime for several user applications. I would like to store this information in a collection and expose the collection to all the user applications. How do I expose an object to multiple applications in Visual Basic?

Technique

You can expose a global object to multiple applications by using the Apartment Threading Model as the catalyst for exposing the object. By creating a standalone ActiveX EXE project that maintains a global reference to an object of a `PublicNotCreatable` class, you can expose the global object to multiple applications by using a public `Connector` class. This `Connector` class allows an external application to create a local reference to the global object and access its properties and methods. By setting the Threading Model of the Standalone ActiveX EXE to Thread Pool of 1 thread, the component will give all instances of the `Connector` class the same reference to any global variables defined in the standard module.

Steps

Complete the following steps to create the Global Collection Manager application and create a test application that accesses the Global Collection:

1. Start with a new ActiveX EXE project. Choose File, New Project. Highlight ActiveX EXE and click the OK command button.

2. Choose Project, Project1 Properties from the menu. Change the Project Name to `GlobalMgr` and then change the Startup Object to `Sub Main`. Make sure the Threading Model is set to Thread Pool of 1 thread, as illustrated in Figure 16.1.

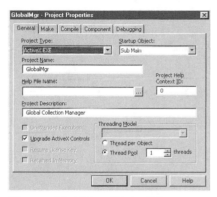

Figure 16.1 The GlobalMgr project properties.

3. Click on the Component tab and select Standalone as the Start Mode. Then, click the OK command button. Change the **Name** property of the Class1 ClassModule to `Connector`.

4. Choose Project, Add Class Module from the menu. Highlight Class Module and click the OK command button. Change the **Name** property of the new ClassModule to `cGlobalCollection`. Change the `Instancing` property of the `cGlobalCollection` ClassModule to `2 - PublicNotCreatable`.

5. Choose Project, Add Module from the menu. Highlight Module and click the Open command button. Change the **Name** property of the Module to `modGlobal`.

6. Choose Project, Add Form from the menu. Highlight Form and click the Open command button.

7. Drop two Label controls onto the form. Table 16.1 lists property changes that need to be applied to the new form and the labels.

Table 16.1 The `frmGlobal` Form and Labels Property Changes

OBJECT/CONTROL	PROPERTY	VALUE
Form	Name	frmGlobal
	Caption	Global Collection Monitor
	Height	1140
	MaxButton	False
	StartUpPosition	2 - CenterScreen
	Width	4965
Label	Name	Label1
	Caption	Number of Items in Global Collection:
	Height	255
	Left	240
	Top	240
	Width	3615
Label	Name	Label2
	BorderStyle	1 - Fixed Single
	Caption	0
	Height	255
	Left	3840
	Top	240
	Width	735

After you have made the property changes, you may save your project at this time. The form should look like the one shown in Figure 16.2.

Figure 16.2 The `frmGlobal` form in the Visual Basic environment.

8. The `Connector` object accesses the `GlobalCollection`, which should be exposed as a property of the `Connector`.

Enter the following code into the `Connector` ClassModule:

```
Option Explicit

Public Property Get GlobalCollection() As cGlobalCollection

    'If the GlobalCollection does not exist,
    If gGlobalCol Is Nothing Then
        'create the GlobalCollection.
        Set gGlobalCol = New cGlobalCollection
    End If

    'Return the GlobalCollection.
    Set GlobalCollection = gGlobalCol

End Property

Public Property Set GlobalCollection(pData As cGlobalCollection)

    'Assign the GlobalCollection.
    Set gGlobalCol = pData

End Property
```

9. The `Connector` object also gives external applications the capability to terminate the GlobalMgr application. The **Terminate** method performs this task by first destroying the `GlobalCollection` object and then unloading the `frmGlobal` form. Unloading the form in turn destroys the `Connector` object.

Append the following code to the `Connector` ClassModule:

```
Public Sub Terminate()

    'Destroy the GlobalCollection.
    Set gGlobalCol = Nothing

    'Unload the form. (This will terminate the program.)
    UnloadForm

End Sub
```

10. The `Connector` object should also enable external applications to create objects and collections on the same thread as the GlobalMgr application. This allows the `GlobalCollection` to retain the objects and collections created, even after the application that created them has terminated. Normally when an application terminates, all objects attached to its thread(s) are destroyed. To avoid the loss of these objects, if they are created by the GlobalMgr application, then they are not destroyed until all references to these objects are set to **Nothing** or the GlobalMgr application is terminated.

Append the following code to the **Connector** ClassModule:

```
Public Function CreateObject(ClassName As String) As Object

    'Provide the ability to create an object on
    'the same thread as the GlobalMgr.
    Set CreateObject = CreateObject(ClassName)

End Function

Public Function CreateCollection() As Collection

    'Provide the ability to create a collection
    'on the same thread as the GlobalMgr.
    Set CreateCollection = New Collection

End Function
```

11. The **cGlobalConnection** ClassModule needs to maintain a private collection that is managed by using the **AddItem**, **GetItem**, **RemoveItem**, and **Count** methods. Also, a private procedure called **UpdateCount** is used to maintain the item counter on the **frmGlobal** form.

Enter the following code into the **cGlobalCollection** ClassModule:

```
Option Explicit

'maintain a private collection
Private pCol As New Collection

Public Function AddItem(Item, ItemName As String) As _
Boolean

    'handle all errors locally
    On Error GoTo AddItem_Err

    'add the item to the collection
    pCol.Add Item, ItemName

    'if it gets here, then OK
    AddItem = True

AddItem_Cont:
    'update the counter on the form
    UpdateCount

    'all done
    Exit Function
```

```vb
AddItem_Err:
    'if it gets here, then not OK
    AddItem = False

    Resume AddItem_Cont

End Function

Public Function GetItem(ByVal ItemName As String)

    'handle all errors locally
    On Error GoTo GetItem_Err

    'get the item from the collection
    'allow retrieval of object references
    If IsObject(pCol(ItemName)) Then
        Set GetItem = pCol(ItemName)
    Else
        GetItem = pCol(ItemName)
    End If

    Exit Function

GetItem_Err:
    Resume Next

End Function

Public Function RemoveItem(ItemName As String) As _
Boolean

    'handle all errors locally
    On Error GoTo RemoveItem_Err

    'remove the item from the collection
    pCol.Remove ItemName

    'if it gets here, then OK
    RemoveItem = True

RemoveItem_Cont:
    'update the counter on form
    UpdateCount

    'all done
    Exit Function

RemoveItem_Err:
    'if it gets here, then not OK
    RemoveItem = False

    Resume RemoveItem_Cont

End Function
```

continued on next page

continued from previous page

```
Public Function Count() As Long

    'Return the GlobalCollection.Count
    Count = pCol.Count

End Function

Private Sub UpdateCount()

    'If the GlobalCollection exists,
    If Not gGlobalCol Is Nothing Then
        'update the GlobalCollection.Count on the form.
        frmGlobal.Label2.Caption = Trim$(Str$( _
        pCol.Count))
    End If

End Sub
```

12. The modGlobal module is used to maintain the global reference to the GlobalCollection object.

Enter the following code into the modGlobal module:

```
Option Explicit

'Maintain the GlobalCollection as a global object
Global gGlobalCol As cGlobalCollection
```

13. The modGlobal module also contains the startup procedure (Sub Main) and the terminate procedure (Sub UnloadForm) to control the execution of the standalone ActiveX EXE application.

Append the following code to the modGlobal module:

```
Sub Main()

    'When we start up, display the form
    Load frmGlobal
    frmGlobal.Show

End Sub

Sub UnloadForm()

    'Provide a procedure for unloading the form
    Unload frmGlobal

End Sub
```

14. The frmGlobal form should maintain its own copy of the Connector object. The form's Load and Unload events are used to manage this.

Enter the following code into the **frmGlobal** form:

```
Option Explicit

'Maintain our own copy of the Connector object
Dim oConn As Connector

Private Sub Form_Load()

    'When the form loads, create the Connector object
    Set oConn = New Connector

    'Start out with form minimized
    WindowState = vbMinimized

End Sub

Private Sub Form_Unload(Cancel As Integer)

    'When the form unloads, destroy the Connector object
    Set oConn = Nothing

End Sub
```

You have finished coding the GlobalMgr application, so save and compile your project now. Your program must successfully compile to test it with your test project.

15. To create a test project to test your Global Collection Manager, start with a new Standard EXE project. Choose File, New Project. Highlight Standard EXE and click the OK command button.

16. Choose Project, Project Properties from the menu. Change the Project Name to **StringMgr** and click the OK command button.

17. Choose Project, References. Place a check in the check box for the GlobalMgr reference and click the OK button.

18. Change the **Name** property of the form to **frmStringMgr**. Drop two labels, two text boxes, and three command buttons onto the form. You also need to make changes, listed in Table 16.2, to the properties of the form and the controls.

Table 16.2 The **frmStringMgr** Form and Control Property Changes

OBJECT/CONTROL	PROPERTY	VALUE
Form	Name	frmStringMgr
	Caption	Global String Manager
	Height	1980
	MaxButton	False

continued on next page

continued from previous page

OBJECT/CONTROL	PROPERTY	VALUE
	StartUpPosition	2 - CenterScreen
	Width	4695
Label	Name	lblKey
	Caption	Key
	Height	255
	Left	240
	Top	240
	Width	735
Text	Name	txtKey
	Height	285
	Left	240
	Text	
	Top	480
	Width	735
Label	Name	lblItem
	Caption	Item
	Height	255
	Left	1200
	Top	240
	Width	3135
Text	Name	txtItem
	Height	285
	Left	1200
	Text	
	Top	480
	Width	3135
CommandButton	Name	cmdAdd
	Caption	Add
	Height	375
	Left	240
	Top	960
	Width	1215
CommandButton	Name	cmdRetrieve
	Caption	Retrieve
	Height	375
	Left	1680

OBJECT/CONTROL	PROPERTY	VALUE
	Top	960
	Width	1215
CommandButton	Name	cmdRemove
	Caption	Remove
	Height	375
	Left	3120
	Top	960
	Width	1215

After your property changes are complete, your form should look like the one shown in Figure 16.3.

Figure 16.3 The frmStringMgr form in the Visual Basic environment.

18. You need to maintain object references to the **Connector** object and the **GlobalCollection**. Use the form's **Load** and **Unload** events to instantiate and destroy the object references.

Enter the following code into the **frmStringMgr** form:

```
Option Explicit

'GlobalMgr object references
Dim Conn As GlobalMgr.Connector
Dim GCol As GlobalMgr.cGlobalCollection

Private Sub Form_Load()

    'create the Connector object
    Set Conn = New GlobalMgr.Connector

    'access the GlobalCollection
    Set GCol = Conn.GlobalCollection
```

```
End Sub
Private Sub Form_Unload(Cancel As Integer)

    'destroy GlobalMgr object references
    Set GCol = Nothing
    Set Conn = Nothing

End Sub
```

19. You need to include functionality for adding, removing, and retrieving strings from the **GlobalCollection**. Insert the following code into the **Click** events of the CommandButton controls on the form:

```
Private Sub cmdAdd_Click()

    'Add the item to the collection.
    'Must specify the Text property of the item,
    'otherwise the control will be passed to the
    'AddItem method instead.
    If GCol.AddItem(txtItem.Text, txtKey) Then
        txtItem = ""
        txtKey = ""
    End If

End Sub

Private Sub cmdRemove_Click()

    'remove the item from the collection
    If GCol.RemoveItem(txtKey) Then
        txtItem = ""
        txtKey = ""
    End If

End Sub

Private Sub cmdRetrieve_Click()

    'retrieve the item
    txtItem = GCol.GetItem(txtKey)

End Sub
```

20. To add functionality that will clear the **Item** text when the **Key** text is changed, insert the following code into the **Change** event of the **txtKey** TextBox control:

```
Private Sub txtKey_Change()

    'clear the item if the key changes
    If txtItem <> "" Then
        txtItem = ""
    End If

End Sub
```

21. Save and compile your project. You can also run your project in the Visual Basic environment as illustrated in Figure 16.4.

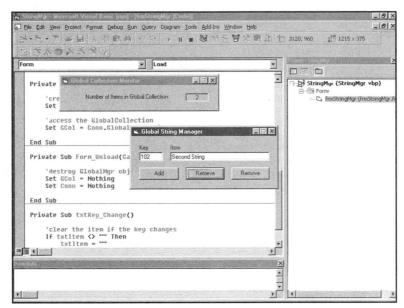

Figure 16.4 The StringMgr and GlobalMgr projects at runtime.

How It Works

When the StringMgr first accesses the **Connector** object, the GlobalMgr application starts up. Then the StringMgr application accesses the **GlobalCollection** through the **Connector** object, which creates the global object for the first time. When you add a string with a key, you can retrieve the string by using the same key even if you terminate the StringMgr application and start up again. As long as the GlobalMgr project continues to run, the **GlobalCollection** will be maintained. You should also be able to access the GlobalMgr from multiple applications and share information between those applications.

The GlobalMgr application is exposing its **GlobalCollection** object by using the **Connector** object and the Apartment Threading Model. A separate **Connector** object is created for each application that simultaneously accesses the **GlobalCollection**, but the **Connector** object is small and should use very few resources.

Comments

This concept of exposing objects by using a global object in a single-threaded ActiveX EXE application can have many uses, depending on your user environment. One function that I have used it for is to pass general lists from one application to another and to maintain client information for multiple ActiveX Document applications.

COMPLEXITY
INTERMEDIATE

16.2 How do I...
Request information from a Web server in an ActiveX document or control?

COMPATIBILITY: VISUAL BASIC 6, INTERNET EXPLORER 4, INTERNET INFORMATION SERVER 4, AND ACTIVE SERVER PAGES

Problem

I know how to create an ActiveX document, but I don't know how to communicate with the server within my ActiveX document. I need to be able to download specific data from the server. How do I request information from a Web server within an ActiveX document or control?

Technique

Whether you are using an ActiveX document or an ActiveX control, the technique is the same. The `AsyncRead` method of either the `UserDocument` or `UserControl` is used to send your request via HTTP. The `AsyncReadComplete` event is used to receive and parse your response from the Active Server Page.

For the server-side scripting language, this example uses Active Server Pages. Other server-side scripting languages could be used, but Active Server Pages was the best choice for this example because the language is similar to Visual Basic.

There are several `Server` objects exposed to Active Server Pages in Internet Information Server. In this example, you use two `Server` objects in your Active Server Page to complete the server-side task. You use the `QueryString` method of the `Request` object to get the data sent from the `UserDocument`. Then you use the `Write` method of the `Response` object to return the requested information back to the `UserDocument`.

Steps

Complete the following steps to create the Active Server Page file. You need to copy this file to your server and then create the ActiveX document that is used to request information from the Active Server Page.

1. To create this simple Active Server Page, you can use whatever editor you choose, but to keep it simple; for this example, use Notepad. From the Start menu, choose Programs, Accessories. Then, run Notepad from the Accessories group.

The Active Server Page receives the request from the **Request** object, and then returns the requested information back to the client using the **Response** object.

Enter the following Active Server Page code into the Notepad editor:

```
<%
'Active Server Page to request a Plan

    'Only variants can be used in ASPs
    Dim ReqStr

    'Get Plan requested from the query string
    ReqStr = Request.QueryString("Plan")

    'Return the selected Plan Info
    If ReqStr = "Plan A" Then
        Response.Write "Plan A;Initial Plan;This is the " & _
        "first plan that you use."
    ElseIf ReqStr = "Plan B" Then
        Response.Write "Plan B;Backup Plan;This is the " & _
        "plan that you use if Plan A fails."
    ElseIf ReqStr = "Plan C" Then
        Response.Write "Plan C;Try It Again Plan;This " & _
        "is the plan that you use if both Plan A and Plan " & _
        "B have failed."
    ElseIf ReqStr = "Plan D" Then
        Response.Write "Plan D;Last Resort Plan;This plan " & _
        "should only be used as the last resort, when all " & _
        "else has failed."
    End If
%>
```

2. Save your Active Server Page file as SelectPlan.asp, and copy this file to a location on your Web server that can be accessed via HTTP.

3. Start Visual Basic and create a new ActiveX Document EXE project.

4. Choose Project, Project1 Properties from the menu. Change the Project Name to **SelectPlan** and click the OK command button.

5. Display the UserDocument by selecting it from the Project Explorer. Drop four labels, one combo box, and three text boxes onto the UserDocument. Table 16.3 contains property changes that need to be made to the UserDocument and its controls.

Table 16.3 Property Changes to UserDocument and Controls

OBJECT/CONTROL	PROPERTY	VALUE
UserDocument	Name	docPlan
	Height	4935
	Width	4290
Label	Name	lblSelect
	Alignment	2 - Center
	Caption	Select Your Plan
	Font	Font: Arial
		Font Style: Bold
		Font Size: 14
	Height	375
	Left	840
	Top	240
	Width	2535
ComboBox	Name	cboPlan
	Height	315
	Left	1440
	List	Plan A
		Plan B
		Plan C
		Plan D
	Style	2 - Dropdown List
	Top	720
	Width	1335
Label	Name	lblPlan
	Caption	Plan Selected:
	Height	255
	Left	600
	Top	1200
	Width	3015

OBJECT/CONTROL	PROPERTY	VALUE
Text	Name	txtPlan
	Height	285
	Left	600
	Text	
	Top	1440
	Width	3015
Label	Name	lblTitle
	Caption	Plan Title:
	Height	255
	Left	600
	Top	1800
	Width	3015
Text	Name	txtTitle
	Height	285
	Left	600
	Text	
	Top	2040
	Width	3015
Label	Name	lblDescription
	Caption	Plan Description:
	Height	255
	Left	600
	Top	2400
	Width	3015
Text	Name	txtDescription
	Height	1575
	Left	600
	MultiLine	True
	ScrollBars	2 - Vertical
	Top	2640
	Width	3015

After you have completed the property changes, your `UserDocument` should look like the one shown in Figure 16.5.

Figure 16.5 The
docPlan UserDocument
in Visual Basic.

6. When the user clicks on the drop-down list and selects an item from the
list, the **UserDocument** should then take the item selected and pass it to
the Active Server Page.

Enter the following code into the **Click** event of the **cboPlan** combo box,
but make sure to replace the hyperlink specified in the code with your
own hyperlink:

```
Option Explicit

Private Sub cboPlan_Click()

    'Handle any errors locally.
    On Error GoTo cboPlan_Err

    'Define local variables.
    Dim Plan As String
    Dim Ptr As Integer

    'Trim the text and...
    Plan = Trim$(cboPlan.Text)

    'You cannot pass spaces in parameters on an HTTP request
    'line. So convert the spaces to plus signs (+).
    Do
        'Find the next space...
        Ptr = InStr(Plan, " ")
        If Ptr > 0 Then
        'If found, then convert it to a plus (+).
            Mid$(Plan, Ptr, 1) = "+"
        End If
        'Loop until no more spaces.
    Loop Until Ptr = 0

    'Use the AsyncRead method to execute our Active Server
    'Page on the Web server, passing the specified Plan as
```

```
        'a parameter, and expecting a byte array in return.
        UserDocument.AsyncRead _
        "http://www.mywebsite.com/SelectPlans.asp?Plan=" & _
        Plan, vbAsyncTypeByteArray

        'Since we are running our request to the server
        'asynchronously, disable the use of the drop-down
        'list until after the response is returned.
        cboPlan.Enabled = False

        'All done.
        Exit Sub

cboPlan_Err:
        'If anything goes wrong, go on to the next statement.
        Resume Next

    End Sub
```

7. Because your response is being returned in a byte array, you need to create a function that converts the byte array to fields. These fields are parsed into a variant array.

Enter the following code into the General section of your UserDocument:

```
Private Function ConvertByteArray(ByteArray)

        'Define local variables...
        ReDim TempVar(0)    'the temporary array...
        Dim Ptr As Integer, Ctr As Integer  'and pointers.

        'For loop through each byte in the byte array.
        For Ptr = LBound(ByteArray) To UBound(ByteArray)
            'The semicolon is the field delimiter. If found,
            'then go on to the next field.
            If Chr(ByteArray(Ptr)) = ";" Then
                'Increment the field pointer.
                Ctr = Ctr + 1
                'If the array is not big enough...
                If Ctr > UBound(TempVar) Then
                    'add another element to the array.
                    ReDim Preserve TempVar(Ctr)
                End If
            Else
            'If any character other than the semicolon, add the
            'byte to the present field.
                TempVar(Ctr) = TempVar(Ctr) + Chr(ByteArray(Ptr))
            End If
        Next

        'Return the finished array.
        ConvertByteArray = TempVar

End Function
```

8. You need to create the functionality that manages the returned data after the `AsyncReadComplete` event is fired.

Enter the following code into the `AsyncReadComplete` event of the `UserDocument`:

```
Private Sub UserDocument_AsyncReadComplete(AsyncProp As
AsyncProperty)

        'Define local variables
        Dim Plan

        'Use the ConvertByteArray function to parse the
        'returned byte array into a string array separating
        'the fields.
        Plan = ConvertByteArray(AsyncProp.Value)

        'Assign the fields to the text boxes.
        txtPlan = Plan(0)
        txtTitle = Plan(1)
        txtDescription = Plan(2)

        'Re-enable the use of the drop-down list.
        cboPlan.Enabled = True

    End Sub
```

9. You need to confirm one last thing before testing your ActiveX document and Active Server Page. Choose Project, SelectPlan Properties and select the Debugging tab. Make sure you have selected the proper options for your system. When you run the project in the Visual Basic environment, if you have checked the check box for Use Existing Browser (as illustrated in Figure 16.6), then Visual Basic launches your Web browser with your ActiveX document loaded automatically.

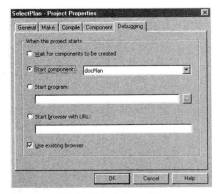

Figure 16.6 The SelectPlan Project Properties debugging options.

10. Save your ActiveX document and compile it. You can either execute the `UserDocument` in Visual Basic or run it within Internet Explorer. Either method should produce the same results.

How It Works

When your ActiveX document is displayed in Internet Explorer, it should look like the one shown in Figure 16.7.

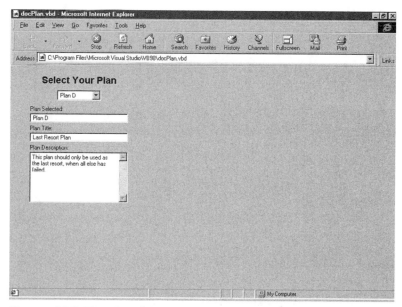

Figure 16.7 The docPlan `UserDocument` in Internet Explorer 4.0.

If the Active Server Page is on the server, and your hyperlink in the `cboPlan_Click` event is correct, you should be able to select an item from the drop-down list and have the Active Server Page return the requested information. This is one of the simplest techniques of requesting and receiving information from a Web server in an ActiveX document.

Comments

If an error occurs on the server, the error message is returned from Internet Information Server in HTML format. You might want to add code to your `AsyncReadComplete` event that can decipher this information if Internet Information Server returns an error messsage.

16.3 How do I...
Use the Class Builder utility to create an object model?

COMPATIBILITY: VISUAL BASIC 5 AND VISUAL BASIC 6

Problem

I need to create an object model to be used in an organizational data application for my company. I have an understanding of class fundamentals, but I would like to use the VB Class Builder utility to create the hierarchy and the skeleton code for the component. I have never worked with this utility before. How do I use the Class Builder utility to create an object model?

Technique

The Class Builder utility is a powerful tool that allows you to design classes and object models in a visual format and specify all properties, methods, events, and enumerations for each class in the hierarchy. When you are finished creating your visual design, the Class Builder utility automatically creates all the class modules and the skeleton code for all the properties, methods, events, and enumerations.

Steps

Complete the following steps to create an object model for the Organization component. This component could be used to create an application that manages data about the organizational structure of a company.

1. Start with a new ActiveX DLL project. Choose File, New Project. Highlight ActiveX DLL and click the OK command button.

2. Choose Project, Project1 Properties from the main menu. Change Project Name to **Organization** and click the OK command button.

3. Right-click the Class1 (Class1) item in the Project Explorer window. When the pop-up menu appears, choose Remove Class1 from the menu. When prompted to save changes to the Class1 file, click the No command button. Now you should have an ActiveX DLL project with no ClassModules.

4. Choose Add-Ins, Class Builder. (If the Class Builder utility is not on the menu, choose Add-Ins, Add-In Manager from the menu and add the VB6 Class Builder utility with a Load Behavior of Startup/Loaded. Then run the Class Builder utility.)

5. Now is a good time to familiarize yourself with the toolbar. Place your mouse cursor over each of the buttons on the toolbar to display the ToolTip text. This helps you learn what each of the buttons on the toolbar is used for.

6. After you have familiarized yourself with the toolbar, then you are ready to create your object model. With the Organization project highlighted in the Classes section, click the Add New Class button from the toolbar of the Class Builder. The Class Module Builder appears. Under the Properties tab, enter the Name property as `Corporate` and then click the OK button. The `Corporate` class then appears in the Classes section on the left.

7. With the `Corporate` class highlighted in the Classes section, click the Add New Class button again. This time, when the Class Module Builder appears, under the Properties tab, set the `Name` property to `President`, and click the option indicator for Public Not Creatable in the Instancing frame, as shown in Figure 16.8.

Figure 16.8 The Class Module Builder.

8. Click on the Object Creation tab and select the option indicator for Property Get on First Access. Then click the OK command button. The `President` class should appear under the hierarchy of the `Corporate` class.

9. With the `Corporate` class highlighted in the Classes section, click the Add New Collection button on the toolbar. When the Collection Builder appears, on the Properties tab, enter the `Name` property as `Divisions`. Set the `Instancing` property to `Public Not Creatable`.

10. Select the New Class option in the Collection Of frame on the lower right. Then click the New Class Properties button below the option. When the Class Module Builder appears, enter the `Name` property as `Division` and set the `Instancing` property to `Public Not Creatable`. Then, click the OK command button of the Class Module Builder. The Properties tab of the Collection Builder should appear as illustrated in Figure 16.9.

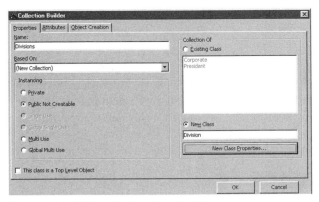

Figure 16.9 The Collection Builder.

11. Click on the Object Creation tab and select the Property Get on First Access option. Then, click the OK command button on the bottom right of the Collection Builder. The Divisions collection should now appear under the `Corporate` class hierarchy in the Classes section.

12. With the `President` class highlighted in the Classes section, click the Add New Property button on the toolbar. When the Property Builder appears, enter the `Name` property as `ID`. Select the Data Type property `String` from the drop-down list. Select the Public Variable option as the Declaration. Then check the Default Property check box at the bottom. Your properties should appear as shown in Figure 16.10. Click the OK command button.

13. Click the plus sign immediately to the left of the Divisions collection in the Classes section. This opens up the Divisions hierarchy and displays the `Division` class as a property under the collection. With the `Division` class highlighted in the Classes section, click the Add New Class button on the toolbar. Enter the `Name` property as `VicePresident` and select the Public Not Creatable option. Click on the Object Creation tab and select the Property Get on First Access option. Then, click the OK command button. The `VicePresident` class should appear under the `Division` class in the hierarchy (see Figure 16.11).

Figure 16.10 The Property Builder.

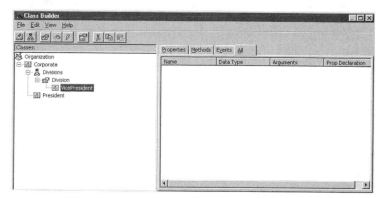

Figure 16.11 The class hierarchy up to the VicePresident class.

14. With the VicePresident class highlighted in the Classes section, click the Add New Property button on the toolbar. When the Property Builder appears, enter the Name property as ID. Select the Data Type property String from the drop-down list. Select the Public Variable option as the Declaration. Check the Default Property check box at the bottom. Then click the OK command button.

15. With the Division class highlighted in the Classes section, click the Add New Collection button on the toolbar. Enter the Name property as Departments and select Public Not Creatable for the Instancing property.

16. Select the New Class option on the bottom right and click the New Class Properties button. When the Class Module Builder appears, enter the `Name` property as `Department` and select `Public Not Creatable` for the `Instancing` property. Then, click the OK command button at the bottom of the Class Module Builder.

17. Click on the Object Creation tab and select the Property Get on First Access option. Then, click the OK command button at the bottom of the Collection Builder. The Departments collection should now appear under the `Division` class.

18. Open up the Departments' hierarchy by clicking on the plus sign immediately to the left of the Departments collection in the Classes section. The `Department` class is displayed below the Departments collection. Highlight the `Department` class and click the Add New Class button on the toolbar. When the Class Module Builder appears, enter the `Name` property as `Manager` and select the `Public Not Creatable` option for the `Instancing` property. Click on the Object Creation tab and select the Property Get on First Access option. Then, click the OK command button. The `Manager` class should appear under the `Department` class.

19. With the `Manager` class highlighted in the Classes section, click the Add New Property button on the toolbar. When the Property Builder appears, enter the `Name` property as `ID`. Select the Data Type property `String` from the drop-down list. Select the Public Variable option as the Declaration. Check the Default Property check box at the bottom. Then, click the OK command button.

20. With the `Department` class highlighted in the Classes section, click the Add New Collection button on the toolbar. Enter the `Name` property as `Positions` and select the `Public Not Creatable` option for the `Instancing` property.

21. Select the New Class option on the bottom right and click the New Class Properties button. Enter the `Name` property as `Position` and select `Public Not Creatable` for the `Instancing` property. Then, click the OK command button at the bottom of the Class Module Builder.

22. Click on the Object Creation tab and select the Property Get on First Access option. Then, click the OK command button at the bottom of the Collection Builder. The Positions collection should now appear under the `Department` class in the hierarchy.

23. Open up the Positions' hierarchy by clicking on the plus sign immediately to the left of the Positions collection in the Classes section. The `Position` class is displayed below the Positions collection. Highlight the `Position` class and click the Add New Class button on the toolbar. When the Class Module Builder appears, enter the **Name** property as **Employee** and select the **Public Not Creatable** option for the **Instancing** property. Click on the Object Creation tab and select the Property Get on First Access option. Then, click the OK command button.

24. With the **Employee** class highlighted in the Classes section, click the Add New Property button on the toolbar. When the Property Builder appears, enter the **Name** property as **ID**. Select the Data Type property **String** from the drop-down list. Select the Public Variable option as the Declaration. Check the Default Property check box at the bottom. Then, click the OK command button.

25. You need to add an **Update** method to the **Corporate** class. The **Update** method is used to update any organizational data changes to the database. With the **Corporate** class highlighted in the Classes section, click the Add New Method button on the toolbar. When the Method Builder appears, enter the **Name** property as **Update** and select a Return Data Type of **Long** from the drop-down list. The Method Builder should appear, as shown in Figure 16.12.

Figure 16.12 The Method Builder.

26. Click the OK command button, and the **Update** method should appear as a member of the **Corporate** class.

27. You can also add a **FullName** property to the **President**, **VicePresident**, **Manager**, and **Employee** classes. Perform the following for each of the classes listed in the previous sentence. With the class highlighted in the Classes section, click the Add New Property button on the toolbar. When the Property Builder appears, enter the `Name` property as `FullName`. Select the Data Type property `String` from the drop-down list. Select the Public Variable option as the Declaration. Then, click the OK command button. Your Organization Object Model should now look like the one shown in Figure 16.13.

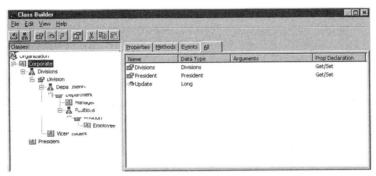

Figure 16.13 The Organization Object Model.

28. Now you are ready to let the Class Builder utility generate the skeleton code for your object model. Choose File, Update Project from the Class Builder menu. You might be able to see Visual Basic doing something behind the Class Builder. After it appears to be finished, choose File, Exit from the menu. Save your project, and you are then ready to add your own code.

How It Works

The Class Builder utility creates all the necessary class modules and the skeleton code for each class module in the object model you design. This is helpful when working with projects similar to the Organization project where object hierarchy is important. When you are finished with the Class Builder, you have a set of modules that are ready for you to add the functional code needed to make your component work.

Comments

You could also use the Class Builder utility to create simple business objects or private classes without any hierarchy. Simply highlight the Project Name in the Classes section each time you create a class for that project. This causes the Class Builder utility to create the class as a top-level object.

GLOSSARY

ActiveX A technology that enables software components developed in different languages to share data and work cooperatively in a networked environment. COM and DCOM are the core technologies of ActiveX.

ActiveX Controls These controls, formerly known as OLE controls, are binary components built using COM. The controls typically contain business logic or GUI functions. ActiveX controls execute on the client computer and use the .OCX file extension.

ADO Acronym for *Active Data Objects*. A high-level abstracted object set that supports data access. ADO is the strategic direction being promoted by Microsoft.

ADSL Acronym for *Asymmetric Digital Subscriber Line*. An older, very high-speed telecommunications technology based on existing copper wire infrastructures. Gaining new popularity because of low equipment costs and monthly fees and its relatively high speed. Operates at different, asymmetric speeds for uploads and downloads. Upload occurs at around 128 kilobits per second. Downloads are handled at a speed of 1.5 megabits per second. See also **ISDN**.

APE Acronym for *Application Performance Explorer*. This utility is written in Visual Basic and assists in the design and performance tuning of distributed client/server solutions.

API Acronym for *application programming interface*. The API is a set of subroutines and functions that provide a programmatic interface to an object, or library of system services.

ARPAnet *ARPA* stands for Advanced Research Project Agency, a government defense agency. The Internet evolved from the ARPAnet.

ASCII Acronym for *American Standard Code for Information Interchange*. ASCII is the standard character set used to store data.

Asynchronous A task that continues without waiting for another task or function to complete.

BBS Acronym for *bulletin board system*. A computer system available via dialup lines that is used to post and reply to topical messages. Falling out of common use and is being replaced by Internet Newsgroups.

Bind Run or create an instance of an object preparing it for use. Objects can be bound two ways. Late binding or dynamic binding occurs at runtime, and static binding happens during compile time.

Bit An acronym derived from *binary digit*.

BLOB Acronym for *binary large object*. Typically used to store images and video.

Boolean A data type that has only two possible values: `True` or `False`. These values are defined as `True = -1` and `False = 0` in Visual Basic. Other languages define `False` as `0` and `True` as "not `False`." This implies that `True` is represented by any value that is not `0`.

Branching A Visual SourceSafe technique in which a shared file is separated into two distinct development paths. Changes to the file are tracked separately for each branch. The distinct branches can be recombined (see **Merging**).

Class A class acts as a blueprint from which an instance of an object is created at runtime. The class defines the properties, methods, and events that control the behavior or the object during runtime. All objects created from the same class have identical methods and properties, but their property values can be unique.

Client A software program that provides access to network resources by working with the information on a server. An example of a client is a browser, such as Microsoft Internet Explorer.

Client/Server A distributed computing model in which client systems access resources on servers or hosts. The client side provides user-centric interfaces, and the servers provide shared resources, such as databases and business logic.

Cloaking A Visual SourceSafe technique used to perform an action on a group of projects while omitting select subprojects.

CodeModule Class Represents the code behind a component, such as a form, class, or document. Each component is associated with one `CodeModule` object. A `CodeModule` object, however, can be associated with multiple code panes. Code contained in a `CodeModule` can be edited.

CodePane Class A code window pane.

CodePanes Collection Contains all the `CodePane` objects in a project.

Cohesion Cohesion refers to the related nature of code in a single routine. Tight cohesion means that all the code in a routine relates to performing a specific task. Loose cohesion describes code that is not focused on a single task. A common example of a loosely cohesive routine is an application initialization procedure that configures many unrelated parts of the program. The only internal relationship in the code is functional. It all has to do with initialization.

COM Acronym for *Component Object Model*. COM provides a defined object interface.

Coupling Coupling is a measure of the external dependencies found in a code routine or module. External dependencies include global variables and calls to other subroutines and functions in the program. Loose coupling indicates that there are no external dependencies. Loose coupling is the goal for each code routine. Tight coupling applies to code routines with high reliance on external data and services. If the code makes external references, the scope of the references must be limited to the extent possible. For example, if a global variable is used, confine its scope to the module level.

CSMA/CD Acronym for *Carrier Sense Multi Access with Collision Detection*. This is the protocol used on Ethernet networks. It essentially means that network interface cards listen before they transmit. If there is a signal on the network line, the interface waits to send and listens for collision signals. See also **Token Ring**.

DAO Acronym for *Data Access Objects*. DAO includes the local and remote data services. The services include Microsoft Jet and ODBC.

DCOM Acronym for *Distributed Component Object Model*. DCOM enhances COM to support transparent use of network-based objects and components.

Delegation An object, such as a control, can modify its behavior by asking another object to handle an event or method on its behalf. This is no different from a manager asking an employee to do something. Instead of handling the event itself, the control or object passes the event on to another object.

Design Time Mode ActiveX controls have both design time and runtime behavior. When a control is placed on a form inside, say, Visual Basic, it is said to be in design time mode. Although the program you are making is not running then, the control's code is executed in response to events such as resizing, painting, and so on.

Differencing A Visual SourceSafe technique that enables code changes, additions, and deletions to be easily compared across different versions.

DLL Acronym for *dynamic link library*. An object or collection of code that is bound to a program either at compile time or runtime.

Encapsulation Enclosing the properties and methods of an object behind a public interface encapsulates the object. An encapsulated object has loose coupling and should have no external dependencies. All the code and data references needed by the object are contained in the object itself, but that does not mean an encapsulated object cannot call or make use of other objects.

Ethernet A common physical networking technology used in both LAN and WAN environments. See also **CSMA/CD** and **Token Ring**.

Event An action that is recognized by an object. Clicking a command button, selecting an item from a list box, and pressing keys on the keyboard are all examples of events.

Event Procedure A code segment automatically invoked in response to an event initiated by the user, program code, or system.

Extranet Typically a private external network involving an organization's trading partners. This network may or may not be implemented over the public Internet.

FTP Acronym for *File Transfer Protocol*. An Internet protocol that allows users to transfer files between computers.

GIF Acronym for *Graphics Interchange Format* (pronounced *jif*). A file format developed by CompuServe for displaying images.

Gigabyte 1024 megabytes. The unit of measure commonly used to refer to one billion bytes.

GUI Acronym for *graphical user interface*. The user is presented with visual images and text for interaction with the system.

GUID Acronym for *globally unique identifier*. Identifiers assigned to COM objects.

Handle A value that points to or refers to an instance of an object.

HTML Acronym for *Hypertext Markup Language*. A tag-based language used for document formatting on the World Wide Web.

HTTP Acronym for *Hypertext Transfer Protocol*. This is the protocol used on the Internet to transmit hypertext documents.

Hypertext Text containing links to other text or documents. Typically seen as HTML pages on the Internet.

IDE Acronym for *Interactive Design Environment*. The IDE is the environment used to design and develop applications. Visual Basic now shares the same IDE used by the other Visual Studio development languages.

IDTExtensibility Class Implemented by Visual Basic as the primary add-in interface.

IIS Acronym for Microsoft's *Internet Information Server*. This is the server-based program that delivers HTML and other Internet content to client browsers.

In-Process Server A component that shares the same virtual memory space as the application that uses the service.

Inheritance Objects acquire, or inherit, their standard properties and methods from their parent class. Inheritance also implies that an object can define properties and methods that it has not gotten from its parent class. Visual Basic does not allow objects created from class modules to define their own individual characteristics.

Instance The actual object created from a class. The class acts as a blueprint for the creation of objects, and each object created from this blueprint is called an instance. The individual instance is often associated with a handle, which is used to refer to the instance.

Instantiate To create an instance of an object. The process of creating or activating an object based on its class.

Interface Wizard A wizard for defining a control's properties, methods, and events. It is accessed from the Add-Ins menu.

Internet A network of networks that are interconnected by using TCP/IP networking protocol. Evolved from the ARPAnet.

Intranet A private internal network that uses the same protocols and technologies as the public Internet.

ISDN Acronym for *Integrated Services Digital Network*. A telecommunications protocol that uses existing copper wire infrastructures. Operates at a theoretical limit of 128,000 bits per second. Typical speeds are often half of the theoretical maximum. See also **ADSL**.

ISP Acronym for *Internet service provider*. An ISP is a company that provides Internet access services.

Jet A Microsoft desktop database engine.

JPEG or JPG Acronym for *Joint Photographic Experts Group*. A compressed graphic file format.

Kernel The kernel is the core of the Windows operating system. It schedules activities to be performed by the computer processor(s).

Keyword A word or symbol recognized as being part of the Visual Basic programming environment.

Kilobyte Actually 1024 (2 to the tenth power) bytes, but commonly used as a reference for "a thousand bytes."

Megabyte 1024 kilobytes. Commonly equated to one million bytes.

Merging A Visual SourceSafe technique in which branched files are merged to restore a single development path.

Method Methods define the tasks that an object performs. An object's methods, and therefore its interfaces, are defined by its class. A Visual Basic class module defines the public and private methods of the objects created with the class. Forms and controls have a predefined set of methods. Custom methods can be added to forms. The standard behavior of controls and forms can be changed by using subclassing and message hooks.

Microsoft Development Objects Model (MDO Model) An extensible information model provided to store and manipulate Visual Basic project data.

MIME Acronym for *Multipurpose Internet Mail Extensions*. A method of encoding binary content into text so it is transferred correctly over the Internet.

Modem Actually an acronym that stands for *modulator-demodulator*. A modem connects two computers together by converting a digital signal to an analog signal that can be transferred over telephone lines. This signal conversion is known as modulation.

MTS or MTX Acronym for *Microsoft Transaction Server*. Codename "Viper." MTS automates the use and sharing of the objects. The automatic features of MTS include thread allocation, dynamic load balancing, ODBC resource pooling, and object persistence for improved performance.

Multithreaded Process A process may have access to multiple threads on which to attach its objects. After an object is created and attached to a thread, it remains attached to the same thread until the object is destroyed.

Multitier Architecture A method for building applications that are segmented into user, business, and data services tiers.

Netiquette The etiquette of the Internet. This includes topics, taboos, and rules, such as using mixed case in messages and postings because all uppercase is considered the equivalent of shouting.

NNTP Acronym for *Network News Transport Protocol*. This Internet protocol is used to distribute articles and replies to newsgroups.

Node Any single computer connected to a network.

Object An object is a self-contained logical entity that has properties and performs methods. Visual Basic creates objects from classes. In the broader sense, forms, controls, and windows are also objects. An object, which contains program code and data, is attached to a thread and is executed only when its thread is given its scheduled time slice by the kernel.

OCX Originally used as a file extension for OLE custom controls; now used for ActiveX controls and active documents.

ODBC Acronym for *open database connectivity*. ODBC provides a homogenous interface to databases from multiple vendors.

OLE Acronym for *object linking and embedding*. This is a method that allows objects to communicate with each other. It is being replaced in the marketplace by COM and DCOM.

OLE Control See **ActiveX Control**.

Out-of-Process A component that runs in its own virtual memory space independent of the application that uses the service.

Pinning A Visual SourceSafe technique that freezes a file at a specific version.

Polymorphism Polymorphism refers to multiple classes that have the same public interface. In other words, the interface is "overloaded" so that it can be used for different purposes based on the object that is bound to the interface. A program can dynamically bind a polymorphic object to an interface class at runtime.

POP Acronym for *point-of-presence*. A point-of-presence is the location used to access a network. For example an ISP or Value Added Network provider will have points-of-presence in many cities. Also an ancronym for *Post Office Protocol*. This is the Internet protocol used to retrieve electronic mail.

PPP Acronym for *Point-to-Point Protocol*. A serial protocol that puts a computer directly on the Internet. See also **SLIP**.

PPTP Acronym for *Point-to-Point Tunneling Protocol*. Provides an encrypted pipeline or tunnel between two machines on a network. See also **SSL**.

Process A process represents the address space and the data necessary for the execution of an object or set of objects.

Property A set of characteristics of an object. Its class defines an object's properties. A Visual Basic class module defines the public and private properties of the objects created with the class. Forms and controls have predefined sets of properties. Custom properties can be added to forms. Some examples of properties are the caption and name of a form or control, or the address and phone number of a customer.

Property Page (ActiveX Control) Each ActiveX control can have one or more property pages. When the control is being used from a programming environment, such as Visual Basic, the user can call up its properties. The programming environment then pops up a Properties dialog box and places all the property pages of the selected controls within it.

Property Page Wizard A wizard for defining a control's property pages. It is accessed from the Add-Ins menu.

RAD Acronym for *Rapid Application Development*. A software design and development methodology for quickly creating applications.

RDO Acronym for *Remote Data Objects*. A high-performance, high-level object layer above ODBC.

Reentrancy Reentrancy is when a thread starts a second pass through the same instance of a method or property procedure before completing the first pass.

Repository Browser Used to view repository data and information models.

RPC Acronym for *remote procedure call*. This is a technique that allows a program on one machine to call or execute a task on another networked computer.

Run Time Mode ActiveX controls have both design-time and runtime behavior. When a program that uses an ActiveX control is running, the control is said to be in Run Time Mode.

SDK Acronym for *software development kit*.

Single-Threaded Process A single-threaded process uses one thread on which to attach all its objects.

SLIP Acronym for *Serial Line Internet Protocol*. A network protocol that connects one computer to a second computer that is actually on the Internet. Commonly being replaced by PPP.

SMTP Acronym for *Simple Mail Transport Protocol*. The primary protocol used to send e-mail over the Internet.

SNMP Acronym for *Simple Network Management Protocol*. This protocol is used to manage network hardware devices remotely. Examples include routers and bridges.

SQL Acronym for *Structured Query Language*. The standard language for working with relational databases.

SSL Acronym for *Secure Sockets Layer*. Enables encrypted and authenticated communications over the Internet. Uses public-key/private-key encryption technology to ensure security and privacy.

Synchronous A task that waits for another task or function to complete.

TCP/IP Acronym for *Transmission Control Protocol/Internet Protocol*. This is the primary transport protocol of the Internet.

Thread A thread is the most fundamental single element or activity within the system that can be scheduled by the kernel. The kernel uses threads to allocate computer processor time slices to specific program code to be executed.

Three-Tier Architecture See **Multitier Architecture**.

Token Ring A common physical LAN network protocol. Network interface cards using this protocol do not transmit on the network unless they own the "token." This implies that the interface card cannot transmit, even if there is no network traffic, until it receives the token. See also **CSMA/CD**.

UserControl A form that represents the ActiveX control you are building.

URL Acronym for *Uniform Resource Locator*. The address that specifies the location of an Internet resource or file.

UUENCODE Acronym for *UNIX to UNIX Encoding*. Commonly used to convert binary files to ASCII representations for transmission over the Internet.

VBA Acronym for *Visual Basic, Applications Edition*. This is the version of Visual Basic that is embedded as a scripting language in other applications. Examples of programs that use VBA are Microsoft Word and Microsoft Access.

VBComponent Class Project components, including forms, classes, and modules.

VBComponents Collection All components contained in a project.

VBE Class The root object that contains all other objects and collections represented in Visual Basic for applications.

VBX Acronym for *Visual Basic Extension*. 16-bit custom controls.

Winsock Acronym for *Windows Sockets*. Provides an API to aspects of TCP/IP network UNIX services.

WWW Acronym for *World Wide Web*. The Web is what most users associate with the Internet. Specifically the Web is the part of the Internet that uses HTML. The Web portion refers the interconnected and linked pages of information.

INDEX

C

Q-R

The Waite Group's C++ Primer Plus, Third Edition

Stephen Prata

The first and second editions of The *Waite Group's C++ Primer Plus* are classics that have sold over 75,000 copies and introduced thousands of users to C++. This new edition includes coverage of the Standard Template Library, one of the most significant additions to C++ since the second edition and a topic C++ programmers will have to master to be competitive in the C++ market. All the listings and examples have been revised to use the new STD namespace and in some of the more difficult areas, such as inheritance, the examples have been made more lucid and straightforward. We've also enhanced coverage of the latest object-oriented programming techniques such as UML, CRC cards, and design patterns. The *Waite Group's C++ Primer Plus*, Third Edition teaches C++ from the ground up, walking beginners through the basics of object-oriented programming while covering the essential elements of C++ such as loops, expressions, functions, classes, and so on. The *Waite Group's C++ Primer Plus*, Third Edition makes understanding and experimenting with important object-oriented programming concepts such as classes, inheritance, templates and exceptions both interesting and manageable. It shows how to handle input and output, make programs perform repetitive tasks, manipulate data, hide information, use functions, and build flexible, easily modifiable programs. This book also guides the reader through complex topics without assuming prior knowledge of C.

$35.00 US\$50.95 CDN   *Programming*   *Beginner - Intermediate*
1-57169-162-6   *Sams*   *850 pp.*

The Waite Group's Visual Basic 6 Database How-To

Eric Winemiller and Jason R. Roff

Visual Basic How-To has sold over 50,000 copies to date and won the *Visual Basic Programmer's Journal* Reader's Choice Award in 1995. This book is written in The Waite Group's proven question-and-answer format. This title has expanded coverage of Visual Basic 6, including Internet topics and lots of al-new How-Tos.

$39.99 US\$57.95 CDN   *Programming*   *Intermediate - Advanced*
1-57169-152-9   *Sams*   *1,100 pp.*

The Waite Group's Visual Basic 6 Client/Server How-To

Noel Jerke, et al.

The Waite Group's Visual Basic 6 Client/Server How-To is a practical step-by-step guide to implementing three-tiered distributed client/server solutions using the tools provided in Microsoft's Visual Basic 6. It addresses the needs of programmers looking for answers to real-world questions and assures them that what they create really works. It also helps to simplify the client/server development process by providing a framework for solution development. This book can save you hundreds of hours of programming time by providing step-by-step solutions to more than 75 Visual Basic 6 client/server problems. It covers in-depth topics like OOP, ODBC, OLE, RDO, distributed computing, and three-tier client/server development.

$49.99 US\$71.95 CDN   *Programming*   *Intermediate - Advanced*
1-57169-154-5   *Sams*   *1,000 pp.*

Dan Appleman's Developing COM/ActiveX Components with Visual Basic 6

Dan Appleman

Dan Appleman's Developing COM/ActiveX Components with Visual Basic 6 is a focused tutorial for learning component development. It teaches you the programming concepts and the technical steps needed to create ActiveX components. Dan Appleman is the author that Visual Basic programmers recommend to their friends and colleagues. He consistently delivers on his promise to break through the confusion and hype surrounding Visual Basic and ActiveX. Appleman goes beyond the basics to show readers common pitfalls and practical solutions for key problems. Dan Appleman revises a successful title with new information on the new version of Visual Basic 6. Appleman is one of the foremost developers in the Visual Basic community and the author of *Visual Basic 5.0 Programmer's Guide* to the Win32 API.

$49.99 US\$71.95 CDN	*Programming*	*Intermediate*
1-56276-576-0	*Sams*	*850 pp.*

Doing Objects in Visual Basic 6

Deborah Kurata

Doing Objects in Visual Basic 6 is an intermediate-level tutorial which begins with the fundamentals of OOP. It advances to the technical aspects of using the VB IDE to create objects and interface with databases, Web sites, and Internet applications. This revised edition features more technical information than the last edition. It specifically highlights the features of the new release of Visual Basic. This is a revised edition of *Doing Objects in Microsoft Visual Basic 5*, the #1 OOP title for Visual Basic programmers and developers. Text focuses on the technical aspects of developing objects and covers the Internet and database programming aspects of the new edition of Visual Basic.

$49.99 US\$71.95 CDN	*Programming*	*Intermediate - Expert*
1-56276-577-9	*Que*	*560 pp.*

Visual Basic 6 Unleashed

Rob Thayer

Visual Basic 6 Unleashed provides comprehensive coverage of the most sought after topics in Visual Basic programming. *Visual Basic 6 Unleashed* provides a means for a casual level Visual Basic programmer to quickly become productive with the new release of Visual Basic. This book provides you with a comprehensive reference to virtually all the topics that are used in today's leading-edge Visual Basic applications. This book looks to take advantage of the past success of the *Unleashed* series along with the extremely large size of the Visual Basic market. The integration of the text and CD-ROM makes this an invaluable tool for accomplished Visual Basic programmers—everything you need to know as well as the tools and utilities to make it work. Includes topics important to developers such as creating and using ActiveX controls, creating wizards, adding and controlling RDO, tuning and optimization, and much more. This book is targeted towards the beginning-to-intermediate level programmer who needs additional step-by-step guidance in learning the more detailed features of Visual Basic. You can use this book as a building block to step to the next level from *Sams Teach Yourself Visual Basic 6 in 21 Days*.

$49.99 US\$71.95 CDN	*Programming*	*Advanced-Expert*
0-672-31309-X	*Sams*	*1,000 pp.*

Add to Your Sams Library Today with the Best Books for Programming, Operating Systems, and New Technologies

To order, visit our Web site at www.mcp.com or fax us at

1-800-835-3202

ISBN	Quantity	Description of Item	Unit Cost	Total Cost
1-57169-162-6		The Waite Group's C++ Primer Plus, Third Edition	$35.00	
1-57169-152-9		The Waite Group's Visual Basic 6 Database How-To	$39.99	
1-57169-154-5		The Waite Group's Visual Basic 6 Client/Server How-To	$49.99	
1-56276-576-0		Dan Appleman's Developing COM/ActiveX Components with Visual Basic 6	$49.99	
1-56276-577-9		Doing Objects in Visual Basic 6	$49.99	
0-672-31309-X		Visual Basic 6 Unleashed	$49.99	
		Shipping and Handling: See information below.		
		TOTAL		

Shipping and Handling

Standard	$5.00
2nd Day	$10.00
Next Day	$17.50
International	$40.00

201 W. 103rd Street, Indianapolis, Indiana 46290   1-800-835-3202 — FAX

Book ISBN 1-57169-153-7

USING THE CD-ROM

The companion CD-ROM contains source code from the book, as well as many third-party software products.

Windows 95/NT 4 Installation Instructions

1. Insert the CD-ROM disc into your CD-ROM drive.

2. From the Windows 95 desktop, double-click the My Computer icon.

3. Double-click the icon representing your CD-ROM drive.

4. Double-click the icon titled SETUP.EXE to run the installation program.

5. The installation program creates a program group with the book's name as the group name. This group contains icons to browse the CD-ROM.

NOTE

If Windows 95 is installed on your computer and you have the AutoPlay feature enabled, the SETUP.EXE program starts automatically when you insert the CD into your CD-ROM drive.

System Requirements

This CD-ROM contains the Microsoft Visual Basic Control Creation Edition. Some of the features of Visual Basic 5 discussed in this book may not be usable with the Control Creation Edition. The Control Creation Edition is provided to allow you to become familiar with the Visual Basic environment and to create your own ActiveX controls.

The following are the minimum system requirements for the Visual Basic Control Creation Edition:

✔ A personal computer with a 486 or higher processor

✔ Microsoft Windows 95 or Windows NT Workstation 4.0 or later

✔ 8MB of memory (12MB recommended) if running Windows NT Workstation

✔ The following hard disk space:

Typical installation: 20MB

Minimum installation: 14MB

CD-ROM installation (tools run from the CD): 14MB

Total tools and information on the CD: 50MB

✔ A CD-ROM drive

✔ A VGA or higher-resolution monitor (SVGA recommended)

MISCELLANEOUS

If you acquired this product in the United States, this EULA is governed by the laws of the State of Washington.

If you acquired this product in Canada, this EULA is governed by the laws of the Province of Ontario, Canada. Each of the parties hereto irrevocably attorns to the jurisdiction of the courts of the Province of Ontario and further agrees to commence any litigation which may arise hereunder in the courts located in the Judicial District of York, Province of Ontario.

If this product was acquired outside the United States, then local law may apply.

Should you have any questions concerning this EULA, or if you desire to contact Microsoft for any reason, please contact the Microsoft subsidiary serving your country, or write: Microsoft Sales Information Center/One Microsoft Way/Redmond, WA 98052-6399.

LIMITED WARRANTY

NO WARRANTIES. Microsoft expressly disclaims any warranty for the SOFTWARE PRODUCT. The SOFTWARE PRODUCT and any related documentation is provided "as is" without warranty of any kind, either express or implied, including, without limitation, the implied warranties or merchantability, fitness for a particular purpose, or noninfringement. The entire risk arising out of use or performance of the SOFTWARE PRODUCT remains with you.

NO LIABILITY FOR DAMAGES. In no event shall Microsoft or its suppliers be liable for any damages whatsoever (including, without limitation, damages for loss of business profits, business interruption, loss of business information, or any other pecuniary loss) arising out of the use of or inability to use this Microsoft product, even if Microsoft has been advised of the possibility of such damages. Because some states/jurisdictions do not allow the exclusion or limitation of liability for consequential or incidental damages, the above limitation may not apply to you.

3. **UPGRADES.** If the SOFTWARE PRODUCT is labeled as an upgrade, you must be properly licensed to use a product identified by Microsoft as being eligible for the upgrade in order to use the SOFTWARE PRODUCT. A SOFTWARE PRODUCT labeled as an upgrade replaces and/or supplements the product that formed the basis for your eligibility for the upgrade. You may use the resulting upgraded product only in accordance with the terms of this EULA. If the SOFTWARE PRODUCT is an upgrade of a component of a package of software programs that you licensed as a single product, the SOFTWARE PRODUCT may be used and transferred only as part of that single product package and may not be separated for use on more than one computer.

4. **COPYRIGHT.** All title and copyrights in and to the SOFTWARE PRODUCT (including but not limited to any images, photographs, animations, video, audio, music, text, and "applets" incorporated into the SOFTWARE PRODUCT), the accompanying printed materials, and any copies of the SOFTWARE PRODUCT are owned by Microsoft or its suppliers. The SOFTWARE PRODUCT is protected by copyright laws and international treaty provisions. Therefore, you must treat the SOFTWARE PRODUCT like any other copyrighted material except that you may install the SOFTWARE PRODUCT on a single computer provided you keep the original solely for backup or archival purposes. You may not copy the printed materials accompanying the SOFTWARE PRODUCT.

5. **DUAL-MEDIA SOFTWARE.** You may receive the SOFTWARE PRODUCT in more than one medium. Regardless of the type or size of medium you receive, you may use only one medium that is appropriate for your single computer. You may not use or install the other medium on another computer. You may not loan, rent, lease, or otherwise transfer the other medium to another user, except as part of the permanent transfer (as provided above) of the SOFTWARE PRODUCT.

6. **U.S. GOVERNMENT RESTRICTED RIGHTS.** The SOFTWARE PRODUCT and documentation are provided with RESTRICTED RIGHTS. Use, duplication, or disclosure by the Government is subject to restrictions as set forth in subparagraph (c)(1)(ii) of the Rights in Technical Data and Computer Software clause at DFARS 252.227-7013 or subparagraphs (c)(1) and (2) of the Commercial Computer Software—Restricted Rights at 48 CFR 52.227-19, as applicable. Manufacturer is Microsoft Corporation/One Microsoft Way/Redmond, WA 98052-6399.

7. **EXPORT RESTRICTIONS.** You agree that neither you nor your customers intend to or will, directly or indirectly, export or transmit (i) the SOFTWARE or related documentation and technical data or (ii) your software product as described in Section 1(b) of this License (or any part thereof), or process, or service that is the direct product of the SOFTWARE, to any country to which such export or transmission is restricted by any applicable U.S. regulation or statute, without the prior written consent, if required, of the Bureau of Export Administration of the U.S. Department of Commerce, or such other governmental entity as may have jurisdiction over such export or transmission.

terms of this EULA; and (2) you may permit your end users to reproduce and distribute the object code version of the files designated by ".ocx" file extensions ("Controls") only in conjunction with and as a part of an Application and/or Web page that adds significant and primary functionality to the Controls, and such end user complies with all other terms of this EULA.

2.   **DESCRIPTION OF OTHER RIGHTS AND LIMITATIONS.**

a.   **Not for Resale Software.** If the SOFTWARE PRODUCT is labeled "Not for Resale" or "NFR," then, notwithstanding other sections of this EULA, you may not resell, or otherwise transfer for value, the SOFTWARE PRODUCT.

b.   **Limitations on Reverse Engineering, Decompilation, and Disassembly.** You may not reverse engineer, decompile, or disassemble the SOFTWARE PRODUCT, except and only to the extent that such activity is expressly permitted by applicable law notwithstanding this limitation.

c.   **Separation of Components.** The SOFTWARE PRODUCT is licensed as a single product. Its component parts may not be separated for use by more than one user.

d.   **Rental.** You may not rent, lease, or lend the SOFTWARE PRODUCT.

e.   **Support Services.** Microsoft may provide you with support services related to the SOFTWARE PRODUCT ("Support Services"). Use of Support Services is governed by the Microsoft policies and programs described in the user manual, in "online" documentation, and/or in other Microsoft-provided materials. Any supplemental software code provided to you as part of the Support Services shall be considered part of the SOFTWARE PRODUCT and subject to the terms and conditions of this EULA. With respect to technical information you provide to Microsoft as part of the Support Services, Microsoft may use such information for its business purposes, including for product support and development. Microsoft will not utilize such technical information in a form that personally identifies you.

f.   **Software Transfer.** You may permanently transfer all of your rights under this EULA, provided you retain no copies, you transfer all of the SOFTWARE PRODUCT (including all component parts, the media and printed materials, any upgrades, this EULA, and, if applicable, the Certificate of Authenticity), **and** the recipient agrees to the terms of this EULA. If the SOFTWARE PRODUCT is an upgrade, any transfer must include all prior versions of the SOFTWARE PRODUCT.

g.   **Termination.** Without prejudice to any other rights, Microsoft may terminate this EULA if you fail to comply with the terms and conditions of this EULA. In such event, you must destroy all copies of the SOFTWARE PRODUCT and all of its component parts.

1. **GRANT OF LICENSE.** This EULA grants you the following rights:

   a. **Software Product.** Microsoft grants to you as an individual, a personal, non-exclusive license to make and use copies of the SOFTWARE for the sole purposes of designing, developing, and testing your software product(s) that are designed to operate in conjunction with any Microsoft operating system product. You may install copies of the SOFT-WARE on an unlimited number of computers provided that you are the only individual using the SOFTWARE. If you are an entity, Microsoft grants you the right to designate one individual within your organization to have the right to use the SOFTWARE in the manner provided above.

   b. **Electronic Documents.** Solely with respect to electronic documents included with the SOFTWARE, you may make an unlimited number of copies (either in hardcopy or electronic form), provided that such copies shall be used only for internal purposes and are not republished or distributed to any third party.

   c. **Redistributable Components.**

   (i) **Sample Code.** In addition to the rights granted in Section 1, Microsoft grants you the right to use and modify the source code version of those portions of the SOFTWARE designated as "Sample Code" ("SAMPLE CODE") for the sole purposes of designing, developing, and testing your software product(s), and to reproduce and distribute the SAMPLE CODE, along with any modifications thereof, only in object code form provided that you comply with Section d(iii), below.

   (ii) **Redistributable Components**. In addition to the rights granted in Section 1, Microsoft grants you a nonexclusive royalty-free right to reproduce and distribute the object code version of any portion of the SOFTWARE listed in the SOFTWARE file REDIST.TXT ("REDISTRIBUTABLE SOFTWARE"), provided you comply with Section d(iii), below.

   (iii) **Redistribution Requirements.** If you redistribute the SAMPLE CODE or REDISTRIBUTABLE SOFTWARE (collectively, "REDISTRIBUTABLES"), you agree to: (A) distribute the REDISTRIBUTABLES in object code only in conjunction with and as a part of a software application product developed by you that adds significant and primary functionality to the SOFTWARE and that is developed to operate on the Windows or Windows NT environment ("Application"); (B) not use Microsoft's name, logo, or trademarks to market your software application product; (C) include a valid copyright notice on your software product; (D) indemnify, hold harmless, and defend Microsoft from and against any claims or lawsuits, including attorney's fees, that arise or result from the use or distribution of your software application product; (E) not permit further distribution of the REDISTRIBUTABLES by your end user. The following **exceptions** apply to subsection (iii)(E), above: (1) you may permit further redistribution of the REDISTRIBUTABLES by your distributors to your end-user customers if your distributors only distribute the REDISTRIBUTABLES in conjunction with, and as part of, your Application and you and your distributors comply with all other

END USER LICENSE AGREEMENT FOR MICROSOFT SOFTWARE

Microsoft Visual Basic, Control Creation Edition

IMPORTANT—READ CAREFULLY: This Microsoft End User License Agreement
(EULA) is a legal agreement between you (either an individual or a single entity) and Microsoft
Corporation for the Microsoft software product identified above, which includescomputer
software and may include associated media, printed materials, and online—or electronic—documentation ("SOFTWARE PRODUCT"). By installing, copying, or otherwise using the SOFT-
WARE PRODUCT, you agree to be bound by the terms of this EULA. If you do not agree to
the terms of this EULA, do not install or use the SOFTWARE PRODUCT; you may, however, return it to your place of purchase for a full refund.

Software PRODUCT LICENSE

The SOFTWARE PRODUCT is protected by copyright laws and international copyright treaties,
as well as other intellectual property laws and treaties. The SOFTWARE PRODUCT is licensed,
not sold.

←